Jean Renoir

HARVARD FILM STUDIES

Jean Renoir

The French Films, 1924–1939

Alexander Sesonske

Harvard University Press • Cambridge, Massachusetts, and London, England • 1980

Library of Congress Cataloging in Publication Data

Sesonske, Alexander.
Jean Renoir, the French films, 1924-1939.

Bibliography: p.
Includes index.
1. Renoir, Jean, 1894-   I. Title.
PN1998.A3R459   791-43'7   79-17406
ISBN 0-674-47355-8 (cloth)
ISBN 0-674-47360-4 (paper)

To François Truffaut

Foreword

Sesonske's book will be published by Harvard University Press. This event means very much to me. I have carefully followed the elaboration of this review of my work. I didn't attend the birth of the child, but I enjoyed watching the child grow up; nearly day by day.

In the beginning I was enchanted by the thought of being the central figure of this story. Little by little, I discovered a new aspect of the question. It can't really be called a story, because everything in it is true. It is an homage to fraternal affection. The Romans built beautiful monuments, temples and arches of triumph dedicated to the memory of an emperor. With Sesonske's book I have my arch of triumph.

Jean Renoir
December 1977

Preface

I first saw Jean Renoir in 1951. He had been invited to introduce *Grand Illusion* to a small audience at UCLA, where I was then a student. I had seen *Grand Illusion* once before, but no other Renoir film, and I knew nothing about Jean Renoir except that he was a son of the painter. He appeared: a rather heavy, florid man, informally dressed, with a decided French accent, who spoke with great charm and vivacity about the making of the film. At the conclusion of his remarks he said, "I have not seen *Grand Illusion* for many years, and I have never seen it with subtitles. It will be interesting to see again." And he sat at the back of the lecture hall as the projection began.

I was greatly impressed by the film, as I had been before. In the final scene the escaping prisoners, Maréchal and Rosenthal, agree to separate if they encounter a German patrol, so they say farewell before attempting the last leg of their escape. They embrace and Jean Gabin, as Maréchal, says, "Au revoir, sale juif." The subtitle accompanying this passage read "Goodbye, old pal." They walk away across the snow and as they recede into tiny black dots the film ends. But just then a great roar arose at the back of the lecture hall and as the lights went on a red-faced man charged down the aisle like an enraged bull, shouting, "Wait a minute! You have not seen the picture!" So we waited while Jean Renoir explained that though the word "Jew" never appeared in the English subtitles, it was in the dialogue as part of a major theme of the film. He had been charming before; now he was intense, angry at the stupidity of the subtitles, concerned that we should "see" the picture without the restrictions imposed by timorous Hollywood magnates on American films. I had been delighted by his first appearance; I think that I have loved him ever since this second unscheduled address.

In 1968 I was a professor of philosophy at the University of California, Santa Barbara, and teaching, improbably, a seminar on the films of Jean Renoir. I had by then, of course, seen many more Renoir films, and in the preceding year I had spent hours talking to Jean Renoir about them. When I asked him to talk to my students he agreed immediately, so I drove to Beverly Hills late one morning, then came back to Santa Barbara with Jean and his wife, Dido. There might have been a simpler method of getting him to our campus, but this way I could spend several more hours with him. As I had expected, my students found him patient, amusing, illuminating, wholly unpretentious. He talked about the works he had done and the work he then hoped to do, displaying in his warmth and tolerance, his humanity and irony, qualities we had found in his films.

Later that night I drove him back to Beverly Hills. The coastal fog and the foul Los Angeles air left a thick patina on my little car, and as we drove down Sunset Boulevard at midnight Jean said, "Now Alex, before you go back to Santa Barbara you must clean your windshield. It's dangerous that way." I said yes, I would. But when I stopped at the door of his house he said, "Wait. I'm going to clean your windshield." I protested: it had been a long day; I knew he was tired; I could very well do it myself. But he hurried across the drive, limping a little as he had for fifty years, returned with a wet rag and then, with more care and patience than the boy at the corner gas station, washed my windshield very thoroughly before saying goodnight and going in to bed.

I tell these two stories in hope that they will explain why I have written this book. There are other, perhaps more logical, reasons, of course. Renoir's films are among the major achievements of this youngest art form. Still, until quite recently they were little known in this country and almost completely ignored by film historians writing in English, despite their originality in both form and content and their influence on the development of cinema.

Jean Renoir worked at this art for over forty-five years. One constant in this long career was that in both style and theme his films were genuinely his, rather than performances executed in accord with the fashions of the moment. This individuality and originality has had its cost in the indifference or even hostility the public has displayed to many Renoir films on their first appearance and the consequent difficulty he had in having his projects financed. But it has also made his works more impervious to the passage of time and changes of fashion than most films and has led to such anomalies as the headline in the Paris Le Monde in 1968 on the occasion of a retrospective showing of Renoir films at the Venice Biennale: "The youngest filmmaker in Venice: Jean Renoir." Or the headline in the Los Angeles Free Press the same year: "37-year-old film premieres," hailing the discovery of Boudu Saved from Drowning by Paul Schrader and the Los Angeles hippie community. Hence it seemed to me that this body of work, one of the great artistic accomplishments of our century, deserved to be treated with the care and thoroughness we readily accord to painters or novelists. Still, if these films had been directed by some other, very different, man, I am not at all sure that I would have undertaken the years of happy labor that have gone into this study.

I have attempted to write clearly and accurately about the films, and to resist the temptation to try to say everything possible about any one of them. Hence I hope that anyone reading this and then seeing a Renoir film will find there much more than I have been able to suggest. I have only sketched out Renoir's place in the history of cinema, for though the overall shape of this history may be clear, the relevant details of the relationship between works and between workers remain obscure—at least to me. Memories are fallible; many films have been lost or remain unseen, and such observed similarities as that between Monte Blue's performance in *The Marriage Circle* (Lubitsch, 1924) and that of Georges Hugon in Renoir's *Nana* (1926) do not seem sufficient to warrant any claim of influence.

I have not often offered overall evaluations of any film, though it should be obvious that I believe all of them interesting and several of them masterpieces.

For most of these films I have tried to show how the cinematic forms that constitute Renoir's style in this period work to enhance, strengthen, sometimes even create the dramatic substance of the film or to convey a comment or point of view on the characters, their situation, or the world they inhabit. This often involves long and somewhat technical descriptions of particular scenes or shots; for I believe these discussions can be effective only if the reader is able to visualize the scene. I know of no other verbal way to show clearly the relation between form and content in cinema.

The photographs accompanying my text are, almost without exception, frame enlargements taken directly from the films rather than the production stills that illustrate most books on cinema. Thus, their photographic quality may sometimes seem inferior; at times I have had rather worn prints to work with. But this is a small price to pay for the great advantage of having illustrations which present the actual images that Renoir arranged and shot. They are, of course, mere photographs and hence lack an essential element of cinema: movement. Still, I have sought to select and order them so they do more than merely illustrate particular scenes from a film. If I have succeeded, the photographs will convey something of the overall look of each film and the development and evolution of Renoir's style. For a few films I have also tried to provide some sense of the superb performances Renoir has drawn from some of his actors. The photographs are intended as an integral part of the text; I presume that the reader will examine them with at least as much care as he does the words I have written. For these frames are themselves representative of the work of Jean Renoir; my words, even if or when illuminating, are still external to this work.

The early stages of my work on this book coincided, not accidentally, with the planning and presentation of the great Renoir retrospective early in

1969 at the Los Angeles County Museum of Art—the first nearly complete exhibition of the films of Jean Renoir anywhere in the world outside of Paris, and the seminal event in the subsequent new recognition of Renoir in this country. Since then similar programs have been presented in New York, London, and elsewhere. His reputation, almost nonexistent except to a few foreign-film devotees, has grown in the United States since 1965 to approach the esteem he has long enjoyed in France. The culmination of this belated recognition came with a Special Academy Award in 1975. In recent years half a dozen books on Jean Renoir have appeared in this country, some translated from French, some written in English. Most of these offer a survey of his whole career and do not include an extended analysis of any one film. They vary considerably in both insight and accuracy, but neither individually nor collectively do they constitute the sort of intense and detailed analysis that I offer here.

I am not dismayed that my work can no longer pretend to introduce the films of Jean Renoir to Americans, as I once thought it might; it is now possible to see them for yourselves. Sixteen-millimeter-film distributors now list almost all of Renoir's French films in their catalogues. *La Chienne*, after forty-five years, has had a successful run in big-city theatres. Even *Tire au flanc* and *Nuit du carrefour* may not be far behind.

Jean Renoir died on February 12, 1979. Though his last film was completed in 1969, these were not years of idleness. He wrote an autobiography and three short novels, and spent the weekend before he died impatiently waiting to begin work on a new book. He was buried in Burgundy, in Essoyes, the village from which his mother and Gabrielle had come so many years ago and where now, in the village cemetery, Pierre-August and Aline, Pierre, Claude, and Jean Renoir have all found their final rest.

A.S.

Contents

Jean Renoir

Prologue
1894–1924

Jean Renoir: born September 15, 1894, at the Chateau des Brouillards, 13 rue Girardon, on the Butte de Montmartre in Paris, the second son of Pierre-Auguste Renoir and Aline Charigot—whatever his own accomplishments, for many Jean Renoir will always be the "son of the painter." The publication of Jean's rambling family biography, *Renoir*, in 1962 only confirmed this image, particularly in the English translation entitled *Renoir, My Father*, for though it reveals perhaps as much of Jean as of "Renoir" it inevitably casts the son in the shadow of his illustrious father. Still, with the later *My Life and My Films* (1974), it remains the primary source of our knowledge of the early life of Jean Renoir.

By 1894 the revolution in painting had been half-achieved. Manet was dead and highly respected; Van Gogh was dead and still unknown. Impressionist painting had gained recognition but the young intransigents who had become the impressionists were no longer a group. Renoir's period of poverty and obscurity had ended. He could afford an apartment and a studio in Paris, a house in Essoyes, the village in Burgundy from which Aline Charigot had come. He had not yet felt any twinge of the arthritis that would cripple him. Each day, as long as the light was good, he hummed happily in front of his canvas.

Jean Renoir was born into a house full of movement, of warmth, of love —a house where the floors were never waxed because "a child might slip and bark his knee." A house full of women: Mme. Renoir, Mme. Mathieu, various models who seemed to be part of the household and who might be found posing nude in the attic studio or peeling vegetables in the kitchen. And Gabrielle, "my beloved Bibon, who for me was the criterion of everything that was good."[1]

Gabrielle Renard: fifteen years old in the summer of 1894 when she came to Paris from Essoyes to live with her cousin Aline and help with the preparations for the new baby. She stayed to become Renoir's best-known model, but also companion, pack-horse, and font of worldly wisdom for Jean Renoir. "The world in those days was divided for me into two parts. My mother was the tiresome part, the person who ordered me to eat up my dinner, to go to the lavatory, to have a bath in the sort of zinc tub which served for our morning ablutions. And Bibon was for fun, walks in the park, games in the sand-heap, above all piggy-back rides, something my mother absolutely refused to do, whereas Gabrielle was never happier than when bowed down under the weight of my small body."[2]

Gabrielle and Jean roamed through the *maquis*, a sort of wasteland of brambles, rosebushes, and nondescript dwellings that bordered the rue Girardon. They ran up and down the rue Lepic, becoming such a familiar sight in the neighborhood that they began to appear in *Le Rire* in the drawings of Renoir's friend Faivre. Gabrielle gave young Jean his first glimpse of the cinema, at the Dufayel department store in 1897—a venture about which Jean writes, "Scarcely had we taken our seats than the room was plunged in darkness. A terrifying machine shot out a fearsome beam of light piercing the obscurity, and a series of incomprehensible pictures appeared on the screen, accompanied by the sound of a piano at one end and at the other end a sort of hammering that came from the machine. I yelled in my usual fashion and had to be taken out. I never thought that the staccato rhythm of the Maltese cross was later to become for me the sweetest of music."[3]

His introduction to the theatre was less traumatic, coming first at the puppet show, the Tuileries Guignol, and a few years later extending to Sunday matinees at the melodramas of the Theatre Montmartre, with Gabrielle, of course—beginning a lifelong engagement with that false world which often reveals the true.

In a long lifetime measured in friendships rather than events, no one ever held a firmer or warmer place in the heart of Jean Renoir than did Gabrielle. The two were parted at the time of World War I, when Gabrielle married the American painter Conrad Slade. Decades later, their lives rejoined in California, where Gabrielle spent her last years close to Jean, pouring forth those memories that played such a large role in Jean's writing of *Renoir*. In the last paragraph of *My Life and My Films*, written when he was nearly eighty, Jean says of Gabrielle, "Certainly it was she who influenced me most of all. To her I owe Guignol and the Theatre Montmartre. She taught me to realize that the very unreality of those entertainments was a reason for examining real life. She taught me to see the face behind the mask, and the fraud behind the flourishes. She taught me to detest the cliche."[4] Perhaps nothing more clearly reveals the depth of his attachment than the final words of *My Life and My Films*, which Jean once thought of using as the title of this autobiography: "Wait for me, Gabrielle."

In the Renoir household everyone served as a model. Eventually Jean would appear in over a hundred of his father's canvases, most of them painted before that summer day in 1901 when the long red curls that Jean hated, but his father called "Real gold," were finally cut in preparation for Jean's being sent to the Sainte-Croix school after the birth of his younger brother Claude.

Jean was baptized in Saint-Pierre-de-Montmartre, a twelfth-century church now dwarfed by its neighbor Sacre-Coeur, then half-built. Over the years the family moved from rue Girardon to rue de La Rochefoucauld, rue Caulaincourt and, finally, in 1912, Boulevard Rochechouart—a series of addresses that form a rough circle around the home where Jean would live while he made many of his films, an apartment on the Avenue Frochot, a quiet tree-lined street protected from the noise and vulgarity of the modern Place Pigalle by the thickness of a billboard and a wall.

But Montmartre was not the whole world for young Jean Renoir. Soon the accents of the peasants of the Midi and the wine-growers of Burgundy became as familiar to him as that of the art dealers of Paris. Each summer the family went to Essoyes, the village of his mother and Gabrielle. In the winter they travelled south to Grasse, Magagnosc, Le Cannet, Nice, finally settling in Cagnes, where they spent more and more time as Pierre-Auguste Renoir's health declined. In 1907 Renoir bought the little farm called Les Collettes in order to save the magnificent olive trees that the whole world would see, in 1959, in *Le Dejeuner sur l'herbe*.

Jean went to school, of course, but occasionally wandered away and came home, less tired from the walk than from the school he had fled, which made his father think he was probably most suited for manual work. At the school of Sainte-Marie de Monceau he had a second, more pleasant, encounter with cinema during Sunday afternoon projections in the parlor, from which he most remembers a comedian called Automaboul, the film being, perhaps, Méliès' *Automaboulisme et autorité*. Later Jean went to school in Nice, then to the University of Aix, in Aix-en-Provence, studying philosophy and mathematics.

Meanwhile his older brother, Pierre, had won a prize at the Conservatoire de Paris in 1907—the same year in which a Renoir canvas sold for 26,000 francs—and had begun his career as an actor. He appeared in his first film role in 1911, in *La Digue*, the first film directed by Abel Gance, but he had small regard for French cinema.

As a child Jean Renoir had dreamed of being a Napoleonic grenadier; his great joy had been to play with the toy soldiers he called "soltats t' l'Empire." In 1913, out of college, uncertain about a career, he acted out a mem-

Jean Renoir, circa 1920.

ory of this childhood dream by enlisting in the cavalry, intending to become an officer. A year later the outbreak of World War I found him a sergeant in the First Cavalry Regiment at Vincennes, but by early 1915 he had quit the cavalry and gone to the front as a sublieutenant in the Sixth Battalion of the Alpine Infantry. Pierre had already been severely wounded early in the war; he would never fully recover the use of his right arm.

"In April 1915" Jean wrote, "a Bavarian sharpshooter did me the favor of putting a bullet through my leg."[5] It did not seem a favor at the time; the wound became infected and only the intervention of his mother saved his leg and, probably, his life. That mission accomplished, Mme. Renoir returned to Cagnes, tired and ill, and died late in June.

When he was able to walk on crutches, Jean was transferred to a Paris hospital. His father had come from Cagnes to live at the apartment on the boulevard Rochechouart, and here these two cripples came to know each other. Renoir painted; Jean watched. They talked about the war and about Renoir's life, and Jean began that discovery of his father he would describe so well forty years later in *Renoir*.

Once recovered, Jean returned to the war, but now in an airplane, first as an observer, then as a pilot of a reconnaisance plane. Injured again in a landing accident, he spent the last months of the war stationed in Paris, now sharing the boulevard Rochechouart apartment with Pierre, who had returned to his acting career.

In these periods of Paris during the war, Jean's passion for cinema grew. He was excited by *The Mysteries of New York*. A friend returned from leave with news of the "revelation of Charlot" and, as soon as possible, Jean hastened to his first glimpse of Charlie Chaplin. He became, he says, "a fanatical cinema fan."

But when the war ended he returned to Cagnes, to Les Collettes, to live with his father and Claude, who had begun to make ceramics. The gloom that had invaded Les Collettes with the death of Mme. Renoir had been dispelled by the arrival of a young, vivacious new model from Nice, with red-gold hair: Andree Heuschling, called Dédée, who posed for many of Renoir's canvases from 1917 to 1919. Jean learned the craft of ceramics and did what he could to ease the last year of his father's life. A few weeks after Renoir died, Jean and Dédée were married. With Claude they stayed at Les Collettes working at ceramics. Alain Renoir was born in 1922.

When Claude was called to military service, Jean decided to move nearer to Paris. He bought a villa in Marlotte, a village near the forest of Fontainebleau, where his father had painted with Monet, Bazille, Sisley, Pissarro, in the days when they were young intransigents. In Marlotte, Jean built a kiln and resumed his craft of ceramics. Cézanne's son, Paul, soon joined him in Marlotte, moving to the property that would later be the setting for *La Fille de l'eau*. Paris and the cinema were near. Perhaps silver images filled the mind of Jean Renoir, but his hands were still shaping clay.

First Films:
Catherine and *La Fille de l'eau*
1924

> *Every artist begins with a pastiche.*
>
> —*Paul Gaugin*

For French film-makers, the end of World War I opened a period of ferment and renewal. France had been pre-eminent in world cinema before 1910, riding a wave of experiment and exploration launched by the Lumière brothers and George Méliès. But then, much of the inventive genius in the art seemed to locate anew in the United States, while French films faltered. After the war Louis Delluc issued an appeal for a truly French cinema devoted neither to recording stage drama nor to imitating the products of other nations. For many French intellectuals the early works of Abel Gance, Germaine Dulac, Marcel L'Herbier, and Jean Epstein seemed a superb response to this plea, recovering for France a place in the first rank of cinema production. But not for young Jean Renoir, who professed to love only American films and scorned the French works he saw. Hence, despite the fascination of film, Renoir continued to work at ceramics until 1924. This career, undertaken more by chance than choice or design, required a combination of craftsmanship and artistry that he loved, and he was not without talent in the art. Yet he abandoned it without regret, once the path to his true métier seemed open.

Fifteen years later Jean Renoir wrote:

The period after the war was something of a golden age for film lovers. This was the great period of American films. The important theaters despised them, preferring pretentious stupidities clumsily played by out-of-date actors or, indeed, the altogether ridiculous Italian films. American films played in little halls, very cheap. They gave us two or three at a showing, and the program changed twice a week. There were several months when I went to the movies three times a day, which meant that by the time I went to bed I had absorbed seven or eight films, fifty by the end of a week and around two hundred in a month.

The idea of working in cinema never occurred to me. It seemed impossible to me that anything worthwhile could be made in France. These American films that I loved so much, these admirable actors whose play enraptured me; weren't they despised and often even unknown to most of our critics? And I, who dreamed timidly of walking in their footsteps without hope of equaling them, how could I imagine having the least chance in this country of mine where everything is done by routine.

As for going to America, I could never have had the self-assurance to consider that utopian project.

One day, at the Colisée, I saw *Le Brasier ardent*, directed and played by Mosjoukine and produced by the courageous Alexander Kamenka of Albatross Films.

The audience howled and hooted, shocked by this spectacle so different from their usual pablum. I was ravished. At last, I had before my eyes a good film produced in France. Of course, it was made by some Russians, but at Montreuil, in a French environment, under our climate; the film was shown in a good movie-house—without success, but it was shown.

I decided to abandon my métier of ceramics and try to make films.[1]

No doubt other factors entered this decision. Among Jean Renoir's circle of friends many had a passionate interest in cinema, and several, including Jean's older brother Pierre, had already worked in film. Still, seeing *Le Brasier ardent* today, one can easily understand how it precipitated Renoir's move from ceramist to cinéaste. Mosjoukine's film is visually alive and exciting, constructed by cinematic means with little dependence on theater. The story may be incredible, the characters absurd, and the style inconsistent, but such apparent flaws may become a source of renewal in art and great delight for the viewer. And *Le Brasier ardent* moves with a lively pace from a disturbing dream to the plight of the detective hero falling in love with the wife whose fidelity he has been hired to investigate. The action unfolds in fantastic or expressionistic sets, interspersed with a few realistic exteriors, using very rapid montage at times and some of those filmic tricks that Renoir then loved. One can well imagine how its combination of burlesque and drama delighted him.

Stirred by *Le Brasier ardent* to declare at last his own choice of profession and having the resources of a considerable inheritance, Renoir, with his longtime friend Pierre Lestringuez, began to plan a film. Jean and Dédée imagined her as a new Gloria Swanson or Mae Murray. Jean and Lestringuez talked of stories and settings, and of Albert Dieudonné, an actor who had played his first film role in 1908 and who, they thought, was very familiar with the technical aspects of film-making. Renoir devised a story, perhaps vaguely inspired by that *Diary of a Chambermaid* which would become the source of a Renoir film in 1946, and engaged Dieudonné as director, entering the film world himself in the guise of producer and scenarist. But given his ambition and ebullience this was hardly enough; he became an actor as well, then began to meddle in the directing of the film. A rumor spread that Renoir had collaborated in directing *Catherine,* provoking Dieudonné to issue a public statement: "I am the sole director of a screenplay which I composed following an outline imagined by M. Jean Renoir . . . with my collaboration. In addition M. Jean Renoir has financed the film and has been my student. I shall see by his future productions if I have reason to be satisfied."[2]

Renoir did not publicly dispute this claim, but when I recently asked if he had directed any of *Catherine* he replied, "Of course—but I had an agreement with Dieudonné that he would get credit as director." Still, their disagreement grew until the production ended in a lawsuit, whose details Renoir professed not to remember.

When completed, *Catherine* made not a ripple in the ocean of films. Renoir recently wrote, "It was a total failure . . . never shown in any cinema."[3] And Catherine Hessling, years after the production, remarked, "*Catherine,* that ought to be hidden from sight. . . . But what an idea to make that, above all with that Dieudonné, who was not a very reliable sort."[4]

In fact the film was shown, but not until 1927, when Dieudonné re-edited *Catherine* and released it as *Une Vie sans joie.* Distributed by Pierre Braunberger, it played in Paris and London.

Every description of *Catherine* that I have seen is quite inaccurate. Renoir's wife, née Andrée Heuschling, did become Catherine Hessling and play the title role, but Albert Dieudonné does not play the male lead and Catherine is not pursued by a villain. Catherine's misfortunes stem mostly from the activities of a group of society women who closely resemble the sanctimonious matrons in Griffith's *Intolerance.* Dieudonné plays Maurice Laisné, who dies just after he falls in love with Catherine during the carnival in Nice, before the film is half over—a role no larger than that played by Jean Renoir, who provides comic relief as a monocled and hypocritical subprefect. There are several passages of rapid cutting, some rather ineptly handled avant-garde techniques, and a climactic chase after a runaway streetcar along the line that then ran between Grasse and Nice.

The finished film is uneven and rather mediocre. However, given Renoir's professed timidity, we may suspect that just such a dubious project was the path he had to take, an experience necessary to encourage him to dare direct a film himself, without further hesitation. For on the whole the making of *Catherine* had been a pleasant adventure involving work within a group of friends. Undismayed by the outcome of their first cinematic fling, these friends soon planned a second one, this time without Dieudonné.

This was to be *La Fille de l'eau*, devised and written by Renoir and Lestringuez, with Renoir becoming set designer, as well as director. Again Catherine Hessling played the title role, but now with Jean's dog as companion for the first half of the film. Their child, young Alain Renoir, has a sunlit moment before the camera, and Pierre Renoir makes a menacingly satanic appearance. Much of the film was shot in Marlotte, in the village cafe, Le Bon Coin, and on Cézanne's property, La Nicotière, where Jean Renoir constructed a village around the existing buildings.

Thus, though *La Fille de l'eau* has little resemblance to his later works, the manner of its making was already that which would characterize Renoir productions. Almost every Renoir film has been undertaken as a work shared among friends, created in a spirit of cameraderie and informality with the usual sharp distinctions of function and hierarchical lines often becoming very blurred in the process. But this informality, which allows everyone to contribute ideas as well as energy and to feel a part of the creative process, has never weakened Renoir's authority nor smudged the stamp of his personality on his films. There is no doubt that a Renoir film is a *Renoir* film, but this personal expression has never been achieved by insistence on a rigid hierarchy on the set. Rather, the relation between this director and the actors, writers, artists, and technicians whom he often called his accomplices was best identified by Renoir himself when he described his role as that of "le meneur de jeu," a phrase which applies to the ringmaster of a circus, the leader of a game, and also the ringleader of an intrigue or conspiracy.

Narrative and Characterization

Jean Renoir frequently remarked that in order to make a film he had to have a story to tell, and for over fifty years he worked tirelessly and endlessly devising and adapting stories, writing and rewriting the scripts for the films he made and for others that were never realized. But he also said that once you have the story it isn't very important. I believe he meant by this that, essential as it is, the narrative element in a film serves primarily as a framework of continuity within which the more important tasks of the filmmaker can be accomplished. This attitude toward narrative developed in the course of Renoir's career, as did his idea of what these more important tasks are; yet it applies strikingly to the narrative of *La Fille de l'eau*. As in many films of the period, the story is melodramatic and hardly credible, making no effort to present either background or motivation for the characters or even any adequately developed setting for its series of events. The story does not establish a coherent world within which the characters act; rather it merely introduces them, then there follows a series of dramatic or comic interactions loosely connected by transitional scenes that often leave both spatial and temporal continuity quite obscure. But this matters little; for all real interest lies in the individual sequences and the glimpses of innocence and terror, delirium and dream, offered there. The story merely provides some plausibility to the order of these sequences, and finally, in its happy ending, a sort of closure to the emotional ups and downs that have ensued.

The heroine, Virginia (Catherine Hessling), a lonely and very innocent young girl, lives with her father and her uncle Jeff (Pierre Lestringuez) on a barge slowly towed through the canals of France. Her father accidentally drowns and Jeff, introduced as a brute, quickly loses the barge through his debauchery. Virginia is saved from Jeff's evil advances only by the intervention of a passing stranger. She flees with her dog and is befriended by a young poacher, Ferret (Maurice Touzé), who lives with his gypsy mother in a caravan near the village where the very respectable Raynal family have their happy home. Virginia becomes a servant to Gypsy Kate and is introduced by Ferret to a life of minor crime. This idyll persists until a growing enmity between Ferret and a fatuous farmer, Justin Crépoix (Pierre Champagne), culminates in Ferret's setting fire to Justin's haystack. Ferret flees with Gypsy Kate and Virginia's dog, not waiting for Virginia to return from fetching water. Drunk and angry, Justin and his friends burn up the caravan and threaten Virginia as they force her to watch the flames. She finally runs blindly through the night, falls over the edge of a quarry, and becomes delirious. The next morning Georges Raynal (Harold Livingston), who once earlier had saved Virginia and Ferret from Justin's wrath, attempts to help her, but she is too wild and terrified to allow anyone near. That night Virginia dreams of being menaced by Jeff and Justin and rescued by Georges, who carries her off on a white horse across the tree tops. While she dreams, Georges finds her asleep and carries her to the nearby miller's house, where kindness and care open a new life for her. But the brutish Jeff reappears and frightens her into giving him money entrusted to her to pay Georges's saddler. Georges discovers that the bill has not been paid and rides sadly away. Virginia, stricken, resolves that she must tell Georges everything. She meets Jeff again instead; but Georges overhears them and a fight ends with Jeff knocked into the canal. Georges and Virginia embrace and set out into the sunset on a visit to Algeria.

When shown in England, *La Fille de l'eau* was given the title *Whirlpool of Fate*. While hardly an accurate rendering of the French, this seems a more appropriate title. The childish heroine moves through the film passive and uncomprehending, almost never taking any part in the initiation or determination of events. She is whirled through life by accident, chance, the whim or decision of others—by fate. And though she begins as a mariner's daughter, nothing in the film establishes any real connection between Virginia and the water of the French title. For those who know how water appears as element and symbol and vehicle of beauty in later Renoir films, it seems sublimely appropriate that his first film should have been entitled *La Fille de l'eau* and that the first images in this film should be of water sparkling in long perspective, reflecting tree-lined banks. But, though visible in many shots in *La Fille de l'eau*, water, in fact, has little significance in the film. Not until eight years later in *Boudu sauvé des eaux* did Jean Renoir find his true child of the water.

All this is not to say that *La Fille de l'eau* was a failure. In 1924 depth and subtlety of characterization or meaning were seldom sought or achieved in film. And Jean Renoir had then no concern for these qualities in his work. In fact, silent film was not very receptive to efforts at genuine characterization, and many successful films made no such attempt. Characters were one-dimensional, pure good or evil, sheer innocence or deceit: stereotypes of some familiar social class, idealizations or caricatures of some single human trait. The characters of *La Fille de l'eau* fit this tradition: Georges is merely good and kind; Jeff a sheer brute. Minor characters function simply to fill a conventional melodramatic role. That Renoir explicitly disavowed any realization beyond this can be seen in his treatment of Jeff, the villain of the film. Jeff abuses Virginia for no reason at all; he wholly destroys the security of her life on the barge and threatens her new life in the village almost as soon as she has accepted it. Yet no genuinely villainous characteristics are conveyed by Pierre Lestringuez, and any possibility for such is denied by Renoir's juxtaposition of a ludicrous scene of Jeff in the village bar with the somber, dramatically lit night scene of the search for the body of Virginia's father. Though such inconsistency undermines effective characterization, it does not hamper Pierre Lestringuez' success in the conventional melodramatic role of villain. Readily identified by the mere sequence of events in the narrative, this role requires for its realization only that Jeff appear truly menacing in his few scenes of conflict with Virginia. As in all melodrama, the mark of achievement is intensity of expression at given moments, rather than integrated overall characterization.

In the one role where something more might have been expected, that of Virginia, *la fille de l'eau*, Catherine Hessling's portrayal endows the heroine only with youthful vitality and charm and a naive innocence that persists through all the traumas of her life. In 1938 George Franju wrote, "Catherine Hessling, with her beautiful blind eyes, her birdlike walk, resembles one of these strange little gypsies of whom one does not know whether to say she is a fairy or a streetwalker."[5] In *La Fille de l'eau*, with her physical maturity masked by costumes and childish gestures, the childlike side of this actress dominates the performance at the expense of both character and credibility. Virginia accepts the abrupt transition from barge to gypsy caravan, with its life of petty thievery, and then to helper in an honest bourgeois home with equal willingness and lack of comprehension. Her response to Georges's love seems to differ little from her earlier acceptance of Ferret's companionship. Within the story, Virginia does acquire some maturity. She accepts responsibility for her action and realizes that she must openly acknowledge Jeff's existence and her relationship to him. But Hessling's performance does nothing to make visible this growth; it is not her acting, but editing and the use of titles that indicate the change. Given Hessling's portrayal of the girl, only the accident of Georges's overhearing Jeff and Virginia seems to keep Virginia from fleeing again. Catherine Hessling's success in the role lies neither in any attempted characterization nor in any sustained portrayal of action, but rather in the striking images that successively convey Virginia's immediate subjective response to the blows that fall.

The characters of La Fille de l'eau are not lifeless puppets or mere types; they do have individuality. But Renoir achieves this by adding quirks to readily identifiable types, rather than by any real presentation of character. Thus, the Raynals are given identity by the attachment of the person to an object: M. Raynal's car, Georges's horse. Justin's individuation lies in his readiness to anger and bluster. But for his main character, Virginia, Renoir does not add quirks, rather he shapes the whole film to give expression to her reaction to the whirlpool of fate.

Treatment: Style and Form

With the later recognition of Jean Renoir, critics began to view his early films with an eye largely for intimations of the future Renoir. Thus, writers ascribe to La Fille de l'eau an "impressionistic vision of nature" or "rustic realism"; they note a concern with food and drink or the relation of classes, while dismissing those scenes that Renoir must have considered his best in 1924 as "démodée" (old-fashioned) or not nearly as moving as the farms, the bistro on the corner, the old walls and paths. There are, of course, similarities between La Fille de l'eau and later Renoir films, but on the whole this first film little resembles Renoir's mature work. The strongest evocation of a later Renoir occurs in the opening sequence of seven unhurried shots that introduce Virginia in her life on the barge. The very first image, sunlit water reflecting tree-lined banks in the long perspective of the canal, remains a surprisingly fresh and vivid glimpse of nature. And the mastery Renoir later developed in creating visual rhythms by combining camera movement with the movement of objects within the action-space of the film seems already present, as he achieves the felt rhythm of this sequence by movement rather than cutting. The essentially dynamic composition of several of these first shots adds force to the flow of movement; the receding perspectives of canal bank and barge activating diagonal lines of force in deep space which overpower the horizontals and verticals that otherwise dominate the frame. A half-dozen later Renoir films are suggested here, as well as Vigo's *L'Atalante*, which must surely have been influenced by these shots.

But this early promise ends abruptly with the title introducing an almost totally static second sequence, and it is never really renewed in the film despite an occasional shot affirming the reality of nature or the beauty of things. One suspects that the rhythm and dynamism of the first sequence was more a function of the setting of barge and canal than a deliberate choice.

But, if one watches *La Fille de l'eau* as film rather than foreshadowing, its most interesting parts remain those that most interested French audiences in 1925, the night scenes of the burning haystack and caravan, and Virginia's delirium and dream. What one notes most, perhaps, is unevenness. For *La Fille de l'eau* is indeed a pastiche, a collection of unassimilated elements borrowed from the films Renoir had admired in the Paris movie halls. Here and there one sees reflections of Griffith and Chaplin, Lillian Gish and Mae Murray. But the dominant influence is that of the Russian emigrés who had made *Le Brasier ardent*. From them Renoir borrows, not so much specific images, gestures, or characters, as the style of editing that dictates much of the form of *La Fille de l'eau* and also a willingness to mix both genres and visual styles without apparent concern for the consistency of the resulting film.

This taste for mixing styles and genres persisted throughout Renoir's career. As he mastered the techniques of film he began to concoct this mixture so skillfully that it became one of the major elements in what has been called Renoir's "naturalism." He perceived life itself as just such a mixture, and he learned to contrive the mixture so well that in later films the flow from burlesque to moments of great dramatic intensity seems as natural as life itself. Rather than merely borrow from the Russians, Renoir found in *Le Brasier ardent* an expression of one of his own basic attitudes. But in *La Fille de l'eau* the joining of styles was awkwardly managed; the joints show, and the great differences in tone destroy the unity of the film, leaving an impression more of a collection of related fragments than of a cohesive whole.

The Russian style of editing, on the contrary, was handled smoothly by Renoir, but proved only very temporary in his career. A rather rapid montage is the essence of this style, with almost every change in point of view accomplished by cutting rather than camera movement. Both rhythm and action are conveyed primarily through editing, rather than being contained within the shots. This mode of editing carves the action of the film into a large number of fragments of very short duration, with frequent changes of camera angle and distance and frequent repetition of the same setup within a sequence. The rapidity of cutting in *La Fille de l'eau* is indicated by the fact that in its hour and forty minutes the film contains about 775 shots and 75 titles. Not many shots last more than ten seconds; often those that do are interrupted by titles. In each major action sequence the cutting pace accelerates with the mounting action; this acceleration reaching its peak in the scene of Virginia's delirium, at whose climax Renoir puts seventeen shots on the screen in just a fraction over three seconds. This was the most rapid sequence of images Renoir was ever to compose; *La Fille de l'eau* as a whole is the most rapidly cut of all Renoir films. For though it worked well in this film and is familiar as the style of many silent film classics, Renoir found such editing not really suited to his temperament nor his developing sense of how a film should be made. He soon began moving toward the very different mode of editing characteristic of his films of the thirties.

However, he does make good use of the Russian style in *La Fille de l'eau*. The film's most powerful moments, the scenes of the burning of the caravan and Virginia's delirium, depend heavily on rapid cutting for their effect. Other factors help, of course: dramatic lighting with stark contrasts of light and dark, and a recurrence of shots with very dynamic composition marked by strong diagonals. The impact of these dynamic shots gains by their contrast with the static composition that predominates through most of the film. The night setting also heightens the power of these scenes. Renoir had already discovered that by shooting his characters against a black background he could destroy the visual action-space that usually provides orientation for the film viewer. Here the threatening figures have no spatial location but simply loom out of darkness, intensifying our identification with Virginia's terror. But, essentially, pace and rhythm give impact to these scenes. The cutting is rapid throughout, quickening in the fire sequence from shots of 2½-3 seconds (40-50 frames) to shots of 1½ seconds (22-26 frames), finally to 1 second shots (16-18 frames)—though not, of course, as regularly and mechanically as this sounds. With shots this short, very little action can be contained within a shot and still remain comprehensible and coherent. Hence, most of our sense of violent action in this sequence comes from the form of the film rather than from what is actually shown. Cutting rhythm is crucial. But this rapid rhythm of cutting has a counterpoint in a slower rhythm of images; for here, as in the preceding scene of the burning haystack, Renoir gives both clarity and rhythm to his film by grouping shots around central, repeated images. Two recurring images, of the burning caravan and of Virginia cowering before it, join with the brisk cutting to give a complex rhythm to this sequence.

The delirium sequence is even faster in pace, beginning with shots seven frames in length and ending in the crescendo of seventeen three-frame shots. All in all, Renoir combines thirty-one shots in just over twelve seconds, including the two thirty-six-frame shots of Virginia that punctuate the giddy flow of her delirious hallucinations. The remarkable thing about this scene is that it remains completely comprehensible throughout, with every image clear despite the pace. Unlike Eisenstein, who carefully coordinated the composition of successive shots to keep the viewer from being bewildered by his rapid montage, Renoir accomplishes this clarity by building the sequence completely of familiar images, repeating frames from shots used in the fire sequence, then repeating these again within the delirium scene. Having seen each image before, the viewer grasps it immediately; three frames (one-fifth of a second) suffice for comprehension. The result has great impact; a very dramatic scene of extremely fast pace, but totally without confusion. Interestingly, though we recognize each image as a repetition, we do not apprehend the sequence as a flashback. Perhaps the rapidity of cutting accounts for this; each image is merely an image, without motion or action. And perhaps these are necessary to give us a sense of reference to the past. Without them we perceive these images as Virginia's present hallucinations, not as memories or thoughts of the past.

Despite the force of these scenes, that portion of *La Fille de l'eau* which most excited audiences in 1925 was Virginia's dream. Though the film was not a great commercial success, its dream sequence was shown separately by Jean Tedesco at the Vieux Colombier, hailed as avant-garde cinema, then reproduced and widely shown in France as an independent short film. Here Renoir does not rely on especially fast cutting, but rather on the photographic tricks that delighted him then. First, a double exposure in which the dream Virginia, clothed in flowing white gown, detaches herself from the real Virginia, still asleep in the rain. Thereafter, Renoir employs slow motion, accelerated motion, reverse motion, uses miniatures to confuse the scale, tips his camera on its side to give the impression of gravity-defying actions. Finally, he photographed his actors on a white horse running on a treadmill against a dead black background in order to achieve the effect of a ride through the treetops. Through all this Virginia moves with unshaken serenity: "The protagonist is an evanescent female figure who appears and disappears across dream forests, who attends impassively to the most strange and incredible things (the passage of a monster across a metaphysical gallery, the resurrection of a hanged man while the cord around his neck changes to a serpent) . . . like a pretty and idiotic little animal."[6] Jacques Brunius called this sequence one of the few true objectifications of a dream on the screen;[7] it does have a dreamlike quality compounded of incongruity, the suspension of the ordinary laws of nature, the jumbling of familiar objects and strange backgrounds, the trancelike state of Virginia, and, above all, a slow flowing movement whose continuity and apparent inexorability set this sequence off from the rest of the film.

Techniques dominate these scenes. Understandably, perhaps, for Jean

Virginia (Catherine Hessling) dreams of Jeff (Pierre Lestringuez), Justin (Pierre Champagne), and Georges (Harold Lewingston).

Renoir began his new career with a consuming interest in the craftsman's side of film-making. Then, as now, he professed disdain for the "artist" who overflowed with emotion and imagination but had no concern for the manual skills required to construct a real object. The willingness with which Renoir became a student of the mechanics of film is reflected in these remarks, written in 1938: "The sole benefit which I derived from my first naive works was rather good knowledge of the techniques of the camera, lighting, decor, and, above all, of trick pictures."[8] Of these techniques, the most superficial and the most easily learned were the tricks that abound in *La Fille de l'eau*. But elsewhere in this film another basic Renoir attitude finds its first expression. While the characters of *La Fille de l'eau* are shallow and undeveloped, the surroundings in which they move—the barge, the village, the canal—have a convincing authenticity. And these surroundings *contain* the action rather than merely providing a setting for it. A full integration of character and environment was to become a mark of the mature Renoir films. This integration was not achieved in *La Fille de l'eau*, where neither characters nor environment are whole—but there was at least a hint of the direction to be taken, a direction that Renoir himself was soon to recognize explicitly.

tragic catalyst within the action.

397 The rabbits become the object of Robert's displaced aggressivity, & therefore his attraction to Marceau? Marceau after all precipitates André's death. Robert's affection for Marceau may have to do with his success at poaching, i.e. women, rabbits and men, and Schmacher's failure to control the rabbits or his wife.

(Note the analogies between sexual relations and animals.)

Is Renoir advocating violence? Certainly the synopsis to the "Versailles" indicate a predilection to resolution through violence.

405 Christine, as the daughter of a conductor, ressembles the music boxes Robert collects, confirm her position as his posess—

405 By doubling his characters, Renoir can have them confronted with their own weaknesses, as Robert, jealous husband who can't act conclusively, is faced with finding

395   The Rules of the Game begins with "Robert refus[ing] to play Claudio", and ends with his frantic & finally tragic performance as Claudio, serving as the ironic master of ceremonies over the last part of the film (ironic in that his action provoked the action and yet he is totally unable to control the course of events, and is perhaps unwilling to) and delivering the last word which seals Andre's fate and judgement on his death.

The "Rules of the Game" is about the failure of will, the cowardice that evade decisive & conclusive action; it is a film about tragic _____ . The "game" referred to is the love chase—cum-hunt, and simultaneously the house duels, all of these serving as evocations of the impending European war.

Simultaneously, Robert's failure is parralled by Octave's, who also serves as a

2

Nana
1926

*From the time that I started working in cinema there have
been two things I hoped to do: to make films free from the
sentimentality that filled the movies I saw, and to destroy the
cliches that pervade both films and life.*
                                                    —*Jean Renoir*

The completion of *La Fille de l'eau* must have assured Jean Renoir of the
correctness of his choice of career and greatly strengthened his confidence as
a film-maker. While this first film did not revolutionize French cinema, nor
make any money, it was shown and seen and praised in reviews. Buoyed by
this modest success and inspired by a chance viewing of von Stroheim's
Foolish Wives, Renoir began planning a much more ambitious work. He
always acknowledged the general influence of Chaplin, Griffith and Stiller
on his early films, but the impact of von Stroheim was more direct and
striking. In 1938 Renoir wrote:

> It was enormous luck which, in 1924, led me into a hall where a film of
> Eric von Stroheim's was being projected. The film, *Foolish Wives*,
> astounded me. I must have seen it at least ten times.
>   Burning with admiration, I understood how I had gone astray until
> then. Ceasing my foolish accusation of the public's supposed lack of
> understanding, I glimpsed the possibility of making contact with the
> public by the projection of authentic subjects in the tradition of French
> realism. I started to look around me and, amazed, I discovered many
> things purely French quite capable of transposition to the screen. I be-

gan to ascertain that the gesture of a laundress, of a woman combing her hair before a mirror, of a street-merchant in front of his cart, often had an incomparable plastic value. I made again a sort of study of French gesture across the paintings of my father and the artists of his generation. Then, strengthened by my new acquisitions, I made my first film worth the trouble of discussing, *Nana*, after Zola's novel.[1]

Renoir has often remarked on his tendency to be influenced by others, to change course as a result of someone else's work or views. Like others, I had assumed that von Stroheim's influence had been to turn Renoir toward naturalism or realism. But *Nana* is less naturalistic, more stylized, than *La Fille de l'eau*. *Foolish Wives* is certainly not a naturalistic film, and while it follows the practice of "realism" in modern literature by stressing the sordid aspects of human affairs, von Stroheim indulges a taste for the bizarre and grotesque that goes well beyond what might sensibly be termed realistic. After seeing *Foolish Wives* recently, I asked Renoir what had so excited him in it, remarking that the film hardly seemed to me to be realistic. "Of course not," he replied, then explained that he had discovered in *Foolish Wives* the possibility of creating within a film a world that might differ greatly from reality but still would be experienced as having a wholeness and coherence like that of the world we live in. This prospect, of creating a world with the feel of authenticity, in which characters might have the solidity of life, had set him to observing closely the details of the life around him; for he sensed that the basis for coherence of the world within a film must be veracity of detail.

I suspect that another discovery Renoir made in his repeated viewings of *Foolish Wives* was the possibility of a visual style quite different from that he had sought to create in *La Fille de l'eau*—a different pattern of constructing and editing action, more continuous, less fragmented. It was not, of course, that Renoir had never seen such a style before, but rather, having now made a film, he saw films in a new light. As he himself remarked about his diminishing taste for American films, "Then, having become a goldsmith myself, I began to discover flaws in the metal."

Narrative and Treatment

Emile Zola's novel of the rise and fall of a great courtesan, before whose rampant sexuality men became willing slaves, strips bare the upper levels of Parisian society during the Second Empire, revealing lust, deceit, cruelty, hypocrisy, and pretension as the reality underneath the surface glamour and decorum. Zola's heroine, Nana, destroys, corrupts, and humiliates the men who surround her, driven by forces she neither controls nor understands—forces vaguely related by Zola to the sordid squalor of the degraded generations from which she sprang.

Jean Renoir while shooting *Nana,* 1926.

As a vehicle for the screen, the novel presents difficulties both in scope and detail. Dozens of characters swarm through its pages, many of them never clearly emerging from the clusters in which they always appear. Such details as Nana's narcissistic adoration of her own nude body, caressing and admiring herself before a mirror while Count Muffat looks on, were beyond the limits of even French cinema in 1926. But Renoir, in his first attempt at transposing a literary work into film, already displays the attitude that marks such efforts throughout his career: he seeks to make a film, not to film a novel. In an interview he explained, "It was necessary either to reproduce the novel completely, with its innumerable characters, or to condense the subject, conserving only the principal persons while still not misrepresenting the character of the work. It is the latter path that I have taken."[2]

Having made this choice, Renoir cuts freely through the novel, eliminating most of the first half and building his film around Nana's moments in the theater and her affairs with three men: Muffat, Vandeuvres, and Georges Hugon. The unending stream of men that flows through Nana's bedroom has disappeared, as have all of the ugly details of Nana's career as a whore and most of the bores whose empty chatter fills the Countess Muffat's Tuesdays. With these go most of Zola's social criticism, except by implication; taken by itself, the film presents the portrait of a destructive woman much more than of a degenerate society.

The film moves swiftly from a rather comic introduction to a series of disasters: Nana (Catherine Hessling) triumphs as Venus on the stage of Bordenave's (Pierre Lestringuez) theatre, displaying more sex appeal than talent. After the performance, the cynical Bordenave brings Count Muffat (Werner Krauss), chamberlain to the emperor, to Nana's dressing room. Nana, half-dressed, postures from behind a screen; Muffat, stiff and formal, "embarrassed to be seen for the first time in his life in the dressing room of an actress," appears transfixed, but recovers sufficiently to perform his first service for Nana, bringing her a comb when her servant fails to respond to her request.

With theatrical ambitions that far outrun her talent, Nana covets the leading role in Bordenave's new production. But the actors respond with laughter and catcalls to her announced desire for the part. This derision leads Nana to persuade Muffat to buy the role for her; but on opening night "La Petite Duchesse" is a flop. When Muffat brings Count Vandeuvres (Jean Angelo) and his young nephew Georges Hugon (Raymond Guérin) back-stage, they find Nana in the midst of a tantrum. Georges immediately falls in love with Nana.

Nana abandons the stage to exploit her true talent, sex. Muffat installs her in a luxurious townhouse, while Georges follows her about like a faith-ful dog as she squanders Muffat's fortune. Vandeuvres calls to rebuke Nana for corrupting Georges, but quickly becomes an aspiring lover himself. At the race track Vandeuvre plots to fix a race and make the fortune he knows it will take to persuade Nana to leave Muffat. But a mistake leads to expo-sure and ruin for Vandeuvres. Scorned by Nana, he warns Muffat of "the golden fly that poisons everything it touches." But Muffat continues up the stairs. Nana, amused when Muffat enters her bedroom resplendent in his chamberlain's costume, then makes him bark like a dog, sit up, roll over, play dead, as her servants watch with ill-concealed disgust. Georges, who has himself been refused by Nana and has overheard her treatment of both Vandeuvres and Muffat, stabs himself with a pair of scissors and falls to the floor in Nana's wardrobe, disrupting her game of humiliating Muffat. Van-deuvres locks himself in with his horses, drinks poison, and sets fire to the stable.

When Nana grows distraught over these events, her "comrades from the theatre" come to console her. They chatter gaily and persuade Nana to ac-company them to the Bal Mabille. Muffat, faithful through every degrada-tion, comes to comfort the grieving Nana but finds her insolent servants banqueting instead. They laugh at his reproaches, tell him Madame has gone to the dance hall. At the Bal Mabille, Nana sits glumly, then gulps drink after drink and joins the chorus to dance a wild can-can. Muffat finds her and admonishes her for living only for pleasure. She cries, "Do you think this amuses me?" and drives him away. Finally she has a convulsion and is carried off by her theatre friends.

As Nana lies ill, Muffat sits dejectedly on a bench amid falling leaves out-side of her house, watching as her servants abandon her, stealing all they can carry. A doctor comes from Nana's room and identifies her ailment as smallpox. The theatre group cringes in fright, but Muffat stolidly climbs the stairs once more, to have Nana die in his arms seeing visions of Georges and Vandeuvres.

Characterization

In his novel Zola describes Nana's performance in the third act of *Blond Venus* in these terms:

> Scarcely was Diana alone, when Venus appeared. A shiver of delight ran through the house. Nana was nude. With a cool audacity, sure of the sovereign power of her flesh, she stepped forth in her nakedness . . . There was no applause, and no longer any laughter. Men leaned forward with serious faces, features sharp, mouths pinched and parched. It seemed as if a wind had passed, a soft, soft wind, heavy with secret menace. Suddenly, in the saucy child the woman stood revealed, full of restless suggestion, bringing with her the delirium of sex, opening the gates of an unknown world of desire. Nana still smiled, but bitterly now; the smile of a devourer of men . . . A wave of lust had flowed from her as from some excited animal; its influence spreading, spreading until it possessed the whole audience. Then her slightest movement flickered the flame of desire; with her little finger she ruled over men's flesh . . . her sexual nature strong enough to destroy the whole throng of adorers and yet sustain no injury.[3]

Sex incarnate, Zola's Nana is a goddess, or, as Muffat suspects, the devil. Incapable of fidelity, with an insatiable appetite for men and luxury, she uses sex as a weapon, a tool, a commodity. Still, the men she devours afford her neither fulfillment nor joy. By turns good-natured, cruel, vulgar, generous, grasping, impetuous, submissive, arrogant, Nana retains a sort of innocence in her inability to recognize or accept responsibility. At last, in the novel, she becomes an almost impersonal destructive force, laying waste to all of Paris.

Renoir's film does not accord Nana the same scope of destructiveness. But the very first shot of Nana announces the great distance between this character and the pure and innocent heroine of *La Fille de l'eau*. The camera angles upward at Bordenave and Nana in the flies of the theatre, preparing for Nana's descent to the stage as Venus. As Bordenave adjusts the rope, Nana's gestures uncover her leg from toe to thigh. This flash of flesh sets the tone for Hessling's performance, but the erotic promise of this first shot remains unfulfilled. Nana cunningly uses her body to attract and control the men who may gratify her whims; the willingness with which they undergo almost any degradation at her hands testifies to the power of the sexual spell she weaves. Yet sexuality seems not at all the key to Hessling's performance; her postures, gestures, movements are feminine, but seldom truly erotic.

This Nana, created by Jean Renoir and Catherine Hessling, becomes neither goddess nor devil, never seems the sheer elemental force of nature that Zole's heroine does. Renoir's Nana may be heartless, coy, tearful, domineering, petulant, sulky or disdainful; but her predominant characteristic seems sheer willfulness, an almost compulsive determination to impose her will on others, to satisfy her slightest desire at no matter whose cost. Yet, even in her most cruel and destructive moments—or when most seductive, if one can judge by the reactions of the men in the film—a sort of childishness pervades the character. In Nana's actions one glimpses a little girl playing at being a woman, simultaneously confident of the power of her gesture and yet innocent of any harm, because it is only play.

Unless we perceive this childishness as a central element in Nana's character, Catherine Hessling's acting in the role must appear ludicrous or totally inept. Every gesture seems exaggerated to the point of destroying credibility, the whole performance greatly overdone. And since no other actor in the film plays in the same excessive style, Hessling's performance cannot be dismissed as merely the sort of overacting demanded by the conventions of silent films. However, if one sees that Nana (not Catherine Hessling!) often acts like a little girl pretending to be a woman, this complicates the character but renders the performance understandable.

If we accept this childishness as integral to the character of Nana, the coherence and seriousness of the film can be maintained, the excesses of the performance understood. A child playing at being an adult overdoes every gesture. Little boys pretending to be men adopt an exaggeratedly masculine stance, speak in an excessively gruff voice. But Nana is not a child, hence the very ambiguous sexuality of the role. Gestures that would be erotic change their character when overdone. In a child this becomes comic. But in the film a woman's body performs the gestures, not a child's; hence the duality of much of the performance, on the edge of both comedy and sexuality. Mae West often overacts in a similar way, yet her voice and her remarks maintain the sexuality of the character while rendering the gestures comic. She seems both genuinely comic and sexual, whereas in Catherine Hessling's performance comedy often seems out of place and sexuality rarely attained.

But *Nana* is not a bedroom comedy, and Nana not a simply, honest whore. Rather, a consistent performance by Catherine Hessling gives rise to a shifting perception of the character portrayed. At first, the combination of childishness, comedy and sex gives Nana a certain charm. She is sprightly, coy, a young actress flustered at the unexpected appearance of a count in her dressing room, and putting on an act to cover her self-consciousness. But the childishness continues where comedy becomes inappropriate; when Nana persists in the same arch gestures while destroying the men who pursue her, she becomes repulsive. When Muffat grovels on the floor under her feet, we feel more repelled by the mindless cruelty of Nana's gay and playful commands than we are disturbed by the humiliation of this once-proud man. Ultimately, she becomes pathetic, destroying herself as senselessly as she did others. When, at the Bal Mabille, she cried to Muffat, "Do you think this amuses me?" the sincerity of this cry points up the falsity of her every other moment. For no gesture or action of Nana's seems genuine or spontaneous; all are posed, acted. Like the protagonist of Dostoyevsky's "Notes from Underground," Nana seems constantly in need of the presence of another person whose reactions will affirm her own reality and power. Every move appears as a contrived production presented to this other, rather than as a natural expression. When none of her admirers is present, Nana's servants provide the audience she requires. She becomes pathetic when we discover that her actions are not contrived to deceive or impress another, but are a necessity welling up from her own insecurity—they are as genuine as she can be!

For many viewers this outline of the character of Nana will seem much clearer than what they find in the film. The performance does get in the way. But my unwillingness to dismiss Hessling's acting as ludicrous stems from my confidence that this performance does embody Jean Renoir's conception of the role. When I remarked once that Hessling's performance seemed quite unlike any other in the film, Renoir responded, "Well, you know at that time Catherine Hessling was my wife. Perhaps I was able to influence her a little more than the others." The character differs considerably from Zola's Nana, but the basic childishness of the characterization is suggested in the novel. I suspect that Renoir found this childishness in Catherine Hessling and built the role upon it.

Thus conceived, this character falls short of full achievement in Renoir's *Nana;* one must work it out, rather than just find it on the screen. Nevertheless, Nana marks a significant moment in Renoir's career, for she is the first edition of a series of women who will live in Renoir films, the later ones more completely, more subtly, more deeply embodying characteristics Renoir sought to bring to life here. The willful destroyer, the little girl playing at womanhood, the performer whose life lies in the creation of a spectacle— from *La Chienne* to *Elena et les hommes*, a dozen characters have their beginning in Nana, though all of them are more complex and more human than she.

The male characters in *Nana* are less puzzling and less interesting. Renoir had learned from von Stroheim that a consistent performance, sustained throughout, could give life to the people in a film, however unreal the characters might be. For *Nana* he appears to have formed a conception of each character and worked out a mode of acting, a transcription in gesture, movement, and facial expression, that would fit or embody the character. Each of these modes tends toward stylization. Understandably, for styliza-

Count Muffat (Werner Krauss)
meets Nana (Catherine Hessling).
With Bordenave (Pierre Lestringuez), Zoe (Valeska Gert), and
François (Harbacher).

tion assures the consistency of the performance, and, beyond that, the
"proper" style should also assure correctness of characterization and the
lack of sentimentality that Renoir sought. In *Nana* he achieves these goals;
yet the result is an almost total disaccord of acting styles that hampers our
acceptance of any real interaction between the characters. Catherine Hessling plays Nana with restless mobility; her movements do not flow but
seem to oppose each other, tend to start and stop. She gestures broadly but
jerkily, almost like a mechanical toy. Her expression, always intense, is also
always ready to change. The rhythm of her performance is ragged and un-

even, surging and subsiding. In contrast, Werner Krauss as Count Muffat seems almost immobile; his style is heavy and slow, his movements ponderous, inexorable. Merely raising his eyes from the floor to meet the glance of another seems to require great effort. Krauss never smiles, seldom gestures except defensively; his most effective change of expression is to open his unblinking, agonized eyes a bit wider.

The character conveyed by this style has both strength and weakness: Count Muffat is stolid, humorless, sure of his own being but also unsure of his actions and totally unable to resist any of Nana's whims. His most typical positions are to stand erect, solid, motionless, but with eyes averted downward; or to walk slowly forward, unblinking, as if to meet his apportioned doom.[4]

Krauss's enormous gravity makes Hessling's effusive performance seem even more excessive and tends to diminish the impact of Nana's cruelty. From his first encounter with Nana, Krauss plays Muffat as a man destined by fate for degradation. His need for self-abasement seems so great that we can hardly blame Nana for gratifying it. In the novel Muffat seems hopelessly ensnared in his adoration of Nana, but also aware that the sinfulness of this liaison cries out for punishment. In the film the religious side of Muffat's character has disappeared, but the very consistency of Krauss's ponderous performance finally gives Muffat an unexpected power and stature. Unlike Emil Janning's Professor Rath in *The Blue Angel*, Muffat transcends his humiliation in the final scenes of *Nana*. Debased and rejected, scorned even by the servants, Muffat still waits patiently, climbs the great stairway again, at the same pace, with the same expression; becoming an image of faithfulness—steadfast, noble, selfless far beyond both the deserts of Nana's caprice and the reach of her sting.

The role of Georges Hugon, played by Raymond Guérin, is stylized in the direction of hesitance and self-effacement, a style that emphasizes the weakness of the character. Georges always appears to be cringing toward the background or to be on the verge of an action he doesn't quite dare to perform. He always walks behind others, with drooping posture, never quite standing erect. His gestures are timid in advancing, quick in retreat—limp, as compared to the crisp gestures of Nana.

Each of these three styles, as adopted by Hessling, Krauss, and Guérin, respectively, provides a core for the characterization, a set of basic traits that persist in the character through a variety of situations and actions. Thus, the stylization assures both continuity and identity for the character. Problems arise, however, when characters meet. Here the puzzle is: how could Nana, whom men adore, possibly be attracted at all by these two, both totally lacking in the vitality with which she crackles and without any overt virility to which her flamboyant femininity might respond?

With the third of the men in Nana's life, Vandeuvres, the problem is reversed. Jean Angelo plays Vandeuvres in a nearly naturalistic manner, supple, graceful, with a slight overemphasis of gesture that functions only to affirm the gestures rather than becoming a pattern of stylization. Handsome, alert, poised, Vandeuvres views the world with an ironic eye which seems to cut through the illusions that envelop Muffat and Georges. He is easily the most attractive and masculine of the trio, and we can readily understand Nana's interest in him. But—how could this man disgrace himself for *her?* We can, I think, understand how the falsity and childishness of Nana could be fascinating to both Georges and Muffat, who in different ways are childish too. But Vandeuvres—worldly and clear-eyed . . . ?

If we simply accept the lines of attraction as they occur in the film, the fall of Muffat and Georges seems inevitable; they cannot help being overwhelmed by Nana. But even granting Vandeuvres' love for Nana, his actions surprise us. Here again, one sees the advantages of stylization: without it Vandeuvres' character seems to fall apart.

Thus, the characterizations in *Nana* cannot really be said to succeed, for their conjunction tends to demolish them. Nevertheless, the film is a considerable achievement. In one leap Renoir had gone from the simplicity of *La Fille de l'eau* to this vast international production, and at the same time he had undertaken that most difficult of tasks in silent film, to make a work whose substance was characterization and whose characters had some degree of depth and complexity.

With the characters basically drawn from Zola, Renoir perceived that stylization was the path to endowing them with life and depth. But given the absence of speech and its individuating value, he may also have felt that stylization would diminish individuality in his persons, leaving, alas, only types, however alive they might be. This, perhaps, led to the adoption of a multiplicity of styles, based on the hope that in this way the people in the film might take on life while remaining distinct individuals. Unfortunately, the experiment does not quite succeed; the clashing styles tend to destroy each other. But in this failure lies the germ of later success. The mixture of divergent acting styles to achieve individuality works brilliantly in later Renoir films—think of von Stroheim, Fresnay, Gabin, Dalio, and Carette in *Grand Illusion*. There, of course, sound plays an essential role. But there, too, we find acting styles rather than the stylization of characters; the style being in the service of the person portrayed rather than providing his basic structure.

After the commercial failure of *Nana*, Renoir never again attempted a serious silent film whose core was character-study. Only when his actors could talk did he return to this problem and make it central in his work.

Style and Form

Faced with the nineteenth-century urban setting of Zola's novel, Renoir and his designer, Claude Autant-Lara, conceived sets and costumes whose stylization contributes to the coherence of the film and helps create that world within the film that Renoir now sought.[5] And, of at least equal importance, Renoir began in *Nana* to develop the style of shooting his scenes that made these elements of decor a dramatic rather than merely an incidental aspect of the film.

In *La Fille de l'eau* the dominant tone of the design had been simplicity. Shot mostly in natural exteriors, the film had used just a few, small interior settings, and the costumes indicated only differences of class and age, not individuality. However, though the space of the canal, village, and sur-

From theatre to townhouse. Nana and Bordenave, Fauchery (Claude Autant-Lara), Rose Mignon (Jacqueline Ford), Count Muffat, Count de Vandeuvres (Jean Angelo), Georges Hugon (Raymond Guerin-Catelain).

rounding countryside is never clearly delineated, there is a sense of spatial openness and freedom in the film, with the action moving through fifteen or twenty different locations. In details of form, though Renoir's editing of *La Fille de l'eau* had been rather avant-garde, the pattern of camera setups was largely conventional. Most scenes begin with an establishing long shot, followed by full and medium shots, then close-ups, with the camera nearly always level and rarely moving. Overall, *La Fille de l'eau* consists predominantly of three-quarter and full shots, long shots occurring where the scope of the action requires them for clarity, with medium to big close-ups for

dramatic intensity and to pick out details of the action. Where two or three characters appear in the same shot, they tend to be in the same plane, the same distance from the camera.

In *Nana* much of this begins to change. Rather than natural locations, Renoir worked almost entirely on immense sets with decor and costumes designed to become expressive elements in the film. Costumes reflect character as well as status: Muffat usually dresses in somber black; Vandeuvres wears a white suit when he is most hopeful of winning Nana; and the neutral gray of Georges's clothes help him fade invisibly into the background in Nana's vast rooms. The two occasions when Muffet departs from his sober dress are significant. When he appears at the theatre wearing a checkerboard cape, the wildness of this attire matches the madness of the action he then undertakes in buying the role of La Petite Duchesse for Nana. And he glistens in his gold-embellished chamberlain's uniform when Nana forces him to play dead dog, the glitter of the gold reflecting the depth of his degradation. The major actions of *Nana* occur in only four locations: the race track and three large interiors—the theatre, then Nana's town house, and, more briefly, the Bal Mabille. These interiors, though very distinct, share the quality of being vast but confined spaces of indeterminate shape and dimensions, each visually quite complex, though in different ways. The spatial coherence that this similarity creates in the film sustains the feeling of melancholy grandeur left by the oppressive, cavernous spaces of Nana's town house in the latter two-thirds of the film. These huge, luxuriously decorated rooms, with monumental stairway, towering draped walls, and ornate mosaic floors, engulf and imprison the people in the film, as Nana engulfs the men who seek her love. However vast they may be, these spaces offer no breath of freedom; they are designed and photographed to appear closed, however remote the point of closure. In the interior sets one feels the influence of German expressionist cinema, as, of course, in the acting of Werner Krauss.

Beyond these surface matters, Renoir's style had begun to change; rather, he had begun to form a style of his own. Over much of the film the cutting remains fairly rapid, though never matching the pace of *La Fille de l'eau*. Parts of Renoir's first film had been edited in a manner close to that Eisenstein would adopt, where the sharp contrast between successive images produces a shock at each cut; in *Nana* editing tends to follow the action quietly. With much less motion created by editing, and more action and motion within the shots, cutting more frequently coincides with movement and becomes invisible. Given some general slowing of pace—*Nana* runs about twenty-five minutes longer than *La Fille de l'eau* and contains about twenty-five fewer shots—the hand of the editor has become much less apparent. More significantly, early in *Nana* one finds the first Renoir shot sustained long enough to include the whole of an action, a scene with Fauchery and Countess Muffat, filmed in a single shot of over seven hundred frames (forty-five seconds). In the edited film this shot is interrupted by an insert after five hundred frames and even then seems rather static after the flow of images that preceded it. But, two sequences later, as Nana persuades Muffat to secure the role of La Petite Duchesse for her, Renoir films the central action of the scene in a single shot of over eight hundred frames. His camera remains motionless, but now Renoir creates enough movement in depth within the action-space of the film to keep the shot alive for its whole fifty seconds. Here, for the first time, two elements of what will become Renoir's mature camera style have been combined: a shot of long duration with rhythmic motion in depth within the shot.

Though there are even fewer shots in *Nana* than in *La Fille de l'eau* which use a moving camera, in these few a new rationale is apparent. Camera movement suddenly has a dramatic or formal significance, rather than being merely a way to follow the action. The first camera movement in *Nana* occurs about a quarter of the way through the film. After her failure in acting an honest woman, Nana storms angrily down a corridor of the theatre to her dressing room, the camera traveling along the corridor following her. Then Renoir repeats exactly the same camera movement, but slowly, in the very next shot, as Muffat, Georges, and Vandeuvres come from the theatre to see Nana. Though both shots could have been filmed with a fixed camera, Renoir instead discovered a formal means to make a dramatic point. Formally, the shots are alike except for the speed of the camera movement, but this difference underlines both Nana's fury and the funereal march of her hesitant swains.

After this event Nana quits the theatre; the following scene finds her established in her luxurious town house. But instead of a conventional establishing shot of this new location, Renoir devised a very different opening for the scene. The shot begins with an iris close-up of an ornate cupid carved on the headboard of Nana's bed. As the iris opens, the camera tilts down to the bed, then slowly tracks back, revealing the immense bed as packages fall on it; continues back the length of the enormous room, disclosing Nana and Georges by the bed, laden with packages; finally, the camera takes in the whole rich and bizarre decor, with the actors dwarfed in the vast space of the hangar in which the set was built. This camera movement is reversed with great effect at the end of the film. Nana, with smallpox, clutches Muffat in fear of death, the two small figures lost at one end of the huge bed. The camera travels slowly forward to medium shot; in this room its movement seems as inexorable as the death that Nana awaits.

Such shots indicate how fast Renoir was learning film techniques, as do the greatly increased variation of camera angles and a new freedom in relation to conventional scene construction. A growing dynamism of frame design or composition also appears. He now begins to divide the frame with horizontals or arrange his actors in depth and photograph them in compositions whose basic structure resembles that of his father's paintings. The tricks that flourished in *La Fille de l'eau* have completely disappeared in *Nana*. This, with the unobtrusive editing, led one French critic to write of Renoir's "disdain for technique." Such remarks are far afield; Renoir was extremely interested in technique at this time and just beginning to acquire that mastery of technique which marks his later work. Despite his own words, Renoir has never disdained technique, but with *Nana* he had begun to feel that it should be subordinated to the needs of drama and expression in the film. He had taken his first steps toward his films of the thirties, where great technical originality and virtuosity become wholly unobtrusive in the finished film.

Noel Burch, in his *Theory of Film Practice,* calls *Nana* "a key film in the development of cinematic language" because of its systematic use of off-screen space, claiming that it "marks the first structural use of it." *Nana* does exploit the possibilities of off-screen space, perhaps even more than Burch's discussion suggests, but I have not stressed this formal aspect of the film because it was not an innovation in *Nana,* nor, I believe, an especially influential element in the film. I do not claim to know what film marks the *first* such use, but a very conscious and systematic structural use of off-screen space occurs in D. W. Griffith's *The Lonedale Operator,* made in 1911, where one can find examples to match almost all of those Burch cites from *Nana.* Though the first awareness of off-screen space in cinema probably dates from 1896, when the Lumiere cameraman Promio first set his camera in a moving gondola in Venice, I suspect that Griffith, much more than Renoir, should be credited with the discovery and exploration of off-screen space. After all, the existence of such space is a presupposition of the famous Griffith last-minute rescue.

Uneven and awkward in spots, *Nana* was still a great advance for Renoir. Influences are apparent, but rather than copying others, Renoir now could assimilate what he found and incorporate it into a coherent, finished work which clearly displays the marks of his mind and hand. This is evident not only in the first appearance of forms and elements of style that he would later develop, but more obviously in the importance in *Nana* of several themes that Renoir would explore throughout his career: First, the question of class or caste, which appears in many Renoir films in the interaction between servants and masters. Here, the most frivolous and destructive of Nana's antics occur with the servants, Zoe and Francis, as silent witnesses. The worlds of servant and master remain separate, but the servants both despise and imitate their masters, as is clear in the climactic scene when Muffat interrupts the servant's banquet. Second, the question of how people meet, the context of their encounters and how, within the encounter, they create a relationship that may endure. Renoir handles Nana's meetings with Muffat, Georges, and Vandeuvres each in a different way. For the first he cuts between Nana, Muffat, Zoe, and Francis, with Nana and Muffat never appearing in the same frame until the end of the sequence, when Muffat brings Nana her comb. When Nana meets Georges, Renoir constructs a little hesitant ballet of movement in the corridor of the theatre. In her encounter with Vandeuvres, he indulges his taste for mixing genres, injecting a burlesque bit of business into a scene that began with Vandeuvres irate and Nana defensive and feigning tears. Taken in by Nana's fake tears, Vandeuvres puts his hand over hers to comfort her. She responds and very quickly they are launched on the old comic routine of piling on hands. But instead of letting this destroy the scene, as it might, Renoir converts it into an instrument to both forward and express the changing relation between Nana and Vandeuvres. As their spontaneous gestures become the first movements in a comedy routine, Vandeuvres and Nana both recognize this and turn their gestures into a game they play together. By the time it is over, they are allies instead of antagonists. The scene ends with Nana kissing Vandeuvres passionately just as Muffat appears outside.

A third enduring Renoir interest which finds its first expression in *Nana* is his love of the theatre and his desire to incorporate elements from the theatre into film. Not merely a desire to make films based on theatrical sources, though he had done that, and certainly not to film theatrical performances, Renoir's wish has been to contain, within a film, action of or from the theatre and do this in a wholly cinematic way while still not vitiating the air of spectacle that pervades the theatre. From *Nana* on, Renoir begins to include in his films not only characters living their lives, but also *performers*, characters who *within their lives* give performances that are deliberately devised, rehearsed and presented to an audience. He explores the relation between life and performance, the way in which one's life enters into the performance or the way in which the acts that shape or express one's life tend to become performances. Though it begins with *Nana*, this interest of Renoir's was not to be fully indulged until the 1950s, with *The Golden Coach* and *French Can-Can*.

In *Nana*, Renoir uses the opening sequence in the theatre for two purposes beyond that of mere introduction: as a light-comedy overture to a film that will steadily darken, and to provide evidence that all of Nana's life is a performance. The device used here, of allowing us to see that a character's actions and movements do not change even though conditions radically alter, is one Renoir would use again. Near the end of *Nana* he stages another spectacle, the dance at the Bal Mabille, which now looks so much like a preview of the finale of *French Can-Can*, nearly thirty years later. In *Nana*, as in the later film, he effectively combines very long shots, with the dancers far off, seen through a smoky atmosphere across scores of spectators in the foreground, and close-in shots that capture first the rhythm and spirit of the dance and then the hysteria that has seized Nana at this moment. And here occurs the first enactment of a major Renoir theme: a character turns to art, a spectacle, a performance, as a refuge from, and sometimes even a solution to, life's problems. For Nana the performance that has been her life now has failed; at the Bal Mabille she attempts to lose herself, her personality, her life as an individual, within the spectacle, the dance— and perhaps she succeeds for a brief moment. She is the first of many Renoir characters for whom, at crucial moments, some sort of performance seems the only hopeful act—it is a recurrent note in his work. *La Fille de l'eau* and

Degradation and death, separated by a spectacle, the dance at the Bal Mabille.

the little match girl have only dreams with which to confront their unbearable reality, but for Renoir art, spectacle, some sort of immersion in the play of a role becomes the central way. Camilla in *The Golden Coach* and Nini in *French Can-Can* are merely the most obvious cases; in retrospect, Batala in *Le Crime de M. Lange* may appear the greatest performer of them all.

Nana played on the Paris boulevards for several weeks and had some suc-

cess in Germany. But though some critics recognized its power and originality, this serious period film, devoid of both the sentimentality of French
commercial cinema and the flashy techniques of the avant-garde, never
really touched the public as Renoir had dreamed it would. With its great
cost, the film was, as Renoir remarked, a commercial disaster, with Renoir
himself suffering much of the loss.[6]

3

Charleston and *Marquitta* 1927

Then I was just learning how to make films. And when you don't know anything at all, you learn a lot very fast.

—Jean Renoir

Jean Renoir's rapid education during the production of *Nana* was supplemented by the film's commercial failure, which very quickly taught him about the cinema business and the hazards of being an independent. But by then he was wholly committed to his life in film and had no thought of changing careers again; having no other alternative, he turned to commercial films.[1] For the rest of the silent film period his major works were financed by others and produced without the freedom he had hitherto enjoyed. But before surrendering to commerce, Jean Renoir had one more little fling: *Charleston*.

In 1932 Renoir told a journalist, "I have made only two films, *Nana* and *La Chienne*—the rest were for sport or commerce."[2] *Charleston* was clearly for sport, an expression of Renoir's interest in American jazz—a film as freely improvised as the music it was to celebrate. Perhaps his intensive labor on *Nana* had created a need for a very different sort of experience, a reaffirmation that film-making could be joy as well as work. As if to cleanse his soul, Renoir made a film as far from *Nana* as possible—short, simple, and jubilant. Using three actors, a single set with one tiny unadorned interior, and each actor wearing a single costume totally inappropriate to the setting, Renoir shot in three days a wholly fantastic little film full of the tricks that still intrigued him even though they had had no place in *Nana*.

There have been several mysteries about *Charleston*. French sources list its original length as 1,200 meters, which would be over an hour in running time. But Renoir remembered it, uncertainly, as only one reel. The only extant prints are those at the Cinémathèque Française, which run about twenty minutes and have neither title nor credits. No one seems ever to have seen a longer version, and there appear to be no reviews from its reputed 1927 release. Henri Langlois speculated that the Cinémathèque print was made up just of rushes from Renoir's shooting, while the film itself has disappeared. Everything written about *Charleston* seems to refer to the Cinémathèque print, or one just like it. Seeing this print, one cannot imagine how it could have gone on for forty minutes more without becoming either intolerable or quite another film.

Faced with these facts, I have tried to unearth the truth about *Charleston*. As nearly as Renoir could reconstruct it, it appears thus: *Charleston* was shot with film stock left over from the production of *Nana*. In addition to Catherine Hessling and Johnny Huggins, André Cerf appears in the role of Hessling's simian companion. The film was never completed; after three days the dancer, Johnny Huggins, was unable to continue. The one-reel film put together from the unfinished shooting may have been shown at the Vieux Colombier, but probably nowhere else. Clement Doucet was to have written music to accompany the film, but since the film was never completed, the music was never written. During the shooting, records of Charleston music were played to accompany the dance.

The Cinémathèque print, then, seems to be all there ever was of *Charleston*, it having been kept, undistributed, by Renoir until he gave it to the Cinémathèque. I suspect that the information that the film was 1,200 *feet* in length was once erroneously printed as 1,200 meters. And in film criticism, as elsewhere, once a factual error is in print it tends to persist forever.

Whatever the truth may be, all we know of *Charleston* is this twenty-minute version. The story is simple: European civilization has been destroyed; Europe lies covered with ice. A black explorer (Johnny Huggins) comes from Africa to rediscover this terra incognita. Finding the ruins of Paris, he lands his spherical flying machine in the deserted city atop a Morris column. But inside the column dwells the last living human in Paris (Catherine Hessling), whose only companion has been an ape. When the explorer lowers a rope ladder and descends to the street, she peeks out from her column, emerges and attempts to be friendly. Finding this stranger a bit wary, she tries to seduce him by performing one of the tribal dances from her era, the Charleston. He watches, imitates her in a few tentative steps, and soon they both dance interminably. Exhausted, he climbs back up to his flying machine. She follows him up the rope ladder, passing en route a tat-

Catherine Hessling and Johnny Huggins meet and dance.

tered poster advertising *Nana*, starring Catherine Hessling, directed by Jean Renoir.

In this home-movie spectacle, Catherine Hessling, dressed in very little more than formal-length black kid gloves, shows much more erotic appeal than she did in *Nana*, miming through comic imitations of a forlorn Griffith heroine and a Hollywood vamp before becoming a marathon dancer. When she needs advice, her telephone call is answered by a chorus of angels—the heads of Jean Renoir, Pierre Lestringuez, Pierre Braunberger, and some friends, attached to tiny beating wings. Johnny Huggins, a black dancer from the "Revue Nègre" on the Champs Elysée, appears in the classical costume of black-face dancers: formal suit, white gloves, battered hat and shoes. He doffs his hat reverently before a cross bearing the inscription *Rue Barré* (Street Closed) and leaves a flower at its base; backs cautiously away from the savage white female who pursues him. But once the dance begins, nothing counts but the Charleston. From a variety of views and angles, using both slow and accelerated motion, Renoir seeks to find with his camera the forms and rhythms of this craze of the twenties. As first Hessling, then Huggins, swing through long routines, Renoir lets the dance have its say, gives it scope to stretch and sway across the screen as his characters lose whatever identity they had and become purely dancers. Simultaneously the film loses its tenuous connections with space and time and becomes merely dance. Silent, the dance sequences seem over-long; but when proper music accompanies the projection *Charleston* becomes an exhilarating and liberating little film. And only then did I perceive Johnny Huggins' real talent as a dancer.

Renoir's first film for "commerce" was *Marquitta*, named after a popular song of the day and commissioned by Marie-Louise Iribe, then the wife of Pierre Renoir, as a vehicle to display her own talents. For obvious reasons *Marquitta* lacked the presence of Catherine Hessling, but Jean Angelo, the Vandeuvres of *Nana*, played the male lead, a prince who discards his mistress and picks up a street-singer, Marquitta, from a Paris corner, only to discard her too when he dislikes her manners and suspects her of stealing the crown jewels. But a revolution dethrones him and, starving, he in turn is picked from the street by Marquitta, now a star. The film ends, of course, with a chase: automobiles along the Côte d'Azur, Marquitta pursuing the prince to keep him from suicide. She succeeds, naturally.

Marquitta has completely disappeared, no fragment of it still existing as far as I can determine. When apprised of this Jean Renoir remarked, "That's no great loss." Renoir once wrote, "In the jargon of cinema, a 'commercial' film is not a film that brings in money, but a film conceived and executed in accord with the canons of the businessmen."[3] *Marquitta* apparently fit this description.

4

La Petite Marchande d'allumettes 1928

I began to make movies because of my love of trick photography. In the beginning I had no intention of writing, of being an auteur, *or inventing stories. My ambition was to make tricks, and I didn't do badly at that from the start.*

—*Jean Renoir*

Having been briefly submerged in the realm of "cinema according to the canons of the businessmen," Jean Renoir struggled to the surface long enough to make two films "for sport" before submitting again to commerce. Jean Tedesco describes Renoir the businessman in these terms: "Chewing a toothpick with a dreamy air, Renoir in conversation with some possible buyers or exhibitors would let his gaze wander like a tyro and his imagination run on about the film that would follow. In venturing into this dangerous underbrush that Louis Delluc called the 'jungle of cinema,' he quickly encountered the sharks and scavengers that flourished then as well as now. He soon understood that there was finally only one reasonable resolution for an artist, that of joyously taking the risks of an independent film-maker. It was then that our friendship became the basis for our collaboration as craftsmen within the frame of the Vieux Colombier."[1]

Tedesco, director of the Vieux Colombier, a leading avant-garde theatre in Paris, dreamed of liberating cinema from its commercial exploiters and building a studio in the attic of his theatre to provide a place where independent films could be made in complete freedom. When invited, Jean Renoir gladly joined in this project. Renoir and Tedesco set to work equipping "the smallest studio in the world." A motor and generator from a wrecked car provided electric current. They invented reflectors, designed lamps, painted the sets themselves, even devised lights with a color temperature suitable to the new panchromatic film. Then, with their studio built, Renoir began his short film *La Petite Marchande d'allumettes*. To complete the handicraft aspect of this film, Renoir and Tedesco developed the film themselves and made the first print in a tiny laboratory built in the kitchen of another friend, Raleigh, who had once worked in Hollywood but preferred to live in France where "the point of view on the question of women was better, more logical."

The choice of Hans Christian Andersen's story reflected both the love that Renoir had kept since his childhood for the Andersen tales and the need for a plot that could be filmed within the narrow confines of the tiny Vieux Colombier studio. Renoir had, as he says, "become a skillful maker of models; the construction of a landscape in reduction or a street in miniature sufficed for my happiness," and *La Petite Marchande d'allumettes* provided ample opportunity for exercise of this skill. Then too, the story provided an ideal role for Catherine Hessling, one in which the childishness that had seemed incongruous in *Nana* could be given free rein.

Treatment

Renoir has so often discussed this film in terms of technique and craftsmanship that critics tend to presume it was undertaken primarily for those technical purposes.[2] They often regard it as aberrant among the films of Jean Renoir, a lovely and fragile fantasy that stands quite outside the main stream of his work. But, far from aberrant, *La Petite Marchande d'allumettes* represents the first full flowering of a tendency that runs through Renoir's films from 1924 to 1970, a tendency to create an atmosphere of strangeness and unreality, to evoke the quality the French call *féerique*. Only this one among Renoir's films has that quality throughout; more often, it emerges within a prevailing naturalism to lend a sense of enchantment to a scene. Further, this film marks the end of the first phase of Renoir's cinema career, a phase marked by his enthusiasm for tricks and by the dominance of the figure of the woman-child, Catherine Hessling. The film abounds in tricks, although such devices never again play a significant role in Renoir films. And after this Catherine Hessling appears only for a brief comic moment in *Tire au flanc*. Though surely not intended that way, *La Petite Marchande d'allumettes* retrospectively seems a farewell homage to this actress and the match girl's death a symbol of the separation of Catherine Hessling from Renoir's creative life—perhaps also of the growth of Renoir's conception of the feminine to include full womanhood.

Andersen's familiar story, short and simple, provided Renoir the occasion for a very free adaption of a literary source, in which he retains the spirit of the original while transforming all of its details. On New Year's night Karen (Catherine Hessling) is thrust out into the snow to sell her matches. She wanders through streets where people pass without seeming to see her, almost making a sale to a handsome young man (Jean Storm). Karen gazes wonderingly through an icy window at the revelers in a restaurant, is pelted with snowballs by some boys, rescued by a friendly policeman (Manuel Raaby). With him she peers, wide-eyed, into a toystore window at dolls, soldiers, animals. Afraid to go home without having sold any matches, she huddles by a fence in the snow, trying to warm herself by lighting matches. Cold and hunger bring on hallucinations. Karen sleeps and dreams of a world where the toys from the window are lifesized and animate. Exploring this enchanted world, curious Karen trips the catch on a jack-in-the-box and releases Death (Manuel Raaby). When Death declares that he has a rendezvous with Karen, the young officer drilling wooden soldiers (Jean Storm) seeks to protect her. They ride through the clouds on a horse, pursued by Death. Catching them, Death strikes the young officer from his horse and rides off with Karen thrown across his saddle. He places her body under a cross, which changes into a rose tree and blooms. The falling rose petals turn into snowflakes; the villagers, finding Karen dead in the snow, remark on the stupidity of believing that one can keep warm with matches.

In filming this tale Renoir divided it into three parts, almost equal in length, each having a very different tone, yet interwoven in that the latter two-thirds of the film repeat, in a changed form, elements presented in the opening section. No portion of the work pretends to be truly realistic—Renoir once described it as an attempt at absolute exterior nonrealism—yet even this unreal aspect of the film, its *féerique* quality, alters from section to section. The mere strangeness and unreality pervading the opening segment gives way to fairyland enchantment through the middle of the film, while a supernatural air prevails through the final third.

The initial section shows Karen lost in the "real" world. From its start—the tiny model village in the snow, a toy train flitting quickly across a viaduct—it is obviously a fairy-tale world, for the shape and structure of these objects is not that of reality. A pointing hand orders Karen from the snowbound cabin, clutching her tray of matches. Once more Renoir uses darkness to advantage, but with a new effect. In the purely visual space of cinema, both sheer blackness and sheer whiteness fail to provide any depth to the space perceived; by filming his snow-covered village at night Renoir reverses normal dark-light relations and creates a spatial oddness which reinforces the unreality of the activity that occurs within this strange space. But essentially it is the action that seems fantastic. People walk to and fro in the street; Karen moves erratically, hesitantly, among them, offering her matches. Yet she appears to be invisible to them, her presence completely unnoticed as each passer-by goes purposefully on his way. This continues for two shots, perhaps forty-five seconds, until the young man appears with his unlit cigarette, looking for a match. But now the invisibility reverses. Karen stands, facing the street; the young man enters the scene from the left, behind her; taps her on the shoulder, cigarette in hand. But she remains totally oblivious, looking leftward down the street until he gives up and walks away. Only then does she turn to look at the space where he has been. Through thirteen shots Renoir conducts a sort of blind-man's ballet, with Karen and the young man alternately seeking each other, but never at the same time.

Karen seems out of phase with everyone, a creature from another clime. Though Hessling's performance here seems often derived from the Chaplin of *The Gold Rush*, she appears neither comic nor pathetic as he does, but like a lost child. When she peers through the frosty window into the restaurant, her look expresses neither hunger nor hurt, just puzzled curiosity. Not until the boys throw snowballs does any interaction occur between Karen and this world. In the first third of the film, only the policeman speaks to her; only with him does she share an experience, as they look in the toy store window. Only he shows concern for her plight, advising her to go home. But we know, as he does not, that home is as unreceptive and unloving to her as is the rest of the world.

Then, having found only rejection, obstruction, or advice she dare not heed, Karen dreams of another world different from this. Her dream fills the last two-thirds of *La Petite Marchande d'allumettes*, but, as Renoir shoots it, its surface is that of fantasy rather than being dreamlike as was *La Fille de l'eau*.

In English "dreamlike" does not mean "like a dream," for most dreams are very real in apprehension—rather, "dreamlike" indicates a certain unreality involving detachment and a sense that one's acts flow in complete independence from one's will. *La Fille de l'eau* achieves this air of unreality through the complete unresponsiveness of Virginia as she moves through the events of her dream. But Karen participates fully in the life of her dream world. She dances and juggles, looking surprised, then pleased, as she falls into the realm of life-sized toys. She explores eagerly, responding to what she finds —pushes a ball, dances with joy at the dolls, parades with the wooden soldiers. And, of course, she is frightened by the jack-in-the-box and responsive to the young officer's declaration of love. We know, certainly, that Karen dreams, but the texture of the film is fantasy rather than dream.

Through the central section of the film Karen plays rather than works— her tray of matches has been left behind. Despair has turned to joy, but her relation to the surrounding world remains one of alienation. Like the villagers in the snow, the toys seem totally unaware of her; they dance and march and drum as if she were not there. But it is not this disconnection that creates the pervading sense of strangeness in this portion of the film. Of course they are oblivious—they are only toys! The oddness, instead, is one of scale, supported by Karen's tendency to move almost as mechanically as the toys and Renoir's trick of fading backgrounds in and out while leaving the foreground constant. However, though it may be "normal" for the toys to ignore Karen, the consequence is to leave her no more at home in the toy world than in that of men—joyful she may be, but still quite lost.

Only at the end of this central third of the film does Karen's presence evoke some response. Then the dream counterparts of the young man and policeman engage her once again. But their attitudes appear quite different now. The young man, now the officer of the wooden soldiers, declares his love for Karen and magically produces a table of food for her. At just this moment the jack-in-the-box disappears from atop the cube where he has drooped and reappears beside the table where Karen prepares to eat. He announces that he is Death; thus the policeman who was the only friendly figure in her waking world has become the only threatening figure in Karen's dream. To underscore the menace he presents, Death walks among the toys and wherever he steps the activity ceases. Soldiers topple over; the heads of the dolls fall forward; the merry-go-round slows and stops. Seeing this, "the young people decide to flee in the clouds" and the eerie chase that fills the final third of the film begins.

Renoir now sets black horses against white frames, rather than the white against black of *La Fille de l'eau*. Again, the effect is to create fantasy rather than dream. In *La Fille de l'eau* the white horse moved slowly, always the same distance away, across the silhouette of tree-tops, his constant pace continuing the cadence of the dream. But for *La Petite Marchande d'allumettes* Renoir galloped his horses across white sand from the forest of Fontainbleu, which photographs as vaguely cloudlike—a totally amorphous space with neither depth nor any clear dimension, wholly lacking coordinates or points of reference which might give clear definition to the motion we perceive. Part of the effect stems from the method Renoir had to adopt to shoot his scene. Seeking to make close-ups of the chase, he tried to photograph it from an auto running alongside the horses, but the auto bogged down in the sand. Finally Renoir shot some footage himself, carrying a camera while mounted on a horse running along beside the horses of the chase. In the film these horses appear sometimes as black spots in a sea of murky white, grow larger, disappear out of the frame, reappear as jagged, jumping shapes too close to be discriminated. Since these shots have no effective background, one cannot tell camera movement from object movement, nor, often, when one shot ends and the next begins. One segment looks almost as if it were done in animation technique, single blurred frames

Karen (Catherine Hessling) awake, and in dream. With Manuel Raaby and Jean Storm.

of Death appearing successively at different points on the screen. Add close shots of Death's grim visage and of Karen and the young officer, tense and wide-eyed, with hair blowing across her face—very real figures in the no-where of this scene—and the whole sequence takes on an air quite different from either the sense of displacement and despair of the snow scenes or the enchanted joy of Karen in toyland. A peculiar ambiguity reigns in this pursuit, which, though given urgency by its rapid pace, has no perceptible goal but the triumph of Death. The dimensionless space through which they run offers the young lovers no escape, within it no location is fixed except by its relation to the two running horses; the only distance defined is that between pursuer and pursued, the only possible outcomes of the chase either eternal pursuit or death. But, when Death takes Karen from her horse, should this be seen as capture or release?

This question is, I think, answered by the conclusion of the film. The horses come together; swords flash. The young man slides from his horse and falls, a tiny figure dropping through measureless clouds. Death catches Karen, rides away with her head hanging by his horse's neck. Dissolve to clouds and bare tree tops. Death, walking, bears Karen's body to earth, lays her on a rock under a cross. As he does, a wisp of her hair remains entangled on his gloved hand. He throws it in the air; carried by the wind, it catches on the cross which turns into a living tree. Death turns and fades into the clouds. Now roses bloom on the tree—buds open; petals turn and spread. Cut to a big blurred close-up of Karen's face. Rose petals fall, turn into snow. In the village once more, prosaic people remark on Karen's death. But the final shot of *La Petite Marchande d'allumettes*, a big soft close-up of Karen's face, peaceful in death, is the most beautiful image of Catherine Hessling that Jean Renoir ever put upon a screen, childish no more. In the death of the child a woman was born.

Had this film been made by Bresson or Bergman, without altering a frame, I am sure it would be discussed as a religious film. But Jean Renoir does not make religious films. Even so, it is hard to evade the scent of salvation that lingers in these concluding shots. Minimally, this scent transforms Death from villain to hero—he rescues Karen from the world—thus confirming at the end of the film the policeman's kindness at its start.

One cannot talk sensibly of characterization here. Karen is a lost child; other characters hardly exist. If the film can be accorded any significance beyond the mere delight of its fantasy, it must be symbolic. And the symbols of death and salvation, rejection and innocence, are too obvious to ignore. Still, Jean Renoir does *not* make religious films! Hence I am tempted to interpret the symbols of *La Petite Marchande d'allumettes* in relation to this stage of Renoir's career rather than religion. There is no doubt that this was a transitional period for Renoir. He had, as it were, served his apprenticeship, learned the game and something of his power in it. And perhaps he had begun to see his actors as the intermediaries through which he might reach the public—that is, he had begun to see that there were things he wanted to say, rather than merely perform tricks, as he once thought. Then too, he had lost his money and his innocence about the jungle of cinema and had been forced to swim in the sea of sharks if he wanted to work. Also, in 1927 he had been injured in the accident that took the life of Pierre Champagne, come to the end of his collaboration with Pierre Lestringuez, and made a film without Catherine Hessling.

In these terms, the death and salvation are quite real. A phase of his career had ended; *La Petite Marchande d'allumettes* forms a sort of commemoration of this end. The child in woman's flesh, which had been *the* image of femininity in all these early films, dies with Karen; and as the rose petals turn to snowflakes, the age of *trucages* in Renoir films dies too. A very different conception of *la femme* soon develops. Whether they portray innocence or experience, destruction or love, the female characters in Renoir films are henceforth women, not children. And a new style, without tricks, will be proclaimed in the very first shot of *Tire au flanc*.

Quite apart from such speculations, *La Petite Marchande d'allumettes* remains at least a lovely fantasy, constructed with delicacy and visual imagination, very nearly maintaining its fairy-tale atmosphere unbroken throughout. In its world of illusion, the sprite-like talents of Catherine Hessling find their proper home; here her reactions seem genuine, her excesses appropriate. The impression she gives of being not quite real, with its hints of both mechanism and unsubstantiality, an impression that marks all of her performances, here seems quite right. In *Nana*, where the reality of the world of the film was unquestionable, this air of unreality imparted a falseness to the character portrayed; in *La Petite Marchande d'allumettes* it forms the basis for her truth.

But however successful the film may have been artistically, its commercial life was doomed. Though it was shown in Geneva in June of 1928, its Paris premiere was delayed for over a year by an unfounded charge of plagiarism brought by Maurice Rostand, who had written a comic opera based on Andersen's tale. Meanwhile, the days of silent films had ended; new

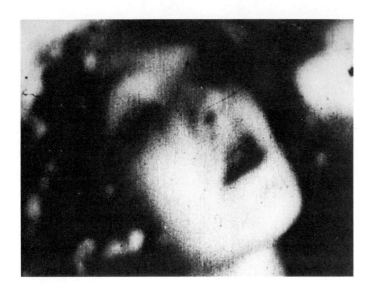

films being shown in Paris had sound. Renoir describes the subsequent events:

> Then there was a very quick attempt to make a sort of soundtrack. Someone said, "We'll put music with it." And they put music with it. I had nothing to do with it; for I was shooting another film at that time. This music is very bad . . .
>
> But you must know that the film was not made to be projected in silence. Originally, a musical score was to have been played, with a small orchestra, at the Vieux Colombier. But that score has disappeared. Hence it is better to see the film silent; for the music added later, by I don't remember what distributor, was truly ridiculous. But, all the same, most of the movements in the film were performed to be in rhythm with some music. Another thing: the subtitles which have been added since are an element for which I am not responsible. The film was made to be projected without subtitles.

Commercially unsalable, *La Petite Marchande d'allumettes* has for forty years been shown in French film societies, a not-at-all-unusual fate for a Renoir film. And no other film was ever made in the little studio atop the Vieux Colombier.

5

Tire au flanc
1928

When I made Tire au flanc, *I was a bit more in control of my
medium, I was beginning to know where I was going. I was
beginning to see that I could indulge certain aspects of my
character without shocking the public too much.*

—*Jean Renoir*

For the purposes of art, the great virtue of military life is that it never
changes. Across the years and national boundaries, Beetle Bailey, the Sad
Sack, and the Good Soldier Schweik would perceive each other instantly as
colleagues suffering the same persecution. And each would immediately
recognize Colonel Bat Guano as the idealization of a very familiar type. The
fact that for generations millions of men conscripted into national armies
have suffered the same indignities when left at the mercy of professional soldiers gives the military comedy somewhat the status held by a tragedy on
Homeric themes in ancient Greece—one can count on audience participation and understanding.

Tire au flanc, a French military idiom that can be roughly translated by
World War II's "Sad Sack," was the title of a military comedy that had
played at the same theatre in Paris for twenty years, depicting life in a
French barracks before World War I. Renoir had agreed to direct a historical film, *Le Tournoi*, but while waiting for the festival at Carcassonne to
develop its full medieval splendor, he and some friends planned another
project, choosing *Tire au flanc* because "it gave us the possibility of doing

something amusing and besides, since the title was very well known, it would be easy to sell."[1]

In 1928, ten years after World War I and several years before the rise of Hitler, Western Europeans could still nourish the illusion that the bloodshed of 1914-1918 had solved some problems and the hope that a lasting peace had been established. In an era of peace pacts and talk about disarmament, one could imagine that armies were obsolescent and national military organizations a quaint survival of a more barbarous past, most useful now to provide colorful elements in a holiday parade. The requirement that a young man do a period of military service was a minor disruption of his life, or perhaps a convenient way of breaking parental ties, but it was not very serious. Hence Renoir's *Tire au flanc*, although it takes an essentially negative view of the military life and mind, breathes a rather gentle antimilitarism and is even a bit tolerant of this dying institution. It displays no savagery or bitterness in its attack, presents no horrifying bill of particulars. Life in the regiment appears to be marked by stupidity, inefficiency, corruption, and boredom; it has, perhaps, a retarding effect on all who enter there—but it might not be a bad place for the idiots who like that sort of thing.

Tire au flanc has been largely ignored by film historians, treated as just another commercial silent film. Renoir himself has occasionally named *Nana* as his only silent film worth discussing. Yet *Tire au flanc* today seems much easier to respond to—perhaps only because comedy found its natural language in silent film. But beyond its merits as comedy, *Tire au flanc* seems central in Renoir's development as a film-maker, revealing more fully than *Nana* the recurring themes or techniques that became elements in Renoir's mature style. And much more frequently than *Nana*, it deviates from conventions to seek genuinely expressive ways of constructing scenes. These departures from standard procedures do not always succeed, but they help make this by far the most instructive of all Renoir's silent films.

Narrative and Characterizaion

The series of actions that makes up *Tire au flanc* hardly merits being called a story. Though there is a linear development through most of the film, it contains few temporal indicators and one has no idea whether the time span of the action is six weeks or eight months. In the midst of this, a half-dozen sequences constitute a mock-documentary on life in the army, presented in quite atemporal documentary style. The events that can be given a temporal order are these: Jean Dubois D'Ombelles (Georges Pomiès) and his servant, Joseph (Michel Simon), are both to be conscripted. Jean, a poet, lives in a houseful of women: his aunt Mme. Blandin (Maryanne) and her daughters Solange (Jeanne Helbling) and Lily (Kinny Dorlay). Hoping to ease Jean's path, Mme. Blandin invites two officers of his future regiment, Colonel

Brochard (Felix Oudart) and Lieutenant Daumel (Jean Storm), to dinner. But the dinner becomes a fiasco and the Colonel leaves feeling abused and irritated and convinced that "le poète" is also "l'idiot." Once mustered in, Joseph falls quickly and easily into army life, while Jean can do nothing right, whether he tries or not. Very quickly he becomes the company Sad Sack. One night Georgette (Fridette Fatton), who is Mme. Blandin's maid and Joseph's fiancée and who has become a *cantinière*, comes ingenuously to the barracks to bid Joseph good-night. The ensuing near-riot ends with both Muflot, "the terror of the barracks," and Jean being ordered to prison. From his prison cell Jean sees his fiancée, Solange, kiss Lieutenant Daumel, but Georgette advises him that it is Lily who really loves him. Vowing to reform, Jean gets out of prison and joins with Joseph as entertainer at the Colonel's annual party, then becomes a hero by extinguishing a fire and finally riding Muflot into a state of submission. In a final scene of a multiple wedding, Jean, in officer's uniform, joins Colonel Brochard and Lieutenant Daumel with the Blandin women at the dining table, while in the kitchen the enlisted men help Joseph and Georgette celebrate their wedding.

Tire au flanc was Renoir's first attempt at filming a theatrical work. Even the original stage version by Mouezy-Eon and Sylvane almost guaranteed that this would be a different Renoir film: the central character would not be female. But in his adaptation Renoir went further, adding a new male character, Joseph, and relating the two as master and servant. In casting Michel Simon as Joseph, Renoir found an actor rather unlike any he had used before—big, with an awkward-appearing body which was yet very well controlled, and with a face that bordered on the grotesque but was capable of a great range of expression. For the central role of Jean Dubois D'Ombelles, Renoir recruited Georges Pomiès, a dancer with no previous film experience—a choice that reflects the growth of Renoir's concern for rhythmic movement in his films and indicates how much he had changed his initial conception of editing.

Whether planned or not, the combination of these two actors with a vehicle that stressed physical action opened a new avenue for Renoir—the possibility of creating characters that were not wholly superficial and who might exhibit some growth and development in the course of the action.

In *Nana* the significant action had occurred much more on the level of gesture than of full bodily movement. By stylizing gestures Renoir had created the only interesting persons yet to appear in his films. But they were limited and the action only revealed their character; they did not develop or grow. Now, in *Tire au flanc*, Renoir had a plot more readily realized in movement than in gesture and two actors with highly expressive bodies. In addition, *Tire au flanc* was a comedy.

Characterization was, at best, difficult in silent film. Deprived of the central characterizing element, speech, most silent films willingly settled for individuated types. But even here comedy had an advantage. In a serious silent film, when the actors spoke, one felt the audience had to know what was said. Thus, the speech had to be simple enough to be conveyed by the mere image or else it had to be communicated by titles that destroyed the visual continuity essential to film. Hence, even the image of speech had to be minimized in serious silent films. But this restriction did not apply to comedy, as Keaton, Chaplin, René Clair and others had discovered. The very sight of a man talking when no sound can be heard can easily be made comic. And a silent-comedy audience knew very well that what a man said didn't much matter; it was what he did that counted. Hence, silent comedy could include rather extensive passages of people talking without the film being disrupted with titles. And though the gestures of speech do not show us exactly what a man says, they do characterize him.

It is not surprising, then, that in the first two and a half shots of *Tire au flanc* Jean Renoir accomplished more in the way of characterization than in all of his earlier films. *Tire au flanc* opens with a close-up, a detail of a painting. The camera recedes, showing the whole painting—a sort of Victorian "Picnic on the Grass,"—and continues back to reveal Georgette and, finally, the Blandin dining room with Georgette and Joseph fixing the table for the impending dinner. Georgette shakes out the table cloth and the screen is flooded with white. Then Joseph and Georgette, on opposite sides of the table, straighten the cloth, Joseph leaning across to kiss Georgette. They change sides of the table; twice more Joseph leans across for a kiss. The camera now reverses its path and moves forward, the shot ending almost where it began, with a close-up of the painting that hangs over the fireplace. This shots lasts almost a minute and is almost perfectly symmetrical in both composition and form, its rhythm created by a combination of camera and object movement, both of these also symmetrical. Within this symmetry we see Joseph as an awkward, loose-jointed young man in love, very open in his affection and much more interested in his lady than in the work he is supposed to do. Neither his face nor his movements have any of the formal elegance and smooth rhythm the shot itself displays.

Fade rapidly to shot 2, which is formally nearly identical with shot 1. The camera recedes from the same painting, starting from slightly farther away, to show the Blandin dining room, with the table now set for dinner, then moves forward again over the table toward the painting. But now Jean Dubois D'Ombelles stands talking in front of the fireplace, with Solange, identified as his fiancée, at its right-hand corner; a bell cord hanging from the ceiling divides the screen in half. This shot lasts for about eighty seconds, with Jean talking all the time. It has the same rhythmic camera movement and compositional symmetry as shot 1, but all of the motion and loving interaction supplied by Joseph and Georgette is lacking, replaced only by the gestures of Jean as he talks and the slight movement of Solange, who walks leftward to stand beside Jean as the moving camera stops at a medium two-shot. Talk has replaced action, and though we have no idea that Jean is saying or even what he is talking about, we begin to know him. He talks with great authority, cocking his chin, gesturing as if for an audience, smiles, nods, completely sure that his words are gems of wit or wisdom, sublimely confident that anyone who hears must be entranced. Solange listens, but without obvious enthusiasm. The formal similarity of these first two shots accentuates the difference between the two pairs of lovers.

Cut to shot 3: the corner of a Victorian buffet projects at an angle from bottom left screen toward the kitchen door, through which Georgette and Joseph appear. Georgette carries a bowl of fruit; Joseph walks very close behind her. They walk past Jean and Solange to the table, the camera tracking with them. Georgette arranges the fruit in the bowl; Joseph stands, not seeming to have any function in the activity. At the first opportunity he kisses her again. In the background Jean starts as if shocked by this action, hastily waving Joseph and Georgette to the kitchen.

This shot has none of the symmetry of the first two—it is almost as if each of these two engaged couples was well-ordered by itself but when put together all went askew. And the difference between these couples is crucial for the characterization in this film. In *Tire au flanc*, as in much of his subsequent work, Renoir develops his characters in pairs, with the contrast playing a major role in the characterization. In these three shots Joseph and Jean are contrasted as movement to immobility, silence to speech, awkwardness to grace, uncertainty to assurance, affection openly expressed to an overt rejection of this expression. We cannot tell whether Jean deplores Joseph's kiss out of prudishness or a master's feeling that servants should carry on their love affairs in private, but we see that the servants touch and kiss while the masters impress each other with words. And that Jean is self-centered and self-satisfied, accustomed to being the focus of attention.

The dinner sequence extends and reinforces these initial impressions of Joseph and Jean. Soldiers parade past the Blandin house and Mme. Blandin, Lily, Georgette, and Joseph all act in response to the martial music—Joseph marching in place with a feather duster over his shoulder as Georgette proudly watches. Jean and Solange both look pained at such frivolous and undignified behavior. Jean, standing by the table, remarks, "They say you've invited a colonel to watch us eat. That kills my appetite." As he talks he takes a banana from the bowl of fruit, thus confirming the impression created in shot 2 of talk that is clever and empty. When the Colonel and Lt. Daumel arrive, Jean takes no part in the confusion and excitement that prevail. He sits indolently at the piano, running his hands gracefully over the keys as the flurry of entrance and introduction goes on behind him. Since Jean does not move, Mme. Blandin at last brings the guests to meet him. Jean stands just long enough to greet Colonel Brochard, who looks very much annoyed; like Jean, he expects to be the center of attention. Jean, oblivious of any fault, assumes that everyone would, of course, be charmed to hear him play. There ensues through seven shots a little duel between these two self-important males, with Jean alternately sitting and standing as Mme. Blandin repeatedly urges him to be respectful to the colonel. This ends when Joseph, crawling by on his knees, moves the piano stool in order to pick up the banana peel Jean has dropped. Jean, sitting down at the piano for the fourth time, falls flat and is immediately surrounded by all the young women, consoling him. Thus defeated in this contest for attention, Colonel Brochard pronounces his judgment on Jean, "Completely idiotic, that boy"; his companion, Mme. Flechois, replies, "He has an excuse, Colonel; he's a poet."

With Jean thus categorized, Renoir returns to Joseph, who is anything but a model servant. Very obtrusively in the background, Joseph tries much harder to overhear the table conversation than to get the diners fed. When Mme. Blandin's request for an office job for her "delicate" nephew prompts the colonel to remark that it seems young people wish to "tire au flanc," Joseph guffaws and knocks the platter to the floor. Hastily retrieving the roast, he stuffs some of the garnish in his pocket and heads for the table, the gravy boat held precariously in his other hand. As Mme. Blandin gazes in amazement at the entree thus offered her, Joseph moves back and forth with the gravy, finally dripping it on the colonel's sleeve. He dabs at the stain, presuming that the colonel is wholly unaware of this, meanwhile pouring more gravy in the colonel's lap. This breaks up the dinner. Through all of this Joseph has an air of complete innocence. Whereas Jean takes it as only natural that everyone should always be attending to him, Joseph seems to think of himself as invisible and always unnoticed—a very proper attitude for a servant, no doubt, but slightly ludicrous when embodied in the expressively ursine form and constantly mobile face of Michel Simon, who can hardly keep from dominating any frame in which he appears.

Through this initial section of the film, the relation between Jean and Joseph remains only that of master and servant, no gesture of friendship marring the perfect sterility of their association. Jean's only recognition of Joseph issues in gestures of disapproval, and Joseph's joy at the Colonel's rejection of Mme. Blandin's plea for her nephew indicates no great affection for his young master.

Having presented his persons, Renoir moves them to a different setting and lets their character become their fate. Appropriately, the barracks reeks with boredom, broken only by the arrival of new recruits. Joseph arrives with the rest, shuffling into the barracks with a silly smile and no expectations whatsoever about how people will treat him. Rather, he responds to them; with a delighted grin he trades his fedora for the kepi of a little soldier and immediately becomes one of the gang. Jean arrives alone, and ele-

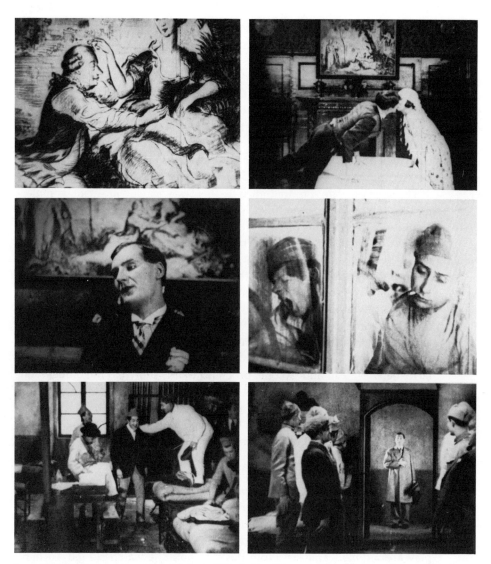

Joseph (Michel Simon) and Jean Dubois d'Ombelles (Georges Pomiès), from Mme. Blandin's to the barracks.

gantly dressed. Watching out the window, Joseph describes Jean to his new companions as a pretentious ass. At the barracks-room door, booby-trapped in anticipation of his appearance, Jean glows with appreciation when a soldier inside shouts, "Attention!" And even though he is nearly torn to pieces in the ensuing scuffle, Jean immediately regains his smug smile and his assurance of his own special status when Lieutenant Daumel arrives to restore order. But the hand Jean extends in relief and friendship is coldly ignored as Lieutenant Daumel orders Corporal Bourrache, "You will teach this man the external marks of respect."

Jean does have a special status, however, though hardly the one he expects. He seems totally incapable of assimilation, failing whether he seeks to avoid or satisfy the standard military demands. The status he achieves is conveyed in a single image, preceded by the sort of cliché Renoir hates but uses here for contrast. The cliché is a three-shot montage of military grandeur, the army on parade. From this Renoir cuts to an extreme long shot from high above the empty parade ground, in the middle of which is a single tiny figure with wheelbarrow and broom: Jean Dubois D'Ombelles.

The skits on army life that encircle this shot provide a caustic commentary on the military scene, but also reveal how the two central characters adapt to their new environment. Joseph, the servant accustomed to making the best of unreasonable orders, treats them here as he did at Mme. Blandin's—he does nothing quite right, but without accepting the invitation to become savage, he goes through the motions and gets out of the way. In a peacetime army Joseph represents the ideal recruit. He disappears into the ranks, survives without pain and without being corrupted, and gives his superiors some excuse for being. But Jean cannot relate satisfactorily to either his comrades or his superiors, and invisibility never seems a possible choice for him. The solution is simple, and it is foreshadowed by the similarity between Jean and Colonel Brochard that is shown in the dinner scene and reinforced when the Colonel turns poet in midfilm. Jean's elevation from the ranks at the end of *Tire au flanc* seems a mere, if belated, case of like recognizing like. The fact that he has apparently made no progress at all in mastering the arts of arms by then provides only one more ironic thread in this military tapestry.

But, however obvious his inability to play the army game, Jean appears affected by it only after being imprisoned. This triumph of military justice —the Colonel punishes Muflot for hazing Jean, and Jean for being the victim of the hazing: "No favors in treatment"—leaves Muflot lounging comfortably in prison, while Jean huddles in a corner away from the rats that play around his water jar. From this viewpoint he watches a gloved hand pick the rose growing outside the window of his cell. Clutching the bars, he pulls himself up to the window to see Solange and Lieutenant Daumel in a passionate embrace.

This low point of his career finds the relation of Jean to Joseph reversed; Joseph stands guard outside Jean's cell, pirouetting on his toes to relieve the boredom. But Joseph proves a more compassionate master than Jean had been and smuggles Georgette into the prison with food for him. As if to affirm that he has learned nothing yet, Jean repeats his gesture from the dinner scene, declaring, "No, I'm too unhappy. I'd rather die of hunger," as he starts to eat. Nevertheless this scene marks the turning point in his character

Crime and punishment. *Center left,* Muflot (Zellas), Georgette (Fridette Fatton), Corporal Bourrache (Paul Velsa). *Center right,* Lieutenant Daumel (Jean Storm).

and in the film. Georgette advises him to forget Solange and think of Lily, and Joseph tells him his comrades are not so bad, even Muflot, "if you know how to take them." Up to now, Jean hadn't "taken them" at all, but simply expected them to take him. So Joseph's advice is essentially to stop being a pretentious ass, pay some attention to others, and respond to them in some way other than the condescending handshake he has proffered to everyone from Lieutenant Daumel to the dummy at bayonet drill. Remarkably, Jean hears this advice. Heretofore, though he expected attention he had always been too immersed in his own performance to attend in return; how else could he have failed to notice Solange's wandering eye before?

Henceforth, Jean and Joseph act as friends. Jean reads self-improvement books in his cell, but the change in him stems more from his new relation with Joseph and Georgette than his reading. Though Jean exhibits a ridiculous naiveté in his expectations about others, Georgette and Joseph are the true innocents in *Tire au flanc*; with great simplicity they expect from everyone the open, good-humored decency they themselves share. Enough adversity drives even Jean to genuinely respond to their concern, and from then on he appears to see others rather than just expect them to notice him.

Critics never fail to identify the shot of Lieutenant Daumel plucking the rose from Jean's prison window as "pure Stroheim."[2] Perhaps, but the little noticed reversal of this scene some thirty shots later is pure Renoir: the recreation of a scene in a form identical in some details, but with the very opposite feeling and effect, as a way of displaying character change. Here Lily stands on a cart outside the window; once again Jean clutches the bars and pulls himself up, but joyfully. Just as Jean and Lily touch through the bars, a guard enters to tell Jean that his prison term is up. Jean beams, reaches out the window to pluck a rose and, as Lily watches through the bars, he presents the rose to the guard and dances happily out of his cell.

The new relationship between Joseph and Jean is best shown in their performance as satyr and nymph at the Colonel's party, but after the prison scene Renoir conveys the change in Jean in three shots: First, a repetition of Jean's entry into the barracks. Muflot has made precisely the same booby-trap arrangements as before, but this time Jean reacts to the real situation and not his fantasy of it, and Muflot is the victim of his own trap. Second, at the Colonel's party Georgette hands a tray of glasses over the counter and Jean, not Joseph, serves them to the enlisted men who are working at the party. Finally, in the film's final shot—a long and complicated traveling shot that begins in the Blandin kitchen and moves through the door to the dining room as Joseph brings a bottle of champagne to the officer's wedding party—the camera, as it moves into the dining room, pauses on the picture above the fireplace, then in a repetition of the opening shot of the film, pulls back over the table, where once again Colonel Brochard sits next to Mme. Blandin, Solange with Lieutenant Daumel, and Jean with Lily. Joseph pours champagne; Jean and Lily drink, exchange glasses. Dropping something, Jean reaches for the floor at the corner of the table; Lily bends toward him and where Joseph and Georgette had kissed over the table as the film began, Jean and Lily kiss under it at film's end. In this first comic treatment of a favorite theme, the interaction of servants and masters, though Renoir does mildly ridicule the bourgeois masters, the two classes come together and when the film ends Joseph has become a better servant and Jean a kinder master.

Tire au flanc is a comedy of action and movement, the tempo of its scenes related primarily to the volume of laughter they are intended to induce. Without any pretentions of being serious, the film nevertheless contains the two most vital characters in Renoir's silent film period. Georges Pomiès' performance as Jean centers on the whirling choreography that erupts in scene after scene, though, characteristically, when the whole barracks joins the dance in response to Georgette's night visit, Jean stands bolt upright in his bed clutching his blanket for half the scene and then remains quite outside the wild barracks melee that follows. The growth of the character is recorded in the coordination of Jean's outbursts of movement with the activities of others. Until the prison scene there is no coordination at all, merely solo moments of frenzy tolerated as unavoidable: "C'est le poète, mon Colonel." "Oui . . . l'idiot." But at the Colonel's party Jean's three performances all occur within the world shared by others. In the ballet to entertain the guests, Jean cavorts as a prancing satyr whose pipes bring the nymph, Joseph, down from heaven. This marks the first, though ludicrous, appearance of a favorite Renoir figure, the nature god whose music has strange power over men. The entertainment over, Jean begins a new dance with a fire hose as partner, extinguishing the blaze started by Muflot and hosing down the guests in the process. Finally, he appears in a pas de deux with Muflot, again the first version of a recurring Renoir scene, the chase carried out in the midst of a party.

But though Jean progresses from idiot to hero, Michel Simon's Joseph becomes the first really credible major character in a Renoir film, warm, awkward, loving and human—and as Truffaut remarks, "promising the most admirable grimaces in French cinema, those of Bruel, Caussat, Colin, Boudu, and Père Jules."[3]

Style and Form

Though its rich repertoire of genuine Renoir characters, themes, and scenes sets *Tire au flanc* off from its predecessors, its style and form most clearly distinguish it from earlier Renoir films. The most obvious formal change is the new freedom with which Renoir employs his camera. A few shots in *Nana* had shown that he recognized the power of a moving camera as a means of expression, but such occasions were rare; camera movement occurred perhaps once in fifty shots. But the initial section of *Tire au flanc*, exhibits more camera motion than all of Renoir's earlier films combined: of sixty-six shots, twenty-six employ a moving camera, and in nineteen of these the movements are large and often complicated—indeed, in this opening section the camera at times seems to have gone wild. At one point, Renoir combines seven separate medium shots in a single shot through the bizarre expedient of joining them by blurred zip pans. But even when most erratic, this camera work remains expressive, for the camera's lurching confusion well reflects the state of the Blandin household as it anxiously awaits the arrival of Colonel Brochard. Most often, the complicated movements are well conceived and executed. The film's first shot, already described, now seems a typical Renoir opening: beginning with a close-up detail which itself has some small significance in the film, the camera then moves away to disclose some characters in the first action-space of the film. But we must note that before *Tire au flanc* no Renoir film had begun in this fashion and that most of his films in the thirties have opening shots of this form.

Truffaut has called the camera movements in *Tire au flanc* "hallucinations of heroism"—a lively phrase, though hard to understand, particularly when the most hallucinated movements occur in scenes at Mme. Blandin's rather than in a military context. I suspect, rather, that they are the hallucinations of a young film-maker who has just discovered the joy of directing a moving camera with the freedom typical of silent comedy.

Most film historians credit the German cinema, and particularly F. W. Murnau, with being the innovator of the mobile camera. But in Renoir's case, the influence seems to have come from a forgotten Hollywood director, Bob Leonard, whose long career included directing all of Mae Murray's films in the early 1920s. "Leonard's films were not very good," Renoir remarked. "They had stock characters and ridiculous stories, but he constructed wonderful scenes with a moving camera." Whatever its source, Renoir's discovery of camera movement linked well with two tendencies he had already shown, that toward extending the duration of a shot and that toward building the basic rhythm of a scene on movement within the shot rather than on cutting. In *Tire au flanc* he seems to be exploring the variety of combinations these tendencies allow, sometimes appearing to try all possible conjunctions of camera and object movement, then again wondering what the effect would be if he just let the camera sit while the action-space was filled with object-movement and then set the camera in motion when everything else stopped. The results are sometimes disconcerting; a blur of motion may convey with great force and economy the strength and impetus of a movement, but some of the blurs in *Tire au flanc* seem unnecessary and unexpressive and detract from the effect of those that do work well. If we accept the concept of a "well-made film" to match that of the "well-made play," *Tire au flanc* would surely not fit it. But it succeeds more often than it fails, and the explorations Renoir carried out here served him well: they prepared him for some elaborate camera work in subsequent silent films, and, more importantly, enabled him to shoot his first great sound film, *La Chienne*, already well in command of the techniques of the fluid camera.

A second important innovation in *Tire au flanc* is the cyclical form Renoir gave to this work. Not only are the first and last images formally almost identical—the camera pulling back from the Victorian painting to show the Blandin dining room, with the very same people seated around the same table, with Joseph serving them again—but the overall spatial pattern of the film and the falling and rising line of the hero's life share this form. At the very center of this symmetry, between sequences in the prison and about equidistant from the two shots in which a rose is picked, Renoir inserts an odd little seven-shot scene, symmetrical in itself, that may seem quite extraneous until we notice its place in this formal structure and see its point: to show, at this low moment in the hero's fortune, the essential similarity between Jean and the Colonel. In a night scene of a little clump of trees, Joseph and Colonel Brochard stealthily approach from opposite sides and wait, Joseph for Georgette, the colonel for Mme. Flechois. In classic silent-comedy style they circle the copse, starting, stopping, and turning in unison, a perfect pre-established harmony assuring that neither will discover the other's presence. Unfortunately, the ladies have not been included in this harmony; they appear, but quite out of phase with the circling males. The colonel embraces Georgette fervently and presents to her the poem he has written for Mme. Flechois; meanwhile, Joseph more quickly discovers he has the wrong partner. Joseph and Georgette run off with the poem, leaving the colonel fuming to Mme. Flechois and at last identified: *le poète, l'idiot.* Around this core the spatial movement of the film goes from Mme. Blandin's to the barracks, to the prison, then to this copse; back to the prison, to the barracks, finally returning to Mme. Blandin's.

Within this large symmetrical pattern, numerous smaller segments also approach symmetry in a number of different ways: single shots symmetrical in composition, small groups of three to five shots with symmetry of movement, character groups, such as the five women, with Georgette as the feminine center of the film and the first loving woman in a Renoir film. In its action *Tire au flanc* is episodic and loosely structured, with most episodes having an air of improvisation (Renoir: "Oh! More than improvised!") that frequently seems nearly out of control. This is the first of many Renoir films in which the actors seem to be having a wonderful time, performing for each other as much as for the audience—a characteristic André Bazin has commented on at length.[4] But this informality on the level of action does not render *Tire au flanc* formless or sprawling, for the underlying symmetries provide a firmness and articulation of structure within which the action can flow almost haphazardly without disrupting our sense of the orderliness of the whole. Here already in *Tire au flanc*, where Renoir's style has just begun to emerge, one can both understand why critics often say he is careless about form and see the error of the charge.

I have spoken a great deal in the preceding paragraphs about symmetry; here I must add that each of these "symmetries" is a bit awry. Renoir had no use for perfection or static form. He claimed to have seen some perfect films, but happily never to have made one, for those he had seen were all "boring." By a "perfect film" he meant one complete, polished, tied together

The joys of army life.

in every detail, so that its audience has nothing to do but watch. In his own films he wanted the audience to have to work, to help him make the picture work; hence each of the circles does not quite close, each of the formal structures has a piece missing here or an odd lump there. But these deviations from perfection of form are not mere assertions of imperfection; they too become expressive elements in the film. Thus, in *Tire au flanc* the deviations from exact symmetry in composition and movement in the opening shot make us more aware of both Joseph's awkwardness and his love, while the formal differences between the first and last images of the film underscore the change that has occurred in Jean in this time. Not that these formal elements alone express much. The actions are central, of course: in the opening Joseph kisses Georgette; at the end Jean kisses Lily. But, given these actions, the form in which they are shown becomes revelatory, and, with Renoir, the departures from perfection of form are usually an instrument of revelation.

The recurring symmetries in *Tire au flanc* are the first example of what Renoir will later describe as his constant effort to attain balance. Symmetry is, of course, a kind of balance, but an essentially static one. In *Tire au flanc* these static forms themselves serve as a balance to the almost runaway flow of motion they contain, but they also achieve a kind of dynamism of their own through their imperfection. Later, when Renoir had further mastered the art of cinema and had the added factor of sound in his control, he began to balance thoroughly dynamic forms—though an overall cyclical form and internal symmetries recur in many of his later films.

One further aspect of *Tire au flanc* deserves mention, since it too marks the first occurrence of a lasting Renoir interest. This is the documentary character of the army training scenes, though here each scene begins with some faithfulness to actual army routine and then lapses quickly into comedy. Judging by audience reaction, the funniest scene in the film occurs when the squad learns to march in gas masks. The corporal orders, "Put on your masks and follow me!" then goes marching away alone, his strange movements somehow suggesting the erratic rhythm of Opale in *The Testament of Dr. Cordelier* some thirty years later. The squad lurches through the woods like a blind beast, then one by one they roll down a hill, bowling over Catherine Hessling and the circle of children she directs. The scene ends with a strung-out chase of Hessling, children, and soldiers down the road until they engulf the little knots of officers who are there to watch the field training; Colonel Brochard having just congratulated Lieutenant Daumel on the brilliance of his company. Renoir says that he wanted this scene to be very realistic, to have the men act the way men really do when they have gas masks on. In this quest for realism he went so far as to have a camera strapped to the chest of a soldier rolling down the hill. "But then," he adds, "in the cutting room I finally realized how funny all this was and left that shot out."

6

Le Tournoi and *Le Bled*
1929

The Jazz Singer was released by Warner Brothers in October 1927, and by mid-1928 producers were striving frantically to include at least a few minutes of some sort of sound in every movie released. The box-office left no doubt that American movie goers preferred the most wretched sound film to the best of the silents. Still, the two biggest and most expensive of Renoir's silent films, *Le Tournoi* and *Le Bled*, were made later, both with big budgets, large casts, and, as Renoir remarks, "lots of horses." Both films were occasioned by particular events: *Le Tournoi* by the *Fêtes du Bimillenaire* at Carcassonne, which revived the pageantry of the fifteenth century amid the best preserved ancient fortifications in France, *Le Bled* by the impending one hundredth anniversary of the French landing in Algeria in 1830. Renoir expressed his feelings about these commercial projects in an interview at about the time *Le Bled* was opening in Paris, "I bitterly regret . . . that I have been obliged to make films of a genre which is far from pleasing to me or according with my mentality."[1]

Retrospectively, however, one cannot regret the time Renoir spent on these conventional melodramas, which pit wicked villains against pure heroes in scenes evoking echoes of Douglas Fairbanks. For these silent films continue Renoir's courtship of the mobile camera: there are shots from horseback with a hand-held camera, a duel filmed in part from the point of view of a rapier (perhaps emulating Abel Gance, who swung his camera through the trajectory of a snowball in *Napoleon*), long traveling shots along the ramparts at Carcassonne and across the vineyards and deserts of Algeria. Meanwhile the directors of talkies had their cameras contained in soundproof booths and their actors confined to the range of an immobile and not very sensitive microphone. In its infancy, the sound film set the visual aspects of cinema back ten years, but during this infancy Renoir took his fluid camera to southern France and Algeria, then did not direct a feature film for two years. By the time he did, the possibility of movement had been regained, and he could turn immediately to the problem of how best to combine sound with the camera techniques he had mastered in his last three silent films.

To my knowledge, no complete print of *Le Tournoi* still exists, the last one having been destroyed by a fire in the Cinémathèque Française in 1959. All that remains is a much shortened version put together for the BBC, which retains the story line of the film while eliminating most of the pageantry that was *Le Tournoi's* chief excuse for being. Set in 1562, when Catherine de Medici ruled in the name of her twelve-year-old son, Charles IX, and tried to maintain power in an uneasy peace between Catholic and Protestant factions, the story mixes politics with pageantry and derring-do, its cli-

Jean Renoir directing Enrique Rivero and Jackie Monnier in *Le Tournoi*, 1928.

Jean Renoir as actor. *La P'tite Lili* (1927) and *Le Petit Chaperon rouge* (1929).

max a tournament of knights in armor played by cadets from the cavalry school at Saumur.

Le Bled does still exist, though I have seen only two of its ten reels. Whereas *Le Tournoi* was only a commemorative film, *Le Bled* had a propaganda purpose as well. Though the French had been in Algeria for a hundred years and making films for over thirty, Algeria had not yet been exploited cinematically. The government of Algeria subsidized the Société des Films Historiques to make a film not only commemorating the centennial but also displaying the charms of North Africa and, they hoped, enticing droves of tourists to the centennial celebration. Thus, the story contrived to show as many variations of the Algerian scene as possible—the city and the country, the north and the south—which gave Renoir an opportunity to indulge his liking for documentary footage. The story involves the arrival in Algeria of two young people seeking fortune and finding, naturally, love. The scenes in *Le Bled* that have provoked most comment include a gazelle hunt in southern Algeria and the use of a trained falcon in a chase after the villain who has carried off the heroine.

Having finished these forgettable films, Jean Renoir went home and again turned actor in a short film directed by his friend Alberto Cavalcanti. Two years earlier, in 1927, Renoir and Catherine Hessling had joined with Cavalcanti in making a ten-minute film based on a popular song, *La P'tite Lili*. *La P'tite Lili* also offered a brief glimpse of young Dido Freire, who would become Mme. Jean Renoir some fourteen years later. Many writers have identified Dido Freire as Cavalcanti's niece; perhaps her appearance in *La P'tite Lili* helped give rise to this mistake. Cavalcanti's actual relationship to Miss Freire was that of *correspondant*; he had come to France from Brazil some years earlier, and when Dido's Brazilian family sent their daughter to France to school they asked Cavalcanti, as a friend of the family, to serve in loco parentis.

In 1929 Renoir and Cavalcanti came together again to make a very free adaptation of Little Red Riding Hood (*Le Petit Chaperon rouge*), with Catherine Hessling in the title role and Jean Renoir playing the wolf. Apparently played broadly for laughs, the film ends, according to Jacques Rivette, with the heroine being carried off in a balloon by the seat of her pantaloons. This short work may have had a therapeutic function for Renoir, as *Charleston* did after *Nana*, being work joyfully done among friends. According to Henri Langlois, *Le Petit Chaperon rouge* is a lost film, only fragments still existing.

After this Renoir played a role in a film made in Germany, *Die Jagd nach dem Gluck*, but did not make another film of his own until 1931. Paradoxically, perhaps, his "success" at the end of the silent-film era worked against his chances of making a talking film. As he recalled it, the completion of *Le Tournoi* and *Le Bled*, both big-budget films made for an organization with vast funds, left him with a reputation as a very expensive director who made films shot in far-off locations and filled with galloping horses. But audiences now wanted to hear voices, and horses didn't talk. Producers turned to the theatre for material, and financiers found money for those films with much dialogue and little movement that contemporary audiences loved, though they now look stilted and confined. Not the sort of film to trust easily to an ex-cavalryman who liked to put his camera high up on some battlements or pretend it was the tip of a sword. So Renoir waited. And worked on his adaptation of *La Chienne*.

Jean Renoir's active career in silent film spanned just five years. In this time he had completed seven films, plus the unfinished *Charleston*; each new work differing quite considerably in form, subject, and genre from its predecessors. Through these diverse works Renoir explored the film medium, mastered its techniques, and began to create his own forms. From a stylistic affinity with the avant-garde, he moved toward a more original but less showy way of constructing his films; his passion for visual tricks cooled, but a new passion for actors grew to replace it. And in the projects that he cared about, though perhaps not in the purely commercial productions, he established that particular relation between director and film that would persist throughout his career, both more personal and less authoritarian than that of many other directors of stature. In every film he took a part in

Jean Renoir on the set of *Die Jagd Nach Dem Gluck*, 1930.

writing the script, even when someone else's name would appear in the credits. Thus he was always, from the very inception of a work, deep inside it, or had it deep inside him. He could not work comfortably from outside, filming someone else's words and ideas. I believe that his success at improvisation stemmed from this internal relation of man and work. When he stepped upon the set, he so carried the whole work with him that he grasped immediately the impact a newly improvised element would have on the whole, whether this be a complete new scene constructed in the inspiration of the moment or a simple change in a line hit upon by an actor. This made him the bane of screenwriters in Hollywood and script-girls everywhere; for he never considered a script inviolable and many times demonstrated his genius by throwing the script away without impairing the unity of his film.

But he did this not at all on the model of the imperious director of Hollywood fact and legend. Genius he may have been, but a hesitant genius, often unsure of himself, asking advice from everyone. Perhaps mere humanity or the example of his father led him to treat everyone involved in a film as a collaborator, but this real uncertainty led him to listen to what others said and gave these others the assurance that they were, indeed, co-workers. And this helped create that atmosphere of freedom and mutual respect that drew from so many "accomplices" the very best they had to give. On the set Renoir made those decisions he found so hard to make ahead of time; it always, at that point, was *his* film. But from *La Fille de l'eau* to the last shot of *Le Petit Theatre de Jean Renoir*, the hundreds of men and women who worked with him usually felt it *their* film, too—and his work profited from this feeling.

This method, if it can be called that, was already established in the silent films. Renoir had no theories about how to make films, but instead an openness—toward both the techniques of the art and the world to be filmed—that allowed him to adjust one to the other without embarrassment and without rigid preconception. And it allowed him to approach the expanded medium of sound film without regrets for the lost art of silent film nor any fixed notions about the limitations of sound. And once he was able to work in the new medium, he discovered the point of his years of preparation; for here at last was his true vocation.

On purge bébé
1931

Michel Simon, indeed! Michel Simon is an actor for whom I have more than admiration . . . But, you know, I've been lucky in my life: what I say of Michel Simon, I could say, for example, of Gabin. In France we have some people like that, who have been invented solely to allow us to make great films.
—*Jean Renoir*

For his first sound film Renoir hoped to adapt a novel by Georges de la Fouchardière, *La Chienne*, with Michel Simon in the central role. Attracted by Simon's stage performance in *Jean de la lune*, he had then worked with him in *Tire au flanc* and now dreamed of Simon in the role of the henpecked cashier, Legrand, whose inner life so contradicted his outer appearance. But, Renoir has said, "*La Chienne* was a film with a sizable budget. *Le Tournoi* and *Le Bled* were expensive and had both taken a long time to shoot. So before I could be entrusted with *La Chienne* I had to give proof to the Braunberger-Richebé studio that I could work rapidly."[1]

Pierre Braunberger did not share with most French producers the feeling that Renoir projects should be approached with caution. Braunberger had returned to France from the United States in 1924 as director of publicity for Paramount in Paris, and soon thereafter Pierre Lestringuez introduced him to Renoir. The two became friends immediately and Braunberger was involved in several of Renoir's silent films. In response to the new vogue for sound, Braunberger and Roger Richebé had renovated the Billancourt studios and equipped them with sound stages. Renoir's proposal to shoot *La Chienne* was welcomed by Braunberger, but Richebé had to be convinced—as Renoir puts it, "I had to pass a sort of examination."

This examination was *On purge bébé*; to pass, Renoir had to complete it within a small budget and a short shooting schedule. He filmed thirty to forty shots a day, and the film earned back its costs within a few months of the day he had started to write the adaptation. Renoir had passed with flying colors, but the exam, like many exams, was of questionable relevance to the real subject. *On purge bébé* showed that Renoir could, if he wanted, make *a* film under conditions imposed by the studio, but that it showed much about making a *Renoir* film is doubtful.

On purge bébé, adapted from a Feydeau play that had been popular on the Paris stage twenty years earlier, resembles many such adaptations of the period, having an abundance of dialogue and not much action. It differs from every other Renoir film in just these respects; even more so in its strict adherence to its source. Renoir departs from the single set of the play only to insert brief scenes that break up the otherwise interminable talk. Except for these omissions, the dialogue of the film follows the play almost word for word.

The French theatre is noted for bedroom comedies, but *On purge bébé* might better be called a bathroom farce. A porcelain manufacturer, M. Follavoine (Louvigny), late one morning awaits the arrival of M. Chouilloux (Michel Simon) from the War Ministry. Chouilloux, Follavoine hopes, will help him put over a big deal. As he explains to his wife:

> Today the government has only one objective—to improve the lot of the soldier. They care for him; they coddle him; they dress him in cotton. So, henceforth every soldier of the French army will have his own chamber pot!—Personal and issued at his induction.—Consequently, shortly there will be a contract made for this new—uh, military furniture, and I, as a manufacturer of porcelain, have decided to submit a bid. And that's where Chouilloux appears as *deus ex machina.*—Chouilloux is president of the examining commission—charged by the state to adopt the model which will become standard. Now you see why I want to treat him tactfully? I have the patent for unbreakable porcelain, no? Then, enter the *deux ex machina*, it's in the bag and my fortune is made.

But as Follavoine dreams about the profit to be made on 300,000 chamber pots, his wife Julie (Marguerite Pierry) interrupts, clad in bathrobe and curlers, to discuss Bébé's constipation. After much talk about purges, slop-pails and chamber pots, Julie goes off to purge Bébé.

Chouilloux arrives to discuss with Follavoine the relative virtues of porcelain and sheet-metal chamber pots and engage in a bowling match in which the two samples of "unbreakable porcelain" pots both break. Chouilloux's polite inquiry about Bébé opens a discussion in which the state of

Chouilloux's intestines are described at length. Finally Bébé himself (Sacha Taride) appears, defies his father's authority, refuses the purge despite a bribe, insults Chouilloux, then says he will take his purge if Chouilloux will too.

None of this anal humor was invented by Renoir; it all comes straight from Feydeau. Renoir's major contribution to the theme was to register loudly on the sound track the unmistakable noise of a toilet flushing. This occurs after M. Chouilloux has refused to cooperate by drinking even a half a glass of the purge, and Julie in vexation has snapped, "Am I to be mixed up in it if his wife makes him a cuckold with her cousin Truchet?" At being called a cuckold, Chouilloux gasps, clutches his throat, and gulps down the whole glass Julie has been pressing on him, then dashes for the bathroom.

Judging by critical comments, this one sound of a functioning toilet was the most noteworthy thing about *On purge bébé.* "That immediately made me pass for a great artist!" Renoir remarked, "The idea of taking the microphone, going to the spot in question and pulling the chain—that seemed a species of audacious innovation." The same sound had of course been recorded by Bunuel a year earlier in *L'Age d'or.* But then the sound was symbolic, while *On purge bébé* had a genuine toilet in use. Renoir did have something further in mind though. In 1938 he wrote, "It was the epoch of false noises; the accessories, the decor being arranged for the sound with an incredible naiveté. These practices irritated me. To mark my ill-humor I decided to register the sound of a flushing toilet."[2] No one seems to have gotten that point, though some have thought that Renoir, like Bunuel, was displaying his disdain for the whole bourgeois world depicted in the film.

While Chouilloux remains in the bathroom, Mme. Chouilloux (Olga Valery) arrives for lunch, accompanied by her cousin M. Truchet (Fernandel). The film quickly ends in almost total disaccord. In the confusion Toto pours his purge on the floor, then shows his mother the empty glass. With everyone else departed in fury, Julie joyfully embraces her good Bébé—two pure and innocent souls cleaving to each other in a world gone mad.

Apart from the sound of swirling water, *On purge bébé* provided the occasion for an early appearance of Fernandel in a few truculent moments as the greatly offended M. Truchet. But there are virtues beyond these. Louvigny and Marguerite Pierry give vigorous performances as the Follavoines; the frequency with which their attitudes and gestures resemble those of characters in the James Thurber cartoons of the 1930s suggests that beneath the ridiculous facade of the farce there lurks more than a glimpse of domestic truths of the period. But Michel Simon proves the delight of the film. The range of his performance is impressive, moving from an initial elegance and official pomposity tinged with irony, through a naive eagerness to tell the world about his intestines, to a collapse into complete distraction at the pronouncement of the word "cuckold," ending with cold hauteur as he dismisses his wife and challenges Follavoine to a duel before departing with complete, if injured, dignity. Apart from his moments of distraction, he moves with grace and fluency of gesture, delivering his lines with more subtely and nuance than anyone else in the film.

In visual techniques, *On purge bébé* is the most meager of Renoir's films, composed almost entirely of full and medium shots, with little camera movement. There are perhaps half a dozen close-ups, including one of the slop-pail Mme. Follavoine carries through much of the film. This paucity of visual variation is credited by Renoir, not to the theatrical material being filmed, but rather to the speed at which he had to work: "Where I would have used the camera with a little more abundance, I was obliged to limit myself in order to complete my thirty to forty shots a day."

Still, one cannot regret the necessity that thrust this project on Renoir at this time. For in the endless talk that fills the sound track—there is no music —Renoir found the revelation that shaped his future work: "At first I was interested mainly in working out the story. Then I became fascinated with techniques and dreamed of making pictures filled with nothing but tricks. Only when the actors began to talk did I gradually realize the possibility of getting to the truth of character. It was when I began to make talking pictures that I had the revelation that what I was most deeply concerned about was character." This realization first occurred during the shooting of *On purge bébé*, of which Renoir said, "It was good. I was content. And then— what I loved above all—it was a great experience with actors; it was very well played."[3]

M. Truchet (Fernandel), Julie Follavoine (Marguerite Pierry), and Mme. Chouilloux (Olga Valery).

Speech was the key to characterization. Renoir soon discovered that when an actor's voice was right, when he *spoke* as the character, then he grasped the role. Here, as in so many aspects of his work, Renoir's approach was intuitive rather than deliberate; having set his actors to talking, he then saw what the import of the talk was for his medium, and also how he, as director, could make the talk most significant in his films without disrupting that sense of collaboration that had heretofore prevailed on his sets.

8

La Chienne
1931

I harbor an immense fondness for La Chienne, *because it was the first and one of the rare films in which I had the feeling of having truly collaborated. A film in which I was set completely at liberty. I can count them on the fingers of one hand. This happened to me once more with Renoir and that was* Boudu.
—*Michel Simon*

Having passed the exam, Renoir assumed he could make his film as he pleased, "In *La Chienne* I was pitiless and, I must say, unbearable. I made the film as I wished, as I intended it, without taking any account of the desires of the producer. I had never shown a single bit of my script, not more than the smallest scraps of my dialogue, and I had arranged for the rushes to remain almost invisible until I had finished shooting the film. At that moment there was a fine scandal. The producer had expected a light comedy; he found himself before a somber, desperate drama which had as its climax a murder not at all to the taste of the moment.

"They chased me from the studio and particularly from my cutting-room, and as I tried to get in there every day, they called the police. Then the producer, having had the film edited as he wished, saw that it didn't hold together and that, loss for loss, it would be better to let me do it. I was allowed back in the cutting room and tried to repair the damage."[1]

Georges de la Fouchardière's novel had been published in 1930 and widely read in France. Renoir quickly saw its possibilities as a film, but had to convince a producer. By the summer of 1931, the novel had lost its currency, and although Fouchardière's reputation as a writer of comic works was obviously known to the producer, Roger Richebé, his novel *La Chienne*, which Marcel Carné described as a "realistic and brutal slice of life,"[2] obviously was not.

Renoir had planned the title role for Catherine Hessling; he envisioned spellbinding scenes between her and Michel Simon. But Roger Richebé had under contract a young actress, Janie Marèze, fresh from a striking success in *Mam'zelle Nitouche*, whereas Catherine Hessling had for some time been out of the public eye. Richebé insisted on Janie Marèze for *La Chienne*. Renoir, faced with a choice between his film and his wife, chose the film. Forty years later he would write, "This betrayal marked the end of our life together."[3]

Apart from this change in casting, *La Chienne* was conceived wholly by Renoir and made in almost complete freedom; hence it provides an accurate index to the state of his art at the time. And, as the first shot of *Tire au flanc* had announced a new visual style, the first shot of *La Chienne* proclaims the emergence of the Renoir of the thirties. Appropriately, sound rather than image conveys this proclamation; for the wedding of sound to the visual style born in *Tire au flanc* gives rise to the Renoir films of that time.

Heretofore, Renoir's opening shots had presented the scene of action, at first with conventional establishing shots, but from *Tire au flanc* on with close shots of a detail, which provided focus and orientation when the camera moved away to show the larger scene. Now, paradoxically, in what is considered the first full flowering of Renoir's naturalism, he chose to frame *La Chienne* in a theatrical setting, though this completely untheatrical film had no integral connection whatsoever with this frame. *La Chienne* opens onto the stage of a puppet theatre. A puppet announces, "Ladies and gentlemen, we will have the honor of presenting to you a great social drama. The spectacle will prove that vice is always punished." A second puppet, a gendarme, reinforces the first, "We have the honor to present you a comedy with moral implications." Here Guignol appears, armed with his club as usual, argues with the others and then beats them from the scene. A beloved character from Jean Renoir's childhood, a most appropriate spokesman for him now, Guignol addresses the audience: "Ladies and gentlemen, don't listen to them. The work we will show you is neither a drama nor a comedy. It has no moral intentions and it will prove to you nothing at all. The characters are neither heroes nor villains. They are just poor humans like you and me." He then proceeds to introduce the major characters, who appear superimposed on the puppet stage: "There are three principals, He, She, and the Other One, as usual. He is a decent fellow, timid, not too young and extraordinarily naive. In intellect and feeling he is above the milieu in which he lives, so that in this milieu he is taken for an imbecile. She is a little woman

78   JEAN RENOIR

who has her charm and her own vulgarity. She is always sincere; she lies all the time. The Other One is 'my Dédé' and nothing more."

Seen now, this prologue appears to be a Renoir manifesto for the talkies, renouncing both the character types and the stories with which film-makers, including Renoir, had heretofore filled the screen—puppets, good and evil, manipulated to demonstrate the dubious clichés of conventional morality. Instead ordinary people—*comme moi, comme vous*—will work and love and die in the mixed genre that most resembles life. Surely, a program for most of the Renoir films from *La Chienne* to *La Regle du jeu*.

Guignol's introduction immediately puts this program into effect. Though perhaps merely a device to replace the printed titles used in silent films this introduction little resembles the titles Renoir had employed for this purpose before. Being spoken, these lines have a different tone. Spoken lines are always in someone's voice, if only Alpha 60 or HAL; always reach us as someone's comment even if the speaker remains unidentified. Guignol gives us a view of the characters, not the truth about them. And the introductions of Legrand and Lulu—He and She—suggest in ambiguity of characterization beyond that obtainable in silent film; rather than merely designating character types, these introductions make complex claims which create questions we can resolve only by perceiving the characters for ourselves.

Narrative and Characterization

Maurice Legrand (Michel Simon), a quiet, middle-aged cashier, finds refuge from the coarseness of his colleagues and the tongue of his shrewish wife, Adèle (Magdeleine Berubet), by painting. But Adèle frequently complains about the mess this makes in *her* house and constantly evokes the memory of her first husband, Alexis Godard, who was killed in the war, "a real man" who would never be such a fool as Legrand.

One evening after a banquet, Legrand refuses to visit a brothel with his colleagues, instead walks home alone. On a stairway in Montmartre he happens upon a drunken pimp, Dédé (Georges Flamant), beating a young prostitute, Lulu (Janie Marèze). Legrand intervenes, knocks Dédé down, and later walks with Lulu, who will not let him take her home but embraces him quickly before they part.

Legrand falls in love with Lulu, furnishes an apartment for her, hangs his paintings on the wall. Lulu accepts all this but cares only for Dédé. Dédé, however, cares only for the money Lulu gets from Legrand. When she returns empty-handed one night, he pushes her roughly away, takes two of Legrand's paintings and leaves. Since the paintings are unsigned, Dédé and a friend invent a painter; a dealer, Wallstein (Mancini), hangs the paintings in his gallery and begins to create a reputation for "Clara Wood."

So Lulu becomes Clara Wood, a celebrity in the Paris art world, and

Dédé changes his style of living—buys a car, new clothes. He pockets all of the money made from the paintings and expects Legrand to provide for Lulu. Earlier, Legrand had taken money that Adèle had hidden away; now he steals from the office safe.

One day a tramp accosts Legrand and identifies himself as Alexis Godard (Gaillard). Having escaped the army and marriage once by exchanging papers with a dead soldier, Alexis now offers to "sacrifice himself" again if Legrand will give him 5,000 francs. Legrand manages to deliver Alexis back into the arms of Adèle and free himself, packs his suitcase and leaves, breathing exultantly, "Ah! Liberty and Lulu!" But at Lulu's apartment he finds her in bed with Dédé. Crushed, he backs out of the door. Dédé storms at Lulu for "ruining everything," dresses, and leaves.

The next morning Legrand returns to find Lulu still in bed, reading. He attempts to explain her behavior; she responds by coldly inquiring, "When are you going to finish that painting? I need it." Legrand can no longer avoid understanding; he calls her a bitch, then finally kills her—driven to this act by her derisive laughter. In the street below the apartment people listen to a street singer; Legrand slips away unnoticed behind the crowd. Dédé arrives in his car, pushes through the crowd and into the building. A moment later he reappears mopping his brow and drives silently away.

Dédé is charged with murder. Legrand loses his job when his thefts are discovered. At Dédé's trial, Legrand faints in the courtroom as the death sentence is pronounced.

Although the major events of La Fouchardière's novel provided the narrative thread of his film, Renoir did not much care for the excessive cleverness of this author's style nor his rather condescending treatment of his characters. Having something quite different in mind, Renoir set out to reconstruct the characters and present them with objectivity and sympathy. So treated, Maurice Legrand emerges in Michel Simon's superb performance as the first of a series of memorable characters who live within the Renoir films of this period.

On its surface, the role of Legrand seems much less appropriate for Michel Simon than those he had previously created in Renoir films. Legrand is closed, turned inward, intent on concealing himself from the world. For the development of both his character and the action of the film, he must be unobtrusive, insignificant, unnoticeable; a man you could meet face to face and immediately forget. Simon's sheer presence as an actor, the mobile expressiveness of his face and body, his size, all seem opposed to such characterization. But now, as Legrand, the face becomes a mask, with pinched mouth, down-turned eyes half hidden by steel-rimmed spectacles, the dynamic ruggedness so evident in Boudu or Père Jules suppressed under a static symmetry imposed by spectacles, mustache, and mousy hair parted in the center. The body too turns in upon itself, stoops, moves slowly, essays a very limited range of gestures; as Legrand, Simon seems to shrink, require less room to live in. His movement subdued, all bouyancy and exuberance suppressed, Simon becomes the inconspicuous cashier, the butt of his colleagues' jokes and his wife's ill-humor.

But beside this pattern of habitual looks and gestures that defines the public person of Legrand, Simon constructs a counterpoint of tone, expression, and action that reveals a very different character, the inner self that Legrand hides from view, strong, assured, and disdainful of his middle-class milieu. In this inner vision Legrand lives as a romantic hero, superior to the petty intrigues of his colleagues, impervious to the bickering of Adèle, his capacity for deep love and decisive action latent under the facade of mediocrity he shows the world. Only in his paintings does Legrand openly express this inner self, but before his affair with Lulu, Adèle alone sees the paintings and she thinks them worthless.

Much of the mastery of Michel Simon's performance consists in his maintaining the precarious balance of outer diffidence and inner assurance so essential to this character. As Legrand, his gestures are all self-deprecatory, withdrawing rather than assertive, pointed downward and inward rather than toward others. Except for Lulu, his hands almost never reach out to touch anyone; more typically, they clasp each other or some object he interposes between himself and others—his hat, a ledger, a palette. Yet on the level of action, he is neither hesitant nor weak; when he chooses to act he does so directly and effectively. A tinge of irony in his voice and a gleam in his eye combine with this boldness in action to let us see and half-believe in Legrand's vision of himself; still, the disesteem everyone feels for Legrand also has firm roots in Simon's performance. It rests not only on his self-effacing pattern of gesture, but also on the disregard for others that makes plausible their failure to perceive the clues which reveal Legrand's inner life to us. Legrand seldom looks directly at anyone, seems wrapped within himself; by what we might call the principle of the reciprocity of attention, this systematic inattention assures that others will take little heed of him. So firm is his colleagues' conviction of Legrand's ineptness that he serves as their model of ineffectuality, a fact which they make no attempt to conceal from him.

But if they are wrong in their conception of Legrand, so is he. However much he may think his usual demeanor a mere disguise, the shy introspective cashier proves as genuine an aspect of Legrand as is the bold hero who lunges across the Montmartre steps to rescue Lulu. This shows in his most intimate scenes with Lulu, away from the crass world he disdains, where he wears no disguise and the warm, romantic inner Legrand may freely emerge. And he is different, indeed; he presses close to Lulu, with his hands constantly on her. He fondles her, holds her arm, caresses her ear. We cannot doubt the reality of his passion, yet his attention seems elsewhere, and these manifestations of love are strangely abstract. Legrand holds Lulu rather as he does the objects he uses as props to fend off the world; we sense neither an outpouring of love nor a celebration of the delights of the flesh. Rather, these tactual expressions of tenderness seem more designed to draw Lulu into his closed inner world than to bring that world out to the surface of his life. The habits of inattention and withdrawal that typify the outer Legrand cannot be discarded at will. They persist throughout his affair with Lulu, defeating his attempt to act out his inner life and win her love. And no doubt they make more inevitable Lulu's account of making love with Legrand: "That doesn't exist . . . I let myself go while thinking of Dédé."

Perhaps a more perceptive woman might have seen the inner Legrand. But not Lulu. She—la chienne, Renoir's first variation on the Nana theme of the destructive enchantress, the devourer of men—exploits Legrand's desire quite pitilessly, flaunts her scorn for his illusions about true love, making it cruelly clear that she has seen only the outer man: "Look at yourself in a mirror . . . Monsieur wished to be loved for himself! Monsieur wanted love! Ah, let me laugh!"

Though Jean Renoir had dreamed of this role for Catherine Hessling, I cannot regret the studio decision to insist on Janie Marèze. For no performance of Catherine Hessling's suggests a departure from the woman-child, wilful and erratic, of *Nana*. As played by Janie Marèze, the winsome bitch Lulu bears little resemblance to Catherine Hessling's Nana. Lulu is not a child; neither petulant nor vindictive, she does not play at love nor collect men just to prove the power of her sexuality, but uses this power to achieve a goal she mistakenly thinks within her grasp. The destruction follows incidentally.

In outward mien and gesture, Lulu appears gentle, passive, even tender, as if indeed her proper role were that of the little wife she begs Dédé to let her be. Wholly submissive to Dédé's every whim, she would soften him by her own softness and acquiescence, sure that such evidence of love must stir awake a better nature than Dédé's usual façade of arrogance. If he allowed it, she would cling softly to him and let the world go by. When with Legrand, she remains equally pliant and passive, yet the whole tone of her reactions alters. Toward Dédé her possessiveness makes every act of submission an offering of herself, a plea for love. With Legrand she is merely submissive. Janie Marèze conveys this difference in her voice, but more essentially in the tension and orientation of her body; Lulu turns toward Dédé and seems drawn to him even when he acts most cruelly, turns away from Legrand even when he is most loving. Bad manners for a whore, even if, as Dédé tells a friend, he never really taught her the business. But though Lulu's metier seems evident and Dédé repeatedly insists that she "arrange" herself with some other man in order to provide the money he desires, Lulu

Maurice Legrand (Michel Simon) finds Lulu (Janie Marèze).

does not see herself as a prostitute. She considers these affairs rather as odd jobs undertaken in a moment of necessity, unrelated to her real life and hardly compromising her honesty and devotion to "my Dédé."

Lulu reveals her view of this situation in a moment of candor as she first walks with Legrand along the bleak Montmartre street, past posters that evoke a Paris night life so different from that these two forlorn figures share —Josephine Baker at the Casino de Paris, the Palace Nudist Bar—Lulu talking only of Dédé to this man who has just saved her from a beating at his hands: "You know he's well-bred. When he came he was very nice . . . Just yesterday he told me that if he had money he would buy me new clothes and then I wouldn't look worse than any other . . . And he has talent, too. You should see him imitate Maurice Chevalier. Only, he has no connections. So I have to help him."

Described as "helping him," her prostitution becomes a bourgeois virtue and need not disturb Lulu's image of herself as a loving wife. Within this self-deception, deceit can readily assume the name of faithfulness, and cruelty become the other face of love. But it also allows some of Lulu's actions to have a genuineness and innocence that Nana could never achieve, and it makes her almost as much a victim as the man she heartlessly deceives.

If we look at *La Chienne* for its treatment of what Renoir has identified as a major concern throughout his career, the way people meet, we see again its depth of insight, its central place in Renoir's early work. Lulu and Legrand meet by accident, from wholly different worlds, with no background to provide identity for each other, no time to prepare a face for the encounter. The misunderstanding is almost total. Legrand cannot conceive that Lulu might have been having an ordinary evening about which she has no complaint; he sees her as a maiden in distress. For Lulu, Legrand's intervention is not an heroic act but an annoyance. Once more being picked up by a middle-aged, well-dressed man, she sees him as just like all the others she has "arranged" herself with before. Neither can distinguish those acts of the other that are characteristic or typical from those that we may call transformational—the rare actions that mark a breaking out of one's old self and the changing of one's life. Legrand believes that Lulu's acceptance of his offer to take her home is transformational, the beginning of a new life for her, but it is, of course, merely characteristic. Lulu thinks Legrand's proposition characteristic—these old men do that with all the girls—but it is of course a complete departure from his whole form of life. These misapprehensions lay the tracks upon which their tragic course will run.

Dédé, the Other One, seems much the least complex of the major characters of *La Chienne*—a vain young punk, nothing more. Jean Renoir wrote in *My Life and My Films*, "Flamant was a remarkable amateur actor whom I had chosen for the part because, having frequented the milieu—the criminal underworld—he had picked up their jargon and behavior." In conversation Renoir put this more bluntly, "I found a young pimp and let him play himself."

Perhaps the small range of situations in which we see him helps account for the lack of complexity, though Georges Flamant's performance endows Dédé with such conceit as to blind him to differences of context. Dédé considers himself far too clever to work; but despite his dubious profession and his contempt for such bourgeois virtues as thrift and honesty, Dédé's notion

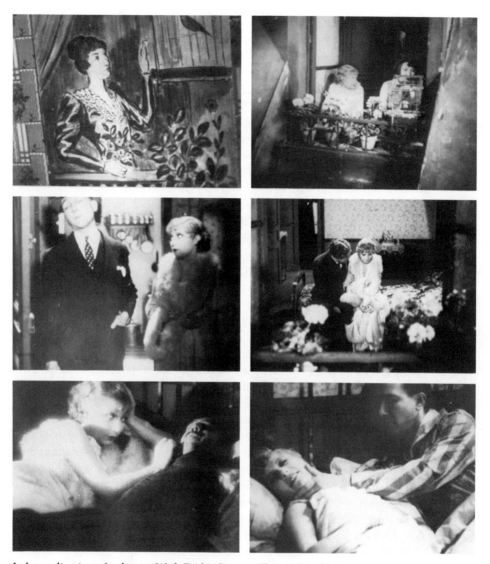

Lulu, realization of a dream. With Dédé (Georges Flamant) and Maurice.

of success still identifies him as thoroughly bourgeois at heart. He asks, "What would I look like with a girl who wears cotton stockings and cheap hats?" tells Lulu that going to the Opera is "out of style," and when Legrand discovers him in bed with Lulu his greatest concern is a loss of income when his car isn't yet paid for. Lulu never speaks to or about Dédé without adding the possessive "mon Dédé," but nothing is clearer than that Dédé is not hers. Rather, he treats her as a commodity to be used as he wishes, acting with brutal confidence that she will submit to any abuse. Only after Lulu's death does he show any sign of feeling for her, repeating with regret during his interrogation, "Ah, oui, c'était une belle fille," but even then shows no remorse about his treatment of her.

Like Legrand, Dédé seldom pays attention to anyone else; but whereas Legrand seems engrossed in himself, the source of Dédé's inattention lies in his constant effort to impress others with his own status. Hence Dédé becomes by far the most mobile character in *La Chienne* in both gesture and facial expression. At first view, Georges Flamant appears to overplay these little self-centered performances in a way which emphasizes the obnoxious traits of this young scoundrel. But then one sees how the overplaying comes from within the character himself and that Dédé is both performer and audience, the exaggerations of expression serving as much to reassure him as to impress others. This realization provides a glimpse into the weakness that underlies Dédé's surface arrogance and makes plausible his collapse at his trial.

Almost everything Dédé says about himself is both false and uttered with great assurance, his conception of the proprieties of speech being that of conformity to his vision of his own eminence rather than the truth. Thus, when questioned about Lulu's death and reminded of a previous conviction for white slavery, Dédé responds with an insolent air, as if correcting a simple mistake, "White slavery? Oh, no, no, no . . . I just gave advice to some young girls who wanted to see the country, to learn things . . . yes, to learn things, *M. le juge*. And well, listen, that was better for them than being servants in a creamery or working in a factory, wasn't it?" And he sees no incongruity at all in telling the examining magistrate, "Put yourself in my place, your honor." His cocksure attitude persists throughout the interrogation; the spell of his own false image so captures Dédé that he cannot conceive of anyone's disbelief in his verbal enactment of it. At the trial his lawyer seeks to defend him by denying this image, but Dédé interrupts; he will speak for himself. He stands and only then does his actual situation seem to strike through to him. No blustering falsehood emerges; in desperation he can only repeat the unbelievable truth: "I didn't kill Lulu. I didn't kill Lulu."

At this point, with Lulu dead, Legrand ruined, and Dédé sentenced to death, the story of *La Chienne* seems over. Despite the frailty beneath his conceit and the pity evoked by his final moment of despair, Dédé remains one of the most negative characters in all of Renoir's mature work, an insufferable young punk whose callous unconcern makes his legally unjust conviction and sentence seem poetically right. But Renoir will not leave it at that; he appends to the trial a brief scene that transforms our final image of Dédé. A priest and officials enter the prison cell where Dédé lies asleep. Someone taps Dédé on the shoulder to awaken him. Cut to a close-up: Dédé, head raised, looking upward, motionless, not quite in profile. The whole array of expressions with which Dédé faced the world—arrogant, sullen, bored, petulant, scornful, cocky, self-satisfied—has been swept away. For once his face seems naked, uprepared before the dawning realization of the import of this moment. This troubling images does not alter our perception of Dédé's character; its revelation is that we, too, are unprepared for it. It jolts our superiority; Dédé too is human and alone.

Renoir has said that only when his actors began to talk did he recognize the possibility of genuine characterization in film. His actors talked in *On purge bébé*, of course; in fact, they did almost nothing but talk. Nevertheless the sort of characterization we associate with Renoir occurs first in *La Chienne*. And the talk is very different in these films. One might say that in *On purge bébé* the action is constructed around the dialogue, whereas in *La Chienne* the dialogue occurs within the context of the action.

In this relation of action to dialogue, *On purge bébé* is Renoir's film that comes closest to being a photographed play. Consequently, one needs merely read the dialogue to gain a rather complete understanding of the film. Talk flows almost without stop; nearly every action is not only performed but also described and commented on. Julie carries her slop-pail around the house and Follavoine waves his chamber-pot; they also tell each other that that is what they are doing. The development and impact of the drama frequently depends more on these descriptions of the action than upon the actions themselves. Lines are often spoken with great relish and dramatic flair; we notice the cleverness of a line or the way it is delivered more than its role in the dramatic situation or the interactions it furthers. This dialogue does, of course, characterize; almost all that we know about the characters we learn from what they say and the way they say it. But these characters have no depth. They have life but no lives. We perceive their thoughts, feelings, and attitudes during the brief period encompassed within the film, but have little sense of any continuity of a life either before or after.

The talk in *La Chienne* has a very different flavor and function. It is not continuous; some important scenes have little or no dialogue. No line in *La Chienne* is included simply for its cleverness; no line is spoken in a fashion that diverts our attention from the context of the action to the manner of delivery, though the manner forms a part of the total context in which the speech is to be understood. The dialogue does, of course, express the thought and feelings of the speakers, but talk and action seldom merely reinforce each other, with each conveying essentially the same information or impression. Much more often, dialogue complements or contrasts with action, each communicating something in addition to that conveyed by the other, or conflicting with or undercutting the impression given by the other. Rarely does the dialogue describe an action we also see in the same scene; only Adèle regularly makes such statements, always as complaints about

Legrand's behavior. Since Adèle alone talks in this way in *La Chienne*, her utterances to serve to characterize her in a way in which similar descriptions fail to characterize in *On purge bébé*. Adèle's remarks evoke a life of constant dissatisfaction and complaint, a querulous, self-assertive character with little sympathy for the interests of others.

Where action is central in *La Chienne*, the dialogue serves as a sort of accompaniment that fills in the background and may reveal the significance of this particular action or show how it fits into the ongoing life of the characters. It may function as a link between scenes or as motivation for a succeeding act. When talk *is* the action of a scene, this talk invariably concerns matters other than what we see while the talk occurs. The lines in *La Chienne* are spoken naturally, without dramatic inflation; their force is utilized within the context of action. When such characters as Adèle or Dédé do dramatize their situation, they project this dramatization into the world of the film and not outward from it. And, whatever its immediate role in the development of the drama, the dialogue constantly combines with details of setting and action to reveal a relationship between characters that reaches beyond the immediate dramatic context and anchors the life of the characters in a precisely observed social milieu. The solidity of this social setting sustains for these persons an encompassing life which includes the moments we perceive; this, then, allows for the depth of characterization Renoir seeks.

The manner in which Renoir embeds his dialogue in the action to create characters within a milieu may be illustrated by the opening sequences of *La Chienne*—three scenes that surround the moment when Legrand's inner self bursts forth in action, fatally upsetting the calm obscurity of his life.

The banquet scene that opens *La Chienne* places Legrand among his colleagues, who appear middle-class, smug and successful, jovial, a bit coarse. Though Legrand wears the same uniform of formal bourgeois respectability as all the others—stiff shirt, black tie, wide satin lapels—almost every line and image in the scene displays his difference. A corny toast, an old cavalry joke, " . . . as we say in the regiment . . . a dry bottom! [*un cul-sec*]" provokes delighted laughter. The camera moves in medium close-up across three laughing faces to Legrand, unsmiling, puzzled, until he belatedly responds, "That's a good one." He seems not to hear the repeated jibes: "Sacré père Legrand. Always up to the minute!" "He won't come; he's too much afraid of his wife," and so forth, each remark accompanied by its own ambient laughter. His quiet remarks refusing to accompany his friends to the brothel contrast markedly to the sounds of festivity that dominate the sequence—glasses, laughter, loud talk, a phonograph playing a popular song —but also have their own tinge of superiority in the mild romanticism expressed in opposition to the worldliness of the others. The final shot of the scene underlines Legrand's separateness. The banquet over, a babbling cluster of men surges past the camera and out of the room, leaving Legrand, alone, bumbling along behind them, solemn, head down, a solitary figure totally apart from the spirit and movement that unite the rest.

The dialogue in this scene relates directly to the action, even constitutes some of it, as in the congratulatory speech and toast. Yet the characterizing power of this talk lies more in the background it reveals by presupposing it —the world of Legrand's work, where day after day he must move in the circle of these men who respect him not at all and whose perceptions so differ from his own.

The next sequence finds Lulu lying on the steps near the church of St. Jean de Montmartre, an arm shielding her face from Dédé's slaps. Legrand, coming down the steps with his old man's gait, stooped, hands clasped behind him, seems to have seen nothing. Yet, when Dédé kicks Lulu, Legrand swerves across the steps, knocks Dédé down with a blow and leans over Lulu, "Are you hurt? I was just passing by." But his courage and concern win little reward. Lulu regards him first with hostility, then cold calculation. When she speaks it is an accusation, "You have hurt him." She moves down the steps to comfort Dédé; caresses his face. Still, a moment later she turns plaintively back to Legrand. "We can't leave him like that. He'll get sick . . . from this cold . . . I don't have money enough to take a taxi." Legrand again responds with immediate action, running off across the square in search of a cab.

Apart from this moment, in which the talk springs directly from the action, the dialogue in this scene has little dependence on what we see. Rather, it provides the context in which the action can be understood. Dédé scolds Lulu for failing to have the money he demands, threatening to leave her if she doesn't get money from Legrand. Lulu reports Dédé's virtues to Legrand, who hardly seems to hear. Legrand pursues a single point: "Can I take you home?" "Let me come with you?" "When will I see you again?" The calm assurance of his refusal to join his friends at a brothel moments before casts a certain irony on these attempts to turn this chance meeting with a gentle whore into an affair. Lulu's footsteps echo in the dark and lonely Montmartre streets; the misperception that leads Legrand to take this moment for the realization of a romantic dream seems mocked by the somber reality of this setting, creating the sort of resonance that led French critics to begin writing of Renoir's "poetic realism."

The third sequence finds Legrand cautiously returning home after his encounter with Lulu. Mme. Legrand, startled awake, storms out of bed and stands in the doorway while light streaming from the bedroom reveals Legrand fumbling with the painting he has knocked froms its easel. As Adèle begins to rail, Legrand answers mildly, "Pardon me, I was trying to be quiet. I couldn't leave. The boss made a speech. The deputy was there." While her tirade mounts in violence and she threatens to give his paintings to the ragman, he methodically rearranges the paintings as if he were quite alone. He pauses only to goad her to greater fury when she proclaims the superiority of her first husband, remarking in ironic tones, with a malicious smile: "You're right. I'm not as dashing as Alexis Godard." Outraged, Adèle sputters, "In any case, you've been warned. Now hurry and get to bed. I want to sleep!" She slams the door. Wholly unperturbed, Legrand again looks sarcastically at the picture of Alexis Godard and mutters, "You must have made a pretty couple," then appears ready to begin to paint.

In this third scene most of the talk comes from Adèle, accusative, strident, unforgiving. Again, Legrand remains silent and unconcerned in the face of an assault. Again, the dialogue reveals more than it describes: the conditions of Legrand's domestic world, the climate for his lonely inturned life. By now the most insistent aspect of the dialogue of *La Chienne* has become Legrand's frequent failure to respond to the talk around him, his apparent obliviousness to much of what he must hear. Thus, behind its more directly characterizing role, Renoir has used his dialogue to separate Legrand from others and display him as lost in the ordinary world. This allows him, in the scene's final shot, to *show* what can't be said. Legrand doffs his jacket, unrolls an unfinished canvas, stands before the painting with his black tie dangling from his hand. In silence the camera rolls forward, moving finally from the wilderness of daily life into Legrand's real world. The scene ends in a close-up of the painting, Christ in flowing robes amid an apparently hostile group in modern dress. This final image provides a sort of punctuation mark at the end of the first section of *La Chienne*, emphasizing Legrand's painting as the quiet center to which he can escape, its Christ figure, strong, gentle, and misunderstood, summarizing all that we have gleaned of Legrand's inner vision of himself.

Treatment

Renoir has called *La Chienne* a "somber, desperate drama" and a mere recital of the events—a murder, an execution, the reduction of Legrand from a respectable citizen to a derelict—seems to confirm this assessment. But despite dark moments, the overall tone of the film is hardly one of desperation. Rather, scene after scene expresses the hopes of the characters, their dreams cherished in a context that seems to promise fulfillment. Legrand dreams of being free of Adèle, of living openly and joyously with Lulu. Lulu allows him to keep her and make love to her, treats him kindly, if disinterestedly, when he is with her; hence his hope seems not altogether frivolous. But Lulu hopes that Dédé will save enough money to enable her to leave Legrand and live only for him, dreams of a home in which she will be Dédé's little wife. Dédé hopes that Lulu will be sensible and stay with Legrand, dreams that Legrand's paintings and Lulu's affairs with other men will support him in the style to which he aspires. The situation is desperate, of course, but only the incompatibility of all these dreams makes it so, and Renoir with his concern to avoid sentimentality and cliché never dwells on the shadows behind the dream.

His cooly observant camera watches Legrand pocket Adèle's savings matter-of-factly in the midst of shaving and walk back to his mirror with quiet satisfaction, then fades to Dédé confidently plotting to sell the paintings he has taken from Lulu's wall. Or follows Lulu as she shows her new apartment to a friend, happily explaining that Legrand paid for the furniture but Dédé came with her to pick it out, for she wanted him to feel at home; then fades to Dédé playing cards and complaining that it's hard to get fifty francs from Lulu, but then asserting that things are much better with Legrand around, demonstrating how he knocked Legrand down when he insisted on speaking to Lulu but then, "He got up and we had a drink and now we are good friends."

The actions observed are indeed dishonorable—deceit, lies, theft—but performed without malice and contained within a world that accepts them as the most commonplace events.

It is perhaps the benign indifference of this surrounding world that restrains the desperation, holds it from breaking through to the surface of the film sooner. This encompassing world provides contrast and comment to the lives and actions of the protagonists, both masks the desperation of their plight and deepens the despair. The moment at which Legrand appropriates Adèle's savings to spend on Lulu may serve as illustration. Renoir accomplishes this scene in a single shot that fades in from the image of Lulu in tears after Dédé has left with the paintings under his arm, responding to her plea, "My Dédé, stay for a while," with an annoyed, "For conversation with madame? And then what else?" Legrand stands by a window of his apartment, in shirtsleeves and suspenders, a towel around his neck, lathering his face in preparation for shaving. Through the window we see across the court and into the Legrand kitchen where Adèle is busy hanging clothes. As he rotates the shaving brush on his cheek, Legrand turns his head slightly, glancing across at Adèle. We hear the sound of a piano, inexpertly played. The camera begins to move, keeping Legrand in the frame, the background shifting away from Adèle, along the wall past a second window where we glimpse an unidentifiable figure at a piano. Legrand walks slowly across the room, wiping his hands on the towel. The piano continues to play with the ragged monotony of a tyro's music lesson. Legrand unlocks a cabinet, quickly whisks the money into his pocket, turns, and retraces his steps, and resumes the methodical soaping of his face. The camera follows; as Legrand stops by the window, it moves forward, the focus shifts. The shot ends with Legrand's shoulder filling the right edge of the frame; in focus across the court a little girl still sits at her piano, patiently repeating again the musical phrases we have heard throughout the shot. Fade!

Thus, slowly paced, unexciting, in the most ordinary looking of events, occurs the crucial step on Legrand's way—without emotion or dramatics, undertaken with the same calm deliberateness that has characterized this unassertive man. Heretofore, he had begun his affair with Lulu, but also had maintained intact his former life—work, Adèle, painting. Now, by this act, he choses Lulu against this life, cuts himself from it, stakes his life on her. And throughout this critical moment, the little girl across the court has been as pervasively present as Legrand, her action as uninteresting as his— the two blending in the incidental harmony of a cosmos in which order reigns. He has moved in silence; she has been wholly engaged in creating sound. We and Legrand have heard every note, as ordinary and unexciting as Legrand's walk across the room, an unfaltering accompaniment to that fatal promenade. Not only do the heavens fail to crack at the downfall of an honest man, but not the slightest ripple disturbs the tranquil surface of the world.

The brief simplicity of this scene, Renoir's total refusal to exploit the incident for dramatic effect, typifies his treatment of the narrative of *La Chienne*. Repeatedly, events that might have been built to peaks of emotion and action are shot unpretentiously and with restraint: Legrand rescuing Lulu, stealing from the office safe, discovering his paintings in Wallstein's window, all accomplished with the quick lucidity of sketches, all afforded only the weight they might have in the encompassing world, rather than within the protagonists' lives. Even the murder is observed with great reticence, our attention drawn away by the insignificant life of the street below. Renoir's thorough rejection of familiar filmic devices which inflate the impact of a scene helps locate his characters firmly within their world and render them so pathetically human—*comme moi, comme vous*. Renoir does not deny the elements of drama, but plays them in low key, allows events to have their impact within a character's life, but understates it—makes us find it rather than thrusting it at us, often conveying in a single image the complex and ironic patterns that constitute the world of *La Chienne*. For example, Dédé complains that Wallstein's friends don't know how to dress, then we see him enter Wallstein's party in that same formal uniform of bourgeois respectability—stiff shirt, black tie, wide satin lapels—that Legrand so gladly shed in order to paint the canvases that have elevated Dédé to this dizzying height of fashion. Or, when Lulu shows off her new apartment, Renoir opens the scene with a close-up of Legrand's painting of a woman in a window with a birdcage, the leaves of a plant filling a corner of the canvas. Later he cuts to a shot of the bedroom seen from outside through the open window, with three geranium pots and a birdcage on the window ledge. Lulu and her friend come forward to the window, where Lulu, the birdcage, and plants momentarily echo the painting with which the scene began—Lulu, as it were, steps into the painting and thus identifies herself with what Legrand most loves. These two images seem a visual metaphor, suggesting that Lulu has assumed the place in Legrand's life that painting held before. The irony of this metaphor becomes apparent only later, when Legrand discovers this same painting in Wallstein's window identified as the work of Clara Wood, and when the same shot through the bedroom window shows us Legrand in the doorway and Dédé and Lulu in bed and, later, Legrand kissing Lulu's hand as she lies dead across the bed.

Perhaps most ironic of all is Renoir's treatment of Legrand's moment of triumph, that instant when he seems about to realize his romantic dream. He has beguiled Alexis Godard into stealthily entering the Legrant apartment in hope of making off with Adèle's money, then trapped him in the kitchen while Adèle's screams fill the apartment with neighbors and gendarmes. Adèle explains: "There was a terrible noise. My husband disappeared." Then Legrand enters from the kitchen in his pajamas, explains solemnly: "The truth is that I was here in bed with this woman when her husband surprised us. She was afraid there would be violence so she called for help. But I am a very quiet man and her husband is a fine, educated man." Adèle regards Legrand as if he had gone quite mad, but with quiet glee he opens the kitchen door to reveal the tramp, Alexis Godard. Adèle gasps, "You're not dead!" and Legrand walks quietly across the room to sit down and enjoy the spectacle. A few moments later he emerges into the rainy street, suitcase in hand, breathing exultantly, "Ah! Liberty and Lulu! Life is beautiful." But between these two shots Renoir has inserted a third, Lulu and Dédé in bed, with Lulu protesting that Dédé must have saved enough money so that she can leave Legrand. Thus once again Renoir shows us the reality before the illusion, and we cannot then hear Legrand's cry as a simple manifestation of joy; for we know that he will have Lulu, but as she really is rather than as he imagines her, and that the liberty he finds will be much greater than he wishes, that he is free of Lulu as well as Adèle—free in fact of his whole former life, for Lulu had already stolen the identity of his inner self by becoming Clara Wood. Thus, by the slightest intercutting of these two confrontation scenes, Renoir gives Legrand's joyful expression of release the overtones of a cry of anguish.

From this point on, the dreams have disappeared from La Chienne, and grim reality dominates. And had Renoir chosen to end his film with the image of Dédé awakened for the guillotine, it might indeed have been only a somber, desperate drama. But again Renoir refuses to conform to the expectations of the period and ends La Chienne instead with an epilogue that not only outrages film conventions about crime and punishment but makes us think again about Legrand's world—and ours. Two old tramps squabble in the street over a tip given one when the other held open the door of an elegant car: they recognize each other as Legrand and Alexis Godard. Walking along the street, they compare notes on the past. "Adèle? Oh, she kicked the bucket years ago," says Godard. The sharing of a smoke displays their

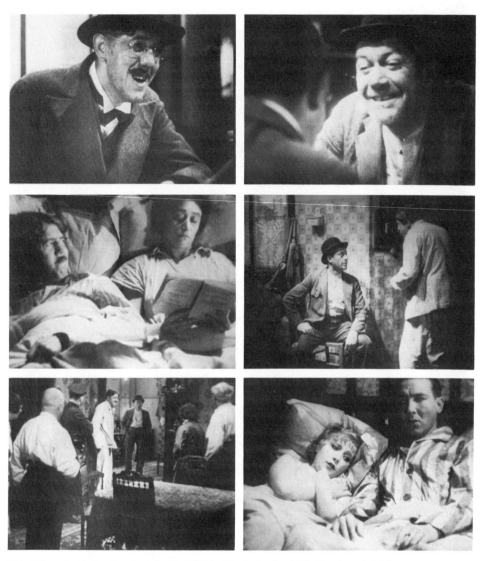

"Ah. Liberté et Lulu. La vie est belle." With Alexis Godard (Gaillard) and Adele (Magdeleine Bérubet).

amity. Legrand offers: "Ah, what I've seen, you know, since I left you. I've done everything, that's plain . . . I've been a ragman, tramp, drunkard, thief. And, to begin, a murderer." Godard laughingly replies, "Well, old man, what do you want, it takes all kinds to make a world." Repeating an image seen earlier in the film, Legrand stands in front of a window looking at the paintings inside; the camera recedes and in the foreground a liveried chauffer carries Legrand's self-portrait from the gallery and puts it in the back of a waiting car. Alexis and Legrand run to hold the car door open for the owner. And, as his painting recedes unnoticed down the street, Legrand turns to Godard: "Ah! Twenty francs! What a blow-out we can have. Let's go. Life is beautiful."—a remark the cashier or painter Legrand had uttered only at that moment of greatest illusion when free of Adèle and not yet faced by the reality of Lulu. But now it reappears as his last words and the final line of this somber, desperate drama. And as the two walk away across the street, the curtain comes down on the puppet stage.

Where we might have left *La Chienne* with a vision of Legrand as a tragic figure, this gay old tramp refutes any such conclusion with his laughter and suggests perhaps that Legrand's inner vision of himself as romantic hero was not false but true—and that the underlying theme of *La Chienne* is not the price of self-deception but rather the impossibility of being a romantic hero in a bourgeois world. I find it an appealing suggestion, for this is of course a theme of *The Rules of The Game*, and its presence in *La Chienne* lends the whole body of Renoir's work in the thirties the cyclical form he loved to give to individual films.

Style and Form

Visually, *La Chienne* carries forward the style Renoir had developed in *Tire au flanc*, applied to a film containing much less physical action and movement but made more complex by the addition of sound. The essentials of this style, a tendency to include the whole of an action within a single shot and to create a clearly defined and coherent space via camera movement, have, as it were, an affinity for sound film; for, as Renoir immediately saw, sound greatly expands the space of immediate awareness, aurally presenting events that need not then be seen. Thus, sound often precludes the necessity for cutting away to show peripheral elements of the action.

Though Renoir had earlier indulged his inclination toward increasing the duration of individual shots, *Tire au flanc* still contained some 560 shots, plus titles. By contrast, the hour and forty minutes of *La Chienne* requires only 302 shots, with each of half a dozen scenes being accomplished in a single shot. The ratio of shots in which the camera moves has risen from about one in fifty in Renoir's first silent films to about three in ten in *La Chienne*. And here, except for a single shot of Lulu and Dédé dancing at Wallstein's party, Renoir never seems to be merely experimenting with camera movements; rather, precisely controlled movements become a very integral element in his presentation of the world of the film. Much camera movement follows the action, of course, but beyond that Renoir has discovered that one way of embedding his characters firmly in their milieu is to provide a very direct and detailed experience of the space in which these characters live. He saw too that this can best be accomplished not by merely

Transformations: Dédé and Legrand.

showing that space in static establishing shots but by moving the camera
through it, thus giving the viewer a sort of kinesthetic sense of the space.
Thus, in *La Chienne*, in the four shots in which Lulu shows off her new
apartment, the camera seems to move a good deal in order to follow Lulu
about, whereas in actuality Lulu's movements have been designed to allow
a full kinesthetic exploration of this intimate space where so much of the
drama will unfold. Even when camera movement remains essentially connected with the action, the moving camera maintains a sort of independence, usually keeping the action within the frame but insisting that there

are other things in the world as well, pausing short of or going beyond a mere centering of the action to notice a cat on the window sill or the little girl playing the piano across the court.

Noticeable, too, is Renoir's growing preference for organizing the action space of his scenes in depth. In a few scenes that use great depth this takes the form of constructing parallel planes of action receding in depth, but this leaves the space between these planes devoid of energy or tension. More frequently, the action ranges through the depth of the space, fully penetrating it and activating the whole field of deep space. Renoir achieves this penetration not only by movement in or out of the depth of the space, but also by mere composition. With a sense of composition probably acquired through living with the paintings of Auguste Renoir, Jean often creates shots whose visual pattern is dominated by the two diagonals of the rectangular screen, but the elements within the scene which form these diagonals in the two-dimensional screen space also range in depth within the three-dimensional action space, thus creating an effect of dynamic penetration of this space. The opening of the banquet scene of *La Chienne* has often been cited as an early example of deep-focus cinematography, but I think this is a mistake. In an interesting variation on what had become the normal form of a Renoir opening shot—a closeup detail, then a camera movement to reveal the larger scene—he includes here both the detail and a long shot of the whole scene in the same image. He does this by shooting the banquet table through a dumbwaiter, an elaborate cake rising to fill the foreground of the frame in close-up as the shot begins. A waiter carries the cake to the table, and the banquet table that had been the background of the image now becomes its whole content. But foreground and background are not in focus at the same time; hence, this fails as an example of the sort of depth-of-field shot that Renoir soon began to seek.

La Chienne also exhibits Renoir's preference for filming conversation in two-shots (shots in which two persons are shown together within the frame), rather than shot-countershot alternation, a silent film form recently rediscovered to solve the problem of photographing talk. The longest scene that approximates the conventional shot-countershot form occurs when Legrand and Alexis Godard discuss which of them will "sacrifice himself" by giving up Adèle; in this second transformational encounter in the film, Legrand welcomes Alexis' attempt at extortion, seizing upon it as a means of completing the change in his life begun when he met Lulu, a conversion of his inner life into outer reality. Here this visual form is exactly right for the conversation: the two speakers oppose each other, each trying to get something from the other, each watching the other carefully for signs of success and altering his own approach in response to the reactions of the other. Hence, the shot-countershot close-ups are not here merely a conventional cinema device, but precisely the appropriate form for communicating the character of this encounter.

Renoir shoots Alexis Godard over Legrand's shoulder, but takes the countershots from a different angle and distance, creating an asymmetry between the opposing full-face shots of Godard and three-quarter views of Legrand and also establishing the independent camera viewpoint that allows us to observe the critical moment when Legrand has the brilliant idea that will free him from Adèle. Legrand then enters with enthusiasm into a conversation heretofore merely endured.

Thus far, Renoir has intercut three shot-forms in this scene, the two opposing close-ups plus a full shot that shows Legrand and Alexis at the table with the bar behind them—seven close-ups of Alexis and five of Legrand, plus six full shots used to disrupt the alternation of close-ups and create a rhythm very different from that of regularly repeated pairs. But once Legrand has his idea, Godard ceases to be an opponent and ceases to appear in close-ups; the last six shots of the scene alternate close-ups of Legrand with full shots as he sets his trap by instructing Alexis on how to enter the apartment.

Hereafter, throughout the 1930s, in his infrequent shot-countershot sets, Renoir will almost always avoid the over-the-shoulder set-ups that predominate in many other films, in which the camera angle and distance approximate the point of view of one of the characters though keeping him in the frame. This is one aspect of Renoir's general avoidance of point-of-view shots, an avoidance that becomes a significant aspect of a style designed to oppose sentimentality.

Though the visual style of *Tire au flanc* carries over into *La Chienne*, Renoir's use of symmetry to give form to *Tire au flanc* does not. *La Chienne* is not symmetrical or cyclical in either visual or dramatic form—all of the relationships in the film are destroyed and none are rebuilt; its end does not resemble its beginning. Nor are there many internal symmetries, Legrand's shaving and theft scene being a notable exception. But Renoir does not substitute for these a tightly knit continuity of action. Rather, he constructs *La Chienne* in a series of relatively self-contained sequences, often leaving us to discover the relation between these within the scene instead of supplying clear connecting links. Thus, after her initial meeting with Legrand, Lulu first reappears in the scene where she shows off her new apartment. In *Scarlet Street*, his remake of *La Chienne*, Fritz Lang takes perhaps ten minutes to develop the affair to the point where the girl moves into the apartment offered by his hero, Chris Cross. But Renoir has little concern for the mechanics of Legrand's infatuation and presumes that his audience can supply whatever details it needs. He bridges these weeks or months with a single line, uttered incredulously by one of Legrand's colleagues, "I say, your story about Josephine Baker, that's like saying you saw Legrand with a pretty girl," and fades to Legrand's painting on the wall of the apartment.

Each sequence occurs later in dramatic time than those which precede it; yet the dramatic development of *La Chienne* is not a point-to-point linear progress. Subsequent scenes not only carry forward the action but also reflect back upon earlier events, deepen our perception of them, and sometimes make us see them in a very different light. For example, we only gradually apprehend the character of Legrand and distinguish his inner vision from his outer comportment; when we do, this alters our conception of his earlier actions. One device Renoir uses to evoke a reassessment of preceding scenes occurs frequently enough to become itself a formal element in the structure of *La Chienne*. This is the repetition of an earlier image in a context that gives it a very different dramatic force and meaning. For example, there are six shots through the bedroom window of Lulu's apartment, each succeeding shot darker in dramatic tone. Legrand, after he finds Lulu and Dédé in bed, walks up the very stairs on which he first saw Lulu, in a shot that simply reverses the flow of images seen when Lulu and Dédé first came along the street and down the stair.

But these aspects of *La Chienne* all involve the development or extension of forms or techniques Renoir had used before. What is new in *La Chienne* is the use of sound as a fully integrated dimension of Renoir's style. I have already discussed the relation of dialogue to character and action; what needs further attention is Renoir's use of music in this film.

There is no score for *La Chienne*—that is, no music written for the film and played as an accompaniment to the action, to be heard by the audience but not within the world of the film. Rather, all of the music is internal to the film, produced within the context of the action and presumably heard by the characters in the film as well as the audience. This use of internal music will be typical of Renoir's films of the thirties, though many also have some external music; it enables Renoir to employ music as one of the major elements in creating the world of the film, the milieu in which his characters live. Typical also, and first occurring in *La Chienne*, is the use of a song to universalize the dramatic situation. The characters of Renoir's films of the thirties are highly individual, neither stereotypes, puppets, nor symbols; they live in worlds whose authenticity we do not question, and they become involved in predicaments that develop quite naturally and are as specific and individual as the characters themselves. But then Renoir will include a popular song whose lyrics mirror the situation within the film, suggesting that this is not merely the peculiar plight of these poor devils but an aspect of the human condition. In *La Chienne*, Renoir uses a song made popular by Eugénie Buffet in the cabarets of Paris in the 1880s—later to be sung by Edith Piaf in Renoir's *French Can-Can*, where Piaf appears as Eugénie Buffet:

> A toi, Oh ma belle inconnue
> Toi pour qui j'ai si souvent chanté
> Ton aumone est la bienvenue
> Fais moi la charité.

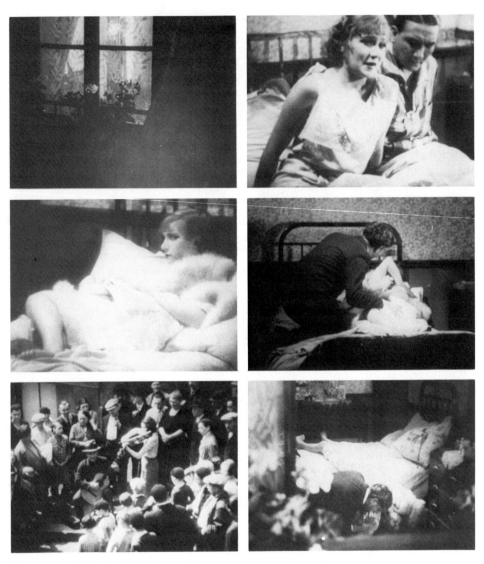

Discovery and death, while the world goes on.

This song occurs during the scene of Lulu's murder. As Legrand pleads, then storms and pleads again with Lulu, who is now beyond subterfuge and deceit, fearing she has lost Dédé, Renoir cuts twice to the street below Lulu's window where a crowd gathers and two street musicians sing. Each time, when he cuts back to the bedroom Legrand's mood has changed. Finally, pleading, Legrand pulls Lulu's arm from over her face—the same attitude in which he first found her on the Montmartre steps—and discovers that she is laughing at him. The laughter maddens Legrand—he shakes Lulu, and Renoir plunges his camera again into the life of the street and the song. This time the camera moves from the singer up the face of the building, finally to look in once again through the bedroom window where Legrand kneels beside the murdered Lulu, kissing her hand. Shot this way, as one event in a world in which people also sing, the murder becomes less dramatic, more poignant; Legrand's grief is more authentically felt through its contrast with the unconcern of those carelessly listening below. The cuts to the street break the suspense and the dramatic effect of the scene in the bedroom, destroy the possibility of building it to a great emotional crescendo. The song places Legrand's anguish in a fully human context, renders him just one among many who do not know their love and who suffer while the world spins on, unmindful—*comme vous, comme moi.*

Almost as if to verify the reality of Renoir's creation, the tragedy of *La Chienne* was, in a way, to be soon reenacted in life. Renoir said, "Shortly after the shooting began, I found myself facing the same situation on the set that I was constructing in the film. Michel Simon and Georges Flamant both fell in love with Janie Marèze. When we had finished the shooting Georges Flamant was sure that his performance as Dédé was going to make him a star, be the beginning of a brilliant career. Like Dédé he bought a new car to celebrate his rise in the world. Fifteen days after the shooting was over, he took Janie Marèze for a ride to show her his new acquisition. She was killed in the accident that followed."

Having finished his film in the form he wished, Renoir felt rather pleased with the result. But the first public showing in Nancy turned into a fiasco. Public and critics both assailed the film and it was withdrawn after two days. Another commercial disaster seemed imminent. But a friend who Renoir admired because he had once been in the Turkish navy then played *La Chienne* in his theatre in Biarritz, proclaiming on his posters "ABOVE ALL, AVOID SEEING THIS FILM. IT IS HORRIBLE." The public flocked to the theatre and praised the film, which ran for three weeks, then opened in Paris, where it had a considerable success.

9

La Nuit du carrefour
1932

My aim was to convey by imagery the mystery of that starkly mysterious tale, and I meant to subordinate the plot to the atmosphere.
　　　　　　　　　　　　　　　　　　　　　　　　—Jean Renoir

Two Renoir enthusiasms had drawn him to this next work: his admiration for the young Belgian writer Georges Simenon and a desire to work with his brother, Pierre Renoir, whom Jean imagined as the perfect embodiment of Simenon's detective hero, Inspector Maigret. After the success of *La Chienne*, the Braunberger-Richebé studio was ready to produce another Renoir film. Renoir discussed the project with Simenon and wrote his adaption of the novel, then assembled a mixed cast of professionals and amateurs, of whom only Pierre Renoir had a wide reputation.

In order to achieve the accents that identify Karl and Elsa Andersen as the foreigners whom most of the other characters despise, Renoir found two Danes for these roles: an actor, Georges Koudria, and a dancer, Winna Winfried. Of the latter Renoir says, "I wanted a very fragile-looking woman in a big, ill-kept, cluttered house. I thought that might be interesting." Two of Renoir's friends, the painter Edward Dignimont and Michel Duran, a writer, became actors for the moment. Most of the minor roles were entrusted to friends who had appeared before in Renoir films. Two new faces appeared among the technicians, Jacques Becker and Claude Renoir. Because of financial problems, several scenes were never shot. Finally, Renoir improvised the last sequence in order to be able to complete the film at all.

Simenon's novel is set in the Carrefour des Trois Veuves, a crossroads around which clusters a garage and two houses, one an old, run-down structure dating from the revolution, the other the new and banal home of an insurance agent, M. Michonnet. When he had decided to make the film, Renoir sought out the crossroads of this name marked on his map on the highway south of Paris, but found that it did not at all match the description invented by Simenon. So he searched the roads around Paris and found, at Bouffemont, 25 kilometers north, a crossroads more to his liking. The company lived together for three weeks at this crossroads, in the rain and fog and the constant noise of the highway, and the exteriors shot at that location give the film its distinctive tone and quality.

Later, André Brunelin described the shooting: "As always with Renoir, there were odd jobs to be done. It was necessary to make the sets with whatever one could find; things had to be painted, patched up. There was not enough money. Never. What was essential was the camera, the film. For the rest you managed somehow. Three-fourths of the company were not paid or poorly paid. What did it matter? Most important was to participate, to do something in which one believed.

"And then, there was the marvelous community of comrades. And their youth, too."[1]

Treatment

This investigation by Inspector Maigret begins at the crossroads with the discovery by M. Michonnet of the murder of a diamond merchant. Michonnet (Jean Gehret) is sure the "foreigners" can be blamed, but Karl Andersen (Georges Koudria), questioned for hours, maintains his innocence. Maigret (Pierre Renoir) pokes about the garage, talks to Andersen's sister, Else (Winna Winfried). Oscar (Dignimont), the garage owner, plays his accordion and watches Maigret. Else smokes, amuses herself with a turtle, lounges on her bed in the old, dilapidated house. The murdered man's wife comes to identify the body and is killed as she steps from the car. Andersen is shot while returning from Paris. Michonnet tries to poison Else, then to strangle her. Maigret uncovers a pistol and veronal in Else's room, cocaine and stolen jewels in the garage. Oscar and his gang fire into the garage at Maigret, then speed away. Police, in a Bugatti, pursue them over dark twisting roads and capture the gang. Else confesses that she is not Andersen's sister, that she came from a "house" in Hamburg. While a doctor treats Andersen upstairs, all the inhabitants of the crossroads are gathered in handcuffs below. Guido (Manuel Raaby), one of the garage mechanics, arrested as he aims a rifle through a window at Maigret, proves to be Else's first husband and the murderer. From upstairs, Andersen calls Else. As she starts up the stairs, Maigret removes her handcuffs, tells her, "Two years will pass quickly. Then you will be free. And he will *really* be free."

No mere description of the plot of *La Nuit du carrefour* could capture the character of the film. Its hero is a detective; its genre, ostensibly that of the *film policier*, usually relies heavily on plot for its effect and treats each incident so as to maximize suspense. Yet in *La Nuit du carrefour* the working-out of the plot, the solution of the crime, seems almost incidental; rather than foster suspense, Renoir allows Maigret to discover the secrets of the garage before we are even sure there is need to be suspicious. An enumeration of the violent deeds committed makes *La Nuit du carrefour* sound like an action-packed adventure story; but the film feels languorous rather than violent. The rifle shots, assaults, attempted poisoning, are all very quickly over. Again, Renoir refuses to inflate these incidents. Systematically, he minimizes their dramatic effect. They occur but create an air of mystery rather than of action and violence: For an instant a rifle shot lights up the rain-drenched night, reveals the silhouette of the rifleman; darkness returns. Or, from the darkness a hand reaches through a broken window, places two bottles on a table in an ill-lit room, withdraws. When Michonnet tries to strangle Else, Renoir shoots the scene through the bannister at the top of the stair; a curtain flaps in the wind in the dark hallway. Even the most rapid action in the film, the pursuit after the fleeing gang, punctuated by shots, impresses us not with the excitement of the chase but the mystery of the night. Renoir allows only five shots for the chase and films most of it from a camera mounted on the Bugatti; we find ourselves propelled down a dark, tree-lined road, turning the corners of narrow streets hedged in by walls and darkened houses. Jean-luc Godard described these shots as "sublime subjective shots traveling forward through the alleys of the sleeping village."[2]

Though over three-fourths of the film occurs in well-lighted interiors, it is not these moments that stay with us. Rather, our impressions of the gray highway, of darkness, rain, and fog in long vistas of the night, an obscure figure by a wall or under the trees, headlights brightening a small area of the dark road, seem to overwhelm these bright interiors and create the dominant tone of the film. A traveling shot past trees along the highway—the sharp black verticals of the trees receding to emphasize the deep diagonal perspective of the road—leads us into the film and holds us there. A shot of three work horses plodding slowly down a rain-swept road becomes charged with mystery and meaning.

The highway sounds that prevail through much of the film help give these exteriors their dominance. This sound provides our first entry into the world of the film. Motors, shifting gears, wheels on the pavement—after a few bars of music these sounds accompany the credits; when the opening shot, traveling forward along the road, fades in, this only adds a visual dimension to an ongoing experience. Asked about this, Renoir said, "Well, I probably didn't have enough money for an orchestra." But intentional or not, this initial use of sound gives the exterior setting a grip on us that it never relinquishes.

The opposition between these dark or hazy exteriors—with deep but obscure space usually shot in strong, simple, and dynamic compositions—and the light interior scenes, whose composition tends to be more static and complex and whose shallow space is often wholly in sharp focus, is but one of a series of strange contrasts that help establish the *féerique* mood of *La Nuit du carrefour*. The two sounds we hear most are the growl and whine of the highway, harsh, heavy, and insistent, and the light melody of the tango Maigret sets spinning on Else's phonograph. This melody provides Maigret a clue to the puzzles when he hears it again played on Oscar's accordion. Then, in the film's final scene, Maigret brings Else, handcuffed, to the room full of police and criminals below and starts the phonograph again as he waits for the mystery to unfold. This popular dance tune, wholly incongruous with the situation, has a rhythm that catches the movement and cutting of the scene and impels it forward as the mystery does indeed unravel itself. Further, the prancing effeminacy of Jojo against the masculine setting of the garage, Else's frail blond beauty and indolence amidst the disarray of the old house, Michonnet's solid bulk verging on hysteria about these foreigners, the doctor appearing out of the night in top hat and white scarf, and, above all, Maigret's imperturbable calm within the confusion of the intrigue—all these create an atmosphere of the bizarre, the unpredictable, which join with rain and dark and fog to form the most vivid impression we carry away from *La Nuit du carrefour*, an impression whose persistence erases the flow of incident and action from the center of our awareness.

The sequence of Andersen's interrogation—the police calm and persistent, Andersen looking ever more weary—Renoir punctuates with shots of a kiosk, the camera gutter-high so that we see only feet approaching and walking away. As fresh headlines appear on the newspapers affixed to the kiosk, a broom sweeps the old papers down a drain, an image of the ephemeral nature of the "news" and of the illusion of importance assumed by moment-to-moment events. In the last of these shots the headline in *Paris-Soir* reads, "Andersen Provisionally Freed; Maigret to Visit Crossroads." Half hidden under the newspaper, a poster announces "Howard Hughes presents *Scarface*." By placing this poster there, Renoir seems to demand that we compare *La Nuit du carrefour* to the American gangster films of the period. A strange demand, since we hardly realize that *La Nuit du carrefour* is a gangster movie until it is nearly three-quarters over, and we never see the gang until they are all in handcuffs. But Renoir's point is not merely to evoke comparison, rather to comment on the American films in a way that shows where the difference lies.

The comment follows from the setting Renoir selects for the *Scarface* poster. The American gangster film, like the press, lives for the presentation of the ephemeral events that constitute its narrative, emphasizing in these those elements that make headlines: conflict, violence, death. Hence Renoir surely does not draw the comparison to show that he can beat the Ameri-

Giving the mystery palpable form. Inspector Maigret (Pierre Renoir) with Oscar and wife (Dignimont and Lucie Vallat). *Below*, Else Andersen (Winna Winfried). *Center right*, Max Dalban, as the elegant doctor, attends Carl Andersen (Georges Koudria).

cans at their own game. A film cannot deny the primacy of immediate events and the importance of the sensational, as does *La Nuit du carrefour*, and be a gangster picture at all.

We begin with a murder; at film's end we know, more or less, who committed what crimes. But we hardly feel that all of the confusion has been dispelled, all of the questions answered. Jean Renoir did not see his task as one of undoing and clarifying the mystery, but, rather, one of expressing it, of giving the mystery palpable form.

That Renoir's only *film policier* should be adapted from a Simenon novel seems quite right. For even in his early works Simenon seemed more intent upon creating the atmosphere of the crime than registering a myriad of details in which clues could be concealed. And he was groping for the truth of character, a process expressed through the person of Maigret, who approaches a crime by seeking to understand the people involved in it rather than by careful induction from the material evidence. Perhaps it was this that attracted Jean Renoir, who was also engaged in seeking the truth of character in his films. And perhaps sympathy generated by this common endeavor accounts for the fact that even now Simenon considers *La Nuit du carrefour* the film that best captures the essential flavor of his detective novels.

Characterization

Anyone first viewing *La Nuit du carrefour* is unlikely to be reminded of *La Chienne*. The films differ in look, in sound, in tone, and certainly in the style of their narration. Still, I can imagine that *La Nuit du carrefour* might have originated with Jean Renoir remarking to one of his companions, "What do you say, let's shoot *La Chienne* over again as a detective film." In order to make a detective film one needs, of course, a detective. And one must begin with a mysterious crime to give the detective employment, then invent enough complication to keep him busy. All this will leave little time for development of the other principal characters or for exploration of their everyday lives. What remains, as the variable element in a *film policier*, is a situation, a set of relationships: an unglamorous, obscure, honorable, middle-aged, middle-class man in love with a prostitute who deceives him and who continues an affair with a former lover. And a resolution: the girl and her former lover are removed from the scene, leaving the man free. *La Chienne*—and *La Nuit du carrefour*.

The similarities do not reach far beyond this, I must admit. But that too is a function of the genre. To give the characters more definition, more background, would begin to undermine the mystery. And if Renoir's purpose was to express the mystery, then this aspect of the conventions of the detective film must be respected. Hence, Guido remains a mere shadow, completely uncharacterized until the dénouement, simply one of the men in the garage, not recognized as the indistinct figure who slips across the dark road with a rifle. Even at the end we know little more about him than that he feels some attachment to Else and will probably share Dédé's fate.

Somewhat more fully perceived, Karl Andersen, like Legrand, is different from the people who surround him. But the effective difference is that conveyed in a word or a glance; he is a foreigner and he wears a black patch to cover a glass eye. He also has a certain dignity the other inhabitants of the crossroads lack. He speaks softly, stands erect, considers himself a gentleman. But, since he is the prime suspect, his honesty and his love for Else cannot be revealed until late in the film. Then we are told he will be free, but we cannot imagine him as a laughing old tramp. And his relation to the crime, of course, is nearly the reverse of Legrand's. Andersen is innocent but suspected and accused; Legrand is guilty but wholly unsuspect.

Else appears to bear a greater resemblance to Lulu, with the bed being the natural habitat of both. Else's beauty and grace, her erotic languor when she receives Maigret in her bedroom, the apparent openness with which she appeals to him, make her the most alluring, thus far, of Renoir's destructive females. But her softness and passivity prove to be feigned, the openness calculated; her complicity in the crimes of the gang casts doubt upon the sincerity of all her behavior. When the plot has been resolved, Else has become a rather attractive puzzle; we have no clear sense of her character at all.

In truth, the demands of concealment in the detective genre forbid the level of characterization Renoir achieved in *La Chienne*. The characters must remain ambiguous and shallow, their identity established externally, by mannerisms rather than significant action. Quite out of accord with Renoir's usual method, most of what we learn about the characters is told in the dialogue, not shown in action and gesture.

However, neither He, She, nor the Other One is the central character of *La Nuit du carrefour*. That role goes to the detective, Inspector Maigret. And, being outside of the mystery, he can be firmly characterized, need not remain ambiguous and obscure. One cannot deny the solidity of the performance; Pierre Renoir's Maigret has depths and shades of character far beyond any other character in the film—alert, intelligent, courageous, perceptive, compassionate yet incorruptible, a character of great strength. Unhurried and unruffled, Maigret maintains an air of professional competence and judiciousness, but without pomp or conceit. Usually unaggressive, he still proves to be in command of every situation, often managing this gracefully by using his pipe as an instrument to deflect attention, control the flow of time and events, impose the rhythm he desires upon the pattern of action and reaction.

Still, impressive though Pierre Renoir's performance may be, Maigret lacks the quality of life that Legrand had. Not that his character needs further elaboration, but that we have no sense of further possibilities for him. Convincing as he is, he exists only within the context of the intrigue and the investigation. He remains, as it were, a fictional person and not, therefore, to be included among the characters we find most memorable among the Renoir creations of the thirties.

Style and Form

Jacques Brunius has written, "There is no Renoir style, or rather there is one for each film; for this man without a style makes films which never lack style."[3] Others have echoed this remark; still, the claim is surely false. There is a Renoir style in the thirties, which develops and changes, of course, but remains recognizable throughout this period. But it is a *style*, that is, a number of related formal tendencies which find expression in rather different ways and combinations when applied to different material. Thus it allows for considerable variation and flexibility; it is not merely a *manner* to be imposed indiscriminately on every subject.

The flexibility of Renoir's style and his willingness to adapt it to various materials are nowhere more evident than in the transition from *La Chienne* to *La Nuit du carrefour*. Here, when the style had just been achieved, one might expect the temptation to resist change, to maintain his style intact, would be strongest. Yet some elements of style prominent in *La Chienne* are almost wholly missing from *La Nuit du carrefour*. For example, no scene in *La Nuit du carrefour* begins with what had become the typical Renoir opening shot, with the camera moving back or away from an initial close-up detail to show a larger portion of action-space in its relation to this detail. In fact, only a single shot in the film has this characteristic form, one occurring late in the scene in which Maigret first explores Andersen's house. And the reversal of this, a shot in which the camera moves in to a close-up detail, frequently used in *La Chienne* at the conclusion of a scene, also occurs only once, very near the end of *La Nuit au carrefour*. The reason for this change seems evident. Such shots clarify and organize the space they reveal, and impose some order on our perception of the objects in it. Hence they become a major stylistic constituent of those films in which Renoir seeks to convey a very clear image of the action-space that contains his characters. But such clarity would subvert his aims in *La Nuit du carrefour*. For similar reasons the frequency of camera movement declines sharply; only about one in seven shots shows camera movement, and only six interior shots display the large and fluid camera movements that convey a kinesthetic sense of the space. With the decrease in camera movement, the rate of cutting increases somewhat; fragmentation of both space and time becomes greater, making it more difficult for us to grasp the wholeness of setting, persons, or actions. *La Nuit du carrefour* is more than twenty minutes shorter that *La Chienne*, but contains some thirty more shots.

These are significant changes that reverse the direction in which Renoir's style had been developing. But they do not destroy the style, for he emphasizes other aspects of it that will not undermine the air of mystery he seeks to create. To compensate for the decrease in camera movement, there is a greater use of depth-of-field in interior scenes and a greater frequency of shots through doors or with a character in the foreground cutting off part of the field while the major action occurs at middle distance. This tends to draw us into the action-space, makes us penetrate beyond the first plane of the visual field and become participants rather than mere spectators, but without either the kinesthetic awareness or the sense of clarity that Renoir achieves elsewhere through camera movement. In *La Nuit du carrefour* there are even fewer close-ups than in *La Chienne*, and shot-countershot alternation has all but disappeared in conversation scenes. Renoir has relinquished none of his desire to locate his characters firmly within their milieu and to give the background a significant role in the action, but he uses means of obtaining this which will not conflict with the dominant tone of the film.

One of the satisfying things about detective fiction is the formal structure that is almost of necessity required by the genre. Given the basic elements— a crime, an investigation and a solution—a detective film can hardly avoid having a beginning, middle, and end. Conjoined with this, the detective's engagement in the action must take a cyclical form: he enters from outside, becomes increasingly involved, solves the crime, then withdraws. Whatever effect the working-out of the plot may have upon the lives of the other characters, the detective-hero is untouched; at the end of the affair he returns to the position of detachment he had at the beginning. Usually, too, there is a reversal and a recognition—the shifting of suspicion from one character to another and a moment when the detective sees how the pieces of the puzzle fall together. In *La Nuit du carrefour* the reversal provides a sort of counter-form to the cycle of Maigret's implication in the affair. The film begins with Andersen being accused of the crime and everyone else presumed innocent; at film's end Andersen alone is innocent and everyone else under arrest.

The span of dramatic time covered in *La Nuit du carrefour* is, of course, much shorter than in *La Chienne*, a few days as compared to months, or years if we include the epilogue of *La Chienne*. This alone makes for tighter continuity, but Renoir handles his continuity quite differently. In *La Nuit du carrefour* he provides more transitional shots, does more intercutting; the sequences of *La Nuit du carrefour* are not self-contained, as in *La Chienne*. Not that Renoir builds a wholly smooth continuity. Rather, once he has provided a transitional shot he tends not to bother doing it again when a similar transition occurs, assuming that we no longer need it. There are certainly gestures in the direction of smooth continuity; however, having given his audience this, Renoir constructs his film of sequences that are much less clear than those of *La Chienne*. He often said, "I want the public to help me make the picture work," and he usually avoided the "perfection" that would leave us with nothing to do but watch—certainly in *La Nuit du carrefour*.

As in *La Chienne*, the major formal innovations of this film occur in Renoir's use of sound. Again, there is no score, no external music; the sources of music in the film are Oscar's accordion and Else's phonograph. But the tango, which has no lyrics, does not function to universalize. Rather, it serves to characterize Else, to provide a link in the plot, to give form and cohesion to the final scene and, in the overall form of the film, to supply a tonal counterpoint to the otherwise dominant highway noises. Some of the street noises Renoir had intended to use in *La Chienne* had been lost when he was barred from his cutting room, hence the highway sounds in *La Nuit du carrefour* became his first large-scale use of natural sound. These highway sounds become much more than mere background noise; Renoir makes them a primary ingredient in his construction of the world of the film and the chief source of our sense of the constant activity that surrounds the often quiet pool of Maigret's investigation.

Renoir's use of dialogue in *La Nuit du carrefour* became, perhaps unintentionally, an even greater departure from the practices of the day than *La Chienne*. A good bit of the dialogue was poorly registered, and reports from the Paris premiere indicate that even at that time it was not fully intelligible. But this seems not to have worried Renoir, for his tendency in this film is to employ dialogue as a third element of sound, along with the music and natural sounds, without much reliance upon the meaning of the words. Recently, Renoir remarked that he would have liked to make a film in which the characters spoke a language no one would be able to understand, for what is essential in communications is conveyed by gesture and the sound of the voices. Such a notion seems already at work in *La Nuit du carrefour*. There are, of course, details that we could not know if they were not mentioned in the dialogue, but surprisingly little of real importance would be missed if one understood only a little of what was said. Andersen and Else speak to each other in Danish, which Renoir does not bother to translate in subtitles. He said of this: "The content of these remarks is fairly obvious. Besides, in a picture of this sort I thought it might help *not* to have the audience understand everything that was said. It adds to the mystery." These remarks could be extended to much of the talk in the film. That one hears the changes in the tone of Else's voice, the constant agitation in the speech of Michonnet, the occasional irony in the calm utterances of Maigret, does make a difference; for such qualities of the sound chart the relations between characters.

It is not that the talk in *La Nuit du carrefour* is often redundant in the sense that it merely reiterates what we are also shown in another way—a use of dialogue that Renoir very much dislikes. Rather, the verbal content of the dialogue turns out not to be very significant; it reveals itself as a conventional element of the ordinary *film policier* and loses much of its point in a film whose aim is to express the mystery.

10

Boudu sauvé des eaux 1932

> Boudu *is my favorite movie. It was the only time in my career that someone gave me money and allowed me to be the producer. I immediately hired Jean Renoir to direct me. We had ideal conditions. We were not tainted by the commercial aspects of cinema. And the results were far beyond our expectations . . . The audience* hated *the film. They screamed and flew into an immediate, absolute rage. When they began tearing the seats apart, the police were called and* Boudu *closed after three days . . . But I have always had the greatest fondness for the character of Boudu. He's a man who cannot integrate into society and so he has to leave it.* —Michel Simon

Renoir's separation from Michel Simon was short-lived. With *La Nuit du carrefour* completed in the spring of 1932, Simon and Jean Gehret became the producers for Renoir's adaption of a play by Réné Fauchois, *Boudu sauvé des eaux*, in which Simon had appeared in 1925. The play chronicles the successful attempt of a left-bank bookseller, M. Lestingois, to make a contented bourgeois of the uncouth tramp, Boudu, he has rescued from drowning. The author, Fauchois, had played Lestingois in the Paris production of the play. But Renoir's adaptation, with Michel Simon turned loose in the role of Boudu, transforms the film into an anarchic romp with Boudu as its center, a work very far in spirit from the triumph of middle-class culture presented on the stage.

Boudu, pulled from the Seine after attempting suicide, becomes an irascible and abrasive guest in the Lestingois home, a constant source of irritation to Mme. Lestingois (Marcelle Hainia) and of frustration to M. Lestingois (Charles Granval) and the maid, Anne-Marie (Séverine Lerczinska), whose nightly trysts are disrupted by Boudu's presence. But just when all have agreed that he has to go, Boudu seduces Mme. Lestingois and a medal is awarded to M. Lestingois for rescuing him. More firmly established than ever, Boudu begins to display some bourgeois habits and attitudes, imagines himself as a bookseller, thinks he wants to marry Anne-Marie. A door opens accidentally to disclose the double adultery in this honest bourgeois household, but since Boudu has just won 100,000 francs, Anne-Marie happily agrees to marry him. Presumably this will make everyone respectable again. The wedding party rows down the Marne, with Anne-Marie's head resting contentedly on Boudu's shoulder. But Boudu reaches for a water lily and overturns the boat. As everyone else flounders ashore, Boudu floats lazily downstream and reaches the opposite bank with the taints of bourgeois culture wholly washed from him. He gladly sheds his wedding clothes and appropriates the ragged garb of a scarecrow, begs food from some picnickers and rolls joyously in the grass, sharing his bread with a passing goat.

When Renoir introduced *Boudu* in Santa Barbara after its American release in 1967, he called the film "an homage to a fantastic actor, Michel Simon," and identified its subject as "loitering," an activity he called "the highest achievement of civilization" even though it may be illegal in most of the places where humans live. Ostensibly, the loiterer in the film is Boudu, who is certainly aimless enough to qualify. But things are never quite that simple with Renoir; *Boudu* demonstrates on several levels that the loitering which society forbids is more a matter of status than of activity. Boudu, with his tattered clothes and scruffy beard, has no address, no profession, no visible means of support; hence, whatever he may do, respectable people will likely consider it loitering. Early in the film, Boudu wanders through the park calling his dog. Women run in fright as he approaches. Boudu asks a policeman if he has seen a dog, "black, with curly fur." The gendarme looks at Boudu and tells him he had better take off before he finds himself in jail. As Boudu walks away, still calling "Black!" a fashionably dressed young woman exactly repeats his action. She wanders over the same path, calling a dog, and asks the gendarme if he has seen her dog, which is "worth 10,000 francs." The gendarme repeats "10,000 francs?" Two more police appear from nowhere, and they all busily go off in search of the dog.

Characterization

When he made *Boudu*, Renoir had just discovered the method of working with actors that he was to follow henceforth. He described this in these terms to *Boudu's* audience in 1967:

Quite late I discovered a marvelous method which I owe to Louis Jouvet and Michel Simon, who used to apply it on the stage. It was well known up to the romantic period and it is called the Italian method—*à l'italienne*. You sit around a table with the actors and you read the dialogue exactly as though you were reading the telephone directory: no expression, absolutely blank. You forbid them to give any expression, and you must be very severe, because any actor instinctively wants to give an expression before knowing what it's all about.

You read a scene about a mother witnessing the death of her child, for instance. The first reaction of the actress playing the mother would probably be tears. We are surrounded by clichés, and for many actors it's as though they had a little chest of drawers, with an answer to a question in each drawer. Drawer number three—Mother witnessing death of child: and you apply the answer. But if you read the lines without any expression, this forces the actor to absorb them; and all of a sudden—you see a spark. One of the actors has a kind of feeling which is going to lead him towards an interpretation of the part which is not a cliché. It will be his own interpretation, having nothing to do with what was done before.

For instance, with Michel Simon this is the way we discovered Boudu; by reading, reading, reading. One day, without realizing it, almost in spite of himself, Michel started reading with the voice of Boudu, with this roughness in his voice. I told him, "Here we are, we've got the part." And out in the courtyard, he was walking like Boudu. A Boudu I didn't expect. I didn't know this Boudu five minutes before. This Boudu was new, a creation by Michel Simon, and perhaps a little bit by myself, not the Boudu which had been done a hundred times on the stage.

The voice grates, fluctuates, wavers, and Boudu's walk forms its perfect correlate. His head bobs unsteadily; his arms flap rather than swinging in coordination with his legs; he changes direction erratically about every third step. When he walks, Boudu appears totally aimless, his movements not quite under control. But first we hear the voice as he lolls under a tree gnawing a chunk of bread and singing "Sur les bords de la Rivière," the words barely intelligible in his raspy tones. According to Renoir, Parisians in 1932 associated this song with luxury and pretty girls singing in a night club; they would have been shocked to hear it growled by a mangy-looking *clochard*.

Michel Simon's performance in *Boudu* stands at the opposite pole from that in *La Chienne*. The role of Legrand demanded not only physical restraint, but also limitation and dissimulation of facial expression, with just that nuance which would reveal the hidden inner state. But in *Boudu* everything is external. Physical uninhibited, Boudu balances across the doorway, stands on his hands, spins on his toes. But also, every inner state has an immediate outer manifestation: expressions of anger, joy, puzzlement, curiosity, discomfort, pride chase each other across his face. Nothing is hidden.

We never feel that this externalization occurs because Boudu has chosen not to conceal his feelings, but rather that the possibility of concealment never occurs to him. Hence this externality becomes a central aspect of his character, achieved via the immediacy of Boudu's reaction to every situation. Further, this immediacy seems an expression of the fact that Boudu lives wholly in the present; he does not dream or worry about the future, quickly forgets the past. His whole being relates to what happens now; he openly displays his response to it. This externality does not, of course, make for any less subtlety in Simon's performance, for the states thus expressed are often complicated and conflicting—combining, for example, innocence, curiosity, malice and resentment. But the transparency of Boudu's life does lend predominance to his voice and walk. With his inner self living, as it were, outwardly, these physical traits become expressive of the whole man.

These aspects of Boudu, the voice and walk, do not themselves manifest his character. But as the elements of his presence established at our first view of him, they become identity marks that first constitute him as a unique individual. So thoroughly do they incarnate his individuality that when his unbridled character does erupt after his rescue, its vehicle seems to be just these physical features. When his independence falters and Boudu becomes tempted by the bourgeois life, his voice and walk change too. After he upsets the wedding boat, we need only see him stagger from the river and weave down a path with the old erratic walk to know that all the traces of middle-class compromise have been erased by the river, that the real Boudu has been born again out of the water, uncorrupted and free.

Love him as we now may, this real Boudu is not always easy to take. The name itself carries a variety of suggestions, all of them activated at some point in the film: *Boue, boueur, boudeur*—mud, scavenger, sulky—and, of course, *boudoir*. But the thrust of the character lies not in suggestions, rather in obstreperous, intransigent action.

Lestingois' first glimpse of Boudu comes through his telescope, as he watches from his window the women walking by the Pont des Arts. Boudu lurches into his circle of vision and Lestingois exclaims, "Oh, how magnificent. I've never seen such a perfect tramp." Struck by this perfection, Lestingois groans in dismay as Boudu climbs over the rail of the bridge, then dashes across the street to rescue him from the river. But what Lestingois does not count on is that Boudu will remain as perfect even after being rescued. The remainder of the film becomes a sort of perverse verification of Lestingois' first cry of admiration.

For a perfect tramp is not a bourgeois gentleman who is down on his luck and dressed in shabby clothes. When rescued, Boudu wholly refuses to conform to the conventions of proper conduct that would have him be grateful to his savior and prepared to begin life anew. Far from thanking Lestingois, Boudu demands, "Why didn't you let me drown?" Prevented from throwing

Boudu, from truculent clochard to
bourgeois groom.

himself back into the river, he reluctantly accepts the necessity of living
again, but with no regret for his suicide attempt and no indication of having
a new purpose in his life. Rather, living wholly in the present, he soon gets
caught up in the role of imposing himself on Lestingois and forgets his
despondency.

Reminded several times that Lestingois has saved him, Boudu presumes
that this action places some responsibility on Lestingois, not himself. Being
urged to have courage and told that he is no longer alone, he insists, by his
refusal to consider anything else, that if he lives it will be with Lestingois,

then demonstrates that the unexpected correlate of this is that Lestingois is going to have to live with Boudu. He accepts revival, but stoutly rejects reformation, and loses no time at all in proving that gratitude and docile acceptance have no part in his make-up. He suspects that Lestingois may steal his braces, throws the shirt offered by Anne-Marie over his shoulder without a glance while muttering that it is too small, rejects Mme. Lestingois' offer of food by saying that he doesn't like soup. He eats sardines with his fingers, spits out the wine and demands water, wears Lestingois' frock-coat but asserts he wouldn't dare go out in it, for the kids would laugh at him. He complains that he has no place to sleep that night, though presumably this makes it a night like any other, and flatly refuses to go to a hotel. Truculent, ill-mannered, disrespectful, he is also affectionate, frank, unashamed of his ignorance ("I can read big letters"), and touchingly simple (asked what he would do if he won 100,000 francs, he replies happily that he would buy a bicycle). When Lestingois explains that a cravat is a piece of cloth that you tie around your neck, Boudu thinks this hilariously absurd and assures Lestingois that he doesn't want one.

Nevertheless, but a few shots later we find him seated at the table wearing a cravat with his new suit, eating with a fork and drinking wine like the others. Truculence no longer necessary, he now has a childlike innocence and curiosity about this unknown world of the bourgeois household and reacts to it with childlike logic. There are new types of objects, such as napkins and women, that he does not understand, and a whole battery of customs that he has never heard of and whose sense he doubts. He is neither slow nor stupid; he misses little of what goes on around him—but he finds it strange. He has no principled objection to bourgeois manners; he is quite willing to try them, but perversely demands that they make sense. And he has some standards of his own: Lestingois may be outraged when Boudu spits on the floor, but Boudu is shocked at the suggestion that he spit in his handkerchief and then put it back in his pocket. Faced with this impasse, he can find nothing better to do when the need arises again than to spit into the copy of Balzac's *Physiology of Marriage* he has in hand—with an expression of guilt, spite, triumph, and relief.

The difficulty is that the actions demanded of him *are* merely conventional; hence Lestingois no more than Boudu can explain their propriety. Lestingois just knows that it is proper to sleep in a bed, even if it is uncomfortable; Boudu only feels the discomfort.

Conventions *are* baffling to the uninitiated, and this bafflement itself is distressing to initiates. If we have lived within a convention, a way of life, our conformity seems as natural as breathing and as little open to question. If someone does challenge or question it, we can think of no rational defense —merely, "that is the way it's done." Hence our usual response to the challenge is anger—a response that is wholly irrational yet quite understandable. The convention is so much a part of ourselves that we feel threatened by the challenge; having no rational defense, we can only attack the challenger.

The middle section of *Boudu Saved from Drowning* may be seen as a head-on collision between nature and convention, with Boudu as the guileless child of nature harried by artificial restraints—or as an uncivilized beast snapping at the hand that feeds him. He is, though, neither of these; he combines innocence and malice, a genuine ignorance of what is expected of him with a delight in seeing how far he can go. The culmination of his contest with bourgeois mores comes when Anne-Marie tells him that she might kiss him if he didn't have a beard. Again ignorant of the proprieties, Boudu siezes a pair of scissors and shears off half his beard, only to be told that he looks worse than ever. Lestingois sets him straight—"Go to a barber." But when Boudu starts out, Lestingois stops him, "You're not going out like that? . . . Your shoes aren't shined." Boudu has accepted the proprieties concerning forks and cravats, but it seems strange indeed that one must polish his shoes before being shaved. Boudu tries, but reduces the kitchen to a shambles in the attempt. He progresses from the kitchen to Mme. Lestingois' bedroom, where he buffs his shoes on the bedspread and wipes the polish off his hands with a bit of madame's lingerie, after giving it an appreciative glance. Finally, he is off to the barber's, his shoes, in a way, shined, but with a trail of shattered conventions in his wake. But this episode appears to be only a final fling before complete submission. When he leaves the barber's with hair cut and beard shaved, the old Boudu has completely disappeared—now he walks with firm purpose, head steady, arms swinging, straight toward the bookshop. He has changed, indeed; for the first time in the film he has set himself a goal and ordered his action in relation to it. From this moment until the wedding scene, he acts like a good, if clumsy, bourgeois. Instead of kissing Anne-Marie he seduces Mme. Lestingois, but this of course is not a violation of bourgeois conventions. The action is approved by the most thoroughly bourgeois character in the film, Mme. Lestingois. He even learns to idle respectably; instead of swinging on the door jambs he leans against the doorway of the bookstore with a proprietary air, smoking a cigar. No one would call that loitering.

Though thoroughly overshadowed by Simon, Charles Granval brings equal conviction to the role of Lestingois. Opposed to Boudu in physical appearance, habits, and outlook, Lestingois lives more in a world of words than of deeds, speaks in elegant phrases that delight Anne-Marie, though his wife no longer seems impressed by them. He thinks of himself as freer and more enlightened than Mme. Lestingois and his bourgeois friends; yet when Anne-Marie asks why he has a piano when no one can play it, he gravely replies, "We have a piano because we are respectable people." But this remark, ludicrous as it seems, expresses just those characteristics of Lestingois that make him the first of what may be called the genuinely civilized characters in Renoir's films—a class that will include, among others, both Boieldieu and Rauffenstein of *Grand Illusion* and the Marquis de la Chesnay of *The Rules of the Game*. All of these characters have a certain self-consciousness and a rather clear awareness of their place within a tradition. They are capable of irony, and they believe that a life should be lived with some style. All this can lend the character an unusual depth and perceptiveness, an admirable objectivity and selflessness, but such characters also, in their concern for style, tend toward lives that become wholly artificial.

They may become so formalized as to lose contact with the most vital realities in their environment; even when they avoid this, they court the danger of appearing ridiculous to the less civilized men who surround them. They exhibit within their own lives a strong sense of propriety, yet tend to be quite tolerant of the improprieties of others. Perhaps this is but one expression of the great attraction they feel for someone wholly outside their own form of life, someone who seems totally un-self-conscious and without style but who has great vitality—the attraction Boieldieu feels for the mechanic Maréchal or de la Chesnay for the poacher Marceau. For Lestingois with Boudu, it is clearly a case of love at first sight.

Lestingois is not of the nobility, as are many of Renoir's most civilized characters; rather, his tradition is that of humanism with its roots in classical literature, its credo that of the Enlightenment. He enchants Anne-Marie when he talks of her running nude through the woods like a Grecian nymph, gladly gives a poor student a volume of Voltaire. He performs an unselfish act of genuine courage in rescuing Boudu and proves good-natured and generous in the face of Boudu's boorish ingratitude. Boudu becomes for Lestingois a sort of second self, free of the inhibitions of "respectable people." The first scene in a Renoir sound film that overflows with affection occurs when Lestingois gives Boudu a lottery ticket and the two talk—their heads close together, Boudu stretched across the table overflowing the orderly space of the apartment—a scene that makes visible the love expressed through action in the rescue. Lestingois willingly suffers all the gaucheries of Boudu—even, we suspect, enjoys them, though he occasionally mutters, "Animal!" Mme. Lestingois' distress at the havoc in the kitchen and her bedroom leads him to assert, "One ought to rescue only people of his own class." Still, he defends Boudu until he discovers Boudu's affront to the whole tradition: his spitting in a "magnificent edition" of Balzac. But even this is forgiven, and Lestingois reacts to the disclosure of Boudu's adultery with Mme. Lestingois with great equanimity, his major concern being that of reestablishing the appearance of respectability.

Lestingois' only interests seem those of literature and love, his only activities either reading or caressing Anne-Marie, usually verbally. Yet an edge of ambiguity cuts across the whole characterization, renders it all slightly suspect. In the film's first scene Lestingois fondles Anne-Marie, then sends her off to the kitchen; alone, he grumbles that she is charming, but he was so sleepy last night—"I'm getting old; my pipes are tired. Soon a young shepherd with a new flute will come." The suspicion arises that perhaps his kindness to the student and his tolerance of Boudu may not be merely the natural expression of a generous spirit, but also in part a campaign to recruit the young shepherd who will take Anne-Marie off his hands.

Still, though Lestingois' humanist virtue may be tarnished and he is the instrument through which Renoir constructs a devastating portrait of bourgeois mores, the portrait is softly drawn, tenderly framed. In *Boudu*, Renoir's work has fully arrived at that stage when, no longer performing tricks or merely telling stories, it creates characters; and however objectively observed, they are all conceived in love.

The domestic setting of *Boudu* holds no prostitutes, no destructive females; though very different from each other, Mme. Lestingois and Anne-Marie are both simpler and gentler than either Lulu or Else. Their difference shows plainly in the rescue scene. Anne-Marie, seeing the crowd, jumps up and down and cries joyously, "Oh! An accident." She watches intently while Mme. Lestingois turns her back and looks bored. As Lestingois and some boatmen carry Boudu toward the bookshop, Anne-Marie exclaims, "Quel courage!" and Mme. Lestingois cries, "You're not going to take that into my house!" While Lestingois works over Boudu, Anne-Marie gazes at him in admiration; Mme. Lestingois looks disgustedly at the dripping Boudu and complains that she has just had the furniture reupholstered. Mme. Lestingois, the proper bourgeois housewife with a maid to do all the work, is idle and empty. She seems to relate to Lestingois only on the level of talk, smiles with satisfaction when she finds dust on the piano. Outraged by almost every action of Boudu, she retires to her bedroom complaining of exhaustion or nerves. And when Boudu tries to explain that he really didn't know about polishing shoes, she coldly asserts that they are a decent bourgeois family and he has acted like a troglodyte. Boudu hardly hears her; his finger keeps edging toward the beauty spot on her bosom that fascinates him. Haughtily she walks away, pulling her dressing gown *off* her shoulders so the beauty spot will be more clearly displayed. She confronts the world from behind a formidable wall of proprieties that conceal her unsatisfied sensual nature, a wall that only the complete irreverence of a Boudu will breach.

Treatment

So often has the symbolic role of water in Renoir's work been cited that we tend to forget how few the films are in which this expressive element actually has a significant place. After a few sparkling shots in *La Fille de l'eau*, water has little part, except as rain or snow, in any film until *Boudu*. Here it is immediately present, in the title and shimmering under the credits, signaling at last the fulfillment of the illusory promise made in the title of Renoir's first film.

The promise here is not illusory. Associated with Boudu throughout the film, water becomes, in the final sequence, central among the group of images and sounds that Renoir commingles with the action to transform *Boudu sauvé des eaux* from a domestic comedy to a universal fable and to impart to the figure of Boudu something of the aura of a mythical being.

Back from the barber, Boudu (Michel Simon) encounters Mme. Lestingois (Marcelle Hainia). Meanwhile, Vigour (Jean Gehret) and Godin (Max Dalban) announce to Lestingois (Charles Granval) that he has been decorated.

This is executed with such unpretentious deftness and so little solemnity as to make the mere statement of the accomplishment sound pompous and exaggerated. Nonetheless, I believe it true.

Other major elements of this magic are the flute music provided by Lestingois' neighbor Vigour (Jean Gehret), the images of Notre Dame that serve as visual punctuation to the action, and Lestingois' repeated evocations of classical mythology. The reedlike tones of Vigour's flute accompany the strange opening shot of the film, acquiring associations that then affect our vision of the images of Notre Dame which introduce the flute theme for the remainder of the film. Water appears intermittently through most of the film, then becomes the dominant image for the final thirty-five shots, evoked with such lyric beauty as to make us forget the other images we have seen, with this itself being a symbol of another transformation performed within the film, that is, the displacement of Lestingois by Boudu as the major figure in the work.

Boudu's opening *is* puzzling. The flute theme begins; fade-in on an obviously false setting: two columns cut vertically across the left half of the frame; behind them a painted backdrop represents a very geometrical formal garden. Anne-Marie, sparsely clad in vines and leaves, skips rope rapidly across the screen; Lestingois, similarly attired, gambols behind her playing panpipes. Anne-Marie hovers behind the columns as Lestingois again gambols across the screen, throws the panpipes down with an effeminate gesture, and leans against one of the columns, which rocks away at his touch. At this he siezes Anne-Marie's arm, pulls her to center screen, and bends her backward in an embrace. Cut to a medium-close shot as Lestingois leans forward to kiss Anne-Marie in a style one might call "Hollywood torrid, ca. 1926," and the camera backs away as the scene dissolves to a normal Renoir opening shot: from a close-up of a bust of Voltaire, the camera recedes to disclose a cluttered corner of Lestingois' bookshop, then pans across the bookstore to Lestingois and Anne-Marie, the flute continuing throughout. Cut to a medium shot as Lestingois caresses Anne-Marie's breast and talks of dancing nude through a moonlit wood as Bacchus presides at the nuptial feast of Priapus-Lestingois and Chloe-Anne-Marie. Cut again, to Vigour by his open window playing the flute, his rather grotesque figure in sharp contrast to both the lightness of the music and the slenderness of the instrument he plays. This shot locates the music heard throughout this time as inside the world of the film and establishes an internal connection between the flute and the opening fantasy. The fantasy endows the flute theme with overtly sexual connotations that may lead us to see Vigour's odd figure as satyric. We may further note the elegance with which the dissolve connecting shots 2 and 3 is conceived: the heads of Priapus-Lestingois and the bust of Voltaire occupy the same area of screen-space and the camera movement is identical in the two overlapping shots, thus this transitional image blends the contradictory cultural bases of Lestingois' humanism: a romantic identification with the nature worship of pagan antiquity and a reverence for the rationalism of the Enlightenment.

Still, what can we make of the opening shots? Lestingois' talk suggests they may represent his fantasy-image of himself as a woodland god, sexually potent and free of all the constraints of society. But what we see is rather a parody of this, a sham-fantasy. It is, I think, a new Renoir experiment, a sort of visual counterpart to the verbal prologue of *La Chienne;* it gives us a view of Lestingois just as the puppet gave us a view of Legrand. It works by allowing the falseness of the image to undercut the content of the fantasy, arriving thus at a rather accurate picture of Lestingois. The difference between a false stage set and a moonlit wood reflects the distance between the real and imagined Lestingois, also perhaps the distance between a Parisian bourgeois home and the ancient culture in which Priapus was a living diety. In imagination Lestingois prances and skips, he acts and does not talk, and he sheds the restraints of convention. In reality he seldom moves, lives in a world of words, and, confronted by the unrestrained Boudu, he clings to the bourgeois conventions and even tries to impose them on this incarnation of the woodland god. Still, his vision is not wholly false; he does recognize his fantasy when he sees it in Boudu and rescues him; by thus giving Boudu life, he acquires for a moment the potency so absent from his sterile daily routine.

The introduction of Boudu appropriately lacks all the cultural trappings that flavor this opening. The first image is simply water, sparkling with light; a toy sailboat enters in close-up and the camera pans with it across the pond to where a mother forces her child to come away from the water. Cut to Boudu, sitting under a tree, caressing his black dog. After a moment he pushes the dog away, tells it, "Go!" The dog trots to the edge of the pond, stops, then runs off along the pond as Boudu chews his crust and sings. Despite its visual difference, this segment bears a strong formal resemblance to the opening introduction of Lestingois, and thus already works toward lending Boudu a mythic status. The first shot shows us Boudu's element and habitat, open space and water—nature—as the classic tradition, civilization, was shown to be the habitat of Lestingois, and suggests what we will discover in Boudu, a child drawn unwillingly from his world. Like the opening fantasy, this has a note of falsity; Boudu is not a child, though he will become childish within the strange confines of a bourgeois home. Then: Boudu caressing his dog, Lestingois with Anne-Marie; like Boudu, Lestingois tells Anne-Marie, "Go!" "Make the soup," he orders, and she moves away, hesitates, then runs up the circular stair—this juxtaposition itself casts a reflection on the bourgeois menage that will soon contain Boudu.

The rescue, a pivotal scene in *Boudu,* is filmed with the restraint that has become almost a Renoir trademark in this period. With complete rejection of dramatic effects, Renoir more than ever achieves his impact through cinematic form rather than melodramatic acting. Having lost his dog, Boudu shambles disconsolately along the Quai Conti in a long and remarkable panning shot, with the space of the quai squashed flat by a lens of much longer focal length than was normal in 1932—the flatness of the shot expressing the feel of Boudu's life after the loss of his only companion. The occasion for the rescue arrives quite accidentally. Like life, Renoir's films are full of such accidents, chance occurrences of little intrinsic moment, but without which subsequent events would be very different. And in Renoir films as in life, these coincidences seldom appear contrived; for, essential as they are, they do not determine the course of the action. Rather, character intervenes as the decisive element; it is the way the persons in the film react to these accidents that shapes the course of events. Here, in *Boudu*, Anne-Marie lazily dusts a desk, picks up the telescope, and gazes out of the window. Coincidentally, Lestingois enters, tells her, "Go—dust the piano," and takes the telescope from her. Then he too happens to point it out the window, at the women on the quai. Eventually, Boudu wanders into his field of vision; Lestingois, smitten, follows with his eye as Boudu impulsively swerves, walks onto the bridge, and clambers over the rail. Lestingois dashes to the rescue.

Sheer chance! Had Anne-Marie been dusting the piano, Lestingois would no doubt have lingered with her and never seen Boudu. But—not to have preferred the telescope to dusting would not have been in character for the amiable servant girl of *Boudu*. Such coincidences provide Renoir with occasions for the exhibition and development of character; they are not the strings on which puppets dance.

Through this sequence Boudu's erratic motion has all flowed from right to left on the screen. Now Lestingois runs left to right across the room and an urgent rush of motion sweeps left to right across the street and to the river, rapid, purposeful, totally counteracting the odd rhythm of Boudu. But when Lestingois dives into the water, at just the moment that should be the high point of the action, Renoir seems to lose interest. He turns his camera away from the river and on to the crowd gathered on the bridge. Through six shots it dallies, almost motionless, on this tightly packed mass that shows such unconcern for the fate of the men in the water below. In the last of these shots, Lestingois' friends Vigour and Godin (Max Dalban) push through to the front of the crowd, Godin exclaiming on the merit of such courage shown by a man of "our class." As if reminded by this, Renoir cuts back to the river and the rescue. But now he shoots it at such extreme distance that the heads of Lestingois and Boudu are mere dots in the water. What we see is river, boats, bridge, open air, and light reflected on the water, the beauty of a warm day on the river, with Lestingois' struggle to save Boudu barely disturbing the surface of this summer loveliness—rather like a cinema version of Breughel's *Icarus*. We do not even see in long shot the pick-up of Boudu from the water; for at that point Renoir inserts another shot of the crowd. Only as the rescue boat nears the shore do we see Boudu and Lestingois at all clearly. But here too the transfer of Boudu from boat to shore shows us only the backs of the mariners who haul him out. The individuals, Boudu and Lestingois, reappear only when Lestingois begins to apply artificial respiration.

Through the twenty-two shots of this rescue sequence we feel most keenly

Rescue and rebirth into the bourgeois world.

the openness, the spaciousness of the scene; we are bathed in limitless space. Renoir seems to say: Once Boudu has leaped into the river, whether he drowns or lives is only an event; what I must show you is the world he has chosen to forsake. But when Boudu, rescued, is carried to the bookshop, we shift quickly from the world he has left to that he will enter, the world of Lestingois. The spatial change is immediate and intense; we are suddenly cut from the unlimited space of the river to an area so confined that the characters must squeeze past the camera to get into the room. Quickly, ten people crowd into a corner of the bookstore, with a pole cutting the space and helping to create a visual jam. When Lestingois complains, "You're all breathing his air," we feel the confinement he protests against.

Through the first eighty shots of *Boudu*, Lestingois has been its central character; we have seen Boudu but know little of him. Now, with the two together, the dominance of Lestingois is reinforced. He completely controls the action-space of the scene. Though he is concerned about Boudu, everyone else attends to him, Anne-Marie with open adoration, Mme. Lestingois with dismay, Vigour and Godin eager to congratulate him on his bravery and tell him of their plan to have him decorated. When Boudu begins to breathe, Lestingois tells Vigour, "Carry on," and moves away to change his wet clothes. But his dominance is such that everyone quickly follows him to the back of the room. When Boudu revives and sits up, he is quite alone.

At the beginning of this sequence Boudu was inert, Lestingois active and dominant. Now, slowly, Boudu begins to move. Through the rest of the scene he exhibits his conditions for accepting life: he will remain Boudu. But while he does this by rejecting rudely every suggestion made, Renoir accomplishes the major dramatic movement of the scene by formal means. At first Boudu's movements are directed by Lestingois, but then he becomes free, explores the room, moves deeper into the space, begins to usurp the center of the screen. As he becomes more active Lestingois ceases his activity and sits quietly at the edge of the visible space. Boudu now roams at will, displacing everyone else, finally sprawling across the table—stretching the limits of the space. As this scene ends, Boudu and Lestingois are joined in affection, but now Boudu firmly occupies the center of the scene and dominates the space.

The extent of this dominance is clear in the succeeding nocturnal scene, which begins with a dark shot of Notre Dame. The tones of Vigour's flute accompany this image, their sexual theme lending phallic overtones to the dark spires and representing the church not as a source of salvation but as the modern vehicle for the pagan rites of fertility. We see then into the four bedrooms of the Lestingois household; in each we can feel the weight of Boudu's presence. Boudu twists and turns, gets out of bed and curls up on the floor. Mme. Lestingois tosses, thrashes her arms, moans. Lestingois and Anne-Marie yearn in frustration toward each other, separated by the presence of Boudu's body in the intervening space. Through the night we hear a mocking whistle: "Auprès de ma blonde, Qu'il fait bon dormir." The scene seethes with sexual tension. Boudu alone seems immune; he tells Lestingois he just can't sleep in a bed. But the flute and the phallic steeples suggest that, here for the first time in close contact with two women, he too is sexually aroused and thus mistaken about the source of his own unrest.

Once Boudu moves into the limited space of Lestingois' home, the film remains almost entirely within these confining walls until the final wedding scene. Boudu fights against the space, acts in ways wholly unsuited to it,

"Faudra changer de conduite, mon ami." Boudu defies bourgeois space and discovers Anne-Marie (Séverine Lerczinska).

but slowly subsides. Now he sings Anne-Marie's song, "Les fleurs du jardin"; his gestures begin to imitate Lestingois'. After Boudu spits on the floor and tickles Anne-Marie as she tries to work, Lestingois tells him, "You'll have to change your ways, my friend." Boudu repeats, as if in mockery, "Faudra changer de conduite, mon ami," but from this point on he does change; he shifts his attention from Lestingois to the two women. We now see him almost exclusively with Anne-Marie or Mme. Lestingois; he offers to kiss Anne-Marie and goes off to the barber's expecting to be kissed on his return. And he is, but by Mme. Lestingois, rather to her surprise. This first sexual experience seems to complete his conversion to the bourgeois life, and it takes only a winning lottery ticket to persuade Anne-Marie to marry him, though she has sworn she will always love Lestingois. Lestingois, quite unperturbed at either his wife's infidelity or this loss of Anne-Marie, benignly welcomes this solution as being in accord "with the morality of the time." Boudu, saved from the water, looks radiantly happy and appears ready to drown quietly in this bourgeois pond. Anne-Marie contentedly rests her head on his shoulder.

Dissolve to a similar shot: Anne-Marie's head on Boudu's shoulder, but now she wears a bridal gown and Boudu a bowler hat. He is dressed in that same uniform of conventional respectability that Legrand wore at the beginning of *La Chienne:* stiff shirt, black tie, wide satin lapels. The perfect tramp has become a model bourgeois, in formal dress, with a wife and wealth, surrounded by those pillars of bourgeois hypocrisy, Vigour, Godin, and Lestingois. Boudu seems to have fully renounced his former life and self, but the radiant joy is gone from his face. The boat moves; light dances on the river and the spatial confinement we have endured for over two hundred shots gives way to open space. The camera, which had almost ceased to move in the last sequences at Lestingois', now glides over the water as Lestingois plays at being Bacchus, presiding at the nuptial feast of Priapus-Boudu and Chloe-Anne-Marie. The flowing movement of the river, the complex motion of the wedding boat and the camera, which come together, then separate, the slowness of pace, the beauty of the scene: all convey a great sense of ease, release, and joy after the tension of the rapidly cut, confined, discovery scene. And Boudu, having won a wife and accepted responsibility and a restricted life, now finds himself on the river, drifting as it will, open and free. Through fifteen leisurely shots Renoir allows us and Boudu to flow with the river, to breathe the warm summer air, to savor the freedom of space and motion. An orchestra at an open-air riverside cafe plays "The Beautiful Blue Danube." Boats pass on the river. The free slow easy flow of time and water reawakens a sleeping Boudu. He looks increasingly distressed. A water lily floats by and he finally reaches out for nature, seeming to have remembered what he had lost. The boat founders, and Boudu returns to the water from whence Lestingois had claimed him. A joyous return—he rolls and bobs like a cork, blows like a porpoise, floats on his back in utter contentment. As in the rescue scene, Renoir pulls his camera far from the action, gazes at the quiet, tree-lined river-bank while Boudu, splashing in the river, almost disappears within the scene. Regaining the land, he lurches, staggers, shrugs off the whole of his recent life. Renoir allows the theme of death and rebirth to be reflected for just five seconds as Boudu pulls up a scarecrow and carries the cross on his back across the path to where he will kick off his wedding clothes and don the scarecrow rags. Then, having discarded wife, responsibility, and 100,000 francs, he flaps down the path in the old Boudu walk, tells a picnicker who offers him food, "I can't eat that without any bread." He rolls in the grass, shares his bread with a passing goat, and sings once more, "Sur les bords de la Rivière." In a final gesture, he flings his bowler hat into the river. Renoir's camera picks it up, moves from it in one last great slow circuit of the river, coming to rest in a frame of reeds and water—forty-five seconds of liquid beauty that express all the joy of paradise regained. And remind us perhaps of Boudu's similarity to the water: he has temporarily taken the shape of the vessel that held him, the bourgeois menage, but when once released his shape flows back to fit the contours of nature. Meanwhile, a little group of sodden bourgeois huddles on the river bank. Anne-Marie asks, "Boudu? Has he gone away or drowned?" And Lestingois replies, "His destiny is to drift with the current." The French phrase that concludes this sentence is *fil de l'eau*; hence, as water was the first image of the film, it is also its last spoken word.

At the film's end we have returned to its beginning. Boudu has rediscovered nature, again the perfect tramp. But now we, and perhaps Lestingois, recognize the truth of that remark of his. Lestingois will once again have both Anne-Marie and Mme. Lestingois with him in the narrow confines of the bookshop. But now each of these persons should have learned something about himself and the others. Do we then return to the beginning? Renoir does not tell us. He ends his film with a last ironic image: the phallic spires of Notre Dame loom against the sky and a line of. *clochards* walks past the camera, singing, "Sur les bords de la Rivière."

The sympathy Renoir shows for all his characters helps make *Boudu* a disturbing film; one can see why French audiences in the thirties might have been hostilely aroused by it. The film does not clearly direct our sympathies, as most films do—it is not simply that its people are complex and neither heroes nor villains, but they are uncomfortably close to us if we happen to be convention-bound, middle-class humans. We would like to think that we share Lestingois' courage and sense of responsibility, his civilized outlook and generous nature—so superior to his friends Vigour and Godin. But we cannot help seeing his emptiness and idleness, and the ridiculousness of some of the conventions that rule his life. Do we share this, too? And like Lestingois, we cannot help identifying with Boudu's love of freedom and we rejoice in his rejection of silly conventions—but he makes us uncomfortable. We wouldn't really want him around; he *is* messy and crude and he takes up too much room. Yet he is so alive, and more genuine, in a way, than most of us. The trouble, perhaps, is that we suspect that Boudu's mocking mimicry of Lestingois, "Faudra changer de conduite, mon ami," is an injunction directed at us, and one we ought to heed. But it is so difficult to really change!

Style and Form

Renoir had previously shown some fondness for cyclical form, but his first full realization of this tendency came in *Boudu*, whose underlying theme of the cycle of death and rebirth makes the form most fitting. Not only dramatic structure but the forms of space and movement in the film return upon themselves; even the sound, to a lesser degree, shares this pattern. The result is a remarkable congruence of form and content, a formal reinforcement of the dramatic development, which imparts to the final section of the film a depth of feeling and an inevitability of movement far beyond what one expects in a comedy of manners. From this congruent flow of form and drama, Boudu emerges as a mythic figure—a status no other character in the film approaches.

The members of the Lestingois household are all firmly anchored in the Left Bank world of the bookshop, so lovingly displayed by Renoir. The pictures on the wall, the dust-catching decorations atop the unplayed piano, the piles of books everywhere, all become familiar. A space form that had now and then appeared in earlier films now becomes a significant element in Renoir's style: Renoir repeatedly shows us in *Boudu* the long, narrow spaces which will henceforth mark his films—shots along a corridor or through a door or window, shaping the space in a way that almost requires that the action develop in depth. By emphasizing this form in his interior space, Renoir can both have the depth he desires and maintain our sense of the confinement Boudu feels in this house. But Lestingois, his wife, and Anne-Marie all live here, and the reality of the setting, its clear location in space and time, assure us of the continuity of their lives.

But Boudu has no such continuity. He lives only within the time-span of the film; he appears at its beginning, loiters briefly in our view, and disappears. He has no past or future. Not, of course, that Boudu is any less real than the others. Simon's exuberant performance makes him one of the most vital characters to grace the screen. But his reality is like that of the water into which he dies and out of which he is reborn again. Though very specific and individual, it transcends the world of the film and achieves the universality of a symbol.

Of equal importance with the cyclical form of the whole film are the numerous occasions in which Renoir achieves a striking congruence of form and content within a single shot. Usually, the impact of form is not merely to reinforce a content overtly presented in other terms; rather, the form itself constitutes a part of the presentation. Thus, the flatness of the space as Boudu walks along the Quai Conti *informs* us of his despondency as well as expressing it, drawing together the series of shots in the park which seemed very disruptive of the continuity of the film but which in their totality display the complete isolation of Boudu from all genuine human contact. This shot is perhaps the first example in Renoir's work of what we might call *epitomizing shots*, shots that concentrate and express the whole state of a character or situation at some particular moment in the film into a single moving image. From *Boudu* on, such shots grace the Renoir films of the thirties. They are often lengthy and involve large camera movements, so that they usually exploit the expressive power of spatial form. In this shot on the Quai Conti, Boudu walks laterally along the quai, apparently oblivious of his surroundings. In the flattened space, his background is a frieze of bookstalls, decorated with a fringe of people; in the foreground an occasional vehicle passes, seemingly so close as to brush the camera lens. Figures pass each other but never touch; there is no penetration of the space in depth. Though the space is flat, its felt character is that of closely packed receding planes. Thus Renoir uses this diminution of the space to heighten our sense of Boudu's isolation, just the opposite of Kurosawa's use of similar lenses in *Seven Samurai* to thrust his characters together in a whirling rage of action.

The final sweep around the river in *Boudu* is also an epitomizing shot, a summation of that call from nature that tore Boudu loose from his bourgeois daze. It is not a generalization of nature, but a loving evocation of just this spot, on this river, on this day. But, as Aristotle knew, it is only through such specificity that true universality can be achieved.

The last few of the shots through the bedroom window in *La Chienne* were Renoir's first approximation to these epitomizing shots. There, however, it was association with the earlier shots rather than the form of the shot itself that gave these images their concentrating power. But we do find in *La Chienne* the first occurrence of a shot form that acquires equal importance and even greater power in Renoir's work in this period, though it occurs much less frequently. These shots one might call *piercing shots*, for they cut through all the masks of the character, destroy all distance between audience and character, and seem to lay bare the very soul of the personage portrayed. In *La Chienne*, of course, the shot is that last image of Dédé, awakened for his engagement with the guillotine. Such shots are almost always big close-ups, with a minimum of surrounding space and environment. They cannot occur until we have had some experience of the character, some background against which the revelation can stand. And they depend greatly upon context; there are only certain moments in the life of a character when such disclosure would be either appropriate or understood. Also, their power in Renoir's films relies upon the very scarcity of big close-ups in these works. They occur rarely; when they do, we are willing to allow their full impact. Given these conditions, every now and then, like a poignant cry, one of these revelatory close-ups will shatter the world of the film and our complacency toward it.

One other aspect of Renoir's style is, I believe, important in making possible such piercing shots. This is Renoir's refusal to employ what is called "star make-up," the cosmetic mask that transforms a face into an idealized image that will always appear the same. Renoir treats the human face as terrain to be explored. He does not seek constancy when photographing an actor; rather, he lets the complexity of his characters be mirrored in the variety of visual aspects and appearances his camera finds in every face. No woman is always beautiful; no buffoon always grotesque. And within this multiplicity of images, which, for Renoir, constitutes each human face, there lurks the possibility of one that will reveal the soul that underlies them all.

In *Boudu* Michel Simon looks different in almost every shot; Séverine Lerczinskà ranges from moments of beauty to other moments where she appears exceedingly plain. Though there are no piercing shots in *Boudu*, one image approaches this intensity. This occurs at the moment when Boudu tells Lestingois he has won the lottery. He has appeared grotesque, ugly, comical, scruffy, but suddenly, in a big close-up, he is quite beautiful—almost beautiful enough to be the woodland god of Lestingois' dreams, beautiful far beyond our expectations of Michel Simon. A revealing shot, surely, but not a piercing one, for this image reveals, not the soul of Boudu, but the depth of his descent (or the height of his ascent?) into the bourgeois world. The deeper revelation will come only with a return to the river; its vehicle will not be a look but an action.

Most of the stylistic tendencies noted in *La Chienne* and *La Nuit de carrefour* continue in *Boudu*. The loose-jointed structure is here articulated by punctuating shots of Notre Dame or boats on the water; deep-focus shots develop leisurely with an internal rhythm created by movement in depth within the shot. Close-ups are few; shot-countershot cutting occurs only when it can be an expressive form within the development of the scene. More often than before, Renoir divides his frame in half with verticals, increasing the complexity of compositions without sacrifice of balance.

What is new in *Boudu* is the application of this style to sunlit nature, trees in the *Bois*, the river and its environs—where the temptation to allow the camera to wander away from the dramatic center of a scene increases. Fortunately, Renoir does not try to resist; and in succumbing, he gives us the strikingly unconventional rescue scene and the lyrical final sequence on the river where the camera lingers for as long as seventy seconds in a single shot in which nothing seems to happen. Renoir's style, with its long-held shots and fluid camera, its relaxed attitude toward tightness of structure and continuity, proves ideal for the exploration and revelation of nature. And nature offers to Renoir an ideal object for some aspects of his style, its unlimited space and infinite variety inviting his camera to flow in open rhythms without having to double back upon itself or recoil from a confining wall.

In *Boudu*, Renoir's exploration of sound continues. As in *La Chienne* the

Nature regained. The perfect tramp
reborn in the river.

dialogue is employed more for characterization than for plot development;
as in *La Nuit du carrefour*, the intonation and rhythm of a voice are as important as the meaning of the words—most interestingly perhaps in the
eight or ten very different intonations with which Mme. Lestingois utters
the name "Boudu." Natural sounds are richer and more varied than in *La
Nuit de carrefour* and play an equally important role, creating to a large extent the background presence of the city. The range of sound includes street
and river noises of an almost startling authenticity, birds in the park, a baby
crying as Lestingois rescues Boudu. To this natural sound Renoir adds much

of the music of *Boudu*, music which is again all internal to the world of the film—Vigour's flute, the riverside orchestra, the whistler in the night, a barrel organ in the street which arouses Mme. Lestingois' sensuality before Boudu returns from the barber—all blend with the natural noises to form the sounds of the city.

In *Boudu* Renoir finds still a different role for the songs he loves to include within his films. Here there are two songs, "Sur les bords de la Rivière" and "Les fleurs du jardin," each identified with a character and functioning within the film as one expression of the domestication and liberation of Boudu. These are not theme songs or leitmotifs played as commentative background music, but, like Vigour's flute, music that plays its part within the character's life.

In one other variation on his use of music internal to the film, Renoir makes the scene of Mme. Lestingois' seduction a kind of musical joke, with a trumpet announcing the triumph of Boudu while the satyr Vigour leads a band down the street to proclaim to Lestingois at this appropriate moment that he has been decorated.

In the three films from *La Chienne* to *Boudu* music occurs only intermittently, filling but a small portion of the sound track; it is all internal, playing a structural role or making a dramatic point within the world of the film. Subsequently, through the 1930s, every Renoir film except *Une Partie de campagne* will contain internal music that helps create the environment of the film and shape its dramatic structure.

The music written for films—usually heard as background music external to the film's world—is subject to fashions that change almost every decade. Scores for films of the 1960s sound quite different from scores of the 1940s. For the first thirty years of the sound era, film music tended to be excessive and nondescript, an emotional bath that gave the audience instructions on how to feel. Movie music was thought successful when it was nearly subliminal, not really heard and remembered but simply existing to reinforce audience emotions. Very often this external music becomes dated and it dates the films it accompanies. Much of the film music of these decades now sounds overdone, banal, sentimental, and it affects the way we see the films. But the Renoir films of 1931-32 seem almost as fresh and undated as the day they were made, partly because the music internal to these films does not date in the same way. It is meant to be heard, and as a part of the world of the film; its validity remains a function of its role within the dramatic setting. Most movie music reflects a manipulative sentimentality that Renoir's films oppose. His use of internal music in these films represents one form of this opposition.

Renoir's internal music also allows him to create a discord between the dramatic events and their musical accompaniment without obvious intervention in the events. With external music, such discord often becomes a sort of blatant commentary from outside. In the Renoir films, the music often does provide a commentary, often an ironic one. But here the discord occurs within the world of the film; the irony appears as a part of that world, not as editorial comment directed at us. We do, of course, recognize the comment as Renoir's—he is the creator of these worlds—but as part of the dramatic substance, integral to it and not imposed from without.

To my knowledge, no complete print of *Boudu* has ever been distributed in the English-speaking world. Inexplicably, all of the subtitled prints seem to lack the segment of perhaps forty-five seconds during which Boudu commits the ultimate desecration of spitting in *La Physiologie du mariage*. *Quel dommage!*

La Chienne, *La Nuit du carrefour*, and *Boudu sauvé des eaux* form a sort of exploratory trilogy within Renoir's work, an introduction to the possibilities of cinema with sound. Together they constitute a remarkably original group within the realm of French cinema in the early thirties. They are original not only in their independence of the trends and fashions of the day and their development of a style very different from those that were dominant in films of that time, but also in their freedom in almost every domain of cinematic form, their rejection of cliché and easy manipulation of audience emotion, the cool unsentimental objectivity with which they observe their very human characters, whose lives are firmly located within a precisely perceived milieu.

But these films are not merely original; they are also formative for the art of Jean Renoir. They provide the field in which ideas and tendencies grow to the point of becoming central elements in his style. His preference for deep-focus cinematography, for example, ran counter to an almost universal gravitation toward the use of faster lenses with larger apertures, and consequently a shallower field of focus, but it admirably complemented Renoir's desire to subordinate dialogue to action and characterization. The mutual support of these two tendencies encouraged his exploration of the varieties of arranging scenes in depth. This in turn results in the emergence in these films of what becomes one rather characteristic look for a Renoir shot, a frame in which a portion of the action-space is blocked by a foreground figure or object, with the center of attention located deeper within the space. This preference for depth also stimulates a conscious awareness of the patterns of motion within a shot, and Renoir began to develop a great sensitivity to the rhythms such motion could impart to his film. He had a rather clear idea of what he wished to achieve: he wanted the background of his action to be felt as an encompassing world that contained the foreground people and events. He thought the background should be a world with happenings of its own, not essentially related to the foreground events by being part of them or like them—a world rich enough that one could shift from foreground to background and pick up the thread of another story or another life as interesting as that one had been following. The people in the background, he thought, should be as real and vital as those in the foreground, though not as demanding on our attention. Yet there must be some connection if the background world was to be felt as containing the foreground action. Renoir began to tie foreground and background together by the rhythms of motion within his shots, thus creating a formal connection rather than a situational or dramatic one.

This conception of the use of deep space is very different from that developed in the early 1940s by Orson Welles. In *Citizen Kane* the persons who occupy the background of Welles' deep space are invariably involved in the same situation or action as the foreground characters, while background figures in Renoir films tend to be much more independent of the central dramatic situation, like the little girl at the piano in *La chienne*. In *Boudu* this provides a startling flash-forward in Renoir's work for those who notice it. As the wedding party rows down the river, another boat crosses the frame diagonally in the background, rowed by Georges Darnoux, who will row down a similar river four years later as Henri in *A Day in the Country*.

In his exploration of the rhythms of motion, Renoir freed his camera both from a strict connection with the central action and from the point-of-view shots that form an important element in classical cinema style. Both of these aspects of Renoir's style served his desire to avoid dramatizing the action of his films and inflating its emotional impact. And this desire reflected his central concern with character rather than action. The avoidance of point-of-view shots tends to reduce our identification with special central characters, to give all of the characters an equal existence in the world of the film, though not an equal importance. The camera's tendency to wander does the same for objects and events: a little girl's piano lesson has the same existential status as Legrand's theft; Bazin remarks of the long, slow view of the river at the end of *Boudu*, "what really touches and moves us is *not* that this landscape has again become Boudu's domain, but the intrinsic beauty of the banks of the Marne, in all their richness of detail."[1]

This style imparts to Renoir's films a surface of naturalness and objectivity: events appear simply to have happened; people seem as real as life. Our responses and sympathies are not controlled and directed as obviously as in most films of the period. We must discover the characters, and many questions about them remain unanswered.

But within this surface naturalness, Renoir does not conceal or deny the existence of the camera. Another aspect of his avoidance of point-of-view shots is that the independence and freedom of the camera involves an acknowledgment of its presence. When it remains strictly tied to the action or the point-of-view of the characters, we may forget the camera and have the illusion of viewing the event itself, unmediated. But when it deserts the action (to drift down the river in *Boudu*) or deliberately turns its back upon it (as it will in the famous shot of Batala's murder in *Le Crime de M. Lange*), the camera declares its presence and that of Jean Renoir behind it. Like the internal music, Renoir's camera style often transforms external comment into internal irony.

As Renoir's style developed, he became one of the great masters of the moving camera, but as he mastered technique he lost the desire to flaunt this mastery. Technique becomes increasingly expressive rather than merely utilitarian, yet the mastery remains unobtrusive. Or rather, as Renoir feels, the unobtrusiveness is a part of the mastery. And however carefully wrought and intricate the formal structures of these works may be, they never become tightly knit, "well-made" films. Hence the legend grows that Jean Renoir is disdainful of technique and careless about form.

But style is not all that develops or becomes clarified in these films. Much of what might be called Renoir's basic cast of characters also emerges, fundamental types that will be embodied in well-defined persons in films to come. Some of these had, of course, already been present in the silent films, for example, the destructive female and the innocent young girl. But after *La Chienne* and *Boudu* several other important types can be identified: The parasite, one who lives off others by combining brashness, charm, and a thorough disregard for others when his own interests are at stake, and who may be always engaged in some sort of performance to impress others. The nature-god, an incarnation of Pan or Priapus, a character whose very presence arouses the instinctual and emotional life of others, but whose innocence and naturalness may conceal a greater wisdom than that of those who think him a fool. The civilized man, whom I have already described in discussing Lestingois. The loiterer, one who prefers idleness to work or good works and doesn't feel guilty about this. The dreamer who accepts the world but whose inner life nourishes visions of a very different self. There are, of course, many other types in Renoir's films, but quite a number of his richest and most interesting characters may be seen as variations or combinations of these.

Whatever we may now think of these three films—*La Chienne, La Nuit du carrefour*, and *Boudu*—by the popular standards of the day they bristled with faults. They are disconnected, the dialogue is often difficult to hear, the camera zigzags through the space and often seems to forget what it was that was supposed to be going on. And they are almost completely devoid of the glamour, the prettiness, the idealized facades given both persons and places in the films that made Hollywood the dream factory for the world. Perhaps, too, the social criticism that is beginning to develop, subtly conveyed in the first two films and rampant in *Boudu*, did not endear these films to middle-class French audiences. Their success was meager. But the subsequent career of *Boudu* provides hope that even in an art form as ephemeral as film has been, quality eventually achieves recognition. Despised by French audiences in 1932, *Boudu* began a new career in French ciné-clubs after World War II, finally crossing the English Channel thirty-three years after its original release, and making it to the United States only in 1967. In America the film was coolly received by the reviewers in New York newspapers, much better appreciated by the more professional critics writing for periodicals, and greeted with cheers of delight by the *Los Angeles Free Press*, which considered its Los Angeles premiere a major event and quickly identified Boudu as the first hippy, born thirty years too soon.[2]

Chotard et Cie.
1933

Nineteen thirty-three was not a happy year for French cinema. The rise of Hitler had thrown a political pall over Europe. France was increasingly bitterly divided between Left and Right; film criticism became more viciously political than ever. The world-wide depression had crippled the French economy; the film industry suffered no less than others. With American films dominating the market, most French studios were in desperate financial straits. Some French directors left the country to work elsewhere. Some did not work at all.

Marcel Pagnol had recently begun to transpose into film his trilogy *Marius, Fanny,* and *Cesar,* warm and human and bursting with the life of the Marseilles waterfront. Purportedly this inspired Roger Ferdinand, a playwright of lesser talent, to engage Jean Renoir to bring to the screen a work of his own, *Chotard et Cie.* Pierre Leprohon writes that Ferdinand worked with Renoir for two months on the adaptation and closely followed the progress of the shooting. Charpin, the voluble Panisse of Pagnol's trilogy, was to play the role of Chotard in the film as he had on the stage. And George Pomiès, the Jean Dubois D'Ombelles of *Tire au flanc,* steps again into the role of a poet unable to adapt to a more orderly form of life.

The plot is that of a pleasant-enough Parisian comedy. M. Chotard (Charpin), wholesale dealer in groceries—the term *épicier* also has the familiar sense of "Philistine"—dominates his little district where business is business and commerce is king, and where the peace is disturbed only by the extravagant activities of a young poet, Julien Collinet (George Pomiès). Chotard's marriageable daughter Reine (Jeanne Boitel) loves Julien, and Chotard agrees to the marriage—hoping to remake Julien in the form of a grocery clerk. But Julien, of course, becomes the "Tire au flanc" of the grocery game, and his father-in-law becomes daily more distressed. One day, however, the Prix Goncourt is awarded to Julien Collinet! He becomes a literary lion, the pride of the district. When Chotard finds that some of Julien's glory even rubs off on him, he discovers that he has a passion for poetry and banishes Julien from the grocery with instructions to stay at his desk and write. While Chotard reads poetry, Julien dances with himself in his room in order to keep from staring glumly at his blank white page, sneaks down to the grocery to work while no one is looking. Caught at it, he admits he has discovered the joy of honest labor; decides that, after all, it's a grocer's life for him. The inscription on the door changes from "Chotard" to "Chotard et Cie."

Among Renoir's films of the thirties *Chotard et Cie.* has long been the one least highly regarded. Georges Sadoul calls it "flat." Renoir himself did not think much of it; when the Cinémathèque was searching for a print of the film and asked Renoir about it, he replied, "*Chotard?* I don't remember it." But in the pamphlet recently published with the *L'Avant Scene* slides, Claude Beylie writes of the film, "it never sinks into the rut of filmed theatre and one finds again intact the verve of *Tire au flanc* and *Boudu*."

I have seen *Chotard et Cie.* once, in a private showing at the Cinémathèque, where the empty theatre did nothing to enhance the film. My impression was of a pleasant but undistinguished work with somewhat the flavor of the Pagnol trilogy, primarily through the presence of Charpin. It seemed memorable largely for the superb Renoir opening shot in which the camera ranges freely through the grocery, disclosing Chotard in the midst of his domain. Yet almost every Renoir film looks different on a second viewing, richer, more complex, more subtly devised, with more going on than one notices the first time through. Hence I hesitate to say much about the film on the basis of this single experience. Still, one suspects that the constant presence of the author-producer may have had a dampening effect on Renoir's love for improvisation and his tendency to reconstruct his source material. Hence, I think it probable that the generally negative opinion of *Chotard* widely shared by French critics reflects a rather just assessment.

However, *Chotard* does mark the first occurrence in a sound film of one of Renoir's loves, a spectacle. Here a costume ball provides the occasion for music and dance, an air of sexual intrigue, further exploration of the possibilities of complex and rhythmic movements within a shot. This scene was perhaps a step along the path toward the *fête de la Coliniere*.

12

Madame Bovary
1934

Madame Bovary is true, even when she is most contrived, artificial in each one of her moments of truth. Everything is composed and formal, except those basic elements that are naturally beyond artifice: the quality of her flesh and her expression, with which one can't play tricks—at least in front of the camera.
—Eric Rohmer

One can speak with confidence about *La Chienne* and *Boudu sauvé des eaux*, but not of *Madame Bovary*. It is the most difficult of Renoir's films of the thirties to discuss, in part merely because it *is Madame Bovary*.

When *Boudu* was first shown, the author of the play, René Fauchois, reputedly exclaimed, "You have betrayed me!" But subsequently he reconsidered: "A very free adaption of my play, Jean Renoir's *Boudu Sauvé des eaux* properly belongs to him. Its merits are an achievement before whose mastery it is only honest to bow." Any criticism of *Boudu* on the ground that, in the play, Boudu ends by being happily married to Anne-Marie, would be thought absurd. But what if Renoir had decided to have Rodolphe respond to Emma's desperate plea by giving her 8,000 francs to save poor Charles from destitution, and then carrying her off to Italy to live the life of her romantic dreams?

Critics have said of Flaubert's *Madame Bovary* that it is a novel "impossible to film." But the justice of this claim rests less on the intrinsic qualities of the work than on its position within a body of literature and a culture.

For every novel is impossible to film if "filming" means producing an exact cinematic equivalent. Fortunately, we make this demand only for those few books that have helped create the conscience of the culture, helped form its perception of the world. For such works one cannot easily deny that the written work is relevant to criticism of the film.

It is not simply a matter of blind deference to the literary tradition or respect due to an acknowledged literary masterpiece. Against this one can well assert the autonomy of cinema. With a work of this stature, the critical fact is, rather, not that everyone seeing the film will know the novel or play, but that our experience of the original inevitably colors our perception of the film. The literary work is a part of our cultural selves and any serious deviation from what we think essential in it is felt as a betrayal, not only of the author but of ourselves and, hence, as a fault in the film.

When the deviation of the film from the original is great enough, we may be willing to grant autonomy to the film, as for Kurosawa's *Throne of Blood*, a magnificent transformation of *MacBeth*. When the film remains close to its literary source but deviates from it in significant details, in tone, in attitude toward its characters or their world, more serious questions are raised.

Renoir's *Madame Bovary* faced inevitable difficulties. The position of the novel in French literature is beyond question, as shown in the words of a critic writing in 1934: "I admire M. Jean Renoir. One day the head of a film company came to see him, or more simply, telephoned. He asked, 'Would you like to make *Madame Bovary*?' And M. Jean Renoir answered, 'Yes.' Like that! As if it were a question of adapting a novel of Octave Feuillet or a melodrama by Bouchardy. *Madame Bovary!*"[1] A work so deeply rooted in the culture makes demands upon its adaptor that lesser works do not.

Also, alas, over one-third of the original film has been lost. Renoir tells of it this way:

Ah, yes. It was very long and much better. To tell you the truth, there too the film has been destroyed in the cutting. And this was not the producers, who fought it as much as they could; but the distributors didn't dare release a film that ran more than three hours. It couldn't be done. It was an epoch when double bills seemed the response to the crisis of the cinema, because there was already a crisis of cinema, exactly as now. The distributors said, 'No. We like your film very much, but it can't be done. It's not possible. It must be cut.' So, I cut it. But strangely, once cut the film seemed much longer than before the cuts were made—it seemed like it would never end.

You know, as it is now, I find the film a little boring. Well, when it lasted three hours it was not boring at all. I had shown it before it was cut, five or six showings in a hall at the Billancourt studios which held about 50 people, and everyone was enraptured. For example, Bert Brecht saw it and he was absolutely enchanted.

Unhappily I am sure that the integral copy has disappeared in the cutting. When they made the cuts in the copy, then in the negative, the cuttings were all thrown out and burned.[2]

One can readily see how a proposal to make *Madame Bovary* would have appealed to Renoir. Though it has a rural locale and is set a hundred years in the past, the dominant theme of the book makes it a fitting culmination of this phase of his work. In *Madame Bovary*, as in *La Chienne, Boudu*, and *Chotard et Cie.*, the conflict between a social milieu and an individual whose life clashes with the conventions of that milieu forms the central thread of the narrative; in each case the social setting is bourgeois and the individual's challenge to it a form of romanticism. Thus, the invitation to make *Madame Bovary* enabled Renoir to explore further his major theme in this period, while its central character combines two of the types that most interested him—the dreamer and the destructive woman.

Renoir's professed reasons for wanting to make the film are rather different from this:

> I can tell you the reason—one always has heaps of reasons for making films. But finally what attracted me, the great reason for this film, is that it was an experiment with people from the theatre. Valentine Tessier and my brother, Pierre, were essentially people of the theatre, and around them we had a troupe composed of many actors from the stage. Max Dearly was above all a man of the theatre. And I was very happy to make a film, to write a scenario for these actors, with dialogue that I thought ought to be well spoken by people from the theatre. At bottom that experiment was a little like what I do now in going to work on location. Simply, it was on a screen. You know, the joy of having certain phrases that one knows ought to be formulated by a throat which is accustomed to pronouncing these words . . . That's a great pleasure.[3]

Renoir's remarks illustrate and affirm his freedom from theory and from commitment to any single view about how movies should be made; but just this is disconcerting to critics who love consistency because it enables them to categorize an artist and then speak freely about him without having to look closely at his work. While other directors were shooting theatrical films and worrying about the audibility of every word of dialogue, Renoir took his camera to Montmartre or Bouffemont or the Pont des Arts and let his dialogue compete with the sounds of traffic or boats or birds or a baby's cry. Now he wished to make a film in which dialogue had a more central role and in which almost every word would be clearly heard. And critics who praised the obscurity of *La Nuit du carrefour* here complained that Renoir has abandoned all his originality in favor of the worst errors of the time.

Treatment

Flaubert's novel remains familiar enough that I will not describe the narrative in detail. Renoir has eliminated the period of Charles Bovary's residence in Tostes and changed the order of some events, but even the cut version of his film includes almost all of the major incidents of the novel: Emma's courtship; the ball at Vaubyessard; the agricultural fair that inaugurates Emma's adulterous interlude with Rodolphe Boulanger, a liaison then carried on while Charles fails in his operation on Hippolyte's clubfoot; the opera at Rouen and Emma's subsequent affair with Léon; her gradual entanglement with Lheureux, and its outcome in her suicide.

During the shooting of *Madame Bovary*, Renoir said, "I have tried to follow the novel closely and to draw a good film from it. No grand scenes: just daily life. No personages in costume: just people who live under the dress they habitually wear. A simple picture without exaggerated relief, a little gray, a bit monotonous. Like life!"[4]

This must have been a rather accurate description of the complete film. Renoir invented some scenes where Flaubert omitted all detail, such as the chance meeting at which the Marquis invites the Bovarys to Vaubyessard. A few details have been added, a few more altered. Occasionally, Renoir has put several incidents from the novel into a single scene. Still, the film displays, for Renoir, a remarkable adherence to the original. In scene after scene Renoir appears almost to have used the novel as his scenario, constructing sequences very much as described by Flaubert, with the dialogue, too, usually taken directly from the book.

Valentine Tessier and Jean Renoir with members of the *équipe* of *Madame Bovary*, 1933.

When I asked if this faithfulness reflected a feeling of respect for a master-piece of French literature, Renoir smiled, "Oh, no. It is just that Flaubert was a very good screen-writer. His novel is full of scenes and images that belong in a film." We are fortunate he felt this way, for only the unusual fact of his fidelity to a source gives the remaining fragments of his film the air of a complete and coherent work. Our familiarity with the novel bridges the gaps in continuity. For example, Léon appears in the film only once before the opera at Rouen. Though there has been some talk about him, we have seen him clearly for only six seconds before he discovers Emma in her box at the opera and goes to declare his love. The connecting scenes have disappeared, but we hardly miss them, for we know who Léon is and that he will appear in Rouen.

But the film as it is falls short of Renoir's description. The incidents portrayed are not great events in the eyes of the world, but they are the grand scenes of Emma's life. What is missing is precisely the daily life that makes these events so important for her, the dull routine she finds so intolerable and which leads her to despise her husband and to long to have lived at almost any time and place but where she is. One can only presume that the seventy minutes cut from *Madame Bovary* supplied this counterpoint of ordinary days which fills the novel between the moments of Emma's reckless endeavors to escape. The first quarter of the film still contains some of this material, but once the Bovarys have been invited to the marquis' ball, Emma's rush toward self-destruction occupies almost every frame for the rest of the film. Hence, one whole dimension of Emma's story is inadequately presented in this truncated version of the film; Emma's boredom seems genuine enough, but in the absence of any real presentation of the days that weigh so heavily on her, there is only poor Charles' stolid insensitivity to blame.

A visual counterbalance to Madame Bovary's despair does remain, though, in the scenes of the Normandy countryside interspersed throughout the film. This countryside does not underlie Emma's boredom the way the missing scenes of village life should; it does, however, provide a context for it. For Renoir shows these landscapes to be spacious and gentle, as if restraining the creatures they contain from any headstrong act. The scenes are beautiful indeed, but their peace and calm is not what Emma seeks; rather, passion, adventure, and romance. Hence, she seems estranged from this land, blind to its beauty, which thus stands as a sort of index to her flight from reality. She moves through this scenery untouched, unnoticing. The most beautiful exterior scenes in the film are perhaps those of the forest through which Emma and Rodolphe ride, but in this setting Emma is wholly absorbed in the romantic ceremony that must precede the seduction she so desires. Only twice does she seem wholly to belong within one of these pastoral scenes. Early in the film, Charles comes home to find his first wife quarrelling with his mother. He intervenes, only to have his wife demand that he swear never to return to the farm where Emma lives. Renoir follows this scene with two shots of Emma on the farm. Here Emma appears to be acting with nature, in harmony with the scene, as tranquil as the countryside itself. But these shots express, I believe, not Emma's world, but only Charles' image of her—so different from his bony, quarrelsome wife. Hence, the only scene in which Emma does seem at one with the land occurs just before her suicide, when she returns home along the millstream after Rodolphe has refused her request for help. She moves distractedly, trailing her cloak, then sinks down to the earth as if finally somehow feeling that it alone could sustain her—a brief reconciliation with these landscapes she has refused to see, before the earth finally claims her in death.

Charles, however, is firmly rooted in the land and the village. Renoir quickly establishes both this connection and Charles' distance from Emma in his opening shots. The first image is of sunlit countryside, an old farm building with tall thatched roof, orchard trees, cows quietly grazing—the camera moving forward through the scene. Dissolve to an interior wall, with the back of Charles' head and shoulders filling the right half of the frame. The camera pans left to show Emma standing by a window, then circles to disclose at last Charles and Emma clearly within the same frame. But while this spatial separation has been resolved, the dialogue reveals the psychological gap that will grow between these two. Emma shows Charles her engraving of Mary Stuart: "Isn't she beautiful? It makes me dream. I would have loved to live in that period. Life was less restricted, sentiments more noble, men more gallant." Charles, out of his depth, can only reply, "Oh, yes, you are right." Emma asks, "Do you go on horseback to visit your patients?" Charles, more comfortable, replies honestly, "Yes, it is more practical than a coach on bad roads." But this prosaic response does not at all fit Emma's need for gallantry. She responds, "I understand, and, well, it is much more elegant," building her false image of Charles as her romantic rescuer.

But Renoir will not let this image stand for a moment in our minds. He fades from this scene to a high-angle long shot of the country road along which Charles rides, past a peasant mule-cart and into the village where Homais stands talking outside his pharmacy. This self-styled rationalist greets Charles with a line that ironically echoes Emma's last remark, "Hello, *mon cher*, slave on horseback. What a beautiful sight." Renoir follows this with two views of Charles in the village square, shot first from inside the pharmacy, then from inside a blacksmith shop. These five shots are full of the life of this countryside: peasants, villagers, a man, woman and child in the pharmacy, the smithies at work. And Charles, firmly in the midst of this milieu, seems in complete harmony with this life, moving at a leisurely pace, doffing his hat to the priest who walks in the street. The two shots

from inside that conclude the scene give the impression that one might look up from any place in the village and see Charles Bovary passing by, as familiar and unsurprising as the leaves on the trees.

With Charles thus secured within his world, the film revolves around Emma. Just as few scenes display the fate of their marriage: one joyful shot of the wedding night—Charles and Emma enter their bedroom and embrace. One happy scene in which Charles gives Emma the scarf she has refused to take from Lheureux and tells her of the coach he has bought. She runs to try it; their first ride finds Emma, acting the great lady, as delighted as a child. They meet Léon returning from Rouen, and he is obviously captivated by Emma's gay vivacity. But the very first image of the following scene indicates the short span of Emma's happiness. For its composition ominously repeats that of the scene in which Charles' first wife quarreled with his mother. A quarrel between Emma and Charles' mother follows, and when Charles intervenes, begging Emma to apologize, she does so coldly, then marches up the stairs, betrayed by this man she mistook for her romantic hero. As if to identify this moment as fatal to the marriage, Renoir employs here the technique of commentative repetition so effectively used in *La Chienne*; the final shot of this scene, with Emma shutting herself in the bedroom alone, repeats exactly the view of this room shown in the happy wedding-night scene.

From this point on, Emma shows little affection for Charles; her life turns toward acting out her fantasies of romance and despair. The second carriage ride confirms the death of love. Emma rides in morose silence, attending neither to Charles nor the countryside. They meet the marquis, and the invitation to his ball transforms her; she becomes bright and animated, but talks only of the change this invitation might make in Charles' career—and, of course, by implication, her position in the world.

The ball becomes undoubtedly the great event of Emma's life, the one occasion when she actually inhabits the world of her dreams without having to create it from her own illusions. For a moment she whirls at the center of attention in the best society, with liveried servants standing at attention. But Renoir also makes this a moment when Emma chooses to punish Charles. In the ballroom, Emma is resplendent, moving with the air of one who belongs, but Charles appears out of place, his clothes ill-fitting. He complains that he would like to dance, but his trouser straps make it awkward. Emma turns on him, "Dance? Why, you must be mad—people would laugh at you. Keep your place. Besides, it is more becoming for a doctor." So as Emma dances, Charles tries unhappily to be unobtrusive and seem interested in something, wandering glumly about examining paintings or sitting alone against a wall. As Emma waltzes by, her slightly decadent-looking partner asks, "But who is this strange body we meet at every corner of the room? He's alone, as if being punished. Do you know him?" Emma looks at Charles as if for the first time, "Me? No, I don't know him"—feeling, we presume, revenged for his betrayal of her earlier.

Madame Bovary is the most somber of all Renoir's films of the thirties. It is not visually gray, as *The Elusive Corporal* will be, but its emotional tone is overwhelmingly dark, despite the sunlit landscapes and the lyrical Milhaud score that often accompanies them. Much of this tone comes from Emma's melodramatic performance of her own life, her frequent pose as a tragic heroine. But also, in every scene that might have been lighter in tone, Renoir included some element to maintain the darkness. The ball provides one example: here, if anywhere, one might expect a joyful scene; it is the only truly gay event in Emma's life. But in five of the seven shots that constitute the scene, Charles is visible—awkward, ill-at-ease, alone, completely lost in this glittering milieu—and the genuineness of his discomfort destroys the light tone of the scene. Our empathy with Emma's joy is thoroughly dampened by the strength of Pierre Renoir's mute performance in these shots. Or again, after submitting to Rodolphe in the forest, Emma is momentarily happy. For once she enjoys her child, Berthe. But Renoir shoots this scene through a doorway, and Charles, returning after the failure of his operation on Hippolyte, steps into the doorway and stops, his black-clad figure blotting out the happy scene inside. At times Charles' well-meant ineptness might be comic, but Emma's constant attitude of contempt for him renders him pathetic instead; hence these moments, too, fail to lighten the tone of *Madame Bovary*.

This near uniformity of tone is untypical of Renoir, who believes the texture of life to be a mixture of light and dark. Probably some missing portions of the film were quite different in tone, thus restoring the balance Renoir usually achieved. I also suspect that it is the destruction of this balance and varied texture in the cutting that led Renoir to describe the cut film as rather boring.

Emma's joy. The first carriage ride, the marquis' ball. Emma Bovary (Valentine Tessier) and Charles (Pierre Renoir).

Characterization

Jean Renoir has often been accused of miscasting major roles in his films, particularly for his choice of Valentine Tessier as Emma Bovary. Critics complain that this actress was much too old and mature to be the Emma Rouault who marries Charles Bovary. Flaubert writes of Emma as a "young girl," not long home from the convent when Charles first calls to treat her father's broken leg, and surely not more than twenty when she married. In

1934 Valentine Tessier was obviously no longer twenty; her full figure and the assurance of her bearing are not that of a young girl. Similarly, Pierre Renoir is patently much older than Flaubert's Charles Bovary could have been at the time of the marriage. Hence neither character ages physically during the film; this creates a notable deviation from the novel, for Flaubert describes the changes in Charles that annoy Emma.

But this is a fault only in the relation of the film to the novel. Within the film, nothing indicates that the age of these persons should be other than it is. If we can overlook this departure from Flaubert, there is a solidity in each performance which more than compensates.

Among the qualities that attract Charles to Emma in the novel are a certain boldness, an air of confidence and refinement. Emma may be incurably romantic, but her sense of her own superiority is not entirely mistaken. She demands more of life than merely remaining a country wife, and her beauty and energy and elegance lead almost all of the men in the novel to share her feeling that she deserves more. Valentine Tessier captures these aspects of Emma admirably; she has an elegance and ease of movement, an air of self-possession and frankness. At first, these combine with a modesty of gesture and the wistful romanticism of her talk to make her seem open and eager for life, yet naive and unaggressive. Right after her marriage, when Charles says, "I am sure there are not many ladies of society who are as elegant as you," her reply, "How could you know? You never went out," is indulgent, not critical—a way of reacting modestly to the flattery she loves. But after her quarrel with Charles' mother, her gestures become more extravagant, more aggressive; her tone becomes sharper. When she responds to Charles' complaint about his tight pants at the ball, "It is because you aren't accustomed to it," her remark is no longer indulgent, but a reminder that he doesn't belong in this social set. Very quickly, Emma starts acting her own life as a melodrama that oscillates between ecstacy and despair. Openness gives way to growing duplicity, an uneasy descent to ignoble actions that she struggles to avoid, then embraces willingly. The assurance of her bearing becomes an instrument of concealment or an arrogant defiance justified by her self-pity and her contempt for Charles. Emma's performances are unconvincing, in that we cannot share her vision of the events of her life and do not feel the appropriateness of her emotional responses. But Valentine Tessier's performance in creating this histrionic woman is almost good enough to be self-defeating. The trouble is, as Tom Milne has remarked, that Emma is a tiresome woman and Valentine Tessier plays her as tiresome —the fault lies not in the characterization but in the character.[5] Only at the end, when Emma plays out her own death, does her performance coincide with the reality of the situation. Even here she would, of course, have her death be an event of greater moment than anyone else's, and she does manage to produce maximum disruption and the greatest possible distress for Charles; but her suffering is genuine.

French critics complain that Emma's character does not develop, that Tessier's performance presents a fixed image throughout. This is true only in the sense that Emma begins and ends as a hopelessly romantic woman, her perception distorted by a thirst for noble sentiments and gallant actions. What remains fixed in her image is the presence Tessier brings to the part, the certitude of her movements which Renoir speaks of as "une espèce de sécurité." Throughout, this security conveys Emma's assurance of her own greatness of soul, her aptitude for being a romantic heroine. But if Emma does not change, in that she dramatizes throughout her life, there is development indeed in the range of her performances, from the simplicity of her portrayal of the virtuous woman when she refuses Lheureux' scarves to the righteous passion of her scornful denunciation of Rodolphe when he rejects her plea for aid. However false to reality, she moves toward an ever greater depth in the emotions she acts out. Perhaps no other character development is possible for a would-be romantic heroine in a world without heroes.

An unsympathetic eye might see Valentine Tessier's whole performance as overplayed, but this again mistakes a trait of the character for one of the characterization. Emma Bovary does overplay almost every moment of her life; no actual circumstance lives up to her performance in it. Everyone fails her, for no one plays his role in her life at a level of dramatic intensity that matches hers. Within the catalogue of Renoir characters, Emma stands at the opposite pole from Nana in this respect; for each of Nana's lovers proved quite willing to demonstrate the depth of his love by sacrificing everything for her. Hence, Nana could destroy them all; but Léon and Rodolphe are hardly touched by Emma's tragic anguish. Emma destroys only herself and Charles, whose steadfast devotion makes him vulnerable.

Emma differs in quite another way from that other romantic dreamer, Legrand. He *under*plays every incident in his life; the habits of unresponsiveness persist even through those moments that he thinks embody his dreams. But, of course, Emma's dramatizing also becomes a habit and plays her equally false. Whatever possibility there may have been for salvaging her situation is lost when Emma cannot resist playing out the role of the deeply wronged, passionate, and sincere woman with each man who hesitates to sacrifice himself for her. The romantic heroine, like the romantic hero, is out of place in a bourgeois world, though for a different reason: The hero, ready to perform noble deeds, finds that the world has no use for them; the heroine, demanding passion to equal her own, finds that the world cannot afford it.

If Valentine Tessier's performance is debatable, no similar questions arise about Pierre Renoir's portrayal of Charles Bovary. Unassuming, practical, quite inept at expressing those things he feels most deeply, Charles possesses just those virtues least likely to hold Emma's love. His devotion, though deep and sincere, is also undemonstrative, largely inarticulate, and thus

Emma's despair. Emma with L'Heureux (Robert Le Vignan), M. Guillaumin (Romain Bouquet), Rodolphe (Fernand Fabre), Léon (Daniel Lecourtois), Justin (André Fouché), and Charles).

unexciting. His attempts to be attentive fall far short of gallantry. His unquestioning trust in Emma's faithfulness presumes that she will be content with a life as unadventurous as his own. In contrast to Tessier's assurance, Pierre Renoir's performance centers on hesitation. He withdraws the gestures he begins, looks away, forever wonders what to do. Thus Charles emerges as slow, steady, stolid, but very unsure; as devoid of ideas as of imagination, wholly incapable of understanding Emma's romantic fantasies and constantly surprised by her reactions to his simple ordinary acts. He seldom talks, is wholly comfortable only with what is conventional and familiar.

The gulf between Charles and Emma is nowhere more apparent than at the Rouen opera. The performance of *Lucie de Lammermoor* seems to our eyes unutterably drab; for Renoir has staged it in the style of 1840, with the singers standing in a row. Emma, completely entranced and absorbed, lives every moment of the performance. Her eyes glow; her face reflects every emotion suggested upon the stage. Charles sits blinking in puzzlement, apparently unresponsive because he has no idea what is going on. He complains that he can't understand the story because of the music. Emma tells him impatiently, "Be quiet! Be quiet!" When the act ends, Emma's emotional involvement has left her utterly exhausted; Charles says, "Yes, it's hot in here. It's the gas."

Charles' sober acceptance of the simplest levels of reality make his perception of the world constantly different from Emma's—and perhaps equally false. And it leaves him quite unaware of where their difference lies. If there is a flaw in Pierre Renoir's performance, it is only that the strength of his characterization of Charles deprives Emma of some of our sympathy. He conveys Charles' dogged devotion and sincerity so convincingly that we may feel Emma more willfully destructive than she is.

The film's secondary characters have probably suffered most in the cutting. Not Rodolphe (Fernand Fabre) perhaps, or Lheureux (Robert Le Vigan), whose roles appear to remain almost intact. Lheureux is a sort of evil tempter playing to Emma's weakness, his gestures always those of subservience, while his proposals are made with the air of an accomplice, shifting as the narrative unfolds from being an abettor of Emma's transgressions to her accuser and prosecutor. Rodolphe, who brings Emma her first illusion of a grand passion, is merely an arrogant young squire amusing himself with a forlorn country wife. His pose of bored worldliness, his romantic dismissal of the morals of society, his fervent declarations of passion, all have a false fluency that only Emma's thirst for romance could mistake for glamor and truth. Léon (Daniel Lecourtois) seems more sincere, but unfortunately no early scenes of the timid clerk who does not dare declare his love have survived. Perhaps most damaged by the cuts is Max Dearly's Homais, who now seems little more than a sketch of the Flaubert character. Renoir could not later remember much detail of the portions that were cut from his film. He did recall, though, a scene in which Homais demonstrated an early form of matches—a chemically coated splint that bursts into flame when dipped into sulphuric acid. This suggests a rather fuller development of Flaubert's pretentious herald of progress and purveyor of intellectual gossip than we now find in the film.

Style and Form

At the center of critical discontent with *Madame Bovary* stands the complaint that Renoir abandoned the style of his earlier works and adopted that of the "theatrical films" of the day. Some critics, I suspect, felt betrayed; others, just dismay. The dismay arose partly from a feeling that Renoir had not merely made a theatrical film, but had drawn it from a novel whose style was more cinematic than theatrical. Thus one disappointed critic wrote: "Imagine a director . . . before such a subject . . . Now, the director opens Flaubert's book and, from the first pages, he ascertains that he has a choice between ten medium shots and as many close-ups. Some close-ups: 'Charles was surprised by the whiteness of her nails. They were shiny, delicated at the tips, more polished than the ivory of Dieppe . . .'; 'and her look came at you frankly with a candid boldness'; 'her neck stood out from a white turned-down collar'; 'the parasol of dove-colored shot silk, through which the sun shone, lighted the white skin of her face with shifting reflections.' It's all done."[6]

But there are hardly half a dozen close-ups in Renoir's film. Hence, one must ask, what is the style of *Madame Bovary?* Did Renoir abandon his own style in this film? And has he opposed the style of the novel in making his film as he did?

Structurally, *Madame Bovary* is built up of scenes that are complete in themselves. Usually they do not flow into each other but are divided by fades or by titles specifying a place and date. Several times a single brief shot of the countryside or the stagecoach on the road provides punctuation between scenes. Fades occur not merely as a convention to indicate the passage of time, but as a formal method of opening or closing a scene. These devices emphasize the separateness of each scene and create an overall rhythm of beginning and ending, opening and closure, which inhibits the building of tension or emotion over any large segment of the film and sustains a sort of emotional equilibrium. Only twice does Renoir intercut scenes and create a continuity that allows a greater accumulation of dramatic impact: when Rodolphe abandons Emma at the time of Hippolyte's operation and in the final scenes leading to Emma's death.

This tendency to create complete scenes and underline the breaks between them was not, of course, new in *Madame Bovary.* It had persisted throughout Renoir's career and is quite marked in both *La Chienne* and *Boudu.* Renoir has said, "personally, I prefer the method which consists in conceiving each scene as a little film apart." No doubt this underlies the repeated complaints that Renoir's films are "disconnected," a characteristic accentuated in *Madame Bovary*, where whole scenes must have been lost in the cutting. Here the disconnection is not merely a lack of smooth continuity between scenes, but the incoherence created when a scene presupposes an earlier one that no longer remains in the film. We cannot know what the overall structure of the complete work might have been, but I would expect it to have had a more complex rhythm and a more varied emotional texture than existing prints show.

Within the scenes, several familiar elements of Renoir's visual style are more apparent than ever. The camera usually remains level. Almost every scene is composed in depth and shot with deep focus; in a surprisingly large proportion of these shots, the main action is seen through a door or window or grillwork: of about two hundred shots that are not country exteriors, some forty have a significant portion of the scene shown through some such aperture, which usually places the action within a symmetrical frame. Though most scenes are shot in depth, the action seldom ranges over the whole depth of the field. Most often, the foreground objects merely form elements of the composition, while the action develops at middle distance or further. This large proportion of deep-focus shots is made possible by an even more sparing use of close-ups than before. There are only three or four true close-ups, with perhaps as many medium close-ups. And, surprisingly, there are only about thirty medium shots. If we identify a shot in terms of the major action, *Madame Bovary* is made up mostly of three-quarter shots or longer; hence, one's overall visual impression is that of action seen at a distance. Again, Renoir avoids the shot-countershot form in filming dialogue, using it only when it has some dramatic point. But Madame Bovary differs from earlier films in its avoidance of close-ups when the shot-countershot form is used.

One visual difference between Madame Bovary and the immediately preceding films lies in the predominating forms of Renoir's composition. Individual shots of *La Chienne* and *Boudu* tended to be dominated by diagonals; in *Madame Bovary* verticals and horizontals prevail. Where doors and windows do not impose a symmetry on the composition, Renoir frequently divides his frame with a central vertical and balances his composition on either side of this. He also often reinforces this symmetry of two-dimensional composition by his treatment of the three-dimensional action-space. Here, where the action-space is usually deep, Renoir photographs it so that our eye moving into the depth of the space is drawn toward the center of the screen rather than a corner. Exterior space receives a similar treatment; for example, roads receding into deep space almost invariably converge toward the center of the screen rather than having an edge from a diagonal, as was characteristic of *La Nuit du carrefour* and *Boudu*. Thus, the overall tendency is toward static, balanced composition, pictorial stillness rather than movement. This gives the exterior scenes their tranquil air. In the interiors the rhythmic movement that fills the action-space tends to offset the stability of the composition; the result is to convey the sense of an ongoing life that is firmly established.

Camera movement, too, is different. The ratio of shots including camera movement is slightly higher in *Madame Bovary* than in *Boudu*, about one in four; yet by comparison the camera seems quite restricted. The difference lies not in the frequency of camera movement but in its freedom. In *Madame Bovary* the camera seems to have lost its fluidity, to have its movement strictly tied to the action. It moves when it has to, but not more than necessary to contain the action. Seldom does the camera seem to explore the space or wander away to see what else may be around. Exterior scenes are somewhat less restricted, but we nowhere feel the freedom of movement found in the last scenes of *Boudu*.

We do find, though, a more frequent occurrence of long-held shots—forty, fifty, sixty seconds or longer—in which the camera hardly moves but merely observes the action developing around it. Characters sometimes move out of the frame, but Renoir neither follows them nor cuts to where they have gone; he simply waits for them to return. This technique lacks the feeling of dynamic freedom developed elsewhere, but it communicates equally well the depth of the world of the film, the sense that life flows on outside the range of the camera's eye.

The manner in which these forms shape and sustain the dramatic action of the film may be illustrated in the two scenes that show the fate of the Bovary marriage. Each scene has three shots; in each, movement and rhythm are created primarily by the motion of the characters within the scene. The first scene opens with a medium shot of Emma by her drawing board, Lheureux showing her the scarves he would like her to buy. Renoir cuts to a long shot as Charles enters behind Lheureux, motions him to leave and takes a scarf from him, then cuts back to a three-quarter shot as Charles puts the scarf over Emma's shoulders. He admires her drawing, her dress, her elegance; she fondly chides him about his ignorance of the world, tells him he will have to take her to museums in Italy. Then he tells her he has bought the coach and goes to the window. Emma follows; the camera moves slightly forward to watch over their shoulders as they look at the coach across the road. Then Emma runs around the drawing board and out of the frame, followed a moment later by Charles at his slower pace. The camera remains fixed, looking out the now-unobstucted window where Emma soon reappears running across the road to the coach; then Charles too enters this secondary frame created by the window and crosses the road. Only as they move off out of this interior frame does Renoir cut to a full shot of them in the coach.

The dialogue is light-hearted. Charles and Emma respond cheerfully to each other, but our sense of their happiness at this point is deepened by the movement within the scene. The overall pattern of movement is balanced, nearly symmetrical. The movements of Charles and Emma are nearly identical; each repeats the movement of the other as if they were quite in harmony. And the doubling of this repetition, first in the large frame of the screen, then within the small frame of the window, brings them even closer together.

The second scene opens on this same room, seen from a slightly different angle. But now Emma plays the piano in the foreground; Charles' mother sits sewing at middle distance, and the servant, Félicité, moves forward out of the background to put a vase of flowers on the piano. Emma instructs her on preparing a punch for that evening. As Félicité moves off, Charles' mother begins to criticize Emma's extravagance. Emma stiffens, replies that Charles is satisfied with his home. But mother continues, "And your Félicité is impertinent. I discovered her yesterday in the corridor with a forty-year-old bearded man who fled when he heard me." Emma does not reply; Charles' mother says sharply, "You could answer me." At this Emma responds, "It makes no difference to me. Félicité is free." This provokes an angry response: "If one does not laugh at morals, one must look after those of the servants. Besides, who knows if you are not taking Félicité's defense in order to defend yourself." Emma stands abruptly, "I demand that you explain yourself." She walks around the piano and past Charles' mother, who asks, "And who is invited tonight to this famous punch that costs tremendously dear?" Emma replies, "The Homais family and M. Léon," then, enraged by the knowing look this provokes, orders, "Get out! If you do not go, I shall." Charles' mother rises angrily and walks off, snapping, "You are insolent and giddy-headed. Maybe even worse." Cut to a shot looking through a door of this room and down a hall, the doorway creating a symmetrical frame for the long space of the hall. Charles comes through a door at the far end of the hall; his mother enters, left foreground, walks down the hall, turns right, and stalks up the stairs. As Emma enters, left foreground, Charles comes to the stairs, calls "Mamma!" then comes forward again to where Emma stands in the doorway. He pleads with her, then gets on his knees, "Tell her something. Talk to her. Be kind." Without turning Emma says coldly, "Very well, let her come down. I shall talk to her." Charles returns to the stair, calls again, "Mamma!" then he too disappears up the stairs. Emma does not move; the camera remains fixed. In a moment Charles returns, standing at the foot of the stairs while his mother reappears and comes forward to where Emma still stands. With frigid dignity Emma extends her hand and says, "Excuse me, Madame"; then takes two steps forward, hesitates, turns, walks carefully around Charles' mother, and, without a word to Charles, marches up the stairs. Cut to a shot inside the bedroom. The camera recedes from the room and down the corridor, leaving the bed framed in the doorway. Emma enters, right, up the stairs, walks resolutely into the bedroom and closes the door in the face of the camera.

I am sure that the dialogue here loses both meaning and impact because an earlier scene showing the attraction between Emma and Léon has been

cut. Still the scene is wholly effective, opening with an appearance of domestic tranquility and ending in complete discord. In both composition and
movement, the first shot matches that of the earlier quarrel between
Charles' mother and his first wife. This formal similarity creates the firm
impression that this is not an isolated incident in Emma's marriage and
establishes the hostility of her mother-in-law as a recurrent element in
Emma's life. The second shot transfers this feeling of estrangement to
Charles and Emma. In the first quarrel he had defended his wife; here his
mother literally stands between Charles and Emma. She enters the hall as he
does, spatially separating him from Emma. When he comes through the hall
he stops where his mother had been, by the stairs, though Emma now
stands in the doorway. When he does move toward Emma, he pleads for his
mother, with no word to soothe Emma's ruffled dignity. In contrast to the
scene with the coach, the movements of Charles and Emma oppose each
other throughout this shot. They never move in unison; in the one action
they both perform, walking from the doorway to the stair and going up, the
movement of each is so timed in relation to the position of the other that the
movements are firmly opposed. The finality of Emma's flight is unmistakably shown by the camera, which has sat patiently waiting as Charles and
his mother have climbed the stairs and come down again, but cuts immediately when Emma goes up the stairs, as if sure there was no point in waiting
for her to return. Brilliantly, Renoir does not follow Emma up the stairs or
even show us her expression, but cuts ahead of her into the bedroom with
its happy memories of the wedding scene, then backs his camera away from
this spot as the marriage has backed away from its gay beginning here. This
movement is then fully confirmed by Emma's still back and the closed door.

Visually, *Madame Bovary* makes no radical departure from Renoir's
style, but displays a greater emphasis on some aspects, such as Renoir's tendency toward extending the duration of his shots and using deep focus, and
a deemphasis of others, the freedom of camera movement and the dominance of diagonals in two-dimensional composition. But its visual style is
certainly not that of the commercially successful theatrical films of the day.
It differs from them at least in its deep-focus photography, its long-held
shots, its avoidance of close-ups and shot-countershot dialogue scenes, and
in its insistent placing of its characters within the scene rather than in front
of it.

Madame Bovary is, visually, within the developed Renoir style. It is more
innovative in its use of sound. Here we find one wholly new departure, external music accompanying parts of the film. *Madame Bovary* is the first
Renoir film to have a score; written by Darius Milhaud, it is a model of
movie music—unobtrusive, melodic, never employed to inflate the emotion
of a scene beyond its dramatic deserts. Some scenes have no music at all,
and several important scenes contain the internal music that had become

characteristic of Renoir films: Emma at the piano, the opera at Rouen, a singer and musicians in the café where Emma has her last desperate meeting with Léon. And at two critical moments—almost as if Flaubert had anticipated that Jean Renoir would be his director—a song sung by a blind man in the street serves as commentary on the scene.

The dialogue of *Madame Bovary* is more extensive, more clearly articulated, and more carefully recorded than in earlier films. We find no long stretches without dialogue; only the short scene of Rodolphe, alone, deciding to abandon Emma, has no talk at all. More than before, persons are characterized by the *content* of their conversation. And the dialogue defines situations rather than functioning as a dimension of action within a situation clearly presented in visual terms. The language of the dialogue is mostly the language of Flaubert, taken directly from the novel—the language of the nineteenth century, more formally structured than the dialogue of, say, *Boudu.*

Thus music and dialogue are both augmented in *Madame Bovary.* But Renoir retains his taste for the authenticity of natural sounds and his desire to create a texture of sound with a depth matching the visual space of his film. Since Madame Bovary was necessarily studio-made, this background of sound is most often not "natural," but created—for example, the crowd noises in the scenes of the opera and the agricultural fair. But a few scenes have a natural setting that provides the ambience of spontaneous sound that often gives a fullness of life to Renoir's films: most notably, the forest scene, where the sunlit trees are almost palpable and the twitter of birds, the rustle of leaves, the random sounds as the horses shift their stance—all the soft noises of the forest—surround Emma and Rodolphe as they enact their highly artificial ritual of seduction.

What then can we say of the style of *Madame Bovary?* I shall pursue no further the question of whether this is a "theatrical film." It is surely not a film in the theatrical style of the mid-thirties. But this whole question is beside the point. What we have here is not a new style for Renoir, or even a radical departure from the old one, but rather a pushing of the style developed over half a dozen years to its classical extreme.

The terms *classical* and *romantic* have long been useful in categorizing works of art and styles, though they can create as much confusion as clarity. I want to apply the term *classical* to the style of *Madame Bovary*, not to its characters or the development of the narrative. What I understand by *classical* is a style that tends toward static rather than dynamic forms, toward equilibrium rather than tension, repose rather than movement, unity rather than diversity; which tends to universalize rather than individualize, to view events at a distance rather than close up, to emphasize harmony rather than contrast, restraint rather than excess, uniformity of emotional tone rather than great variation. The feeling I associate with the classical is

Seduction. Emma and Rodolphe Boulanger.

that of control as opposed to spontaneity; the overall appearance, that of formality as opposed to formlessness or, better, informality.

If classical and romantic are poles, Renoir's own stylistic tendencies fall between them. He has often said that he has tried to be classical, but his natural preference seems to be for compositions and structures that are very dynamic yet balanced, for characters that are highly individual yet achieve a sort of universality, and for a varied emotional texture without great peaks and depths. Certain elements of his style tend toward the romantic:

the freedom of camera movement, the varied flow of motion in scenes, the air of spontaneity and improvisation, the preference for natural sounds and images. Some classical tendencies are his aversion to fragmentation and his desire to comprehend an action within a single shot, his pervasive concern for balance, his reticence about using close-ups, and the objectivity with which his characters are observed.

In *Madame Bovary* the classical tendencies are stressed, the romantic ones suppressed, creating the most formal of all Renoir films, the most controlled, the least overflowing with movement and life. One consequence of this stylistic emphasis is the creation of a greater distance between audience and film than we are accustomed to, so that the events of the film seem removed from us. This stylized distance combines with settings, costumes, and the formality of gestures and language to set the action of the film unalterably in the past. As Armand Cauliez has written, "Whether one chooses or not, it seems though that one is in 1850."[7]

The care Renoir took to maintain this style and its distance and to preserve the unity of his scenes may be seen by comparing his treatment of the street singer in *La Chienne* with the blind singer of *Madame Bovary*. In *La Chienne* Renoir cuts from Lulu's bedroom to the scene below, plunging us fully into the careless life of the street and breaking off the mounting tension of Legrand's cruel awakening. In *Madame Bovary* the blind beggar first appears when Emma is at the heighth of her passion for Léon. Léon and Emma sit on the bed in a hotel room in Rouen, viewed in one of the few medium close-ups of the film. They compete in declaring the depth of their love. Emma tells Léon she is his slave; he calls her "my heroine." Emma kisses Léon, pushing him back down on the bed. As they embrace Léon's hand begins to unbutton her dress. The camera cuts chastely away to a table across the room, then lifts to the window above, moves forward through the curtain and tilts to look down into the street below as the blind beggar, followed by a pushcart, walks across the frame, singing in his raucous tones:

> Often the warmth of a lovely day
> Makes a maiden dream of love

The camera remains in the room; the singer is viewed at a distance. And though his song has let the world into this dim room and likened Emma's grand passion to the fleeting fancies of every young girl, the mood of the scene has not been broken. The camera can cut back to Emma—who now smokes a cigarette and idly caresses Léon's head while she talks of death as desirable after one has just been happy—without our feeling any interruption of the scene.

The blind beggar appears once again, at the end of the film. Emma, dying, has been given the sacrament. She clings to the cross until the priest pries her hands loose. The raucous voice breaks into the scene, and Renoir cuts to the street where the blind beggar walks, coming forward out of the

Emma and Léon in Rouen.

darkness like the grim death Emma awaits, singing the same song. But here the song affirms that life goes on outside this chamber; it also carries the resonance of Emma's futile passion and her talk of death and happiness. Here again, the two cuts to the street do not interrupt the scene; rather, they add to its growing power. For the beggar appears as a spectre from Emma's past, a sort of gruesome accumulation of all her blind folly, now returned to claim its due.

Critics who do not like *Madame Bovary* talk of its coldness; those who do, of its beauty. The remarks are related. The distance imposed by Renoir's classical style can be seen as coldness, but this distance and the repose of *Madame Bovary*'s composition also make us more consciously aware of its pictorial beauty, the play of light and shadow, the rhythm of movements, the balance of masses in a scene. The film is very carefully composed throughout, but the compositions are not designed to call themselves to our attention; they build the world of the film rather than detaching themselves from it. Only when we lift a frame from the stream and look at it alone are we struck by its visual design. Within the film the harmonic flow of classical composition maintains the distance of the scenes and gives a feeling of permanence to the world created. But it is more likely to make us explicitly aware of individual objects on which Renoir seems to turn his eye than of its own forms. Thus, one remembers the piled-up sacks of grain at Père Rouault's but not the structural role they play in the visual depth of the scene. Or the white horse dappled with sunlight and shadow, but not its compositional relation to the dark figures of Emma and Rodolphe.

But, one may say, this is *Madame Bovary;* perhaps it is an interesting idea to take a story whose central character is the most hopelessly romantic individual in French literature and frame it in a coldly classical style, but what does it do to the novel? I hope by now that the question answers itself; for that, of course, is exactly what Flaubert did. Rather than deliberately making a theatrical film, Renoir was seeking a cinematic equivalent of Flaubert's style. If so, the style would, of course, be classical; Flaubert may have started his career as a romantic, but *Madame Bovary* is the masterpiece of nineteenth century literary classicism—written with a mania for formal perfection, its characters observed with an objectivity which forbid the intrusion of any shade of the writer's opinions or feelings.

Just how well Renoir succeeded in finding an equivalent to Flaubert's style, we cannot really tell. A style is not defined simply by the character of the components of the whole; we must also know how they are fitted together. Hence any real assessment could, I think, only follow on the recovery of the complete film.

13

Toni
1935

In Paris they consider Toni *a foreign film.*   —*Jean Renoir*

Nominally, France had been among the victors of World War I. But the nation had suffered enormously. Most of the war had been fought on French soil; hence the conquered nation, Germany, actually sustained much less physical damage than France. French agricultural areas were blasted by artillery, churned by tanks, strewn with mines, divided by barbed wire and trenches. Industry had been destroyed, and almost a generation of your Frenchmen had been killed.

The French working force was decimated. But a ready supply of replacements stood nearby. An isolationist America had cut to a trickle the flow of immigrants that could come seeking work and freedom and streets paved with gold. In the early 1920s France replaced the United States as the refuge for the underfed, underprivileged, unwelcome populations of southern and eastern Europe. Some three million were soon in France, from Poland, Italy, and Spain; most of them working in heavy industry, some on the farms of southern France. Before the rise of fascism, most of these immigrants were not refugees fleeing from political repression, but men who came seeking work. Hence, many of them did not harbor any great nostalgia for the land they left, but felt like the railroad worker who says, early in *Toni*, "My country is the one that offers me something to eat."

French industry centered largely in the north, but many Italian, Spanish, and Corsican immigrants came to the Midi—southern France. Some worked on the land; many clustered around Marseilles, the industrial center of the south. One spot where work could be found was Martigues, a small port on the southern shore of the great saltwater lagoon, the *étang de Berre*.

In the early 1920s the police superintendent of Martigues was Jacques Mortier, who had been a boyhood friend of Jean Renoir. Mortier was not an ordinary police officer, but a novelist as well. Sometime in the late 1920s he related to Renoir the details of a murder that had been committed while he was at Martigues, a crime of passion involving Latin immigrants.

Renoir has said, "I carry my ideas for years. I am no good for telling a new story. I have to digest an idea before being able to do something with it." So the story of the murder at Martigues digested while Renoir made films whose characters lived within the French bourgeois milieu. Then, by some fortunate coincidence, late in 1934, when the idea was ready, Renoir was offered the chance to make a film under conditions rather different from those he had worked in before.

By late 1934 the studio system in France was near collapse. Mismanagement and corruption had combined with the depression to bring most of the big studios near ruin. Film production became the province of "independents," some of them fly-by-night impressarios who did not always manage to keep one step ahead of the sheriff or their creditors. Georges Sadoul writes of this period, "The French monopolies and international combines were succeeded by promoters with neither integrity nor great capacity, with checks without funds, phantom companies established in furnished rooms, productions without capital or security, bankruptcies, even swindles." In this chaos Marcel Pagnol retired to Marseilles with his profits from *Marius* and *Fanny*, opened his own studio, and offered Jean Renoir the chance to make *Toni* at a time when *Madame Bovary* was being treated coldly by critics and public alike.

Madame Bovary had been a film requiring great control, careful research, and elaborate preparation. Well-known actors spoke, in clear and slightly formal French, lines that every literate Frenchman would already know. *Toni* seems designed to be as different from this as possible. Renoir's idea was simple enough, but, in 1934, quite radical. At a time when most films were made wholly within the studio, he conceived of reconstructing an actual event in the locale of its occurrence and filming it without any of the aura that seemed inescapable in commercial cinema—a film shot completely on location, played by relatively unknown actors and townspeople speaking the dialects of the region.

There was, of course, resistance. Renoir has said: "The producer, Pierre Gaut, is a good friend of mine and played an important role in the shooting. All the same it was necessary to convince the producer of *Toni* that he was interested in trying to make a film out in the open, without stars, with events which, being taken from a true story, inevitably involved a certain brutality."[1]

In writing the scenario Renoir enlisted the collaboration of another friend, Karl Einstein. Renoir describes him in these terms, "He was a man with a wide-ranging mind. It seems to me that to bring to the cinema people who are not of the cinema, but who have great ability in their own field, can from time to time enrich a film, give it a certain nobility—as Karl Koch has done in several of my films before the war. Karl Einstein was an art critic. He had written some of the best books on abstract painting."[2]

Leaving Paris behind, Renoir took with him only a few technicians and one actor, Max Dalban, a regular Renoir bit-player since *Tire au Flanc*. Renoir's nephew, Claude Renoir, would here shoot his first film as director of photography. A few familiar names remain—Georges Darnoux, Marguerite Renoir—but cast and crew alike consisted mainly of the southerners whose accents and gestures would give *Toni* the authenticity Renoir sought.

With Marcel Pagnol in Marseilles, Renoir found a group of actors who had little experience in cinema but a background in the Marseilles music halls that Georges Sadoul calls, "l'inégalable école des caf' conc' marseillais."[3] The principal players of *Toni* were drawn from this group, supplemented by recruiting bit-players from among the workers of Martigues, including an American black who happened to be working there and whose presence makes *Toni* one of the very few 1930s films in which a black man is treated as simply another person.

Narrative and Treatment

Toni Canova (Charles Blavette) comes to Martigues from Italy to work in the quarry. He becomes the lover of Marie (Jennie Hélia), in whose rooming house he lives, but tires of her and falls in love with Josepha (Célia Montalvan), a young Spanish immigrant whose uncle owns a nearby farm. Toni wants to marry Josepha and persuades his companion Fernand (Edouard Delmont) to go with him to talk to Josepha's uncle, Sebastien (André Kovatchevich). But while Toni and Sebastien talk about the marriage, Josepha is seduced by Albert (Max Dalban), the blustering, craven foreman of the quarry. Told by Sebastien that he will respect Josepha's wishes, Toni finds Josepha with Albert in the drainage ditch.

In a double wedding marked by drunken song and no great joy, Josepha married Albert, and Toni despondently weds Marie. Two years later, Albert, tired of marriage, neglects Josepha, and Sebastien, near death, asks Toni to be the godfather of Josepha's baby. Albert and Marie both resent this, but Toni promises. Marie tries to drown herself in the lagoon when

Toni goes to Sebastien's funeral despite her objections. Rescued by fishermen, Marie rejects Toni, who goes to live in the hills with a group of Corsican charcoal burners.

From his hillside, Toni watches Josepha's house like a hunter, dreams of carrying her off someday. Albert runs the farm negligently, argues about money with Gaby (Andrex), Josepha's cousin. Gaby and Josepha plan to run away together after taking Albert's money. But Josepha awakens Albert when she cuts the billfold from around his neck. He beats her, and she kills him with the gun he has carelessly discarded. Toni, discovered by a gendarme while arranging Albert's body to look like a suicide, confesses that he killed Albert, then escapes. Josepha confesses. But Toni is shot and dies by the tracks as a train arrives with a new group of immigrants.

"Pas de grand scène: du quotidien." Though this statement of intention had been made about *Madame Bovary*, its realization awaited *Toni*, where Renoir so completely immerses this complicated plot in the daily life of his characters that it loses all of its air of melodrama and appears as simple as the surface of their workaday life.

From the first frame, the world of immigrant laborers holds the center of attention in the film; drama emerges only as events that at first seem merely a common part of this world take shape to form a coherent narrative. The first sound is a guitar: single notes in a simple melody accompany the credits, then flow into the rapid rhythm of a song. Three men in a railroad car huddle together in song, stop, and pass a bottle between them. In the song the words easily heard—*marina, cucina, generale, esposata*—are recognizably southern Italian, but others seem strange and the rhythm not quite Italian. Under the song, the railroad clatters and a whistle screams as Renoir cuts to a shot of the train crossing the viaduct which bridges the narrow inlet connecting the *étang de Berre* to the Mediterranean. Two men working on the roadbed watch the train pass, then in the accents of immigrants complain about, "The Spaniards moving en masse"—a new load of foreigners "come to steal the bread from our mouths." At the Martigues station, passengers hurry from the train. The stationmaster's whistle blows; the train moves on. The immigrants straggle through the town, mostly men, a few women, here and there a child. As they walk by, two policemen at a corner stop one of the men at random: "Your papers, please." "Is this the first time you've come to France?" "No, no. I'm just coming back." "OK, go on." Papers checked, the man moves back into the flow of immigrants. Traffic noises: auto horns, truck motors. Snatches of conversation: "There's good air here, no?" "Yes. It smells of oil." "The smell of oil is the smell of work here." As they stroll under the bridge, the three men from the opening shot sing again. Not a Corsican song this time, but a French verse about leaving one's home, then an Italian chorus, "Addio Napoli . . ." The camera follows them along the road and then halts; the uneven file of immigrants moves out of the frame. The song fades under the strong, sharp image of the viaduct, black grillwork cutting the bright sky; a few reeds beside the empty road stir in the breeze that ruffles the water. Cut to a path leading downhill to a white house; the immigrant who had been stopped by the police walks down the path, knocks at the door. Marie opens the door and Toni says, "Bon jour, madame. They tell me you take in boarders?" "Yes. Do you have a job in the quarry?" "Not yet, madame—but I will." They enter the house and the camera resumes its movement, panning past the house and across the tree-dotted landscape to stop on an image of soft hills with the lagoon shining in the distance, the chorus of the song rising again as the camera pans. Fade!

The five minutes of this opening sequence create the background of *Toni* —a context of men seeking work and the region that affords it, a mixture of tongues and temperaments and successive layers of immigration, with early comers suspicious of new "foreigners." The voices sing of departure, of sailing away from homelands, but in a tone of hope. As they walk past the bridge, a boy asks his father if they will be happy here. "Yes, my child," comes the confident response.

The story evolves almost accidentally, as if the camera had simply followed a man randomly selected by the police on the corner—anyone else would do as well. The immigrants move off past the bridge—Where now? Well, what became of that fellow whose papers were checked?

What distinguishes *Toni* from earlier Renoir works is not so much the solidity and vividness of the background, but its persistence as the center of the film; the shift from seeing the group of immigrants arrive to observing the life of one individual among them seems not to take us away from this supporting context but deeper into it. The principal characters do not emerge from the setting but remain wholly within it. But above all, Renoir maintains the social milieu as the real object of his lens through much of *Toni* by allowing the dialogue to carry the development of the narrative while the images reveal the daily life of the community.

The opening sequence forms a sort of prologue to *Toni*. There follows a second shot of that same path leading down to Marie's house. Early morning: two tall young men swing down the path, singing raggedly as they go, their rhythmic walk almost turning into dance. Near the house, two men wash by a pump; a third, Fernand, fills a coffee pot. At the door he meets Marie, regards her lovingly, tells her he is starting the coffee. The ragged song, Italian perhaps, or Spanish, drifts softly in the morning air as the young men move further along their way. In a bedroom Marie prods Toni, "Wake up, Toni, It's late." "What time?" "Six o'clock." Toni sits up sleepily. "You might say 'Good morning.'" "Good morning, Marie." "No kiss?" Without enthusiasm, Toni kisses Marie. "Oh, la la. That annoys you. When you came here a foreigner I didn't have to ask you. You held me in your arms, wanted to kiss me all day." Toni complains that he feels sick: "I didn't sleep well. I tossed and turned all night. And if I touched your leg it felt like it was burning up." As they talk Marie combs her hair, walks around the bed and sits with her back to the wall. Toni begins to dress, "Look at my nightshirt; it's soaking wet." But Marie has others ideas about what is wrong, suggests that some other woman has been pursuing Toni: "Some cat who thinks she can take what she wants. Maybe Josepha? She arrived not long ago and couldn't speak a word of French, and already she's chasing all the men in the neighborhood [elle lécha toutes les collines]. Or Alinda—you know, with Alinda you won't be the first."

In the kitchen Fernand pours coffee for Marie; the guitar player picks out a few notes on his instrument, as if to see how it passed the night. Fernand and the guitar player eat; the black quarry-worker pours coffee. Toni, behind Fernand, drinks from a bottle. Marie listens in the background. Fernand scoffs at Toni about the rabbit he brought from Sebastien being tough. The guitar player remarks that it is not the rabbits that make Toni visit the farm so often, but that young chicken Sebastien keeps. They rise and set out for work; shoulder to shoulder Fernand and Toni push their bicycles down the path.

Here the dialogue tells us the events of a year in the story, disclosing the relationship between Toni and Marie, Marie and Fernand. The first mention of Josepha, Alinda, and Sebastien occurs, characterizing them in important ways. But visually the scene flows down the path and into the life shared by these people, so bound together in their interplay of familiarity and respect. The close texture of their communal life, its warmth and solidity, shows through the images of the scene. Only when Marie complains to Toni is the talk of any consequence; otherwise, the point is just to be talking to someone, rather than to say something to him. Renoir captures here precisely that vitally important aimless chatter that fills our lives, affirming by its mere occurrence a comfortable relationship between persons, rather than transmitting information back and forth. This talk displays a surface camaraderie, but the substance of the fellowship is revealed by the significance of gesture, by the organization of space and the coordination of movement. The grouping of four men around a table, the blending of two figures by the pump, the tilt of Fernand's head, show us more than the dialogue tells.

This casual handling of the narrative persists through much of *Toni*, often treating the details of action as no more interesting than objects that happen to exist within the scene or the Provençal hills within which these pulses beat. Josepha smiles at Gaby, talks sweetly trying to lure him into helping her with her laundry cart. Gaby, uninterested, picks up a tiny black kitten to fondle while he tells Josepha how busy he is. Sebastien calls Gaby away; Josepha pulls her cart down the path. The camera lets them go, stops to watch the black kitten tumble cautiously from the wall. Or, Toni and Fernand work in the quarry while Toni tells Fernand about his desire to marry Josepha, but Renoir shoots them from above, looking down into the quarry, and places there heads low in the frame so that the bustling activity of the quarry far below fills two-thirds of the screen. Even when it is action and not talk that carries the narrative, the images may reduce this action to mere incident within a wider scene. Marie, desperate at Toni's insistence on attending Sebastien's funeral, runs after him, catches him in the wood, and seeks reconciliation. Then, angry again when he still insists on going, she tells him: "Remember the kittens you drowned last year. That did something to you . . . Now you are pushing me under as wickedly as you did the kittens." She whirls dramatically and marches off to drown herself. But Renoir has cut from the intensity of the angry close-up to a very long shot in which Marie's tiny figure moves amid the grace of the trees, dark against the shimmering surface of the lagoon. And when she rows out to complete her act, the shining, tranquil face of the lagoon almost fills the screen; the dark figure of Marie in her little boat, reflected in the water, seems merely a dramatic accent in the peaceful scene.

In *Madame Bovary* Renoir's classical style had placed the action at a distance. In *Toni*, by embedding the narrative so deeply in the social and physical setting, he draws us into the world of the film. Yet the emphasis on milieu rather than dramatic action lends a sort of impersonality to the narrative, reinforced by enclosing the action within shots of the arrival of a trainload of immigrants—as if it were not the individuality but the universality of these few humans that was being shown. The simplicity of the milieu and its working-class characters adds to this effect, as it adds a deceptive air of simplicity to the plot.

These aspects of *Toni*, combined with the fact of its being shot wholly on location, mostly in natural exteriors and apparently with natural light, have prompted critics to call *Toni* the first neorealist film, a forerunner of the surprising Italian cinema that blossomed in 1945.[4] Others have denied the connection, seeing political commitment, the denunciation of an unjust social order, as the central thread of neorealism. Renoir has never claimed any direct influence; he once wrote: "Our ambition was to have the public imagine that an invisible camera had filmed the phases of a conflict without the human beings unconsciously swept along in this action being aware of it. I was probably not the first to attempt such a venture, nor the last. Later, Italian neorealism would push this system to perfection."[5]

Toni does lack the political overtones of neorealism. An important change occurs in the milieu on which Renoir focuses—the inhabitants of Marie's boarding house are hardly Parisian bourgeois—but the coolness of his view remains. *Toni* is neither a cry against injustice and oppression nor a eulogy of the noble worker. The conventions of the peasants and workers of

Martigues do not appear a vast improvement over those of that kind-hearted bourgeois, Lestingois.

But, apart from its political neutrality, *Toni* does hear the stamp of neo-realism and, ten years before the liberation of Rome, pointed toward a new cinema. The essence of neorealism is a convincing air of truthfulness at two quite different levels: the truth of the look of a certain environment at a particular time and the truth of a condition of life. The level between these, that of the story, truth on the level of narrative, is relatively unimportant, though both *Toni* and *Rome: Open City* reconstruct actual events. These essential things, the real appearance of the world, the truth of a condition of life, are not in fact easily known. We seldom really look at the world and we avoid learning the truth about our own lives. What convinces us that the neorealist films sees more clearly than we do is its unadorned look, a bareness and simplicity which shows that nothing has been added and nothing concealed. How appropriate that Jean Renoir, so committed to demolishing both cliché and illusion, should be among the first to make a film having this look.

In fact, the existing prints of *Toni* probably look more like the neorealist films than they rightly should. The masterpieces of neorealism, *Rome: Open City*, *Shoeshine*, *La Terra Trema*, *The Bicycle Thief*, are all predominantly somber in tone, sweeping darkly to their unhappy conclusions. *Toni*'s world never has the grimness of postwar Italy; yet, in its present form, the last twenty-five minutes of the film are wholly serious in tone. And though the events that lead to Toni's death all seem unnecessary, even accidental, the unbroken gravity of tone gives the last third of *Toni* an air of inevitability, of destiny. Yet, again, Renoir's original conception has been damaged by cutting; this time by the producer, who found one late scene unacceptable. Josepha, beaten by Albert when he discovers her taking his money, cowers under the kitchen table, but, when Albert turns away, she stealthily picks up the pistol he had arrogantly tossed on the floor and confronts him with it when he turns. Toni and Gaby, coming down from the hill, hear a shot and enter to find Albert stretched dead on the floor. Josepha goes to get her baby and prepare to leave with Gaby, but Gaby promptly departs, leaving Josepha to Toni, but taking the money he had persuaded her to steal from Albert. Josepha returns, distraught to find Gaby gone, but Toni tells her that they will fix Albert's body to look like suicide. At this point the present film cuts to the woods where Albert's body lies under a tree with Toni standing over it to arrange the pistol in Albert's hand. As he does this, Toni talks to Albert, "Now, Albert, Josepha is all mine," attracting the attention of the passing gendarme.

But as Renoir originally shot *Toni*, several minutes of film stood where the cut is now. Toni and Josepha put Albert's body in the laundry cart, cover it with dirty linen and pull it along the path toward the woods. As they walk they meet the charcoal burners with whom Toni has lived on the hillside. These Corsicans follow along behind the cart, talking and laughing and singing an accompaniment to this stroll through the woods—creating a sort of mock cortege in marked contrast to the somber, wet, formal funeral of Sebastien, which was accompanied only by the peal of the church bell. This scene, seven minutes before the end of *Toni*, would sharply break the increasingly serious tone of the film, reinstating the rhythmic recurrence of song and give the conclusion of *Toni* an ironic cast it now lacks—particularly since this would mesh with a small ironic touch still in the film: The black kitten Gaby petted early in the film has become a cat. In the scene where Albert quarrels with Gaby and Josepha, he complains about his dinner and tells Josepha to open a can of sardines. Then he gets up, roughly throws the black cat squalling from the mantle and fastens his money to the cord he puts around his neck. Later, when Toni and Gaby find Albert dead, the black cat is on the table eating from the tin of sardines.

These images, the cat crouched on the table behind Josepha with the gun in her hand, and the happy Corsicans singing as they follow the laundry cart through the woods, would form a celebration of Albert's death in contrast to the sadness that surrounded the death of Sebastien—mingling a rather truthful irony and irreverence with the tragic movement of the film. They would also restore the social milieu to the center of the film just when the narrative has taken it over, and thus make the repeated arrival of immigrants at the end of the film seem less arbitrary. But one can only speculate about how the film might appear then: we shall never see it to know.

Characterization

The neorealism of *Toni*, like the formalism of *Madame Bovary*, grows from tendencies already present in Renoir's developed style. But the characters do not; *Toni*'s focus upon a group of men sharing a common life, upon comrades essentially characterized by the quality of this shared life, has little precedent in Renoir's sound films.

Strangely, perhaps, only the force of this camaraderie in *Toni* makes obvious the extent of its absence from earlier films. From *On purge bébé* to *Madame Bovary*, the intensely felt relations all involve a male and a female in a liaison that tends to thwart the sharing of one's life with anyone but the sexual partner. Friendships occur, of course, in these films—Lestingois and Vigour, Charles Bovary and Homais—these men support each other at moments of sorrow or joy, but their daily lives go on quite apart. These lives intersect; they do not mingle. And these films offer no glimpse of lives truly shared. The garage of *La Nuit du carrefour* or the grocery of *Chotard et Cie.* provide hints perhaps; at moments Lestingois and Boudu seem strongly drawn together—but no more than that. Within these films deep

The death of Albert and Toni, but
without Albert's funeral cortege.
Gaby (Andrex), Josepha (Célia
Montalvan), Albert (Max Dalban),
Toni (Charles Blavette).

human relationships are always sexual in nature; companionship between
men or between women appears as a negligible element in life.

Yet Renoir was surely aware of the possibility of camaraderie, of the role
it could play in a man's life. All the reports of his own life in these years
make it plain that he intensely shared his work and his life with others, immersed in a circle of companions who worked together, ate together, then
spent endless evenings filled with talk and laughter and red wine, or walks
along the river bank. And among Renoir's accomplices, one, at least, held a
special place: Jacques Becker, Renoir's assistant for eight years. These two

revealed themselves completely to each other, shared thoughts and dreams, food and drink, sound and silence, and discovered such secret joys of intense friendship as the magical efficacy of the absurd phrase from Dumas that they whispered to each other when things seemed at their worst: "Le graisse t'oie il est tres ponne avec des gonfitures" ("Goose fat is very good with jam"). One cannot read Renoir's memoir in Jean Queval's *Jacques Becker* or Becker's brief note in Leprohon's *Jean Renoir* and still doubt the import of such companionship in Renoir's own life.[6]

Yet none of this shows in the films before *Toni*, perhaps because 1931-

1934 is the period of what might be called Renoir's bourgeois films—films whose action develops within the social context of the French bourgeoisie. This bourgeois culture, with its stress on competiton and its emphasis on family more than community, tends to separate people rather than unite them. And the relationships felt to be deepest and most significant within this culture are precisely the exclusive male-female sexual alliances that dominate the 1931-1934 films. Hence the focus upon such relationships is quite appropriate, and the repeated failure of the relation is one aspect of the generally critical light these works cast on this bourgeois milieu.

In calling 1931-1934 Jean Renoir's bourgeois period, I do not imply that he had ever deliberately undertaken a series of films exploring this bourgeois background. More likely Renoir, like most everyone else at that time, simply took the bourgeois background for granted. Though labor made impressive gains in France after 1918, the dominance of the bourgeoisie was almost unquestioned. If the Renoir films of this period did not simply reflect the world, that was because they were more critical of it than most of his audience would be. But once *Toni* appears, it reveals the narrowness of the social background and the very limited range of social possibilities these films present.

And once *Toni* appears, Renoir films are never the same. From *Toni* to *The Rules of the Game*, every film allows male companionship a significant role, both in the social setting and the narrative, with this camaraderie becoming the central relationship in several films, relegating male-female associations to a secondary place. From this expansion of the social context, these films gain a greater fullness of life; they delve more deeply into a larger range of characters than do the bourgeois films.

The techniques of characterization also undergo a change. From 1931 to 1934 Renoir achieved depth of characterization primarily by contrast; he revealed his characters by showing how they differed. But repeatedly, these differences prove so great they defeat the efforts of the characters to build a common life. As the contrasts disclose the characters to us, we also become aware of the inevitable failure of their attempts at union. We know that Legrand's dream of "Liberté et Lulu!" is merely a dream, and that no effort will succeed in making Charles Bovary the lover Emma longs for. But in *Toni*, similarity as well as difference becomes a major element in characterization, and harmony rather than contrast marks the interaction among several characters. This does not entail a loss of individuality, but these individuals are more like each other than are the characters of *La Chienne* or *Boudu*.

One result of this focus on a cooperating social group is to give the impression of a fuller presentation of minor characters. We probably see the guitar player in *Toni* no more often than Dédé's friend in *La Chienne*, the black quarry-worker no more than Lestingois' friend Godin. Yet we feel we have penetrated much more deeply into their lives, for we see the pattern and flow of their days, their work at the quarry, their home at Marie's; whereas we see Godin and Dédé's friend only at odd moments that have no felt connection with their daily lives.

In contrast to the bourgeois films, neither duplicity, contempt, nor malice, nor great romantic dreams abound in *Toni*. They are not wholly absent, but seem incidental rather than the very stuff of life. Instead, sympathy, a sort of gentleness, an intuitive understanding of each other and a great tolerance and willingness to accept what befalls them characterize Toni and Fernand, the major figures among the men at Marie's. Marie, dark and intense, shares most of these qualities but with less patience, less willingness to let whatever will, happen. She listens more to an interior voice, much more often dramatizes her life. The spontaneity of Toni and Fernand is one aspect of lives lived more on the level of action than of thought. Marie thinks more, and this proves her undoing, for her imagination builds Toni's persistence in keeping his promise to Sebastien into a much greater threat to her marriage than Toni's actions warrant—though perhaps at bottom it is Josepha rather than Toni whom Marie misunderstands. The group at Marie's share a regard, a consideration for each other, a concern for the effect of their own actions on others. Though Marie and Toni quarrel and separate, this concern persists—it is love that dies, not kindness.

The group at Sebastien's farm—Sebastien, Josepha, Gaby, and later Albert—are much more self-centered, more willing to use others callously. Josepha, the most innocent of Renoir's destructive females, hardly seems aware of the import of her acts, though their self-serving aim is clear. Time and again the camera catches her combing her hair, straightening her dress, preparing a smile for an approaching male—always as a prelude to asking some favor. Toni, the willing victim of this coquetry, accords it greater seriousness than Josepha seems capable of, confirming what earlier films suggest—that the destructive female can destroy only with the cooperation of her victims. Gaby and Albert respond to Josepha quite differently, Gaby with his own display of self-serving charm, Albert by treating the sexual basis of her appeal as its only content. Josepha's underlying innocence seems apparent in the seduction scene. When Albert refuses to be turned away by her plea that he be nice, but responds with his alimentary metaphors, "That's it, the sauce without the roast . . . I adore hor d'oeuvres, but I'm in the habit of having complete meals," and persists in his demand, she succumbs neither from desire nor fear, but simply because she doesn't know what else to do.

But "innocence" is perhaps not the right word; Josepha shares with the other characters of *Toni*, rather, a great simplicity. Their ideas, like their lives, hardly reach beyond the circle of hills within which they live. Their acts seem almost wholly controlled by emotion and convention; thought does not so much inform these actions as rationalize them. Not that, like

Boudu, their lives are completely external. They plot, plan, try to mislead each other, but act on these plots so artlessly that no one less simple than they could be deceived. This simplicity does not prove to be a wholly admirable proletarian virtue; *Toni* is not a paean to the joys of the simple life. Rather the characters are all victims of it; their inability to think beyond the surface of their own situation converts trouble into disaster. And true love fares no better here than in Montmartre. Toni, who loves passionately, dies a useless death; Fernand, who loves patiently, serves but does not win Marie, and Marie, who loves deeply, cannot hold Toni. Gaby and Josepha, who do not love at all, fare at least as well as the others.

Albert, the northerner among these southern European immigrants, seems less simple than the rest; at least he believes this and treats the others with condescension, a mixture of sarcasm and glib talk. At bottom weak and cowardly, he affects a surface bluster and bravado that he mistakes for cleverness. Max Dalban, as Albert, seems often to be acting, as compared to the complete naturalness of the performances of Blavette and Edouard Delmont. But this, again, is a trait of the character, who performs for others to mask his own weakness. In earlier films Dalban had played worldly minor characters. As Albert, his only major role, he turns this worldliness, so out of place among the workers of Martigues, into a facet of the defensive facade of a character who is regarded as an outsider by all and never really wins acceptance within their clannish lives.

The fact that Albert seems less simple than the others leads us too easily into taking him for the villain of the film. But while he is hardly admirable, he seems no more blamable for the events that lead to Toni's death than several others. Albert's seduction of Josepha is primarily an assertion of his own manhood, prompted more by Toni's truculent denial of Albert's freedom—"Play around as much as you want, but leave *our* women alone."— than by any great desire for Josepha. Since everyone knows that Toni lives with Marie, his denial of Albert's right to pursue Josepha has indeed an air of arrogance. If Albert were as simple as Toni, he might have taken this outburst of Toni's for what it was—a direct expression of Toni's own intention. Being more complex, Albert sees it instead as a derogation of himself and a challenge which, in his role as outsider, he cannot ignore. The marriage required when Toni discovers Albert with Josepha is one nobody wants; Sebastien states his distaste for it while pouring the wine that will seal the marriage contract. When Fernand tells Toni that, after two years of marriage, Albert has been running around, we may, like Toni, think that Albert's villainy has been confirmed. But Gaby's confession that Josepha has been his mistress all along should put Albert's actions in a new light. It doesn't, though; we tend to accept the view that Albert's bluster and cowardice and the fact that he is an outsider establish him as a *salaud*. But Albert is no more cowardly than Gaby, no more faithless than Josepha. If we resist the common view of his viciousness, Albert may seem as much a victim of the simplicity of the others as he is the cause of their plight.

With their simplicity, the one trait shared by all the characters of *Toni* is a need to talk, about everything or nothing, and at a great rate, the words tumbling over each other. Toni grows more silent as he lies in wait in the hills above Josepha's house, but otherwise talk abounds as an accompaniment to every action. Some critics feel the talk excessive; others criticize Renoir because of the rapidity of the dialogue. But I deem it one of the most realistic aspects of the film; my own experience in working with Italian immigrants in the 1930s is that they talk all the time, with the mere act of talking much more important than the content of anything said.

Style and Form

If we analyze the neorealistic look of *Toni* terms of style, the most apparent stylistic trait is a complete absence of ornamentation. But what does that mean? Ornamentation in a spectacle like *My Fair Lady* may be obvious, but how is *Toni* less ornamented than another dramatic film about simple people in a lower-class setting—John Ford's *The Informer*, for example, made at about the same time?

The comparison is illuminating, for, beside *Toni*, *The Informer* looks almost baroque. It is filled with dramatic lighting that creates arresting highlights and mysterious pools of shadow, camera angles which accentuate emotions without showing anything that could not be seen in a level shot, portentous symbols like the clock that ticks away Gippo's life, external music used to heighten tension and build emotion, camera movements that thrust the reactions and feelings of the characters at us, artistic compositions, make-up that accentuates the personality or status of the characters, and such tricks as superimposition. These are perfectly legitimate means of cinematic expression, and Ford handles them well. But none of these techniques is necessary to the presentation of characters and events in a film; in its avoidance of them all, *Toni* exemplifies the absence of ornamentation.

Several of the Renoir tendencies suppressed in *Madame Bovary* here reassert themselves. The camera regains its freedom and fluidity, no longer seeming compelled to attend only to the action. Dynamic compositions with dominant diagonals reappear, along with a much greater frequency of close-ups and medium shots. The use of deep-focus continues, but without the devices which put the action of *Madame Bovary* at a distance from us. There are few shots through doors or windows, few compositional foreground objects. Instead, Renoir keeps the space alive by movement or, as in the remarkable shots in the quarry, by engaging our interest in action both in the foreground plane and in the deep background. All this gives *Toni* a much more pervasive feeling of movement than *Madame Bovary*.

Exteriors. The quarry, the farm, the woods, the lagoon, the hillside. Toni with Fernand (Edouard Delmont), Josepha, Marie (Jenny Hélia), the charcoal burners.

There is no interior space in *Toni* that Renoir explores and displays with the care he used to establish the locales of *La Chienne* or *Boudu;* here, the exteriors constitute the major setting of the film: a countryside as peaceful as that of *Madame Bovary* but more varied and richer in its visual forms. Our sense of place in *Toni* is founded on these exteriors; our empathy with the lives of the immigrants rests heavily on our feeling of acquaintance with the land that shelters them. Half a dozen sites define the area: the viaduct and the road that runs along the edge of the lagoon, the quarry with its rugged, rocky walls, the sandy shore of the lagoon where thick clumps of

reeds drift over the dunes, the graceful little wood near Marie's with its gentle slopes, the hillside where the charcoal burners live, the path past Dominique's farm, where Josepha pulls her laundry cart and Toni digs a bee-sting from her back. In several scenes Renoir immerses the action so deeply in its setting that it becomes a minor element within the frame. And he seems deliberately to have refused to shoot any two scenes at the same time of day, so as to show the difference time and weather make. A clear early morning at Marie's, a bright early afternoon in the quarry with the sun glaring on the white walls, a misty dawn on the hillside, a hot late afternoon at Sebastien's farm when Albert finds Josepha naked under her thin dress and seduces her, a downpour by the farm, a bleak drizzle in the sad little cemetery, a night by the charcoal burner's campfire . . . the simplicity and lack of ornamentation in *Toni* does not prevent visual variety and richness in the exterior settings, but rather allows these exteriors to create the atmosphere of the film. The exploratory camera movement typical of Renoir occurs in *Toni* almost exclusively in exterior shots.

The richness of *Toni's* soundtrack more than matches this wealth of scenery. With his love for spontaneous, authentic sound, Renoir here achieved nearly a complete naturalness in this dimension of his film. Not that we hear only natural noises in *Toni*, but both music and dialogue appear to be completely uncontrived, simple, natural events within the world of the film. The music, produced wholly by the guitar and the voices of the immigrants at Martigues, is not merely internal to the world of the film, but internal to the lives of the characters and thus itself a characterizing agency in the film. It is personal music, created with no air of performance or of presentation to an audience; yet, with the words of the songs usually having a direct connection with the lives of the singers, it achieves the universalization Renoir desires. The homogeniety of this music, its similarity in sound and rhythm throughout, forms one facet of the apparent simplicity of *Toni*, though the auditory texture is diverse and complex. Of the ten minutes of music in the film, very little accompanies the action that constitutes the story of *Toni*; it occurs, rather, as punctuation and as a mode of imposing a rhythmic organization on the narrative. The multilingual songs reinforce the variety of accents heard in the dialogue and reassert the prominence of the encompassing social milieu. And the music combines with the railroad sounds as a central element in the opening and closing scenes, which give an overall cyclical form to *Toni*. Thus, this simple, internal music has much greater significance in the film than any external score could have.

The naturalness of the dialogue is more debatable. The abundance of talk appears to me just what one should expect in this setting. The variety of the speech patterns unquestionably plays a major part in establishing this milieu and indicates again Renoir's greater concern for the authenticity of the sound than for its ready intelligibility. Almost every character speaks with a different accent, a sprinkling of Spanish or Italian terms, a variation in vocabulary. When excited, Josepha speaks French in completely Spanish rhythms; Toni's speech has an Italian cast. Fernand sounds like a typical Marseillaise, with very expressive intonation, pronouncing final *e*'s to impart a strong rhythm to his speech. Sebastien talks in more formal phrases, Albert with a crisper pronunciation and a more complex vocabulary.

Some critics find some of this talk too "literary." Here the question is ultimately one of characterization; not whether the lines are literary but whether this character might plausibly utter that literary line. Some characters do tend toward self-dramatization, notably Marie. But southern Europeans have long been characterized as "passionate," meaning not that they feel more deeply than brooding northerners, but that they act out, dramatize, their feelings more. We forget that where there is an oral tradition of poetry or song, the least literate people often speak in "literary" phrases.

I suppose the most literary line in *Toni* is the last line spoken by Fernand as he stands over Toni's body beside the railroad track, "Toni, three years ago you too arrived, so full of hope." That it is literary quite suits its role in confirming the cyclical pattern imposed by the beginning and end of the film. But even this seems hardly out of character, for Fernand has been the most thoughtful of these men, with a habit throughout the film of describing events with more generality and in a wider perspective than the others do.

Armand-Jean Cauliez has called the sound in *Toni* "montage rather than sonorization."[7] I think this true of the dialogue, in the sense that it often informs us of things not seen rather than merely presenting the auditory dimension of events we witness. But it also has importance as mere sound. The dialogue of *Toni* dominates the soundtrack probably as much as that of *Madame Bovary*, but with a rather different impact. The music, the sound of traffic and trains and water, expand the space of the film, give depth and reality to its world but have little import in the development of the narrative or characterization. The dialogue, of course, does, but seems to accomplish this in passing. So little of this talk seems the result of deliberation or settled intention; it just gushes forth without premeditation. It contrasts sharply with the dialogue of *Madame Bovary*, where lines are spoken deliberately, clearly—well-spoken lines whose speakers savor them as they come. There are no well-spoken lines in *Toni*, but simply the sound of human voices.

The incoming train of immigrants at the beginning and end of *Toni* suggests an overall cyclical form, but in the existing prints this appears to be imposed as a framework upon an essentially linear development through the rest of the film. But here again the elimination of the mock funeral procession has seriously distorted the film. For were this scene restored, the flow of visual images would become essentially cyclical over the whole length of *Toni*. Not, of course, with mirror-image symmetry, but with patterns of recurrence grouped around a central point to articulate the cycle.

The center of this formal structure, occurring almost precisely halfway through the film, is Sebastien's death and funeral. This also forms the pivotal point of the plot, since it changes all of the relationships in the film. Sebastien's death makes Albert master of the farm and the foreman, as it were, over both Gaby and Josepha as well as the quarry. It also leads to the separation of Toni and Marie. That this scene also forms the center of a cyclical visual pattern can be seen once we recognize that the scenes at the charcoal-burners' hut in the second half of the film are the inverse of the quarry scenes in the first half. Both scenes show the locale of Toni's work—as he tells Fernand, while he lies on the hillside he is not idle but, like the hunter, busy watching for the game he seeks. And visually they are counterparts— the quarry scenes, brightly lit, show the depths of the quarry; the scenes at the charcoal burners' are dark and show the heights of the hillside. Each of these is followed by a scene at Sebastien's farm. Were the mock funeral restored, the scenes of quarry and farm would be preceded by, and the scenes of hillside and farm followed by, a scene in which Toni and Josepha pull the laundry cart along the path through the woods. And at either end of this pattern stands the arrival of a train of immigrants at Martigues and a shot of these immigrants walking under the viaduct singing the same song.

It appears then that Renoir conceived and executed this film with a clearly articulated, balanced, and regular formal structure in mind, though unfortunately this structure did not survive the producer's whim. But once we see what it should have been, it may appear that Toni is as classical as *Madame Bovary*.

14

Le Crime de M. Lange
1936

There is no Socialist majority, there is no proletarian major-
ity; there is a Popular Front majority . . . It will be the object
of our experiment . . . to discover whether it is possible to get
out of this social system the amount of order, well-being,
security, justice that it can produce for the mass of workers
and producers.
　　　　　　　　　　　　　　　　　　　　　　—Leon Blum

Madame Bovary carried Renoir's style to one of its limits; *Toni* marked a
new level of social awareness. But neither film had any obvious connection
with the contemporary world in which Renoir lived; both were set in a
space and time remote from the Paris of the 1930s. In this they differed from
earlier films; for, though neither *La Chienne*, *La Nuit du carrefour*, nor
Boudu provide any direct reflection of political events, they do breathe the
life of France and of Paris in the early thirties.

Hence, if this period, 1933-1935, marks the end of Renoir's bourgeois
films, it also seems a moment of withdrawal from contemporary society.
However, his turn in *Toni* toward presenting a group of comrades who
share their life and work proved a prelude to a much deeper plunge into the
political life of his time than had ever before been reflected in his films.

Not that Renoir had been unconcerned before; rather, until 1935, a certain distance separated his own political commitments from the content of
his films. But this distance was to diminish for the rest of the thirties; a
diminution so clearly felt that critics soon came to regard Renoir as cinema's

spokesman for the Left. He had long delighted in ridiculing the bourgeoisie; now his work stepped beyond mere criticism to advocate the program of the Left. Indeed, the times were ripe for it; for the period of *Madame Bovary* and *Toni* also rocked with the scandal known as the Stavisky affair, which led to the dismissal of the Paris Prefect of Police, M. Chiappe, familiar to filmgoers as the man who suppressed Bunuel's *L'Age d'or* in 1930. The separation of M. Chiappe from his prefecture touched off riots in the Place de la Concorde on February 6, 1934, led by such fascist paramilitary groups as the Croix de Feu. Three days later equally bloody Communist-led riots erupted in the worker's quarter. The Radical government of Daladier fell, and Doumergue returned to form a National Government—"to restore both order and the honor of the Republic." But the parliamentary panic created by the riots subsided; the interminable political bickering recommenced; and nine months later M. Doumergue in turn resigned with little accomplished, but with many Frenchmen now alarmed by the power of the fascist leagues. The stirring idea of a union of all the Left was in the air.

Jean Renoir had been in Berlin at the moment when Hitler came into power; he had witnessed the brutality of that event. Not surprising, then, to find him moved by the appeal for a Popular Front against fascism in France. The official birthdate of the *Front Populaire* was July 14, 1935, a day when the Left sought to recapture this national holiday from the reactionaries, although an alliance of the Left had been taking shape for months before. The official program of the Popular Front, was published on January 11, 1936—just two weeks before the Paris premiere of *Le Crime de M. Lange*. Thus, all of the work on this film was accomplished in the shadow of this political movement. And it requires no great imagination to find in the film an allegory of the political events of the day.

France in 1935 was so politically divided that every person in public life had to make some choice. Jean Renoir undoubtedly became the film director of the Left; he emerged as the central figure within a group of cinema workers actively engaged in promoting the program of the Popular Front. Documents from that period amply testify that he attended Communist Party rallies and wrote and spoke in support of the Left. He agreed to supervise the production of the film financed by the Communist Party for the May elections, *La Vie est à nous*, and was for a while a leader in Ciné-Liberté,[1] the cinema wing of the Popular Front. But merely calling attention to Renoir's engagement with the Left seems misleading. For one thing, the French Communist Party at the time was, publicly at least, wholeheartedly in support of the Popular Front. Whatever its long-range plans, its avowed program in 1936 was nationalistic and moderate—down with the two hundred families and up with the workers, of course, but specific demands were for paid vacations, a forty-hour week, and so forth, not for violent overthrow of the government.

Jean Renoir, 1935.

Renoir's deep attachments have always been to people rather than ideologies; significant changes in his work have been influenced by particular persons or specific events rather than by adherence to a political party or program. If his memories are accurate, even then, when the danger of fascism was acute and he willingly joined with the only force in France actively fighting it, Renoir's concern was with the general goal of opposing Hitler much more than with day-to-day partisan plans. Of course, if one is politically involved, some of the daily events must enter one's life. But Renoir's implication in such events flowed from his companionship with men strongly attached to the Left, rather than being a consequence of any explicit commitment to political activism or lasting endorsement of an ideology. The political spirit of his films comprises an artist's revelation of his epoch rather than the political exploitation of an art. As Thorold Dickinson says, "Politics are not a preoccupation with him; they were thrust upon him."[2]

Thus, Renoir stubbornly refused to be wholly political. Even when most engaged, the focus of his films remains on character rather than polemic or political action. His sympathies are usually apparent; yet even those characters who represent the political views he most opposed are viewed with warmth, as well as a detachment that renders political orientation as one aspect of a human life; Renoir does not cast his human figures in the reductive mold of politics. This helps his films of this time survive their period with almost undiminished impact; one need never have heard of the Popular Front to find *Le Crime de M. Lange* an absorbing and wholly comprehensible film. However central the politics of the thirties may have been in the genesis of the film, or however important political references may have seemed to French audiences at that time, the film transcends the politics of the moment, for its characters represent more than just the clash of political ideas.

Narrative and Treatment

Among Renoir's companions in the early 1930s was one Jean Castanier, whom Renoir has variously described as a "spherical Catalan," a "painter who was too lazy to paint," and "a man who loved to talk and so preferred to work with a group and design sets to painting." The idea for *Le Crime de M. Lange* originated with Castanier, who describes its beginnings in this fashion: "At the beginning of 1935 I took to Jacques [Becker] the idea of a film which could be called *Sur la cour*. It was a story very much of the people, about a likable little world of print-shop workers and laundresses who form a cooperative. Jacques hoped to direct the film and proposed the scenario to Des Fontaines." But the producer, Halley Des Fontaines, though a friend of Becker, did not want to trust the direction of a feature film to Renoir's meticulous assistant, who had made only two short films of his own. Hence, Des Fontaines asked that Renoir direct the film and Jean agreed. Castanier continues: "Jacques was angry with everyone in that affair; with Des Fontaines to be sure, with me a bit, but above all with Renoir. He couldn't understand how Renoir had agreed to do a film that he, Jacques, wanted to make. In the group that we formed with Renoir, no one had an idea that was just his. We worked together in the spirit of a community. What was essential was to make a film that interested us, to make it together; it mattered little whose signature was on it. And if there was ever a film that was the collective work of a group it was that one, which was finally called *Le Crime de M. Lange*. Be that as it may, Jacques didn't understand and he abandoned us."[3]

This account exaggerates a minor difference between himself and Becker, Renoir feels; however, Becker did not assist on *Le Crime de M. Lange*, though he was back at Renoir's side immediately afterwards for the shooting of *La Vie est à nous*.

Renoir and Castanier wrote a script but Renoir felt it lacked something. "I thought of asking Jacques Prévert if he would lend a hand to help perfect it and he agreed." So Prévert joined the *équipe*. Halley Des Fontaines describes this stage of the production: "It was not without trouble. He [Prévert] was then very lazy. Renoir and I were obliged to lock him in an office to make him work. We let him out only at meal times. Meanwhile he slid the pages of his scenario under the door as fast as he wrote them."[4]

The publication of the first treatment of *Le Crime de M. Lange* by Renoir and Castanier, in André Bazin's *Jean Renoir*, indicates that the overall structure of the film, the essentials of the story, the central characters and the spirit of the production were all conceived by Renoir and Castanier before Jacques Prevert lent his hand to the proceedings. Arizona Jim and Ranimax Pills are missing, though M. Lange already has his passion for "les Cow-Boys," and this early treatment fails to indicate either the role to be played by the courtyard or the richness of the character of Batala. Still, as Francois Truffaut remarks, "Renoir's film is already there; it awaits the contribution of two other men of genius: Jacques Prévert and Jules Berry."[5]

From 1933 to 1936 the spirit of live theatre in Paris was sustained by a group of avant-garde artists of extreme-left political persuasion, known as the *groupe Octobre*, which included both Jacques Prévert and Jean Castanier. By the time Renoir had shot his film, so many friends of Jacques Prévert had also joined the company that some critics call *Le Crime de M. Lange* a film by the *groupe Octobre*. These recruits included not only actors, but also Pierre Prévert as Renoir's assistant and composer Joseph Kosma, who wrote the song Florelle sings, then continued composing for Renoir films throughout the rest of his life. And however perfected the scenario may have been when Prévert slid the last page under the door, its fate was that of all scripts on a Renoir set: it served as a starting point for the shooting and not as a blueprint. So Renoir contrived to continue Prévert's collaboration. "I asked him to come on the set with me. He came every day, very agreeably; and constantly I said to him 'Well, *mon vieux*, there we must improvise.' And the film has been improvised like all my films, but with the constant cooperation of Prévert. I am sure that it would be impossible in this film to know the origin of ideas, if it were Jacques or I who found this or that. Practically, we found everything together."[6]

Surviving both Prévert and improvisation, the central thread of *Le Crime de M. Lange* remains as Castanier describes it: a story about a likable little world of print-shop workers and laundresses who form a cooperative.

In an old gray building enclosing a paved courtyard, Valentine Cardet (Florelle) manages her little laundry, while her former lover Batala (Jules Berry) runs a publishing house of dubious stability. The concierge, M. Besnard (Marcel Levesque), is an old veteran of the Indo-China campaign; his son Charles (Maurice Baquet) loves a little laundress, Estelle (Nadia Sibirskaia), and complains about having to sleep in a room walled off from the court by a billboard advertising *Javert*, the detective magazine that Batala hopes to publish. Amédée Lange (René Lefèvre), assistant to Batala, spends his nights writing western stories about his hero, Arizona Jim, but seems oblivious to most of the events that happen during the day—including Valentine's effort to interest him in love.

Batala, accused of a swindle, has a brilliant idea: he briefly introduces Lange to the complaining capitalist, M. Baigneur (Jacques Brunius), then explains that Lange, "a genius," is writing *Arizona Jim*. Having placated

M. Baigneur with an option on this great work, Batala enthusiastically tells Lange, "Good news! We are going to publish *Arizona Jim*," then quickly charms Lange into signing away his rights to his own work. When the first issue appears, Lange gazes at *Arizona Jim* with pride and pleasure, then becomes outraged when shown where Batala has inserted plugs for Ranimax pills. Confronted with this perfidy, Batala soothes Lange, then discovers a forgotten letter threatening legal action to collect one of his debts. Batala sends his secretary and mistress, Edith (Sylvia Bataille), off to offer herself to M. Baigneur, hoping this will somehow save him. Then he turns to seducing Estelle, who has come to his office with laundry. This episode ends as an inspector from the *Sureté Nationale* comes looking for Batala, who packs his bags and leaves on the first train.

Valentine has lured Lange into bed at last; there they hear a radio report of a train wreck in which M. Batala was killed and a priest has disappeared. The print-shop workers and Batala's creditors meet; when Louis, the print-shop foreman (Marcel Duhamel), proposes that they form a cooperative, the representative of M. Meunier, the principal creditor, objects. But a gangling young man appears, introduces himself as M. Meunier, *fils* (Henri Guisol)—"Papa is sick"—and declares that he loves cooperatives.

The cooperative flourishes, with *Arizona Jim* as its major and hugely successful publication. All of the members of the little courtyard community

Jean Renoir and friends, 1935. Photograph by Claude Renoir.

pose as characters for the photographs that adorn the cover—with Lange appearing as Arizona Jim. At one such photographic session, M. Baigneur and Meunier, *fils*, run breathlessly into the court, Meunier announcing, "Something extraordinary! I had an idea!" They will make a movie of *Arizona Jim*, with, of course, a role for the beautiful girl whom Meunier would like to impress. Valentine proposes a party to celebrate.

At the party Lange has an idea for the film and goes to the office to write it down. There he finds Batala, dressed as a priest, rummaging through the cupboard. Batala tells Lange of his plans to return, take over again, and publish *Javert*. Reminded that things improved as soon as he left, he raises an eyebrow, "You should kill me," and strides out, leaving Lange staring glumly at the pistol Batala had called a pious relic. In the courtyard Batala meets an astonished Valentine, draws her into a corner. Above, Lange seems to awaken, moves across the office, runs down the stairs. He shoots Batala without another word, then asks dazedly, "Is he dead?" Meunier, told that Lange has killed a man, says, "If it were me, I'd start moving," and offers to drive Lange and Valentine to the frontier.

As this sketch indicates, a central thread of *Le Crime de M. Lange* might have been borrowed from *La Chienne:* a romantic dreamer, considered a fool, whose real life lies in the world he creates at night, is robbed of his work by a cynical scoundrel and finally, is goaded to murder by a victim who himself provides the weapon, with the crime going unpunished within the film. But this common plot, somber and wholly centered on its dreamer in *La Chienne*, receives very different treatment in *Le Crime de M. Lange*. Often the screen seems overflowing with life, and an air of gaiety pervades much of the film.

After *Toni*, no single character, however important, dominates a Renoir film as Legrand dominates *La Chienne*. The visual focus of *Le Crime de M. Lange* is not a person but a place, the courtyard with its surrounding complex of laundry, print-shop, and conciergerie. The life of the film flows through the court; the lives of the characters meet and mingle there. Rather than the isolation of each character within his own illusion, a sense of community and camaraderie pervades this film, with Lange's illusion becoming a reality for the court.

Being Renoir's primary instrument for establishing the social focus of the film, the court becomes a structural element within the action itself. The people in the film have an essentially topographical relation to each other; their encounters depend not upon class or profession or even preference, but upon the fact that they work and live around the court. In all of Renoir's films no locale is more firmly identified nor more clearly linked to the lives of his characters. Valentine's *blanchisserie*, on the ground floor, holds the work and the talk of most of the women in the film. Its door faces that of the conciergerie, with the foot of the big curving stair between them. Batala's office and the composing-room of the print-shop are across the court, on the second floor. The room where Charles lays recovering from his broken leg, walled from the court by Batala's billboard, is beneath the composing room where the workers and creditors meet after Batala's presumed death. At this meeting the intervention of Meunier, *fils*, allows the creation of a cooperative; the first act of cooperation follows almost immediately— the removal of the billboard from Charles' window.

No one plans this event as a cooperative enterprise; it simply becomes one through the interpenetration of the areas around the court. Lange, upset at discovering that Batala had tricked him out of the rights to *Arizona Jim*, leaves the meeting and decides to liberate Charles. The concierge objects. His protest brings heads out of the windows all along the court; Meunier and the printers run down to help Lange and a dozen hands pull the billboard down. As the light floods into Charles' room, the area of action spreads across the court. Printers lift Estelle through a window and bring her to be reunited with Charles—a meeting prevented by Charles' mother as long as he was sealed off from the court. Thus the removal of the billboard becomes an expression of the life of the cooperative, which begins as an association of the print-shop workers but quickly involves the whole of the court. Even the concierge becomes a Mexican general on the covers of *Arizona Jim*.

Renoir's cinematography creates the unifying role of the court and exhibits the interpenetration of its spaces; camera positions and camera movements repeatedly include within a single shot both the courtyard and some interior space. The camera looks out of a composing-room window down at the court, or moves from the court through a window into the laundry, or roams across the court looking in the windows. Many camera movements are complex and return upon themselves, the culmination of these cyclical shots being the now famous 360° pan that follows Lange through the print-shop, sweeps the whole court, and ends with Batala's murder.

But the court is not simply the center of a unified small world; it also evokes the larger society. Unknown children play in the courtyard; a man throws open a window and shouts at the drunken, singing concierge, "I work all day! I'm tired!" In the background of half a dozen shots a man works repairing bicycles in a corner of the court. Other people—other stories waiting to be told. The few scenes outside the court occur in readily identifiable Paris locales, thus containing our little realm within the larger city. Renoir's desire to create characters within a vital and encompassing world succeeds so well in *Le Crime de M. Lange* that time, place, social setting, and action all seem simultaneously expressed in almost every frame and gesture of the film.

The time and place are very much the Paris of the Front Populaire. Though singularly lacking the virulence that marked much oratory of the mid-thirties, the satire touches all of the types who aroused the wrath of the Left: evil employers and shady financiers who exploit the workers, complacent priests who deplore the social unrest of the day, military minds lost in dreams of former glory, corrupt police. And success within the film entails the realization of the goals of the Popular Front: reform of the social structure, with cooperation replacing authoritarian exercise of power, and the liberation of workers from oppressive conditions of labor. The film no longer seems revolutionary because throughout it remains focused upon the minute complex of the court rather than the larger society in which the struggles of the Popular Front raged. However, the outcome of *Le Crime de M. Lange* is not merely the death of Batala, but a verdict affirming the justice of such an act of violence against an oppressor. Hence, in its time it appeared as militant and unconcealed support for the Left.

But a Left more tolerant than some supporters of the Popular Front preferred; *Le Crime de M. Lange* is no *Potemkin*. Its contending forces are individuals, not classes. And among these individuals, only Batala remains wholly evil. But he seems as eager to swindle the financiers as to exploit the workers, while even Lange would pick up a few of Batala's tricks if he could master them. Thus neither class solidarity nor class consciousness marks the little world *sur la cour*. And it is no revolutionary group that judges Lange innocent, but the most simple and ordinary citizens. Social criticism may abound in *Le Crime de M. Lange*, but not doctrinaire oversimplification or social despair.

The social emphasis of the film also transforms the import of the unpunished crime. In *La Chienne* Legrand's murder of Lulu occurs as an individual shudder of violence, a reaction wrung unwillingly from a victim viewing the wreckage of his life; and Legrand's escape from the law is an accident compounded of Dédé's arrogance and the continued failure of everyone to perceive the real Legrand under his mousy skin. But Lange shoots Batala as a deliberate act in defense of the community, and his freedom follows acquittal by his peers. To achieve this treatment of the crime, placing it in a social context and reflecting a social reaction to it, Renoir departs, for the only time in his career, from a linear temporal development of his intrigue and encloses the action of his film in what might be called a context of justification.

Flashbacks are conspicuously absent in Renoir films. He finds his persons in the midst of life, reveals character in action, then shows how this character responds to and creates its world, how in the interplay of coincidence and opposing purpose a man's character may be decisive in shaping the flow of events even though he may be swept away in them. Quite unconcerned with psychological explanation of how a character came to be what he is, Renoir's attention centers, rather, on how persons relate to each other, given that each is as he is. Hence, his focus remains on the present moment

of his character's lives. The past does enter Renoir films but in the dialogue
—as reminiscence or complaint evoking an era different from this present,
as in *Grand Illusion* or as a reminder of how things came to the state they
are in, as in *Toni*; or as a distraction from a disturbing scene, as in *The
Rules of the Game*. But this past remains subordinate to the present, perhaps illuminating but never displacing it, never evoked with an immediacy
that interrupts our sense of the present, as flashbacks often do.

Never, it seems, except in *Le Crime de M. Lange*, which begins at the end,
in the Hotel de la Frontière where a gendarme tells some men at the bar
about: "Lange, Amédée Paul François, born February 3, 1900—the year of
the Exposition. Wanted for murder!" The men glance at the handbill, "A
man like any other [*un homme comme un autre*]," and go on drinking.
Soon Meunier's car stops at the Hotel; Meunier says, "Here we are. Not
very fancy, but the patron does well in the kitchen. Down there are the
dunes; beyond the dunes the frontier. Once there you're free, so they say.
[*la liberté, comme on dit*]." Meunier drives off; Lange, walking as if in a
daze, enters the hotel with Valentine. In their room Lange collapses on the
bed while Valentine admires the whiteness of the sheets. Downstairs the son
of the patron whispers urgently, "Papa, listen . . . Call the police." Startled,
the patron mutters, "What? A murderer? A murderer in my place?" and
while the boy keeps insisting that "the police will come . . ." the men gather
at a table and talk:

"Denounce them? Why?" . . . "What you want is the reward, obviously."
. . . "Sure, he wants his picture in the papers with the police." . . . "All the
same, you can't just let them loose on the road. That would be too easy."
. . . "And is it too easy to kill someone?" . . . "Oh, you never killed anyone." . . . "Yes! In dreams. It was a rat . . . This fellow; maybe he killed a
rat, too." . . . "But all the same, we haven't the right . . ." . . . "You haven't
the right! Watch your own ass, first." . . . "And if it's his mother that he
killed?" . . . "His mother? . . . Why not God the father while you're at it?"

As they talk Valentine comes through the door. Silence! Valentine begins,
"The man you're talking about is upstairs asleep. If you want to turn him in,
it's easy."

"We didn't say that." . . . "We were talking about it." . . . "We were discussing it."

Valentine sits at the table, "Yes, he did kill. I'll tell you what happened
. . . His mind was always somewhere else. At night, while everyone slept,
he wrote stories, impossible stories, with an old fountain pen."

Dissolve to Lange seated in his room, writing *Arizona Jim*—completing
an episode that includes, almost as an afterthought, "Arizona Jim killed one
or two of them." The story then unfolds swiftly until Batala lies dead in a
corner of the court. We return then to the hotel: Valentine completes her
story just as Lange reappears looking as harmless and puzzled as he did in

Hotel de la frontière. Valentine (Florelle) tells of the nocturnal adventures of M. Lange (René Lefèvre).

the opening scene. Dissolve to footprints in wet sand; the camera tilts up to show Lange and Valentine walking across the dunes away from the border. Two men from the bar wave as the fugitives recede, having reached *la liberté, comme on dit.*

Some critics describe the whole central action of the film as a flashback; others treat it as the present time of the film and call the opening sequence a "flash forward." But neither of these correctly identifies the structure of Renoir s film. There are no flashbacks in Renoir films, but he does frequently frame his work in prologues and epilogues. In *La Chienne* the puppet prologue places the "somber, desperate drama" within the context of the human comedy; the epilogue affirms this by shattering any impulse to see Legrand as a tragic figure. *Le Crime de M. Lange* almost reverses this; the hotel scenes frame the comic characters of the court in a world of more prosaic people and events. Lange, introduced as a murderer, appears mild and gentle, almost incapable of any action, let alone a killing; thus the question posed is not, "What will happen?" but "How could this man be a killer?" The men at the bar, poor devils *comme moi, comme vous*, react to crime as we all do: "Un assassin? Un assassin dans ma maison?" but they realize that, outside of the fantasy world of Arizona Jim, killing a man is not simple, though it may be easy. And they also know that judging a man's actions is not simple either. Their talk presupposes the relevance of context in determining the moral import of action, thus setting the stage for Valentine's proposal, "I'll tell you how it happened, and if you find that you have to turn him in . . . well, you turn him in. If not . . . "—a proposal we cannot help but accept. Thus, the hotel scenes that frame the film eliminate some suspense, make character dominant over mere story, and leave the verdict to ordinary people with ordinary moral sensibilities.

All this may suggest that the film has the tone of a moral treatise; but while serious questions do occur, the treatment of these is anything but heavy. Much of the film skirts the edge of absurdity. Only excellent performances keep several characters from seeming simple caricatures rather than the foolish but credible humans they are. After the dissolve from hotel to court, we soon forget the enclosing context and nothing in the film reminds us of it. Instead, we are wholly engaged in the life of the court; the moral question returns only with the return to the hotel. But by then no decision needs be made; for Lange's act of violence has become so inevitable and right that we can imagine no conclusion to the film other than the completion of his flight across the frontier.

Thus, the verdict of the men at the Hotel de la Fontière affirms our sense of justice and allows the film to end on a note of hope, as a comedy should. But the final shot on the dunes provides no happy ending, Hollywood style, for *Le Crime de M. Lange*. Lange, like Arizona Jim, has slain the villain and saved the cooperative, but Paris is not Arizona and its citizens do not greet the news of Batala's death by naming Lange sheriff. Lange and Valentine are free, "so they say," but exiled from the court that held their lives, and, after the shock of his real encounter with death, we are not sure Lange will ever again write with the same careless delight, "Arizona Jim killed one or two of them." Hence the final image of these two lonely figures receding on the windswept dunes conveys as much of sadness as of joy. We can know only that they have salvaged a few more moments together; not, surely, that life will be pleasant and serene. The music that accompanies this final scene is that of the song Valentine sings earlier, recounting the life of prostitutes and hungry tramps; its final line, "C'est une triste vie," hardly identifies this as a joyous moment. Renoir insists, at most, on the *possibility* of happiness, making hope worthwhile—its actuality is never assured.

Oddly, some critics note a progression from the pessimism of *La Chienne* and *Boudu* to the optimism of *Le Crime de M. Lange*. Odd, because both *La Chienne* and *Boudu* end in joy—where in cinema is joy more deeply expressed than in *Boudu's* recovery of the freeom of nature?—whereas *Le Crime de M. Lange* offers only hope amid the destruction of all that had brought joy into the world of the film.

Quite often the comic surface of Renoir's films masks a vision of the world very darkly toned and suffused with sadness. One aspect of Renoir's genuine realism is his awareness that the cosmos offers no guarantees to human endeavor, that the odds are high against any enterprise turning out exactly as we hoped or planned, and that, even if it does, we may regret it. Optimism seems hardly *le mot exact*. Yet, beside this insistence that nothing is ever certain to come out all right in the end, one feels an assurance that life is endlessly interesting, that men do occasionally learn from experience, and that every moment is worth living and some are sweet indeed. We have a glimpse, now and then, of how fine life might be, in the affection between Fernand and Toni or the love of Charles and Estelle. But this may only deepen the sadness; for the obstacles that defeat this possibility are human blindness, willfulness, ignorance, or, perhaps more often, merely custom, inertia, or forgetfulness. This dark underside of Renoir's vision, seldom absent in any film of the thirties, grows more insistent as the decade passes, finally approaching despair as the whole world of *The Rules of the Game* takes on the rhythm of a danse macabre.

Characterization

At the center of plot and interest in *Le Crime de M. Lange*, though hardly its hero, stands Batala, the evil genius whose presence poisons the world of the court. Among major characters in Renoir films, none appears more negative than he. Valentine calls him, "The worse bastard I ever met." Only once, when conversing with the priest on the train, do we find him not exploiting or manipulating someone, and even here this encounter generates in Batala the idea of using the priest to abandon his own identity when the wreck occurs.

The unrelieved villainy of Batala's character might be attributed to Jacques Prévert, whose vision of the world has always been less tolerant than Renoir's. Still, Batala's place in the lineage of Renoir characters is far too clear for that. For Batala lives as Dédé, the arrogant pimp of *La Chienne*, dreamed of living: well-dressed, "respectable," familiar with important people, a man with "ideas" and the ability to carry them out—with each idea aimed at exploiting someone for his own, Batala's, pleasure or benefit. And despite his higher status, Batala does not shun stooping to Dédé's profession when necessary. Remembering Baigneur's remark, "I'd rather have her fall into my bed than be struck by lightning," he sends Edith to Baigneur without hesitation; when she returns with only a few francs to show for her favors, he throws them down in dismay, asking, "Is that all?" but, of course, he pockets them as he leaves to catch his train. At the station his advice to Edith might be an illustration of Dédé's claim that what the law called "white slavery" was just some pretty girls who wanted to learn things: "If you are intelligent you can always find something to do. . . . I knew a fellow . . . a terrific guy . . . oh, a phenomenon. He lived off women. He knew psychology and he had noticed on . . . When a train leaves there is always someone on the platform who cries. He observed that when it is a pretty girl who cries—think, what a business! You understand? With a little platform ticket and then a little handkerchief in her hand . . . you can do ravishing things, n'est-ce pas?"

Edith pays for the advice, of course, as Batala picks up his cigarettes, makes a final gesture illustrating the allure of a handerchief in the hand of a tearful woman, and exits, leaving her to cope with the waiter.

Wholly self-centered in intention and motivation, with complete disregard for the wants or welfare of others, yet supremely confident that everyone will succumb to the charm he regards as his gift to women, in Jules Berry's superb portrayal Batala represents the perfection of one familiar Renoir character type. Like Dédé, like Rodolphe in Madame Bovary, his actions are performances for an audience, with calculated effects. Hence, if his heart is black, Batala's exterior designedly conceals it. He moves with grace, seems single-mindedly attentive to each person he approaches, talking with a vivacity and charm that both flatter and disarm his hearers. Yet not always insincerely; for he is his own most appreciative and convinced audience.

Batala first appears coming across the courtyard, eyeing with polite suspicion the gentleman who greets him: "M. Buisson. I represent M. Meunier of Lille . . . Six months ago M. Meunier loaned you 300,000 francs for new presses . . . I have found that you used most of this money for personal ends . . ." Suspicions confirmed, Batala invites M. Buisson to his office, but turns on every step of the stairs, gestures, talks, and by the time they reach the top he has negotiated the size of the bribe, stuffed 7,000 francs in Buisson's pocket and dismissed him with cheerful advice for M. Meunier, "For the liver—Vichy!" In the composing room he meets Lange, looks at the text of some ads, and, finding a page of Arizona Jim under it, reads a line and pats Lange on the head, "Quel drôle de monde la-dedans." In the corner he puts his arm over the shoulder of the artist drawing illustrations for *Javert*, "That's very good, but . . . your bloodstain is too small . . . I can't see your corpse either . . . Remember, a crime is full of small details."

In his progress from courtyard to office, covering in reverse exactly the route that Lange will travel, gun in hand, late in the film, Batala has cajoled, flattered, caressed everyone he meets. Above all he has handled, had his hands on, each person he encounters—hands exerting a slight pressure on Buisson's shoulder, patting Lange's head, embracing Edith, holding Valentine. He has bribed a threatening creditor, jollied unpaid employees, placated an irritated mistress, and made advances to an old flame. Jules Berry's hands, constantly mobile, dance about each intended victim; every utterance is accompanied by gestures expressive enough to convey Batala's intention, the words serving only to fill in details. The utterances themselves are often slightly incoherent, consisting of exclamations, half sentences, repeated meaningless syllables, with the timbre of his voice more effective than the words in creating the impression he desires.

This incoherence may stem from the fact that almost all of Berry's lines were improvised during the shooting. Renoir reports: "Jules Berry never could say the lines as they were written. Prévert and I would give him his lines but he always changed them as he spoke. It was not so much a matter of bad memory but rather it was just not possible for him to use the words of other people. So Prévert and I tried to give him the feeling that he was speaking his own lines rather than those of an author. Berry was a very fine actor, one who lived his roles. He was so much Batala that while we were shooting he forgot he was Jules Berry."

The resulting, slightly disconnected speeches leave gesture and facial expression as the prime constitutive elements of Batala's character. This enhances the authenticity of the character; for this manipulator of others, Berry's hands form the perfect instrument of characterization. Repeatedly, they direct the maneuver essential to Batala's success, gently and smoothly separating people from each other, isolating them to be dealt with one at a time, each in turn becoming the exclusive object of his deceptive charm. These hands stand out in the performance, but the symbol of Batala's impact on the life of the court is the billboard over Charles' window, which isolates him from the court, allows his mother to come between him and Estelle, and brings him into conflict with his father.

Though relying heavily on exclamations and gestures, Batala also employs various props in his manipulations. Thus, Baigneur's dog merits attention when Batala suspects that his visit may not be quite friendly. Baigneur has entered with an affected air of suaveness, eyeing Valentine as he passes, holding the dog affectionately under his arm. Batala seats Baigneur politely and bends to the dog, pats her head, remarks, "What a pretty little dog [*joli petit chien*]." Baigneur corrects him, "It's a female, Daisy." Batala

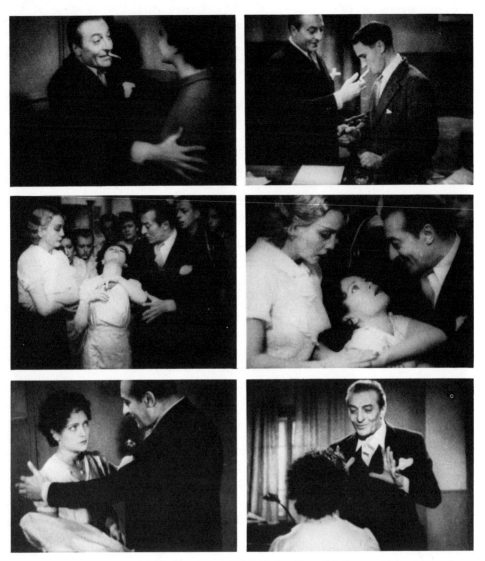

Destructive charm. Batala (Jules Berry) with Edith (Sylvia Bataille), Lange, Valentine, and Estelle (Nadia Sibirskaia).

tries again, "Ah, a daisy bitch—excellent breed." Coldly, determined to maintain his anger, Baigneur replies, "Daisy iș her name." "Oh, that's English," Batala says, still eagerly, but Baigneur snaps, "She's Belgian!" Having exhausted the possibilities of using the dog against her master, Batala turns to Baigneur, "Now then, M. Baigneur, what good wind brings you here?" With equal politeness Baigneur explains that the makers of Ranimax pills have gotten exactly nothing for their money and that the word "swindle" seems appropriate ("le mot exact"). Batala makes soothing sounds and gestures, remembers in desperation the manuscript page he saw in Lange's hand and, immediately attributes to this wholly unknown work all the qualities necessary to placate Baigneur. With a magician's wave of the hand, he produces another prop, Lange. Lange enters on command to be ceremoniously introduced; he stands a moment, pats the dog, fidgets. Batala waves him out and Lange leaves, wholly mystified by this little episode—repeated almost exactly by Truffaut in *Stolen Kisses* thirty-two years later.

Batala now has his plan. "You saw M. Lange?" he asks the equally mystified Baigneur. "A genius! A genius! He's doing an immense work." Baigneur is dubious, "Really? That boy?" But Batala now is in full flow, "Imagine, him with his insignificant look . . . He's writing *Arizona Jim!* . . . Something like . . . like *Les Miserables*. With *Arizona Jim* Ranimax pills will go around the world. Think of it—Jean Valjean or Don Quixote taking Flaconnet salts or Ranimax pills. It's prodigious!" Batala leans forward to become confidential, but steps on Daisy. Undaunted, he apologies and continues, "I have exclusive rights to *Arizona Jim*. If you don't buy it, you're a fool." "A fool," Baigneur repeats and emerges a moment later with an option in his pocket, and his eye, this time, on Edith.

Dogs and people function as occasional props for Batala, but with such innocents as Lange he needs only his hands and his standard instrument of manipulation, a cigarette. A constant smoker, Batala also uses cigarettes for pacification, persuasion, camouflage, distraction, betrayal. Lange, ecstatic at the prospective publication of *Arizona Jim*, stammers his gratitude, "No, no, no. I'm dreaming. It's impossible," but still starts to read the paper Batala has asked him to sign. Batala stops him immediately with an elaborate ceremony of the presentation and lighting of a cigarette. Lange, who doesn't smoke, is completely distracted. Returning to business, Batala jokes, "Just sign it. Don't bother to read it. It's useless. It's all bunk, red tape. Idiotic!" Lange happily helps him along, "Idiotic but necessary," and blithely signs away his cherished work. Later when Lange complains about Arizona Jim taking Ranimax pills, Batala again quickly disarms him with a ritual cigarette and Lange's accusation dies.

On the train, Batala politely inquiries of the priest, "Will the smoke bother you?" "Not at all," the priest replies, "I myself, from time to time, have an innocent cigarette." Batala remarks, "A priest is a man like any other [*un homme comme un autre*]," and the two soon nod in agreement about the evils of the age: "Quelle époque!"

When next we see Batala, he has adopted not only the cassock of a priest but the gestures and vocabulary as well. All that wit and energy and talent, with its compulsion to destroy what it cannot dominate, now stands wrapped in the cloth of sanctity. Surprised by Lange in his old office, Batala turns with a gesture of revelation, but the light on his face shows him as purely demonic. "It's my costume that shocks you?" he asks, posing to show it off. Seeing surprise and anger still in Lange's face, Batala resorts to his old reliable device, "Have a cigarette—an innocent cigarette." But Lange and the court are no longer his. Lange does not even acknowledge the offer, but Batala seems not to see the significance of the refusal. Lange will not be manipulated; yet Batala stages his finest performance in this scene, alternating between the roles of the priest and the old Batala. He accepts the 12,000 francs Lange offers him, remarking, "For my poor? A priest has no needs; he has responsibilities," praises the virtues of work with a gesture of benediction, gleefully spreads his hands as he proclaims, "I want it all! It's all mine!"

Here the moral-political edge of the satire cuts deepest, as this priest-charlatan, swindler, seducer, big-business man states his view of the cooperative: "Ha! Cooperatives! But what's that, a cooperative? It's ridiculous, old man, it's . . . it's all screwed up—chaos! I swear! Everybody's in charge! The bill-poster gives his opinion. Oh, no! What's necessary is authority, someone who gives orders, a man! Me! Ha! And then if I feel like it, I'll throw everyone out the door!"

So swept along by his own performance that he hardly notices how Lange fails to respond, Batala cannot resist the ultimate dramatic gesture of suggesting to Lange the solution of his problem: "You should kill me." Uttered as a mocking denial of Lange's power to intervene, this is heard by Lange instead as a real possibility; "Who would miss you?" he asks. And in the most revealing and memorable image in the film, Batala sweeps his black hat through the air in a magnificent gesture, his face alight with the joy of his own performance, a delight in his way with women and a sense of his own consummate charm. "Les femmes, mon vieux!"—the perfect exit line, and he literally dances into the shadows and away. So superb is this performance, and so convincing to Batala himself, that when, a few moments later, Lange shoots him in the corner of the court, Batala's reaction is not so much fear or anger as sheer astonishment that anyone could do this to him—at the shot he cries, "Are you crazy?" voiced in the idiom of literary circles, "T'es sonnée, toi, mon vieux?" If Lange's fantasy life as Arizona Jim has led him to act as defender of the community, quite a different fantasy has driven Batala into the corner where he dies.

Though cynical and ruthless, Batala is also sentimental about his conquests, warm and enthusiastic about all of his projects, and more than half convinced of their genuineness: "Nothing is impossible with a man like me." Though Lange is the author of *Arizona Jim*, it is Batala who exhibits a genuine literary flair; hence young Meunier's remark that he loves *Arizona Jim*, especially the parts about Ranimax pills, may not be mere idiocy but perhaps rather shows an eye for style and a genuine basis for Batala's dubious

Batala.

schemes. The incantation with which he describes his illusory detective magazine, *Javert, hebdomadaire litteraire et policier, une enterprise magnifique*, reveals both the con man's guile and Batala's dream. But the dream withers; the schemer prevails, and, with all his energy and talent, Batala remains a deceiver cruelly deceived, a half-step ahead of the failure of his last idea. He learns a whole new repertoire of ecclesiastical gestures and phrases, but cannot see the uselessness of his own life and dies playing out the irony of his final role, a false priest who believes in the possibility of his own salvation. Whether or not one takes this as an image of laissez-faire capitalism, Jules Berry's creation of Batala remains one of the truly great performances in French cinema.

The character Lange, hesitant, awkward, shy, never calls attention to himself as Batala does and seldom dominates a scene; hence René Lefèvre's performance is less noticeable than Berry's. But it seems no less perfect, though constructed of almost opposite elements. Berry's facial expression changes rapidly; his reactions are both quicker and more effusive than those of others. Often he seems to register three different expressions before anyone else has begun to react. His hands constantly move; his body seems always prepared for action. Alert and attentive to others, he manages also to register Batala's inner reactions in brief expressive asides. Lefèvre's reactions, in contrast, are slightly slower than those of others and less diverse. His expressions range only through variations on the slightly puzzled, uncertain, but friendly smile with which Lange naturally greets the world, or an equally puzzled but grave expression that appears when he is troubled. His hands are characteristically still, his bodily movements slow and ungraceful. He usually looks away from the person he addresses, invariably becoming most animated and attentive at the mention of Arizona or Mexico. He talks clearly but with a flatness of tone and grammatical formation that increases his air of being not quite in touch with others. "Il est toujours ailleurs," as Valentine says.

Valentine describes Lange as a dreamer. The women in the court think him mad. Batala, trying to discourage Valentine, tells her that Lange needs cold compresses. But Lange is the most innocent and gentle of creatures, his strangeness more an estrangement from the world than any actual deficiency of his own. It is not, however, the estrangement of a Legrand, who held his colleagues and their world in contempt. Lange seems happy with his fellow-workers, but the workday world that forms the center of their lives provides for him only an interlude separating the nights when his fantasies of Arizona create a world much more exciting than the Paris that surrounds him. Renoir shows this nocturnal life of Lange in a single shot, the first cyclical shot of the film—an epitomizing shot, though here it functions as introduction rather than summary: Dissolve from Valentine in the Hotel de la Frontière to a medium shot of Lange at his desk. He begins to read aloud what he has written; the camera moves over his left shoulder to the wall behind him, where a cowboy hat, gun, and leather vest hang. As Lange continues to read, the camera pans right, over his head and past gun belts, rifles, chaps, a large map with Arizona heavily outlined, bridles and an Indian head-dress. It then pans left at a lower level across Lange's bed, where the little black dog lies, returning past another cowboy hat to Lange wildly waving his arms. During this exploratory camera movement Lange has read, with increasing excitement in his voice: "Straddling the limb the Negro-killer smiled and pushed the poor Negro into the void. All the fine gentlemen broke into laughter. And a shot rang out. The rope broke. The Negro is saved. 'Hands up!' And all the fine gentlemen reached for the sky. Arizona Jim . . . Arizona Jim . . . killed one or two of them . . . and set off again at a gallop . . . carrying off the Negro . . . in a cloud of dust."

As he ecstatically recites the final phrase, "un nuage de poussière," Lange's action matches his imagination: he claps his hands and stamps his feet in a rhythm as rapid as the music that accompanies the shot. An alarm clock rings; the sound of church bells interrupts the music, signalling the beginning of the day and the end of Lange's nocturnal fantasy. Cut to the street, where M. Besnard slowly pushes open the gate to the court.

The development of Lange's character through the first half of the film builds upon the traits comically ascribed here: a childish enthusiasm and naivete, a concern for justice and the fate of the downtrodden, an inattention to the normal activities of the ordinary world. The sweet innocence of Lange's look, the awkwardness of his gait, his hesitancy in almost every situation, convey the unworldliness which assures us that, for Lange, Arizona Jim is more real than Batala. Lange describes to Valentine the hardness of life in Arizona, where bandits rob the poor, but to her question, "What about here? Who robs the poor?" he replies, "I don't know. I never go out." Her repeated suggestion that she likes only love stories leads him only to fondle the dog and repeat bemusedly, "D'amour." His reactions to people are as different as possible from Batala's manipulative and performed responses, and thus less flattering. His attention wanders; he never touches anyone except to shake hands. Only once does he act independently and decisively, and this in a scene evocative of Arizona Jim: everyone stands looking at the injured Charles; Lange climbs into the cab and orders it to the hospital. Otherwise, he seems so unsure of himself that most of his actions appear to be suggested by others: Valentine asks why he doesn't have Batala publish his "Indian Stories"; a few shots later some pages of Arizona Jim happen to be under the copy Lange shows Batala. After Valentine's talk of love, Lange asks Estelle for a date, and though it was obvious in Batala's office that Lange did not smoke, he comes to his date equipped with cigarettes, ready to imitate Batala as a way to overcome Estelle's resistance. He fails, of course; manipulation is not his forte. Estelle takes the cigarette he offers, then throws it away, saying, "I never smoke," and breaks off the date, leaving Lange standing uncomfortably on the curb while she rides off on a bus. To hide his discomfort, Lange takes a cigarette himself, then a fat streetwalker succeeds where he had failed, using the cigarettes to create a relationship within which he will accept her invitation, "You walking alone, cheri? . . . Come and have a little fun." Lange throws away his cigarette and follows her, not so much from desire as from indecision once again resolved by someone else's suggestion.

Unexpectedly, this leads to self-knowledge and growth. Heretofore,

Lange has denied what was apparent to all, his shyness with women; now to impress Charles, he combines his adventures with Estelle and the whore into a single event, boasting of his conquest of Estelle with the help of "des Camels." Charles' violent reaction finally awakens Lange to what everyone has known, that Charles loves Estelle, and he admits his boast was just invention. "But why did you lie?" Charles asks; a chastened Lange answers quietly, "Because I'm a fool."—doubly, he may see, a fool to claim to be someone he isn't and a fool to be so unobservant of the life of this boy he calls his friend. This moment of self-awareness occurs midway through the film. Thereafter, Lange does not cease to be a dreamer, but he stops being a fool.

He now notices the world around him, and, the opposite of Batala, he acts in ways which bring people together. Not as a strategy but in sympathetic response to the situations he finds, the dreamer unites where the schemer divides. Called on to speak at the party, Lange can only say how happy he is that they are all there together. After the first "death" of Batala and the awakening of Lange, lovers come together; the cooperative flourishes; Lange's episodes of *Arizona Jim* bring even the concierge and his wife into the community, while the missing Batala becomes the masked bandit. Lange may finally have found the answer to Valentine's question, "What about life here? Who robs the poor?" But in drawing everyone into his story, he has lost the distinction between the real world of the court and the fantasy world of Arizona Jim. He is, to be sure, in love with Valentine; his voice is firmer, his walk more assured, but the map of Arizona hangs on the office wall and Lange wears chaps and a leather vest. Posed in his cowboy regalia by the fake desert scenery in the courtyard, Lange, with his sweet gentle look, hardly appears a hardened rider of the purple sage, but he so identifies with the role that he opposes the idea of making a movie, because "we'll have to use those phony sets."

Young Meunier's response to the request that he say a few words at the party well expresses this blurring of the line between fantasy and reality: "I want to say a few words to congratulate Arizona—no, no—Arizona Jim—no—to congratulate the author, the author, of *Arizona Jim*." This blur makes possible the murder of Batala; for when Batala returns, he comes, indeed, in the guise of the masked bandit. His appearance does not disturb the fantasy, but confirms it; his priestly garb and ecclesiastical gestures have as little relation to reality as Lange's cowboy hat. Just a few hours before, Lange had written of the masked bandit odiously. abusing Estelle. Now, with a mocking laugh, this Batala in disguise sweeps from the office, and Lange, immobile by the window, hears him a moment later in the court with Valentine. Arizona Jim—no, "l'auteur d' *Arizona Jim*"—takes the gun from the desk and moves toward the court. Lange is as astonished by the murder as is Batala; for Arizona Jim has killed the masked bandit, but there in the corner of the court lies Batala, *un homme comme un autre*. Lange asks dazedly, "Is he dead? How easy it is!" The fantasy shatters, destroying with it the Lange who had become a central figure in the life of the court. We cannot know what man will be reborn in that walk across the dunes.

The moral import of Renoir's films more often emerges from his conception of characters and his expressive use of cinematic form than from the plot or story. *Le Crime de M. Lange* is perhaps more explicit in its moral attitudes than other Renoir works, but many of his films show the same moral outlook. Details differ, but each in its way reveals the price we humans often pay for our separateness, and for our avoidance of love by imposing on it our conditions, our image, our pride, and our fear. Thus the most profoundly moral events in a Renoir film occur at the rare moments when love penetrates the masks, and a character cannot help but see himself aright. In those terms Lange becomes, perhaps, the ultimate Renoir hero; he not only has his moment of insight, but henceforth every action of his, including his crime, is an act of love.

If Batala is the most evil of Renoir characters, Valentine stands near the opposite pole. Loving and supportive of Lange, kind and understanding with the girls who work in her laundry, she defends the young lovers, Charles and Estelle, and organizes the party that celebrates the joy the cooperative has brought to the court. The most sensible major character in the film, she talks sympathetically with Lange when others regard him as a fool, encourages him to publish his stories and urges him to complain to Batala when Ranimax pills appear mysteriously in the hands of Arizona Jim. She has already seen through Batala. In their first encounter she tells him, "When I think that I used to sleep with you, it gives me *mal de mer*." When he appeals to her to help an old friend adrift, she merely fingers the expensive cloth of his coat and remarks that he probably wants a little extra money for the sleeping car. She refuses to be used, repulses him verbally at every meeting and tells everyone that he is a *salaud*. But she does not always treat him so harshly. She lets him hold her while he extols, "Javert, . . .," invites him into her office when he comes to the window. Such behavior may demonstrate how free and strong Valentine is, but Batala, not a man to be impressed by mere words, and even more self-confident than she, is not discouraged from renewing his advances. Thus Valentine innocently becomes instrumental in Batala's death, when, his voice rich with nostalgia and desire, he greets her, "Toujours belle, Valentine!" and cannot resist drawing her into the shadows under the window where Lange stands. She is also, of course, Lange's defender at the Hotel de la Frontière.

In conception, Valentine is a major figure in this film, a character whose good sense and forthright acts contrast strongly with other characters. Unfortunately, Florelle's performance makes Valentine the least credible person in the film. Virtue and strength are not inherently incredible, but now and then a note of falsity in gesture or intonation shakes our belief in this character. Only a minute difference separates an authentic gesture from a false one—a matter of exact timing and slight degrees of emphasis—and often Florelle overshoots the mark. Perhaps her theatrical style ill-befits the naturalistic scene of this film, but her laughter seems forced, the toss of her head exaggerated, her movements sometimes calculated rather than spontaneous. She is most incredible when she sings to Lange; here Renoir's penchant for inserting a song into the texture of his film has gone awry. Usually, these songs provide a background to the action, but this one occupies the foreground and interrupts the movement of the film. For Florelle sings, not in the manner of Anne-Marie singing as she dusts, but as if on a stage and with an accompaniment of external music. Even Lange looks uncomfortable.

In Renoir's films of the thirties, this is the only occasion when a singing character is accompanied by background music. Renoir says of this, "Jean Wiener was doing the music for this film, but I had just met Kosma and wanted to use some music of his. And I thought it would make the character of Valentine more interesting and a little mysterious to suggest in the song that she had once been a prostitute. Also I used this music to create a contrast in the sound of the film. It is unreal, of course—but everything in the film is unreal."

This is true, and the song, coming immediately after Edith has walked from the railroad platform with the man she has caught with her tears and hankerchief, suggests not only Valentine's past but also Edith's future. Still, all the other unrealities in *Le Crime de M. Lange* fit together so persuasively that we do not notice their incredibility, while this one shouts for recognition.

Florelle's performance seems the major flaw in the film, but does not greatly weaken it. The scenes move so swiftly and with so much life that our doubts about Valentine hardly disturb our immersion in the world of the court.

No similar problem mars our view of Edith or Estelle. Sylvia Bataille plays Edith as a young woman with a tough exterior and inner doubts, in love with Batala, jealous but wholly unable to cope with him. She shrugs in bewilderment when he treats her as a confederate instead of a lover, telling her that Baigneur is "tres amoureux de toi," and that he has lots of money. She has no defense against his attempt to send her to Baigneur, despite her repugnance for the task; he knows precisely how to override her hesitant protests by just presuming her already hardened and experienced enough to play that game. She isn't, of course; she returns quickly and almost empty-handed. In the catalogue of Renoir characters, Edith is a fledgling destructive female, but learning fast. Finding Batala about to abandon her, she asks, "What will I do now?" and follows his advice so well that she never

Edith, abandoned by Batala, follows his advice.

returns to the court. Though she tells Batala that Baigneur disgusts her, the man she picks up in the railroad station so much resembles him that some critics think the roles were played by the same actor. And the look behind her tears as she walks off with him is cold and hard enough to make us wonder about the poor man's fate.

After Valentine reminds him of love, Lange watches Edith walk up the stairs, but it is Estelle he asks for a date. Despite his denials of shyness, Estelle may be the only female whom Lange could approach. Both Edith and Valentine appear strong and assured; Estelle, tiny, frail, with a small voice —a *blanchisseuse* and most insecure—seems so vulnerable, so mild and unaggressive that even Lange feels confident in her presence. Events confirm the appearance of helplessness: Estelle faints in Batala's arms when Charles has his accident; she walks away puzzled, hurt, forlorn, but unprotesting when Mme. Besnard denies her request to see Charles; she appears transfixed by terror when Batala locks his office door and turns with his wicked smile. Finding herself pregnant, she wants to die, plans to leave without seeing Charles, and is saved only by Lange's removal of the billboard—for both Charles and the little black dog demonstrate their love immediately. Through these scenes Nadia Sibirskaia makes Estelle a timorous little animal, ready to turn and run if a threatening hand is raised. But even she can resist Lange's awkward attempt at seduction. Despite her curly hair and fair skin, he tells her she looks Mexican, thereby making himself feel like Arizona Jim and able to act confidently. But Estelle's honesty and Lange's innocence soon turn this project upside down; instead of Lange seducing Estelle, she describes the enterprise to him. Here Renoir cuts to a big close-up and, in a moment that pierces the surface of the film and reveals the depths of a soul, Estelle tells of a painful incident in her childhood, then, in medium shot, with her voice husky and sad, tells Lange how she said, "no," to Charles who asked so nicely, so sweetly, and promised to love her forever. Heretofore Estelle has been merely a pretty little laundress; now, in the park with Lange, she appears far more beautiful. The curving brim of a hat frames her small symmetrical face, with its wide eyes and prominent cheekbones; she has an intensity and seriousness not visible before. Then she turns her head, raises her chin—the light cuts her nose in half; one cheekbone is high-lighted, the other dull. The wide eyes become catlike. The symmetry of the face vanishes; the hat that had been a foil for that symmetry suddenly accentuates the lopsidedness. Estelle lowers her head and her beauty reappears, but not until we have seen its fleetingness and, as it were, her mortality, and perhaps felt with a pang the deep sadness of her life. A sadness banished by the cooperative, however—if the political allegory of the film makes Estelle the most pitiful victim of ruthless exploitation, she and Charles, the injured innocents, become the joyful symbol of the reign of love once the exploiters are expropriated.

The women in Le Crime de M. Lange are not comic characters. But social satire colors the conception of the male roles. All the fascination and menace of power are concentrated in Batala; the three capitalists—Buisson, Baigneur, and Meunier, fils—appear more ludicrous than hateful. Buisson, readily corruptible, proves to be a lackey, a yes-man not averse to a bit of blackmail on the side. Baigneur, whose supercilious air and precise diction create an air of superiority, is in fact more susceptible to Batala's blandishments than his dog, Daisy, and pays more attention to the passing girls than to the fortunes of les pillules Ranimax. Meunier, an amiable young moron who hates bow ties, agrees to the cooperative simply because Buisson opposes it. Several notches lower in status, Inspector Juliani (Sylvain Itkine), though more recently a croupier, still uses his official title when he thinks it might be impressive—a habit that costs Batala his business.

The texture of the film, achieving a sense of genuine life by weaving together absurd people and incredible events—requires a credibility in these minor parts, the attainment of which seems no more a function of internal consistency and the skill of the actors than of the solidity and authenticity of Renoir's construction of the containing world of the court. The workers provide the core of this authenticity, without themselves developing individual identity; the flow of motion in print-shop, laundry, and courtyard seems wholly natural, though its rhythm is often as intricate and precise as a ballet. André Bazin has noted how Renoir and his actors seem to forget the camera and become their own audience, playing for each other with an obvious delight in the performance and a sort of complicity that may leave the spectator feeling left out of the fun.[7] In Le Crime de M. Lange the vitality of the court flows over us; we can hardly help joining in—at least to the extent of happily accepting all of its absurdity as the very breath of life.

The secondary and background characters fill the world of the film almost to overflowing, without ever competing for the center of our attention. But the one performance which, surprisingly, grows to major proportions is that of Marcel Levesque as M. Besnard, the concierge, who, through the whole final segment of the film, almost single-handedly provides a counterpoint to the confrontation of Batala and Lange.

Marcel Levesque was a well-known actor in French silent films, playing substantial roles as early as Feuillade's *Les Vampires* (1915), but he disappeared from the screen with the coming of sound. Recalled from oblivion by Renoir, his performance in *Le Crime de M. Lange* becomes almost as memorable as that of Jules Berry. Through sixty-eight minutes of the film, M. Besnard seems just one of several satiric sketches that collectively condemn the bourgeois-capitalist society in which Batala flourishes. He wanders stiffly around the court, muttering about his misery and refusing to admit any responsibility, whether for the plumbing or the billboard that keeps the light from his son's room. Whenever possible, his talk reverts to the "militaire" and the Indo-China campaign, which left him an expert on Indians and blacks, as well as Southeast Asians. A firm believer in authority, he gladly anticipates Batala's need for money and defends the billboard even after Batala is presumed dead. His promotion to being a Mexican general seems appropriate; one critic calls him "certainly one of the *Croix de Feu*."

An amusing portrait of an old imbecile—but then, in the thirteen minutes of the party scene, M. Besnard becomes the source for the rhythm on which the scene is built. Explaining "everytime it's late and I'm drunk, I think it's Christmas Eve," he sings "C'est la nuit de Noël," which then serves as the musical accompaniment for Batala's death, while his drunken lurching through the courtyard creates the rhythmic motion that Renoir uses to balance the tense and almost motionless encounter of Lange and Batala. Though the concierge, in a sense, does nothing in the scene, he plays a cru-

cial role in this denouement of the film. His surprised cry, "Un mourant!" brings Valentine into the court where she finds Batala and immediately becomes the object of his "pilgrimage." A few moments later M. Besnard almost stumbles over Batala stretched across the little fountain. Drunk as he is, the habit of subservience is so ingrained that his start of recognition, "O-oh, Bata—," stops in mid-word and he finishes "Monsieur Batala." Batala grimaces, "I'm dying. Find a priest." The concierge reels away, shouting, "Un prêtre!" But ever since he had left the party to care for his garbage pails, M. Besnard has been completely lost in this courtyard that is his own domain, and now the revellers inside shut the doors and windows against one more idiocy from this drunken fool. Totally out of touch with the world, he staggers through the court, "Un prêtre! Un prêtre!" The camera follows him from door to window to midcourt, then, in the last of those circular pans, makes one final sweep of the court to Batala, now dead facedown in the corner, a black rag thrown across the familiar gray cobblestones.

In this thirteen minutes, the two performances by Jules Berry and Marcel Levesque combine with the visual rhythms of the scene to give the sequence a unity and power that lifts it above the rest of the film. The final shot, with its search of the empty courtyard, both a last glimpse of this place which has held the life of the film and a return to the unmasked bandit who would have destroyed it, while the drunken cry "Un prêtre!" still echoes over the stones, brings to a rather stunning conclusion that strand of satire linking army, priests, and evil employers as enemies of the people. And if *Le Crime de M. Lange* began with a plot from *La Chienne*, it ends with a foretaste of *La Regle du Jeu*, thus earning its reputation as the pivotal work in the Renoir films of the thirties.

Style and Form

In both *Madame Bovary* and *Toni*, some aspects of form are presented so consistently that they must become apparent to every viewer—for example, the distancing classicism of *Madame Bovary* and the starkly unadorned surface of *Toni*. But *Le Crime de M. Lange* seems a reversion to the style of *Boudu*, where, however important the form is in shaping our impression of persons and events, it seldom becomes an object of explicit awareness. Most of us think about the happenings in films very much as we do the events in our lives, so we are little more inclined to notice the formal dimensions of these happenings than we are of this morning's shopping trip or last night's date.

The enclosing scenes at the frontier cast the development of *Le Crime de M. Lange* in an overall cyclical form that we cannot help but notice, but apart from this and the characters and story, audiences seem aware primar-

"Un Prêtre." The death of Batala. M. Besnard (Marcel Levesque) and Batala.

ily of the rapidity of the flow of events and the vivacity of the life portrayed. The cyclical form is familiar—Renoir has often sought closure in a
shot, a scene, or a whole film. Here he imposes a spatio-temporal circularity
on a linear narrative via the temporal discontinuity of the opening scenes;
the closure occurs not within the lives of the characters, but in the form in
which the narrative is cast. Hence, it might seem more arbitrary than the
cyclical forms of *Boudu* or *Toni*, were it not reaffirmed by myriad smaller

"C'est la nuit de noel." M. Besnard sings. Meunier, *fils* (Henri Guisol) and M. Lange say a few words. Meanwhile, Batala returns.

forms within the film. Most obvious, perhaps, are the recurrent camera movements that loop back upon themselves; but a wealth of additional internal cycles and correspondences supplement these. One type is a circle within the action, as in that party scene which both begins and ends with M. Besnard standing up to sing, "C'est la nuit de Noël." Another is the sort of linking correspondence, already noted, between the path of Batala from courtyard to office early in the film and the reversal of this path by Lange at film's end. A counterpart to the shots with the looping camera are those with minimal camera movement, but where the movement within the shot forms a cyclical pattern. The shot that introduces M. Baigneur provides a fine example of this: with the camera positioned near Batala's office, viewing the length of the composing room, the shot opens on a quiet scene, four men working at their tables in the depths of the room. Then the scene springs to life: Valentine enters from lower right and walks into the composing room; Louis comes up the circular stair as Lange leads Baigneur down the stair in the far background, upper left screen. The four men working become six, then seven, as they move apart and out from behind the machines. Lange and Baigneur thread their way through the room from background to foreground. Louis and Valentine circle; Louis recedes into the background while Valentine goes down the circular stair. Lange and Baigneur exit, right foreground, exactly where Valentine entered. The seven men at work have merged back into four; the last frames of the shot look almost exactly like the first few. This shot displays the rhythm and timing of a dance in an intricate pattern involving a dozen characters, but its aural accompaniment is conversation about Batala's publications: *La cuisse de Paris*, *Les grandes manoeuvres de la môme Cracra*. Within the solid background of work that sustains Batala's flimsy enterprises, Renoir creates revealing glimpses of Baigneur, Valentine, and Batala and immerses us in the teeming life of this little community—all in a single shot whose form reinforces the structure of cyclical forms that underlies the unity of the film.

As one further example of cyclical structure, I may cite a larger pattern involving both dramatic and visual forms. *Le Crime de M. Lange* develops initially through a series of encounters, each involving two persons. This isolation of people in pairs—characteristic of Batala's organization of the world—prevails in neither the Hotel de la Frontière nor in the court during the period of Batala's feigned death. But it dominates the early development in the court, and Renoir casts the whole opening segment of twenty-five shots into a cyclical pattern by linking these encounters in a loose version of the form of *La Ronde*, where one of the two persons in each encounter appears as a participant in the succeeding one. Through four shots, whose action might be called the choreography of the court, the camera moves with M. Besnard from the street through the court, in the door and up the curving stair, until Valentine passes the concierge on the stairs. There follows a series of two-person scenes—Valentine and Lange, Charles and Estelle, Estelle and Lange, Lange and Valentine, etc.—punctuated by the flow of workers into the court and marred by the discord that arises when three characters, Valentine, Batala, and Edith, come together in the same shot. The sequence concludes with the choreography of the composing room, described above, achieving its closure with the movement of Valentine down the circular stair. In its cycle it has introduced the court and all of the characters and has identified the significant relations between them. As it ends, the arrival of Baigneur adds a new twist to the intrigue.

The locale adds one more dimension to these cyclical patterns. The building completely surrounds a courtyard paved with cobblestones laid in concentric circles. The arcs of camera movement here seem merely to echo the form of the setting itself. This and the cyclical forms that precede it prepare us to accept the bizarre and brilliant camera movement of the murder scene as absolutely right. Two earlier shots have a special role in this preparation: first, the loop of the camera from the billboard up and across the second-story windows and then back to the billboard to catch Meunier, whom we have just seen in a window, running into the frame to greet Lange; second, the circle of the camera around the court following the drunken concierge with his garbage pail.

The climactic moment begins in a corner of the court, where Batala mocks Valentine's love for Lange, "le soleil de Mexique . . . " The camera lifts diagonally up the face of the building to the window where Lange stands. As he moves, the camera follows across the office and composing room, with Lange reappearing at each window. The camera lowers as he runs down the stairs and meets him as he comes through the door and pauses. Cut from three-quarter to medium shot, then, as Lange moves forward, the camera turns its back on him, panning 180 degrees around the court to complete the circle begun in the preceding shot and reframe Valentine and Batala a second before Lange enters the frame and shoots Batala. André Bazin wrote: "This astonishing camera movement, apparently contrary to all logic, has perhaps some secondary justification, psychological or dramatic (it gives an impression of vertigo, of madness; it creates suspense) but its reason for being is more essential; it is the pure spatial expression of the whole construction of the film."[8] But it becomes such a pure expression only by being the dramatic consummation of the whole encompassing structure of cyclical forms.

Thus, the overall cyclical form created by the frontier scenes is merely a shell containing a rich organization of similar forms, with the sweeping circle of the murder scene at its center. I add only one final remark about this proliferation of cycles. The final shot in the court, with the concierge shouting, "Un prêtre!" and the camera finally turning its back on him to make one last circle of the court and end on Batala's corpse, is both the visual and dramatic counterpart of the choreography of the court with which the story began.

None of these circles is perfect, of course; we hardly expect that from Renoir. But in their overlapping, enclosing, opposing relations to each other they build the coherence of the film and its feeling of unity within diversity. The dramatic development, though complex in detail, is relatively simple in total structure. The first half of the film presents a series of two-person en-

Le crime de M. Lange.

counters in which the attempt of one person to establish a certain relationship always fails. The only persons who succeed are Batala and the plump streetwalker, who do not seek to create relationships but to manipulate others. Through this series of failures, our sense of the vitality of the life of the court is sustained by a different sort of success, the success of the recurrent cyclical forms in achieving completion and closure. Once Batala leaves the court, the two-person encounters give way to group scenes and mutually supportive relationships spring up all over—Lange and Valentine, Estelle and Charles, the workers and the financiers, the print-shop cooperative and its enthusiastic audience of *Arizona Jim* fans. Now the cyclical forms reinforce the joyful expression of accomplishment generated within the dramatic development. For example, our sense of the triumph achieved when the billboard comes down is surely enhanced by the closure of the looping camera movement and the convergence of all the physical motion within the scene just before the panel pulls away from the wall.

The return of Batala brings these two segments of the dramatic development into conflict; his divisive presence threatens the unions achieved within the court—a situation visually expressed by Renoir's alternation between the happy group scene of the party and the tense two-person encounter between Lange and Batala. And the cyclical forms that appeared almost randomly before now seem purposive, as the camera moves in everwidening arcs toward that climactic shot which encircles and thus unites the whole court in its rejection of Batala's proposed return.

The elements of visual style characteristic of Renoir appear in *Le Crime de M. Lange* in variations appropriate to this film. The fluid, exploratory camera finds its home in the courtyard; in these exterior scenes two out of three shots involve camera movement and, more than ever before, complicated, zigzagging, or looping movements bring as much action as possible into a single shot. This high ratio of moving-camera shots drops sharply in interior scenes, where Renoir relies instead on deep-focus cinematography, often creating a long, narrow action-space in which foreground and background simultaneously hold significant components of action. Not only the men in the printshop, but the women in Valentine's laundry as well, provide Renoir scope for a further exploration of the camaraderie of work and the creation of rhythm within a shot by the movement of people engaged in cooperative activity. This internal rhythm, with that of the looping camera, provides the major rhythmic structure of the film. With less than 200 shots in the eighty-odd minutes of the film, cutting rhythms play a subordinate role, but Renoir's concatenation of many short scenes, each usually completed in from one to six shots, makes for great rapidity of development.

Within this familiar visual style a few surprises occur, and most of them appear to be parodies of the film conventions of the day. For example, a first "establishing" shot establishes nothing, but quickly cuts to a characteristic Renoir opening shot that begins with a close-up of a bottle of homemade gin. The shots of the car speeding down an empty road are clichés of the chase, but done as intentional clichés, with overly dramatic music, obvious cinematography, and no one chasing.

One visual innovation wholly integrated into the film is the dance of *Arizona Jim* covers, which conveys the reality, progress, and success of the cooperative in a single montage-set. As everyone's face finally shows up on a cover, Renoir condenses time, action, and development enormously within a singly witty scene, while fully maintaining the pace and tone of the film.

Once again, the greatest departure occurs in the dimension of sound rather than sight. On the sound track, the hand of Prévert shows most clearly. Except for *On purge bébé*, Renoir films of the early thirties are not marked by verbal cleverness. Critics of the time who admired the theatrical films that held the field often found Renoir's dialogue dull and welcomed his collaboration with Prévert, generally regarded as the best French screenwriter of the day. The dialogue of *Le Crime de M. Lange* does have an unfamiliar wit and caustic bite, imparting a crackle to the rapidly-spoken lines, a quality rare in Renoir films after *On purge bébé*. Varieties of word play run through the film, with frequent repetition of words or phrases in contexts where the repetition evokes something of a revelation: *un homme comme un autre, quelle époque, une innocente cigarette, quel drôle de monde— drôle de mort.*

Also, the content of the dialogue plays a larger role in characterization. Renoir's tendency had been to use dialogue as one dimension of sound and to define and reveal his characters more by action, gesture, and intonation than by words. Now, with Jacques Prévert writing the dialogue and standing beside Renoir on the set, the weight of characterization shifts a bit toward description and conversation.

In this respect an illuminating comparison might be made with the Prévert-Carne *Le Jour se lève*, where Jules Berry plays a role very similar to that of Batala, but where, until late in the film, this reputedly evil character is defined essentially by descriptions given by Arletty. In *Le Crime de M. Lange* someone else, at some time, describes almost every important character, but these descriptions are sometimes wild—as when Mme. Besnard describes Lange as "un vrai satyre"—and, even when accurate, they serve more to confirm than to constitute the characterization. Intonation still carries much weight in creating character; Lange's voice grows firmer and more assured with his success, then, when he shoots Batala, he suddenly reverts to the puzzled, hesitant tone of the beginning. And Batala's voice dominates the sound track, as his visual presence dominates every scene he is in; it is the richest, most expressive sound in the film.

Apart from the unobtrusive, lyrical Milhaud score for *Madame Bovary*, the earlier Renoir sound films have no background music. Now, suddenly, in *Le Crime de M. Lange*, loud and sometimes unmelodious music breaks in to accompany the action or sustain the emotional tone of a scene. Perhaps the necessity for this grows from the montage of *Arizona Jim* covers, which requires supporting music that will suit the animation-like technique of the scene. The score as a whole has little coherence despite repetition of the chase music and the two songs. I am not sure how this sounded in 1936; now, much of the music sounds comic or overdone. Audiences laugh at the dramatic burst of musical sound when Batala turns from the locked door to a terrified Estelle. I believe that much of this external music is best heard as parody; only as such does it really cohere with the rest of the film. Fortunately, Renoir does not allow its presence to prevent him from enriching the world of the court with its own internal music. Someone, somewhere in the court, practices on a violin, church bells ring, and the party scene provides its own music as the uncoordinated voices of the cooperative take up the concierge's "C'est la nuit de Noël"—a song much more tellingly integrated into the action of the film than Valentine's "Au jour, le jour."

Le Crime de M. Lange had only indifferent success on its release in France and, like several other Renoir films, has at times been suppressed by the censors. Despite the degree to which its biting social comment is covered over with the sprightly facade of a farce and warmed by Renoir's humanity, the French filmgoer was uncomfortable with a film that posed a serious moral question, and certainly with one that gave a verdict in favor of murder—not that he might not agree with the verdict, but rather he did not expect that sort of thing in a film. Critics did not treat the film harshly, nor were audiences outraged as they had been at Boudu. But neither did they welcome it with joy. Like other Renoir films, it somehow survived and in the 1960s finally reached the United States, where Bosley Crowther pronounced it a "complete antique" which would not stand comparison with the technically more expert films of a later day (1964). But the American discovery of Renoir in the late sixties has brought a new generation of prints with better subtitles and has stirred greater critical enthusiasm, as in Penelope Gilliatt's, "See it, instead of any of the week's barren releases . . . After mediocre films M. Lange is like friendship after days of garbage on the telephone."

Recently, many critics have ranked Le Crime de M. Lange among the most significant films of the 1930s—clearly reflecting that period and the social consciousness stirring then, a film whose style and technique set it apart from its contemporaries. Pierre Leprohon writes: "The richness of such a film shows better retrospectively the absolutely original position of Jean Renoir in the cinema of his time. And precisely by that technique which he pretends to despise."[9] And in L'Encyclopédie du cinéma one finds: "They were even going so far as to indicate an economic, social, and political solution to the problem posed by exploitation: Le Crime de M. Lange is the only French film in which a cooperative organization has been seen taking into its own hands a production enterprise and making it prosper . . . [it] remains—from this particular point of view—the most 'advanced' film, not only in the work of Jean Renoir, but in all of French cinema until today."[10]

But in 1936 the one indubitable result of the release of this film, following on the heels of Toni, was to confirm for many the suspicion that Jean Renoir had become the cinematic spokesman for the Left, a reputation that was no doubt instrumental in his next engagement.

15

La Vie est à nous
1936

*At this time, the working masses no longer have a choice be-
tween bourgeois democracy and the dictatorship of the proletariat, but only between bourgeois democracy and fascism.*
—*Dimitrov*

*I found myself engaged without having sought for it. I was
the witness, voluntary or involuntary, of events which were
always stronger than my will. External facts, acting on me,
induced my convictions . . . What I see around me determines
my reactions. I am the victim, happily, of the environment.*
—*Jean Renoir*

In January of 1936, all Europe seemed poised on the threshold of fascism.
Right-wing dictatorships already ruled in Italy, Germany, Portugal, Austria, Poland, Yugoslavia, Greece, and Bulgaria; the remaining democracies,
weak and plagued by recurrent crises, seemed incapable of collective or effective action. Only the Soviet Union stood firmly opposed to fascism,
though itself considered an even graver threat by many Western European
capitalists, with the cry of anticommunism often camouflaging right-wing
bids for power. In France the paramilitary Croix de feu had grown from
sixty thousand members in 1933 to two million in 1936, and Colonel de La
Rocque seemed to have ambitions to become the French Hitler. A height-
ened sense of both danger and camaraderie grew among those on the Left,
and the Popular Front was born. Many Frenchmen who had not been politi-

cally active shared Jean Renoir's feeling that "any action that could be taken against Hitler was a duty."

In preparing for the May elections, the leaders of the Communist Party decided to commission a propaganda film to show at public meetings. Jean-Paul Le Chanois has said, "The idea came from Jacques Duclos, who had immediately seen the immense possibility of cinema . . . Pierre Unik and I had shaped up a first state of the project."[1] Reportedly, Louis Aragon first suggested that Jean Renoir be asked to supervise the work; at any event, he seemed the natural choice. He had just finished a film with obvious sympathy for the Left, the credits of which included many members of the militant *groupe Octobre*. Both his habit of-working with a group of comrades and his preference for constructing his films in relatively self-contained episodes lent themselves to this propaganda effort. And he was the acknowledged leader of a band of cinema workers with both talent and a leaning toward the political Left.

Renoir has said, "Some of my young friends asked me to help them make this film and I agreed. A few of them were Communists, but most of us weren't. The film is a collective work; I was to play the part of the producer, in the American sense of the term. At first I was not going to direct any of it. But the film was made quickly and with lots of confusion; as the work went on I did work with the actors one or two times. I directed the sequence with Nadia Sibirskaia, and I might have directed the scene of the schoolboys. I am not sure, but I remember that I selected the location for the scene in the street. Several of us, Le Chanois, Zwoboda, Cartier-Bresson, Jacques Becker and I, each directed some and I supervised it all. No one was paid for working on this film; everyone had other jobs, so it had to be made between jobs or after work. I don't think of it as my film, in the same sense as the others, because I didn't edit it. Oh, when we saw the rushes I would give some advice on the editing. I remember we made up a little dance for Colonel de La Rocque. But after the shooting I was working on another film, and I had nothing to do with editing this one. I never did see the finished picture in 1936. Then, of course, the Communists made a pact with Hitler, and we learned from that."

Something of the spirit in which *La Vie est à nous* was made is indicated by Nadia Sibirskaia: "One other time, Renoir invited us to a congress of the Communist Party. I hesitated a little, because I had never been political, but Renoir told me to take it or leave it. So I took it, out of friendship for him. All of Renoir's friends were there and then a big likable man I didn't know. I went toward him; I took him by his lapels, 'What's your name?' Everybody around me laughed; I didn't understand. And the big likable man told me, 'Me, I know you.' Ah? Finally someone did me the favor of telling me that I had just met Maurice Thorez. Thorez found that very funny and invited me to take a place beside him on the platform. I was completely panic-stricken.

Jacques Becker in his brief role as an unemployed film fan.

I hid, but someone found me and finally I accepted the place of honor. But afterwards, they wanted me to speak. Think of that, with my voice. I refused. That's how I too am in *La Vie est à nous*."[2]

Le Chanois says that the work was done in total freedom, "We had some conversations with Jacques Duclos who indicated the Party position in the Popular Front and in the campaign. But no one imposed a line of conduct on us." A report by Maurice Thorez to the Eighth Congress of the Parti communiste français purportedly supplied the outline for a script elaborated in collaboration by Le Chanois, Jacques Becker, Pierre Unik, Jacques Brunius, and Renoir. Some reports also claim that a Party leader, Vaillant-Couturier, had a hand in the script, but this has not been confirmed. Appropriately, *La Vie est à nous* was a collective work throughout. Scores of actors and technicians, the singers of the Chorale Populaire de Paris, hundreds of workers, gave their time to the project—cheered, no doubt by the Popular Front victory in the Spanish election of February 16, 1936, while the film was in the making. Still, on the question of whose film it is, Le Chanois says, "My feeling is very clear on that question; it was truly Renoir who made the film."[3]

The film was financed by contributions and cost about one-tenth of the usual budget for a French film at that time. Le Chanois remembers, "No one who worked on the film was paid. Still we had to have money for film, the lab, the studio, etc. So the Party took up collections at the end of its meetings; and as the people who came weren't very rich, they gave us mostly coins. So much that one day someone brought to me—on the sixth floor without an elevator—an enormous potato sack filled to bursting with coins that André Zwoboda and I spent one day and one night sorting and counting. There must have been fifty kilograms of coins that came to about 60,000 francs."[4]

Completed several weeks before the May election, *La Vie est à nous* was not distributed as a commercial film, but was projected without credits in private viewings at political meetings before the election. Reviews in 1936 described the film as banned by the censors, but Le Chanois claims it was never submitted for their approval: "First, because it seemed useless; this was before the 1936 election and the Popular Front victory and the film had no chance of passing. And then because the film had not at all been made for commercial distribution." Besides, given the political tension of the period and the film's treatment of Col. de La Rocque, one doubts that *La Vie est à nous* could have been shown publicly without provoking a violent reaction from the Croix de feu.

La Vie est à nous was accurately described by critics in 1936,[5] but seems to have disappeared after the election. Writers in the postwar period refer to it only vaguely, usually misdescribing it and identifying it as a short film running fifteen minutes. In 1969 a print was discovered by L'Avant-Scène, and *La Vie est à nous* then had its first public showing in Paris.

Jean Renoir first saw the film on July 2, 1973, a few days after a print had finally reached Los Angeles from Paris. "I was very happy to see this picture at last," he said. "I am glad to see the faces of so many old friends, a lot of them now dead. And it showed me again the faces of French workers. It's technically not very polished, that's evident. But for a picture made by twenty people, in such confusion, perhaps it's not so bad. And maybe something like this is more interesting now than it would have been then. We can accept the technical crudeness in an old picture—it has become a documentary now."

Conceived as a propaganda vehicle and therefore designed to achieve a particular political purpose at a specific historic moment, *La Vie est à nous* differs in both structure and content from Renoir's narrative films. Those films tell a story; this one presents an argument. Pierre Bost wrote in 1936, "*La Vie est à nous* is the first film-essay that has been offered us."[6] The term is not inappropriate, but one might add that the film is an essay written with passion and intended not only to inform but also to persuade. *La Vie est à nous* seeks to define the situation in France in 1936, propose a mode of action in response to this situation, and move its viewers to adopt this mode of action. To do this, it combines documentary footage with fictional scenes in a manner that tends progressively to obscure the distinction between them, its power as propaganda depending heavily on just this blurring of the line between actual and imaginary events.

Here too Renoir's previous predelictions were readily adapted to the task. Though all his earlier works are narrative fictional films, he had always had a tendency to include documentary elements in them, the riches of Algeria, the streets of Paris, the quarry at Martigues. Le Chanois says Renoir's influence was decisive in making *La Vie est à nous* this mixture of documentary and fiction. "Being a man of fiction films, he could not be content just to work out a documentary; he had to introduce the element of actors, of imagination, of play." Shooting fictional events in actual settings had long been Renoir's habit, but *La Vie est à nous* goes far beyond this, achieving a dramatic articulation of a political discourse by creating a dialectical interplay between dramatization and actual events—not an inappropriate method in a film commissioned by the PCF. Critics have found this the most original aspect of *La Vie est à nous*.

The film begins in classical documentary style: a sequence of unstaged shots accompanied by an anonymous commentary. The commentary describes the bounty of France, "one of the richest and most beautiful countries in the world," citing numbers of bushels of wheat, gallons of wine, acres of forests, etc. The images show the French countryside: long shots of sea, mountains, forests, vineyards; close shots of a tractor, a plow turning the earth, pine branches swayed by the wind, these edited in the Russian style of montage, with each image held for only two or three seconds. Apart from their succession there is no discernible temporal relation between the shots; so they become, in effect, timeless. Ordered and edited so as to create a rhythm of movement as well as a cutting rhythm, these shots also have a rhythmic relation to the commentary, which makes these words without an internal speaker seem to belong to the timeless images themselves and thus be heard as objective and indubitable, as happens in such documentaries.[7]

After twenty-eight shots—sixty-five seconds—cut to a low angle shot of Jean Dasté, speaking the lines of the commentary, with a rough outline of France on a blackboard behind him. This shot, held for nine seconds, totally changes the relation between the commentary and the preceding images. No longer do the words simply accompany merely factual pictures; rather, now the pictures have become illustrations of this man's speech. Cut again, to the back of the room, and a long shot reveals a classroom of schoolboys listening to their teacher—with a striking resemblance to the schoolroom of *Zéro de conduite*, complete with M. Huguet. The flow of pictures of France continues, progressing from nature to agriculture to industry, architecture, art, fashion, but now interspersed with shots of Dastè and the schoolboys, listening, laughing. What began as purely documentary images have become a part of this fictional scene, with the commentary not addressed to us, the viewers of the film, but to the schoolboys. Its objectivity dissolves; even if the words are true—and they do report authentic statistics of production—we can no longer hear them as telling us *the* truth about France, for this poor schoolroom shows us things that these words do not say.

The class ends; the boys file out as Dasté/Huguet mutters, "poor kids."

The kids emerge into the street, talking of the class, "You heard the teacher. He said that in France there was the most wine." . . . "and iron." . . . "and women's hats." But now the dialectic begins. In the first sequence a documentary dissolved into fiction; now a fictional scene achieves documentary status. For the boys may be acting, but the street is real and contrasts starkly with the description of France we have heard—poor, torn up, with piles of dirt lying about. Talking of the richness of France, the boys walk past a crumbling wall, a boarded-up shop whose sign proclaims "Closed because of bankruptcy," and stop for a moment by the littered yard of a miserable house. The opening documentary images seemed timeless; this street does not. This is Paris, 1936; and the reality of the cheerless street finally penetrates the boy's talk. One says, "Yes, old boy, France is a very rich country." Another repeats, "Very rich," thinks for a moment, then, "Still, at my house mama often says that we are poor. How does that happen?" "Well, that's not surprising. It's because your father has no work." "But, no—when he did work we were still poor. There has never been enough money at our house."

Thus, out of the dialectic of documentary and fiction, the underlying question of *La Vie est à nous* emerges. Each half of this opening sequence contributes a partial truth; their conjunction poses the problem: If France is so rich, why are we, its people, so poor? The answer opens the propaganda barrage; in a low angle close-up, a young woman proclaims, "France does not belong to the French; France belongs to the two hundred families."

A chorus repeats the question and the answer; we see a cartoon of the two hundred families by Jean Effel—the only image in the film that attacks the army and the church—then an album of family photographs, the de Wendels, Renault, a few others, the reputed masters of France. These factual images lead again to fiction: directors of industry, with Jacques Brunius as chairman of the board urging that sacrifices must be imposed on the workers in order to increase dividends. The wall behind Brunius becomes a back-projected industrial scene; he moves off screen and, reversing the process of the opening sequence, fiction gives way to documentary as newsreel shots of economic strife appear: workers smashing machines, farmers dumping milk, burning wheat. In an insert Brunius calmly loses a million francs at a gaming table; back at the board room the directors chant in chorus for the *compression* of the workers. Cut to a crowd of workers standing behind the bars of a fence, chanting, "Du travail et du pain!"

The mixture of documentary footage and actors playing roles has become not merely fact and fiction, but fact and political claim or interpretation. The facts, for an audience in 1936, must have been inescapable: economic depression, strikes, sabotage, unemployment. France *is* naturally rich; yet many of its people do suffer from want. The political claim, that this suffering follows from exploitation by the two hundred families, sounds a famil-

Schoolboys, fascists, and French workers. *Center left*, Colonel de la Rocque.

iar note of socialist doctrine. But in 1936 this note has darker undertones: the next montage connects the idle rich and fascism, moving again from fiction to fact, from the garden sport of shooting imaginary workers to the real bombs dropped by Italian planes on Ethiopia. This sequence breaches the boundaries between fact and fiction in a different way. A single doctored shot of Colonel de La Rocque appears four separate times in views of a Croix de feu parade, making the colonel appear as a cretin shuffling forever on the edge of the procession. With a shot of Hitler ranting we hear the sound of a barking dog. Both these scenes have the same implication: the threat is real, but its triumph not inevitable. The sequence ends with a direct affirmation of this implication. The Croix de feu march by; a bourgeois looks on and says, "There's nothing to be done against those people." A worker pushes to the front, "Nothing to be done? Yes! There's the Communist Party!" The rest of the film develops this response.

This first one-third, roughly, of La Vie est à nous defines the situation its (1936) audience faced. Since it is their world, here and now, that is defined, it need not *inform* them of what they already know; rather, it reminds them of what this signifies. Thus, fact and fiction can play the same role: each comments on the state of the world; describing it is not necessary. Thus, too, fact and fiction can be equally "objective"; the schoolboys acting their scene show as clear a truth about France as do the Croix de feu legions marching through Paris. Each scene functions to elicit recognition or acknowledgment, not to convey new information; success in this function depends upon the fact that the audience lives in the very world that the film displays. Very few of those attending political rallies for the Left in 1936 would have had a perception of the world situation very different from that of those who made the film. Hence the fictional elements early in the film would have had, in the eyes of its audience, the sort of objectivity I have claimed. This fact becomes important for the propaganda function of La Vie est à nous, for the rest of the film relies heavily on fictional scenes that may not have coincided so readily with the preconceptions of its audience. But, once established, the objectivity of the fictional scenes tends to persist, especially in as skillful a mixture with fact as this film presents.

Having identified the fascist threat and equated it with exploitation, war, and death, La Vie est à nous records the reaction of the Left, suggesting in its editing that the Parti communiste français is solely responsible for this reaction. Headlines in L'Humanité, the Communist newspaper, call for counterdemonstrations to the February 6 fascist riots. But where the earlier shots of February 6 had shown groups of men moving menacingly in the dark and the damage left at dawn, the February 9 demonstration is shown in still photographs emphasizing injured workers and aggressive police. Then, intercut shots of L'Humanité's front page and crowds in the Paris streets. In the Croix de feu scenes men marched four or six abreast, with yards of space separating them from those watching on the curb. Now a mass fills the street from side to side, moving in an irresistible flow—the whole city appears to have risen to L'Humanité's call! These powerful crowd images evoke for the first time what will become the film's theme: union, united action.

After obligatory shots of Lenin and Stalin to offset the earlier images of Hitler and Mussolini, we see the old French communist hero André Marty, who led a mutiny in the French navy in 1919, then Marcel Cachin, editor of

L'Humanité. But here again, at the end of this documentary sequence, the distinction between actual events and acted scenes becomes purposely obscure. The shot of Cachin in the *L'Humanité* office follows several shots of men selling the paper in different locales. Are they actors or news vendors? We can't tell, but it does not matter; the truth we recognize, that men read *L'Humanité* throughout France and that therefore we are not alone when we do, loses no force at all from the admission that these sales may have been staged for the camera. Cut to the *L'Humanité* office: Pierre Unik brings a bundle of mail to Marcel Cachin, who opens an envelope and, in a real action performed just for the film—that is, spoken to the film's audience— reads the current *L'Humanité* circulation figures. These numbers lose their abstractness in the next scene, obviously acted, in which a little *L'Humanité* vendor is attacked by three belted fascist bully-boys. Bystanders spring to his defense, rout the fascists, and all join in an effort to restore to the newsboy his papers and his dignity. We are not alone.

Now Marcel Cachin becomes an actor, playing himself, as he opens and reads the letters, written by *La Vie est à nous*'s scriptwriters, which introduce the three fictional episodes that form the center of the film. Each episode relates the action of the PCF to a different segment of the French population; each shows Party members as compassionate and effective; each begins with trouble and ends in a scene of union and joy.

First, a factory episode, directed by Jean-Paul Le Chanois, including in its cast Charles Blavette, Max Dalban, and Madeleine Sologne in her film debut. A mettlesome timekeeper, "who has nothing to do but spy on the workers," has an old workman fired. The communist cell among the workers organizes a strike, demanding that old Gustav keep his job, that the timekeeper be removed, and that no reduction be made in the piecework rates. The workers unite; management accedes. A cheer for old Gustav; a hoot for *le chrono*.

Second, a farm episode, directed by Jacques Becker, with Gaston Modot, Eddy Debray, Léon Larive. A poor farmer and his distressed family see their worldly goods about to be sold at auction. But a Communist nephew, Phillipe, shows up with some friends who forcibly suppress any inclination by others to bid, while Phillipe, bidding three francs for a cow, buys back everything for 112 francs. The bailiff leaves; Phillipe and his friends happily carry the furniture back into the farmhouse.

The two episodes show the PCF at work on its home ground, among those classes, workers and peasants, which it claims to represent. The message—the power of united action, the human value of solidarity—offers the PCF as defender of the weak in a world where the strong yield only to strength, not sentiment or justice. The good accomplished stems from the effort of a few Party members, but their connection with the larger PCF and its hierarchy is suggested by the letters to *L'Humanité*. The third episode differs, with its protagonist a middle-class professional-intellectual, its story not of a problem solved but a life saved, its point not to demonstrate the effectiveness of the Party but to show how one may come to choose its path.

This episode, directed by Renoir, with Nadia Sibirskaia and Julien Bertheau, concerns a young unemployed engineer, René, too sensitive to impose further suffering on his girl by continuing to be dependent upon her. As she cooks an omelette, he sneaks out the door behind her, then grows shabbier and hungrier as he walks the streets. A job washing cars ends abruptly when a Croix de feu dandy complains that his car is not finished soon enough. A soup kitchen closes, turning René away. Starved and alone, he sinks weakly into a doorway where two passing Party members find him, lift him to his feet, and help him to a PCF gathering where food and sympathy soon revive him as a chorus sings an appeal for union. Regaining strength he finds camaraderie and even work; he takes over a spotlight as a spoken chorus proclaims, "Comrade, you are not alone!"

Watching this episode in 1973, Jean Renoir remarked that he didn't find it very good; it is looser, slower, its development less assured than the others. But perhaps this reflects a difference in the relation of the PCF to the classes in question. The workers and peasants being naturally the exploited classes, *La Vie est à nous* could simply assume the relevance of the Party to their condition and be content merely to show the humaneness and efficiency of the Party's work on their behalf. But the middle-class professional-intellectual must be freed from the illusions of his class and made aware of his condition and his need for union with his fellows.

It seems obvious that in 1936 *La Vie est à nous* was not intended merely to confirm the choice already made by Party militants, but to win new adherents to the Left. It was aimed at that portion of the middle-class susceptible to persuasion by the Left. To these persons *La Vie est à nous* offered René as a character to identify with; to succeed it had to persuade them that their condition was analogous to his. And that, of course, is the thrust of the film, on two levels: first, to suggest that economic conditions are so precarious that no one can feel secure; second and more centrally, to show that fascism threatens all and exists as a clear and present danger that can only be met by united action.

Thus far the appeal has relied more on suggestion and feeling than reason; song and images and dramatization have all affirmed that we are not alone and have urged us to unite in action. But political conviction requires some rational basis, too. Hence the third episode flows naturally into direct political discourse, a statement of the Party's position and aims. The top PCF leaders, from Vaillant-Couturier to Maurice Thorez, appear successively, each presenting a portion of the argument for a Communist vote. This fragmentation works well, producing the feel of a large rally while sub-

Confounding fact and fiction. Actors Georges Spanelly and Charles Blavette, Eddy Debray and Gaston Modot, Nadia Sibirskaia and Julien Bertheau. Communist Party leader Maurice Thorez. The faces of French workers.

jecting us to only a few minutes of political speech. An intercutting of speakers and audience reveals all the major characters from the preceding three episodes among the listeners, once again confounding fact and fiction. For there stand Marcel Cachin and Jacques Duclos and Thorez, speaking for an election in which we (the film's viewers in 1936) will vote, but speaking also to René and Phillipe and old Gustav.

Having made the argument, *La Vie est à nous* ends with a powerfully moving flow of image and sound. The fictional characters reappear within a human stream that floods across the screen, singing the "Internationale," this intercut with images of France which echo the opening montage. But these images no longer appear as the establishment view fed to schoolboys; rather they hold the promise that France can be *à nous* if we will act together.

The propaganda power of *La Vie est à nous*, which can still be felt today, though 1936 seems several lifetimes behind us, depends upon our feeling as genuine the scenes of union and fraternity that recur through the last two-thirds of the film. Each episode ends in a scene of unity and friendship; the film ends with the coming together of all the characters in a hopeful political union. The ending has great force, not only because of its rhythmic sweep but also because of our sense of the genuineness of this union. Here, perhaps, lies the deepest level of that mingling of fact and fiction which marks *La Vie est à nous*. Le Chanois has said, "The fraternity of *La Vie est à nous* was not an invention of the scriptwriters, but rather it was precisely that fraternity among us which allowed the realization of the film."

After *La Vie est à nous* had been first shown publicly in 1969, Michel Capdenac wrote: "*La Vie est à nous*, it is the film of a hope and of a collective dream . . . one of those rare lost paths which lead us back to the source, that of reality . . . For Renoir's film is also this: a contribution to a movement whose power prevented the immediate establishment in France of a regime of fascist terror. And this is why in *La Vie est à nous*, in its admirable epilogue where two human rivers join and intermingle in a space at first desolate and desert-like, punctuated only by factory chimneys, where the crowd flows bit by bit to flood the whole horizon, one rediscovers the epic breath, the lyricism and that mastery of the image which would at the same time give its force of impact to [his] *La Marseillaise*. The two films form the panels of a superb dyptich whose immortality Renoir's mastery and sensibility assures."[8]

I have tried to describe *La Vie est à nous* in its own terms, that is as a propaganda film of 1936. Viewed within the context of Renoir's work, the film confirms, above all, his openness and flexibility, his unwillingness to be wedded to a single style, not even to his own. He had tried and abandoned the Russian style of montage years before; the direction of his development had been steadily away from the fragmentation characteristic of that style, as well as its expressionistic camera angles and frequent close-ups. But here, where it seemed appropriate, he readily returned to this style. Though it was Jacques Brunius who assembled and edited the opening documentary shots, the form of the montage was decided by Renoir. The closing sequence employs the Russian style even more effectively. The stylistic pattern throughout *La Vie est à nous* is, generally, montage *à la Russe* for the documentary portions of the film, while the fictional episodes, whoever directs them, approximate the style of Renoir. Thus Jacques Becker's farm episode begins with a very fine and typically Renoirian opening shot. This combination of styles does not damage or unbalance *La Vie est à nous*, rather, it contributes to its articulation and, by contrast, intensifies the power of the final scene. Moreover, this mixture of styles appears to express quite precisely the historical situation of the film. The Russian montage affirms the connection of the PCF with the Soviet Union. But within the Popular Front the PCF took a nationalistic stand, for the moment, at least, suggesting its independence of the Komintern. In the 1936 election the Party and *La Vie est à nous* called for the triumph of the Parti communiste français, not world communism. As the Party asserted its Frenchness, so the film, refusing to submit completely to the Russian style, may in its mixture of Eisenstein and Renoir suggest a distinctly French socialism.

Apart from the continuity of actors—Dasté, Dalban, Brunius, Blavette, Nadia Sibirskaia, and others familiar from earlier Renoir films, as well as Gaston Modot, Eddy Debray, and others making their first appearance in a Renoir work—three scenes in *La Vie est à nous* have a direct connection with later films. Two scenes in *Les Bas Fonds* come straight from *La Vie est à nous:* Jacques Brunius' moment at the gaming table is clearly the ancestor of the much more elaborate Casino sequence, and the bailiff's inventory of the Baron's furnishings surely originates in *La Vie est à nous*'s farm episode. Most striking, perhaps, is the resemblance between the documentary shots of the February 6 riots, with their suggestion of an indeterminate crowd of people moving uncertainly in the dark, and the opening scene of *La Regle du jeu*. When I spoke to Renoir of this, he nodded, "When I made *La Regle du jeu*, I probably had that in mind."

16

Une Partie de campagne
1936–1946

There is nothing so mysterious as a river. Away from other human beings, lost in the overhanging foliage, fearful of breaking in on the sound of the water gliding over the weeds . . . we lay on our stomachs in the skiff, silent and motionless, our faces near the surface of the water, watching the movements of a large fish, which in turn was watching its prey.

—*Jean Renoir*

In that warm, rambling reminiscence entitled *Renoir, My Father*, Jean Renoir slowly reveals Pierre Auguste Renoir as a man combining great simplicity with a need for complication in his life, and a clear-eyed unsentimental view of the world with a deep-rooted humanity. Everyone who knew Jean Renoir well must have found in him this same conjunction of traits—a combination that led some critics to accuse both father and son of a *fausse bonhommie*, as if the very combination showed that the simplicity and humanity could not be genuine.

But without such unlikely combinations there would be no human comedy. Apparent inconsistency is the very stuff of life. In the life of Jean Renoir these traits underlay a certain rhythm of production, a recurrent swing from complex, large-scale conceptions requiring great numbers of people, great technical proficiency, and the resources of a big studio, to intimate works of a simplicity that seems (falsely) to deny the intervention of all technique and artifice. By mid-1936 Renoir had moved from the outside into the very center of the contemporary social and political turmoil. The final step, *La Vie est à nous*, became not merely the making of another film but a leap into the political arena itself. Now, once again, he felt the need to reverse direction, to live or work for a moment in a simpler vein.

Political events may themselves have suggested the move. The Leon Blum government, brought to power by the Popular Front victory, finally took office in June and survived its first crisis, precipitated by the sit-down strikes of late May and June. For a moment one could even imagine that this union of the Left in France would be the rallying point about which the democratic forces of Europe might gather to check the march of fascism, that this election, following the Popular Front victory in Spain, would demonstrate that bourgeois democracy still stood as a viable alternative to dictatorships of the Right. The moment was brief indeed; on July 18 the Franco rebellion broke upon Spain, bringing the civil war that would end Spanish democracy and also prove to be the rock upon which the French Popular Front would shatter. But in this moment, in early July, Jean Renoir took his little company to the banks of the Loing River and began shooting *Une Partie de campagne*.

Many Renoir films have a checkered history, marked by false starts, mutilations, and difficulty in finding an appreciative audience, but none appears quite as confused as that of *A Day in the Country*. The film origi-nated in Renoir's idea that "it would be interesting to write a story that would run thirty-five or forty minutes and which I would make exactly like a big film."

For his subject Renoir had chosen a short story of Maupassant's, a gentle nineteenth-century tale of seduction in a natural setting along the banks of the Seine, with few and unsophisticated characters and no great events. Set in an unhurried past and touched by no echo of industrial strife or political intrigue, this film would not merely take Renoir away from the problems of 1936, but would be, in a way, a return to a quieter moment of his own past. For he had decided to shoot the film near Marlotte, the village where his father had painted and from whence his own cinematic career had been launched—the locale where *La Fille de l'eau* had been conceived and shot.

Renoir has said, "I wrote the script thinking of spots where I could shoot it, because I knew that section of the Loing, near Montigny, very well. I though that the Loing, at that spot, could represent the way the Seine had been near Paris at an earlier time. Now, it is impossible to find such places near Paris. Above all, the great reason for choosing these exteriors was that I knew them absolutely; I knew at what time the light would be directed agreeably at which group of trees. I knew the smallest details of that coun-tryside."[1]

Thus envisioned, *Une Partie de campagne* should have been a brief and pleasant respite in mid-career, and the finished film appears to be just that;

no Renoir work seems more unstudied, more a pure flow of life caught unaware. Watching *Une Partie de campagne*, one can imagine it being shot in three or four carefree afternoons, but actually the shooting was interminable. It never ended but simply stopped. And the film would not be finally edited and released for another ten years.

On July 15 Renoir and his company were on the banks of the Loing, expecting to spend a week shooting exteriors. But 1936 was the rainiest summer in memory and early in September the exterior shooting had not yet been finished. The modest sum budgeted for the film had long since been exhausted. They waited for the sun to shine; Renoir went back and forth from Paris trying to raise money.

"We couldn't work," Renoir says, "but we were in a beautiful place. We had good food. When it rained the actors played cards. But the rain kept on, so once again I modified the scenario and adapted it to rainy weather. That is why there are some scenes of rain that were not originally planned and why I did not shoot all the scenes that were planned." Sylvia Bataille has remarked about the tension created by enforced idleness,[2] but Renoir says, "Everybody was happy but Sylvia, who was having some problems in her personal affairs." One day Renoir returned from Paris and announced that he could wait no longer to begin work on *Les Bas Fonds*. The resulting uproar subsided when Braunberger declared the shooting of *Une Partie de campagne* over. Back in Paris, a montage of the footage shot so pleased Braunberger that he persuaded Renoir to extend it into a feature film. Jacques Prévert was asked to write a scenario. But Renoir, continuously busy and not overly pleased with the Prévert script, never managed to shoot another foot of film for *Une Partie de campagne*. And, thinking that two scenes were still missing from the film he had envisioned, he put off making a final montage.

The war began. Renoir left France, with *Une Partie de campagne* still unfinished in its boxes. One day after the war it occurred to Braunberger that the two missing scenes could be replaced by explanatory titles. But the one print of the preliminary montage had been destroyed by the Nazis. Henri Langlois had managed to save the negative, though, and with Renoir still in the United States, Marguerite made a new montage. The titles were added; Joseph Kosma wrote a score, and in May 1946 *Une Partie de campagne* finally emerged as a finished work.

That a masterpiece should result from such a chaotic history seems unlikely. Even those who worked on the film doubted that it could be salvaged. Sylvia Bataille remembers: "After the war, when Braunberger showed us the montage of the film without music, no one believed that it was possible to release that. You understand, we still had the memory of the initial project, and this was a memory without joy, almost painful. But truly, when Kosma had added his marvelous score, the film was completed in a single blow, without flaws—a real surprise!"[3]

Narrative and Treatment

One summer day in 1860, M. Dufour (Gabriello), a Parisian hardware merchant, borrows the milkman's cart and takes his family to have lunch in the country. At the restaurant of Père Poulain (Jean Renoir) on the banks of the Seine, mother (Jane Marken) and daughter Henriette (Sylvia Bataille) enjoy the swings, grandmother (Gabrielle Fontain) pets a kitten, M. Dufour and Anatole (Paul Temps), his clerk and future son-in-law, look at the river. When lunch is ready they find the place they have chosen occupied by two young men, Henri (Georges Darnoux) and Rodolphe (Jacques Brunius). Gallantly, the young men cede their place, and the family eat and drink to the bursting point. Lunch over, the two young men provide fishing poles to keep M. Dufour and Anatole amused, and they invite the ladies to go rowing. On the river Rodolphe and Mme. Dufour play at courtship and move unerringly toward the consummation they both desire. Henri and Henriette row slowly in a silence punctuated by the talk, simultaneously inconsequential and serious, in which they reveal themselves to each other. They stop at an island; in a secluded spot they listen to the song of a nightingale. The silence, the song, the river, and the trees move Henriette to tears; for a moment she fights Henri's attempt to kiss her, then abandons herself to his embrace.

The Maupassant story ends with a brief scene, two months later, in the Dufour hardware shop. Henri, passing by, stops for a moment, and Mme. Dufour tells him that Henriette has married Anatole. Renoir wrote this scene into his script; it is one of the two never shot. But he did add and shoot a new concluding scene: years later, Henri, returning to his "private room" on the little island, finds there Henriette and Anatole, long married. Henri and Henriette exchange a word about their memories, then Henri, alone on the bank, watches Henriette and Anatole row away.

Images of flowing water enclose these two segments of the film; trees and river fill the screen at both beginning and end of each episode. Renoir's camera, unobtrusive as ever, moves with the assurance that nature extends everywhere beyond its eye, revealing a serene and undramatic site where boys fish, seminarists walk, children play, and Père Poulain offers a repast for two francs fifty. The Dufour's country excursion creates a momentary eddy on the river bank; the water flows on unconcerned, still reflects the shimmering leaves. Seeing the film, one feels not so much absorbed by the drama as immersed in the scene; however remote the setting in space and time, the continuity of nature that encompasses Henri and Henriette offers its embrace to us.

In Maupassant's story the natural setting exists only as background, and a narrator's often condescending voice places every event at a distance. The events are the same in the film, but Renoir has replaced cold observation with a celebration of nature, and the distant impersonal voice with an affectionate eye. As always, literary material has been a source for ideas, not a model to be scrupulously followed. But here the mere passage of time may have been instrumental to the change. Maupassant, writing a contemporary tale, could view with a cynical gaze the follies of his world; we, from our lives set in the murderous twentieth century, see 1860 as a more tranquil era when time moved at a gentler pace and the sweetness of life could be tasted in simple days marked by simple joys.

How much of the charm of Renoir's film lies in the way it evokes this feeling! And how much of the feeling depends upon nature having been brought into the foreground of the tale! Nature lovingly perceived, and within its ambience the human antics, ridiculous, tender, sad, achieve the complexity and resonance of actions rather than remaining mere events observed. Maupassant's work is more a vignette than a story; from this sketch Renoir has created a world which seems close enough that we can breathe its soft air and be filled with warm nostalgia for a benign unremembered past. Though picnic and seduction form the central actions of the tale, these must share our attention with the langorous warmth of a summer day, the deep shade of trees overhanging the river, wind bending reeds, the roll and throb of a nightingale's song—and the flood of joyful recognition evoked by these lends grace to the absurd humans found within the scene.

Most often, perhaps, it is myth that prompts such forceful recognition of an unexperienced past. But this time the source seems less arcane; for we recover here, no doubt, the world of the impressionist painters. "Which Renoir have we here? Is it Auguste, Jean, the father, the son? I no longer know." Critics and public alike have found in the poetic surface of *Une Partie de campagne* an homage to Pierre Auguste Renoir and his companions *en plein air* and a confirmation of their feeling that, given his heritage, Jean Renoir must be an impressionist film-maker. Many images do indeed call forth such a response, most unmistakably that almost enchanted instant —following four spatially confined interior shots in which Rodolphe and Henri have voiced their snobbish contempt for these Parisian "milkmen"— when Rodolphe rises from the table and pushes open the blinds: the world floods through the window. The shallow space bursts open as the compositional center of the shot leaps to the deep exterior, with the interior scene becoming a mere frame for the young girl from Pierre Auguste Renoir's "La Balançoire." But if one finds mere homage in such moments, we may note that the second half of the film begins with an image which parodies a long tradition in painting, culminating in Manet's *Déjeuner sur l'herbe.*

Impressionistic moments abound in *Une Partie de campagne*, from liquid sparkling under the titles to the final quiet frame of leaves reflected in water. Images of trees and river repeatedly display the sensitivity to variations of light and the indistinctness of outline characteristic of impressionist painting; costume, setting, gesture, all seem to stir an uncertain memory of a Renoir canvas we cannot quite identify. So compelling is the limpid radiance of these exterior scenes, so tenaciously do they persist in our mind's eye, that they have had an inordinate weight in forming the popular image of "Renoir films," fostering that confusion of father and son that may prevent us from seeing the films clearly. For even here the label "impressionist" is not completely apt. Renoir does not merely show the surface of either his characters or their world. He envelops us within the transient beauties Maupassant viewed at a distance, altering almost every detail of Maupassant's sketch; yet beneath these surface impressions, a fundamental link with the author remains as the driving force in the film, an instinct that overpowers the cautions and reservations of reason. And not only in the human realm are such deeper forces discernible. With all their captivating shimmer of indefinite forms, almost every impressionistic image of *Une Partie de campagne* affirms that Jean Renoir's deepest pictorial debt to his father is compositional; repeatedly, the crossed diagonals of composition create a dynamic tension and movement within soft-textured images of verdure and gently undulant water reflecting bright sky. Thus Jean Renoir carries to the level of sheer form the theme of vibrant and powerful forces underlying nature's summer skin.

And thus the impressionistic moments may mislead us—if we are to be more than impressionistic in our account. For, important as they are in establishing the tone, the atmosphere, the appearance of the world of the film, they convey only a part of its reality. Our sense of the vivacity of that world and the harmony of its creatures, our assurance of its kinder heart than ours, is sustained by the rhythm that provides the pulse of the film and functions as the formal counterpart of the élan that pervades our, or at least

my, experience of *Une Partie de campagne*—a joyful impetus that sweeps us through the film as a leaf is carried along the river, now sailing smoothly with the current, now caught momentarily in a quiet pool, then swirled forward again into midstream. So fully does this rhythm pervade the film that one critic calls it the real subject, a remark that at least reflects Renoir's success in incorporating the totality of his cinematic material into its creation. For however easy this rhythmic flow may seem in apprehension, its construction partakes of every aspect of the film—camera and object movement, cutting pace with its shifts of light and dark and transitions in direction and speed of motion at the cuts, the alternation of voices and of speech and silence in the dialogue, the shifting contours and limits of the action-space, the flow of interaction between characters. And, of course, the music; for the marvel of Kosma's "marvelous score" is how it mirrors and sustains this construction of often indefinite impressionistic images in a compelling rhythmic flow. The melody, when hummed by Germaine Montero, has an indistinctness which resembles that of the images it underscores, while its rhythm so sharply catches that of the movement and flow of the world of the film that it seems a very part of it—one almost has to be reminded that here the music is external to the action of the film.

If "impressionism" implies a concern only with ephemeral appearance, the mere capture of a transient moment in all its transience, then Renoir as film-maker and *Une Partie de campagne* as film are more than impressionistic. The transient moments occur, right enough, more feelingly perceived than by any other director of the thirties, but Renoir seldom reveals mere transience. Rather, almost every such fleeting impression in a Renoir film either appears as a contrast illuminating some intransient, intransigent reality of character or soon acquires depth through our growing awareness of its role in shaping these very human lives. I think of Lulu at the window with the flowers in *La Chienne*, the rescue and the river in *Boudu*, and of course the sunlit meadow and river bank of *Une Partie de campagne*. Usually, too, some dimension of these scenes transcends mere appearance, functioning as expression rather than merely conveying some impression— the space of *Boudu* or the rhythm of *Une Partie de campagne*, which seems to pulse far beneath the surface play of light and shadow.

Yet in this film the surfaces so catch our eye, surfaces of both nature and character, that we may easily fail to see anything else at all. Comic gestures divert us from the serious tones of speech; the rhythmic flow entices us to merely drift along. And then the closure that Renoir achieves for the sequence on the river works so well that the lyric movement and emotional intensity of the final moments tend to overwhelm any resonance left from the early scenes—so much so that Pierre Leprehon can write seriously, "The episodic personages of the first part are there only to initiate the adventure of the boaters."[4] Indeed, we may seem left at film's end with only a poignant vision of Henri and Henriette and the unfeeling beauty of the river, and this may prompt us to dismiss the film as merely a sentimental vignette, "interesting only in its form and even in the nuances of form," as one French reviewer wrote in 1946.[5] But the irony typical of Renoir films of this period is hardly absent here, nor is a darker vision of the world than these sunlit banks suggest—a vision we shall never comprehend, however, if we take half the film to be mere initiation and treat the other half as something out of *True Romance*. For however Renoir may indulge his penchant for mixed genres, and however deep his immersion in nature may appear, *characters* remain the center of his concern and only a clear perception of these characters will bring us to the truth of the film.

Characterization

Characteristically, Renoir's adaption of Maupassant's tale does not expand the action to render it more dramatic; rather, every alteration serves to give depth and life to characters that Maupassant has merely sketched. Where Maupassant had created one character, Renoir develops two contrasting pairs, and does it, so to speak, within the bounds of the original story. But the characters owe more to Renoir than to Maupassant. Rendered more sympathetic by his warm and lucid regard, they appear within the context of Renoir's concern for the relation of man to nature and to the myths of our tradition, and their actions reflect his awareness of the complex and devious roots of human behavior. The characters do not develop; the film affords no span of action in which character development might occur. Rather, like the trees and the river, they are simply there in the sun—sadder and funnier than the trees, often as beautiful as the river.

An honest bourgeois family out of their natural habitat, the Dufours by their very appearance display their allegiance to the proprieties of their class and the degree to which their lives are ruled by custom. On this hot summer day, on a country excursion, they come swathed from head to toe in bulky clothing—hats, ruffles, frock coats, corsets, silk—delighted to be "face à face avec la nature," but quite unprepared for the meeting. Père Poulain, the country innkeeper on a working day, dresses in shirt-sleeves. The young idlers, Rodolphe and Henri, contemptuous of those in commerce, are lightly clothed, bare-armed and comfortable. But, like Lestingois, the Dufours would not think of "going like that." To dress according to fashion, despite the heat and the country, is an unconsidered necessity of their status in life; it would never occur to them to do otherwise. If asked, I suppose they would proclaim that they wear hats because they are respectable people. In consequence, they soon *look* less reputable than anyone else. Because they must dress uncomfortably, they must also relieve themselves somehow of the discomfort. M. Dufour's collar is askew before they reach the restaurant. Mme. Dufour must be unlaced; M. Dufour unbuttoned. By the time lunch is over they verge on total disarray.

Film-makers have always recognized cinema's capacity for exploiting the expressive possibilities of dress. Silent films, Renoir's like the rest, regularly used distinctive clothing both to identify the types that people its worlds and to achieve some individuality within the types. Comedian, cowboy, or Latin lover, each had some article or style of dress that was uniquely his. The advent of sound diminished film's dependence upon costume for characterization, but costume can still provide the most direct and immediate cue to social role or status and individual temperament, in the real world as in film.

Renoir had used clothing as an indicator of both status and idiosyncracy in *Madame Bovary*, had shown its connection with both dream and deceit in *La Chienne* and *Le Crime de M. Lange*, and its role in the rituals of the bourgeoisie in *Boudu*, where it serves as a vehicle for both the temptations and the absurdities of bourgeois life—Renoir's ultimate comment on the connection between clothing and character coming, perhaps, at the moment when Boudu abandons his wedding garb for the scarecrow's rags. In *Une Partie de campagne* Renoir employs his costumes to conceal as much as to reveal. Of course, the Dufour's clothes and the bourgeois status they symbolize do play a part, even to the double role of Henriette's hat, which not only serves as the bait needed by Rodolphe and Henri to hook their prey, but also inadvertently hooks Henri, whose sentimentality first awakens as he imagines Henriette pinning flowers on it that morning. Further, much of the comedy stems from the incongruity of the Dufour's garb; neither M. Dufour nor Anatole would seem nearly as ridiculous if their clothing fit the setting, and them, a bit better. And Henri's simple and comfortable apparel weighs heavily in our assurance that he would be infinitely preferable to Anatole as a lover for Henriette—for almost nothing that Henri says or does bears this out.

M. Dufour *is* gross and awkward and excitable; this, combined with the rapid deterioration of his excessively formal attire, may make him appear a purely comic figure. Yet, until he founders on food and drink, he seems the person most fully alive in his little world, and perhaps the most intelligent and best informed as well. His fondness for technical terms gives his talk a slightly affected air, but he knows what he is talking about, and, in Gabriello's fine performance, he evinces an enthusiasm for this day in the country in almost every speech and gesture, and he speaks almost every line with a different shade of expression. Early in the film, Henri confesses to Rodolphe that he has the soul of a "père de famille," but it is M. Dufour who exhibits such a soul, and we may well doubt that Henri could ever approach M. Dufour's care for his family.

In the first scene the contrast between the overdressed Dufours and a barefoot boy (Alain Renoir) fishing from the bridge strikes a comic note that may deflect us from noticing the warmth and ease of the relationships within the Dufour family—especially if we do not comprehend the French dialogue that expresses their delight at being in the country. M. Dufour, who calls his family "mes enfants," chooses the restaurant but solicits agreement from his wife before turning off the road, "Ça t'va, Mme. Dufour?" He helps her down, and after all these years of marriage still becomes excited at the sight of her leg as she steps from the milk cart, and finds a reason to embrace her a moment later. He shows concern for his mother-in-law, telling her to stay in the milk cart until it is in the shade, helping her at the picnic, responding to her questions. He willingly pushes his wife on the swings before going off with Anatole to look at the river and explain to him the mysteries of nature. He accepts Henriette's suggestion that they have lunch on the grass, then comforts the others when it appears that Rodolphe and Henri have taken their place. One could ask no more of a *père de famille:* M. Dufour is kind, helpful, attentive, obviously the head of the family but not at all authoritarian.

Though frustration leads Mme. Dufour to go off to the woods with Rodolphe, there is no hint of general dissatisfaction with her husband. Her pique is momentary, a consequence of the wine and fresh air that have made her amorous at just the moment when M. Dufour has grown somnolent after lunch. She remembers with pleasure how they had gotten lost in the forest of St. Germain the year before, and she would gladly repeat that experience now. But M. Dufour merely opens one eye and grunts. Still, when her "crise de nerfs" has made sleep impossible, he rouses himself and goes off to cure Anatole's hiccoughs—maintaining his good humor even in the face of that deepest of feminine jabs, "If you were a man . . ."

Anatole, as awkward as M. Dufour but without his excuse of size, shares M. Dufour's good humor, enthusiasm, and willingness to be helpful, yet seems wholly inept. Critics call Paul Temps' "exaggerated" performance the major flaw in the film, but fail to mention Anatole's role in maintaining the balance so dear to Renoir and in avoiding the temptation to sentimentality that arises so often. Anatole's ineffectuality is one aspect of the contrast between innocence and experience that marks each of the three pairs whose dialogue largely carries the characterization in the first half of the film. And Anatole's is the innocence of ignorance, his excesses those of uninformed enthusiasm—one may at least hope he will improve.

The contrast between Rodolphe and Henri takes a rather different form. These young idlers view the arrival of the Dufours with a dismay expressed in the petty ill-humor of their talk: "Say, it's some milkmen." "Why should I give a damn about that?" Learning that the milk cart carries a family, Rodolphe exclaims, "Zut, alors. That's the end of everything. There's nothing left to do but pack our bags." . . . "They will certainly have lunch on the grass [*dejeuner sur l'herbe*], these Parisians; they always picnic on the grass. If this keeps on we'll have to go at least to Corbeil to find some peace." They decline Père Poulain's offer to fry the fish they have caught: "Since the factory has been there, the fish tastes like oil." Henri suggests, "Give them to the Parisians; they will be delighted." Smug in their assumed superiority, they drink their absinthe and complain that the Parisians, having found their retreat, will multiply like microbes.

Despite this scorn, Rodolphe cannot resist pushing open the window to see what the Parisians look like; Henri hardly deigns to notice. By the swings the Dufours talk to Père Poulain and confirm the young men's prejudices. They *are* delighted to have fried fish and they *will* picnic on the grass—"We didn't come to the country to shut ourselves up inside." But their delight seems so genuine, their shared pleasure in the country scene so pure that the young men's carping talk seems mere snobbery. Henriette swings with a joy as childishly innocent as that of the boys whose heads peer over the wall. Rodolphe, enchanted, blinks his eyes, strokes his mustache, tells the servant, "Quiet! Don't bother me! We are extremely busy." His disdain wholly dissolved by the sight of Henriette, Rodolphe displays a more dangerous innocence than hers, akin to that of Boudu or the nature god he will mimic later in the film—the innocence of one fully conscious of his sexual nature but untouched by concern for the social consequences of the encounter he contemplates—the innocence before the Fall, which cannot doubt that such joy is good.

Once conceived, the project of seducing the Dufour women becomes for Rodolphe an enterprise to be savored. His petulance forgotten, the boring afternoon instantly transformed by this delectable sport, he watches and plans and devises an appropriate way to talk about the affair. Like M. Dufour, he loves to speak in obscure technical terms which Henri, like Anatole, sometimes fails to understand. The seduction itself, merely the consummation of the game, is not that important; he delights in every moment of the chase, whether lying in wait, gallantly returning Henriette's hat, or expansively assuring Mme. Dufour and Henriette of his rapture at their presence, while Henri only shrugs and rolls his eyes. Rodolphe's joyful innocent desire becomes the moving force in the action of the film, as Henriette's innocence becomes the basis for its emotion.

If Rodolphe acts with the innocence of nature, Henri may seem to speak with the wisdom of experience. Less impulsive than Rodolphe, he professes no interest in the pursuit that excites his friend: "What do you want of me, old chap? I have the soul of a family man. Whores bore me, society women even more, and the others—I find that too dangerous." "You are afraid of disease." "No, of responsibility. Suppose that you happen to please that young girl who swings so prettily? . . . What if she falls in love with you? . . . I can't at all see you working in the dairy. Naturally you won't follow

up, and then on the other side there will be perhaps a life shattered, wasted, what? It's hardly worthwhile, old man."

This sounds so reasonable, an admirable expression of temperance based upon mature self-awareness, a characterization reinforced by Henri's calm indifference as Rodolphe exclaims and gesticulates about the Dufours. In one interpretation of the film, this virtuous restraint is simply overrun by passion when Henri sees Henriette; he really falls in love with her, with the most honorable intentions, which are, alas, thwarted by fate. Leo Braudy even says that Henri goes with Henriette to protect her from Rodolphe and that they merely kiss in the woods.

But many details suggest a very different description of Henri and reveal the traits that underlie his appearance of virtue. He is, for example, the more cynical and snobbish of the pair. Both are dismayed at the arrival of the Dufours. Rodolphe, with characteristic ebullience, laments and complains, but a mere glimpse of Henriette terminates his negative refrain. Henri, speaking without the tinge of passion that colors Rodolphe's remarks, compares the Parisians to microbes and declines a part in Rodolphe's game. But even after Père Poulain's praise of Mme. Dufour has "made his mouth water" and quieted his qualms, since it is the mother he will "take," he still speaks disparagingly of "that sort of people."

Again, after Henri declares his indifference, this conversation occurs:

Rodolphe: "We know! You are the man for eternal liaisons. . . . La belle Hortense, you kept her for fifteen months."

Henri: "Oh! but she was a beautiful girl."

Rodolphe: "Agreed. But what a fool! At the end of a week, I would have had enough of her."

Arrival. The servant (Marguerite Renoir) greets M. and Mme. Dufour (Gabriello, Jane Marken) and Anatole (Paul Temps). Henriette swings; Henri (Georges Darnoux) and Rodolphe (Jacques Brunius) watch and talk. Pere Poulain (Jean Renoir) serves an omelette.

Henri: "What I asked of her had nothing to do with intelligence."

This self-satisfied reply sounds neither enlightened nor virtuous—particularly if we note that Henri's praise of Hortense ("mais c'était une belle fille") echoes exactly Dédé's belated praise of Lulu in *La Chienne*. A common enough remark, perhaps, but combined with Henri's physical resemblance to Dédé, Renoir may intend it to cast a shadow over our conception of Henri.

Note too how Henri fumbles at making his drink, until Rodolphe takes the bottle from him, exclaiming, "Stop, wretch! You'll never learn how to make a purée." But when Rodolphe looks away, Henri quickly pours a glass of absinthe which he swallows at a gulp. A wholly trivial act, though it shows a sort of insensitivity and self-indulgence, particularly when "absinthe before 1914 was more than a drink, it was a ceremony." But this incident is an exact counterpart of Henri's "theft" of Henriette from Rodolphe, suggesting that the latter act is not a rare case of virtue overcome by passion, but rather an instance of a recurrent pattern in Henri's behavior.

The Renoir films of the thirties might serve as a treatise on the cigarette as an instrument of social interaction. From film to film, cigarettes serve to express or create a relationship between characters, from the manipulative practices of Batala to the warm reunion of Legrand and Alexis Godard, the camaraderie of *La Grande Illusion*, or the recognition of their shared condition by Marceau and Schumacher in *La Règle du Jeu*. But not in *Une Partie de campagne*, except for the brief moment when Rodolphe uses a cigarette to open the conversation with Henriette and Mme. Dufour. In the hands of Henri, a smoke is rather a sort of self-indulgence, never shared, and a way of avoiding or delaying interaction. In all of Renoir's films only one character, Joseph, the malevolent servant of *Diary of a Chambermaid*, more regularly uses a cigarette to shield and separate himself from others.

Enticed by the prospect of sex without responsibility, Henri joins in Rodolphe's *partie de pêche*, but he joins in quite a different spirit. Where Rodolphe will have a joyful afternoon whether or not the game succeeds, Henri has interest only in the seduction itself; the pursuit seems to bore him. Rodolphe appeals to the women's femininity at every moment; Henri just sits. When Henri has managed to switch partners, Rodolphe remarks, "I'll be a sport and take the mother," then proceeds to pay court to Mme. Dufour as if she were, indeed, Juliet. But Henri merely gazes soulfully at Henriette and tries to persuade her to come alone to the country. On the river, Henriette in ecstasy says, "It seems as if it would be wrong to make a sound, to break this silence." Henri replies, "Silence? Listen, the birds are making a racket." In the woods his wooing consists in persistently putting his arm around her waist, finally forcing her to the ground and flinging himself upon her. If Henriette succumbs to this "courtship," is it not to the river and the nightingale and those strange stirrings within, rather than his charm? The irony is that she will mistake this for love.

I prolong this list of details illuminating Henri's character only because so many viewers do not notice them, partly no doubt because much of the dialogue does not appear in the English subtitles. Henri is not so blinded by passion that his earlier reservations are swept from his mind. Rather, he finds Henriette charming "for a shopkeeper's daughter" and knowingly sets out to seduce her. When Rodolphe suggests a boat ride on the river, Henri says to Henriette, "We could go to the factory dam. You'll see, it's very pretty," naming as his destination just the spot that Rodolphe had earlier, with a suggestive gesture, identified as the ideal place for the seduction. Five shots later, Rodolphe reproaches Henri, "Look here, if I understand, you are poaching in my waters." Henri shrugs, "So what?" A moment later Rodolphe reminds Henri of his renunciation, "In short, responsibilities frighten you less and less!" Henri jokingly kicks Rodolphe and replies, "I'm beginning to get used to them." At this point Henri knows very well what he is doing.

But, if not a sincere and honorable young lover, Henri is not simply a cold-hearted seducer, either. Both insensitive and self-indulgent, he is also sentimental; that is one form his self-indulgence takes—he is ready to yield to excessive emotion and allow it to shape his responses to events. When struck by Henriette's poise and fresh young beauty, he poaches her from Rodolphe without qualm or hesitation. This seems only a change in the game plan, not the game, but soon his moonstruck silence leaves no doubt of the rush of feeling flooding over him. Both Mme. Dufour and Henri have professed to be more reasonable than their companions; one of the ironies of *Une Partie de campagne* is that they are the first to be swept away by emotion. Henri, once smitten, seems willing merely to gaze at Henriette, if that is what she wants, until Rodolphe's skiff sweeps by with Mme. Dufour announcing happily that she is going all the way ("jusqu'au bout"). Thus prompted, Henri allows his feeling its head and becomes intent on going all the way, too. Not coldly, then, but with great fervor, he guiltlessly seduces Henriette despite his earlier disavowal of such an act. The irony is that he does not recognize this as love.

M. Dufour and Anatole, by the river's edge, peer into the water. They talk of nature's secrets, M. Dufour knowingly, Anatole in utter ignorance. Renoir cuts from this scene to Henriette and Mme. Dufour seated under the cherry tree, where they too talk of nature. Both Anatole and Mme. Dufour remark that there are such funny things ("des drôle de choses") but the similarity ends there. The rapacious side of nature attracts the men. They look for the "fresh water shark," the pike, which could bite a finger to the bone; Henriette finds a golden caterpillar. Tentative, tremulous, her voice filled with wonder and sympathy, she marvels, "How wonderful the country is. Under every blade of grass there is a heap of little things, which move, which live—so natural." Mme. Dufour, as ignorant as Anatole, has only old wive's tales as answers to Henriette's questions, but she responds instead to her mood, with a warmth and understanding that make this the tenderest scene between two women I have ever seen upon the screen.

With Henriette's head on her mother's shoulder, the two seem as close in spirit as in body. Yet as the scene ends, their paths diverge. Henriette asks, "Did you feel a sort of tenderness for the grass, for the water, for the trees—a kind of vague desire? That catches you here, and mounts; that almost

Tenderness. A kind of vague desire. That catches you here and mounts; that almost makes you want to cry.

makes you want to cry. Tell me, Maman, did you feel that when you were young?" But as she talks, her own description draws her deeper into her feeling, away from her mother; her eyes have moved to seek a distant star. Mme. Dufour smiles a secret, knowing smile; her eyes too turn outward as her thought delves within, "But, *ma petite fille*, I feel it still. Only, I am more reasonable." Each for a moment seems lost in contemplation of that Panic energy that surges through pike and caterpillar and human alike.

Just here, sentimentality might easily have overrun the film. Sylvia Bataille and Jane Marken are so convincing, so authentic; they catch us so completely in the intimate tenderness of the scene. If left to linger over its feelings, inflate them with nostalgia, imagine this as just the moment when the young girl on the swing reaches womanhood . . . But Renoir allows no such indulgence; pausing for the merest rhythmic beat, he cuts back from the close-up. An excited Anatole runs into the background, shouting "Eh! Come and see! Some boats that look like owls—such funny boats." Henriette, a girl again, echoes, "Oh, some boats, some boats!" and runs toward Anatole. Mme. Dufour jumps up, catches her skirt on some brambles, and the bourgeois matron reappears, "Oh! Oh! My skirt! Oh! The country is so messy."

This quiet moment under the cherry tree defines the point in Henriette's life at which Henri will appear, displays her open innocence, her intelligence, her eager sensitivity—her assurance and her vulnerability: traits that will both attract Henri and lead her to be his willing victim. Her sentimentality, that gentle cheat which will contrive "true love" from a nightingale's song, seems fresh and pure compared to his—self-enlarging rather than merely self-indulgent, and providing an imaginary liberation from her bourgeois milieu.

Mme. Dufour, shallow, sensuous, inconstant, and seemingly self-conscious of every tone and gesture, still shows a depth of sympathy with Henriette that Nana or Lulu or Emma Bovary could never reach. Archly feminine, she blends impatience, laughter, a perhaps pretended frailty and a firm idea of what she wants into a coquettish charm that flatters the surrounding males even as it demands attention from them. When aroused, she tickles M. Dufour with a blade of grass, speaks her desire in a sweet, soft voice, then changes quickly from an earthy seductress to a shrill complaining bitch when he fails to respond, only to turn coy and girlish instantly when Rodolphe and Henri approach.

Thus, each in her way, these two women come to the moment when the tempter appears. Whatever the plan, it is fitting that Rodolphe and Mme. D. should find each other. Her skittish sensuality invites his extravagant gallantry; his mock-serious courtship addresses itself precisely to her neglected pride. In the woods his satyric dance responds to her frustration without even raising the question of infidelity—and perhaps parodies that other Rodolphe who led an unhappy woman to the woods in *Madame Bovary*.

Henriette has a crueler fate. The girl who ran to see the boats also runs to ride them. Anatole, wondering and inept, might have shared with her an innocent discovery of the river, but Henri's moody silence lures her deeper into sentiment. The smooth glide along the water, the closeness of the trees, the nightingale—romantic bird—arouse again that vague desire; she gently

The tempter appears.

wipes a tear from her eye. Henri's desire, explicit and persistent, can hardly fail to impose its form on hers. After she submits, Henriette turns her face away from Henri's kiss; the big close-up that results cuts through the flesh like the pike's tooth, to the quivering soul within. One dark, moist eye gazes out in mute appeal: an image whose power and beauty banish any comic residue that may have lingered, and any illusion about the pure joy of adolescent love.

The first half of *Une Partie de campagne* displays the characters in sexually segregated pairs: Rodolphe talks to Henri; Mme. Dufour and Henriette sit under the cherry tree; M. Dufour and Anatole peer into the river. Then the three pairs come together and two new pairs form—Henri and Henriette, Rodolphe and Mme. Dufour—while the comic pair, Anatole and M. Dufour, disappears. Henceforth the moving force within each pair is sexual, but the major contrast in the film opposes the growing tension within the human interactions to the calm beauty of the nature that surrounds them. All of the growing tension finally concentrates in Henriette's brief attempt to avoid Henri's kiss.

Before our era of explicit sex, movies had a dozen ways of showing that a kiss is not a kiss. Renoir here uses two of them, one purely conventional, the other as original and compelling a sexual metaphor as I have seen, one which resolves the tension with astonishing ease by absorbing it into nature and then diffusing it. First, a dissolve from the big close-up to a full shot of Henriette lying on the grass with Henri beside her, neither looking at the other. Then cut to nine brief shots of windswept river-bank and sky, shots taut with an impulsion to movement checked and restrained. Trees and reeds bend in the wind but hold fast, building a sense of confined energy and great resistance which bursts with the cut to three long shots traveling swiftly backward down the rain-drenched river. This long, smooth undulant movement over the rapidly receding face of the river, pierced by the myriad needles of the rain, brings relief, then elation, then an almost incredible sense of closure to the scene.

Whatever Renoir's original intention, this closure assures us that Henri does not see Henriette again until they meet in the elegiac epilogue. Thus, it cannot be a cruel world that has thwarted true love, but his avoidance of responsibility, as he foresaw. In the epilogue the sun still shines on the river, but a change of angle and rhythm and the lingering weight of the preceding closure render the light less joyful. Henriette's clothes are dark; the childish zest has left her face and voice. Henri once more lights a cigarette to avoid or hide a response. He sadly contemplates the tree, his self-indulgent sentimentality now also self-imprisoning. Henriette's strangled "I think of it every night" reflects the way her sentimentality, once liberating, now matches his, tying her to a delusive past, blinding her to whatever joy there might be in the present. But which life is wasted?

Once more Renoir tempts us toward sentimentality, then mocks the temptation. His slowly moving camera might be an extension of Henri's gloomy gaze, but then it finds the boat, and the sight of Henriette rowing wholly destroys that mood. The camera still moves, across Henri's empty skiff to the river, whose beauty still survives—sparkling water still reflects the trees. Sentimentality is a human invention—as Rosenthal will say of boundaries in *La Grande Illusion*, "La nature s'en fout."

The piercing close-up of Henriette, before the rain, is the most remarked

image of *Une Partie de campagne*, but another haunts my memory. In the final shot of the first half of the film, Mme. Dufour and Henriette again sit under the cherry tree and Henriette calmly, unhurriedly reaches up to pick a cherry, her expression so strikingly resembling that of Gislebertus' *Eve* at Autun that it hardly seems coincidental, even though Renoir denied any conscious intent to create such a resemblance. "I might have seen a postcard from Autun" he said, "but I certainly wasn't thinking about it." This fleeting evocation of the Fall, as brief and unemphatic as the appearance of the cross in *Boudu,* and similarly made ironic by Rodolphe's remark that the cherries

"sont pas fameuses," may merely foreshadow the end of innocence that Henriette's encounter with Henri will bring. Or, seen within the context of Renoir's work, with its recurring contrast of nature and convention and its repeated intimation that bourgeois culture has corrupted both the energies and myths of our tradition, it may have the full resonance of that image at Autun, where Eve, half-reclining, almost absent-mindedly picks the apple with her left hand while her pensive abstract gaze, turned outward yet somehow deep within, questions the world in which such a simple natural act could be so fateful.

Water, nature, beauty, life—in discussions of Renoir, these four terms have so often been associated that it may be useful here to sketch the pattern of water symbolism—or rather, map the river's flow—through Renoir's films. Leo Braudy has argued against the simple identification of water images with a purely positive love of nature, contending that Renoir shows as much awareness of the destructive forces of nature and water as he does of its beauty and beneficence.[6] Of course, this is true; more than that, beauty itself may be the destructive force—the river and the nightingale have a larger role in destroying Henriette's innocence than does Henri's crude assault. More centrally, Renoir does not often employ symbols in his work—elements or images having a ready-made significance to overlay the force or meaning of a scene and give it depth and profundity. Rather, whatever symbolic force an image has, it acquires within the film, through its relation to the flow of action and movement within which it appears. The river may suggest life or death, hope or resignation; the mere fact of its being a river does not predetermine this.

But as evidence, Braudy claims that "suicide in Renoir's films invariably takes place in rivers."[7] And that, of course, is false; there are no *successful* suicides by drowning in Renoir films. Suicide attempts succeed by other means—poison, hanging, deliberately exposing oneself to gunfire—means that take one's fate out of nature's hands. The leap into water always ends not in death, but in rebirth. A new self emerges, or the old self awakens into a new life, not necessarily better or happier, but different. Thus Marie in *Toni* and Harriet in *The River* slip into the water in moments of despair; rescued, they show a new acceptance of the conditions that made them desperate, order their lives around a new center. Boudu comes from the river unchanged, but all the circumstances of his life have been altered; he explores this new milieu until it nearly drowns him, then drops back into the river to reclaim his old life. These recurrent failures of suicide by drowning suggest that the river—nature—rejects such attempts; water can be a destructive force, but it is not malevolent. We may think it evil, as men regard the swamp in *Swamp Water*, or use it in evil ways, as in Scott Burnett's attempt to drown Tod Butler in *Woman on the Beach*, but the water itself has no such character. It offers beauty or death, change or sameness, without discrimination—it is we who choose. But for Renoir its usual association is with life, not death: a life where the factors that determine one's happiness are human decisions and character, not the impersonal forces of nature. Thus, throughout Renoir's films the water imagery usually occurs as a context of change, most often a change that involves a loss of innocence. In rather different ways *Boudu*, *La Règle du jeu*, *Swamp Water*, *The Southerner*, *The River*, and *Dejeuner sur l'herbe* all display this connection. *Une Partie de campagne* is the central work on this theme. The Fall from innocence has no supernatural overtones in Renoir—his gods are nature gods;

innocence and experience are equally natural, equally unavoidable. And, however poignant, a loss of innocence may be a condition of growth.

The river shows how beauty and destruction can be elements of the same flow; the most beautiful images in *The Southerner* are of the flooded, rampaging river. The river's counterpart, life, holds the same duality within its flow; we may drown in the flow of life as easily as in the river, as Henri and Henriette do. And, like the river, life will flow on undisturbed, still reflect our choices and evasions, still contain the elements of beauty and death, still offer the possibility of rebirth, if we wish and choose. Thus the image of calm liquid beauty with which *Une Partie de campagne* ends does not merely mock the self-pitying sentimentality of Henri and Henriette. Though ironic and unhappy, the ending is not hopeless, as it is not hopeful—life and the river persist; one may stagnate, or move with the flow and be renewed.

17

Les Bas Fonds
1936

How can we accept Jouvet as a high tsarist official, or believe Gabin's Parisian banter displays the "restlessness of the Russian soul"? Or take the banks of the Marne for those of the Volga? But it is just that which Renoir has the impudence to ask.
                                                                    —*André Bazin*

The idea of filming the well-known Gorky play *The Lower Depths* was proposed to Renoir by Alexander Kamenka, the Russian emigré whose Albatros Films had in 1924 produced *Le Brasier ardent.* In the mid-thirties the French had a taste for films with a Russian flavor. The rise of Hitler and the Popular Front had created within the Left a new sense of solidarity with the USSR; and perhaps the sight of deposed grand dukes provided a distraction from the disintegration of politics in Western Europe. What better in this climate than that the film director of the Left should adapt a work by the most popular of Soviet writers?

Jean Companeez and Eugene Zamiatine had already written an adaptation of *Les Bas Fonds* for Kamenka, and among the emigrés in Paris one could have found a completely Russian cast. But Renoir abandoned the Companeez-Zamiatine scenario, wrote a wholly new script with Charles Spaak as collaborator, and cast his film almost entirely with French actors, including Jean Gabin in his first role in a Renoir film. Gabin was not then a star, according to Renoir. "He thought his career would be helped by an appearance in a different sort of role," Renoir remarked, "He had seen some of my films and liked them; so he let it be known through his agent that he would be interested in a role in *Les Bas Fonds*."

Despite this cast, Renoir could not simply make *Les Bas Fonds* as a French film, set in his own country; even without considering the pressure from political leaders, a French *Lower Depths* would have disappointed audience expectations at the time. Gorky's work was too familiar, its Czarist Russian setting too much the established locale of the play. So it became the only Renoir film of the thirties whose action occurs in an imaginary land, with actors wearing the uniforms of one country but speaking the language of another.

Narrative and Treatment

The Baron (Louis Jouvet), reprimanded for gambling with government funds, goes back to the casino and loses again. Returning home he finds there a thief, Pepel (Jean Gabin). The two then spend the night playing cards. The Baron awakens that morning to be told that his creditors are removing his furniture, that he has been given an indefinite vacation without pay, and that a thief who has been arrested claims to be his friend. The Baron assures the police that he indeed gave Pepel the bronze horses he is carrying, and Pepel, freed, continues on to his squalid lodgings in a doss-house (*asile*) owned by Kostilev (Vladimir Sokoloff), who also disposes of the goods that Pepel steals. Pepel has been the lover of Kostilev's wife, Vasilissa (Suzie Prim), but now dreams that the love of Vasilissa's young sister Natacha (Junie Astor) would save him from his sordid life.

Soon the Baron comes to live at the doss-house, joining the eternal card game and the empty exchange of cynicisms, memories and dreams. An old woman dies. Vasilissa asks Pepel to free her from Kostilev. Luka, an old pilgrim, tells the alcoholic actor (Robert Le Vigan) that he can be cured.

Kostilev and Vasilissa, fearing the police, try to win favor with an inspector (Gabriello) by arranging his marriage to Natacha, who unwillingly goes to a restaurant with him one Sunday. Pepel finds them there, blackens the inspector's eye, and takes Natacha from him. Kostilev and Vasilissa beat Natacha; Pepel bursts into their apartment and intervenes, chasing Kostilev down into the yard, where he dies after Pepel strikes him. Vasilissa denounces Pepel to the police. Pepel goes to prison; Vasilissa, happy to be free, leaves town.

Natacha waits for Pepel. In the doss-house the actor hangs himself. Pepel returns, and he and Natacha take to the open road.

The action of Gorky's *The Lower Depths*, first produced by the Moscow Art Theatre in 1902, takes place wholly in a dingy and sordid basement doss-house and the adjoining junk-littered yard in a Russian river town, a squalid setting that offers a last refuge on earth to some of those "at the bottom of life"—Gorky's original title. But the very first shot of *Les Bas Fonds* indicates that Renoir's film is quite differently conceived: the Baron, dressed in the uniform of a government bureau, stands in a well-lit, elegantly appointed room, with tapestries, paintings, mirrors, classical statuary, in a scene that has no counterpart at all in the play. Whatever world we are in, it seems far from that of *The Lower Depths*.

This departure may seem less arbitrary if we remember that Chekhov once wrote Gorky, "How the Baron has gotten into the night lodgings and why he is a Baron is not made sufficiently clear either." Still, Akira Kurosawa's 1957 version of *The Lower Depths* shows the power that can be achieved in cinema by staying close to the text and setting of Gorky's work. Kurosawa's film transposes the play to Japan, but follows Gorky's text almost scene for scene. In a style that resembles Renoir's in its long takes and deep-focus cinematography, Kurosawa creates his wretched doss-house as the locus of a world, as integral to the film as Renoir's court in *Le Crime de M. Lange*, while the superb ensemble acting of Kurosawa's cast achieves some of the most memorable moments in cinema. By comparison, Renoir's *Les Bas Fonds* may appear to be merely variations on some themes from Gorky. Renoir himself remarked, when first seeing Kurosawa's film in 1977, "That is a much more important film than mine."

Renoir had always been free in his adaptations; even so, a first viewing of *Les Bas Fonds* suggests that here he had only mixed a few moments from the play in with the film he really wanted to make. Less than one-fourth of the film's 236 shots occur in locales that we actually see in the play. The scene that opens the play appears almost halfway through the film, though the first, nearly fatal, confrontation between Pepel and Kostilev has taken place in the film's second scene. Some characters have simply disappeared; others have had their roles completely changed. Lines are taken from one character and given to another. Yet when it is all over, we may be quite surprised at how much of the play is tucked away somewhere in the film—almost all of the major actions, many of the ideas.

The asile, suitably dreary, gloomy and oppressive, its inhabitants lost souls with no hope, but only illusions to make life bearable, has lost the dominant position it had in the play. The film neither begins nor ends there, and its most effective scenes occur elsewhere. Visually, it remains the most interesting locale in the film, with its chiaroscuro lighting and dramatic shadows, its rough bricks, rude stairway, and old wooden posts that often divide the screen vertically or project diagonally across the frame, and its length that lends itself so well to deep-focus cinematography. But the heart of the story no longer resides in the lives of the derelicts who cluster there; except for the actor, we discover very little about any but Pepel and the Baron. For the dormitory has become a mere way station, a place to go to or from, one place among many—the river bank, the casino, the jail, the

Baron's house, the restaurant—and Renoir's concern centers more on how one moves in or out of the lower depths than upon what life is like when you are there.

It remains true that for many the only way out is death. But Renoir merely notes this in passing; the deaths simply provide a sort of punctuation in a story whose center lies in the relationship between Pepel and the Baron —a relationship of little importance in the play.

The worlds we find in Renoir films have open possibilities: a Sunday excursion may lead to a ruined life or a pleasant memory; one may look out the window and see the perfect tramp, or walk blithely up the stairs and find Batala. However difficult, men can learn and undertake effective action; hope is not merely a delusion. Even in those films with a cyclical structure, where the end resembles the beginning, the people should have or could have learned and changed. Faced with the closed world of Gorky's play, a world in which events occur, people come and go, but no one ever changes, Renoir must reach outside that stultifying context and make the most significant moment of his film one that had long been his concern—the moment when people meet and a new relationship may be formed, a moment when new possibilities are easiest to see, if not to grasp, and the openness of the world can be most readily confirmed. The pivotal movement of the film begins when Pepel and the Baron meet, a movement of two lives coming together from opposite social poles, joining briefly, then separating again—a movement symbolized by the bronze horses that the Baron gives Pepel, the horses standing side by side but facing in opposite directions.

The uneasy imposition of the open Renoir world, with its possibilities for change and hope as well as disaster, upon the closed and desperate world of Gorky's Lower Depths helps make of Les Bas Fonds the most uneven Renoir film of the 1930s. Critics complained at that time, but Henri Langlois asserted that the faults would seem less serious when time had altered the expectations of the French audience of 1936: "We will see then only the profound qualities of the work. Qualities which derive from the style and personality of Renoir."[1] Thirty years later, Pierre Leprohon wrote, "In 1937 . . . we expected Gorky; we hardly found him there. Today we expect Renoir; we do find him. That is the secret of the 'revival' of Les Bas Fonds."[2]

Indeed, once we cease looking for Gorky, Les Bas Fonds reveals itself as a Renoir film. The unevenness remains, but now may be felt as Gorky impeding the development of a Renoir theme, rather than as Renoir betraying Gorky. For almost all of Renoir's departures from the play bring Les Bas Fonds closer to the preceding Renoir films. The central theme of two lives coming together, then parting, echoes Boudu, where, too, circumstances bring one character to give up his form of life and come to share a very different life with another. The arrival of the Baron to live in Pepel's world brings to the film the camaraderie now characteristic of Renoir's films and wholly missing from Gorky's *Lower Depths*, where each character remains essentially alone and separate, wrapped in his own protective shield of cynicism or memory or illusion, each perhaps dreaming of escape but each also denying the dreams of the others. The closing scene of the film, with Pepel and Natacha on the road, resembles that of *Modern Times*, as often noted, but also that of *Le Crime de M. Lange*, affirming that however precarious the future, selves and lives can be changed in the Renoir world.

These Renoir elements so crowd the film that some critics identify as its least persuasive scenes those closest to Gorky; they find Renoir unconvincing in his portrayal of the asile, where despite the genuineness of the atmosphere the impression conveyed is of actors posing rather than characters living out their lives. In part this stems from the mere proliferation of other locales: words and gestures that become revelatory of character when the characters are continuously present lose this capability when they occur in isolated episodes.

Kurosawa, by the sheer vitality of the life in his *Lower Depths*, manages to overthrow the despair and pathos that permeate the play; only minimally altering Gorky's text, he still imposes upon it a vision less hopeless than that of traditional interpretations. By contrast, Renoir defeats the play by enclosing it in a world less harsh, often undermining the power of the play's darkest moments by cutting from them to scenes with a very different tone. Nowhere is this more destructive of the impact of the play than in the film's final scenes. The play ends with the actor's suicide, an event which prompted Chekhov to write, "The actor's death is terrible; it is as if you were hitting the spectator on the head all of a sudden without preparing him for it." But Renoir allows the Baron to report the death of the actor, then dissolves from the asile to Pepel contentedly eating by the roadside, and ends his film with Pepel and Natacha walking happily away from their meeting with two policemen—that phase of Pepel's life when he always feared arrest now safely behind him.

If the film were simply an adaptation of the play, this ending would be outrageous. But Renoir's transformation makes it appropriate. Once he has shifted the dramatic focus from the derelict group, the actor's death becomes no more significant than his life. And only Pepel's freedom could bring to a conclusion the central theme of *Les Bas Fonds*.

Characterization

It happens again and again in Renoir films: In the army, Jean Dubois D'Ombelles finds that he can do nothing right, while his awkward servant, Joseph, goes through the military routines with the greatest of ease. Soon Joseph stands guard outside the cell in which Jean languishes. Chotard, the grocer, reads poetry while Julien Collinet sneaks down to work in the warehouse. Lange, the dreamer, pins his map of Arizona on the office wall when he takes over Batala's desk. And so it goes; one symptom of the openness of Renoir's world, a measure of its multiple possibilities, is this tendency of characters to exchange role or status. The change may be short-lived or accidental or more imaginary than real—Boudu leans against the doorway smoking a cigar and imagines that he has become a bookseller. Or it may be carefully planned, complicated, and ironic—Maurice Legrand schemes to restore Alexis Godard to his old status as Adèle's husband, and to cast Adèle as a faithless woman while he, Legrand, goes off to take the little whore, Lulu, as his faithful wife; he succeeds only in exchanging roles with Godard.

That a major theme in *Les Bas Fonds* should be an exchange in the lives of two characters is hardly surprising. Yet the only inkling of such possibilities in Gorky's *Lower Depths* lies in old Luka's insistence that a man can do anything, if he wants to enough, and that anything that one believes in exists. Perhaps Donald Ritchie is correct in seeing that in the play, and Kurosawa's film, the problem lies in believing or in wanting; none of these poor wretches can do it.[3] If we allow this, then perhaps the world of the play is not as closed and hopeless as it seems; rather just these characters cannot find their way free in it. But then the fault may lie not so much in will as in imagination. None of these characters can conceive of their lives as really different; their dreams are only dreams. The cynicism they exhibit toward each other reveals this.

If we accept this reading of the play, Renoir's transformation seem at least consonant with Gorky's view, for Renoir provides occasions when Pepel and Natacha can glimpse the possibility of a new life and can then, perhaps, believe and want enough. The role of Luka has been so reduced that his words have little impact; perhaps Renoir has compensated by incorporating Luka's vision into the lives of Pepel and Natacha. Such an interpretation would give some credence to this statement by Renoir: "I have tried to make a bitter and tender picture of the very soul of that 'poem on the loss of class' that Gorky wrote thirty-four years ago."

"A poem on the loss of class"—whatever else Renoir found in the play, this stirred his interest. He would not, however, diffuse his perception of this loss across a dozen inmates of the asile, but rather create one character whose whole life becomes an embodiment of this theme. The Baron has so merged his identity with his class that he has no other name, but unlike the actor he does not lament the loss. In the upper-class world of his birth he is addressed as "Monsieur le Baron" or "mon cher Baron." When his ties to rank and privilege have all been severed, his new roommates at the asile ask, "What shall we call you?" and he replies, "Baron, if you don't think that's too funny"—seeming to cling to this last remnant of status even after all else is gone, or perhaps merely having been called "Baron" for so long no other name could ever seem his own. But Louis Jouvet's "astonishing performance" endows the Baron with much greater depth and complexity than this episode suggests.

In Gorky's play the Baron seems the most degraded character of all; having fallen from higher than the rest, he has been carried further down. He shows not even the pretense of pride; he sponges off Kvashnya and Nastya, the prostitute; he cheats at cards and will roll on the floor and bark like a dog if Pepel will buy him a drink. Only his cynical reduction of everyone else to the same level suggests even a perverted remnant of self-respect. Renoir diminishes or abolishes this aspect of the Baron, endowing him with a past and a capacity for warmth and dignity unsuspected in the play. The cynical lines remain in those portions of the film taken directly from the play, creating some tension between the essentially negative character the Baron then displays and the sympathy he evokes in scenes added by Renoir. But rather than destroy the character, this tension renders him more human and more interesting than the Baron in the play. Renoir's Baron, aloof, viewing himself and others with a detachment that frees him from the grip of both convention and self-pity, moves through the world as if it were a dream. With slow but often expansive gestures, a somnambulistic walk in which his arms swing together instead of alternately, smile and speech both often emerging as if through a mist, Jouvet creates a Baron whose presence is equaled only by that of Gabin's Pepel.

By itself, the first shot of Les Bas Fonds reveals more of the Baron than we ever know of the derelicts in the asile: the Baron stands, erect and serious, his uniform carelessly buttoned, before a draped window and a paneled wall. The camera circles left, keeping the Baron center screen in a medium shot, as an off-screen voice speaks with authority: "Far be it from me to think of demanding an account. We are not shopkeepers. You serve the state, mon cher Baron, with a zeal that equals your patriotic fervor . . . but money has disappeared—much too much money, yes?" The Baron listens politely, appears unimpressed, responds with a condescending smile. The camera reverses direction, remaining focused on the Baron but displaying more of the room as it moves—sculpture, sumptuous furniture, a tapestry with nude figures. The voice continues: "You have used it for the public good, I am persuaded. However, the disappearance of these thirty thousand roubles is—regretable, you understand? Someone less liberal would ask you for full details . . . would be astonished that you have no memory of this use, yes? You have other things in mind, mon cher Baron, but it's troublesome all the same. Secret funds, you will tell me once more. But, mon cher Baron, the secret funds are not, alas, inexhaustible. I warn you that despite our old friendship, henceforth it will be impossible for me to close my eyes."

As the camera ends its swing, the Baron's figure fills the right half of the

screen; in the upper left we finally see the speaker, a tiny gesticulating figure reflected in a mirror. The Baron's demeanor has made it evident that politeness, rather than fear or respect, has kept him standing; when at last he and the Count appear in the same frame, the image seems to express the Baron's view of the encounter, reducing the reprimand to the idle buzzing of a fly.

Jouvet forms the still center of this remarkable, long-held shot, which not only exhibits the Baron in his milieu but defines his situation and his attitude toward it. Renoir's circling camera reveals three-fourths of the elegantly appointed room, the Count discharging his distasteful duty; yet also catches every nuance of the Baron's reaction to the Count's words—his aristocratic hauteur impervious to any suggestion of guilt, his boredom, his distance from this scene in which he should be deeply involved, his disdain for the whole affair. Renoir says of this opening, "For a shot like that you need a good actor and a good cameraman. I thought it would be interesting to have a little pantomime for Jouvet. He is so good; his gestures and the rhythm of his speech are so strong. I thought it might be interesting to have this shot where he says nothing and does almost nothing, but shows so much."

But not only Jouvet "shows so much"; the very form of the shot conveys a central facet of the Baron's character. The Count circles and talks; the Baron stands, unmoving and unmoved, more an observer than an actor. This passivity persists throughout the film; the Baron's indifference to the opinion of the world finds expression in his willingness to let its activities go on without him. He neither participates in nor opposes whatever occurs, but merely acquiesces, usually in a manner that deviates from accepted behavior. Wholly unconcerned with his own fate, he has as little sympathy for the conventions and duties of aristocracy as he later shows for the dreams and illusions of the downtrodden. But the effect of this detachment or disdain differs in the two realms. Amid the derelicts of the lower depths, this aspect of the Baron's character appears destructive: his scoffing cynicism helps drive the actor to suicide and leads Nastia to assert that even with holes in his shoes he is a real baron. But in the upper strata those he scorns or derides are secure enough to regard him as simply eccentric, and his actions seem merely self-destructive. Even his servant, Félix (Léon Larive), when told by his departing master, "I know I owe you a lot of money, but surely you must have stolen enough to make up for it," stiffly replies that M. le Baron should not trouble himself about it.

The glimpse we get of the upper-class world makes the Baron's scorn and detachment appear healthy and honest, for neither concern nor honor seem important to those so devoted to maintaining appearances. Sonia, the singer who smiles so nicely, later admits that she cultivates the Baron only because he is so generous when he wins: "He gives and gives; all one need do is take." She will drop him if he loses. The Count's reprimand in the opening shot, with its rhetoric of zeal and the public good, becomes sheer hypocrisy when, in the casino, he blandly accepts ten thousand roubles which both he and the Baron know has been taken from "les fonds secrets." The Count smiles as the Baron proclaims, "Dettes de jeu, dettes d'honneur." The Count's messenger, come to inform the Baron of his dismissal, recoils with shock, "M. le Baron!" when offered an egg. In this context the Baron's suave disregard of convention, wealth, and position may seem politically significant and courageous, thus laudable. However, his lack of concern extends not merely to aristocrats and their entourage but to almost everyone; he expresses it as freely in the asile as the casino, and there it has the appearance of arrogance and malice. But the Baron acts consistently; in neither world has he any ambitions or designs of his own. His unkindness is disinterested; his destructiveness more akin to that of Boudu than Batala.

One passion, gambling, consumes and overturns the Baron's upper-class life. A great discovery settles his fate: that a three-kopek game in the asile intrigues him as much as the thousand-rouble game in the casino. If he has lost his class, he has also found his life. He sheds luxury and prestige as easily as Boudu slips back into the river, and with no more regret. When Pepel, finding existence in the lower depths unbearable, proposes to leave the asile and asks the Baron what he will do, the latter replies without hesitation, "Oh, I'll stay here." He has no desire to go; unlike Gorky's Baron, his descent from aristocracy has not been degrading but liberating. Though Renoir speaks of a "poem on the loss of class," Les Bas Fonds is not, it seems, an elegy.

But detachment and arrogance form only a part of the Baron's character —and not the part to which we most respond. Jouvet's sardonic look, his tone—caustic, facetious, superior—create a barrier behind which the Baron watches the world go by. Though his relations with Felix and the women in the casino seem quite cordial, the distance remains. Only with Pepel does warmth and affection mix with the Baron's candor, perhaps because the circumstances of their first meeting present Pepel to the Baron as a colleague—another unsuccessful thief. Renoir often says that a French farmer can understand a Chinese farmer more easily than he can a French banker; the *fraternité des métiers* has been a continuing theme in his films. But this episode in *Les Bas Fonds* may seem an ironic prelude to the meeting of von Rauffenstein and de Boieldieu in *La Grande Illusion*. Still, how fitting for the world of *Les Bas Fonds*, where, despite the gap that separates them, persons at both ends of the social scale, in the flophouse and the casino, tend to be exploitive or manipulative in their relations with those of their own class. In such a world, perhaps the only open and honest interaction is found in the fraternity of thieves.

A thief, Pepel is; he makes no secret of his profession. But again Renoir's vision differs from that of Gorky. Pepel has none of the Baron's aloofness, but Renoir detaches him from the life of the dormitory, removes him from those scenes in which defeat and distrust find expression. He may live in the asile, but it does not define his life as it does that of the others. Renoir conveys this difference in many ways, beginning with our very first glimpse of Pepel as he pensively extinguishes the light in his room and walks, silent and alone, through the dormitory—his space-time world merely overlapping that of the derelicts who sleep or smoke or just lay open-eyed. Even less do their lives coincide. Pepel, in almost every scene, shows a strength of character far beyond the others. If he appears confused at times, uncertain how to escape his apparent fate and easily aroused to violence, even these traits distinguish him from the derelicts. They are not uncertain but lost, and wholly incapable of the energy and passion expressed in Pepel's violence.

By removing him from the despairing life of the asile, Renoir avoids in Pepel the uneasy interplay of humanity and cynicism that marks the Baron; by recasting some lines he endows Pepel with depth and intelligence beyond that of Gorky's character. But above all, openness, honesty, and self-awareness set Pepel apart. He deceives no one, not even himself. Trying to part cleanly with Vasilissa, he allows neither her anger nor her seductive poses to deter him. He declares his feeling for Natacha but accepts her hesitation without rancor or petulance. And, most surprising, when interrupted while ransacking the Baron's house, he responds to the Baron's banter without pretense or aggression, acting as if this were an ordinary occurrence in a thief's life.

Gabin's relaxed performance, natural and restrained apart from his moments of anger, creates a character of a constancy quite lacking in Gorky's Pepel. Toshiro Mifune, in Kurosawa's *Lower Depths*, incarnates a thief who is blunt and outspoken but also anxious, derisive, tender, blustering, fearful, suspicious, bold, cunning, thoughtful, hopeful, desperate—a superbly nuanced performance that explores the full range of the Gorky character. But Gabin and Renoir eliminate most of the negative traits from this range and extend its positive side to build a wholly sympathetic character whose clear outlines are blurred only slightly by the occasional lack of fit between the dialogue taken from Gorky and that invented by Renoir and Spaak.

Goffreddo Fofi has noted that *Les Bas Fonds* marks the first appearance of Gabin in "his classic role," the role which creates "the principal character of the French cinema" in the late thirties.[4] Unmistakably from the working class, masculine and forthright, strong yet gentle, this character seems pinned between love and violence, trapped in some situation he can neither control nor evade. Repeatedly in this period Gabin played variations of this role, variations in which neither courage nor charm slow his progress to an inevitable death. Fofi writes: "Romantic, anarchic, predestined, with tragedy written on his face, a total rebel who believes in nothing but love and, sometimes, in his 'mates', Gabin is not so much a Popular Front character as one who represents the agony and the end of the front and the approach of war. In every film . . . he wears a metaphysical cap of desperation and defeat . . . Even love, the only apparent road to salvation, escapes him in every film, right up to the final tragic solution which occurs in every case."[5]

An apt description of *Quai des Brumes* or *Le Jour se Lève*, but not *Les Bas Fonds!* The persona of the classic Gabin character is there indeed, decent and vulnerable, with the situation designed for his defeat. But the world was not ready; the Popular Front had not yet reached agony, though already driven in that direction by the Spanish war. Perhaps this delayed Gabin's emergence as "the tragic hero of contemporary cinema." Not until *La Bête humaine* would he fully play out this role in a Renoir film. For at the end of *Les Bas Fonds* Pepel wholly escapes the Gorky text to become, indeed, a Popular Front character—the reformed thief, his love beside him, sets forth as a strong and honest worker who will help rid the world of its rottenness.

Gorky's play offers no such exit from the lower depths. If not death, his Pepel faces at least prison and despair. But where *The Lower Depths* explores one depressed milieu, *Les Bas Fonds* concedes that a world surrounds it, and Pepel's encounter with the Baron averts his fate. Before they meet, the film's opening links these two and shows their shared condition: each immersed in a life he cannot leave and cannot gladly live. Renoir then bridges the Baron's time at the gaming table with Sonia's song "Les bandits s'en vont en expeditions . . . Plaignez les pauvres garçons" cutting into the song an image of Pepel sidestepping the police on a dark street. Since the Baron gambles with "les fonds secrets", these shots and the song relate the two bandits, Pepel and the Baron, in their separate midnight expeditions. The image of the Baron which reveals that he has lost again—gaunt, immobile with his unlit cigarette—precedes a cut from the casino to a dark room in the Baron's house, and the link closes as Pepel pries open a drawer to find only a revolver—he, too, is a loser, his big haul come to nothing. "Pleurez les pauvres garçons."

In the lineage of Renoir characters, these two are descendants of Lestingois and Boudu. But, as usual in such descents, the blood lines become obscure. The Baron, of higher class than Lestingois, lacks his culture; Pepel has much more of the social graces than Boudu, but lives as a criminal rather than a tramp. Still, there are similarities in the first encounters of these two pairs. The Baron's style precludes his exclaiming, "Magnificent! A perfect thief!" but both his speech and actions show that he, like Lestingois, has succumbed to love at first sight. Like Boudu, Pepel reacts with suspicion, but quickly accepts the Baron's guileless air as genuine and relinquishes the revolver with no more assurance than the Baron's word. Soon, like Boudu, he is eating his host's food and wearing his clothes. Lestingois literally carries Boudu into his bourgeois world; the Baron, however, can offer Pepel a new life only symbolically, with the gift of the bronze horses. A rescue does occur, but it reverses that in *Boudu*; Pepel saves the ruined Baron from suicide and later welcomes him to the life of indigent idleness in surroundings which he, Pepel, will soon leave.

In their first encounter, each opens the eyes of the other to the possibility of change. They drink as colleagues, but each reveals that he cannot conceive of his own life as different—the Baron by his question, "Has it ever occurred to you that a life like that isn't worth living?" (one of the several remarks that show his suicidal mood)—Pepel by his answer, "A life like that? What do you want; it's the only life I know." But by dawn they are comrades and each sees the other not as *un homme comme un autre*, but as *un homme comme moi*. That is, a man whose life might be mine. Each shares something of his life with the other, and Renoir reveals by repetition the difference their meeting has made. As the night ends Pepel plays his cards: "There, and there, and there. And you've lost!" "What were we playing for?" "Your share of paradise." Pepel divides his last cigarette and gives half to the Baron. We know that when the Baron loses, he cannot light his cigarette, but now he does light it and says regretfully, "Pepel, what a pity I've met you so late! Why didn't you come to rob me sooner?" Pepel leans forward as the Baron lights his cigarette, too, then spreads his hands, "Ah, if I had only known." A moment later the Baron declares, "I'd like to make you a present. Pick out something as a souvenir." Pepel returns to the sight of *his* loss, the dresser he had pried open, and chooses the bronze horses.

Each glimpses a new possibility: the Baron of a life without things, Pepel of a life without thefts. But surely it is less painful to lose one's share of paradise than ten thousand roubles from the Chancellery. But that is just the point; the possibility recognized by the Baron is that of loss without pain, by Pepel that of gain without fear. Next day each reaffirms his revelation: within the elaborate ritual of his awakening, the Baron asks Félix, "Tell me, Félix, have you ever thought of sleeping on the grass?" and Pepel, the horses on his shoulder, gives the apples he has stolen to a child and tells him, "If anyone says Pepel is a thief, you tell him that's a lie."

Thus far the whole structure of the film has emphasized the sudden, surprising warmth and ease of the interaction between the Baron and Pepel, set against the contrast of their lives and characters—a contrast punctuated when Renoir provides for Gabin a shot that matches the opening shot of Jouvet: again, a long take of a single, standing man, with the dialogue implicating an off-screen authority figure in the scene. But this time we see the speaker, and the camera does not move; Pepel's gestures provide the movement in the shot as he explains why he should be freed. We can imagine the off-screen Commissar listening with as much rapture as the Baron hearing the Count. But then the Baron appears and Pepel is freed.

At this point Gorky's play interrupts Renoir's film, and the two seem almost indigestibly mixed thereafter. The first thirty-six minutes have been almost pure Renoir, with a few moments from the play rearranged to fit the Renoir themes. There follows a sequence which resembles the opening scene of the play, fifteen shots presenting the squalid, squabbling life of the asile. But now these derelicts cannot demand our attention as the principals of the film; they only provide the framework for the new possibilities open to the Baron and Pepel—the world the Baron must enter and Pepel escape.

But we hardly hear its voices before Renoir cuts outside to where Pepel argues with Kostilev and then welcomes the Baron as he comes through the yard. The Baron's life has already changed, with all his fine clothes gone "jusqu' à le souvenir," and his black mood gone with them. He greets Pepel with a happy smile and soon joins the card game, the revelation of his night with Pepel already become the substance of his life.

This central strand culminates in the final major scene between Pepel and the Baron on the river bank, a scene related to Pepel's coming change of life as the first scene was related to the Baron's. Renoir says of this scene, "It wasn't going well and I saved it by finding a snail and putting it on the back of Jouvet's hand. Then when the film was shown, I knew from the audience reaction to that scene that the film would be a hit and that Gabin was going to be a star. I had never felt such a warm response from an audience for one of my films."

And rightly so, for there had never before been two Renoir characters who conveyed such warmth and affection for each other throughout a film —all the more noticeable here in contrast to every other relationship in *Les Bas Fonds*. The improvised addition of the snail seems a perfect example of

Renoir's "genius on the set," for it does save the scene and allow it to deepen both the characterizations and the affection we feel between these two. From the first moment, each has accepted the other just as he is, without regard to the past or concern for the future; that acceptance is a key element in their affection. But here is a scene in which they speak directly and seriously of their past and future. They could not simply look at each other and speak those lines; that would jar against all of their preceding scenes. Nor could they simply look away from each other and speak the lines; that would bring into question the acceptance so basic to their mutual regard. The snail solves the problem admirably; it becomes the visual center of the scene, with Jouvet watching it as they talk, and the conversation becomes a sort of aside to this bit of nature study, allowing a serious interchange to occur without disturbing the casualness which has characterized their relationship.

They lie in the grass near the river. Pepel awakens and relates a dream, then expresses his disgust with life in the asile, where everything is rotten except the Baron. The Baron watches the snail and, dreamily, describes his life as like a dream in which all he does is change clothes. Pepel responds with an account of his life: "My path was traced for me by my father when I was a kid. Poor old man spent all his life in prison and advised me to do the same." He declares that he can evade that advice only if Natacha will love him; then he can become a new man with a new life. He asks the Baron, "What will you do?" The Baron replies, "Oh, I'll stay here. When you told me it was nice sleeping in the grass, I doubted it. But now I'm convinced." They lie back down.

This dialogue reaffirms what each had earlier discovered and confirms the contrast that underlies their divergent paths—the Baron's passivity and Pepel's active willingness to take responsibility for his life. Pepel's speech is not an account of what happened to him, as the Baron's is, but rather an assertion of his determination to effect the envisioned change. For the Baron, once shown by Pepel's talk of sleeping on the grass that another life was worth living, the realization of this required only that he let it happen. For Pepel the change will never happen until he acts to achieve it. His speech here is the first such act. There remain two obstacles: Natacha's hesitation and the hold that Vasilissa and Kostilev have over her. The remainder of the film portrays their removal.

Perhaps Pepel and the Baron would not so dominate *Les Bas Fonds* if the third major character, who comes between them, were more convincing. Dramatically, Natacha plays a prominent role in the film, necessary for both the death of Kostilev and Pepel's escape from the lower depths. But Junie Astor's performance destroys almost every scene she is in. Speaking of her, Jean Renoir remarked, "She's terrible, isn't she? She was a friend of the producer. He asked me, as a special favor, to give her that part in the film. I

Meeting—the moment which may change one's life. The Baron (Louis Jouvet) and Pepel (Jean Gabin).

worked hard with her but it didn't do much good. I think of her as almost anti-cinematic. Her face has nothing. Some faces are beautiful, made for the camera. Some are not beautiful but interesting; they show you something even if they are ugly. But Junie Astor had a face that showed nothing to the camera. It is empty."

Feeling this way, Renoir managed to shoot his film with only half a dozen close-ups of Junie Astor. Each one confirms his description, her blank face conveying nothing of Natacha's presumed inner life. Her movements are awkward and unnatural; she shows little sense of the rhythm of interaction of the scenes she is in. She merely recites her lines, often seeming eager to get rid of them as quickly as possible. Consequently, Natacha has no real life at all, though we can divine what she should be like. Hence we can describe, for example, the crucial moment early in the film which establishes the pattern of relationships: a deep-focus shot up the stairway of the asile; in the foreground Pepel strangles Kostilev while Vasilissa stands above, arms folded, complacently watching. Between them Natacha looks on tensely, then drops her lamp. Pepel releases Kostilev and turns; he and Natacha look at each other. From the top of the stairs Vasilissa sees this, realizing, presumably for the first time, the attraction between Pepel and Natacha; she turns and goes with Kostilev into their room. Then two close-ups extend the long moment of silence that marks the new awareness Pepel and Natacha have of each other. Pepel picks up the lamp and offers to replace it. Natacha denies she dropped it purposely, and Pepel remarks, "It's lucky for me that you are so awkward." Natacha recoils from his touch and, responding to her own fear of having revealed herself by dropping the lamp, harshly expresses the wish that he be locked up that night. Pepel answers gently that God doesn't listen to his saints any more than the others and goes about his night's work. The pattern of emotion seems clear enough, but Natacha is a blank to be filled, rather than a living presence. Fortunately, we hardly notice her when Gabin is on the screen, and he is able to carry his role despite the absence of any believable love object.

But Junie Astor's weakness hampers Renoir's attempt to create a third milieu between that of the Baron and the lower depths—the bourgeois world of the Kostilevs. The Kostilev apartment, above the asile but wholly different from it, with a clutter of bric-a-brac and tasteless objets d'art, functions—with the bustling restaurant and its band, officious maitre d'hôtel, and overdressed clientele—to establish a visual basis for this second gross departure from Gorky's play. But the four principal characters at this level—Vasilissa, Kostilev, Natacha, and the inspector—fail to coalesce into a credible group as do the Baron, the Count, and Félix in the upper class realm or the derelicts in the asile. Each of these characters, except Natacha, has some plausibility, but their interaction creates no firm sense of a shared world distinct from that of the lower depths, perhaps because the incompatibility of acting styles casts doubt on every scene. Junie Astor's failure as Natacha weighs heavily in our perception of the scenes in Kostilev's apartment and the restaurant. She is so obviously acting, and acting execrably, that we almost cannot help viewing the others as actors, too, rather than characters. Gestures and expressions which might otherwise be accepted as aspects of character become instead doubtful elements of a performance. Thus, though he hardly lacks acting ability, Gabriello's performance as the

Before meeting the Baron, Pepel rejects Vasilissa (Suzy Prim), strangles Kostilev (Vladimir Sokoloff), and looks at Natacha (Junie Astor).

inspector remains just that, a comic performance that fails to create a character with a life of his own. We are amused by the performance and accept the inspector's role in the dramatic development of the plot, but find no *person* there to whom we can respond as we do, for example, to Pepel or the Baron or even the actor. Suzy Prim's scheming Vasilissa and Vladimir Sokoloff's miserly Kostilev fare somewhat better; they at least have moments of authenticity. But these occur, mainly, in the context of the asile rather than the bourgeois settings. In her scenes with Gabin, Suzy Prim does convey Vasilissa's intensity and vanity, her self-centered ruthlessness and her deviousness; her characteristic pose, with arms folded, seems the natural expression of this character's orientation to her world—self-enclosed, displaying a sort of rejection of others, an attitude of "Well, do something, I'm waiting." Kostilev *looks* authentic, surely, but some critics accuse Sokoloff of being "too Russian," in a film where everyone else is too French. As a consequence, Sokoloff's performance appears the opposite of Junie Astor's: she conveys nothing; he overstates everything. Hence Kostilev's character traits are too clear, and this combination of greed, hypocrisy, a cringing weakness, combined with a domineering air toward subordinates, tends to collapse into incoherence through its sheer explicitness. We cannot, at times, tell whether it is meant to be comic or serious.

The play of the ensemble that comprises the derelicts of the lower depths is much more consistent. They do interact without calling each other's roles into question, and they do convey some sense of both vitality and despair. But having become merely the background for the action of the film, these roles are so reduced that only Jany Holt as Nastia and Le Vigan as the actor achieve any individual identity. Still, these two pathetic creatures, as close to Gorky characters as the film gets, add some human density to the play of more shadowy figures that surrounds them, and this group, aided enormously by the solidity and visual power of their setting, creates what strikes us as the real world of the film. The Baron's presence in the asile creates a peculiar resonance; for here, where everyone looks for escape, he has already made his. We may find in this an ironic comment on the notion of escape, a comment to be repeated by Renoir. Here, it only deepens the despair and thus adds to the credibility of these scenes.

Though I have said that Renoir defeats Gorky's play by enclosing it in a different world, one might respond that the play reciprocates and defeats Renoir's film through the dominance of the asile setting, even though it has ceased to be the center of the drama. Note how critics persist in describing *Les Bas Fonds* as if its focus were this group of society's dregs, though they have only a peripheral relation to the action.

Style and Form

Once we cease to think of *Les Bas Fonds* as essentially Gorky, its own identity may be more readily discerned. The central dramatic line, encompassing the fall of the Baron from the aristocracy to the asile and the rise of Pepel from the asile to the world of respectable work, develops within a clearly articulated formal pattern constructed of relatively complete and independent segments, each segment having a distinct and determinate spatial context while their concatenation creates a forward moving but rather indeterminate temporal flow. Such formal structures are characteristic of Renoir films and probably the source of critical complaints about editing and continuity. As compensation for his departures from conventional continuity, Renoir has always, so he says, sought to achieve balance in his films. When he succeeds, we experience this balance as a quality of the work not only in its overall structure but also within a myriad of smaller balances achieved throughout the film. These internal or secondary balances may extend over an aspect of the film as large as its total pattern of sound or as small as the composition of a single shot. Usually they include some balance both among and within characters, and very often involve repetition or reversal of an action, a gesture, a pattern of images. In short, Renoir seeks both a balancing in motion within the film, a sort of equilibrium that pervades but does not impede the flow of the work, and an encompassing balanced form that reinforces our sense of the unity and closure of the film.

Among Renoir films of the thirties the most obvious failure in achieving such balance is *Les Bas Fonds*, this despite the evidence of efforts throughout the film to attain it. One aspect of this failure, the inadequacy of Junie Astor, vitiates both an intended balance of characters and a sort of triangular dramatic equilibrium of the three social realms. But the imbalance of *Les Bas Fonds* goes deeper than this, being rooted in the conflict between the film and the play.

Renoir sometimes fashions his films via the proliferation of variations of a single formal pattern that serves not only as an overall form but also recurs in smaller compass throughout the work—for example, *Le Crime de M. Lange* with its abundance of cyclical forms, where shots, actions, characters return upon themselves and eventually the whole film comes back to where it began. *Les Bas Fonds* exhibits a similarly repetitive formal structure, but with a symmetrical rather than cyclical form as basis for the variations, with segments of the film repeatedly being shaped into two matching halves. Within the central dramatic movement, nothing returns to its origin. Except for Kostilev, every major character wants to change his life; in the course of the film, every life does change. The ninety minutes of the film break into two halves, each concerning one such pattern of change. The first half contrasts the Baron's aristocratic milieu to Pepel's world of the asile and ends almost exactly at the temporal midpoint of the film, when the Baron walks into the yard to take up residence with Pepel. The second half contrasts the lower depths with the bourgeois milieu of the Kostilevs and ends with Pepel starting a new life. Each half contains three scenes of the milieu being contrasted to the asile, one long and revelatory conversation between Pepel and the Baron, one scene in which Pepel attacks Kostilev, one scene in which Pepel encounters two policemen on the road, one prison scene involving Pepel and Natacha, etc. Thus, the overall form of the film is roughly symmetrical, with the terminal points of this form being the open-

The lower depths, derelicts living in despair. *Upper right*, Nastia (Jany Holt). *Lower left, rear*, the actor (Robert Le Vigan). *Center*, the Baron finds a new life in the depths. *Lower right*, the bourgeois milieu of the Kostilevs.

ing shot of the Baron and the Count, locating the Baron on the edge of his old world, about to topple off, and the final shot of Pepel and Natacha, ⌊locating Pepel on the edge of his new world, about to venture in.

In each half, many segments are themselves symmetrical or fall into symmetrical groups. For example, in the matching scenes that display the social world of the contrasting milieus—the casino in the first half, the restaurant in the second—the significant action occurs at the still spatial center of the setting and is contained within a symmetrical pattern of an entering and a withdrawing movement through the extensive space of the locale, accompanied by music internal to the world of the film. And the casino scene has as its center the precisely symmetrical inset of Sonia's song, with its own symmetrical central inset of Pepel and the police. Or again, the first scene between Pepel and the Baron, symmetrical itself in that it begins and ends at the same location by the dresser and is divided in two by the dissolve from night to dawn, is flanked by scenes of the Baron and Félix, these forming a triangular whole in which the scenes with Félix show the effect that his night with Pepel has had on the Baron. In the first scene he is morose and sardonic, in the last almost gay.

Renoir constructs the dramatic development of *Les Bas Fonds* in a series of two-person encounters—the Baron and the Count, Pepel and Vasilissa, Natacha and the inspector, and so forth. Often he groups these encounters in threes, shaping the development into a series of progressive triangles, as when Pepel meets Vasilissa and rebuffs her, has his violent encounter with Kostilev, then is himself rejected by Natacha. Some such symmetry characterizes almost every sequence of the major characters. Almost always this is a dynamic symmetry, a symmetry within which change occurs and the action moves forward. Thus, the camera moves through the varied scene at the garden-restaurant, following the head waiter to the room where the inspector offers to make Natacha "une petite reine," but it moves outward from that room and back through the same space with Natacha and Pepel toward a scene in which Natacha confesses her love for Pepel—this scene itself made symmetrical in its alternation of two-shots and close-ups.

These symmetrical patterns find echoes elsewhere in the style of the film, in the balance of dark and light musical themes, in the patterns of camera movement, in the composition of individual shots. Among such familiar compositional patterns as that which achieves balance by dividing the screen vertically into two equal halves, we may note one striking and unfamiliar composition that recurs throughout *Les Bas Fonds:* two characters face each other in medium or three-quarter shot, while between them in the background another figure occupies the center of the screen. The final shot has this composition, with Pepel and Natacha on the road while between them two police recede into the distance. Renoir cannot resist including a nature god even in *Les Bas Fonds*, using this compositional form to place a Pan figure in a fountain between Pepel and Natacha when Natacha finally admits her love.

Formally, Renoir embeds the story of the Baron's fall and Pepel's rise in a complicated structure characterized by repeated symmetries, with the elements of this structure tending to create and maintain a balance throughout the work. Thus fashioned, the story contains characters and events from

Gorky's *The Lower Depths*, assimilating these in its balanced form even though its own tone and movement differ greatly from the play. The working out of this story constitutes what I have called "the Renoir film" as contrasted to "the Gorky play." But *Les Bas Fonds* contains both; we find the play spliced into the carefully balanced structure of the film and the resulting whole palpably lacks balance.

The "play" here comprises essentially four scenes in the asile which have only a background relevance to the story of Pepel and the Baron, but present a condensed version of that world of lost souls created by Gorky—disheveled, distraught creatures wandering aimlessly through this vast rude room with its everlasting card game, bickering pointless talk, and hopeless dreams. These scenes not only interrupt the "film," but create a rival center of interest, both formally and thematically, whose inclusion in *Les Bas Fonds* upsets its pattern of balanced halves.

Formally, these sequences discompose the ongoing film from their first inclusion. *Les Bas Fonds* is constructed largely of two-shots, medium to full, with occasional groups of close-ups and rather frequent long traveling shots with large and complex camera movement. These traveling shots often involve intervening structures, that is, the action occurs at three-quarter or full-shot distance, and as the camera moves some structure intervenes between lens and action. Such shots had occurred occasionally in earlier Renoir films; here they become an element of style and, with the symmetrical two-shots containing a central background figure described above, constitute one more phase in Renoir's continuing effort to place his characters firmly within a diverse encompassing world. In *Les Bas Fonds*, scenes usually begin with traveling shots and are organized in groups or patterns of dynamic symmetry, combining balance and change, creating a dramatic momentum of development reinforced by the kinetic momentum that Renoir's mobile camera generates. In contrast, the scenes in the asile feel essentially static; the flow of the film seems to stop here. Both symmetry and dynamism largely disappear. Group shots rather than two-shots predominate, and though the camera does move, it seems both less fluid and less resolute in its movements. As no action occurs in these scenes but merely aimless talk and pointless motion, so the camera too seems to have lost purpose.

The thematic disruption echoes this formal discontinuity. Renoir's film concerns possibility, insight, and change, the power of love and the venom of hate in a context where actions have effects and character shapes action. But the asile houses a world where action seems futile and interaction empty, where there is no encompassing background, and character is reduced to habits of gesture and speech. Each scene ends with things left quite as they began. The open, indeterminate Renoir world, where virtue may triumph, but so may vice—Pepel escapes the lower depths, though with only

The Renoir film and the Gorky play. Pepel finds love and freedom. The actor kills himself. Two endings clash.

forty roubles, "for two" as the Baron says, but so does Vasilissa, in comfort and style—confronts here the closed Gorky world and a very different vision. The confrontation destroys the equilibrium of *Les Bas Fonds*.

Perhaps this unbalancing effect would not be so great if the scenes in the asile did not hold our eye so well. We may not believe in the characters, but Renoir's group compositions within the striking Lourié set produce the most interesting images in the film. Hence the broken flow of the story cannot easily outweigh these scenes and regain the disrupted balance. Though Pepel does escape, the despair of the asile prevails in our retrospective conception of the film.

Unequal, imbalanced, *Les Bas Fonds* remains. The film is richer for containing both these visions, but less coherent. The dual ending points up this incoherence. Renoir provides one ending for each world; the actor's death concludes the Gorky play, Pepel's new life the Renoir film. But they follow each other and are mutually destructive. The poignance of the actor's death dissolves in the triviality of Pepel eating by the roadside, while whatever sense of freedom might have been expressed by Pepel's jaunty nod to the police is undercut by the dark scene of the actor's death, with its enormously greater visual power. Once again, Junie Astor's ineptness adds to the debacle.

But we should not overstress the lack of balance. Before the play intervenes, the first thirty-six minutes of *Les Bas Fonds* give us first-rate Renoir work, visually inventive, with strong contrasts, a compelling rhythmic flow, superb camera work, effective and economical characterization, and fine performances by Jouvet and Gabin. The opening scenes form a much more accomplished realization of the pattern first used by Renoir in *Boudu Sauvé des eaux:* a prologue followed by parallel scenes presenting the two central characters, then a scene in which they meet, with the meeting having a profound influence on their subsequent lives. I have already noted the resemblance between the meeting of Pepel and the Baron and that of Lestingois and Boudu; the introducing scenes have a similar resemblance. In each film these parallel scenes have a striking contrast—of space in *Boudu*, of lighting in *Les Bas Fonds*—combined with similarity in dramatic form. Both Pepel and the Baron set out on midnight expeditions; each walks through a large room, meeting on the way a woman he gently and firmly rebuffs, then after a traumatic event each faces another woman for a moment, then turns away. Each then talks to yet another person, with the conversation expressing some dissatisfaction. Then they meet.

In *Boudu* this opening development seems uncertain and rather uneven; in *Les Bas Fonds*, though more complex, it flows with a compelling rhythm and a feeling of complete mastery. Despite the later loss of balance, these opening minutes of *Les Bas Fonds* seem finely wrought and moving enough to justify the award to the film of the Louis Delluc Prize for the best French film of 1936.

Despite a mixed critical response, *Les Bas Fonds* was well received by the public. No doubt, one reason for its success was that the film's uneasy mixture of hope and despair precisely caught the mood of this moment when the euphoria of the Popular Front victory was over and the grim political reality of 1937 confronted France. Thirty-two years later, François Poulle would denounce *Les Bas Fonds* for just this attunement to its times, declaring, "In fact, with *Les Bas Fonds* begins the French *film noir* of baleful memory."[6] And while *Les Bas Fonds* is not a film noir, the charge may be historically accurate; the Gabin tragic hero does have his roots here, and what lingers after the film is over is the dark and desperate atmosphere of the asile.

18

La Grande Illusion
1937

> *In 1914, man's spirit had not yet been falsified by totalitarian religions and racism. In some respects that world war was still a war of respectable people, of well-bred people. I almost dare say, of gentlemen. That does not excuse it. Good manners, even chivalry, do not excuse a massacre.* —Jean Renoir

The idea for *La Grande Illusion* had its origin, Renoir tells us, in his rediscovery of an old comrade of World War I, Pinsard, who had become a general and commander of the air base at Istres near Martigues, where Renoir was shooting *Toni* in 1934.

"I saw him again and that reminded me of his escapes. I said to Pinsard, 'Well, old chap, tell me your stories of escape. Maybe I could make a film of them.' "[1] But, as Renoir has also said, "I am no good with a new idea. I have to carry it for years." So he wrote down Pinsard's tales, talked to other men who had been prisoners, and remembered his own experiences in the cavalry and as pilot of a reconnaissance plane. He wrote a scenario for "Les Evasions de Capitaine Maréchal" but didn't much like it. Meanwhile, he was making other films and digesting the idea.

At some point Renoir took his story to Charles Spaak and asked him to collaborate on the scenario. A new version emerged that pleased Spaak and Renoir, as well as Jean Gabin, who had become an accomplice of Renoir with the shooting of *Les Bas Fonds*. The script was offered to the producer of *Les Bas Fonds*, Kamenka, but he couldn't persuade the financiers to back the production. Renoir says, "If it weren't for Gabin, I could never have made *La Grande Illusion*. Fortunately, he loved the story and the role of Maréchal; so we went together all over Paris looking for a producer. I don't know how many offices we tried, French, American, Italian. They all refused. 'No more war stories,' they said. Or, 'You can't raise these delicate questions in a film,' or they didn't like it because it wasn't much of a love story. Nobody wanted it. Finally we found somebody who was interested, a man named Albert Pinkovich, who was the assistant to a financier, Rollmer. Rollmer had dreams of doing something in the movies. Pinkovich and Rollmer made *La Grande Illusion*, I am sure, only because they weren't in the cinema. All the professionals were sure it couldn't be a success."

In the years that Renoir had carried the idea, both he and the world had changed. As the world plunged toward a new war, what started as an adventure story became "simply a cry, the affirmation of a conviction. I had the desire to show that even in wartime the combatants can remain men." The early treatment published in Bazin's *Jean Renoir* contains many scenes still in the finished film,[2] but the tone of this version is much harsher than that of the film we know, and it ends on a scene of disillusionment that perhaps originally gave point to the title, *La Grande Illusion:* Maréchal and a companion, Dolette, have escaped and reached Switzerland. Safely there, they agree to celebrate the next Christmas Eve together at Maxim's. The final scene occurs at Maxim's, where in the midst of the revelry marking the first Christmas after the war an empty table awaits two men who never appear, Maréchal and Dolette. As the world became ever more sharply divided, this scene, which suggests that even the wartime companionship of two individuals is an illusion, may have seemed inappropriate to a film that insisted on the humanity of men. The scene disappeared, though the idea would find expression twenty-five years later in *Le Caporal épinglé*. Without this scene the title became more ambiguous; critics have wondered what the great illusion might be. Even Renoir later remarked that he had chosen that title because he didn't want to say anything precise.

Of course, no script is ever final on a Renoir film, but this time the last-minute changes were to be cataclysmic, altering not mere detail but the whole shape of the film. For as Renoir was preparing to shoot his exterior scenes in Alsace, Eric von Stroheim, recently returned to Europe hoping to salvage his career, was offered a part in *La Grande Illusion*. Renoir and Spaak were stunned by the news that von Stroheim was to join the cast, for their script included no appropriate role for him. Legendary accounts of the first encounter of Stroheim and Renoir have circulated, but the most reliable report is probably that given by Renoir's meticulous assistant, Jacques Becker, to André Brunelin, which makes the meeting sound like a scene from Fellini's *8½:* "In reality when Stroheim was told the name of his director it had to be repeated twice. He hardly spoke French and Renoir very poor English. Jacques Becker served more or less as an interpreter. Renoir literally stammered in embarrassment. 'Explain to me my role,' Stroheim demanded. 'Later,' said Renoir, 'there's no hurry.' And he made a show of laughing in order to ease the situation."[3]

Since there was no role, this provided ample opportunity for Stroheim to share in the creation of his character. He did so eagerly, with his influence most evident in Rauffenstein's appearance. Any acquaintance with Stroheim's own films will verify his obsession with uniforms. In *La Grande Illusion* the uniforms are sober and authentic, all except Rauffenstein's, which verges on the fantastic. Françoise Giroud vividly describes the collaboration from which Rauffenstein emerged:

> Stroheim painfully talked broken French. Together [with Renoir] the two men talked German . . . With Renoir's assistants Stroheim would work in English. Then began an astonishing collaboration. This commandant, episodic and colorless, suddenly began to take on a new dimension; slowly his form emerged. First, the physique: Stroheim saw him as rigid, enclosed in an orthopedic apparatus and always wearing gloves.
>
> We began to run around the city of Colmar to find an understanding orthopedist who could create in two or three days the singular object that we demanded. Once the appearance of the character was fixed, his past must be known in order that his present would ring true. He would be an old flying ace, shot down in combat. His back broken— hence the apparatus—burned all over—hence the gloves. Then the decor came into view: the strange Gothic chamber, the camp bed, the solitary geranium. Stroheim wanted sheets of black crêpe de Chine. Renoir resisted. From the profusion of ideas that Stroheim stirred up, Renoir chose the best, rejected the worst, adapted, softened, began always by reflecting before saying, 'Not that.'
>
> All of the commandant's scenes were made over; some were completely reinvented. Renoir and Stroheim discussed them in German. Stroheim wrote his text in English—it was the language that he knew best—we translated them into French; Renoir recast them all.[4]

This flowering of Rauffenstein gave to *La Grande Illusion* a new balance and center of interest. Heretofore the relationship between Marechal and Boeldieu had dominated the script and carried its theme, but now a whole new dimension arose in the interaction of Boeldieu and von Rauffenstein, allowing a much more complex pattern of associations and a much more profound exploration of the theme of human union and separation.

The addition of Von Stroheim to the cast moved *La Grande Illusion* some way toward finding its dramatic form. But the shooting brought even more changes. Like Rauffenstein, Rosenthal also looms much larger in the film than he did in the shooting script. About this change Renoir says, "Well, the assistant to the producer was a very interesting and intelligent man, Albert

Renoir at Chamonix, late 1936, shooting the final scene of *La Grande Illusion*:
Photograph by Sam Levin.

Pinkovich. He was a Jew—he had once studied to be a rabbi—and he had
an understanding of Jewish ways and traits. He was always on the set, and
when we were shooting he would come and stand by me and tell me how a
Jew would act and what he would say in that situation. He was very good
and he did it only to amuse me, but he was so authentic that I soon began to
think that I should use what he told me in my film. That's how Dalio's part
began to grow."

As usual, other chance events had their impact. In the script there are some
thirty shots of airplanes, air fields, aerial combat; none of this remains in
the film. When I asked Renoir about this, I received a familiar sort of response: "No, none of that was ever shot. We couldn't get the planes for it.
One day the producer told me that he just couldn't get them; he was happy
because they would have been very expensive—but I was furious. Only I
thought it over a little and by the next day I saw that the film would be better without them. I often have fortunate accidents like that. If I had shot
those scenes and spent all that money, I probably would have used them.
And, you know, the film changed so much in the shooting that I didn't
know how it should end. I didn't decide how to do the last scene until the
exterior shooting was almost all over—maybe I had even edited some. It
was only then that I saw how the end should be."

And, Renoir adds, the film had changed so much that his collaborator
didn't know it: "Spaak helped me with the script, of course, but he was
never on the set. Then when I showed him the final cut he didn't recognize
the film he had written. It was so different that he said I shouldn't leave his
name in the credits. But I left it, of course."

The film took shape in the shooting, but other problems persisted. Renoir spent four weeks shooting exteriors in Alsace; he later said: "Of course shooting in Germany was out of the question for me in 1937. I shot these scenes in certain parts of Alsace extremely influenced by the Germans during the period which followed the war of 1870. The quarters, the barracks in which we shot, were artillery barracks constructed by Wilhelm II at Colmar. The last chateau is a chateau constructed by Wilhelm II, the Haut Koenigsberg. These are buildings of an absolutely German influence."[5] But while Renoir was shooting, his amateur producers might have been talking to the professionals. For they then expressed doubt that the film should go on. Renoir stopped to edit some scenes already shot, hoping to convince them that he should be allowed to continue. He succeeded and was then able to complete the shooting with four or five more weeks of interiors in the studios.

Narrative and Treatment

La Grande Illusion is Renoir's best-known film; a sketch of the narrative should suffice as a reminder:

Lieutenant Maréchal (Jean Gabin) and Captain de Boeldieu (Pierre Fresnay), shot down behind the German lines by Captain von Rauffenstein (Eric von Stroheim), are invited to dine with Rauffenstein's squadron before being taken to a prisoner-of-war camp. Later, in the *offizierslager* at Hallbach, Maréchal and Boeldieu are quartered with an engineer (Gaston Modot), an actor (Julien Carette), a teacher (Jean Dasté), and Rosenthal (Marcel Dalio), son of a rich banking family whose parcels now feed them all. Each night they work at digging a tunnel; each day they smuggle out the dirt to dump in the garden. With costumes sent from Paris, the prisoners plan a revue for their own entertainment, but on the eve of the performance their captors celebrate the German capture of the fortress of Douaumont, so they decide to invite the camp commander and his officers to their show. But during the revue Maréchal interrupts to announce the recapture of Douaumont. Put into solitary confinement, Maréchal does not return until the tunnel is almost complete. A few days later they all await nightfall to escape, but their plans crumble when the German guard announces that all officers are changing camp that day.

Many months and several camps later, Maréchal and Boeldieu rejoin Rosenthal at the offizierslager at Wintersborn, a fortress high on a mountaintop, reserved for prisoners who have escaped from other camps. Rauffenstein, no longer fit for combat, serves as camp commander. He makes a confidant of Boeldieu, fellow aristocrat and career officer, sharing with him his gloomy view of the future of their class. Maréchal, Boeldieu, and Rosenthal talk of escape. Boeldieu conceives a plan; he takes it upon himself to create the situation in which Maréchal and Rosenthal can get away. A noisy disturbance in the camp leads to a general roll-call; Boeldieu does not answer to his name but appears high in the fortress, playing a flute and leading the guards a chase until Rauffenstein pleads with him to return and, when he refuses, reluctantly shoots him, then learns that Maréchal and Rosenthal have escaped. Boeldieu dies in Rauffenstein's room.

Maréchal and Rosenthal make their way across the countryside, cold, hungry, hiding in ditches. Rosenthal injures his ankle, slowing their progress. They grow bitter, argue; Maréchal marches off alone, then returns. Taking refuge in a barn they are discovered by Elsa (Dita Parlo), a farm wife whose husband and brothers have all been killed in the war. She feeds and shelters them while Rosenthal's ankle mends. On Christmas Eve they make a crèche for Lotte, Elsa's daughter; when the evening ends Maréchal and Elsa discover they are in love. But the war goes on; Maréchal and Rosenthal must complete their escape. They leave and cross safely into Switzerland.

"I made La Grande Illusion because I am a pacifist," wrote Jean Renoir in 1938, when pacifism was equated with cowardice, defeatism, even treason, not only by fascists but by many across the political barricades as well.[6] Still, the public response exceeded that accorded any other Renoir film—a smash hit in France, an international triumph, La Grande Illusion even received a special jury prize at Venice, where it would have embarrassed both Renoir and the Italian dictator to have had the film awarded the Mussolini Cup. Banned by Hitler, praised by Franklin Roosevelt—"Every democrat in the world should see this film"—the success of La Grande Illusion, like the failure of La Règle du jeu two years later, seems detached from at least some of its intentions, and due perhaps more to its hopeful tone, the depth of human sympathy expressed, and the quality of its performances than to any general acceptance or even recognition of a pacifist theme. For, like every other Renoir film, it fits only awkwardly the categories it tempts us to assign. A war film, as the New York Times reviewer called it? An escape story? A pacifist film? Yes—and no.

The war lurks there somewhere, of course; almost every frame acknowledges its existence. And yet . . . no trenches, no mud, no exploding shells. Idle heroes and no villains—expecially no villains. "La guerre en dentelles," Premier Plan charges. Indeed, as the film unfolds the war seems only to provide a background that recedes physically ever further from the scene; it still breathes heavily on the men at Hallbach, but has become a dismal memory and a distant fact at Elsa's farm. The protagonists, who begin as combatants, are reduced—or elevated—to being mere men. Still, on another, deeper plane the film reverses this movement; the war grows ever closer until the final scene thrusts it to the foreground again, calling the whole hopeful development of the film into question.

This physical distance from battle deprives Renoir's pacifism of its clichés.

Many antiwar films make their plea by providing a surfeit of the horrors of war; Renoir's does not. Nor does he win our allegiance to peace with thrilling combat scenes. As James Kerans has said, he does not fight the war for peace.[7] Rather, he provides some glimpses of brave and honorable men—citizens, soldiers—interacting within the vague ambiance of the conflict, leaving us to find and feel in this display of life the futility and wastefulness of war. Unlike *La Vie est à nous, La Grande Illusion* neither proclaims nor sings its message; hence an Italian writer can denounce it both for being "defeatist, quietist and anti-heroic" and for failing to reveal this content to its viewers,[8] while a French critic from the Right praises Renoir for "exalting that which constitutes for us the essence of intelligent nationalism."[9] Obviously, *La Grande Illusion* offers more than doctrinaire pacifism.

From Pinsard's description of his escapes, Renoir might have drawn a picaresque film, unified by the continuity of its hero's actions in his quest for freedom. *Le Caporal épinglé* will approach this in 1962. But far different winds were blowing in 1937. Escape remains a major motif, but Pinsard's adventures survive only in the brief interchange when Rauffenstein welcomes Boeldieu and Maréchal to Wintersborn: "Captain de Boeldieu, four attempts to escape . . . Lieutenant Maréchal, five attempts to escape . . ."—almost like a footnote to remind Renoir how far this work had come from its original idea.

Memory and history, hope and pride, converge in the currents from Renoir's life and work that flow together in this film. Pinsard's reminiscence aroused old memories of camaraderie in arms; in the film's opening shot Gabin wears the very uniform that Renoir had worn in 1918. Camaraderie had become a major theme in Renoir's work, imparting to the films of 1934-1936 more warmth than had been evident before. This camaraderie of shared work or kindred temperament posed no problems; it showed the sustaining spirit of unity without questioning its possibility. But the very insistence of *La Vie est à nous* on its message: "Comrade, you are not alone," creates that question. And the dormitory of *The Lower Depths*, where men without work live together but remain alone, offered perhaps so negative an answer that Renoir turned aside to find the fellowship he needed in a fraternity of thieves. But now, he says, "I discovered that if you put some men together in a room and keep them there, you can do lots of interesting things." So the gambit declined in *Les Bas Fonds* was accepted for *La Grande Illusion*; the story of escapes becomes instead a study of men in confinement, facing up to the question of camaraderie.

But an offizierslager is not the lower depths, of course. The asile of *Les Bas Fonds* defined the lives of its inhabitants, but an oflag merely holds its captives in suspension from their life in the inaccessible world. Unlike criminals they have no sins to repent, no rehabilitation to achieve; they need only await war's end. For most, this period comprises an unreal, inadmissable portion of life; their thought and talk must evade it and turn to the past or future, or the present elsewhere, to seem relevant. Hence the prisoner-of-war camp, the oflag, may, like Thomas Mann's Magic Mountain, become a reflecting surface for the world, a metaphor for history.

The fortuitous conjunction of two Renoir projects probably influenced both at this time. *La Marseillaise*, that "chronicle of some events contributing to the fall of the monarchy," was planned before the shooting of *La Grande Illusion*. The finished films, set some century and a quarter apart, appear as two points in a single sweep of history, with the social upheaval initiated in 1789 finally finding its completion in Rauffenstein's prophecy in 1917 that "whoever wins this war, the end of it will be the end of the Rauffensteins and Boeldieus."

Some of this history Renoir had lived through. He had known Europe before and after 1914 and served in World War I as an officer in both cavalry and air force—the two romantic services where one could still imagine himself a descendant of knights in armor. Perhaps this helped shape his treatment of aristocrats, which suggests some regret at their passing. But here again, Renoir's love has individuals as its object; the social cost of the aristocratic regimes seems apparent enough.

La Marseillaise makes its historical claims openly; in *La Grande Illusion* they are a matter more of resonance than direct statement, achieved through the interaction of fictional characters rather than the reconstruction of actual events. Hence, history remains subordinate both to character development and to the concrete exploration of the more abstract theme of human union and separateness.

The 1914 war did mark the end of the Europe of *la belle époque*, its conventions and illusions giving way to new ones as the aristocracy ceded its power and its place—the change that Rauffenstein laments. Some critics take this lament for the substance of the film, finding support for this in the power of Stroheim's performance. But this interpretation, like that which discounts the first half of *Une Partie de campagne*, diminishes the film; for one of the achievements of *La Grande Illusion* is precisely that it transcends the heroics of its middle section and in doing so affirms more tranquil virtues. Then a temptation toward sentimentality dissolves in the irony or honesty of the admission at film's end that these virtues, too, may fail to affect the contemporary world.

Elsewhere, Renoir's irony provides a frequent counterpoint to the optimistic surface of the film, functioning as one aspect of the richness in detail that offsets a simplicity of dramatic structure. On its surface *La Grande Illusion* moves in a straightforward linear development, without distraction of subplots or secondary complications. Two brief initial sequences form a prologue that introduces the context and the central characters, with a single dissolve sufficing to transform Maréchal and Boeldieu from combatants to prisoners of war. The film then divides into three sections, each presenting a different form of community. The scenes at Hallbach, essentially "some men together in a room," repeatedly combine cooperation and individuality —unity in diversity—in an interplay of nationalism and human sympathy which carries two parallel developments: the escape plan that fails and the gradual drawing of Boeldieu into the inclusive unity whose possibility this portion of the film displays. At Wintersborn, in scenes dominated by the relationship of Boeldieu and Rauffenstein, the exclusive community of this pair points up the separateness which prevails. This escape succeeds, but only at the cost of Boeldieu's life. *La Grande Illusion's* final third finds Maréchal and Rosenthal, without uniforms or confining walls, separate and reunite, then come together with Elsa and Lotte in a simple union dependent upon neither nation nor class—a community created by the war and destroyed by its shadow. The final scene sends Maréchal and Rosenthal back toward the beginning: "You'll go back to a squadron, me to a battery." "Someone's got to finish this whore of a war—let's hope its the last."

The scenes at Hallbach begin with displays of apparent distrust and strict discipline. Weary prisoners stand in line, guarded by old soldiers with fixed bayonets. In harsh French, a German officer reads the camp regulations: "Here you are under the authority of German law . . . German discipline . . . It is strictly forbidden to dress in a slovenly manner, to gather in groups, to speak loudly of matter injurious to the German nation . . . It is strictly forbidden to talk to the guards." At his side the camp commander punctuates this reading by intoning, "Streng verboten!" Behind them soldiers come and go, saluting the backs of the German officers before passing by. In a moment an English officer about to be searched will snap, "Take your hands away! Don't touch me! You want my watch?" drop his watch to the floor and grind it under his heel. And Boeldieu will complain that the search could be carried out more politely. But between these scenes Renoir inserts four shots which show that life in the camp hardly conforms to this first appearance. Sloppily dressed French soldiers stand in a group and sing at the top of their voices, warning the new prisoners to hide their gold. The German officer who had just barked the regulations waves the singers away without rancor. Soon we shall learn that the French prisoners call him "Arthur," with some fondness, and that he tells them how the cabbage served as food to guards and prisoners alike sits on his stomach. So much for regulations!

After this introduction, every scene at Hallbach speaks more of brotherhood than enmity, showing the conditions common to guards and prisoners more than their differences. Distinctions of nation, race, and class are facts in this world, but so is human sympathy; and at Hallbach, it frequently prevails. The guards are guards, of course; they will celebrate a German victory and will beat or shoot a prisoner who escapes. But most of them are old; they are weary of the war and tired of eating food that tastes like old shoes. And they know their captives are men. The guard who finds Maréchal despondent in solitary confinement, his food untouched, waits patiently through an outburst of rage and frustration, leans his rifle against the wall and sits beside Maréchal on his bunk, searching his pockets for some offering that will restore this prisoner's sense of connection with the human world. He finds three cigarettes, then a harmonica; silently, he leaves these on the bunk. Absent-mindedly Maréchal picks up the harmonica; outside the cell the old guard listens, smiles as he hears the first few notes, then walks away singing "Frou-Frou"—the same song Maréchal sang in the film's opening shot. Sympathy and humanity do penetrate the barriers of nation and language.

The symbols of fellowship are familiar: cigarettes, food, music. If for Renoir a proffered cigarette seems a tentative move toward community, shared food often marks its achievement and music its celebration. The party in *Le Crime de M. Lange* is merely the most obvious example. *La Chienne* begins with a banquet; *La Vie est à Nous* ends in song. And the dual endings of *Les Bas Funds*—interrupted and inconclusive as they are— find the derelicts singing to Alyosha's accordion, and Natacha and Pepel picnicking by the roadside. Even the Lestingois' unplayed piano remains an indication of music's role in human community—and its silence one more symptom of the bourgeois failure to achieve it.

Success seems closer in *La Grande Illusion*; at Hallbach, both French and Germans eat and sing together. Among the prisoners, Renoir's "men in a room," a common nationality and tongue underlie a camaraderie in which differences of class and metier become complementary rather than divisive. Men may talk of a personal past, but they act in concert toward present reality. Only Boeldieu resists absorption in this brotherhood; in a group where every action is cooperative, he plays solitaire. One difference, of course, is that a career officer finds a prisoner-of-war camp a normal part of his world. Boeldieu accepts this present life, never talks of the outside, pre-war world, but keeps up the conventions, insisting on his rights, maintaining his proper distance from others. He needs no reason for escape: "For me the question doesn't arise. What's a golf course for? To play golf. A tennis court, for tennis. Well, a prison camp is for escape." The others do have reasons, reasons tied to that real, outside world they try to recreate in their revue, which, by chance, occurs at just the time when the nationalism aroused by the fall of Douaumont has undermined the sympathy that usually unites guards and prisoners at Hallbach. Characteristically, Boeldieu, the realist, does not attend the revue; so he is not even present at the musical climax of this segment of the film, when the recapture of Douaumont evokes a singing of "La Marseillaise." This spontaneous chorus of the French national anthem, serious, joyous, defiant, does piognantly express

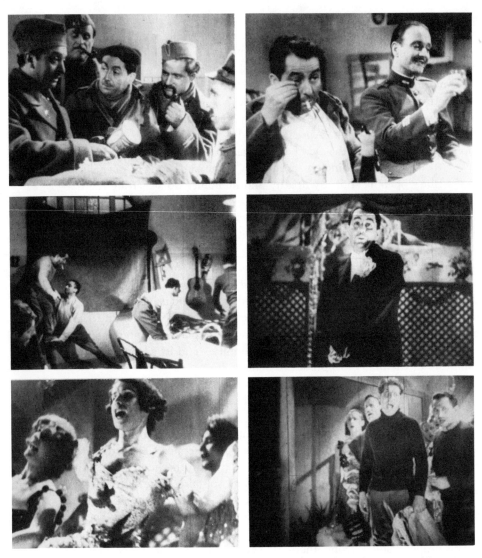

Hallbach. Some men in a room. *Upper left*, Rosenthal (Marcel Dalio), the engineer (Gaston Modot), the actor (Julien Carette), the teacher (Jean Dasté). *Upper right*, the actor and Boeldieu (Pierre Fresnay). *Lower right*, Maréchal (Jean Gabin) and Rosenthal sing "La Marseillaise."

the feelings aroused at such moments, but Renoir renders it ironic and ambiguous by the execrable pronunciation of the British soldier who requests, "The Marseillaise, please"—reminding us that the Allied prisoners are also separated by nation and language—and by having some of these singers still dressed as chorus girls, thus comparing this musical event to those that preceded it. The comparison casts no doubt on the genuineness of the momentary unity felt by the prisoners, nor the sincerity of the patriotic song. It does, perhaps, question its value. For though "La Marseillaise" marks the moment of greatest solidarity among the prisoners, it also marks the deepest penetration of the war into its place, dividing the room into two hostile groups. The German officers hastily confer and leave; armed guards hurry through the streets. But the music of the revue had excluded no one, drawing German and Ally into its warm nostalgia and producing a moment of open affection between prisoner and guard—what André Bazin calls an "inspired instant of pure cinema"—when the actor flips his coattails at a "chorus girl," then calls to the *feldwebel*, "Tu piges, Arthur?"

The following scene underlines the question; as guards carry Maréchal back into his cell after his dash for freedom, the bells announce the German reconquest of Douaumont. But now no one cares; both guards and prisoners read the bulletin without emotion. And the simple music of a harmonica will show that the sympathy between guards and prisoners has survived. By now it is clear that whoever holds Douaumont, the war will go on—the difference it makes will emerge only later in the film, when Elsa shows Maréchal and Rosenthal a picture: "My husband—killed at Verdun."

The terrible ambiguity of war, which arouses both the worst and the best in men and engenders both the greatest hate and the deepest love, underlies the ambiguity that runs through *La Grande Illusion*. At Hallbach the distance of the prisoners from their own world makes dreams of escape inevitable, and the persistent memory of patriotism makes attempts at escape seem necessary. Yet, like the Baron of *Les Bas Fonds*, they have already escaped—both the war, which imposed its violent reality on them, and the narrow confines of their old lives. Hence in some ways one may feel that life is more, not less, real here, and that the relationships are more natural and genuine—a suggestion expressed in Renior's central symbol of community, when the teacher declares, "I have never eaten so well in my life." One illusion holds that escape will be to something better. But what? Back to the *Bouffes du Nord*, or an unfaithful wife? Hence these scenes contain a suicidal, self-destructive note, twice clearly struck. The teacher returns from his reconnaissance to report that an escaped prisoner has been caught and killed "in the garden behind the building"—precisely where their tunnel will emerge. The prisoners look serious—and go on with their plan. Later, when emptying the dirt from their digging, Maréchal asks the engineer what he is planting. The latter replies, "Dandelions. I dream of having a salad of dandelions with bacon." But the French idiom, "manger des pissenlits par la racine," equivalent to the American "pushing up daisies," is here intimated, suggesting a sort of death wish in the persistent effort to escape. Hence the concluding scenes at Hallbach have their own ambiguity. When the tunnel is complete, Arthur appears and announces the change of camp, frustrating the escape attempt but perhaps thus doing more than the prisoners to assure the fulfillment of his wish that they should soon return to their wives. Like the policeman/death figure in *The Little Match Girl*, Arthur's reappearance here may be the culmination of the theme of cooperation between guards and prisoners, rather than its reversal.

Traveling dissolves and traveling music bridge the months between Hallbach and Wintersborn, the flow suggesting that, from camp to camp, life does not change. But the first image at Wintersborn bears no resemblance to the opening shots of Hallbach: Instead of weary prisoners, a crucifix hangs before a Gothic window. This symbol of compassion precedes the introduction of new prisoners to the camp and, indeed, they are greeted compassionately. Rauffenstein bows, extends his hand to Boeldieu, "Delighted to see you again, Boeldieu." Then with great sincerity, "I am very sorry to see you here." The official business transpires in relaxed, not very formal, talk. Rauffenstein sits on his desk, smoking, hands copies of the regulations to the three prisoners, remarking, "They make good bedtime reading." He leads a tour of the fortress, chatting with Boeldieu about old times along the way. Demolder admires the ancient architecture; Maréchal avers that among "Maxim's" he prefers the restaurant to the machine gun. Rauffenstein regrets that he cannot offer Boeldieu a private room; Boeldieu regrets that he could not accept it.

How much more humanized these first formalities appear. But again Renoir includes another image to contradict a first appearance. Behind Rauffenstein's cordial demeanor we glimpse cold stone walls, guns, and patroling dogs, with no singing prisoners in view. As at Hallbach, these secondary images prove more revealing. Here sympathy and cooperation do not prevail; each man's private world tends to exclude the others. Boeldieu's cards and Demolder's dictionaries compete for the space of the table; the Senegalese works on his painting, but when he finishes Maréchal and Rosenthal hardly glance at it. Most significantly, Wintersborn is the only locale in the film that has no shot of men eating together: Rauffenstein eats alone, and the Russians' promise of a shared repast becomes an angry conflagration from which Demolder is forcibly ejected. And, except for the improvised concert of the escape, Wintersborn is the only locale whose sound does not include music.

Denied the symbols of a community, Wintersborn also lacks its substance. The scenes in the fortress form a negative counterpart to those at Hallbach, with a thematic reversal finding expression in a reversal of action. Fellowship hardly flourishes here; its very existence seems dependent upon ties with the past. The contrast of nature and convention, a recurrent Renoir theme, receives in *La Grande Illusion* a much more subtle elaboration than in the simple confrontation of *Boudu*. The conventional distinctions that separate men yield to natural sympathy at Hallbach; at Wintersborn the other pole of this dichotomy seems dominant. Appropriately, then, the central relationship here involves the two most formal characters yet en-

Wintersborn. Von Rauffenstein greets the new prisoners: Boeldieu, Maréchal, and Demolder (Sylvain Itkine).

countered in a Renoir film, Boeldieu and Rauffenstein, two men for whom life without style and order is unthinkable. The sympathetic brotherhood begun at Hallbach still unites Maréchal and Rosenthal, and they alone seem firmly oriented toward the future. For Boeldieu and Rauffenstein, the common code and culture of their international elite weighs more than sentiment in a fraternity that looks to the past. "This is war; sentiment is out of the question," Boeldieu declares at Hallbach just when sentiment had finally

broken through his shell of cold reserve. At Wintersborn he denies his sentimental tie to Maréchal at the moment when his action confirms it. Once
again, the climax brings all the prisoners together for a musical event, but
now Boeldieu, absent at the Hallbach revue, holds the spotlight and provides the music—assuming the role of the actor whom Boeldieu had earlier
disdained. Maréchal and Rosenthal escape, but the stars of the performance
are Boeldieu and Rauffenstein, and the rules of their game decree that Rauffenstein must kill the one he loves while those he disdains are freed.

In Elsa's barn, Maréchal stands tensely by the door, grasping a thick club.
Woe to he who enters. But once more the first impression of a new locale
proves false. A cow comes through the door, followed by Elsa, frail,
blonde, unafraid, more concerned that Rosenthal's ankle is *kaput* than that
these two strange men should suddenly appear. One of her first gestures
offers food to them; one of her last provides a package for the road. Like
Rauffenstein, she describes *les richesses* that the war has brought her, and
both early and late in the last segment of the film the image of Lotte alone at
the big table conveys the cost of those "greatest victories." Elsa shares with
Arthur and Rauffenstein the role of keeper of a property, but one whose
points of interest are not guns and walls and prowling dogs but rather a
cow, a water pail, and blue-eyed child. The prisoners, now confined by
Rosenthal's injury rather than a captor's arms, here fully share in the community they find. Elsa enforces no regulations, German or French, makes
no demands, but merely offers warmth, safety, and finally love. The familiar pattern repeats: the characters gather; music is played; soon some will
depart. But a celebration, not a performance, occurs this time, and no an-
tagonisms result from this event—love, not death, prevails. Once more Renoir touches lightly on a deeply-rooted cultural symbol, when Lotte asks if
she can eat the Christ child; and indeed, for a moment the communion of
this little group seems beyond the reach of the war and the world. But only
for a moment; the final departure confirms the presence of the world and
the necessity of confronting it.

Perhaps only here can we discern the full contours of the movement that
lies at the thematic heart of *La Grande Illusion*. At Hallbach a shared condition moves men toward fraternity, but the context of nations at war defeats
this flow. The departure scene, appropriately, is one of frustration, with
French, German, and British remaining quite apart. In this portion of the
film, effective fraternity, ultimately, is national. At Wintersborn national
solidarity breaks down as differences of metier separate man from man
among both French and Germans. The camaraderie begun at Hallbach
falters as the presence of Rauffenstein draws Boeldieu away: despite his
attachment to Maréchal, the only scenes in which Boeldieu seems really
comfortable are those with Rauffenstein. But international unity also fails:
the Russian invitation comes to naught; Boeldieu and Rauffenstein are

Elsa's farm. Maréchal and Rosenthal find refuge with Elsa (Dita Parlo), a water pail, and a blue-eyed child.

eternally separated by the very code of the profession that unites them. Appropriately again, the final moments here are of despair, expressed in Rauffenstein's romantic gesture of clipping his geranium.

The divisiveness of Wintersborn persists through the moment when Maréchal and Rosenthal separate, to the accompaniment of the same music that had separated them from Boeldieu. Only with Maréchal's silent return does true community emerge, a movement culminating on that Christmas

Eve in a union in which differences of metier, nation, language, and race all dissolve. Hence, departure from Elsa's, no longer escape, brings both hope and pain—hope in that this little community has shown the conditions in which, indeed, this "whore of a war" might be the last; pain in that this possibility requires separation from the community to fight for its extension. Hence, too, the power of the final shot: two small figures bobbing through a field of snow, where the conventional Swiss border is real enough to halt pursuer's bullets, yet the unmarked sweep of snow suggests a world in which such potent fictions need not be, but where the love these figures now embody will suffice to turn away wrath and war.

As in *Le Crime de M. Lange*, the final image, two lone figures receding in vast open space, conveys possibility more than achievement, hope more than happiness—a hope which, in 1937, was a grand illusion, but also a grand affirmation of the only human answer to despair.

Characterization

Renoir's original conception of this film, as a tale of a soldier in a series of adventures, seems evident in the title of his first script. The transformation of "Les Evasions de Capitaine Maréchal" into *La Grande Illusion* begins with Renoir's decision to adopt a familiar literary device and double his hero, thus creating two characters, Maréchal and Boeldieu, highly differentiated yet indissolubly linked together, sharing the adventures. Given Renoir's concern for character over story, and his own dual career in the French army, this development may have been inevitable. But not the next. When Eric von Stroheim joined the cast, a second, unplanned doubling occurred—as Boeldieu is a second Maréchal, Rauffenstein becomes a second Boeldieu—and again the linking of character provides a dual perspective on their common situation. The last term in this schema grew from Albert Pinkovitch's camera-side chats with Renoir, which occasioned the final doubling of the first pair, Maréchal and Boeldieu, into two pairs, Rauffenstein and Boeldieu, Maréchal and Rosenthal. Thus unusual doubling and redoubling, accidental as it seems, shapes the central dramatic structure of *La Grande Illusion* and underlies the richness of characterization that marks this film. It also underlies our strong sense of the equality of the characters in the world of the film.

Many critics identify Boeldieu and Rauffenstein as the central characters of the film, but this surely responds to a few dramatic moments at the expense of the whole. For few other films so firmly resist our tendency to divide the cast into one or two stars surrounded by supporting players; after forty years, *La Grande Illusion* remains a superb example of ensemble playing.

The role of Maréchal provides the one great deviation in Jean Gabin's career as the tragic hero of French cinema in the late thirties. In a film with

two tragic heroes, Maréchal represents an affirmation of life and the saving power of love. He shares some positive characteristics with the Gabin tragic heroes, but wholly lacks the "metaphysical cap of desperation and defeat" that fits them so tightly. If the ill-starred heroes of *Quai des Brumes* and *Le Jour se lève* symbolize the hopelessness of the ordinary man's common aspirations, Maréchal affirms the resiliency of these aspirations and the inestimable value of the common men who share them.

With exemplary economy, Renoir requires just four shots—two minutes—to introduce both Maréchal and Boeldieu and develop the contrast between them. *La Grande Illusion* opens in a French *bar d'escadrille:* First, a close-up of a phonograph record; from this black disc the camera tilts up to the head of Lieutenant Maréchal, who leans over the machine, coat unbuttoned, hat on the back of his head, rapt, softly singing, "Frou-frou, frou-frou," to the music, lost not so much in thought as in the movement of the spinning disk. He wanders through the room, asks for a ride to Epernay to see "Josephine," grumbles, "Well—I say—it's the wrong time," when told by Captain Ringis: "There's a fellow from the General Staff. You'll have to take him out." But he quickly shrugs off his disappointment: "So—she'll wait. At your orders, captain."

In Ringis' office, Boeldieu stands, erect, hat straight on his head, monocle in eye, an aerial photo held in a gloved hand. He speaks coldly, with a haughty air, never moves. When Maréchal and Ringis disagree about the photo, Boeldieu's response drips with irony: "Touching unanimity! This precision gives a rich idea of the perfection of our photographic work."

In every movement and word Maréchal appears casual, relaxed, spontaneous. He speaks in the familiar *tu* form, his broken sentences sprinkled with slang. Moved by impulse, by his momentary experience, without serious plan or set purpose, he drifts through time as he drifts through the bar, showing little more concern for his casual affair than for "Frou-frou." Open and direct, he looks squarely at the men he addresses, using the same tone to a truck driver and his squadron commander.

In contrast, precision marks Boeldieu's every gesture and phrase; his speech matches his carriage and appearance, being equally formal and correct, without superlatives or slang. He speaks with biting wit and a superior air. Cold, impersonal, immaculate, he treats Maréchal and Ringis as mere information sources. Hardly glancing at them as he speaks, he regards the photo as he utters his ironic barbs. Perhaps Boeldieu's view of the world, as much as of the photograph, finds expression in his remark, "It is that gray smudge that troubles me"; in his life he conceals all the gray smudges of impulse and sentiment under a meticulous style, an air of cold efficiency, and an irony that displays both his scorn for almost everything and a rejection of all the imperfections of life. His manner is that of the dandy, of whom Baudelaire wrote, "The characteristic beauty of the dandy consists, above all, in his air of reserve, which in turn arises from his unshakable resolve not to feel any emotion."[10]

In his first appearance Rauffenstein seems to fall somewhere between these two. Entering the German equivalent of the *bar d' escadrille*, hatless, cigarette in mouth, helmet slung over his shoulder, he tilts backward to down his drink in one gulp, scratches his ear, calls for music, requests a bowl of Herr Freissler's famous punch to celebrate his second kill. When Boeldieu and Maréchal arrive, Rauffenstein becomes the gracious host. On seeing Maréchal's wounded arm he murmurs, "Je regrette," and though he may recognize Boeldieu as "one of us," until they are seated he is more solicitous of Maréchal than Boeldieu. Boeldieu remains properly military; when Rauffenstein extends his hand, Boeldieu salutes, then hesitantly shakes hands. Maréchal appears confused in this context, more human than military. He shakes Rauffenstein's hand without hesitation, bows to the officers, acknowledges Rauffenstein's regret with the slightest nod, seems rather ill at ease until he discovers a fellow mechanic from Lyons at the table.

Through this scene Rauffenstein acts with assurance, at ease with his men, friendly but without the informality seen in Maréchal's squadron. Always military in his bearing, he seems yet more relaxed than Boeldieu and allows a great range of expressive intonation in his voice: very warm as he calls, "Herr Bredow," cold and clipped when giving orders, jovial as he calls for a celebration, soft with regret to Maréchal. In both speech and action he seems more natural and human than Boeldieu, more formal than Maréchal. Rauffenstein appears here generous, gallant, sympathetic, but strictly military in a romantic vein, with notions of knightly honor, perhaps, and of respect for a brave enemy. International in his language and experience, he assumes without question his connection of common class with Boeldieu; yet remains proud of being a combatant for his nation. Boeldieu apparently shares few of these traits; his attitude to the war seems coldly practical rather than romantic; he remains rather distant with Rauffenstein, though less so than he had been with Ringis and Maréchal.

In the opening sections of *La Grande Illusion*, Maréchal, Boeldieu, and

Rauffenstein each have a separate entrance, with each first seen alone in close-up or medium shot. But Rosenthal first appears as one of a group of prisoners, inconspicuous among the singers, and throughout this section of the film he remains just one of the men together in the room. This difference influences characterization; for, unlike Boeldieu or Rauffenstein, Rosenthal is deeply social and gregarious, more anxious to affirm his identity with others than his separateness from them. His role in the two major communal events we see at Hallbach underlines this aspect of his character: he acts as host at the dinner and provides the costumes for the revue. All his actions are tied to the group: even the reception of the goods he receives in the mail becomes a collective activity. The suggestions of anti-Semitism in remarks by Boeldieu and the Actor, which tend to separate Rosenthal from the group, obviously wound him. He undertakes to give with bravado an account of his international background and his ties to France, but utters the words with his back to his hearers and grows progressively more agitated as he speaks. Open, warm, and sympathetic, it is Rosenthal, who voices the group's concern for attempting their escape without Maréchal— prompting even Boeldieu to admit he can be touched by emotion.

While thus locating Rosenthal firmly within the group, Renoir also marks him as different—of the four, only Rosenthal is usually called by name— and provides formal links between him and both Maréchal and Rauffenstein, preparing for Rosenthal's role later in the film. When the group dines, Rosenthal invites his comrades to the table in a shot that echoes the opening image of Maréchal: First, a close-up of a dinner plate; from this white disc, the camera tilts up to the head of Rosenthal, leaning over the table. At this repast Rosenthal plays precisely the role which Rauffenstein had played earlier, but again a difference reflects a contrast in character: at Rauffenstein's table conversations are exclusive, two by two; at Rosenthal's the general conversation includes the whole group.

Significantly, where Maréchal had been ill at ease at Rauffenstein's table, Boeldieu's haughty air seems out of place at Rosenthal's. The Hallbach scenes develop this opposition between Maréchal and Boeldieu, but also bring them together. Perhaps a single shot, the opening shot at Hallbach, most simply expresses their difference: Dissolve from the traveling interlude to Boeldieu and Maréchal standing in the second rank of a line-up of prisoners. Both are weary. Maréchal, hatless, lets his head hang sideways and forward, eyes heavy-lidded; Boeldieu's head is more erect, but with eyes mere slits and mouth sagging. Boeldieu starts to yawn, stifles it, conceals it with a gloved hand. Maréchal yawns too, but without concealment or restraint, eyes closed, mouth gaping wide. Boeldieu observes this vulgarity with quiet contempt, raises his head, and regains his lofty air.

Maréchal immediately becomes one of the group of prisoners; Boeldieu's aloofness creates suspicion. Hence the Engineer must ask Maréchal if "ton

Maréchal.

copain capitaine" can be trusted, before revealing the existence of the tunnel. Maréchal's assurance allows the work to go on, but does not change Boeldieu's relation to the group. At night, when the digging starts, Maréchal watches with interest, asks questions and, chafing under the restraint of his wounded arm, assumes for himself the post of listening by the window. Boeldieu sits on his bed playing solitaire, doing his best to ignore the actor's antics. He does ask if the tunnel is solid, but refrains from seeming interested, does not notice the signal—a tin can—though it falls right beside him, and does not move from his bed to lend a hand until the actor is dragged feet first from the hole. He agrees to join the digging next night, but even then in a manner that belittles the effort: "I've heard that crawling is very wholesome exercise."

Henceforth, Boeldieu becomes part of the group, though never fully participating in its life, as Maréchal does. Boeldieu withdraws completely from the preparation for the revue, looks out the window while the others work on costumes, does not even attend the performance. But, after the fall of Douamont, he does accord to Maréchal his words of highest praise, "tres chic," when the latter suggests they invite the German officers to the performance. Still, the degree of Boeldieu's commitment to these men and the strength of his feeling for Maréchal emerge only after Maréchal's solitary confinement, and then involuntarily. The prisoners talk of the impending escape and Rosenthal says, sadly, "For me, there's one thing I'll always regret; that's to leave without Maréchal." Boeldieu looks up and, for once, allows himself to admit some feeling: "That's very painful for me, too. Indeed, it troubles me." Then he throws down his card and resumes his mask of indifference, "But this is war—sentiment is out of the question." But when a dirty, exhausted Maréchal comes through the door a moment later, though Rosenthal sheds a tear, it is Boeldieu, whose every action has heretofore been deliberate, who first reaches his side, and the words of greeting that tumble out lack their usual cold precision.

Maréchal wears no mask; he hides neither the naive optimism which prompts his belief that the war will soon end, nor his ignorance of the Rosenthals or the meaning of *cadastre*. His human feeling shows in every scene —from his amused tolerance at being searched: "Ja, ja, old man. I've got nothing. If I had known I was coming here I'd have taken a little something with me," to his cry of despair in the dungeon: "I want to see the light and talk to someone—hear someone speak French, French, you hear, speak French!" In the theater, when Maisonneuve dons wig and dress, Maréchal expresses the wonder which strikes them all immobile and silent: "Oh—a real girl!" And it is he who demonstrates the transcendence of nationalism over mere fellow-feeling by disrupting the harmony of the revue to shout, "We've retaken Douaumont!" and stand glaring defiantly at the German officers.

When Boeldieu and Maréchal arrive at Wintersborn, the year they have spent together has had some effect. Maréchal now speaks with a touch of irony—"C'est un bien joli château, mon Commandant. Et puis, c'est ancient. Et puis, c'est gai."—while a shade of warmth can be heard in Boeldieu's voice. Maréchal has lost his optimism; Boeldieu has learned to value his lower-class comrades. And the attachment between these two has obviously deepened, though it is not a subject on which Boeldieu will permit discussion. Rosenthal now works alone, drawing his map; in the fortress from which "no one escapes," he maintains his hope of eluding his captors.

Rauffenstein, of course, has suffered from the war; as the symbol of his experience a chin plate and steel corset hold his shattered body together. Physically these make no apparent difference: Rauffenstein's neck is no stiffer, his back no straighter at Wintersborn than in his opening scene. However, they mark the change from combatant to prisoner, which once again allows him to meet Boeldieu as an equal. But the terms of Rauffenstein's imprisonment are harsher: when the war ends the stone walls will no longer confine Boeldieu, but Rauffenstein will remain forever encased in his steel fortress. Hence those aspects of the dandy which were not apparent in his first scene are accentuated now. As Henri Agel has written, "Dandyism is the last state of heroism in decadence."[11]

Fifteen years earlier, in such films as *Foolish Wives*, Stroheim had become the exemplar in cinema of a certain incarnation of the dandy: cold, pitiless, self-centered, sensual, engaged in a ritual of elegance that kept him aloof and untouched by the cares and emotions of ordinary men. Even earlier, in propaganda films of World War I, Stroheim's portrayal of the Prussian officer had made him the essence of "German brutality" (*la barbarie allemande*), billed as "The man you love to hate." Renoir recalls this career in *La Grande Illusion* when Rauffenstein tells the new prisoners that at Wintersborn he applies French regulations, "Pour que l'on n'accuse pas la barbarie allemande."—recalls it both to remind us of the stereotype created by Stroheim and to insist that this will not be repeated here. Rauffenstein, like Boeldieu, does perform the rituals of the dandy, though he explains his white gloves as necessary because he has been burned all over, and he shows his fine contempt for "un Maréchal et un Rosenthal" and the French Revolution that bred them. But he is neither pitiless nor cold. He shows sympathy for his men; his voice retains its great range of emotive intonation; he expresses openly to Boeldieu his feeling about the world and his position in it. If the credo of the dandy is never to be astonished and never to be moved, Rauffenstein fails on both counts: he is genuinely astonished at Boeldieu's promenade along the ramparts, and he is often moved.

Now the primary object of this emotion is, of course, Boeldieu. Merely a gallant foe and a fellow aristocrat in their first encounter, at Wintersborn Boeldieu represents much more to a Rauffenstein whose former life is beyond recovery, whatever else the war may bring. When Rauffenstein laments that he was a combatant but is now "un fonctionaire, un policier," he mourns more than his role in the war. His cavalry life of international equestrian competition, with its attendant café society, has been shattered with his spine. Forever inaccessible, this life yet appears again in the person of Boeldieu, who can chat in English of the Prince of Wales Cup and remembers Fifi at Maxim's. For a moment, in his prison, as they smoke and talk of Blue Minnie and Count Edmond de Boeldieu, Rauffenstein can regain the prewar life that will never return. Need we ask why he makes an exception of Boeldieu?

Rauffenstein.

In the single long tracking shot which first reveals his presence at Winters-born, Renoir encapsulates Rauffenstein's character. To the background sound of a lone bugle, the camera descends from a gaunt crucifix before a Gothic window to an altar where stands a portrait of General von Hinden-burg, then moves past a small cabinet holding a single geranium and across the table where cluster the personal effects of this yet unseen commandant: a champagne bucket and bottle, a pistol resting on a leather-bound copy of *Casanova*, a watch, a photograph of a woman, a volume of Heine, a nude statuette, binoculars, an atomizer, whips and spurs, swords . . . As the camera comes upon an emaciated orderly blowing into a pair of white gloves, an off-screen voice complains in harsh German, "Open the window. It stinks in here—enough to make you vomit!" The orderly springs to attention, opens the window, then reports respectfully, "We have only two pairs of white gloves left." The off-screen voice, less harsh, replies: "It's too complicated to get more. Try and make them last until the war is over." The camera follows the orderly as he offers "Herr Major" more coffee, then tilts from a white gloved hand up to Rauffenstein's face, supported by his chinplate. His voice now warm and gentle, he responds: "Since you baptise this slop with the name of coffee, I resign myself. It'll warm my guts." The shot ends as the orderly hands Rauffenstein the list of new prisoners, including the name "Boeldieu." The capping gesture to this catalogue of effects and intonations, seen through the door a moment later as the new prisoners wait, is the image of Rauffenstein spraying himself with perfume before going out to greet Boeldieu.

The crucifix with which the tracking shot begins is a symbol of compassion, but the rest of the shot complicates its meaning; for it reveals the command post of a military prison established in a chapel. One may see this as the dandy's defiance, setting up his profane ménage in God's domain, or alternately, an appropriation of the chapel to the romantic, aristocratic nationalism of the Junkers—a confident assertion of *Gott mit uns*. Or, with Rauffenstein, as both.

Though Eric von Stroheim had created cinema's image of the dandy, in *La Grande Illusion* it is rather Pierre Fresnay who brings this role to its perfection. The emotion that Rauffenstein openly displays, Boeldieu insistently denies. Though his cold style never falters, he preserves a latent, inner fire discernible only in his irony until the moment arrives for his final heroic gesture. His credentials as a snob were firmly established at Hallbach, yet now he assures Rauffenstein that the word of a Rosenthal or a Maréchal is "as good as ours." He will risk his life to help Maréchal and Rosenthal escape, but he firmly rebuffs every effort by Maréchal to express his feelings —"I'm doing nothing for you personally. We risk getting sentimental."— and engages him instead in the ritual of elegance, to help him wash his white gloves. When Maréchal complains that, after eighteen months together, they still speak with the formal *vous*, Boeldieu coolly replies, "I say *vous* to my wife and *vous* to my mother." This remark rejects the familiarity Maréchal seeks, yet still allows that Boeldieu's relation to Maréchal may be as deep as that to his wife or mother—deep enough, it proves, to claim his life. Maréchal's plaintive "You can't do anything like the rest of us do" identifies, of course, a mark of the dandy, who, above all else, will not be ordinary.

The escape plan Boeldieu devises remains wholly within this vein—bizarre in its outward appearance and singularly complex in its motivations. This man of icy reserve who shuns display and whose "competence in theatrical matters is highly debatable" will perform in the glare of spotlights with more style and finesse than the actor's turn in the revue. The man who declared at Hallbach, "I hate fifes," will offer a solo concert, piping a children's song on a pennywhistle flute. Should we wonder at Rauffenstein's amazement?

Though "duty is duty," this performance reaches further than the proprieties of war and Boeldieu's relation to Maréchal. It includes, of course, the dying class of the Rauffensteins and the Boeldieus. Rauffenstein speaks with regret of their passing from the world, but Boeldieu merely responds, "Perhaps there is no longer a need for us." He is, as he claims, a realist, willing to face the end of his world without complaint, but also without concession—to find for himself a "bonne solution" and choose his identity and his fate, thus making explicit in his performance the implicit suicidal undertone of the Hallbach escape attempt.

In the script of La Grande Illusion in the Harvard Library, a few pages, perhaps carried over from an earlier script, spell Boeldieu's name "Bois le Dieu." Even more strikingly, on the page where Boeldieu and Maréchal wash the white gloves, a marginal change that appears to be in Renoir's hand uses this same spelling. Bois le Dieu: God of the Woods! A familiar figure in Renoir films, of course: Boudu, Rodolph, Jean Dubois D'Ombelles —but who would expect to find him here, concealed within the consummate figure of the dandy, the least natural of men! A reversal of this concealment had been hinted at in Boudu, when Lestingois dresses Boudu in a frock coal, the ritual vestment of Baudelaire's dandy. But where Boudu had laughingly rejected the garment, Boeldieu chooses the woodland god's instrument to play his dying song.

Renoir's nature god is, we know, a god of love, whose piping stirs an erotic flow within the human breast. But when the god becomes a dandy, love and death mingle in his tune. Perhaps his power is perverted by the social context of his life, which drives him to deny sentiment, enthrone style, and treat the contest of nature and convention as a holy war. Love does arise around Boeldieu. His own love for Maréchal finds expression at last in the thin tones of "Le Petit Navire," but this act of love and of duty is also Boeldieu's own means of escape into death. He has observed the affection between Maréchal and Rosenthal—"I know your preference."—so his action may be tinged by the reaction of a rejected lover, as in its completion it becomes an action rejecting the love so patently offered by Rauffenstein.

For Renoir the nature god signifies freedom from conventional restraint. And "Bois le Dieu" does play this role in the escape. His action frees Maréchal and Rosenthal, and, as he stands atop the fortress, it brings Rauffenstein to plead that they face each other as mere men. Where Boeldieu's expression of love came in the sound of a flute, Rauffenstein's declaration is made in a foreign tongue, English, the language of *their* world: "I beg you, man to man, come back." Renoir says that he told Stroheim to speak these lines like a man pleading with his mistress to return. But Boeldieu's style will not permit him to turn back: "It's damn nice of you, Rauffenstein, but it's impossible!" And Rauffenstein's honor as a marksman will not allow him to miss, though it also does not require him to kill. So the chapel becomes an infirmary for the final act of the performance. A dying Boeldieu can be softer: "Francais ou Allemande, le devoir, c'est le devoir . . . pour un homme du peuple, c'est terrible de mourir à la guerre. Pour vous et moi, c'était une bonne solution." Despite the god of love, in the world of gray smudges the dandy must choose death. Hence, in this context, the final image of Rauffenstein cutting his geranium becomes not merely "the supreme expression of a ritual of elegance" or a sentimental romantic gesture expressing Rauffenstein's grief, but a precisely appropriate sacrifice of nature at the death of the nature god become victim of the conventions he embraced.

Boeldieu and Rauffenstein are heroes; their training and temperament demand it. Maréchal and Rosenthal are not; if they perform heroically, it will be in response to men, not style. So, while the aristocrats play out their game of death, the common men gamble for life. Amid the isolation of Wintersborn, they work together, braiding their cord, smoking, openly avowing their mutual regard. Rosenthal defends Boeldieu as "épatant" (splendid); Maréchal, agreeing, says, "but we don't have the same education. Listen, if you and I happen to fall into the shit, we'd just be a couple of poor stiffs— but whatever happened to him he'd still be *Monsieur* de Boeldieu." Rosenthal describes his family background in terms quite different from the catalogue of properties defensively cited at Hallbach: "I'm very proud of my rich family. When I invite you to my table, that gives me an occasion to show them off. People think that our great fault is avarice. Grievous error; we are often too generous. Alas, in the face of that quality Jehovah has overly endowed us with the sin of pride." Maréchal responds: "Oh, that's all bunk. Me, I don't give a damn for Jehovah. All I see is that you've been a good pal."

This amity carries them through the escape. Free of the fortress, they huddle together against the cold, move cautiously through the bleak frozen countryside, disagreeing about how to go. In *La Grande Illusion* the path to the final test leads through the reduction, or ascent, from combatant to prisoner to mere man. At its end Boeldieu and Rauffenstein could not shake their identification with their world of noble status and war, could not overcome the habits of adherence to the conventional values of the fortress: duty, honor, ascetic denial. Maréchal and Rosenthal have less to overcome but that renders the test no less severe.

Starved, frozen, their movement all but stopped by Rosenthal's ankle, they rage at each other:

"You slipped! We know you slipped. And if we get nabbed, dragging along like this, you can explain that you slipped! Clumsy! We've got nothing left to eat; might as well give up right now!"

"Gladly! For I'm fed up, too. Fed up! Fed up! If you only knew how I detest you!"

"I swear that it's mutual! Shall I tell you what you are to me? A burden! A ball and chain tied to my leg! For a start, I never could stand Jews—you hear?"

"A little late to find that out. Shove off then! Why are you waiting to get rid of me? You're dying to!"

"You won't have to tell me that twice!"

"Clear out—clear out! Quick! So I won't have to see your ugly mug any more!"

"Fine! I'm off! Try to shift for yourself. So long!"

"Good-bye! I could sing, I'm so happy!"

Ugly with frustration and exhaustion, they glare at each other, then as Maréchal strides away, each absurdly chants Boeldieu's song of love, "Le Petit Navire." But the words die in Maréchal's throat. Cut to Rosenthal, seated on his rock: shattered, abandoned, his desperate bluster dissolved, he weeps pitifully; the skirt of Maréchal's black coat edges silently into the frame. Rage spent, both the voices and the words have changed. Plaintively, Rosenthal asks, "Why did you come back?" Tenderly, Maréchal replies, "Let's go. Come on, mate," as he helps Rosenthal to his feet.

The crisis past, the other values of mere men can oppose those of the fortress: loyalty, humor, brotherhood. Now each acts with concern for the other, Maréchal wanting to stop, Rosenthal insisting he can go on. At the sound of a step in Elsa's barn each tries to protect the other.

Maréchal's colloquy with the cow captures the spirit of life at the farm: "Don't be afraid, it's me. You don't give a damn if a Frenchman feeds you, hey? You smell like my grandfather's cow—that's a good smell here. You were born in Wurtemberg and me, in the Twentieth in Paris, but that doesn't keep us from being pals, you see. You're a poor cow and me, a poor soldier—but we each do our best, don't we?"

Those values of ordinary men, thus far little noticed in the film—home and work, wife and child, joy and tenderness—now make their stand against the fortress. At Wintersborn the great crucifix hangs unnoticed over its altar; at the farm Rosenthal's potato-Jesus delights a child, his Jewishness can be fondly asserted—"mon frère de race"—and the bells in the valley sound of Sunday morning calm. The actions are simple and most unheroic: Maréchal feeds a cow and chucks a hatchet into a chopping block; Elsa scrubs the floor; Lotte counts her fingers; Rosenthal winds a phonograph. The insignificant pursuits of peace—but in them the drifting Maréchal finds a compass, and his good-fellowship blossoms into tenderness. Though we are left at film's end with only a forlorn hope that Maréchal will, indeed,

Boeldieu.

ever return to Elsa, we cannot doubt the depth and truth of his feelings. The gulf between the fortress and the farm, the militaristic world of the past and Maréchal's, and Renoir's, humane hope for the future, finds direct expression in the words of love that are evoked in each, in the contrast between Rauffenstein, smartly uniformed, gun in hand, calling to a distant figure in the darkness, "I beg you, man to man, come back," and the simplicity by which Maréchal, in his nondescript refugee clothes, child in his arms, conveys all his love, his hope, his gratitude: "Lotte hat blaue augen."

The performances of Fresnay and Stroheim, Gabin and Dalio in these roles seem little short of perfect. Despite the comparative rigidity entailed in their commitment to a noble style, the characters Boeldieu and Rauffenstein are built of nuances whereby an inner life shows through the style: the tilt of an eyebrow, the slight upturn at the corner of a mouth, the minute ways in which Fresnay conveys Boeldieu's repugnance at being touched—so that when he extends his hand to Maréchal before the escape it becomes an extraordinary act of deep attachment. Stroheim's voice achieves subtleties of expression in three languages, from his agonized plea to Boeldieu in English to the harshest German in the film a moment later as he orders the pursuit of the fugitives—this flexibility of voice provides a counterpoint to the stiffness of body throughout the role.

For Maréchal and Rosenthal a much greater range of physical reaction is permissible, hence Gabin and Dalio indulge in broader gestures, construct their characters more of actions than intimations. Maréchal's overt expressions range from despair and rage to the joy and tenderness with which he regards Elsa on Christmas morning. Not that these performances lack nuance, but the nuances add depth to the characterization rather than being its primary constituent. Dalio's success in creating a warm, generous, slightly defensive but wholly sympathetic Rosenthal is perhaps measured by the virulence of the attack on the film by the French anti-Semite Céline in *Bagatelles pour un massacre*.

The second tier of characters, Elsa and Lotte, Demolder, the other men in the room, have the same authenticity as the central quartet. Gaston Modot's engineer is judicious in his actions, reasonable and careful in thought and speech, yet claims to be moved by the "spirit of contradiction." Carette's actor, whose performance in the revue demonstrates how far he stands from the top of his profession, nevertheless acts at every moment, any word or event evoking the outbursts that are his mode of combating boredom for both himself and his comrades. At Hallbach the actor and Boeldieu create two poles of stylization of self—effusive and reticent—against which the naturalness of the others shows itself. Jean Dasté, once more a teacher, creates a character at once the most sensitive and the most ineffectual of the prisoners. Unsophisticated, unadventurous, a bit inept, yet thoughtful, considerate, tolerant; he represents the characteristics of that profession both maligned and admired in France since the Revolution, dedicated, underpaid men sometimes called "saints without hope."

André Bazin writes that Renoir's "realism is not that of the copy, but of the reinvention of that which is exactly known, outside of all convention, to create detail which is at once documentary and significant . . . Accuracy of detail is with Renoir as much a matter of imagination as of observation or reality, from which he always knows how to disengage the revealing but nonconventional act."[12] His concern for the nonconventional act is one aspect of Renoir's war on clichés, but he often succeeds with such subtlety and so little fanfare that his viewers supply the clichés he avoids. Thus, the moment when the teacher discovers the fallen signal is, as played, precisely right for this ruminant, soft-spoken character, but it is described in the *l'Avant-Scène découpage* as the usual cinema cliché. The *l'Avant-Scène* description reads: "Dead silence. They are all very upset by the news. Suddenly the teacher jumps; he has just noticed that the tin for the alarm has fallen on the bed. The teacher: 'Oh! The alarm!' "[13] But in the film the teacher neither jumps nor speaks in exclamations. He slowly looks up and without change of pace or expression, softly and slowly says, "Oh, the signal," expressing urgency only in his intonation.

This tendency of viewers, and reviewers, to demand the clichés that Renoir refuses to provide accounts for the charge that Dita Parlo is not a very convincing farm wife, as it accounts for much of the talk about Renoir's miscasting. It is no more true, surely, that every *bauerfrau* is fat and homely than that every young lover is handsome or every Prussian officer cold and cruel. Dita Parlo's performance, is unexceptionable: her speech is simple, clear and direct, her stance and movements slightly lacking in grace. Her face, with its eloquent pale beauty, shows both the sadness of her lonely life and the cheer Maréchal and Rosenthal bring to it. And, in a film in which love speaks obliquely and in a foreign tongue, its most joyful expression is Elsa's hesitant, smiling, shy, "Le . . . café . . . est . . . prêt."

Style and Form

Before *La Grande Illusion*, Jean Renoir had shown a tendency to shape his films into cyclical or symmetrical wholes, with the symmetry involving both cinematic form and narrative content. But he had also often included in these films matching or parallel sequences, characters, actions, or shots, as well as repetitions of a phrase, a gesture, a composition or a camera movement, in ways which established a network of internal references within the film and helped to create the density and richness that distinguish these works.

This use of parallels and repetitions, heretofore an important but subordinate element in the totality of a Renoir film, in *La Grande Illusion* becomes the organizing principle of the whole: Two parallel introductory scenes; three large parallel central sections; one pair of characters splitting into two parallel pairs, with a complex variety of smaller parallels and repetitions, where the repetitions are often also reversals, a repeated form with a contrast in meaning. There are perhaps twenty parallels in the film and as many repetitions and internal references.

The introductory scenes are parallel not so much in their presentation of characters as in their depiction of the two opposing sides in this war. The predominant moral perception of the film, that men on both sides of the line are equally human, finds its first expression in the juxtaposition of these two scenes, and most simply in two images: two rooms traversed by a moving camera. These two rooms, where men eat together, share music and drink, a white-clad barman stationed by the door, nearly identical phonographs and very similar pictures tacked carelessly on the wall. But the French sit scattered in groups, while the German room holds a single large table. And the German side shows no counterpart of the mocking poster tacked to the French bar, proclaiming: "Alcohol kills. Alcohol drives you mad. The squadron leader drinks it."

Rauffenstein's lunch precedes the meal at Hallbach, and this parallel pair of convivial scenes stands in contrast to two later images: Rauffenstein eating alone while his orderly stands by and Lotte alone at the big table at Elsa's. Also, Rauffenstein's drink at the beginning of his role matches that at its end, not only in the tilt of his body backward, the neck unbending, but also in that each drink follows an action of shooting down Boeldieu, though the first is taken in celebration and the second as fortification against death.

I have already noted the parallel openings of the three central sections, each followed by several scenes of interaction, then by a departure from this locale. These parallel developments allow for a rich array of contrasts and cross-references: The engineer asking Maréchal if Boeldieu can be trusted; Rauffenstein asking Boeldieu, "The word of a Maréchal?" when Boeldieu has replied to his request for assurance with a diplomat's truth which preserves both his honor and his comrade's hope of escape, since the forbidden cord is not literally in the room. Two scenes of unpacking a crate, each followed by a moment of stunned silence: where even these incursions from the outer world reinforce the difference between Hallbach and Wintersborn, unity and division. Soldiers before a bulletin board announcing the fall of Douaumont; Elsa, Maréchal, and Rosenthal before a wall with pictures of her dead husband and brothers, where we shall miss the parallel if we cannot identify Douaumont as the fort whose fall opened the battle of Verdun, in which half a million men were killed or wounded. Boeldieu telling Rauffenstein "Duty is duty," thus justifying his own death; a German soldier in the window telling Elsa, "Duty is duty," thus leaving Maréchal and Rosenthal free. Three scenes with talk of departure while someone else is being left behind, at Hallbach with regret, at Wintersborn with embarrassment, at Elsa's with tears and a promise to return.

Etcetera. The central formal structure of three parallel developments reflects of course the central theme of three possible forms of human community. If *La Grande Illusion* appears richer and deeper on a fourth or tenth viewing, its intricate texture of parallels and repetitions, references and reversals, must contribute to this.

The familiar Renoir visual style shows no radical transformations in *La*

Grande Illusion, but rather complete mastery. Long takes in deep focus with characters ranged in depth through the space, large and supple camera movements, dynamic compositons that form and reform as the camera glides, a total integration of characters and setting, few close-ups or shot-countershot exchanges, a rhythmic flow of movement that appears completely uncontrived—*La Grande Illusion* looks so natural and sweeps so smoothly past our eye, our impression is that no one would think of doing it any other way. But this appearance veils a dozen or more shots brilliant enough to stand out as virtuoso pieces if our engagement with characters and action did not make the technique seem inevitable and necessary and therefore unexceptional. Typically, though not exclusively, these shots open a scene, presenting and exploring setting, people, and situation simultaneously. Some are epitomizing shots that summarize a character or context in a single moving image. One such, obviously, is the long traveling-shot which first reveals Rauffenstein in his chapel/chamber at Wintersborn.

Almost the whole of *La Grande Illusion* is a model of economy in development, and several brilliant single shots demonstrate the falsity of the view that condensation of time always occurs in the cutting, while the actions conveyed in a single shot must have the same duration as they would in the real world. The first shot of Maréchal in solitary confinement provides an example: Maréchal works patiently gouging a divot from the wall with his spoon; the camera pans right and pulls back, then pans left again with the old guard who enters and watches in puzzlement, then asks, "What are you doing there?" Maréchal answers calmly and seriously: "There? A hole! Yes, I'm digging a hole to escape," and gestures to show himself disappearing out the hole. The astonished guard leans forward; Maréchal pushes him aside and dashes out the open door, closing it as he leaves. Rather than cut outside with Maréchal, Renoir lets his camera run on in the cell where the old guard now stands, back to the camera, looking through the little window in the door. We hear Maréchal, "Foutez-moi la paix . . . " and the sound of scuffling. The old guard stands aside; the door opens again and four guards carry an unconscious Maréchal to his bunk as the bells announce the recapture of Douaumont. This whole scene takes sixty-five seconds, a brevity accomplished by conveying the major action of the shot only by sound, thus allowing our imagination to apprehend in twelve seconds events that would take many times that long.

In the single shot showing almost all the preparations for digging the tunnel, all in one minute, forty-five seconds, camera movement rather than sound becomes Renoir's instrument of condensation. The camera restlessly prowls the room, changing direction a dozen times, so that we see fragments of action and assume them to be completed while we look away—but this fragmentation occurs without the experienced discontinuity of cutting.

For economy, consider all that is conveyed in two minutes, forty-five sec-

onds, in the theatre when the costumes arrive: the scene begins with a moving camera surveying a rather absurd chorus line of British soldiers singing "Tipperary," an orchestra assembling, and various soldiers working on sets and props, before coming to rest on Arthur inspecting the crate of costumes while Rosenthal and his friends wait. Arthur holds up a corset as the actor asks, familiarly, "Well, Arthur, you found nothing?" "No, I found nothing. Amuse yourselves." And Arthur departs. The prisoners crowd around the crate; Rosenthal holds a dress against himself, saying: "Be careful! These are objects one must handle cautiously, and with closed eyes." As they unpack the case, the dialogue reveals the duration and weight of their imprisonment: "Real dresses, mates!" . . . "How short it is. A little girl's dress." . . . "Eh! Say, you don't know that women wear short skirts now?" . . . "Just below the knee!" . . . "It's true! My old woman wrote me, but I didn't believe it."

Maréchal tells the actor, "Put one on—so we can see how it looks," but Rosenthal objects, "He's not shaved," and hands a dress to a young soldier. "Here, you, Maisonneuve, with your angel face." Maisonneuve carries off the dress as the others continued to rummage "Corsets!" . . . "Easy! Easy!" . . . "It's not only dresses that are short. They cut their hair, too." . . . "Short hair! Oh—one must imagine he's going to bed with a boy!" . . . "Really, when we're not there to watch them, women act like fools." . . . "I'm sure mine hasn't cut her hair. Bah! All those tricks are for high class whores" (a discussion to be continued in Truffaut's *Jules et Jim* and then in Renoir's novel *Les Cahiers du Capitaine Georges*). "Oh, shoes!" . . . "We'd forgotten how small they are." . . . "Stockings!" . . . "Of silk like I've never touched."

Maisonneuve calls in a falsetto, "Fellows, I'm ready." Maréchal replies:

Rosenthal.

"Let us dream a while. If we see you, that'll spoil what we imagine." But Maisonneuve emerges, in blond wig and dress; Maréchal says softly, "It's a real girl!" The ambient hubbub gradually subsides as Maisonneuve walks slowly forward, a vision of a lost world, evoking memories and dreams. The camera pans across the faces of soldiers frozen in silence, to end with a long shot of Maisonneuve gesturing weakly in the center of the group. The final twenty seconds pass in absolute silence except for Maisonneuve's repeated, soft, plaintive "It's funny . . . It's funny, isn't it?"

Some few scenes deviate from Renoir's usual unfragmented style, most prominent is the escape scene, where fifty shots fill only seven minutes, with added music intensifying the pace. Renoir usually shoots conversations in medium or three-quarter group or two shots with little cutting. The three exceptions in this film, shifts to shot-countershot format, all have an expressive basis. When the engineer, washing Maréchal's feet, leans forward to ask if Boeldieu can be trusted, Renoir cuts from two-shot to shot-countershot close-ups, then shows the two united in the same frame again after the assurance has been given. Similarly, when Rauffenstein performs his official task of citing the escape records of his new prisoners, Renoir shifts to this style, but uses group shots for the rest of this otherwise informal welcome. But the major scene employing a shot-countershot style is the conversation in the chapel that serves as Rauffenstein's chamber between Boeldieu and Rauffenstein, the two most stylized characters in the film. Here the form not only fits the characters, but this conversation articulates a central theme of the film and gains impact from cutting and close-ups that it would not have if the whole film were in this style.

The scene begins in long shot, Boeldieu and Rauffenstein standing together under the big crucifix. They walk forward, talking of Boeldieu's cousin Edmond, pause, walk again, smoking together. Boeldieu: "He's doing well. He's very happy. He was wounded. He has one less arm and has married a very wealthy woman." Rauffenstein, not without irony: "That is a very fine career." Cut to a reverse shot; back to the camera, they walk to the window at the end of the room and sit with the geranium between them on the window sill as the camera moves forward to three-quarter-shot distance. Boeldieu lifts a trophy from the window sill. Now they speak in English. Rauffenstein: "You recognize her?" Boeldieu: "Blue Minnie? Of course. You were riding her when you won the Grand Military at Liverpool in 1909." Rauffenstein: "The Prince of Wales Cup." Boeldieu: "I remember."

These remarks, this language, reaffirm their common past, their class ties in the prewar military aristocracy. That done, Renoir cuts to a medium shot of Rauffenstein in profile, now speaking French again: "I am going to tell you something, Boeldieu. Believe me, my present metier is as repugnant to me as it it to you." In matching medium shot Boeldieu replies, "You are severe." Cut to Rauffenstein: "I was a combatant, and now I am a functionary, a policeman. But it is the only means still open to give me the air of serving my country." Here, at the most intimate moment yet between these two, Renoir includes three rare point-of-view shots. First, Boeldieu, silent, full face, looking not quite directly at the camera. Then Rauffenstein, leaning forward toward the camera: "Burned all over—the reason for my gloves. Backbone fractured in two places, silver plates, a knee-cap of silver, too. The misfortunes of war have brought me these riches." The direct, personal character of this talk, expressed in these face-to-face point-of-view shots, makes Boeldieu, with his great distaste for emotion and self-exposure, withdraw from the implied intimacy. He asks—still in a point-of-view shot, for his question is as revealing as Rauffenstein's confession—"Allow me a question? Why have you made an exception of me, inviting me to your quarters?"

There follow three pairs of close-ups, two pairs of medium shots, then an unmatched pair—close-up of Rauffenstein, medium shot of Boeldieu—before the final shot in which the camera moves from a close-up of Rauffenstein back to a two-shot almost identical with that in which they spoke of Blue Minnie. That exchange, in English, had shown the similarity between these two; now, these six shot-countershot pairs display their differences and also constitute the film's central meditation on the world of 1914. In the close-ups Boeldieu is shot full face, looking up, speaking almost directly to the camera, never losing his air of irony and skepticism. Rauffenstein, three-quarter face and looking slightly down, an angle that reinforces the condescension of his remarks, speaks with utmost seriousness.

Rauffenstein: "Why? Because you call yourself Boeldieu, career officer of the French army, and me, Rauffenstein, career officer in the imperial German army." Boeldieu: "But my comrades are also officers." Rauffenstein, with disdain: "A Maréchal and a Rosenthal, officers?" Boeldieu: "They are very good soldiers." Rauffenstein: "Yes, a pretty present from the French revolution." Boeldieu: "I'm afraid that neither you nor I can stop the march of time."

Rauffenstein moves forward, stubs out his cigarette, picks up the scissors that lie beside the geranium and snaps them as he replies, "Boeldieu, I don't know who will win this war; the end, whatever it will be, will be the end of the Rauffensteins and the Boeldieus." Boeldieu responds with his ironic smile, "Perhaps there is no longer a need for us." Rauffenstein: "And don't you find that a pity?" Boeldieu, enigmatic: "Perhaps," looks away and changes the subject by remarking about the geranium.

The two minutes and forty-five seconds of this nearly symmetrical scene take twenty-one shots; a single shot suffices for the immediately following conversation between Maréchal and Rosenthal. A little later, Renoir will use only three shots for the two minutes and twenty seconds of the equally important scenes between Maréchal and Boeldieu before the escape, scenes which seem wholly informal though they center around the ritual of washing Boeldieu's white gloves and end with Maréchal refusing the offer of Boeldieu's cigarette: "English tobacco hurts my throat . . . everything separates us."

As usual, the most important and effective music in this Renoir film is internal, produced and heard within the world of the film. This includes not only the revue, "Le Petit Navire," and the Christmas music at Elsa's, but also much of the background sound at Hallbach. Here a few scattered shots and a continuity of sound create a whole new dimension of the war: drill-field commands echoing across flat open space, the sound of marching feet, male voices singing as they march, and two lines of dialogue—an old woman's, "Poor kids," and Boeldieu's, "On one side children playing at soldiers . . . "—these sounds surround the prisoners at Hallbach with young men who will soon fill up the trenches and the graves at Verdun.

Renoir's concern about the quality of sound in his films and his experimental approach to it show clearly in these lines by Françoise Giroud:

> The day when the arrival of Stroheim was announced at Colmar we had rented the city theatre. Jean Renoir asked von Stroheim to join us there to help in the projection of the work of the last days. He arrived, clean-shaven, wearing a monocle, and escorted by a terrifying nurse who wouldn't let him an inch out of her sight.
>
> There is nothing more sinister than a cold and empty theatre. There were a dozen of us, wrapped in mufflers, seated in the balcony. The lights went down. The projection began. The screen remained empty, but the noise of boots resounded, the sound of a hundred men marching in cadence . . . The sound grew louder, approached, approached closer, invaded the room, burst our eardrums, withdrew, disappeared, returned . . . There was still no picture on the screen. Five minutes, ten minutes, twelve minutes . . . the German boots continued to thud. Finally the lights went back on. We were all silent, as if stunned. The sound was far from being mastered as it is today; its use in France was still rather rough. That it could have such power, such dramatic significance, these nuances—we didn't really know that. Under Renoir's impetus the engineer of sound, Joe de Bretagne, had just made this innovation.
>
> "There," said Jean Renoir to Stroheim, "that's all that I have to show you."
>
> "I think that I am going to have a fancy for working with you," responded Stroheim.[14]

La Grande Illusion does contain background music, rather sparsely, with most of it supportive and unobtrusive. What may appear as the only flaws in the film were probably not noticeable in 1937: The music accompanying the escape seems somewhat too mechanical and insistent, and, more importantly the central theme, which Kosma had borrowed from Stravinsky's First Symphony and which swells as Rauffenstein contemplates cutting his geranium, tends to divert the sentimentality of his gesture from the character to the film.

I have left until last the most radical innovation of *La Grande Illusion*, so radical that thirty years later an American studio would proudly announce that they had done it for the first time. In its use of language *La Grande Illusion* may still remain unique, being not merely a multilingual film, but one in which language becomes a major dimension of subject matter. Beyond being a mere element in Renoir's search for truth, his insistence that each character speak his own tongue proves essential to a central theme: the role of language in human affairs.

In the contest of nature and convention, language is a convention become natural; hence, it stands on both sides of the division. Speech is as natural to man as walking, but each separate language imposes its own conventions on us, uniting some in a linguistic community that divides them from others, and sustaining all the other conventions that constitute our distinct cultures. And for most of us most of the time, nothing plays so decisive a role in our perception of character as how, and what, an individual speaks. These familiar facts take dramatic form in *La Grande Illusion*, which explores many facets of our life as talking animals, and speaks itself, of course, for the common humanity that underlies our linguistic differences.

Maréchal and Boeldieu are separated by the language they share, as they finally acknowledge: "Tout nous sépare." Boeldieu and Rauffenstein distinguish themselves from their fellows, French and German, by the third language, English, which bridges for them the chasm of the war (an innovation improvised by Renoir when he discovered that Fresnay, like Stroheim, spoke excellent English). In the parallel conversations at Rauffenstein's table early in the film, Rauffenstein switches from French to English without question or explanation, knowing that a "de Boeldieu" will of course understand; beside them Maréchal is surprised to find his German neighbor speaking French and seeks an explanation. The moments when Boeldieu and Rauffenstein speak English are quite distinct and always have reference to the prewar world of their class—until the final moment when Rauffenstein calls in English, "Boeldieu, have you really gone mad?" futilely evoking that world in his appeal for Boeldieu's return. Their common language drives Maréchal and Rosenthal apart when they translate frustration into attacks on each other; they come together again in silence. The camp commandant at Hallbach repeats in German, "Streng verboten," even though he apparently understands French well enough to know when this injunction is appropriate; the language confirms the ascendance of German authority here. The English officer who has dropped his suitcase replies, "I don't speak French," to Maréchal's frantic efforts to inform him of the tunnel.

In all these cases, language proves as much an instrument of division as of unification. But it also serves to create an instant bond between the new prisoners at Hallbach and the old hands, and to establish Maréchal immediately as one of the men together in the room—the same speech patterns that separate him from Boeldieu unite him with the actor and the engineer. And Maréchal in his dungeon feels the despair of one cut off from the sounds of his own speech.

Among the facts that most interest Renoir is that love can transcend the barriers of language. And repeatedly, late in the film, he employs the most divisive aspects of language—the fact that different languages *are* different

The language of love: "I beg you, man to man, come back." "Streng verboten." "Le . . . café
. . . est . . . prêt." "Lotte hat blaue Augen." "Au revoir, sale juif."

and mutually unintelligible, and the fact that a common language may be
used to create barriers rather than destroy them—to express the closest ties
developed in the film. The camp commandant's harsh "Streng verboten,"
repeated mockingly by Maréchal through the film, becomes an expression
of love and pure joy when Lotte wants to eat the baby Jesus. Almost no
avowal of love is made in the speaker's native language, but nevertheless
they are made and understood. Maréchal and Elsa sit side by side, each
speaking words the other cannot understand to convey the emotion evoked

by the necessity of parting, but each hears the love and pain expressed—and recaptures it again at the moment of leavetaking in simpler terms: "Lotte hat blaue augen." . . . "Blaue augen." And finally, Maréchal's whole journey in understanding and his growth in love is summarized in an ugly phrase made joyful by experience and affection: "Au revoir, sale juif."

The first image of *La Grande Illusion* is of a phonograph record, the last, of a field buried in snow. Tone changes from black to white; perspective, from close-up to extreme long shot; movement, from a spinning in place to the slow forward progress of two men moving together. These changes might be seen as symbolic of the distance covered in the film, in the life of its hero, in the world portrayed. And the greatest illusion may be that it cannot be, that we must forever spin in place, that this is merely a hopeful dream from a world long dead.

Like many another Renoir film, *La Grande Illusion* has had a long life in film societies and universities. But it has also had an astonishing commercial career, with four grand openings in Paris, in 1937, 1946, 1958, and 1972, all of them triumphant, though the 1946 revival was the occasion for a critical controversy begun when the critic Georges Altman deplored the presentation of such a film while the memories of Dachau and Buchenwald were still fresh.[15] The 1958 revival followed the discovery of a new negative that had been seized by the Nazis and recovered during the war. Reissued in complete and integral form, *La Grande Illusion* was voted by an international jury at the Brussels Exposition as among the six greatest films of all time. Its Paris opening in October 1958 brought with it a memoir by Françoise Giroud, who had been the script girl, listed in the credits as Gourdji. This memoir contains a description of Renoir, the director, which has been echoed by many another Renoir collaborator and which I can confirm as an accurate portrayal of Renoir at work on *Le Petit Theatre de Jean Renoir* in 1969:

> He was *le patron*—exacting, indefatigable despite an old war wound that made him limp, sometimes hard and sparing of no one, expecting each to do his best, but setting the same value on the intelligent effort of a mechanic who levels the rails for a traveling shot on uneven ground as on the imagination of his cameraman Christian Matras . . . or the keen virtuosity that Stroheim must display to play a role in a language he didn't understand. Respecting only one heirarchy, that of professional competence, he gave us all the chance to understand how fifty individual efforts could fuse into a collective effort and give each one the pride of having fully participated.
>
> Is that a grand illusion? It is his, and I must not be the only one to whom he has communicated it.[16]

19

La Marseillaise
1938

What is exciting in our metier is that we can from time to time try to restore to the facts their true sense, to disengage them from all the rubbish, all the dust, that masks and deforms them.
—Jean Renoir

Allons, enfants de la patrie,
Le jour de gloire est arrivé.

While the camaraderie of the Popular Front still endured and memories of making *La Vie est à nous* remained fresh, Jean Renoir's friends of the Left dreamed of a film spectacle celebrating and solidifying this union of "the people." Conceived within Ciné-Liberté and supported by the recently revived leftist labor federation, the Confédération générale du travail, a proposal emerged for an enterprise unique in the short history of film—a commercial film financed and produced outside of the normal channels, a film by the people and for the people. As Renoir went to work on *La Grande Illusion*, plans for *La Marseillaise* grew—plans whose eventual outcome would move a fascist critic to proclaim: "*La Marseillaise ou La Grande Désillusion.*"

Posters and pamphlets sought support for a truly national film: "The film of the union of the French nation against a minority of exploiters, the film of the rights of man and of the citizen. For the first time a film will be produced by the people themselves, by a vast popular subscription. Two francs for a share of the partnership! Two francs for a ticket of subscription! Two francs which will be deducted from the price of a seat in the hall where the film will be shown. Subscribe!"[1] Who but Jean Renoir would be a fitting director for such a project? And when the Chorale Populaire sang "La Marseillaise" as often as "L'Internationale," the story of the marching song of the Army of the Rhine flooding across France with the Revolution seemed an appropriately unifying theme.

But while Renoir was making *La Grande Illusion*, the Popular Front writhed and withered. Its *jour de gloire* had already passed. The policy of nonintervention in Spain made mockery of the common front against fascism. In late February of 1937 Premier Blum announced a "pause" in the program of social reforms; a few days later the police fired into a left-wing mob attacking a cinema where a *Croix de feu* program played. Now the Popular Front government had worker's blood on its hands. A new wave of strikes occurred. Shortly after *La Grande Illusion* has its Paris premier in early June, the Blum government toppled; the Popular Front triumph had lasted barely a year.

Still, *La Marseillaise* was launched with great enthusiasm. *L'Humanité* and other organs of the Left described the preparation and aspirations of the film; public meetings were organized to promote its production. The word even reached London, where *World Film News* of July 1937 carried a story, "Citizens of Paris Make a Film," in which Marie Seton gave a totally inaccurate account of the film-to-be, distributing leading roles to Maurice Chevalier and Jean Gabin and describing scenes with no resemblance at all to the film Renoir would actually make.

Renoir and his historical advisors read the pages of history—documents from the period of the Revolution—Renoir making his acquaintance with the citizens and courtiers who would people his film. He says of this: "Usually I told stories that happened in an environment that I knew, where I had lived, where the documentation was already in me. But *La Marseillaise* was an historical film and I had to learn a great deal about the style, the fashions, the speech and the people of that epoch. And as a result of my reading, I can almost say that I didn't have to write the dialogue in *La Marseillaise*; almost all of it is taken from existing documents."[2]

Shooting would begin in the fall, with scenes set in Marseilles to be shot in Antibes. In 1937 the rue Thubaneau, which had housed the Jacobin society of Marseilles in 1790 and heard the first singing of Rouget de Lisle's *hymne* in 1792, was not yet the disreputable little street adjoining an Arab quarter that it is today, but still the city was not a promising location. Renoir explains: "Of course Marseilles no longer has any resemblance to the Marseilles of 1790. But I thought the streets of Antibes would more nearly correspond to what those of Marseilles must have been." Other locations were to be in Alsace, Provence, Fontainbleau, and the mountains of Haute

Provence. The money raised by subscriptions fell far short of the budget for this ambitious project, with its scores of actors and hundreds of extras in costume. So the visionary people's film became just another cinema production—"Yes," Renoir says, "Along the way the film became an absolutely normal enterprise and was distributed normally."[3]

However, if the business side lost its revolutionary character, on the set the film remained a vast cooperative undertaking of artisans at work together—Claude Beylie calls it "Un cinéma de batisseurs"[4]—in which the élan sustained within the *équipe* perhaps rekindled something of the spirit that nourished the Revolution. To achieve authenticity of speech, Renoir found a different pool of actors for each of the distinct groups in the film: the Comédie-Française for the measured, classical enunciation of the court, old friends like Nadia Sibirskaia, Gaston Modot, Carette, Séverine Lerczinska for the more common speech of the people, and the meridional actors he had known while making *Toni* for the southern rhythms of the citizens of Marseilles—hoping to mingle these varied sounds from the present in a convincing evocation of the past. "The film was very easy to make," says Renoir. "I had only very good actors; even the small roles are interpreted by someone very good. But the parts of this film that gave me the greatest pleasure were the scenes played by my brother Pierre and Lise Delamare. When I wrote and shot the scenes at the Tuileries I had the feeling that it might really have happened that way, that there I was close to reality."

Narrative and Treatment

At the Cinémathèque française, Lotte Eisner recalled how Jean Renoir had once described his idea for the opening of *La Marseillaise:* A quiet country scene, with a river flowing past verdant fields. Two peasants sit silently on the bank, fishing. In the river a corpse floats into view, moves slowly with the current. Then another—and another. When half a dozen bodies have drifted downstream one of the peasants turns to the other: "Jean, something must be going on in Paris."

Renoir says he didn't use this scene because he thought the public probably wouldn't have liked it. And given the superb opening he did devise, we may be grateful. Still this grisly joke does suggest the spirit in which Renoir undertook his task of filming an historical epic. His eternal war on clichés would have a new dimension; to the clichés of cinema and daily life, he now added the clichés of history. And among the first of these was that of the solemnity of great events. "Precisely, when I made this film I was trying with all my might to avoid solemnity. I think that it is only after the fact that things take on this solemn air. People who accomplish something aren't solemn at the start. Only after they have succeeded do they become conscious of the importance of their mission. And it was the same with these

Marseillais. They started out with ideas about what was wrong in France, but they didn't at all suppose that they would end by bringing down the monarchy. They were even convinced they were only going to deliver the king from bad advisors, and hence far from imagining that they were going to lead him to the guillotine."[5]

The popular conception of history sees the climactic event of the French Revolution as the storming of the Bastille; so Renoir begins his film of the Revolution after the Bastille has fallen. The names we associate with the Revolution are Mirabeau, Danton, Marat, Robespierre, but none of these appear in Renoir's film. He chose rather to make this film "by the people and for the people" also a film of the people, the relatively anonymous ones who took a hand in great events without leaving their fingerprints large on the pages of history. Their traces can be found, of course, but only by reading diaries, chronicles, court records—as Renoir did. He says: "In studying the history of these men who took such a part in the assault on the Tuileries, and thus in the downfall of royalty, we found among them very simple, human, normal people. Of course they were, above all, revolutionaries, but that didn't keep them from eating or drinking, from being too hot or too cold. They had their jobs and professions; there was a painter, a customs clerk, a mason, a dock worker. They were as much alive as if we had just come upon them in some street in Marseilles."[6]

Since the "story" would be familiar to everyone before the film began, Renoir could indulge his penchant for discontinuity. Labeling his work "A chronicle of some events contributing to the fall of the monarchy," he merely collected these events together, with little attempt to provide connecting links. The assault on the Bastille had shown that the old regime could not survive without change; the battle of Valmy, turning back the Prussian invaders, had assured that the change would extend to the creation of a French republic. *La Marseillaise* hangs between these two events, beginning as news of the Bastille reaches the King, ending as the French revolutionary army approaches Valmy. Renoir spans three years in half a dozen widely scattered scenes, linked by an insistent drumbeat that seems to drive France toward her fate. To call this a series of tableaux would belittle the life that fills the screen; still, compared to earlier Renoir films, the term may be appropriate. Yet these scenes reach far beyond the mere pageantry of court and country in revolutionary France. *La Marseillaise* is a film of ideas, with a continuity of ideas more than of actions, and each early scene both shows developing events and reveals the currents of thought which swept France toward the First Republic. Then, having created the setting of the Revolution, Renoir allows half a dozen "patriots" in Marseilles to fill the foreground of his space; from the background, the first strains of the Rhine Army's marching song filter through the talk in a recruiting hall. Thereafter the progress of these men and this song on their route from the Mediterranean to the Tuileries and beyond becomes the central thread of the film.

The sequence of events is this: The king is informed of the fall of the Bastille. In Provence a peasant is arrested and escapes to the mountains where he hides with some patriots from Marseilles. In Marseilles some citizens sieze the forts that overlook the city. In Coblenz aristocratic emigrés praise the king of Prussia, scoff at the revolution, and plan a triumphant return to France. The Marseillais recruit a battalion of volunteers to go to Paris; they leave singing a song brought from Strasbourg by a Jewish peddler and enter Paris to the same tune. Louis XVI decides to présent the Brunswick Manifesto to the Assembly. The Marseillais hear of the counter-ultimatum by the Paris Commune, demanding that the Assembly depose the king. On August 10, 1792, Louis XVI reviews his guard, then agrees to take refuge with the Assembly. The Marseilles battalion leads the assault on the Tuileries, then marches toward Valmy.

The opening scene of *La Marseillaise* reflects Renoir's approach to history —authentic and revealing in its details, reticent in its statement, refusing to reproduce that which we most expect. A royal guard stands in the palace at Versailles as the film opens. The medieval tapestry behind him teems with life and movement; the richly dressed guard stands rigid and immobile—the two together perhaps present a capsule history of the ancien régime. A new guard replaces the old, assuming the same lifeless, frozen stance. The camera pans left to the squad marching down the hall, changing the guard at each station. A trumpet fanfare sounds and is answered by a second, echoing, fanfare from a distance. A group of women sweep across the hall in the foreground like leaves blown by the wind, their scattered flow contrasting to the strictly ordered, mechanical goose-step of the guards, with this single image of the court and its inhabitants suggesting a class devoted to frivolity and sterile formalism.

The camera watches the guards recede down a long hall. At its far end the duke de La Rochefoucauld-Liancourt enters, comes forward around the guard, disappears through a door on the left. In the background the changing of the guard goes on. Characteristically, Renoir has left his camera idly watching the routine life of the palace; incidentally it happens upon the messenger who heralds the end of that life. Cut to the waiting room where La Rochefoucauld asks to see the king. An insolent young man-in-waiting, Guémenée, doubts that the king should be disturbed after having performed the labors of Hercules in the hunt, but yields to the duke's insistence. The door opens and Louis XVI can be seen deep in the room as Guémenée and La Rochefoucauld enter. Cut to a full shot of Louis XVI (Pierre Renoir) and his servant, Picard (Léon Larive). The king sits in bed eating, a heavy, middle-aged man in night clothes, with a scarf tied around his head. He talks of his hunger and hunting, asking Guémenée to reach the wine, Rochefoucauld

to pass the chicken, finally, between bites, asking, "What is it?" Rochefoucauld replies, "Sire, the Parisians have taken the Bastille." In close-up Louis takes another bite, then looks up: "Oh! It's a revolt." Rochefoucauld knows exactly what is up: "No, Sire, it is a revolution." The scene fades without showing the king's reaction to this distinction, but history records that on July 14, 1789, the entry which Louis XVI made in his diary was a single word: "Nothing."

He was not the only one. Renoir has said, "The principal cliché for all the great events in life is the belief that one turns a page, that before it was black and afterward it is white. That's hardly true. Life is not made up of clean cuts in a film which unreels, but of dissolves. In fact, for most of the provincial nobility, and even some Parisians, the fall of the Bastille changed nothing at all. There were some who weren't even aware of the event." So in *La Marseillaise* Renoir attempts to portray the gradual spread of the seminal idea of the Revolution:

> In *La Marseillaise* I was following an idea. I wanted to express, not the birth of the idea—for it had existed for a long time—but rather its rebirth, the development and growth of the idea of the nation as opposed to the idea of the feudal system. It was a question of moving from a condition in which people were the subjects of a personal power, obeying a seigneur or a king—perhaps because they loved that seigneur and he was very good—at any rate loyalty was felt to the person of the lord. And for the people of the nation what was important was the person of the king. Then progressively—for a new feeling takes time to develop—from this personal attachment to an individual the people passed to feeling a personal attachment to the ensemble of citizens, that is, to the nation. That is the story of *La Marseillaise*.[7]

But of course ideas alone don't make a film; so Renoir also fills *La Marseillaise* with precise details about the world of revolutionary France in which the idea was growing.

Renoir speaks with affection of the source of some of these details:

I had two marvelous assistants. One was Carl Koch, a German, who knew well the German side of Marie Antoinette and all that concerned the German influence on the court. The other was Corteggiani. Corteggiani had a passion for mechanisms and their history. For example, he knew perfectly, to the point of being able to describe, draw, break down and reassemble all the firearms used since Agincourt. All of them! It was he who helped me give the troop movements the precision they have. For example, for the changing of the guard at Versailles; that is exactly as it happened. Koch told me, for that same opening shot at Versailles, about the fanfares which accompanied his Majesty's awakening, coming from both sides of the canal. There was one troupe of musicians on one side of the canal and another responded from the far side.

One can't say all that in a film; it would take too long. So I didn't say it. But that is the reason why the fanfares, from the beginning in the vestibule, answer each other, one louder because it is closer, the other less loud. Thus, those reasons that one doesn't show are no less there, and I think that when you have reasons that you don't state but that are deepseated and exact, that gives a certain life to the scene represented. I have always been greatly attracted to that sort of precision. It is at the same time extremely enriching for the film and for oneself, and very amusing.[8]

But sometimes the reasons that aren't shown are useful for understanding. Only one sequence of *La Marseillaise* depicts, rather than merely talks about, the conditions that underlay the revolution. This sequence opens with shots of pigeons in a field. An old peasant, Cabri (Eduard Delmont), kills a pigeon with a sling and is promptly siezed and marched off to a feudal court where an arrogant nobleman declares, "It is my heritage as seig-

neur to mete out justice." He proposes to send Cabri to the galleys, since "The pigeon is mine and there are witnesses." The village mayor protests: "The galleys for a pigeon. You think that is just?" The count replies that the pigeon is merely a symbol of "the order it is my duty to defend." Those of us who have only a smattering of French history may agree that it doesn't seem just, but still wonder why Renoir couldn't find a more forceful illustration of the oppression that leads to revolution. Leo Braudy identifies Cabri as one of the many poachers in Renoir's works and thus as a symbol of the protest of nature against restrictive conventions. He writes, "The rescue from court of Cabri, the poacher in *La Marseillaise*, becomes one of the first events in the French revolution, because it focuses popular animosity against the limitations of feudal law. Class conflict in nature becomes the conflict between the landowner's fences and the poacher blithely leaping over them."[9]

But Cabri is not a poacher; he leaps no fences. When arrested he complains: "The pigeons were devouring my harvest. I have nothing but that to live on."

Under the old regime hunting rights belonged to the king, who shared them with the nobles by issuing licenses, *capitaineries*, which entitled the seigneur both to feed and hunt his game on the peasants' fields, without interference or payment for any damage done. A peasant could be sent to prison or the galleys for hunting, even on his own land and to protect his only resource. How much these hunting laws imposed a burden on the peasantry and aroused their anger is indicated by the fact that on August 4, 1789, when the National Assembly set about abolishing the feudal system, their very first specific decree dealt with pigeons and declared, "Everyone shall have the right to kill them on his own land." The second specific decree abolished *capitaineries* and gave every proprietor the right to destroy any kind of game on his own property.

Cabri's flight to the mountains and his talk with Arnaud and Bomier about the simple natural life do suggest the role that Rousseau's conception of nature played in kindling the Revolution. But the scenes of Cabri's arrest and trial, far from being merely symbolic of other abuses, are a documentary presentation of the major grievance felt by perhaps 85 percent of the French population against the ancien régime. Renoir says that the details come directly from a court record.

Documentary moments abound in *La Marseillaise*, though not all are as readily recognizable as the demonstration of how to load a muzzle-loading rifle in twelve counts, which may serve not merely as an amusing bit of antiquarian lore, but also explain how any of the Marseillais could escape alive from the Tuileries. There is, for example, the unlikely moment when the nobles sing to the king in the Tuileries. About the latter Renoir says, "One improbable thing that excited me when I read it, is the song 'Oh, Richard, Oh, My King.' When Louis XVI agreed to review the guard, the gentlemen who were in the vestibule went to their knees and sang 'O Richard, O mon Roi.' That looks like a nice effect by a director to give a sort of rhythm and solemnity to the descent of the king to the courtyard. Not at all! It happened exactly like that. The song is taken from 'Richard Coeur de Lion,' a popular opera at that time, by Gretry. All the fashionable people knew it by heart and readily sang the grand air, "O Richard, O mon Roi." So when Louis XVI came out, instinctively they all sank to their knees to intone that air, because they all knew it and it seemed to them to respond to something in that situation."[10]

Yet along with such precision of detail goes a certain carelessness about other aspects of history and, of course, the inclusion of fictitious characters and events. For example, the seizure of the fort in Marseilles actually occurred on April 30, 1790, but the film dates it some months later, and the actual seizure was achieved by means more simple than the ruse Renoir devised for his film, which allows him to involve all of his central group of characters in the action. Thus we find in *La Marseillaise* some counterpart to that blending of fact and fiction which had characterized *La Vie est à nous*.

But of course, the "facts" in *La Marseillaise* are facts of the late eighteenth century and, necessarily, have been reconstructed for the film. But a substantial proportion of the factual material appears in the dialogue, where the exact repeatability of utterances and the timelessness of truth make authenticity easier. By taking the lines of his dialogue from documents of the Revolution, Renoir could achieve in the talk and ideas of his film a level of veracity which the images merely approximate, with the idea of the Nation, the fraternal union of all Frenchmen, as the unifying concept. The early scenes combine to present the central conflict of the era, opposing a passionately held idea to an entrenched order and class. The transformation, or radicalization, of the idea appears in the clamorous disorder of the *Société des amis de la constitution* in Marseilles, the Jacobin Club, where the oratory modulates from a defense of the king—while denouncing the "handful of troublemakers who compromise the Revolution"—to a labeling of the king and queen as M. and Mme. Veto and an accusation that M. Veto betrays because he is a straw man, Mme. Veto because she is an Austrian.

Two interlocked developments express the growing public fervor through which the idea of the nation gave birth to its actuality: the amplification of the song that would become "La Marseillaise" from a single voice in the background to a vigorous chorus of the Marseilles battalion greeted by the cheers of a Parisian throng, and the amplification of movement from the lone figure of Cabri climbing the mountain to the ragged lines of the Marseilles battalion strolling toward Paris, then to the flow of Parisians toward the Tuileries and, finally, the march of a revolutionary army toward Valmy.

These are the movements that dominate the film and carry its message of liberty and fraternity, but interspersed in their flow are glimpses of the opposing force, the dying order of the old regime. Renoir and his film stand firmly on the side of the Revolution—"I shot the film in a state of great enthusiasm for democratic ideas, that's evident"—yet he represents the court and the aristocrats lucidly and objectively.

By 1789 the French nobility had become a privileged class that performed small service in return for its privileges. Most had achieved nobility by the purchase of patents from a needy king. Some served in administrative posts; most lived as rural seigneurs, lords of a small domain. The most arrogant clustered at Versailles, where they helped bankrupt France by their extravagance. Some nobles fled from France soon after the Bastille fell; others followed later. These emigrés formed a counterrevolutionary group in exile, doing their best to enlist foreign aid against the Revolution. Louis XVI publicly accepted the constitution, but privately joined the appeal for armed intervention. Many emigrés stayed in the Rhineland, believing that when the Revolution failed they would quickly return to France and visit a terrible vengeance on the republicans.

These emigrés become the subject of one of the most expressive scenes in *La Marseillaise*, one reminiscent of *La Grande Illusion*: some men and women together in a room, confined by their own choice perhaps, yet held in suspension, away from their real life in another land. The scene opens on a sign: Hotel Stadt, Coblenz; the camera recedes to include in its frame St. Laurent, the deposed commander of the forts of Marseilles, then follows him as he walks through the room. Like Captain de Boeldieu, these "prisoners" keep up the appearances, dress in ruffles, powdered and curled wigs, *culottes*; the women wear jewels, though one of the men complains of the holes in his shoes. Some play cards; one toys with a yo-yo; another holds a monkey in his arms; some merely stand and talk. The scene creates an impression of idleness, emptiness, endlessly repeated conversations—of yearning for the old France that remains home. A woman asserts: "The time for regret is past. Soon we will be back in France," and talk turns to the triumphant Prussian army of the duke of Brunswick, which will restore the old regime. Illusions multiply: the march to Paris will be merely a pleasant promenade; the populace will kneel in joy before the comte d'Artois and acclaim the white flag and the fleur-de-lis; at the sight of the invaders, the Revolution will collapse—one doesn't make war with weavers, cobblers, and lawyers. Their nation is merely a gathering of the rabble against people of quality, a swarm of little people who have neither the knowledge, experience, nor talent for great affairs. St. Laurent protests: "The French have not always been beaten. The man who relieved me of my command had a very different concept of the nation. If they have many like him our path will not be easy."

A woman interrupts this political conversation: "Can you help us settle a dispute of great importance? At Versailles, in the third figure of the gavotte, does one look to the right or to the left?" One of the speakers starts to answer, stops in dismay, "Why, I've forgotten." Several arise and they try to remember the dance by dancing.

One may feel that the conclusion of this scene merely confirms the emptiness and futility of the life displayed. But Renoir's insight reaches deeper than that—goes indeed to the heart of the Revolution. For despite its reliance on talk about nature and natural rights, this revolution was essentially a struggle over which conventions to adopt, which forms would constitute the tradition. "St. Just sent people to the guillotine to impose the metric system. It's fantastic," says Renoir. And the term *sans culottes* relates to a disagreement about whether men would wear long pants or knee-breeches. But of course, nothing is more crucial in human life than the rules, the conventions we live by.

For the nobility, by 1792, a style of life was at stake, a style that was their life. And the dance at Versailles is the purest expression of that style and the ancien régime—a mere form, but one that gives birth to harmony and beauty if all agree and execute it gracefully. The dispute about the gavotte is indeed of great importance. For these emigrés, displaced from their land, if they have really forgotten the steps of the dance, the Revolution has already won. So the end of the scene becomes ludicrous, sad, and profound: the duke of Brunswick forgotten, they raise their hands, move in rhythm. The scene fades on this effort to recapture the formal elegance which had become their only excuse for being.

Here, as elsewhere, *La Marseillaise* reflects faithfully, if incompletely, the era of the French Revolution, even to the culinary revolution encouraged by the Marseillais' taste for tomatoes. But some critics also claim that *La Marseillaise* represents more than any other Renoir film the era of its making, the time of the Popular Front. Some critics of the thirties saw the film largely in terms of contemporary politics: "When the mayor of Marseilles cries, "The aristocrats have raised the cost of living," one must translate, "Down with Bonnet."[11] But by now we must ask how true or relevant this is.

No doubt *La Marseillaise* emerged from the Popular Front. The facts of its origin are plain, though Renoir says he had long been thinking about a film on the Revolution. Renoir and his confreres saw clearly the parallels between 1792 and 1937: France torn by dissension, in economic distress, with a strong popular movement striving to shift power toward the unprivileged classes while an external threat was growing across the Rhine. Renoir has said, "When I shot the scene of the emigrés praising the King of Prussia, of course we knew that some Frenchmen were ready to welcome Hitler and thought he would 'restore order'." In evoking the union that had created the nation in 1792, *La Marseillaise* sought to sustain a union which would save the nation in 1939. Of course! Yet a remark about the film often repeated

since it appeared in a fascist journal in 1938,[12] that when a Marseillais asserts that a priest is not necessarily a reactionary this refers to Maurice Thorez' hand extended to the Catholics, now seems ridiculous, or at best irrelevant. It diminishes the film by diverting attention from it—which was perhaps its original intent.

In 1790 the "Civil Constitution of the Clergy" and the requirement that priests and bishops be elected and take a civil oath became one of the most divisive issues of the Revolution. The Jacobin Club of Marseilles grew progressively more hostile toward the church—no work purporting to reflect currents of thought in 1792 could omit reference to this issue, however the world might go later. In 1938 the dialogue of *La Marseillaise* seemed resonant with echoes of the contemporary twentieth-century world. But these echoes have faded with the years, perhaps to their proper level. However consciously Renoir may have included lines pertinent to his own time, he also took care to root each one firmly in the facts of the revolutionary period—and these roots now seem much more pertinent to the film.

When *La Marseillaise* was reconstituted in a nearly complete version in 1967, critics wrote that it had lost none of its power over the years. But in 1938 few seemed aware of this power; neither commercially nor politically did the film have much success. It was, perhaps, a victim of the political turmoil of its time; too direct in its statement for some, too oblique for others. We may now feel that Renoir's engagement with the Popular Front was fulfilled in the film's espousal of the democratic ideals of the Revolution; we no longer search for more obscure meanings. Perhaps this attitude was necessary for the release of the film's latent power.

Characterization

Fleeing from the aristocrats, two revolutionaries go to the mountains of Provence where they live with nature and wonder why they should want any other sort of life. Fleeing from the revolution, a dozen nobles go to a hotel in Coblenz where they complain that it is not Versailles. In simplistic terms, the Revolution was a confrontation of the people and the court; *La Marseillaise*, unlike other Renoir films, characterizes classes more than individuals and treats individuals as representative of their class. Hardly a frame in the film fails to contribute to Renoir's depiction of the contending groups and their divergent conceptions and styles of life. The Jacobins shout at each other, mill about in confusion, prance singing through the streets; sometimes their meaning is lost in the tumult of the moment or the passion in a voice. The courtiers move and speak with decorum, disagree politely, hardly ever raise their voices; they enunciate clearly and distinctly. The Marseilles battalion straggles toward Paris, strung out in threes and fours, inventing new verses for the rousing song they sing; the nobles kneel in unison and reverently chant, "O Richard, O mon Roi." The people speak often of the nation and its citizens; St. Laurent asks Arnaud to explain these strange terms and still professes not to understand. Later, facing a firing squad, a young man addressed as "citizen" hotly denies the term, "I am no citizen. I am Armand de Hoffenberg," and proudly dies. Even though they are equally assured of the rightness of their cause, none of the Marseillais displays the air of superiority with which the least of the courtiers moves and speaks—an air conveyed by gesture, a characteristic tilt of the head, the tone and rhythm of speech. On one side diversity, vitality, spontaniety, disorder are held together by a common purpose and ideal; on the other a uniformity of manner and style, a rather rigidly ordered exterior, mask a multitude of individual differences.

In the vocabulary of 1792 in France, a *patriote* was a revolutionary and an *aristocrate* anyone opposed to the Revolution. Most of the patriotes were bourgeois and relatively prosperous. The ideology of the Enlightenment and the philosophes channeled their anger against an extravagant and decadent ruling class into specific political action. In 1791, some 70 percent of the members of the Jacobin Club of Marseilles were bourgeois, though the proportion dropped rather sharply by 1794. Working-class members of the club were much more likely to be artisans than laborers.

Renoir's revolutionaries in *La Marseillaise* fit this picture: a custom's clerk, a mason, an artist who supports the revolution by painting the heroes of antiquity rather than the pastoral scenes preferred at Versailles. Though Bomier, the mason, wonders what sort of revolution it is that will accept supporters only if they are free from debt, it was in fact that sort of revolution. As Renoir has said, an urban proletariat did not yet exist.

Through most of the film, a small cluster of men share our attention: Arnaud (Andrex), Bomier (Ardisson), Javel (Paul Dullac), Ardisson (Fernand Flament), Cuculière (Alex Truchy). In this sense they are the major characters of *La Marseillaise*, yet their roles differ greatly from what we might expect of Renoir heroes, who usually act in situations where their choice has some effect. But these Marseillais are the common men of the revolution; they have already chosen to be *patriotes* and thus relinquished further choice. Hence their action hardly differs from that of the men who surround them. But their talk becomes the thread which leads through the labyrinth of history. Thus their central role in the film is as a chorus commenting on the events that transform France from monarchy to republic—most of the ideas that inform *La Marseillaise* find expression in their voices.

Consonant with their role as chorus, characterization rests more on saying than doing. On the level of action, they are hardly distinguishable; all are courageous, devoted to their cause, loyal to each other, stout-hearted fighters on the side of liberty. Usually they act together, whether sitting in the gallery of the Jacobin Club, marching with the battalion, or waiting in Paris for decisions to be made. Arnaud and Bomier do first appear in the mountains; their descent to the city to join the Revolution may symbolize Renoir's belief in nature as a source for the renewal of civilization. But once in Marseilles they become simply members of a revolutionary group. As choristers, though, each member has a distinct personality, a voice of his own. Arnaud, analytic and judicious, with a theoretical turn of mind, functions as leader of the chorus, propounding the pregnant ideas of the era, those of the nation, the citizen, representation; he describes the effect of the Rhine Army song on the Marseillais, and provides a reasoned account of revolutionary events. Arnaud, too, makes the summarizing statement at film's end, asserting the lasting value of their actions even should they fail at Valmy: "The Prussians can't wipe out what we have given the world. Before we arrived, men just stared at liberty, like a lover forbidden to approach his beloved. Now, thanks to us, he has embraced her. To be sure, she is not yet his mistress, but they know each other and will be reunited." Andrex, who had played the weak and self-serving Gaby in *Toni*, gives a completely different sort of performance as Arnaud, confident, articulate, affirmative, compassionate, prepared for battle yet preferring to advance the Revolution by reasoned discussion. He moves with grace and poise, speaks with assurance, a handsome and vital spokesman for the Revolution and one whose commitment seems based on clearly grasped ideals.

By contrast, Bomier seems more impulsive than thoughtful, more readily moved by specific people and events than by ideas, more commited to his comrades than to abstractions. Where Arnaud talks of ideas, Bomier talks of food and women, his mother and his debts. Among the chorus, only he is shown having an ordinary life apart from politics, and planning for his life after the revolution. Effusive, garrulous, changeable, he doubts and questions more than the others but acts in concert with them. The romantic of the group, he expresses a Rousseauian view of nature, recalling the mountains in his dying moment. Javel, the painter, seems the least rationally motivated of the group, dogmatically anticlerical and ready to give credence to any rumor. Arnaud calls him an incorrigible pessimist, and indeed his view of the revolution seems more negative than the other's, more simply a matter of opposition to the church and the nobility than adherence to a positive goal—an attitude that persists to the final line of dialogue in the film: "Twenty thousand slaves and five thousand traitors can't defeat twenty million free men. Vive la liberté." Ardisson is forthright and simple in speech, Cuculière the youngest and quietest of the group. Though all speak with the rhythm of the south, they differ in the pitch and pace of their voices, the clarity of their thought, the degrees of emotion expressed.

Thus, the individual identity of these heroes emerges from the dialogue. But the overall movement of La Marseillaise runs from speech to action and from individual debate to mass endeavor, from Cabri killing a pigeon to an army washing over the Tuileries, leaving a rubble of corpses in its wake. Hence Renoir's chorus, since its members also engage in the action, becomes entangled in the currents of history and eventually engulfed, swallowed up, so that our final impression of the film is more of the sweep of a mass movement and collective effort than of individual speech or act. Renoir succeeds for a while in humanizing history, but ultimately history triumphs. So La Marseillaise becomes a most unusual Renoir film, in which characterization finally bows to the flow of dramatic events. The Marseillais of the chorus, since they have no control of the action but merely dance to the tune of those powers that remain in the background (the Assembly, the Paris Commune, the pamphleteers), seem particularly susceptible to being submerged by events, but other characters fare little better. Some appear briefly, then vanish: the count and the village mayor, the emigrés at Coblenz, Jenny Hélia as a fiery orator at the Jacobin Club, Carette and Modot as volunteers at Valenciennes. Each is vital, authentic, and highly individual, small gems of performance by fine actors; yet they are mere suggestions rather than full-blown persons. Cabri, St. Laurent (Aimé Clariond), and Louison (Nadia Sibirskaia) have greater latitude and achieve greater depth. Still, the central conflict in La Marseillaise opposes an idea or ideal to an order and a class; hence each of these characters becomes representative of one or the other and thus loses some of his identity as the film achieves its epic scope. Renoir has sometimes said, "I don't see why you always have to follow the same people in a film," and in La Marseillaise he refused to do so. Yet the film remains coherent through his shifts of focus because all those he follows can be assimilated to the central opposing forces. But a consequence is that they all may seem merely accidental occupants of the camera's field of view; any one of a hundred others would have served as well and the story remained the same—there were five hundred Marseilles volunteers, scores of emigrés, thousands of peasants oppressed by the hunting laws.

One group resists this erosion of identity. Partly because they are not accidental figures in this field, but rather the very center of the historic storm, the court, and especially the king and queen, provide sturdier images than the commoners do. Though appearing in less than 30 of the film's 360-odd shots, Lise Delamare and Pierre Renoir create enduring characters, not easily displaced in our minds by the rising cadence of events.

When Louis XVI became king of France at the age of twenty, his young wife soon earned the nickname "the Austrian" among some members of the court. By 1789 much of the French populace thought of Marie-Antoinette as *L'Autrichienne* and neither trusted nor liked her. A victim of court intrigue, she learned the game herself and often exerted more weight in political decisions than her lackadaisical husband. She became a principal in negotiations carred on after the Bastille fell. Always a partisan of the French alliance with Austria, she became a determined foe of the Revolution, secretly abetting its enemies while publicly accepting the constitution she considered a tissue of absurdities. She identified France with the monarchy, and when convinced that the survival of the royal family depended upon armed intervention, she betrayed the plans of the French generals to the Austrians, an act which later helped bring her to the guillotine.

Renoir's Marie-Antoinette fits this historical account quite nicely. Like the common people of the Revolution, Renoir did not find Marie-Antoinette to his taste at all: "Everything that I learned about her displeased me." So his portrait lacks warmth. We see a woman confident of her ascendance over the king, rude to others in the court, conscious of her power and ruthless in using it, calculating and, above all, cold.

Marie-Antoinette first appears in *La Marseillaise* as the king considers the Brunswick Manifesto. When a minister, Leroux, voices doubts about the manifesto, she curtly challenges him, "What do you know about it?" and quickly emerges as the strongest personality in the room, ultimately winning with a tearful and artful plea. This reduces the king to a state of contrite confusion in which the question of the manifesto is settled by default. But before this Marie-Antoinette gives the most lucid account of the royalist position to be found in the film. Leroux has remarked that the publication of the Brunswick Manifesto may arouse the public to a pitch of fury that will threaten the very existence of the monarchy. Marie-Antoinette replies: "You are right, Leroux. The curtain is about to rise on the final act of this tragedy. My opinion is that we should ring it up. In a war the best defense is to attack. I wish to end this false situation: a king who yields, subjects who won't be subjects, who no longer obey, a war we are obliged to wage against our natural friends, our own kin. To protect our lives we make detestable compromises with men we despise and principles we think blasphemous." She proposes to settle the affair by provoking an attack on the Tuileries: "The revolutionaries may enter the palace, but none will leave alive. With them, as with us, the most active elements, I dare not say the best, will always be in the lead. This extermination will be the end of the sinister comedy."

The scene in the Tuileries on August 10 opens with Marie-Antoinette planning the extermination with La Chesnaye, the commander of the guard. But her dependence on him does not prevent her from rebuking him sharply when he suggests that the crowd of nobles will hinder the defense, "You speak out of turn! . . . These are reliable men [les hommes sûr]". Intent on developing events, she is shocked to find the king calmly eating. Throughout this scene she seems much better informed and more capable than the king. Much more alert and in command, so much so that when les hommes sûr kneel and sing, we suspect this gesture may be more a response to the personality of the queen than the person of the king. This too, accords with the historical account; Mirabeau, a leader in the early days of the revolution, reputedly said, "The King has only one man on his side and that is his wife."

The frivolous and extravagant side of Marie-Antoinette does not show in La Marseillaise. We have only a sketch, but a powerful one, of a proud and arrogant woman, unwilling to cede her place in the world. For the emigrés at Coblenz and for most of the court, the assertion of their position and even the gestures in which they embody it have a tinge of the absurd; performances teeter on the edge of the comic, characters on the edge of credibility—as perhaps the whole life of their class did in 1792. In contrast, Lise Delamare gives to Marie-Antoinette acerbity, dignity, and considerable presence, making her the film's clearest and most forceful representative of the ancien régime.

But if Marie-Antoinette is historically sound, the Louis XVI created by Jean and Pierre Renoir seems much more disputable. Instead of the tyrant of popular history, we encounter a man misplaced by fate, an amiable, curious man whom ill-fortune miscast in the role of a king. Human, too human and quite lacking that air of superiority the other nobles share, he occasionally works himself up to appearing impressive in his uniform and speaking with some authority, but his mind seems elsewhere. The hunt, food, everything interests Louis except politics, and there his lack of interest seems matched by his ineptitude. For a moment his discussion of the manifesto written by the emigrés and signed reluctantly by the duke of Brunswick seems sane and sage: he reads it perceptively, expressing shock at finding "our person" cited in a manifesto directed against his subjects, stops at the words "crushing total destruction"—"subversion, strange word. Unfortunately it is clear. He says just what he means." When Marie-Antoinette speaks of ending the sinister comedy, he replies that in this affair, "we are also actors, and that is obviously a less comfortable position than that of a spectator." He speaks calmly and judiciously, but as he begins to talk of M. Brunswick the king's voice begins to rise until he comes to the point, "What bothers me most in this affair is that I will have to take him hunting." Surprised, Marie-Antoinette replies that that is only natural, but he bursts out: "He shoots badly! I have it from your brother and his minister . . . " Both voices fill with passion as the queen objects, "How can you believe a man who washes his teeth, and in public, every day?" and the king hotly defends this peculiar practice, claiming it good for the health, even asserting, "If it weren't for these troubles that engage us at present I would try this brushing myself." Then he reverts to his central complaint: if M. Brunswick comes to France, a few days of hunting will be spoiled.

Quel drôle de monde. The monarchy hangs in the balance, but the head that bears the crown worries more about toothbrushing and the hunt. Should we not praise the queen for her effort to settle the issue on more relevant grounds? Yet Renoir aligns our sympathy with Louis XVI throughout this incongruous exchange and confirms it at the end by allowing us to glimpse the cold gleam of triumph behind Marie-Antoinette's tears.

Objectively, perhaps, Louis' willingness to give more weight to the disruption of his hunt than to the *foudroyant subversion total* of the city should be as chilling as Marie-Antoinette's plan to exterminate the revolutionaries. But it isn't. For hers is a political action expressive of a ruthless determination, while his reaction seems merely ingenuous and, oddly, nonpolitical. This strange detachment from the politics of his own life persists throughout the scenes of August 10. While the queen plans a defense of the palace, Louis XVI wonders about the new food the Marseilles battalion has made popular in Paris. When she asks in dismay, "Sire, do you eat in such circumstances?" he replies calmly, as if it were the most important question of the day: "Why not? The stomach is an organ ignorant of the subtleties of politics. I ordered tomatoes. We heard so much about this vegetable the Marseilles battalion brought to Paris and I thought I'd try it. Would you like to have my impression? It's an excellent dish that we have been wrong to neglect."

Talking of tomatoes, Louis XVI speaks as one knowing and confident in his judgment. But reviewing the guard a moment later he seems more a country cousin than a reigning monarch. Uneasily wiping his face, he looks uncomfortable when the nobles in the vestibule kneel and sing, embarrassed as he waves awkwardly to the cheers of "Vive le Roi" from loyal troops, and wholly bewildered when he wanders into the National Guard sections and the men shout: "Vive la Nation!" "A bas le Roi!" "A bas Veto!" Nowhere in this scene does Pierre Renoir invest Louis XVI with the presence of a king or the air of a man who understands his situation. Back in the palace,

Louis XVI (Pierre Renoir) considers the Brunswick Manifesto. Marie-Antoinette (Lise Delamare) prevails.

his crooked wig troubles him more than the impending attack. Louis Jouvet as Roederer dominates this scene, showing what a truly regal presence might be like: aloof, dignified, properly respectful, yet completely confident and wholly in command. Confronted by this presence and the demand that he make a decision, the king merely shrugs with inept uncertainty. But when pressed by Roederer to take refuge with the Assembly, he stands and utters a single word, "Marchons!" Marie-Antoinette turns to Roederer, "M.

Roederer, you have won," but the latter replies disarmingly, "No, Madame, it's the king's good sense." Thus simply does the monarchy fall.

Renoir has said, "When I read that in some chronicle, this 'Marchons!' struck me. I said to myself, but why didn't he say 'Allons-y'? Or 'Vous avez raison'? No. 'Marchons!' There are frequently words of this sort with Louis XVI. This 'marchons' I think, has a sort of symbolic value. It could almost mean, 'Marchons à la mort.' "[13]

Perhaps Renoir is right in finding in Louis XVI a sort of quiet acquiescence in the inevitability of his own death, but I hear in this "Marchons!" rather an echo of that song the Marseillais also brought to Paris, and which surely was as much discussed as their tomatoes. Heard this way, "Marchons!" has a different symbolic value, an acceptance not of death but of the revolution by this essentially nonpolitical man who could not have deeply regretted the end of his political career.

Every other significant character in *La Marseillaise* lives largely within the political struggle, but Louis XVI's involvement seems more as victim than participant; his intentions relate more to private activities than public events. This air of living his real life outside the political arena contributes to making Louis XVI the most memorable character in *La Marseillaise*. The action that dominates the final section of the film overshadows the characters who engage in it; it is the revolution that triumphs, not the chorus of Marseillais. But though he is destroyed as king by this action, Louis XVI, as character, remains outside it to the end. As the royal family walks toward the Assembly, the children run to play in a pile of leaves. The king raises the dauphin from the ground, looks up at the trees and remarks with a touch of sadness: "So many leaves. They have fallen early this year."

Renoir says: "These words, which I did not invent, seem to me rather poignant. And they tend to confirm that aspect of a knowing victim which I believe I found in Louis XVI."[14] Yet this knowing victim has a kind of freedom no other character shares. Having accepted his fate, he lives his life beside it, as it were, being aware of the leaves on the trees while those who have mounted the tiger of political action are wholly occupied with staying on. Thus Louis XVI, of all the characters in the film, has a life apart from the action and a character that survives it. Whether the king was actually such a man, I cannot say, though Renoir believed he was. But the credibility of Pierre Renoir's performance is such that we cannot doubt that, however he was, this is how he might have been.

Style and Form

Many of the recurring formal structures in earlier Renoir films have this in common: they achieve some sort of closure or balance, or create a moment of rest amid a flux of action and movement. And they themselves become a part of the balance that Renoir constantly seeks. Typically, the world of a Renoir film is open and indeterminate, marked by movement and change, with a thickness or depth that sustains a sense of diversity and contingency. His people may not learn or change, but the possibility remains; their actions issue from choice or character rather than fate or external forces. Renoir then balances the openness of his world by displaying it in forms that achieve closure, giving a more determinate structure to our experience of the film than to the world portrayed, giving his films a beginning, middle and end, though usually the lives of his characters have neither origin nor completion within them; their past remains unknown, their future unpredictable. This balance of closed forms and open content offers the satisfaction of closure and the pleasures of freedom and indeterminacy. But beyond this, the very proliferation of closed forms becomes a factor in the openness of the Renoir world. For every closure leads to a new opening; for every end there is a new beginning—the rhythm of the film and its world absorbs these and flows on, rich enough to promise renewal after every pause. So the final closure in films like *Boudu* or *Toni* or *Le Crime de M. Lange* contains its own promise of renewal. In a Renoir film the completion of a cycle is seldom a closing of the hinge of fate.

In its form *La Marseillaise* seems an exception among Renoir films. Renoir's most familiar formal patterns seem absent. *La Marseillaise* is neither cyclical nor symmetrical in overall form; shots or sequences that pivot on a formal center and end as they began are almost wholly missing. No parallel scenes; few repetitions or internal echoes. No exchange of roles; no meeting from which dramatic movement flows—the three notable meetings in the film, though they do effect the characters, have almost no effect on subsequent events. And a form that Renoir had generally avoided, the shot-countershot construction of conversations, here occurs repeatedly and without any obvious expressive basis.

Precisely those forms that achieve closure are conspicuous by their absence in *La Marseillaise*. Instead, most scenes involve both material change and formal openness; many end without reaching equilibrium or coming to a stop. In the opening scene all movement flows toward the king; yet the scene ends on a close-up of La Rochefoucauld, though a final shot of Louis XVI would have both shown the reaction we expected to see and added symmetry to the shot-countershot set which completes the scene. Even the scene at Coblenz which creates an impression of empty lives caught in endless sterile repetition is formally open. It progresses from talk to action and ends with the beginning of the dance. Through the film Renoir transforms this lack of full closure in individual scenes into a positive forward impetus by an even more fluid camera style than before and by two new formal devices, the repeated drumbeat used as transition between sequences and the proliferation of dissolves, heretofore used sparingly by Renoir.

In this absence of familiar forms, *La Marseillaise* becomes in its felt movement the most linear of Renoir films, despite its loose continuity and its broken narrative line. The complex movement of earlier films gives way to a constant forward progression. Perhaps this explains the repeated shot-countershot sets, which give to dialogue scenes a greater feeling of forward progression than do the group shots or two-shots of *La Grande Illusion*.

In shifting to these open forms, Renoir does not abandon his search for balance. Rather, the balance is, in a sense, reversed. Formerly he created free characters in an open world and displayed them in forms that achieved closure. Now he chooses open forms to display characters whose world has closed upon them. The nobles, committed to a dying culture, can do little more than go on with the dance. The revolutionaries have already chosen the revolution; they are now fixed in its grip. They are all caught in the currents of history—not that history is necessarily determined, but these characters do not hold its reins. Where before, a multiplicity of closed forms had confirmed the openness of Renoir's world, here a concatenation of open forms becomes a relentless progression in which the characters are merely swept along. Perhaps this sharply reflects the patterns of revolution, where the dream of freedom is projected into the future, while "revolutionary discipline" becomes the order of the present.

One can view the historical events of the film from either of two perspectives: from the point of view of the nobility, they mark an end, a closing, the death of the old regime; for the revolutionaries, a beginning, an opening, the birth of the nation and a new era. Thus, however objective Renoir's treatment of the court, his choice of an essentially open overall formal structure puts him squarely on the side of the Revolution. Not only does the film move quite steadily forward; it grows in scope and power. The conclusion of the film seems neither an end nor a closure; rather, it propels us toward the future with a force that its makers hoped would reach to the Europe of 1938.

Perhaps the best metaphor for the overall form of the film is that of a river, flowing onward, increasing in volume and power as it flows. Within this open forward flow, Renoir builds a pervasive rhythm of motion and rest which intensifies as the film proceeds. Many scenes open with lengthy shots containing large and complex camera movement, often only loosely conjoined with some object movement within the scene, as in the opening shot where the camera motion roughly coincides with the marching guards, but four different centers of interest emerge during the shot. Frequently, there soon follows a shot-countershot set with motionless camera and minimal object movement, but where cutting maintains the forward impetus of the scene. The camera moves and stops; talk and action alternate.

Within the open visual forms, the dialogue often reaches a dynamic closure in which a line both terminates one discussion and leads to a new scene. These, and such moments as the repetition late in the film of the opening image of guards before a tapestry, augment the rhythm of the forward flow. For the first third of La Marseillaise, this rhythm persists on a relatively small scale, with neither motion nor rest being long sustained or intensified. Characters move in and out of the frame more often than they penetrate the depth of the visible action-space, and the recurrent shot-countershot sets fragment the moments of rest. Yet the movement is steadily forward, from the fall of the Bastille to the call for a Marseilles battalion.

Then, fifty minutes into the film, a pattern of motion continues for three and a half minutes. For the first time in the film, there are five consecutive shots containing large camera movements, linked to object movement in deep space. This pattern begins when Bomier's mother tells him how he can join the Marseilles battalion; he embraces her and dashes out the door. The camera pans through the room in this shot, then from a reversed perspective crosses to a window and tilts down to watch Bomier prance down the narrow street into the depth of the action-space, singing as he goes. Dissolve to another window, where the camera moves with Bomier as he passes by and into the recruiting hall. Through two more shots the camera roams through the room as Bomier signs up for the battalion. Meanwhile, the first strains of "La Marseillaise" sound from a neighboring room where the Montpellier battalion dines; the song continues through the rest of the scene.

This sustained flow of motion and moving sound opens the second movement of La Marseillaise, a central portion of the film wherein the rhythm of motion and rest is greatly augmented. The most sustained moment of rest in the film follows immediately: ten consecutive shots without camera movement and only small motions within the frame, as Arnaud, Bomier and

The Marseilles battalion marches to Paris. *Upper left*, Jenny Hélia as an orator in the Jacobin Club. *Lower left*, Louison (Nadia Sibirskaia) and Bomier (Edmond Ardisson). *Lower right*, Arnaud (Andrex).

Cuculière talk about the Rhine Army song. Bomier declares, "There is something wild and grandiloquent about it that doesn't please me at all," and argues that it ignores the rules of harmony. But Arnaud brushes aside such quibbles: "The song bowled me over. It seemed like an echo of my own thoughts." As Bomier declares that the song will be forgotten in two weeks, this tranquil scene dissolves to the central shot of the film, the longest and most complex—a single shot in which the Marseilles battalion departs for Paris and the song that will become "La Marseillaise" moves into the foreground of the film.

This fine epitomizing shot begins high in the air, level with a tree-borne banner proclaiming the departure of the battalion. As the crowd which fills the space below lustily sings "La Marseillaise," the camera moves forward and down, then roams freely through the square, changing directions a dozen times as it both registers the vastness of the throng and sorts from it half a dozen groups of familiar faces. No technique of photographing this scene which fragmented the crowd into separate shots could equal Renoir's achievement here, where his fluid camera moving in deep space to capture the event in a single shot combines with the music in which he celebrates community to perfectly express the concept that forms the core of the film and the backbone of the Revolution: the nation, the fraternal union of all Frenchmen. We know, as the Marseillais did not, that their marching song was destined to help unite all France into the nation they dreamed of; in this shot their concept of *nation* is made manifest as the song sends them forth to their fate. And in this essentially fluid shot, Renoir creates a new alternation of motion and rest; the crowd stands and sings while the camera moves, then as the camera comes to rest the battalion is called to formation and moves with the crowd through the frame.

This shot releases the flood of motion that propels the Marseillais across France toward Paris: twenty-four shots, thirteen dissolves, with the camera moving freely in seventeen of these shots, while the ragged line of the marching battalion usually moves diagonally in deep space rather than in and out of the frame. Movement seems almost continuous here, though the alternation of marching and camp scenes and of talk and music maintains a rhythm in the flow—a flow that encompasses a montage of the beauties of France, a further exploration of political attitudes in 1792, instructions about the weapons of the revolutionary army, new verses for the song as well as advice on how to keep your feet in shape while marching. Music predominates over talk and serves with the repeated dissolves to amplify and intensify the movement of the film while maintaining its rather leisurely pace.

Yet there is a different sort of complication here, another combination of movement and rest. I have spoken repeatedly of the felt movement of *La Marseillaise*, its constant forward progression, and of how spatial movements, of camera and characters, contribute to this. However, this felt movement or progression of the film is not itself spatial but rather a progression through time and events, essentially a felt temporal flow. But here the progression becomes spatial, while the temporal flow of the Revolution seems held in abeyance. The march of the battalion toward Paris has somewhat the air of a stroll in the park while the world stands still, a fact noted in the film when near the end of the march a Marseillais remarks, "I wonder what's happening in Paris."

This suggests a modification of remarks about the constant forward progression of La Marseillaise. This progression divides into three movements, with the first and third dominated by the temporal flow of historic events and the second consisting essentially of a spatial flow while history marks time. Here again Renoir has welded form and content into an expressive whole: the northward march of the battalion and its song becomes the vehicle for a critical revolutionary fact, not indeed a specific datable event like the fall of the Bastille, but rather that major spatial non-event, the spread of revolutionary ideals through the French populace—a non-event underlying Roederer's proclamation, "Action is useless; resistance impossible. All Paris marches."

The combination of spatial movement and temporal rest continues after the battalion reaches Paris, in the scenes of welcome and through the skirmish with the aristocrats on the Champs Elysées, with the spatial movement through Paris stopping at the Tuileries gate. The very next image renews the temporal flow and opens the final movement of the film. The king's hand holds a magnifying glass over the Brunswick Manifesto as he asks, "What sort of a bird will hatch from this egg?" We swirl again in the currents of history. Where the central section began with a surge of motion, the final segment opens in immobility: twelve shots with little action before Louis XVI stands and beings to walk about the room. But from this still beginning, the final movement of La Marseillaise mounts to a crescendo of mass movement and violence unequaled in any other Renoir film. A flurry of pamphlets evokes the debates of August 1792. A second scene in the palace is filled with people and movement and leads to the tragicomedy of Louis XVI reviewing his guard when both his wig and his troops are askew, and thence to the sad little procession of the royal family through long rows of trees toward the Assembly and the guillotine. In the calm before the final storm two images evoke Auden's "Musée des Beaux Arts": "About suffering they were never wrong/ The old masters . . . ": the dauphin plunging into a pile of fallen leaves while his parents march à la mort; children playing marbles in the street while thirty yards away the mob batters at the Tuileries gate.

The gate gives; the Marseillais enter and the National Guard troops hesitate only a moment before joining them with a cry of "Vive la Nation!" On the stairs of the palace, Arnaud tries to persuade the Swiss to do likewise. La Chesnaye gives the order to fire. The battle breaks in a barrage of nearly motionless images; in eight seconds, eight shots of loyal troups firing abruptly accelerate the pace of the film. Cut to the courtyard, where men run in disarray past abandoned cannon, beginning a flow of movement that carries to the film's end, sustained again by dissolves between shots. The revolutionaries swarm over the palace, and Roederer returns like a messenger in Greek drama, carrying the news of the king's deposition. Having

The fall of the monarchy. *Patriotes* storm the Tuileries, then march to Valmy. *Lower left*, the chorus of Marseillaise: Ardisson (Fernand Flament), Arnaud, Cuculière (Alex Truchy), Javel (Paul Dullac).

swept out the monarchy, Renoir cuts forward a month in time to the road near Valmy and finally allows himself a symmetrical scene as the final one in the film, with Arnaud's last speech as its center, flanked by close-ups of Javel, Ardisson, and Cuculière and beginning and ending with marching troops and running horses—a closure that brings the film to its conclusion without impeding the flow of historic events.

La Marseillaise is the noisiest of Renoir films, full of crowd and battle noises, with a greater density and volume of sound and much more external music than any other Renoir film of the period. For its last twenty-five minutes, the sound of *La Marseillaise* is an almost continuous barrage of bells, trumpets, drums, gunfire, and shouting crowds, ending with a parade of drummers past the camera as the army moves on Valmy. This final image and its accompanying sound identify at last the drumbeat used in transitions earlier in the film and thus create another element of closure in this essentially open ending. This identification also completes our perception of the very unusual pattern in the relation of sound to image in *La Marseillaise*. As we know, the central characters of the film form a sort of chorus, hence much of the dialogue is, in a way, commentative sound, though it originates within the world of the film. Most of the extensive external music reverses this relation. It doesn't originate within the world of the film, hence is straightforwardly commentative; yet it is music from the revolutionary era and thus has historic overtones and connections. Further, the rich pattern of sound in *La Marseillaise* contains a collage of French accents, including even the German of Alsace, with this variety of voices then forming a kind of commentary on the diversity of peoples who joined to make the Revolution. The identification of the transitional drumbeat as the sound of the revolutionary army approaching Valmy then competes this pattern of sounds which are both internal and external, both elements within the overlapping worlds of French history and *La Marseillaise* and a commentary on their events.

20

La Bête humaine
1938

Another very clear idea, that of balancing the two murders, one at the beginning, the other at the end, had very much tempted Zola. But finally he renounced it and expanded on the outcome of these events. Me, I've clung to that idea, because, I repeat, a film is a small thing, much smaller than we think.
                                                                    —Jean Renoir

In 1937 Jean Renoir declared: "After I finish *La Marseillaise* I want to make some comedies. And I'll make them."[1] But the hazards of the movie game proved less predictable.

Jean Gabin had always wanted to drive a locomotive. By 1938, as the leading male star in France, he could choose his roles. A film entitled "Train of Hell," directed by Jean Gremillon, was scheduled, but the producer Robert Hakim finally rejected this project and proposed instead the role of Jacques Lantier in Zola's novel *La Bête humaine*. Renoir once said, "I made *La Bête humaine* because Gabin and I wanted to play with trains." Elsewhere he remarks: "*La Bête humaine* is not a subject that I chose. Robert Hakim proposed the project to me and convinced me that I should do it."[2] We might have divined this without Renoir's confession; for of all Renoir films of this period only *La Bête humaine* fits snugly into the mold of the most popular French films of the day. Appearing between *Quai des Brumes* and *Le Jour se leve*, *La Bête humaine* shares with these Carné-Prévert productions a dark atmosphere, an air of hopelessness, and the presence of

Gabin in his classic role of doomed tragic hero—a *film noir*, hardly a category one associates with the name Jean Renoir.

Black was an appropriate color for 1938, especially for partisans of the Left. Europe's dance of death was in full swing, but, like most of his contemporaries, Jean Renoir went about his work as if the world were sane. The Spanish Civil War and the Russian treason trials had already undermined the solidarity and confidence of the Left. Early in 1938 the second Popular Front government resigned; the Radical Camille Chautemps, who had been premier during the Stavisky scandal in 1934, remained as head of the new government composed wholly of Radicals. His new air-minister, La Chambre, called for vigorous action to revive the French Air Force, outstripped by Hitler's Nazi Luftwaffe since 1935, but a new wave of strikes in the aircraft industry crippled this belated effort. By February 11, when Renoir's *La Marseillaise* had its Paris premiere, the Left was already too much in disarray to respond to this appeal for union; in London, Prime Minister Chamberlain refused to listen to the misgivings of his foreign secretary, Anthony Eden, about the slowness of British rearmament. The next day Adolf Hitler threatened the Austrian chancellor with invasion and scoffed at the idea that France or England would lift a finger for Austria. On February 20, Anthony Eden resigned, no longer willing to be identified with Chamberlain's policy of appeasement. Jean Renoir was flattered that the attacks on *La Marseillaise* in the reactionary press resembled Herr Hitler's vilification of the Western democracies.[3]

On March 10, Premier Chautemps resigned; hence France had no government at all on the weekend when the German army lumbered across the Austrian frontier. France and England did not lift a finger. Most of the Nazi tanks broke down; still Hitler drove through cheering crowds to Vienna and on March 13 declared the dissolution of the Austrian republic and the annexation of its territory to the German Reich; the usual Nazi atrocities soon followed. Prince Stahremberg and his actress wife, Nora Grégor, fled to Switzerland. On March 14 Léon Blum formed a new government and promptly declared that France was prepared without reservation to honor her commitments to Czechoslovakia. But a week later Neville Chamberlain had decided to abandon that small country should Hitler threaten, and on March 24 he publicly declared that England was under no special obligation to the Czechs. Blum asked for plenary powers and was defeated; he resigned after less than a month in office.

On April 13, Edouard Daladier formed a new "Government of National Defense." As foreign minister he chose Georges Bonnet, whose eagerness for appeasement matched that of Neville Chamberlain. On April 14, Jean Renoir announced in *Ce Soir* that he was beginning work on a new film, *La Bête humaine*, and would not write his column for some weeks.[4] He had first read *La Bête humaine* twenty years earlier; now he quickly wrote a "rather superficial scenario with very bad dialogue" following the central thread of Zola's novel. Meanwhile the British signed an agreement with Mussolini, effectively giving Italy a free hand in Spain. In Czechoslovakia the Nazi Party of the Sudetenland demanded local autonomy for the German regions.

On May 28 Hitler ordered preparations for an attack on Czechoslovakia, and on June 12 Premier Daladier reaffirmed France's pledge to aid the Czechs if Hitler attacked. As an air of impending doom hung over Europe, Jean Renoir read Zola's notes to *La Bête humaine*, expressing the writer's desire to produce a work conveying a sense of fatality. Renoir did resist the producer's suggestion of a famous femme fatale, Gina Manès, for the role of Séverine and asked that Simone Simon return from Hollywood for the part, again casting a performer in a role outside her usual range—another technique for destroying clichés. After *La Marseillaise*, Jacques Becker had left Renoir to pursue his own career; still, as Renoir gathered his *équipe*, many familiar names reappeared: Gabin, Carette, Jenny Hélia, Corteggiani, Léon Larive, Kosma, Lourié, and others. Young Alain Renoir became an assistant cameraman.

The British sought to negotiate a settlement of the Czech question with Hitler; late in July, France and England sought to promote a compromise between the Czech government and the Sudeten Nazi Party. Jean Renoir and his nephew Claude, with Gabin, Carette, and Fernand Ledoux, became students of the *chemin de fer*, determined to make a film that the *cheminots* would not disavow as false to their metier. With the cooperation of the national railroad, the Société Nationale de Chemin de fer, and the railroad workers' Fédération, they rode the engines, prowled the yards, watched the workings of the station. Gabin, to become the engineer, Jacques Lantier, learned to put a locomotive through its paces. Carette, who would be the fireman, Pecqueux, practiced stoking the fires.

On August 3, Lord Runciman arrived in Prague to mediate the Sudeten question. On August 8, Jean Renoir and Jean Gabin arrived in Le Havre to meet the Normandie, bringing Simone Simon from America.[5] Shooting began on *La Bête humaine* in mid-August, at about the time that Lord Runciman's mission broke down as Hitler provided the Sudeten Nazi Henlein a mounting series of demands. At Le Havre the SNCF provided Renoir with a locomotive and ten kilometers of track where the film crew could operate as they pleased. Renoir complained in *Ce Soir* about the exaggeration in journalistic accounts of Gabin's prowess as a locomotive engineer; still, of the work scenes, only the shot of Lantier's suicide was done with mock-up and back projection—not from a fear that movie audiences could tell the difference between an actual locomotive and a studio set, but rather because Renoir was sure his actors would be better in an authentic setting. "Gabin and Carette could never have played so realistically in front of an artificial background, if only because the very noise forced them to communicate by means of gesture."

With the eyes of Europe on Czechoslovakia, the eyes of the *cheminots* of Le Havre were on Renoir's crew; Renoir wrote, "For fifteen days we have been working in the station at Le Havre, thanks to the kindness of the company's agents. Not only do they tolerate us (and when one knows how much hard work cinema involves, the fact that they tolerate us is already a great deal) but they help us even more with their advice . . . Not a gesture, not an act has not passed through the screen of friendly criticism by these benevolent collaborators."[6]

But if this collaboration was benevolent, that of France and England on the European scene was fatal. In the end, Chamberlain and Daladier collaborated in forcing the Czechs to accede to all of Hitler's demands. Returning from Munich, both Chamberlain and Daladier drove through cheering crowds; a few days later Jean Renoir took time out from editing *La Bête humaine* to write in *Ce Soir* that there was now less reason to be proud of being French.[7]

In its dark tone, its pessimistic mood, its air of fatality, *La Bête humaine* differs from every other Renoir film of the thirties. I have included this historical sketch to indicate how these qualities fit the moment of the film's making. That Zola's novel was appropriate to 1938 was not a decision of Renoir's. Still, *Les Bas Fonds* had shown that Renoir could shape any material to express his own vision; hence the darkness of *La Bête humaine* may

Renoir, Gabin, and coworkers discuss a problem in shooting *La Bête humaine*. Photograph by Roger Corbeau.

reflect Renoir's reaction to the debacle of European politics. But his full response to the danse macabre of the bourgeoisie awaited another year and *La Règle du jeu*.

Narrative and Treatment

On a visit to Paris, Roubaud (Fernand Ledoux), deputy stationmaster at Le Havre, discovers that his young wife, Séverine (Simone Simon), has been the mistress of her rich and influential old godfather, Grandmorin. Wild with rage, Roubaud forces Séverine to ask Grandmorin to meet her on the train. Meanwhile, Jacques Lantier (Jean Gabin), a locomotive engineer, has been held over in Le Havre by a hotbox—an overheated bearing—and visits his godmother and her daughter Flore (Blanchette Brunoy) in Bréuté, where he nearly strangles Flore in a strange fit of compulsion. Despite Flore's avowal of love he leaves her, asserting that he cannot trust himself with women and thus it is best he never see her again. On the train to Le Havre he sees Roubaud and Séverine as they come from the compartment where Roubaud has killed Grandmorin, but at the inquiry he responds to an appeal in Séverine's eyes and says he saw nothing. Determined to keep Lantier silent, Roubaud and Séverine befriend him. An ex-convict, Cabuche (Jean Renoir), who has reason to hate Grandmorin, is arrested for the murder. Lantier and Séverine become lovers. Roubaud, repulsed by Séverine, neglects his work and spends his nights gambling. Lantier and Séverine plan to kill Roubaud, but when the moment to strike arrives, Lantier cannot do it; Séverine leaves him. Later, Lantier dances with Séverine but she tells him that since he cannot free her from Roubaud their affair must end. Lantier follows Séverine home, where he swears that he now has the will to kill Roubaud. They wait for Roubaud to return from the café, hear a step in the hall. Séverine kisses Lantier to give him courage but instead this rouses his compulsion and he kills her. Next day on the run to Paris, Lantier tells his fireman Pecqueux (Carette) that he has killed Séverine, then he leaps from the cab to his death.

Filmgoers may easily misread the title of Zola's novel. Though his central character is a compulsive killer, the analogue of Zola's title, *The Human Beast*, is not *The Scarlet Empress*, referring to an individual, but *The Male Animal*, whose reference is to the species. Zola wrote in a letter in 1889, "As for the title, *La Bête humaine*, it has given me a good deal of trouble; I searched for it a long time. I wanted to express this idea: the cave man remains within the man of our nineteenth century; there is something in us from this far-off ancestor."[8]

The novel is one of Zola's Rougon-Macquart series, that vast "natural and social history of a family under the Second Empire." It ends with Lantier and Pecqueux fighting and falling under the wheels of the locomotive, leaving a wild train, filled with drunken, singing soldiers but with its cab empty, hurtling madly across France—a symbol of the plunge of the Second Empire into the Franco-Prussian War of 1870. Before this symbolic finale *La Bête humaine* is a novel of murder, suicide, bribery, jealousy, and rage, depicting a society corrupt from top to bottom, from the "president" Grandmorin, who specializes in debauching young girls, to the crossing guard Misard, slowly poisoning his wife because she has hidden a thousand-franc legacy from him. Descriptions of the railroad pervade the novel, Zola having spent months on documentation. The railroad company pervades the lives of the characters, functioning as Zola's symbol for the industrialization of France. The direst events of the novel litter the railroad embankment with dismembered corpses, including that of the locomotive, *La Lison*. Even the honest and innocent worker Cabuche is destroyed by his chaste passion for Séverine, when Jacques Lantier commits his compulsive murder then disappears into the night, leaving Cabuche to be found with the body. Lantier, as one of the Rougon-Macquart, carries the weight of his family's degradation. Zola attributes Lantier's compulsion to kill to a hereditary failure, a "spoiling of his blood" by generations of drunken ancestors, but Lantier's compulsion seems no more destructive than those that drive all the characters of *La Bête humaine* to their sordid ends. Roubaud's murderous rage, Aunt Phasie's stubborn choice of dying rather than revealing the hiding place of her legacy, Mme. Lebleu's obsessive determination to discover her neighbor's infidelity, are all as irrational and uncontrollable as Lantier's *fêlure*.

Renoir remarked that Zola's novel contains enough material for a dozen films. But he was content to draw from its welter of improbable and melodramatic events the central thread which links Lantier, Séverine, and Roubaud in a web of passion and crime—a story of starcrossed lovers, heavy with the weight of destiny. Writing in *Cinémonde* of Zola's remarks about fatality, Renoir says: "This fatality works powerfully in the novel and I hope it will be visible in the film. In this aspect Zola's *La Bête humaine* reaches back to the great works of Greek tragedy . . . Jacques Lantier interests us as much as Oedipus Rex. This railway mechanic trails behind him an atmosphere as heavy as that of some member of the family of Atreus."[9]

But such predestined or fated characters fit uneasily into Renoir's own conception of the world, and he could not refrain from creating a counterpoint to the dark and fate-filled life-space which closes on Lantier, Roubaud, and Séverine. In the environment and activities of the railroad, Renoir found a world of work and achievement that transcended the narrow circle of the doomed, a sort of second foreground for the film in which a sane and hopeful worker's milieu provides a contrast to the madness that overwhelms the central characters.

In the trajectory of Renoir's engagement with the Left, *La Bête humaine* appears as a further fall away from the active commitment of 1936. Perhaps in reaction to the failure of the Popular Front, from Zola's overtly poltiical novel Renoir drew a nonpolitical film. Indeed, he cites the change of setting from 1869 to 1938 as a reason for avoiding Zola's political criticism, writing late in 1938, "France today is not that of Napoleon III and, such as she is, with her qualities and her faults, I consider her worthy of being defended to the end by all of her children."[10] The reduction of Zola's epic canvas to a spare triangular composition eliminated most of the social contrasts of the novel. A mere echo remains of Zola's recurrent theme of the corrupting influence of money, while only symbolically can any reference at all be found to the political life of 1938.

Not that Renoir's political opinions had greatly changed. From 1936 to 1938 he wrote occasional pieces, including a Wednesday column in the leftist *Ce Soir*, and through 1938 these essays continue to speak for the Left. Rather, the proposal to make *La Bête humaine* became the occasion for another polar swing in Renoir's work—not only from light to dark, complex to simple, but more importantly from a film of ideas to a film of action. In both *La Grande Illusion* and *La Marseillaise* articulate characters discuss their situation rationally, see themselves with some objectivity, and act in ways that reflect the ideas they hold. In contrast, *La Bête humaine* becomes in Renoir's hands a film without ideas, where the actions have no rational basis but simply surge forth from some dark interior well. Ignoring the whole ideological level of the novel, Renoir shows no concern for the sociological or psychological implications of Zola's famous passage on Lantier's heredity. Though he cites this passage twice, it serves merely to make plausible Lantier's compulsion to kill. Renoir's *La Bête humaine* is a tragedy, not an exposé.

Still, he would not be Renoir if nowhere in this film were there a sign of his continuing adherence to the Left. I find this sign in the railway scenes; nonpolitical though they are, they mark the point of Renoir's deepest penetration into a working-class milieu, reflecting that general article of faith of the Left: if there is hope, it lies in the working class. Renoir expressed some of this attitude in *Ce Soir:* "The profession of the railroad man is not a lark; it is a grand metier. For some it is even a priesthood. These men put the safety of their passengers and respect for the timetable before their own private life and their comfort; they spare themselves no trouble; they endure the weather, the cold, an irregular life. They impair their health and they do not complain, their metier has such a grip on them. Their finest recompense, when, majestically, their engine ranges alongside the platform in a great station, is to say, 'They'll be happy; they arrived on time.' "[11]

But if the easy competence of the *cheminots* brings a note of hope to *La Bête humaine*, the mechanisms of the railroad serve Renoir in other ways.

Zola begins his novel with Roubaud at the window of la mère Victoire's, overlooking the gare St. Lazare, watching the trains as he waits for Séverine. In the chapter that follows, Zola uses both description and dialogue to divulge the past life of Roubaud and Séverine and the events leading up to this afternoon in Paris, then moves quickly to Séverine's fateful disclosure that Grandmorin had given her the serpentine ring. But Renoir, with his dislike for flashbacks and explanatory dialogue, places this scene far inside his film and conceives a very different opening. La Bête humaine begins with a cinematic tour de force, a distillation of the railroad run from Paris to Le Havre, a sequence of such authenticity and power that French writers declared it "éblouissant" ("dazzling"). Both the film's milieu and the metier and camaraderie of Lantier and Pecqueux are established in this first four minutes, which also initiates what André Bazin called "the organizing principle in La Bête humaine," the metaphor of man and machine;[12] for the trajectory of the locomotive endlessly swallowing its dual ribbon of rails here conveys to the film audience that compulsion which later comes to be felt in the lives of all the central characters, while Renoir's opening image of the firebox of La Lison becomes a visual expression of that consuming inner flame which drives each character toward his fate. This opening sequence tells no part of the story of La Bête humaine, yet foreshadows its development and also creates the ambiance of relentless forward motion that pervades the film.

Renoir's script had carried hints of the diverse threads that are woven together in Zola's novel, but while shooting and editing he pruned these all away, replacing much of his "very bad" dialogue with lines taken directly from Zola, simplifying and reorganizing his scenes to give the film a tightness of construction and a rhythmic flow not at all discernible in his original scenario. In this process he reduced the film to little more than two counterpointed motifs, the destructive interaction of Roubaud, Séverine, and Lantier and the working life of the railway men, so interlocked as to avoid all feeling of digression and allow the linear drive created in the opening sequence to carry through the whole film.

For the last shot of this opening journey, Renoir pointed his camera at the roof of the station, with the silhouette of the locomotive moving slowly against a background of ironwork and glass—a majestic closing moment for this initial symphony. Once in the station the story quickly begins; Lantier discovers the hotbox that will keep him in Le Havre, and as Roubaud stops to greet Pecqueux a woman passenger appears to complain about Turlot, the sugar king whose threat will send Séverine to talk to Grandmorin.

Historically the railroad had been an instrument of both liberation and brutal power. In the nineteenth and early twentieth centuries the train whistle heard from afar at night brought a magical romantic evocation of distant climes and of the possibility of escape from a confined and limited

Paris to Le Havre. Jacques Lantier (Jean Gabin) and Pecqueux (Julien Carette).

life. Yet the source of this magical sound was steeped in corruption and callous exploitation. Some echo of this background resounds in Renoir's railroad images. The train en route dominates the screen early in the film. Initially the movements of Lantier and Pecquex seem dictated by the forward rush of their machine; they make no decisions, but function as mere instruments of its progress. The locomotive in motion appears as a demanding master, controlling its servants, who are also silenced by its roar—perhaps thus evoking critical reference to "brutal strength rendered inarticulate by industrial society."[13] In the station, at rest, the locomotive still requires attention, but now tendered more from love than from compulsion. Far from inarticulate, the *cheminots* project an image of pride in their work and service to their public, the passengers. The railroad scenes do not present this work as alienating or degrading, but as a context of warm camaraderie and felt accomplishment; the men respect each other and their machines. Corruption comes from outside, from Turlot and Grandmorin in their network of money and power.

Generations destroyed by degrading labor may lay behind Jacques Lantier's *fêlure*, but when in its grip he begins to strangle Flore, the sound of a passing train frees him and spares her life—suggesting perhaps that men may be saved as well as destroyed by work.

As Jacques Lantier becomes entangled with Séverine, the railroad images reflect the change in his life. Dynamic shots of charging locomotives give way to views of the yards and freight cars standing amid dark pools of shadow. Lantier loiters behind a boxcar waiting for Roubaud to leave; he betrays his love, *La Lison*, by embracing Séverine in her silent cab. They make love in a tool shed and lurk in the shadows of the marshaling yard, waiting to kill Roubaud. Silent and still, no longer master, the railroad becomes witness or accomplice as the movements of Séverine replace those of *La Lison* at the center of Lantier's world. Yet as the characters become fixed in the one-way track of their obsessions, the less frequent images of the moving train, which originally expressed compulsion, become moments of liberation, used by Renoir to achieve some semblance of balance in the mood of the film and to check the mounting intensity of the drama.

Almost every shot occurs within sight or sound of the railroad. Renoir has said, "It seemed to me that I would have betrayed Zola if I hadn't at every moment recalled that our action occurs in the world of the railroad and not somewhere else." But the function of this setting transcends mere fidelity. A sense of fatality weighs on the world of the film, and these recurrent railroad images help sustain it by suggesting the pervasive presence of some obscure overbearing power. Yet the railroad also provides a Renoir counterpoint to this, its liberating flow of motion implying that fatality is not the final word in this world.

Characterization

Renoir in 1951: "What helped me on *La Bête humaine* were the explanations the hero gives of his atavism: I said to myself, 'No, that's not very beautiful, but if a man as handsome as Gabin said it . . . in the open air, with a great deal of horizon behind him, and perhaps some wind, it could take on a certain value.' That's the key which helped me make the film."[14]

Renoir refers here to one of Zola's most famous passages, which speaks of the "great smoke" that rises in the head of Jacques Lantier, "deforming everything," and of how he came to think that he was "paying for the others, the fathers and grandfathers who drank, the generations of drunkards who had spoiled his blood." In Zola's novel Jacques Lantier never utters this explanation. Rather, the lines describe his thought as he lies in the dark, face down on the grass beside the railroad line, devastated by the compulsion to kill that had seized him at the moment when Flore, Zola's "virgin warrior," had yielded to his embrace. Lantier had fled, leaving Flore unaware of his attack and feeling spurned and perplexed. He wanders in distraction, recalling the history of his *fêlure*, that madness which overwhelms him in the presence of some women and has driven him to forsake a normal life and find peace only in the cab of his locomotive *La Lison*.

All this history Renoir compresses into a single scene and a few lines of dialogue, leaving Lantier's background and his flaw much more obscure than in the novel. This obscurity seems foreign to a Renoir film; it is one of several elements which set *La Bête humaine* apart from the others. François Trauffaut has noted that Renoir's is a cinema of understanding. Usually we neither need nor are given any background for a Renoir character; we feel close to them from the first, with every gesture revealing them to us. But throughout *La Bête humaine* Renoir attempts to find single images, a gesture or a line, which will express aspects of a character or a life that Zola describes at some length. Hence the full import of these images may be readily accessible only to viewers familiar with the novel—which would include much of the French audience in 1938. Without the novel as guide, the characters must be unriddled; their opening scenes do not really open them to our view. Thus Jacques Lantier in the cab of *La Lison* appears a model of competent masculinity, cool, confident, his hand firm on the controls. A glance or a gesture tells Pecqueux what must be done; men and machine move in perfect harmony. At Le Havre, Lantier blends easily into the casual camaraderie of the *cheminots*; his concern to see his locomotive through the machine shop seems only normal in this *grand métier*. Pecqueux's suggestion that Lantier would eat better if married and Lantier's response, "I'm married to *La Lison*," seem merely part of the banter that often goes with satisfying work. Not until his godmother at Bréuté asks about his "attacks" do the shadows in Lantier's life appear. Too brusque, too insistent, his denial evades the question rather than responding to it. A moment later, with Flore, the answer shows itself perforce.

Renoir transposes this scene from night to day and converts into images Zola's description of Lantier's inner turmoil. Jacques finds Flore by the river; the uncertainty each feels makes their meeting awkward. Flore runs away and up the railroad embankment. He catches her; she resists, then yields. They kiss but as Lantier looks up his eyes become fixed and blank; his hand moves from Flore's breast to her throat. She cries in bewilderment,

"Jacques!" His face contorts with fury as he tries to strangle her. Close behind them a train passes; Jacques looks up, blinks; his grip relaxes. He stands and walks away. Cut to an open field, with trees and a vast expanse of sky. Jacques dazedly walks across the field, sits on a hillock. Flore follows and sits beside him as he speaks those thoughts from the novel about the rage that overcomes him and the curse of his drunken forebears. They exchange avowals of love, and Flore declares she will risk becoming his wife, if he wants. Then in the image Renoir describes—a close-up of Gabin before a great reach of sky, with the wind ruffling his hair—Lantier responds, "You're mad! Don't talk of it," and declares it best he never see her again: "I think that women, for me . . . "

This image of Lantier renouncing his pure true love, handsome, deeply troubled, but honest and open as the wide sky behind him, closes the door on the simple workman of the opening scenes. Renoir fades from this image to the Roubauds' arrival in Paris, and we next see Lantier about to board the train on which he will meet Séverine. Henceforth an undercurrent of tension and concealment blurs our vision of Jacques Lantier as his compulsion and Roubaud's crime combine to shape his life.

Early in the novel it becomes apparent that Zola's hero does not merely feel a blind compulsion to kill; he is also fascinated by death. He both abhors and cherishes his *fêlure*, the common root of both guilt and desire. He flees from his urge to kill Flore but a brief glimpse of the murder of Grandmorin in a passing train leaves him filled with envy of this unknown man who had "dared", who had "gone to the end of his desire." Never this clear in the film, this side of Lantier still lurks beneath the surface of Renoir's hero, subversive in its intimation that not Séverine's beauty but her crime captivates him.

But guilt and love inevitably mingle in this affair. Séverine's first approach, prompted solely by fear, evokes no response from Lantier. Distressed by a cinder in his eye, he looks but curiously at this fashionable young woman, different in every way from the Flore he has loved and foresworn, and he makes no reply at all to her idle talk, having as yet no inkling of her crime. A few moments later in the station, with the murder revealed, the desperate plea in Séverine's eyes proclaims her guilt to Lantier and he lies to shield her.

Roubaud had sworn to Séverine that his act would create something "solid" between them. Now the confession in her eyes extends this circle of guilt to Lantier. How snugly this noose fits Lantier's neck, how willingly he thrusts his neck into the noose, shows most plainly in the five long, close two-shots at Mme. Victoire's, where Séverine describes Grandmorin's murder, and Lantier's hidden shameful self can no longer be denied but surfaces in the avid, tense manner of his insistence that she repeat every detail.

In 1959 Renoir would transform the Jekyll and Hyde story into *The Testa-*

ment of *Dr. Cordelier*, where the two halves of a divided self split into two characters, embodying the polarities of intelligence and instinct, nature and convention, and, more ambiguously, good and evil. Cordelier is the culmination of a long series of Renoir characters who harbor a second self not acknowledged by their everyday world: Legrand, Lange, Emma Bovary, Pepel—even Lestingois gives life to his imagined self in rescuing Boudu. Jacques Lantier becomes a sort of middle term in this series, with a violent, atavistic inner self quite unlike the romantic projections of Legrand or Lange, yet never openly accepted by Lantier, as Cordelier initially accepts his evil alter ego, Opale.

But Lantier's acceptance of his other self may be concealed within his love for Séverine. Torn between guilt and desire, he has renounced women. But Séverine offers a guilty love—to share her crime appeases his own urge to kill and leaves him free to love, creating the illusion that his divided selves can be reconciled. But, as with Cordelier, acceptance of his violent self does not tame it; he can neither choose to kill, nor stop himself from killing.

"Jacques Lantier interests us as much as Oedipus Rex." Like Oedipus, Lantier's fate lies in the fact that, unlike Legrand and Lange, his hidden self remains hidden from himself. Unwittingly, his eager questions about the knife that slaughtered Grandmorin lead his hand to snatch a knife to murder Séverine. Reflecting surfaces abound in *La Bête humaine*, but these serve less as symbols of self-awareness than as reminders of how seldom any character really sees himself. Jacques Lantier does twice. In the dark yard where, with Séverine, he waits to kill Roubaud, he stoops to grasp an iron bar and for a moment views his own reflection in a puddle. Roubaud walks dully by, but Lantier, having seen himself about to commit that

crime, cannot do it. Later, after killing Séverine, he stops to leave the knife on the sideboard; his glance catches itself in the mirror. He looks away, then back and for an instant sees himself—a look of recognition and self-hatred, hard and cold as a serpent. This look perhaps leads Renoir's Lantier to suicide; Zola's hero, by contrast, was filled with joy and pride after his crime and never felt remorse.

Jean Gabin plays Lantier superbly, so well that Truffaut calls *La Bête humaine* Gabin's best film. A deadly seriousness marks his performance; only in his locomotive does he seem at ease and only when he talks of *La Lison* does joy break through. Even his rare smile is cautious and measured, and beneath his careful impassivity in many scenes we feel a driving inner tension, often conveyed by the tightness of his mouth, the reticence of his eyes, the abruptness of a gesture. That this anxiety bespeaks a dual self resembling Cordelier seems overtly indicated by Pecqueux's remark as Lantier lies dead beside the tracks, a line that echoes a similar last line in Stevenson's *Jekyll and Hyde:* "Poor fellow, he never looked so calm."

Though Renoir has likened Lantier to Oedipus, Roubaud may better seem to fit that mold. As the film begins, it is Roubaud who holds the envious position, who has the most to lose. He first appears warm and courteous, upright and honest in his work, with courage enough to tell the arrogant Turlot, "I treat all passengers alike." Asked by a friend, Cauche, to play cards at the cafe, Roubaud responds that he's not much for cards "and there's my wife who waits for me." Cauche nods and answers, "Ah, happy man!" Roubaud's complacent acceptance of that description shows in his smile as he stands in the doorway looking fondly at Séverine. But hubris, the pride that blinds, lies in that smile, unmasked by Séverine when she turns away from his embrace, apparently more concerned with her hair than with his love. We seldom see him smile again.

Roubaud waits for Séverine at Mme. Victoire's, overlooking the trains, watch in hand, as befits a railroad man. His questions disclose a tinge of suspicion mingled with hunger at the root of his impatience, but Séverine's charm and her "petit cadeau," the knife, quickly soften him. She reports that the affair with Turlot was easily settled by Grandmorin. Roubaud remarks, "He has a long arm," echoing a line of Louis XVI in *La Marseillaise*. This was a weak joke in *La Marseillaise*, for Louis XVI had precious little influence for a king. But in *La Bête humaine* it becomes a sad and tragic truth; Grandmorin's arm has reached much further than Roubaud suspects. As they talk Séverine mentions her refusal to go to Doinville with Grandmorin. Roubaud asserts, "There's something bizarre about you and Grandmorin." Then, "I had a funny idea—you may be his daughter." Startled, Séverine repeats, "Sa fille! Sa Fille!" jumps from her chair and peers in the mirror, not to discover who she is but to be reassured of what she isn't—Grandmorin's daughter. Her excitement excites Roubaud, but she fights off his embrace, complaining about men. Then, incautiously, "This ring he gave me, I could throw it out the window." Roubaud's suspicion flares back to life and soon explodes in anger: "You've slept with him!" He beats an admission from her and soon has forced her to abet his planned revenge.

Critics of the film have said that Roubaud is too sympathetically shown at the start and that his later acquiescence in Séverine's liaison with Lantier casts doubt upon the authenticity of his jealous fury at Grandmorin. But Renoir's Roubaud seems neither so simple nor as much a brute as Zola's character. The opening scenes present not just a proud and capable Roubaud; they also show the complaisance and fragility of his self-image, as controller of his life, model workman, and happy husband, a middle-aged man vital and virile enough to have won a beautiful young wife and now fill her world. Roubaud's wild rage flows not merely from his knowledge that Grandmorin has seduced Séverine—he had even thought it funny that

Roubaud (Fernand Ledoux) with Séverine (Simone Simon).

Séverine's mother might have slept with Grandmorin—but rather from the abrupt destruction of his self-satisfied image. His life and marriage suddenly appear in a wholly different light—a light reflected in his anguished cry as he bangs the bed upon the floor, "An old man's leavings!" His proud tie of love with Séverine bluntly severed, his rage must forge another tie of blood. But such ties, he soon discovers, bring despair not joy: "If we can't forget, it will be terrible, the two of us in this house."

Her duplicity once revealed, Séverine can never, for Roubaud, regain her innocence. Hence, when he joins her in courting Lantier, this may not be mere prudence but, subconsciously, a further getting even with Grandmorin by taking on his role, Roubaud now giving his "leavings" to another, younger, man. And that slow downfall of Roubaud, so carefully depicted by Zola, follows step-by-step. His good humor disappears; his smile becomes a sullen gaze. His jaunty walk degenerates into a dejected plod. Grandmorin's money, which he "respected" but would never touch, now feeds his obsessive gambling. Renoir completes this fall with an image of total despair: Roubaud slumped in the bedroom doorway, stunned by the sight of Séverine's corpse, the last vestige of his fatal act swinging from his hand: Grandmorin's watch, a reminder of the railroad man Roubaud has been and of the forces that destroyed him.

Though Fernand Ledoux had appeared in a score of films, he had no great role before Roubaud. After shooting *La Bête humaine*, Renoir wrote: "This film is the first I have had the pleasure of shooting with this actor. I think he may well surprise everyone. Not that he does surprising things. On the contrary, what he does always appears to just happen. Even I who, necessarily, have seen these scenes shot, I forget during the montage that I'm dealing with an actor. It's Roubaud!"[15]

Jean Renoir's writings about *La Bête humaine* remain the best revelation of the rationale that underlay his purported miscasting of actors:

Many friends have been much surprised that I asked the producers to bring Simone Simon from Hollywood to interpret this role. They object: she's marvelous in fantasy; her grace and elegance are inimitable; she can, better than anyone, animate a musical or a light comedy. But she's not a tragedienne. Well, for years I have had a conviction to the contrary . . . It's a curious convention which holds that a tragedienne must be a tragic figure from the beginning of the film. I've happened, in my life, to have been near the heroines of some frightful, passionate affairs. Usually they were gentle little women, smiling and wholly harmless in appearance.[16] . . . When one reads in Zola his descriptions of Séverine, the way she walks, sits down, her pretty indulgences, her immense desire for something indeterminate that will never happen, it is impossible not to think of Simone Simon; and if we had put in the film an actress typed as a vamp the whole thing would have tumbled down. From the first scene, one could have predicted this creature was going to generate drama. The thing would have been so evident that it would have been useless to shoot the film beyond the first reel; the public could perfectly well predict without going further everything that would happen . . .
There is another reason that led me to ask Simone Simon to take this role; it's that she has talent, and the form of that talent is that which most captivates me. Not one of those clamorous, ostentatious talents. Never, after an "expression," does she turn toward the audience blinking her eyes, with the air of saying, "What do you think of that?" It is a discreet talent and it's that which is its strength. She glides over the ef-

fects; she is modest; she never overplays. And because of that she has known how to be my dear Séverine, this curious little character, passive and yet destructive, this tiny center of the world who is all the women who trail misfortune behind their Louis XV heels.[17]

On the eve of shooting *La Bête humaine*, Renoir had written of Zola's Séverine:

Séverine is an odd little woman and for fifteen days we have had all sorts of experiences with her. I mean the real Séverine, that of Zola, not Simone Simon . . . Séverine has really exaggerated with us. I say us because, Gabin and I, we no longer know very well which of us two is the lover of Zola's heroine. She has lied to us, made us believe that she was pure when she has had lovers. She made us believe that she had an unhappy childhood, while when she was in short skirts her best times were spent in leading old gentlemen on. She made us believe that she thought only of us, while she was tied to her husband by the vilest interest, by an infamous secret. And we went on thinking we were fortunate. We didn't dare touch her for fear she would break. We even came to avoiding gross words in front of her. Our language became so chaste that one couldn't recognize it any longer.

Then one day she went too far, and Gabin killed her. I say Gabin, because, me, I'm not a man of great resoluteness.[18]

In the film we first see Séverine by the window, looking as soft and gentle as the kitten she holds, with an air of childish innocence quickly belied by the confidence with which she evades Roubaud's embrace and responds to his suggestion that she go to talk to Grandmorin. When she was young, he remarks, she was scared to death of Grandmorin. "Oh, scared to death! You exaggerate, as usual," she replies with great assurance: "To be sure, all the others were afraid, even his daughter Berthe. If they knew he was coming, they all ran away. But I waited, steady, my nose in the air, and he would pat me on the cheek. I got everything I wanted. He never scolded me." As she talks she stands, steady, nose in the air, getting what she wants from Roubaud, now as then quite conscious of her appeal.

At Mme. Victoire's she enters flushed from running, senses Roubaud's irritation, and quickly becomes again the artless loving child, calming him with practiced ease. But the thoughtless disclosure of her stupid, oft-repeated lie about the ring undoes that game. When Roubaud asks suspiciously, "What did you say? That ring *he* gave you? Who?" her annoyance dissolves; she turns in wide-eyed guileless innocence, but now this just feeds his rage. Her confession once made, Séverine never again plays the simple child for Roubaud. They speak frankly through the rest of the film; a relationship of comfortable hypocrisy gives way to an honesty in which hatred thrives. Though she protests his plan, once murder is done she becomes quite practical about the deed, approaching Lantier without hesitation, urging Roubaud to burn the money, which his bourgeois conscience will not let him do. As he hides it in the floor she still thinks of Lantier, "A fellow like that can be persuaded, influenced."

These three, then, come together quite by chance, which soon becomes another name for fate: Lantier, open and honest but driven by his compulsion, fearful of women but with an unacknowledged fascination for death or guilt; Roubaud, complaisance shaken but with his image of control restored by murder, still self-deceived in thinking that this act, this "accident," can leave his life unchanged; Séverine, outwardly passive and pliant, but self-centered and confident of her skill at manipulating the world. None chooses what to do; each perhaps has an illusion of choice, but every fatal step flows rather from some circumstance that elicits an irrepressible response. Séverine must influence Lantier; Roubaud must join this venture to preserve his illusion of control. And Lantier must share Séverine's guilt and hear the details of her crime. The strength of these reactions creates our sense that these three are fated, doomed; that had these chance events not happened these characters would have found another path to the same end.

From scene to scene the pressures run: Séverine, slapped into honesty with Roubaud, replays her act of ingenuous innocence for Lantier. Convinced of her guilt, he still accepts her pose as troubled child and offers his protection—perhaps her pose helps calm his fear; it is women, not children, he has an urge to kill. Both Séverine and Roubaud find Lantier's presence comforting; it assures them of his silence and avoids their being "the two of us in this house." Séverine's sexual coldness is plain enough in the novel— "Usually she surrendered with a complaisant docility . . . This seemed without pleasure for her"—but less clear in the film, being suggested by her response to Roubaud and by her startled reaction to Lantier's first declaration of love, when she asserts that love is not possible for her. Now, in her new honesty, she identifies Roubaud's sexual assaults with their act of murder and tells him, "Never again." Deprived of his "wife who waits for me," Roubaud seeks solace at the café; Séverine turns to "friendship" with Lantier. In the novel Séverine's frigidity and Lantier's compulsion are, as it were, complementary; each is the other's cure, and their first act of love is a joyous revelation for both. In the film, the rain and the added layers of clothing this requires may be symbols of the obstacles the consummation of this love must overcome, and the final image of this scene—the lover's embrace, their faces lit by the sun—seems an attempt to show this sudden joy, described at length by Zola, and not, as it may now appear, a cliché Hollywood image of eternal bliss.

The love she has discovered only increases Séverine's contempt for Roubaud when she finds him taking money from the floor, and this drives him to swear their crime has bound them in a tie she never will escape. Love also leads Séverine to confess her crime, so as to make Lantier wholly share her life. But this confession arouses Lantier's fascination with death, rekindling the flame that love had, perhaps, extinguished. And his excitement forces her to reconstruct the crime; this then becomes the seed of a new crime, the plan to kill Roubaud. Once conceived, though Lantier will act, emotionally it will be Séverine's crime. In the dark yard she is the active force. Lantier squints into the gloom; Séverine sees clearly and describes Roubaud's path. As he approaches, she must act; she kisses Lantier passionately enough to impart to him all of her determination, her very will. When he cannot strike, it is not merely his failure but a thwarting of their love, a denial of its power. The weakness underlying his apparent strength proves unequal to the hardness hidden under her surface fragility. Hence the affair must end.

At the Railwaymen's Ball, Lantier seems propelled toward Séverine by the remarks of Pecqueux's friend, Philomène. But Séverine has already launched another venture with young Dauvergne, and the apparent ease of this transfer creates doubt about the depth in her of any emotion beyond her longing for her own comfort. She treats Lantier quite coolly; almost matter-of-factly she asserts, "Our path is barred." Yet her admission, "Tonight I wanted to dance only with you," is encouraging enough to draw him after her into the dark and heavy atmosphere of the apartment to try again to kill Roubaud. There, his show of resoluteness leads her once again to take this crime as her own, once more to try perversely to make him mortal with a kiss. This time she does; his hand finds the knife it has longed for and plants it in her throat, repeating the act he had so avidly insisted she describe.

Graham Greene once wrote of Carol Reed's *The Stars Look Down*, "Here one forgets the casting altogether; he handles his players like a master, so that one remembers them only as people." This happens often with Renoir, not least in *La Bête humaine* where the actors seem wholly absorbed into these three characters, so immersed in, so weighed down by, the narrow frame of their world.

Three secondary characters supply the major contrast to the heavy atmosphere of immobility and powerlessness that surrounds the central trio: Flore, forthright and independent, a "vision of fresh youth and robust health," as Renoir says; and Pecqueux and Cabuche, both capable of movement and choice and endowed with a life that overflows the narrow frame. The warm and faithful friendship of Pecqueux, relaxed yet showing genuine concern, creates the one sustained positive note in Lantier's life, conveyed in a performance restrained enough to lead a usually hostile critic from the extreme right to say of Carette that "under a firm and precise direction he has left in the dressing-room his usual little repertoire, so deplorably trivial,"[19] while the editor of *Premier Plan* writes simply, "Carette, once more, is perfect."

But Jean Renoir provides the surprise of the film in his most ambitious acting role to date as Cabuche. Cabuche is a quarry worker in the novel, but in shooting the film Renoir omitted the one line from his original script

Séverine and Jacques Lantier plan to kill Roubaud—and fail.

that referred to the quarry and endowed Cabuche with the clothing and lan-guage of a poacher. Many years later, Renoir remarked, "Probably because of the romantic idea that a man living in the woods must be a poacher, on this occasion I fell victim of the cliché." Though arrested in an act of official arrogance, Cabuche in the novel is freed to avoid official embarrassment. Renoir uses him to show the degree of Lantier's complicity in Séverine's guilt. Lantier tells Roubaud and Séverine that he knows Cabuche is innocent and says, "If he is condemned, I'll have to do something." But then Lantier and Séverine become lovers and we hear no more of Cabuche, apparently abandoned by Lantier and left to an unknown fate. In Jean Renoir's vigorous performance, Cabuche seems, even more than Flore, a creature from another world, vital, truculent, simple, blunt, and free, but capable of genuine feeling. Given Lantier's constant tension and the doubt created about the depth and honesty of Séverine's emotions, the most authentically tender moment in *La Bête humaine* comes when Cabuche describes his days with Flore's sister, Louisette.

Style and Form

Like *Toni*, *La Bête humaine* begins and ends with an episode of trains. The final sequence creates a sense of closure in both films; in *Toni* this completes a cyclical structure that now begins again, but in *La Bête humaine* we feel that the thread of these lives has run its course; the tale has ended and will not take up anew. One factor in this difference is that the last scene in *Toni* repeats the first, but in *La Bête humaine* the final railroad run reverses the opening scene, the train traversing the same landscape but in the opposite direction. This end pattern of two matching scenes, with one containing a reversal or contrary of the other, is repeated through the film, becoming its dominant form.

The matching pairs vary in scale, from single shots to large sequences, but the pattern of reversals runs throughout. Thus the first scene with Séverine begins with Roubaud standing in the doorway looking at her, smiling, while the last scene with Séverine ends with Roubaud standing in the doorway looking at her, weeping. In large scale, the early scenes in the railroad yards and dormitory, showing the railway men at work, are matched by the late scene of the *bal de nuit*, the *cheminots* at play. In each of these scenes Jacques Lantier's concern centers on his "love"—first *La Lison*, then Séverine. But in the first, Lantier and *La Lison* are wholly integrated into the life of the railway men, while in the latter Lantier and Séverine seem wholly isolated amid the dancers. And the outcome differs drastically, of course: the repair of *La Lison*, the death of Séverine.

Perhaps most obvious in this array of matching pairs are the murder scenes, but even here one may not notice how precise the pattern is. There are two murders in *La Bête humaine*, but also two attempts that fail. Four attempts: two compulsive, two deliberate; of each type, one succeeds, one fails. The first, in daylight and open air, occurs when Lantier kisses Flore and compulsively begins to strangle her, but the train intervenes. The last, at night in the dark apartment, occurs when Séverine kisses Lantier and is killed, compulsively, by him, with the act vaguely perceived through an open door. Between these two occur the deliberate attempts: First, with Séverine watching, Roubaud kills Grandmorin inside a train, with the act concealed behind a closed door. Then, with Séverine watching, Lantier stands beside a train, prepared to kill Roubaud, but lacks the will.

Each deliberate attempt at murder grows from a scene at Mme. Victoire's, and each of these in turn begins with a man on the balcony overlooking gare St. Lazare. He checks his watch against the trains, meets Séverine at the door—a kiss, a meal, then a confession from Séverine. But in the first, a burst of violence forces the confession, which leaves Roubaud determined on the crime; in the second an act of love evokes the confession and leads Séverine to think of murder.

Other examples might be cited, but the structure should be clear. Repeatedly a later scene will match an earlier one, usually with some repetition of detail, always with some reversal of effect. Though not arranged as symmetrically around a center as are the pairs of matching scenes in *Toni*, most pairs here are divided between the first and second halves of *La Bête humaine*.

The structure of recurrent repetition and reversal contributes strongly to the sense of inevitability or fate that so pervades *La Bête humaine*. The remarkable opening sequence, which both introduces this structure and creates the feeling of compulsion, lays the groundwork for this feature of the film.

Characteristically, movie scenes of rapid travel achieve their effect by editing, with quick, accelerating cutting used to convey speed. But Renoir avoids this convention altogether, using only thirty-one shots in the four and a quarter minutes of this sequence—a cutting pace somewhat more rapid than the rest of *La Bête humaine*, but certainly no faster than that of the average film of 1938 and intolerably slow beside comparable scenes by Eisenstein or Abel Gance. Instead of rapid cutting, Renoir relies upon the rhythm of movement within his shots to create our experience of speed and irresistible momentum, in particular upon a carefully formed relationship between the movement we perceive in the screen-space, the two-dimensional surface of the screen, and the movement we recognize in the action-space, the three-dimensional space of the world of the film.

A whistle screams; we see in close-up the blazing, open firebox of *La*

Lison. The receding camera reveals Pecqueux stoking the fire, then Lantier, and, finally, the countryside flashing by as the locomotive races down the track. This first shot establishes the real movement of the scene, the event within the action-space, as the forward motion of the train. The visual correlate of this motion, on the left side of the screen, is a flowing of images of the countryside from the center toward the edges of the screen. As the camera pulls back through the cab, the visual correlate of its motion is a movement of images in the cab from the edges toward the center of the screen. Thus the backward movement of the camera on the train counteracts the camera's forward travel with the train, creating tension in the shot, but raising no question about the objective motion in the scene.

Ten shots follow which all contain some similar internal contrast, with this contrast reinforcing our awareness of the rapid forward movement of the train. Of these ten shots, eight make up four matching pairs, with the second shot a reversal of the first. Three of these pairs alternate medium shots of Lantier and Pecqueux, with the background motion, right to left, left to right, reversed from shot to shot. Thus Renoir begins the structure of reversed matching pairs very early in the film and makes it unmistakable here, where the abrupt change in visual motion renders each cut highly visible. Late in this series of ten shots, he sets his camera facing forward beside the boiler as the engine flashes by standing freight cars, a station, an underpass. The solid, black bulk of the boiler steadily fills two-thirds of the screen, contrasting to the rapid center-to-edge motion in the left third of the frame. Riding thus, we move with the train into a tunnel and the screen goes wholly black for twenty-six frames in a sort of visual punctuation mark that concludes this opening movement of the sequence.

Now, out of the tunnel, the second half of this reversed matching pair begins. The reversal starts with a new image which omits all of the internal contrasts of motion that marked each preceding shot. Renoir now sets his camera ahead of the engine, shooting straight down the track, and we rush forward through the space; all across the screen, images flow toward the edges of the frame, engulfing us. In the first twelve shots the omnipresent locomotive served as buffer between us and that devouring space; now it swallows us alive.

Finding a dramatic pretext in the scooping-up of water from a trough between the tracks, Renoir now combines seven shots in which the camera faces steadfastly forward, alternating between the cab and the front of the train. Here no reversal occurs at the cuts; the thrust of screen-space and action-space coincides, and our sense of forward movement heightens steadily until the train sweeps through a long ironwork bridge. Within this funnel, the varied image gives way to an almost uniform pattern of ironwork and track flowing inexorably off the edges, while the white rectangle of the bridge's end grows in the center of the screen. Coming at the end of this series of shots, this image becomes hypnotic and wholly compulsive in its creation of a sense of irresistible forward momentum thrusting us inexorably along those predetermined tracks. The compulsion becomes so strong it must be broken, and Renoir inserts three alternating shots of Lantier and Pecqueux before cutting back to the tracks ahead of the train, where we are caught once more in that compelling flow. A long curve looms ahead. Thus far, the sound has been the whistle, roar, and clatter of the train, but at the center of the curve music begins and suddenly, magically, releases us. This external music, not heard within the world of the film, creates a distance between audience and image and frees us from the compulsive movement of the film. Once we are freed, the images change, too. Lantier looks at his watch—a first act of free will not dictated by the forward rush of *La Lison*. A moment later even the camera is freed, panning away from the hypnotic tracks to view a passing tower. The station at Le Havre appears ahead, and Renoir fades to the final image in this sequence, the majestic entrance of *La Lison* shot against the station roof. Lantier and Pecqueux dismount and the story beings.

In the structure of *La Bête humaine*, the symphonic opening plays a double role. It introduces, both internally and as a whole, the pattern of reversed matching pairs, and it creates the dominant mood of the film, that sense of compulsion which becomes fate when it invades the character's lives. And it still remains one of the most effective bits of pure cinema ever created.

Once the story starts, it moves steadily forward, prompting critics to note the "rigor" of the film's construction, purportedly surprising for a Renoir film. Besides the structure of matching scenes, they mean, I think, that the camera keeps steadfastly at its work, not wandering off to see what else might be going on, and that the passages from scene to scene are both elliptical and very clear, with no waste motion of transitional images when dialogue has already bridged the cut. Though the camera moves more frequently than in any earlier Renoir film, resting stock-still in less than half the shots, we do not feel its fluidity, for it remains almost as tightly tied to the action as to the tracks of the moving train.

La Bête humaine seems the darkest of Renoir's works of this period, not merely in mood, but visually as well. Though several bright exteriors appear early in the film, its last third occurs essentially at night, and the momentum of action tends to leave these dark scenes in our memory. Smoke and rain, dim rooms, somber yards, faces half in shadow, lighting that dramatizes shadows and accentuates the darkness: these are the impressions that remain. Occasionally Renoir achieves an effect through lighting alone, as in the scene of Grandmorin's murder, when Roubaud cautiously peers out of the compartment and down the dark, empty aisle. A shiver of light from outside slices through the car windows, streaking down the silent cor-

The death of Séverine. *Lower right,* Pecqueux and Philomene (Jenny Hélia) at the railway-men's ball.

ridor toward the camera. Compulsive and fast, it precipitates the murder to come, slashing through the car as Roubaud's bright steel will slash through Grandmorin's flesh. Visually it is a striking shot, quick, clean, and premonitory.

Most of the music in *La Bête humaine* is external, much more than usual for Renoir, with all of it justified, as far as I am concerned, by that moment of distance and release in the opening sequence. But once again at a critical moment Renoir puts his music inside the world of the film, in a popular song that reflects the action, "Le Petit Coeur de Ninon." This scene has probably evoked more comment than any other formal invention of Renoir's.

Séverine has left the *bal du nuit*; Lantier follows and finds her in the apartment. She sits before a mirror, another mirror in her hand, with this doubling of the mirror imagery perhaps symbolic of the depth of her self-absorption. In a scene where only a few sparse lines of dialogue break the silence, Lantier asserts his readiness to act, finds Roubaud's pistol. They wait in darkness, mistaking another's footsteps for Roubaud's, silently kiss as Séverine seeks to breathe the iron of her soul into his. Then Lantier, maddened, pursues her to the bedroom and her death—the only sound, their footsteps and her scream. Here Renoir cuts back to the ballroom, to Pecqueux and Philomène and the fickle little heart of Ninon, which may be offered to all but possessed by none. In the midst of the song he cuts again to a close-up of Séverine's hand hanging by the bed, the camera moving across her body to the gash in her throat and then to Lantier still standing over her. At this cut the song continues and now fills the silent apartment, bringing a recognition that sound from the outside world has been audible in this apartment all along, but blocked by the intense absorption of the characters in themselves, and ours in them. The cut back, with its intruding sound, marks the moment of release for Lantier. He walks away from Séverine, stopping at the sideboard for that deadly glance of self-awareness, and out the door—the song continues throughout the scene.

We find here, I think, the subtlest of the reversals that form the structure of *La Bête humaine*. In the opening scene Renoir used the intrusion of external music to release his audience from the compulsion of the rails; now in the climactic scene the intrusion of internal music releases his character from the compulsion of his madness. The external music brings us back to its world and ours, the world of the film audience; the internal music returns Lantier to its world and his, the world of Pecqueux and Philomène and *La Lison*—but a world, now, without Séverine, a world he can no longer bear.

21

La Règle du jeu
1939

*What is interesting about this film, perhaps, is the moment
when it was made. It was shot between Munich and the war
and I shot it absolutely impressed, absolutely disturbed by the
state of mind of a part of French society, a part of English
society, a part of world society. And it seemed to me that a
way of interpreting this state of mind, to the world hopefully,
was not to talk of that situation but tell a frivolous story. I
looked for inspiration to Beaumarchais, to Marivaux, to the
classical authors of comedy.*   —*Jean Renoir*

After completing *La Bête humaine*, Jean Renoir wrote an account of his
career for the magazine *Le Point*. Published as "Souvenirs" in December
1938, this remained for years the most authoritative description of his first
fifteen years in film. Renoir acknowledged the growth of a preference for
deep focus, affirmed his French roots, and concluded with another hopeful
expression of an old Renoir dream: "Film making is the metier of craftsmen,
and it is these craftsmen grouped together to protect themselves who will
perhaps make French cinema the best in the world."

He had not only hypothetical groups in mind, but his own new attempt to
form a cooperative production company that would allow him to work
without the recurrent need, so costly in time and energy, of convincing
some producer that a new Renoir project deserved backing. Thirty-five
years later Renoir would complain mildly about the waste and frustration

his metier entailed: "When I think of the fruitless efforts that have filled my life, I am amazed at myself. How many humiliating concessions! How many useless smiles! How many denials and, above all, how much wasted time! I am a speedy director. If instead of exhausting myself in unavailing visits I had spent that time making films, I would surely have a dozen more to my credit."[1]

But now, late in 1938, bubbling with ideas for his next film, he joined with his brother Claude and three old friends to form the Nouvelles Editions Françaises (NEF),[2] a production company within which he hoped to make two films a year. Even more involved designs underlay the scheme, for the creators of the NEF envisioned it as a French equivalent of that earlier American cooperative, United Artists. But realization of such hopes awaited the success of their first venture, a new Renoir film provisionally entitled *Les Caprices de Marianne*.

La Bête humaine opened in Paris just after Christmas and was an immediate hit, playing to full houses for months at the Madeleine. Renoir's reputation was at its peak; yet even while shooting *La Bête humaine* he had been turning away from its dark romantic realism, which so well expressed the mood of the moment but did not match Renoir's own orientation toward the world. So, seeking inspiration for his next film, he looked to French classical comedy. Meanwhile, Europe continued on its path toward war, and the resonance of this impending disaster would combine with Renoir's return to the classics of the French comic stage to create that state of mind from which *La Règle du jeu* finally emerged.

Renoir's response to Munich had been clear and strong: "This four-power pact has a flavor of white slavery that would be rather amusing if it weren't for the consequences . . . Have you seen those faces, fat, smiling, and satisfied, those pretty creases under the chin, those unctuous rolls of fat on the neck, and those uniforms. The most handsome is Goering. In the place of Daladier and Chamberlain, humble representatives of our so-called democracies in that foreign hut, I would have felt rather humiliated. . . . So, the Germans will enter the Sudeten villages. Will our papers publish, as they did for Vienna, photographs of those fine jokes that the Hitlerites will not fail to practice on the Jews of that region?"[3] Still he too was touched by that wave of relief which swept Europe—shop girls waved tricolored flags to welcome Daladier back to Paris; souvenir umbrellas and pictures of Chamberlain appeared in the Bon Marché; at Périgueux, his constituents greeted the foreign minister with shouts of "Merci, Bonnet!" Léon Blum, the hesitant conscience of the Left, wrote of the mixture of "cowardly relief and shame" he felt at the dismemberment of Czechoslovakia. Renoir was reassured enough to propose to his friends the formation of the NEF, a project which presupposed that life would go on as usual for some time.

But uneasiness remained and subsequent events quickly undermined the guilty euphoria of early October. The complete demise of the power of the Left soon became evident. Only the Communists voted against the Munich pact, adding fuel to the violent anti-Communist campaign mounted by the Right immediately after Munich. By the end of October, Daladier too had denounced the Communists at a Radical Party congress and soon abandoned the Popular Front alignment to seek a new majority in alliance with the Center and Right. On November 24 the police used tear gas to drive strikers from the Renault factory; a general strike called for November 30 failed miserably. The illusion of a left-wing threat to the power and privilege of the bourgeoisie was officially over.

The policy of nonintervention in Spain, that lie which had poisoned French political life since 1936, also approached its end as the fascist victory grew near. Franco began his final offensive on December 23. Amidst pleas for aid for the Spanish government, the French Chamber of Deputies began its last debate on "nonintervention" on January 13—and was still debating on January 26 when Barcelona fell. Despite howls of rage from the extreme Right, nearly half a million refugees were allowed to cross the border into France. The French deputies began to think of those reasons which would allow them to save appearances while quickly recognizing the new Franco government. On February 25 the headline of *Le Populaire* proclaimed: "The Chamber of May 1936, the Chamber of the Popular Front, has recognized General Franco." Léon Blum left the meeting "overwhelmed by an almost intolerable disgust and anxiety."

Meanwhile, late in January, Jean Renoir left Paris to work on his script. A reporter asked him, "Just what will *The Rules of the Game* be like?" Renoir's answer came without hesitation, "An exact description of the bourgeois of our time."[4]

Much had changed since his first hasty sketch of *Les Caprices de Marianne*. As usual Renoir wrote and rewrote his scenario and it gradually took the shape of the film we know now. Initially he planned to retain two of his leading players from *La Bête humaine*, casting Simone Simon as Christine and Fernand Ledoux as Schumacher; Pierre Renoir had agreed to play Octave. But Simone Simon demanded a fee of 800,000 francs, almost one-third of the projected budget and more than Camille François, the general administrator of the NEF, was willing to pay. Searching for a new Christine, Camille François found a young actress and persuaded Renoir to attend the play in which she was performing. At the theatre Renoir seemed only mildly interested until his wandering eye found an elegant woman watching from a box. Between acts he disappeared; when he returned he was jubilant. He had found Christine, exactly what he was looking for—the woman in the box. She was Nora Grégor, wife of Prince Stahremberg, an Austrian nobleman and political leader, who had fled when Hitler overran his country. Before her marriage Nora Grégor had been on the stage and in

Jean Renoir, 1939. Photograph by Sam Levin.

several movies, playing a substantial role in Dreyer's *Michael*, shot in Germany in 1924. Renoir was not disturbed by the fact that this Christine was rather older than he had envisioned and hardly spoke French. Despite the protestations of his colleagues, she was signed for the role.

When the plans for *La Règle du jeu* expanded to include several weeks of shooting at Sologne, Pierre Renoir withdrew from the project. Though he occasionally worked in film, his career centered on the stage and he refused to leave Paris for shooting on location—for this same reason Louis Jouvet had declined the role of Boildieu in *La Grande Illusion*. So Jean Renoir began seeking a new actor to play Octave, and managed not to find one. A few years ago he said, "I really didn't look very hard. I was just waiting for the moment when Pierre would say, 'Why don't you play the role yourself, Jean?' He didn't have to ask me twice."

By late January the cast had been essentially settled: Nora Grégor, Dalio, Roland Toutain, Jean Renoir, several who had played in *La Bête humaine*, Carette, Corteggiani, Jenny Hélia, Léon Larive, Claire Gerard, and other old friends of Renoir. Gaston Modot, Paulette Dubost, and Mila Parély would be added later. Karl Koch, André Zwoboda, and Renoir went to

Marlotte where they could work in peace on a "final" script. The success of *La Bête humaine* made fund-raising easier, and soon *La Règle du jeu* was announced as the great French production of 1939. On two huge adjoining sound stages at the Joinville studio, the set designers, Lourié and Douy, began to build one of the most beautiful and costly sets ever created for a French production.

Renoir returned from Marlotte with a detailed script for only one-third of the film and a mere sketch of the events at the chateau, but ready and anxious to begin shooting: "In reality, I had this subject so much inside me, so profoundly within me, that I had written only the entrances and movements, to avoid mistakes about them. The sense of the characters and the action and, above all, the symbolic side of the film, that was something I had thought about for a long time. I had desired to do something like this for a long time, to show a rich, complex society where—to use a historic phrase—we are dancing on a volcano. My ambition when I made the film was to illustrate this remark: we are dancing on a volcano."[5]

So, he was ready to begin the dance. But again fate intervened. Three years before, as the Spanish Civil War was beginning, Renoir had sat with his company on the banks of the Loing, waiting for the rain to stop so he could shoot *Une Partie de campagne*. Now, as the remnants of the Republican army straggled across the Spanish frontier, he sat with his company amid the marshes of Sologne, waiting for the rain to stop so he could shoot *La Règle du jeu*.

The rain fell for a week, two weeks. The actors played cards; Renoir worked again on his script. Expenses mounted, both in Sologne and the idle studio at Joinville. Clearly, the original estimate of the budget would not suffice, so Zwoboda went to Paris to negotiate with Jean Jay, director of the Société Gaumont, for an advance on the rights to exhibit *La Règle du jeu* in the large circuit of Gaumont theatres. At last the weather cleared and Renoir could begin shooting his exterior scenes in the gray misty beauty of Sologne, which, he says: "my father regretted that he had never been able to paint. How well I understand the sincerity of those regrets before these beautiful lanscapes of Sologne, in astonishing colors, of a grace so melancholy and yet so gentle."

The shooting went slowly, being largely improvised, and now Jean Jay was there, with a hand in the affair, and urging Renoir to hasten back to Joinville, to use that set that was costing so much. Renoir shot all the exterior scenes that required actors, then wrote a very complete script for the rest and went back to Paris, leaving Zwoboda, Corteggiani, and a small crew to capture the stunning details of the hunt scene.

In mid-March, despite the guarantees given at Munich, Hitler's army overran Czechoslovakia and the Führer went to Prague to declare its annexation to the Reich. At last Neville Chamberlain discovered that Herr Hitler was not a gentleman, and Chamberlain extended to Poland the assurances of British support that he had denied the Czechs—an ironic decision, perhaps, after Poland had hastened to claim her share of the spoils at the time of the Czech dismemberment. France declared a partial mobilization. At the Joinville studio a few electricians and mechanics disappeared. The distant gunfire which had formed an unheeded background for the bourgeois life since October 1935 drew a little nearer.

In an interview years later Renoir was asked, "Did you also discover only later all those things in *La Règle du jeu* which made one feel the approach of the war?" He replied, "Ah! No. I thought of it then, but in an extremely vague way. I didn't tell myself, 'It's absolutely necessary to express this or that in this film because we are going to have war.' But, knowing that we were going to have war, in being absolutely convinced of it, my work was impregnated with it, despite myself. But I didn't establish a relation between the pressing state of war and the dialogue of my characters, such and such words."[6]

In the studio the work still went slowly, with Renoir sometimes changing the dialogue for every take of a shot, sometimes doing fifteen or twenty takes of a complex shot before getting just that expression he sought. Chris-

Renoir, while working on the script of *La Regle du jeu*. Photograph by Sam Levin.

tine's role diminished; Geneviève's and Lisette's grew. Jean Jay watched the rushes and was dismayed at Renoir's performance as Octave. Renoir offered to start all over with Michel Simon as Octave, but, with the film two-thirds finished, Jean Jay refused and asked merely that Octave's role be reduced. Renoir ignored the request, built his role and his film as he felt it should be, with all the disorder and complexity he felt necessary to reflect the world he knew: "When I made *La Règle du jeu* I knew where I was going. I knew the malady that gnawed at the contemporary world. That doesn't mean that I knew how to give a clear idea of that malady in my film. But my instinct guided me. My awareness of danger furnished the situations and the lines, and my comrades felt like I did. How anxious we were! I think the film is good. But it's not so difficult to do good work when the compass of anxiety indicates the true direction."[7]

With the last frame shot, Renoir had expended himself in his work, had gotten everything he wanted for it, had made it exactly as he wished. Marguerite took the miles of film that had been printed and began the montage. Early in July a complete version was projected—113 minutes. Jean Jay insisted that the film be cut: it was too long; the role of Octave had to be reduced. Renoir refused. The opening was scheduled for two Gaumont theatres in Paris; Jay predicted a commercial failure if the film was not cut. Renoir: "Je m'incline devant le commerce." Thirteen minutes were cut from the film before its release. Not until April 23, 1965 would a complete print of *La Règle du jeu* be commercially shown in Paris.

On July 7, 1939, Hitler was threatening Poland; Britain was rearming. Those who had sighed in relief at Munich now asked, "Why should we die for Danzig?" *La Règle du jeu* opened at the Colisée, preceded by an interminable documentary consecrated to the glories of the French Empire—marching troops and waving flags. The audience cheered. But as *La Règle du jeu* unrolled, the applause turned to expressions of fury. As Renoir watched, a spectator set fire to his newspaper and tried to ignite the back of his chair, declaring that any theatre which showed such a film ought to be destroyed. Whistles and boos drowned the dialogue. Wholly disconcerted, Renoir left the theatre. Later René Clair asked, "In fact, mon vieux Jean, what exactly was it you wanted to do?" and Renoir could only reply with a line from the film, "I don't know; I no longer know." Thirty-five years later he would give this account of the violent reaction to his film: "I depicted pleasant, sympathetic characters, but showed them in a society in process of disintegration, so that they were defeated at the outset . . . The audience recognized this. The truth is that they recognized themselves. People who commit suicide do not care to do it in front of witnesses."[8]

Attempting to save something from the debacle, Renoir cut the film again. It shrunk from a hundred minutes to ninety, then eight-five. But each time an offending shot was removed, audiences found a new one to hoot at.

Its run at the Colisée ended in three weeks. On September 1, Hitler invaded Poland; on September 3, England and France declared war. In October *La Règle du jeu* was banned by the censors as "demoralizing."

Narrative and Treatment

Any brief account of the narrative of *La Règle du jeu* must seem complicated to the point of unintelligibility. I offer such an account, knowing this danger, but trusting that the discussion that follows will make more sense of it.

Inspired by his love for Christine de La Chesnaye (Nora Grégor), André Jurieu (Roland Toutain) has flown the Atlantic in record time. Landing in Paris he blurts out over the radio his disappointment at her absence from the airport. Christine hears him, but turns from the radio to ask her maid, Lisette (Paulette Dubost), about her marriage and her lovers. Christine's husband, Robert, the marquis de La Chesnaye (Marcel Dalio) assures her of his understanding and is moved by her expression of confidence to break with his mistress, Geneviève de Marras (Mila Parély), but in the face of Geneviève's unhappiness he proves too weak and sympathetic to complete the break. André Jurieu, in despair, runs his car into an embankment; his friend Octave (Jean Renoir) then undertakes to bring André and Christine together again. Octave visits Christine, whom he has known since her childhood in Vienna, and persuades both Christine and Robert to invite André to a hunting party at their chateau, La Colinière. Christine's maid, Lisette, scoffs at the idea that she should leave Madame and live with her husband Schumacher (Gaston Modot), the gamekeeper at La Colinière.

At La Colinière Schumacher catches a poacher, Marceau (Carette), snaring a rabbit, but the marquis intervenes and hires Marceau as a servant. The guests arrive, greeting André as a hero; Robert proposes a party—*une grande fête*—in honor of André. Marceau, coming to the kitchen to begin his work as servant, also begins a flirtation with Lisette.

After the hunt Geneviève decides to leave, since Robert seems bored with her, but Christine accidentally sees Robert and Geneviève in a farewell embrace. Next morning Christine talks with Geneviève and confirms that she has been Robert's mistress; she asks Geneviève to stay for the party that night. Schumacher catches Marceau and Lisette in an embrace, but is chased from the kitchen by the major-domo, Corneille (Eddy Debray).

At the fête de La Colinière, Geneviève clings to Robert; Christine goes off with another guest, St. Aubin; André searches for Christine. Schumacher finds Marceau and Lisette together and pursues them. André fights with St. Aubin; Christine tells André that she loves him. Schumacher chases Marceau through the salon, shooting at him as he goes. Robert finds Christine with André; as Robert and André fight, Octave leads Christine to the terrace where they talk of Vienna and Octave's failure. A shot from Schumacher interrupts the battle between Robert and André. Corneille trips Schumacher and ends the chase. Robert tells both Schumacher and Marceau that he must fire them, but Lisette declares that she will stay with Madame rather than leave with Schumacher. Robert and André talk about André's future with Christine. Lisette finds Octave and Christine on the terrace and gives Christine her hooded cloak to protect her from the cold. Schumacher and Marceau meet and console each other; seeing Octave and Christine, they mistake Christine for Lisette. In the greenhouse Christine tells Octave that he is the one she loves. They plan to leave together; Octave goes to the chateau for Christine's coat. Schumacher swears to kill them both and takes Marceau along as he goes to get his gun. In the chateau, Lisette tells Octave that Christine will not be happy with him. André appears; Octave tells him that Christine is waiting and gives André both Christine's coat and his own. Schumacher mistakes André for Octave and fires. Octave and Marceau leave the chateau. Robert explains to the guests that a deplorable accident has occurred.

In a subtitle that forms a preface to his film, Renoir calls *La Règle du jeu* a "divertissement"—a word which suggests the baroque music and classical French comedy that helped inspire the film. Renoir says: "What happened with *La Règle du jeu* is what happens with all my films, with everything I write, with everything I do. Generally and always, all my life, I am pos-

Renoir directing Dalio in *La Regle du jeu*. Photograph by Sam Levin.

sessed by certain general ideas. These general ideas are extremely strong, but in the beginning I never find the vehicle which will permit me to convey them. I don't know how to express these general ideas—they are there; they are very strong; they possess me, but how to materialize them, to give them a form, about that I know nothing. And then very often, when I have confidence, I find a little idea, an idea purely of plot, purely vaudevillesque. For example, in this project, the idea of trying to imitate a comedy by Musset, as an exterior. Then when that happens, this minor idea absorbs, then can serve as a vehicle for, my general idea. Then I'm happy and my work goes well. Such was the beginning of *La Règle du jeu*."[9]

Renoir speaks of reading Marivaux and Beaumarchais "very attentively," not intending to follow them, but to help himself establish a style. Marivaux, the most romantic of the classical comic playwrights; Musset, the most classical of the romantics; Beaumarchais, watchmaker, adventurer, who rescued the French stage from the doldrums of the *drame bourgeois* on the eve of the Revolution—When Renoir wrote in *Le Point* of the necessity that a French artist ground himself in the tradition, this was not a grand generalization, but rather an exact description of Renoir's own creative need and activity at that moment.

"You spend an evening listening to records and the result is a film. I cannot say that it was French baroque music that inspired me to make *La Règle du jeu*, but certainly it played a part in making me wish to film the sort of people who danced to that music."[10] Such a remark suggests that Renoir's turn to classical comedy occurred more or less through coincidence or accident. But, retrospectively, viewing *La Règle du jeu* in the context of all Renoir's work in the thirties, it appears much less a matter of chance.

From *Toni* to *La Règle du jeu*, Jean Renoir made nine films. Five of these concern essentially lower-class characters—workers, farmers, derelicts. The other four involve a contrast and interplay of classes; three of these four are historical, that is, set in the past. These nine films explore two themes that recur throughout Renoir's career: the contrast of nature and convention and the question of how people meet—Renoir's concern with the encounter which may change one's life.

These themes had persisted as Renoir moved from the bourgeois films of the early thirties to those which present larger groups of a lower class, but from *La Grande Illusion* on they are subordinated to the question of class, or "caste" as Renoir sometimes calls it. But these three themes are not distinct; they might better be seen as variations on a single theme. For the encounter which changes one's life is that between persons not bound by the same conventions, persons in whose lives the relation of nature to convention differs. And the difference between classes is a difference in forms of life, that is, in the conventions which shape the lives of members of each class. The meetings that change not lives, but history, are the encounters or confrontations of classes, for the outcome of these may be a change in the conventions which dominate a society. Hence one may see both the change in theme and the occurrence of the historical films in the late thirties as merely two aspects of the expanding social context of Renoir's work—from an emphasis of individual relationships in the bourgeois films to a concern with small communities in the mid-thirties and thence to the creation of worlds containing multiple classes. From this perspective, *Une Partie de campagne* and *Les Bas Fonds* appear as transitional works, for though the former involves only individual relationships, the individuals come from different classes, and though the Baron in *Les Bas Fonds* has lost his class, Renoir's invention of his former life provides the community of derelicts with the background of an opulent upper class.

Some critics see *La Règle du jeu* as part of a trilogy with *La Marseillaise* and *La Grande Illusion*. If so, then *La Règle du jeu* too is an historical film, though set in the present, being the final strand of a thread perceived in French history from 1789 to 1939. The thread is the relation of classes, and the substance of the trilogy is the transformation of the French middle class from revolutionaries to parasites. *La Marseillaise* shows the revolution of 1789 as an action by the middle class—craftsmen, painters, lawyers, clerks —the restrictions on enlistment in the Marseilles battalion make that evident. Neither peasant nor proletarian plays a significant role, for then it was the middle class who had the energy, the ideas, and the will to overthrow a nobility that had become a burden while remaining arrogant. Scenes at Coblenz and the Tuilleries display the nobility of the day, whose lives are empty of everything but style, performing acts that are merely conventional —ceremonial or ritual gestures whose only significance lies in identifying and uniting the class. Hence the importance of remembering the fourth figure of the gavotte. For *La Marseillaise* Renoir sought inspiration in history, searching for the truth of a past he had not known.

By 1916, the dramatic time of *La Grande Illusion*, the middle class had become the backbone of the nation; they fought its wars and filled its major roles. In *La Marseillaise* a nobleman scoffs at an army of lawyers, clerks, and carpenters, but by 1914 the French army had become just that, and the prisoners in *La Grande Illusion* include a teacher, an engineer, a locksmith, a professor, a mechanic, an actor, and a banker's son. Boildieu and Rauffenstein represent the remnant of a fading upper class, performing their ritual of elegance and the ceremonies of military life, saved from sterility by the fact of the war, which makes their sole acknowledged motivation, duty, a useful one. Here Renoir's source was memory—his own, Pinsard's, other veterans'; for they had lived through that event and played the roles themselves.

After twenty years of peace and power, in 1939 the upper bourgeoisie had grown rich and idle and adopted the life of style, but without the traditions

Jean Renoir directing a scene in *La Regle du jeu*. Photograph by Sam Levin.

of either the military or the royal court. Duty no longer called; work was no longer necessary; as with Boildieu and Rauffenstein, life was more performed than lived. Within this sterility, only one motive retains its power: love—but the rules forbid that it be serious. Hence the major activity becomes the ritual of courtship, the game of love.

If Jean Renoir saw the bourgeoisie of 1939 in this way and thought of making a "gay drama" about them, then a search for inspiration could best go to only one source: that strand of classical comedy that began with Marivaux, in which the force which sets every character in motion is love, and the characters have no other occupation to interfere with this pursuit.

If we ask, to what game does the title of Renoir's film refer, the title of Marivaux's best-known play seems the most obvious answer: *The Game of Love and Chance*. By 1939, between Munich and the war, this had become the game of love and death. But we need not seek that change merely in history, for the same transformation occurs on the French comic stage between Marivaux's *The Game of Love and Chance* (1730) and Musset's *Les Caprices de Marianne*, first performed in 1851.

In 1716, after nineteen years of exile, a troupe of Italian players appeared in Paris at the Hotel de Bourgogne. In 1720 this group presented Marivaux's first successful play; for twenty years thereafter he wrote his best work for the *Nouveau Theatre Italien*, transforming elements from the commedia del' arte into rhythmic, sprightly, graceful diversions decorated by an exquisite and sophisticated banter that quickly added to the French language the term *marivaudage*, a style once described as "an introduction to each other of words which have never made acquaintance and which think they will not get on together." Within a symmetrical grouping of masters and servants typical of the commedia, Marivaux brings to the fore young people whose sole preoccupation is love and fastens his attention on the growth of love in society. The adoption of mask or disguise is frequent; in *The Game of Love and Chance*, masters and servants exchange roles, then face each other as matching pairs in false guise. The masks are not adopted for deceit, but to evoke an interplay of truth and falsity, illusion and reality, in the belief that this will bring forth a revelation of the truth of the heart. When this truth is found, when love is avowed, the play is over. The broad comic action that runs rampant on the commedia stage, Marivaux minimizes to make room for a closer inspection of love than French comedy had ever seen, but love in a context where desire is generally subordinated to the maintenance of the social order. To this end, Marivaux abandons all the extravagant adventures, the music, and much of the complication of the commedia del' arte. As a central comic element, however, he joyously retains the servants Harlequin and Columbine, although his Columbine is usually called Lisette.

If its title echoes Marivaux, the prefaces and first sounds of Renoir's film evoke Beaumarchais, whose *Le Mariage de Figaro* (1784) had shown that dancing on a volcano is not an exclusively modern pastime. The first sound, the music of Mozart, accompanies the prefaces: two subtitles, the second of them a song from *Le Mariage de Figaro*, "If Love Has Wings, Is It Not to Fly?" In this context the first subtitle, denying any pretension to social criticism, surely suggests Beaumarchais' long preface to this play, where the playwright ends by ironically denying that his play reflects the truth of the contemporary world. But earlier in his preface Beaumarchais had asserted: "Vice and abuses, they never change, but disguise themselves in a thousand forms under the mask of the prevailing morals; to tear off that mask and show them bare, such is the noble task of the man who devotes himself to the theatre." We must, I think, read Renoir's preface in the spirit of Beaumarchais, a critical spirit quite far from the gossamer elegance of Marivaux.

Like Marivaux, Beaumarchais examines love in society, but a society where the abuse of privilege is the rule. Again, a symmetrical grouping of masters and servants interact. But where Marivaux had reduced the intricacies of action to display the subtleties of sentiment, Beaumarchais revived the *comédie d'intrigue* with its complicated, quickly moving plot. The relation of masters and servants has become itself a matter of intrigue as Beaumarchais constructs his plot of overlapping triangles, real and imagined, and transforms Harlequin into Figaro, confident, resourceful, clever, and ready to assert his own worth against that of the nobility. In *Le Mariage de Figaro* the dénouement occurs in the park, during a *grande fête*, with an exchange of clothing by mistress and maid as the instrument of deception. All ends happily, but not before Figaro has delivered the famous soliloquy that prompted Louis XVI to declare that one would have to destroy the Bastille in order to keep the presentation of this play from having dangerous consequences. For Beaumarchais might well have described *Le Mariage de Figaro* as "an exact description of the nobility of our time." The nobility were greatly amused, leading Beaumarchais to remark, "There is something more outrageous than my play, and that is its success." However, one horrified member of the upper class declared, "Their own caricature has been held up before them and they reply, 'That is it; it is very like.' " The Parisian bourgeois of 1939 would not make the same mistake about *La Règle du jeu*; perhaps the rumble of the volcano would be more audible then.

Musset's debut in the theatre, the opening night of his first play in 1830, was as great a disaster as the premiere of *La Règle du jeu*; the young poet swore that he would never again face that "menagerie." For nineteen years he was content to create an "armchair theatre," writing plays to be read rather than performed. Thus *Les Caprices de Marianne*, written in 1833, was not performed until 1851. Renoir attributes "la petite idée" which began to shape *La Règle du jeu* to Musset and based his first scenario on *Les Caprices de Marianne*.

In Musset's play, Coelio, a downcast lover, enlists his friend Octave, a dissolute and cynical buffoon, to plead his cause with Marianne, the convent-reared young wife of a self-centered, jealous, middle-aged judge, Claudio. Marianne's virtuous rejection of Coelio turns into passion for Octave, and her modest obedience gives way to reckless fury. One night Marianne expects Octave at her window, but he sends Coelio instead. Coelio runs into the garden to be killed by Claudio's hired assassin. In a final scene, Octave mourns the death of Coelio and the waste of his own life. Though *Les Caprices de Marianne* derives from traditional French comedy in both its characters and language, its movement departs sharply from the usual succession of temporary obstacles that delay a happy ending. Rather, every comic exchange moves toward the fulfillment of Coelio's prediction that he has nothing to do but die. Once Octave's irony penetrates Marianne's cold exterior, this "comedy" sweeps inevitably toward death and despair; by 1830 the strict classical division of tragedy and comedy had dissolved in the romantic identification of love and death.

"I'm not very inventive, but I have a good memory," says Renoir. Having read Marivaux and Beaumarchais, his memory held the details of that reading as the *petite idée* from Musset began to grow.

La Grande Illusion had begun with the idea of a character suggested to Renoir by his friend Pinsard. A doubling and redoubling of that character had determined the form of the film. A similar but more complicated process appears to have formed *La Règle du jeu*. Here the doubling involved not merely a character but a group, and the redoubling became the superimposition of two dramatic forms.

For personnel, Renoir began with four characters from *Les Caprices de*

Marianne: virtuous wife, jealous husband, despairing lover, interceding friend. The doubling of this cast, and simultaneously the doubling of their caste, may have been suggested by the matching pairs in Marivaux, but it is carried out in the spirit of Beaumarchais, yielding a second husband, wife, and lover among the servants. With two matching sets Renoir could then work variations on the types found in Musset and rearrange their qualities, confronting each with its opposite. Thus Christine, the faithful wife, confers with Lisette, the faithless one; Schumacher becomes the jealous husband, allowing Robert to be a tolerant one, surprised by his own jealousy. André Jurieu, the despairing lover, languishes while Marceau, the bold one, thrives. Like Beaumarchais, Renoir fills out the sets by overlapping them; Robert, the husband of the upper set, becomes the friend in the lower one. But in all his actions the marquis displays a rather simple faith, whereas Renoir's Octave retains some of the cynicism of his namesake, Coelio's friend.

With the characters doubled, Musset's linear plot would no longer do. Most simply, doubling the personnel suggests doubling the plot, with parallel developments replacing the straight line. But, as with characters, the doubled plot invites variations, and again Renoir's variations confront each original action with its opposite. In *Les Caprices de Marianne* wife rejects lover, friend intercedes on lover's behalf, husband forbids wife to see either lover or friend. In *La Règle du jeu*, Christine rejects André but Lisette welcomes Marceau while rejecting her husband, Schumacher; Octave speaks to Christine on André's behalf, but Robert aids Marceau by acting against Schumacher; Schumacher forbids Marceau to speak to Lisette, but Robert invites both André and Octave to the chateau.

Thus, by doubling the elements derived from Musset, Renoir brings his intrigue to a boil. But its resolution requires another doubling, the imposition on this structure of the plot from *Le Mariage de Figaro*, with its fête and its mistaken identities, false jealousies, misunderstood discovery, and double disguise.

None of these devices occur in *Les Caprices de Marianne*. Though Coelio dies by mistake, Claudio's anger has its basis in Marianne's real defiance. Claudio proposes to kill the man who loves Marianne, and does. In *Les Caprices de Marianne* everyone has his reasons, and the emotions which motivate the action do not stem from misperception. But in *Le Mariage de Figaro* jealousy is as often baseless as warranted. Suzanne slips Count Almaviva a note making a rendezvous, then Suzanne and the countess exchange costumes to trap the count. Figaro discovers that the pin which sealed the note belongs to Suzanne; his falsely based jealousy sends him to the park, where he sees the count and countess, but like the count he takes her to be Suzanne. In return, the count sees Figaro and Suzanne, and takes her to be the countess; his falsely based rage leads to the unmasking, which ends with the count contritely asking pardon of his wife. In *La Règle du jeu* not a pin but a telescope becomes the instrument for a misunderstood discovery and, treating Beaumarchais as he had Musset, Renoir matches the falsely based jealousy of Schumacher and Marceau, who mistake Christine for Lisette, with its opposite, the falsely based confidence of Robert and André, who mistake Octave the lover for Octave the friend. The second disguise in *Le Mariage de Figaro*, of Suzanne as the countess, serves mainly to provoke a performance by Figaro, but the second disguise in *La Règle du jeu*, André dressed in Octave's coat, returns us abruptly to the climax of *Les Caprices de Marianne*—the lover, sent by a self-doubting Octave, killed by the husband's hireling, while Octave lives on in despair. But a climax here made doubly ironic by the doubling that has gone before.

I suggest no mechanical derivation of *La Règle du jeu* from Renoir's classical sources; he does not work that way. No doubt the structure of the film emerged as much from improvisation as design, but an improvisation that often touched those memories of Figaro and Marianne. In characters, structure, and action *La Règle du jeu* has roots in those classical comedies Renoir had read; and attentive readings of Marivaux, Musset, and Beaumarchais will reveal many more details of concurrence.

Still, all this does not yet yield *La Règle du jeu*. First, the nineteenth-century characters must be dressed in modern garb, the eighteenth-century comic forms filled with the indifference and despair of 1939.

Coelio, Musset's hapless lover, laments at not being born in the days of tournaments when he could display his love for Marianne by wearing her colors in some bold exploit. Renoir, taking or leaving a cue from Beaumarchais' song, "If Love Has Wings, Is It Not to Fly?," gives his lover wings for a bold exploit of the 1930s, a trans-Atlantic flight, as romantic and hazardous as a medieval joust, equally dependent on contemporary technology, equally linking love and death, and perhaps reminding audiences, between Munich and the war, that the French view of aviation had remained romantic while the Germans methodically manufactured airborne death. Perhaps also recalling the last such scene at Le Bourget, welcoming Daladier back from Munich. As in Musset, Renoir's action begins with a go-between: quite literally at first as the camera follows the cable from a Radio-Cité van to a reporter describing Jurieu's flight then through her intervention as agent of that electronic intermediary which here intrudes its shameless message, "André loves Christine", as Renoir cuts with André's voice from the darkness of Le Bourget to the bright luxury of Christine's room. In response Christine flicks off the radio, showing no sign of regret at having missed that rendezvous. In Robert's study the radio plays on. Musset's Claudio, declaring that his dishonor was public, vowed vengeance, but Renoir's Robert de La Chesnaye hears the public proclamation of his wife's disloyalty to a would-be lover, then dismisses it, saying, "Men are so naive."

Since Robert refuses to play Claudio, the plot requires some other device; 393

From the darkness of Le Bourget to the bright luxury of Christine's room. André Jurieu (Roland Toutain), Christine (Nora Grégor), Lisette (Paulette Dubost).

once more Renoir proceeds by multiplying entities, matching one electronic go-between with another, the telephone, to prepare for an opposite message —the end of love—and displacing Claudio's jealousy to Geneviève. Two scenes at Geneviève's confirm the intimations we have had about the world of this film—a world of the rich and idle, whose conversation revolves around a single topic, love; but a world whose measure Geneviève reveals in Chamfort's precept, identifying love in society as "the exchange of two fantasies and the contact of two skins." An elegant dissolve on this *mot* brings Robert and Geneviève to face the end of their affair, linking Geneviève's professed cynicism about love with her hurt reaction to Robert's new fantasy, a ripple from the pebble of sincerity dropped in the pool of lies by André at Le Bourget. Seen through the window, the Palais de Chaillot provokes further remembrance of the conflicts that ravaged the French community. In 1937, as one further blow to the Popular Front, the construction on the place du Trocadero had become a cause célèbre when strikes delayed the completion of the Palais far beyond the scheduled May 1 opening of the Paris Exhibition. Perhaps, too, in 1939, the sight of the Palais stirred unwelcome memories of France's less than heroic role in the Spanish war, for when the Paris Exhibition finally opened, its most conspicuous exhibit was Picasso's *Guernica*. But nothing from that world seems to penetrate this room or these lives. As Robert and Geneviève play out their game of love, two placid Buddhas watch, condemning by their beauty and symbolic wisdom the shallowness of lives lived by Chamfort's *mot*. In these shallows, the ripples die.

Renoir's exposition begins with an airplane landing, ends with the crash of an automobile. Thus far each act of the modern hero, André, whether seeking love or death, employs some mechanical device. This suicide manqué demonstrates again the soullessness of such aids—as the radio had carried André's plea to Robert and St. Aubin but failed to move Christine, so now André emerges unscathed while Octave doesn't "know if he is alive." Though André's attempt at self-destruction fails, the crash may symbolize an action necessary before André can enter the world of the de La Chesnayes, a stripping off of his armor of twentieth-century machinery. Hence Renoir completes the scene in an almost empty frame—gray sky and a fringe of grass—where André turns to human aid and Octave retreats from his declaration that André can kill himself "but all alone, without me."

To the twentieth-century machines that define André Jurieu's milieu, Renoir opposes the mechanical trifles that surround Robert de La Chesnaye, matching a close-up of the radio in Christine's room with one of a musical doll, a "romantic negress," in Robert's study, as later André's trans-Atlantic flight will be matched by Robert's presentation of his Limonaire. Symbolically, these "instruments musicaux et mécaniques" evoke the eighteenth century, nostalgically an age of order and decorum, when everything knew its place. Clocks had been made from the thirteenth century and portable timepieces from the fifteenth, but the watch was essentially an invention of the eighteenth century, when the clockwork mechanism captured the imagination of an era as the airplane did earlier in ours. Grandfather clocks appeared as the proudest possession in many a home, and God became the celestial watchmaker, a divine craftsman whose intelligence creates a world of infinite precision where Pre-established Harmony rules.

The correspondence of two clocks was Leibniz' best known illustration of Pre-established Harmony and the construction of clockwork musical instruments may be the most aesthetic expression of that eighteenth-century idea. At least they have that role in *La Règle du jeu*. For Renoir desired to make a comedy, a frivolous story, which would express the state of mind of 1939, as the epoch neared its tortured end. The dark and fate-filled dramas that best expressed the spirit of the time, *Quai des Brumes*, *La Bête humaine*, *Le Jour se lève*, all moved their tragic heroes unwillingly toward a destined end. The fate of Western Europe had loomed nearer since Renoir had shot *La Bête humaine*; how could he express this in a comedy? But, of course, seen dramatically, Pre-established Harmony is the comic counterpart of Fate! So the doubling of Musset's characters creates two clocks that run in harmony, two sets of troubled lovers whose comic tribulations will intersect at the appointed time.

The eighteenth century is the spiritual realm of Robert de La Chesnaye;

Two placid Buddhas watch. Robert de la Chesnaye (Marcel Dalio), Geneviève de Marrast (Mila Parély).

André Jurieu, the twentieth-century hero, rejects all the connections to which the marquis clings. As he asserts to Octave his claim to Christine, André scornfully describes Robert's eighteenth-century milieu: "If you desire Christine's happiness, let her come with me—because, me, I love her! Anyway, it's a shame to see her with that idiot de La Chesnaye, with his hunts, his chateau, his mechanical birds [*oiseaux mécaniques*]." But is there more sanity in André's sign of love, his dash across the ocean in a twentieth-century *oiseau mécanique?*

In the empty frame, without machines, André can only plead "If I don't see her again, I'll die." Octave's response, "I'll make it my affair," sets Renoir's upper echelon in place: wife, husband, mistress, lover, friend. Octave's entrance into the mirrored opulence of the hotel de La Chesnaye begins another movement of the dance, a quartet following a series of pas de deux, but a dissonant quartet. Octave, with battered hat, lumpish walk, a manner somewhat less than gracious, seems out of key in this elegant decor. He blurs the line between master and servant by embracing both Lisette and Christine, destroys the prevailing formality by calling everyone *tu*, sprawls on the bed with Christine, chases Lisette around the room. With truculence and charm he extracts from both Christine and Robert the agreement he desires, to invite André to the chateau, overcoming Robert's reluctance with the oft-quoted line," on this earth there is one thing that is dreadful; it's that everyone has his reasons." *Bien sur!* but in *La Règle du jeu* the reason is always the same: I love her/him. The difference lies in the acts each character believes this reason justifies; they range from suicide to murder and include inviting André Jurieu to La Colinière.

At La Colinière, Renoir completes the doubling of his cast with the entrance of Schumacher and Marceau and the conversion of Robert from husband into friend.

Schumacher waits by the steps at La Colinière, unaware that Lisette has

"I'll make it my affair."

already voiced distaste for married life. Robert, who knows, refuses to intercede. To Schumacher's renewed complaint, "My wife always in Paris, me here; that's no life," he replies "If your wife wants to stay with you and leave her service with Madame, that's her affair, not mine." With Geneviève, Renoir had added a fifth member to Musset's set of four; this conversation names the correlative term in the doubled lower set. Lisette's attachment to Christine makes Madame a figure in this design; with appropriate ambiquity, a perfect match: husband, wife, Mistress, lover, friend.

Lover enters soon. To the sound of distant gunfire, Robert sits in an open field, once more confounding Schumacher by denying his request to protect young plants from rabbits with wire fencing: "I don't want fences and I don't want rabbits. Arrange it, my friend." Schumacher walks away muttering, shoots at a cat, finds a rabbit caught in Marceau's snare. Perhaps from sheer frustration, he decides to wait. Marceau's first appearance signals his affinity with Robert. He arrives on a bicycle, takes off his coat, changes hats, and transforms himself into a comic copy of the marquis. Surprised by Schumacher, he smiles disarmingly, "You want my rabbit?" Grimly, Schumacher marches him across the fields.

Like Lestingois rescuing Boudu, Robert plucks Marceau from the grasp of Schumacher, ignoring the gamekeeper's incredulous, "Is M. le Marquis joking?" Obviously Robert has never seen a more perfect poacher and is dazzled by the sight. Unlike Boudu, Marceau is not ungrateful to be saved and does not resist a chance to change his life. He happily reveals to M. le Marquis the tricks of the poacher's trade; they quickly join in league against Schumacher. For a moment they simply bask in mutual affection, then Marceau reveals his dream. Boudu suspects that Lestingois had rescued him because he wants a servant; being rescued, Marceau confesses that a servant is what he has always wanted to be.

But, as in *Boudu*, a perfect poacher is not a bourgeois gentleman's servant in disguise. The costume changes, but instinct remains the same. Novices in the game of love, Christine and André spend long hours together in friendship before André is moved to action—and that most indirect. But Lisette and Marceau need no such novitiate. Marceau reports to the kitchen, neatly dressed but wholly unprepared for Corneille's query as to what he knows how to do. Though he becomes an instant "spécialiste" in matters of dress when Corneille offers that, he betrays his real speciality when a mere exchange of glances serves to launch his amorous adventure with Lisette. Both clocks now run in proper parallel.

Meanwhile, the guests arrive at the chateau. One needs no reason for following conventions, doing the done thing. These bourgeois gentlefolk conform magnificently, discuss the weather, play games, exchange cliches as if they were bons mots, maintain a surface of perfect amiability while gossiping in pairs. They greet André as a hero, prompting Christine to confess her role in his exploit and refute the gossip by a public display of "amitié." And as Robert's reassurance had sent Christine spinning round the room, so her grasping of the nettle inspires him to propose the Fête de La Colinière. Charlotte, huge and undisguisable, exclaims in delight, "We'll all come in disguise!" André Jurieu, much less pleased, feels like taking off, but Octave dissuades him.

In classical comedies, the action often pauses in midstream, giving way to a ballet or spectacle whose style and content only vaguely fits with what has gone before—an irrelevant and diverting interlude before finally unravelling the threads of the intrigue. In this nest of oppositions called *La Règle du jeu*, Jean Renoir again converts a classical device into its opposite, building a spectacle into the intrigue but interrupting his divertissement with an interlude more serious than the activity it delays, and of deadly relevance. Until its very end *la chasse*—the hunting scene—does not advance the plot at all. As if to underline this fact, Renoir brackets the scene with two declarations that momentarily arrest the plot. Both André, before, and Geneviève, after the shooting denounce the affection displayed by Robert and Christine and signal their retreat from these amours. A second bracketing has St. Aubin and La Bruyere exchange polite disclaimers at the start but angry accusations at the end. In a field strewn with slaughtered game, they heatedly dispute the etiquette of the hunt—the living game means nothing if the rules of the game are breached. These exchanges show perhaps how thin the veneer of civility is; within the double brackets Renoir displays the savagery that smolders underneath.

Each in his place, these gens du monde wait quietly as the ritual begins. With Schumacher in charge, the beaters move with measured tread, white figures accenting the beauty of the birch woods. Rabbits nestle in the grass, quiver, leap and run; a pheasant gabbles. Faces harden; eyes grow more intent; gun barrels elevate. Christine shrugs; Schumacher points. A rabbit scampers and the holocaust begins. The sky rains pheasants. Rabbits tumble dead. The sound of gunfire fills our ears; each hunter with a grim elation fires. Ten seconds pause, and then—a final rabbit stretches, stiffens, dies. His quiver rends the heart. It's over! Dogs run through the field, and cultivated conversation reappears. André kisses Jackie and discovers he's not cured. The plot resumes, but the world is not the same.

Of course, as Renoir says, the whole hunt prepares us for the death of Jurieu, but more than that the awful beauty of the scene transforms the game of love into the dance of death—and, perhaps, just that death that haunted Europe between Munich and the war. With such power, this interlude becomes the thematic center of the work; henceforth the darkness that both begins and ends the film will underline, and undermine, our laughter.

The hunt scene also best defines the matrix in which masters interact with servants. The servants at table have been seen to emulate their masters, in gossip, snobbery, and in their fine concern for propriety—"les convenances sont les convenances." The hunt indicates the limits of servant participation in the life of the leisure class. We have seen Schumacher patrolling the grounds of La Colinière, with shotgun slung on shoulder, guardian of his master's domain, charged with repelling marauders large or small, poachers or stray cats. At the hunt Robert proclaims the order of the day and, in effect, blesses the affair, "Messieurs, je vous en prie, fleurissez-vous!," then Schumacher preserves its form, places the hunters, commands the beaters, with horn and voice directs the procession of men and game toward the

The ritual begins. Schumacher (Gaston Modot).

guns, assuring that protocol prevails. But he neither wears nor carries his shotgun this day. The utilitarian task of rabbit control may be his, but ceremonial killing is the province of the masters, reserved for the upper class.

The hunt, of course, reflects on the film's final scene. If we have attended to the rules of the killing game, it may appear that the death of André Jurieu occurs quite in accord with the etiquette of *la chasse*. As a utilitarian act, clearing the master's domain of one more invading rabbit, it falls quite properly to a servant, and quite precisely to Schumacher. But if, as Renoir says, it also is a sacrifice on the altar of God so that the bourgeois life may continue for a while, then Robert, the master, must authenticate the rite—as he does by proclaiming the death an accident. Hence, perhaps, the propriety, in this bourgeois world, of the general's final verdict on the deed: "No, no, no, no, no. This La Chesnaye does not lack class."

The day wanes; the shooting ends; the hunters stray in groups toward the chateau. Geneviève draws Robert aside, perceives he's bored, requests, for old time's sake, a "bel adieu." Octave, Christine, and others meander by the marsh. A pocket telescope reveals the intimate life of a squirrel, the plumage of a gallinule—then, as Octave jostles Christine's arm, the intimate life of Robert de La Chesnaye: he and Geneviève in their farewell embrace. Christine, of course, cannot see its finality.

Having let his plot languish, Renoir inserts between the hunt and the fête some scenes to wind it up again. Christine, determined to unearth by stealth the truth of her discovery about Robert, visits Geneviève and performs admirably the role of knowing wife intent on diverting the attention of her errant spouse so that she may carry on her own affair. Geneviève, startled by Christine's confessed awareness of her liaison, discloses all that Christine wants to know—but not what Christine fails to apprehend, that the affair has ended. Falsehood performed creates its own truth: Christine's request that Geneviève remain, plus her feigned indifference toward Robert, restore Geneviève's hope and revive the dead affair. Octave decides to dress up as a bear. Schumacher, a faithful spouse, gives Lisette a warm and rainproof cloak; Lisette destroys his efforts by remarking that it doesn't flatter her, then enters the kitchen where Marceau is shining shoes. Marceau at once converts the shoes into an aid in his seduction of Lisette, and recruits one of Robert's musical dolls to the same end. A comic routine ends in an embrace as Schumacher looms in the background. He parts them roughly, only to be ordered out by Corneille, waving an angry finger as he leaves, "Next time I see you talking to my wife, I'll take a shot at you."

Thus, when the fête begins Renoir has reactivated both sides of the intrigue; both clocks have been rewound. Already the appearance of a reconciliation of rivals, a change of partners, has occurred—but a false appearance here; that figure in the dance is not yet due.

Music remains a primary Renoir symbol of community, and the fête de

La Colinière celebrates the community of the rich and idle bourgeoisie—but this community and this celebration shelter the agents of their own decomposition, and music sets them free. We enter the fête with its show in full swing. On stage all the members of the upper echelon of the intrigue, with others, perform "En Revenant d'la revue"—a Boulangist song that outraged the Right in 1939 by seeming to ridicule the French army. André cracks a whip over his tame bear, Octave. When the curtain closes, Geneviève flings her arms around Robert, and Christine, though she has invited Geneviève's diverting of Robert, reacts to its actuality with blind resentment, clutches the hand of St. Aubin and leads him from the frame.

The rest remain for a curtain call, then Robert and André both ask, "Where is Christine?" Octave starts to search for help in removing his bearskin (*peau d'ours*). Backstage, four guests prepare for the next act, three dressed as ghosts, the fourth as Death. The piano plays all by itself; the curtains part on a darkened room, and the danse macabre begins. Ghosts spill out into the audience while Death cavorts upon the stage. Spotlights play about the room; Corneille and the chef stand by the wall, Death's reflection dancing in a mirror at their side—a premonitory image, for through a mirror Death will strike at André Jurieu.

The danse macabre on the stage precipitates its lethal counterpart, a dance of death enacted through the halls and gardens of the chateau, with the principals in almost constant motion, changing partners as they go— moving, of course, in perfect Pre-established Harmony. The new act upon the stage releases the main characters from their roles as performers in the show without making them part of its audience; hence, they are now free to continue their own performances in the game of love and chance, but still within the exhilarating atmosphere of the fête. The servants, not privileged to sit in the audience, watch from doorways; thus they, too, are not immobilized by the show and can enter in the dance. In a doorway Lisette kisses Marceau, while Schumacher stalks them through the hall. Marceau slides silently from the frame; Lisette would follow, but Schumacher grips her hand. André watches from a corner while Christine carries on with St. Aubin.

Octave futilely seeks help with his *peau d'ours* from Christine, St. Aubin, Robert, André, and St. Aubin again. His furry bulk shelters Marceau, as Schumacher, towing Lisette, searches the room. Looking for aid, Octave leads the camera from group to group, disclosing the current state of the intrigue. One may take this passage as a comment by Renoir on a director's relation to his work. He determines the beginning and the end of the creatures in his film, but once the characters step into their world they take on a life that flows out of his control; he can only keep his camera on them as they go.

As if to confirm that things are out of hand, Renoir's matching pairs grow bigger, wilder now. Two confrontations of Robert with Schumacher each lead to the exposure of Christine in the arms of another man, with André switching roles from scene to scene. Two awkward, sprawling brawls erupt, bearing no resemblance to the titanic battles that decorate American films, where men with fists of iron and jaws of steel silently exchange clean and well-timed blows. Renoir's antagonists push and kick, mutter, sputter, and call each other names, lurch and stumble through the room. At the end of the first fight, Corneille with perfect equanimity snaps his fingers to summon a salvage crew. No doubt these seriocomic scrambles are more true to the life of Renoir's characters than a John Wayne fight would be; they may also be a Renoir comment on Hollywood films or, perhaps, on the earlier roles of Roland Toutain, who was a sort of French Douglas Fairbanks.

On each occasion, Marceau triggers the action. First, he waylays Robert in the hall to ask for help in evading Schumacher. Here the spiritual kinship of this pair, marquis and poacher, shows most flagrantly: Marceau explains his plight, "Ah! Monsieur le Marquis, women are very nice; I like them a lot; I even like them too much—but that makes trouble." Robert responds, "You're telling me!" They talk of women and Marceau offers his advice, "Me, M. le Marquis, with women—if it's to have them or leave them or keep them—first I try to make them laugh. When a woman laughs, she's disarmed; you can do what you want with her. Why don't you try that?" Robert replies sadly, "My poor Marceau, that takes talent." Marceau nods sagely, "Bien sur!"

In this scene Robert's attempt to halt Schumacher fails when Robert is called away for his performance in the show. Schumacher, who has now lost both Marceau and Lisette, then inadvertently leads André to Christine and St. Aubin.

The second furor begins when Marceau stumbles as he tiptoes from the kitchen behind Schumacher, interrupting Lisette's falsely innocent prattle about the beauties of Alsace with the clatter of a platter on the floor. This leaves no time for talk; at the moment when Robert comes from the salon, Marceau, Schumacher, and Lisette burst through the kitchen door, and Marceau seizes Robert as an obstacle to thrust at Schumacher. This time the chase sweeps through the gun room, drawing Robert in its wake to his discovery of André and Christine, with its resulting hullabaloo.

Between these two hectic, violent scenes Renoir inserts a symmetrical triptych, two quiet yet troubled duets flanking Robert's solo performance of presenting his Limonaire. The first duet, to our surprise, and probably to hers, has Christine declare her love to André, though her defiant air suggests the words are really meant to reach and hurt Robert. André beams his pleasure, then, to her consternation, asks what they should do. She imagines a romantic elopement but, abruptly, André has become a defender of the rules: "I must go tell La Chesnaye." "What for?" "Because it's the thing to do." Her ardor fades as he explains, "After all, I can't run off with the wife of a gentleman who welcomes me to his house, calls me his friend, to whom I give my hand, without at least an explanation . . . After all, there are rules!"

The second duet once more completes a matched, opposing pair. Again a man and woman talk of leaving the chateau. But now he, Schumacher, swears that they will go, "It's idiotic . . . to work in someone else's place when you can be the master in your own," while she, Lisette, with no intention of departing, sweetly acquiesces while furtively making signals to Marceau, whose slipping starts the chase again.

Between these duets, and at the very center of the fête, Robert, as his world collapses, stands on the stage beside "the culmination [aboutissement] of my career as a collector of mechanical musical instruments": the Limonaire, an orchestrion, or mechanical orchestra—garish, ornate, and wonderful. To its loud, thumping, wheezing rendition of Die Fledermaus, the camera cuts from an inglorious romantic nude and pans across three prim mechanical figures to the glowing face of the marquis. Twenty-some years later Renoir would recall this as "the finest shot I've done in my life. It's fantastic—that mixture of humility and pride, of success and doubt."[11] In the film the Limonaire represents as great an accomplishment in the field

of clockwork music as André Jurieu's flight does in the world of modern *oiseaux mécaniques*. And once again, when a lover achieves his greatest success, Christine fails to appear to share his triumph. But Robert does not seem to miss her at all.

Through all this melee Octave has been absent—last seen as Geneviève began to tug at his *peau d'ours*. He returns with Geneviève while Robert and André fight. Christine, distraught, clutches at him, and he leads her from the room. Though the mood may change sharply from shot to shot, or moment to moment, the dominant tone throughout the fête has been that which Renoir calls "burlesque"—full of sound and movement and tending to make ridiculous the most serious or delicate of human affairs. The reappearance of Octave begins a modulation to the darker, quieter tone that will dominate the final sections of the film.

From the bright, chaotic room, Renoir cuts to Octave and Christine in the dark stillness of a porch. The battle continues inside, but its noise drops to a subdued background uproar as Christine's voice becomes the dominant sound, expressing her exasperation at André's response to her avowal of love—"He talked to me, talked—about propriety." As these outdoor scenes recur and then prevail, the background sounds diminish and the voice of Octave becomes more prominent as, unwittingly, he intervenes again in this affair. By reawakening memories of her father and of the simple joy of experiences shared in Vienna, Octave drains off whatever residue remains of her sudden passion for André. When, a few minutes later, he insists, "I must talk to you about André," she hardly listens and responds to his explanation about modern heroes: "Look at the moon with its halo. It will rain tomorrow."

But Octave's evocation of Christine's past has also touched his own. In a joyful imitation of her father, he strides across the terrace to the plaudits of an imagined throng, stands at the top of the steps, and raises his arms to conduct an unseen orchestra, "as in a dream." The background music of a single piano from the fête amplifies, penetrating Octave's dream and confronting it with his own reality. He drops his arms, sits on the steps as the stone semicircle of the terrace that his gesture had converted into a concert stage reasserts its dark emptiness and becomes a mirror of his life.

With Octave and Christine on the terrace—she released from her momentary love for André, he sunk in the despair of promise unfulfilled— if Preestablished Harmony prevails, then someone else must also leave the chateau. Hence two lines of action intersect again and destroy each other to create a new figure in the dance, a change of partners in which enemies become friends. Marceau scuttles like a rabbit through the room; behind him Lisette struggles with his pursuer, Schumacher, each shouting at the other. Geneviève tipsily watches this and the brawl between André and Robert. André, enraged, chokes Robert as Schumacher frees his hand from Lisette, draws his gun, and fires. The bullet breaks a lamp by Robert's side, jarring him and André from their fury long enough to notice that Christine has disappeared, and long enough for Geneviève to descend upon Robert, effectively terminating his combat with André. On their next circuit of the house, Schumacher and company now draw Corneille in their wake. New shots set off hysterics in Geneviève, moving Robert to shout, "Corneille . . . stop this comedy!" With perfect logic and straight face Corneille replies, "Which one, Monsieur le Marquis?" At the height of the confusion the Limonaire, too, goes mad, adding a dreadful cacophony to the din and completing the reduction to chaos of Robert's clockwork world.

But once the choice is indicated, Corneille moves quickly to quell Schumacher. Robert and André now cooperate to quiet Jackie and Geneviève and share a cigarette. The fête has ended; the guests retire to bed. Robert apologizes because "my staff was a little excited tonight." But some reply that they thought it part of the show, and Charlotte, the perfect guest, responds, "Those people have to have a little fun like the rest of us," a line to rejoice in were it not for its cruel and bitter suggestion that some members of this class responded thus to events in Ethopia, Austria, Spain, and Buchenwald.

With peace restored, Robert has one more task, to fire Schumacher: "I can't have my guests under the constant threat of your firearms." And as Geneviève had intervened to disrupt the conflict between André and Robert, now Lisette withdraws to effect the reconciliation of Schumacher and Marceau: "If Madame will still have me, I'll stay in her service." Hence Robert must also sack Marceau: "It's difficult for me to throw Schumacher out and leave you here with his wife. That would be immoral." The room empties, leaving Robert and André to talk about Christine. Each gives the same account of his excess: "I love her!" but Robert adds, "I love her so much I want her to go with you, since her happiness, it seems, depends on that."

But the drama now has moved outside, where Christine shows no interest in Octave's defense of André. Lisette, delighted to find Madame, gives up her cloak; Octave explains that, in our epoch, everyone lies—government, radio, cinema, newspapers—"Then why insist that we others, simple individuals, shouldn't lie too?" Marceau, departing, finds Schumacher in tears and, weak as Robert, cannot help but sympathize: "It's not with you she's married—it's with Madame!" *i.e. w/ her freedom, only!*

For the last time in this phase of his career, Renoir calls on that familiar gesture of amity: Marceau offers Schumacher a smoke. Marceau entered the film as a comic copy of Robert; now, about to leave, he foreshadows in comic patter Robert's authentication of André's death. Freed from his disguise as servant, he shares with his erstwhile foe his plans for poaching by the rules: "I've got an idea. I'm going to get a license as a game dealer. A cop stops me, 'What've you got there?' 'In my basket? Ten wild rabbits and a license—and I'm going to sell them, and au revoir, monsieur!'"

Nearby, another strand unravels. Throughout the film, Octave's role in this milieu has been that of a court jester, privileged to speak his mind and tolerated by the masters for the amusement he provides, yet not a full participant in the rituals of their world. His abstention from the hunt, his promenades along the hall, have shown this, as has, most clearly, his symbolic presence at the fête as a performing bear. Hence, with Christine at wit's end, he reacts exactly as his role demands, with an amusing performance to distract her. But at its climax this performance has shattered his

"A failure, useless, a parasite."

own protective facade and forced acknowledgment of his failed career. Now he spits in the water and asserts that's all that he can do: "It's not very agreeable to realize once more that one's a failure, useless, a parasite."

He has so well succeeded in comforting Christine that now her sympathy flows to him. He pulls her hood about her head and they walk across the footbridge, past Marceau and Schumacher in the shadows, and to the greenhouse where Christine's need for love finds a third object, more likely than the other two. Throughout the film she has been most responsive and alive when with Octave—whether love or shared nostalgia, we feel a warmth in their encounters that she has not shown for either André or St. Aubin.

In this calm moment the figures in the dance have grown absurd. Friendship triumphs, but Lisette has spurned both Schumacher and Marceau; Robert and André have both lost Christine. Octave, jester and accommodating friend, has really made it his affair.

But Pre-established Harmony cannot fail; the lines have crossed again and, in the dark, Marceau and Schumacher bristle at the perfidy of this Lisette. Note the precision of the clockwork here, and how it still remains Renoir—that is, coincidence provides occasion, but character determines the act. Marceau has first suggested: "You've got your revolver. Take a shot at him." But there are no bullets: "I shot them all at you." So they wait and watch. When Christine and Octave kiss, Schumacher groans, "Lisette!" then seethes, "I'm going to kill them both!" Marceau, ever sentimental, cries, "Ah, no! Not her!" but Schumacher, frustrated throughout the film, remains righteous and firm, "Ah, yes, yes, both of them! I'm going to get my gun." He starts to leave but Marceau, in anguish, cannot help but cry again, "I swear, not her." This second protest then makes Schumacher insist, "Come with me." Hence neither remains to notice that this "Lisette" is, in truth, Christine.

In the chateau, Robert and André, in full accord, agree there's no need to worry, for Christine is with Octave. Behind them Octave signals to Lisette, "Bring me her coat!" Lisette begins to argue, but Octave pays no heed. He goes on looking for his hat until she says, "Madame won't be happy with you," then, too late, reveals her motive, "Will you take me with you?" Too late because Octave, hat in hand, has glanced into the mirror and impaled himself upon the glance. He had left the greenhouse a young lover, joyous, filled with hope; now he perceives a middle-aged failure, a parasite, a man ready to betray his friend. Again the clockwork is perfect; delayed by Lisette's chatter, Octave turns to find André, "Where is Christine?" And, now, he can only answer, "Waiting for you." Soon André runs into the garden where Schumacher awaits. Pre-established Harmony stands transformed to Fate.

Thus, this intricate invention unwinds to its appointed close, with its eighteenth-century forms absorbed and justified by their expressive force. That ancient comic device revived by Renoir, the *quiproquo*, or mistaken identity, exactly fits the world he wants to show—where everyone lies mistaken identity is the normal state, for real identities are carefully concealed. And where life has become theatre—as in that leisure class wholly devoted to the pursuit of form and style, with mind and heart exhausted in the elegant and empty performance of symbolic gesture and expressive rite—a faith in Pre-established Harmony implicitly survives in the belief that the world will continue to sustain this mode of life. A faith displayed in 1939, perhaps, by those who purchased souvenir umbrellas and waited for the miracle that would resolve the "Danzig question." That such Pre-established Harmony would turn to Fate was not a hazardous prediction between Munich and the war.

Though it took us twenty years to see it, it now seems inevitable that this divertissement would become the *aboutissement* of Jean Renoir's prewar career. For the uniqueness of his films had always lain in their interplay of form and character, in the vitality of the characters these forms revealed, and in the critical light these creations cast upon our troubled world. In these works he had repeatedly used accidental conjunctions as occasions for the exercise of choice, converting dramatic contrivance into the most convincing characterization. Now, in the most complex work he had yet devised, he sought to express the state of mind of 1939 in a clockwork comic structure with cogs of character and chance. Marceau's "I swear, not her," Octave's glance at the mirror, are only two among many moments when coincidence and character combine both to develop character and to keep the intrigue on its track. Take the moment when Christine becomes "Lisette." Octave has revealed the anguish which underlies his jester's life, but

The figures in the dance have grown absurd. Marceau (Julien Carette) and Schumacher. Christine and Octave. André and Robert.

ends in embarrassment: "Oh, la! la! What a beautiful night, eh? Well, look there, the moon, eh?" They both deny they are cold, but, being Octave, he must *do* something to break the mood, so finds the most available gesture, covering Christine with the hood of Lisette's cloak.

These moments combine into the appearance of Pre-established Harmony but do not create its turn to Fate. That requires something more: the intervention of that mysterious and sinister character, Berthelin.

Berthelin, played by Renoir's expert adviser on firearms, Corteggiani, first appears in the background at the moment Christine decides to describe her role in André's flight. It is he who finds the hunting horn and plays those fanfares that provide a transition from the chateau to the hunt. And it is he who derails the Limonaire to produce its awful din at the climax of the chase. But between these moments, three actions give Berthelin his special place in *La Règle du jeu*. He gives Christine the telescope through which she will see Robert and Geneviève; he calls Robert away just when he would halt Schumacher's pursuit of Marceau, and, centrally, he appears as Death to lead the danse macabre. For the eighteenth-century, a celestial watchmaker had fashioned a wondrous world; in our time Death directs the infernal machine.

Renoir shot two endings for his film, then decided to use them both. The first, derived from *Les Caprices de Marianne*, has Octave lament that Lisette did not let him go to Christine; then Octave and Marceau depart from the chateau. But, as Renoir saw, this scene does not conclude his film, does not provide a closure to a work whose subject is a class. Hence, the ending we know, one final ceremony for that class, with a transformation into shadows at the close.

The interlopers have all been expelled—Octave, André, Marceau—only the proper masters and servants remain. As they come from the greenhouse, Jackie's weakness seems to lend Christine strength, confirming, perhaps, the falsity of her confession of love for André. By the time she climbs the steps, Madame's mask has slipped firmly into place; she bids her guests good night with the air of one who is, as the general has said, a model hostess. Cut to a long shot, with the camera not quite squarely facing the chateau—a view we have seen before when Octave stood before his phantom orchestra. Robert turns from the door and walks to the top of the steps; Schumacher stands midway up the steps, with back to camera and shotgun slung from his shoulder. He walks further up the stairs as Robert begins to speak: "Gentlemen, it is a question of a deplorable accident, nothing more. My gamekeeper Schumacher believed he saw a poacher, and he fired as was his right. Fate willed that André Jurieu should be the victim of this mistake." Then in medium close-up Robert completes his speech with a brief eulogy of André and an invitation to come in from the cold. Cut to a medium shot of the general and St. Aubin, who says, "New definition of the word 'accident'." The general has the last word, the same word he has repeated through the film: "No, no, no, no, no! This La Chesnaye does not lack class, and that's become rare, my dear St. Aubin, that's become rare." They leave the frame; the camera remains fixed on the wall of the terrace with its line of cypresses and balustrade; in the background shadows move, left to right, across the front of the chateau. Monsigny's music, which began softly when Octave and Marceau departed, swells as the film ends.

Of the eight major characters in *La Règle du jeu*, six are absent from the

"It is a question of a deplorable accident, nothing more."

final ceremony. Those present, Robert and Schumacher, are performers, not observers, of the rite whose function does not serve their double set of dancers but the class that assimilates them all, the masters by membership, the servants by adherence. The deed is done, the marauders repelled, Christine returned to the fold; the rite confirms the rule that rules them all, the sacrifice of reality to appearance, and thus reaffirms the rightness of their lives.

IRONIC

If "reality" is real, then appearance must accommodate it, else it will not present itself as appearance but as fantasy. The tales we tell, the games we play, if they will convince us, must take up those shreds of reality we can't avoid. The game of love and death disguises them to conform to the image that the world, and we, mistake for self. Thus Robert's speech becomes both true and false, both accurate and wholly counterfeit. Octave's performance had earlier transformed the terrace into a concert stage on which his failure could no longer be concealed. To St. Aubin, Robert now makes it a platform on which to camouflage success. But for Robert it seems, rather, the stage of a Greek theatre, with its altar placed before the double doors—a set where one may appropriately speak with the ambiguity of an oracle and where, in the final scene, dire events can be attributed to Fate or to the gods.

". . . a deplorable accident . . ." To call an event an accident is to disallow a charge of blame. Robert does not deny the shooting nor the deliberateness of Schumacher's aim. Renoir speaks of André's death as a sacrifice, "It is necessary to kill people in order to appease the gods." A sacrifice, a rite performed for the good of the community, is a deliberate act, but one which does not merit blame. But the rules of our game do not permit talk of human sacrifice; we use another word. When workmen die to appease the gods of corporate profit, we call it an industrial accident. Andre's death restores the wholeness of the bourgeois community. And is anyone to blame?

". . . my gamekeeper Schumacher . . ." Schumacher was gamekeeper when the fête began, but this wild night relieved him of the post. Yet, there he stands, in an attitude of contrition; so, surely, when Robert speaks, he speaks the truth: "my gamekeeper Schumacher." And if our lesson from the hunt is true, that servants do not engage in ceremonial killing, then Schumacher must lose his job before being free to perform the sacrifice—as it is only by being fired that he is freed—of Lisette, the chateau, his hatred of Marceau—and set loose to kill André.

". . . thought he saw a poacher . . ."—of his wife, while the poacher by his side, who had shown that such poaching might succeed, confirmed the sight.

". . . and fired, as was his right." As unemployed gamekeeper? As deceived husband? or, more ultimately, as receiver of that chilling order from Robert: "I don't want fences; I don't want rabbits. Take care of it, my friend."? This order, the hard face behind his shotgun in the hunt and the fury of Robert's attack on André, all belie the soft urbanity of his normal manner and expose the violence that it overlays. And what but the deadly accuracy of Fate, working through the self-doubt of Octave, the self-concern of Lisette, the self-denial of Robert, could set before Schumacher's sights, not a harmless trifler with his unfaithful wife, but a poacher in dead earnest, despoiling the master's domain? Robert appears to tolerate this theft, but Schumacher has not merely acted on his own. Marceau, a kind of double of Robert, an alter ego rather less well bred, has urged the deed. The substitution of André for Octave as victim has been matched by the substitution of Marceau for Robert as surrogate master for this act.

"It's a question of a deplorable accident, nothing more. My gamekeeper Schumacher thought he saw a poacher and fired, as was his right. Fate willed that André Jurieu should be the victim of this mistake."

Could truth better be concealed beneath a "truth"? This La Chesnaye does not lack class.

Characterization

Jean Renoir once remarked that none of the characters in La Règle du jeu were worth saving. Perhaps that merely makes them more like the rest of us, comme vous, comme moi. But Renoir has also described them as sympathetic, and it is abundantly clear that the love he lavishes on his creations extends to these ridiculous creatures, too. The characterizations are unusually rich and complex: not merely are there eight major characters instead of a pair of stars, but they have the density and inconsistency of life. In part, this complexity stems from the background of the film, as I have sketched it above. Some characters have behind them, or within them, not only a series of Renoir characters from earlier films but also persona from the layers of classical comedy superimposed in this film.

When asked who is the principal character in his film, Renoir replied: "There isn't any! My conception at the beginning—and at the end—was to make a film d'ensemble, a film representing a society, a group of persons, almost a whole class, and not a film of a personal affair."[12] His failure to obtain the services of a star must have helped in realizing this conception; his players, expert as they are, were accustomed to secondary roles and to sharing the screen. Roland Toutain was best known at this time, having just appeared in the greatest commercial success of 1939, Three from St. Cyr.

Robert, the marquis de La Chesnaye, may not be the principal character of La Règle du jeu, but he is the master of the chateau and organizer of its events. Yet even here, at the formal center of his life, in those actions he undertakes as marquis—ceremonial acts, of course, since in the Third Republic "marquis" is at best a ceremonial title—he seems unwilling or unable to exercise the authority that should be his. Even when he impulsively suggests the fete for André, he then asks the general when it should be, and it is Christine who decides. Repeatedly, Robert responds to questions concerning action with "Ask my secretary," "Ask Madame," "It's her affair, not mine." When Geneviève says, "It's a good thing you're a weak man," he laughs and agrees: "I get that from my father. The poor man had a very complicated life"—a pleasant sally that avoids facing the fact of his own weakness and is thus another witness of it. Robert's weakness suggests the failure of nerve of the French bourgeoisie in 1939, but the external lineage of this character may also be related to this trait.

In his role as husband in the intrigue, Robert derives, of course, from Musset's Claudio, but Renoir does not give him any of the traits of that embittered and suspicious man. A somewhat closer kin may be Beaumarchais' Count Almaviva, but the real progenitors of Robert de La Chesnaye are Renoir characters: Lestingois, Louis XVI, the Baron in *Les Bas Fonds*, Boildieu, and, naturally, Rosenthal—civilized men whose ability to act has been curtailed. Boildieu and Rosenthal are prisoners; the Baron no longer resides in the world; speech has largely replaced action in the life of Lestingois. All these characters feel attracted to a less cultivated, less inhibited man—Maréchal, Pepel, Boudu—and all become involved in some attempt to change the life of this friend. Yet the marquis' closest affinity may be to Louis XVI, another master in a decadent milieu whose weakness undermined his formal authority. Louis' warmest interactions are with his servant Picard, his deepest interests far from the affairs of state.

Robert's weakness links to other traits we usually admire: tolerance, sympathy, an apparently genuine concern for others, a pervasive warmth that makes him an attractive character. When Octave complains that "everyone has his reasons" and wants to disappear into a hole, Robert responds: "But, of course everyone has his reasons—and I, I'm for everyone exposing them freely. I'm against barriers, you know; I'm against walls." An admirable attitude, but since Robert seems to have no convictions of his own, the reasons others give usually suffice to win him over. But though Robert may seem unable to refuse anyone, his encounters with his gamekeeper belie this, for he refuses Schumacher at every turn.

Stanley Cavell seems to find these refusals manifestations of fear,[13] but I do not think this obvious in the film. Schumacher has the appearance of strength, both in his size and in the assurance he shows in his own domain. Robert's response to this apparent strength may be rather a symptom of resentment of his own weakness, creating a need to challenge and oppose the strength he finds in Schumacher in order to unmask it and demonstrate that weakness is everyone's normal state and strength a false façade. This may be the underlying motivation for that order: "I don't want fences; I don't want rabbits. Take care of it, my friend," issued in the context of Schumacher's admission that he has not been able to control the rabbits. But whatever its motivation, this order exposes the fatal inconsistency in Robert: a professed inability to hurt anyone and a desire for openness, but also a real inability to decide between exclusive alternatives where the lack of a decision implies that someone will be hurt. Though Schumacher grumbles to his companion, "He said that he doesn't want fences and he doesn't want rabbits . . . How do you try to arrange that?" the climax of the film shows that, implicitly or symbolically, he understands well enough; for the logical conclusion of that conjunction, "no fences and no rabbits!" is, of course, "Kill them!"

Asked by Dalio, "Why did you choose me, who had always played burlesque parts or traitors, to play a marquis?" Renoir replied, of course, by restating his determination to destroy clichés and noting that he, Dalio, was just the opposite of the cinema cliché of a French aristocrat. But also: "The character of the marquis was not made up out of thin air but came from my memories; I have known aristocrats who were just like you. And there is another thing; I thought you were the only actor who could express the feeling of insecurity which is the basis of the character."[14]

Dalio, whose Rosenthal in *La Grande Illusion* had seemed completely genuine, achieves this expression of insecurity by creating a Robert de La Chesnaye who is completely false—not that he is consciously insincere, but he has been so absorbed by the life of style and yet remains so doubtful of his position in it that every move and every gesture comes as a performance, slightly overdone, slightly self-conscious, slightly apologetic for its aggressiveness, and, therefore, slightly inauthentic. Thus his final gesture at film's end is as true/false as the speech he has just concluded. He speaks of André Jurieu with real tears in his eyes, then turns at the door to welcome his guests back into the chateau, but performs the gesture like an inexpert actor, too broadly, and undercuts the apparent concern he has just expressed.

A servant's conversation reveals the base of the marquis's insecurity and the precariousness of his status within the world of this elite. His chauffer calls him a "métèque"—a pejorative term applied to foreigners. When Lisette asks, "What does that mean?" the chauffeur replies, "Simply that La Chesnaye's mother had a father named Rosenthal, who arrived straight from Frankfort, that's all." The cook (Léon Larive) defends La Chesnaye as a "man of the world" even though he is a Jew. The appropriateness of Robert's insecurity was quickly enough demonstrated in July of 1939 when the anti-Semitic right-wing press violently attacked *La Règle du jeu*, taking Renoir's casting of Dalio as a French marquis and the Austrian Nora Grégor as Madame la Marquise, as an insolent and deliberate provocation. The world had changed enough to allow a Jew, Léon Blum, to become premier of France, but not enough to keep the champions of French "purity" from hating and despising him.

This scene in the kitchen, with its reference to Rosenthal, illuminates the historical transition from *La Grande Illusion* to *La Règle du jeu*. Robert de La Chesnaye is a descendant of Rosenthal who has achieved the social status of a Boildieu. He combines the elegance and devotion to style of Boildieu with the humanity of Rosenthal—he says *vous* to his wife, but *tu* to Octave —but in this unstable compound he fails to be as genuine as either of his predecessors.

Renoir and Dalio call the marquis "un amateur en tout," using the term in both its senses: lover and dilettante. In this respect, and others, that marvelous shot of the marquis before the Limonaire is, as Renoir and Dalio agree, the summation of the life of La Chesnaye.

I have stressed the role of matched opposing pairs in the structure of *La*

Humility and pride. Success and doubt.

Règle du jeu, but this does not mean that each scene is opposed to only one
other. The scene of Octave on the terrace, imitating Christine's father, most
obviously matches the film's final scene, but in quite another way it works
in opposition to the shot of the Limonaire. The two shots are sensual oppo-
sites: Octave, back to the camera, alone on the dark terrace with the thin
sound of a lone piano; Robert, facing us, on the brightly lit stage before the
gaudy machine whose raucous tune evokes applause from the audience of
guests. But they are also matched as the failure and success of a similar aim;

for the *aboutissement* of La Chesnaye's career is to conduct by merely presenting it, the mechanical orchestra of the Limonaire. Seen thusly, this ironically matched pair indeed illuminates the life of the marquis. Octave has failed to achieve an artistic career and to have that "contact with the public" that he thinks would be "staggering" ("bouleversant"). He stands on the terrace with arms raised to bring his phantom orchestra to attention, then expresses his failure and despair, wholly and unambiguously, in two simple gestures. He drops his hands; he sits down on the step. In contrast, there is nothing unambiguous in Robert's success. He stands by his monstrous possession with a glow of a sublime joy, waves his hands in a way which both deprecates his accomplishment and appreciates the response of his "public," wipes his face in a gesture of anxiety: "Humility and pride, success and doubt." For a moment as he gestures for the lighting and playing of the Limonaire, Robert becomes a participant, a conductor of this event, but then he can only step aside into the merely formal and external relation of possessor, and the doubt and insecurity immediately invade his manner; his contact with the public becomes only that of chief spectator rather than creator of that which they enjoy. Hence, though he opposes success to Octave's failure, it is the hollow success of mere possession rather than achievement.

For the marquis's life is consumed by his possessions—the chateau is filled with tapestries, instruments, trophies of the hunt—and his relation to the persons in his life remains almost as formal as that to his *oiseaux mécaniques*. Wife and mistress are numbered among his possessions, to be enjoyed or displayed and then set aside—hence his confession to Marceau that he sometimes wishes he were an Arab; for the harem ideally fits the conception of women as possessions. His relations to Christine are extremely formal. They sleep in separate rooms; in the morning he goes to her door, asks, "Vous permettez?" and kisses her hand. Hence the need for Berthelin's telescope if she is to know the details of his intimate life. Only Octave and Marceau seem to break his barrier of formality; perhaps that is why Robert calls Octave "un dangereux poète."

If the marquis's character is ambiguous, Christine's is enigmatic; though she whirls at the center of the film's intrigue, we seldom know what she really thinks or feels. From the beginning, Nora Grégor's involvement in this work has been controversial; conflicting stories describe her original appeal to Renoir. André Zwoboda said, "She had that which Renoir loved above all; an incontestable class, a style, the gestures and bearing of a great distinction."[15] Some accounts have Renoir falling in love with his Princess Stahremberg, then his ardor cooling in his struggle to extract a competent performance for her. Renoir did, in fact, fall in love during the making of *La Règle du jeu*, but the object of this affection was not Nora Grégor but his script girl, Dido Freire, who would later become Mme. Jean Renoir.

Renoir himself once said of Nora Grégor: "The reason I insisted on her for this role was her accent. I had the impression that her accent would create a little barrier, a curtain, between her and her surroundings, surroundings which are purely French."[16] Years later he would write, "I was content to profit from the appearance of Nora Grégor, her look of 'birdlike' sincerity, to build the character of Christine."[17]

To me this last remark seems most apropos. For with her sometimes stiff and foreign gestures, this "look" places Christine among the marquis' prize possessions, his *oiseaux mécaniques*, and thus roots her dissatisfaction with her life in his tendency to regard all of his surroundings with the eye of a *collectioneur*. For, despite an occasional profession of happiness, her dissatisfaction seems apparent even before the relevation in the marsh. She can "think of nothing else" but children and caring for them, and her formalized marriage does not seem about to result in that. She confides in Lisette, but displays real warmth and spontaneity only with Octave. The fervor of her greeting when he first arrives, the note of desperation in her reaction when he threatens to leave, suggest a life otherwise devoid of the camaraderie these moments with Octave provide. *The* rule of the bourgeois game, which Christine knows very well, may be the lie, the insistence on appearance at the expense of reality, but there are other rules as well. Well bred as Christine may be, she comes from that Bohemian Viennese milieu where camaraderie, *amitié*, is possible. When Lisette says of friendship with a man, "You may as well talk of the moon at midday," she utters no universal truth but another rule of that world where the only occupation is the game of love—a rule that Christine doesn't understand, though André does.

Though he includes no shot to make this clear, Renoir's conception of Christine was of a woman "not too young, rather innocent, rather romantic," who thinks of love as pure and eternal—a woman "belatedly romantic" in that both her age and the epoch in which she lives make romanticism inappropriate, a foreigner in a milieu where love is "the exchange of two fantasies and the contact of two skins." Nora Grégor's performance does not clearly project this romantic image, but does not deny it either. She often seems cold and stiff, hardly a siren who would have all the available men at her feet, but she does have that air of distinction Zwoboda noted, and a combination of physical awkwardness and social grace which makes her different and therefore, perhaps, a fertile ground for the fantasies that pass for love.

Christine's remark to Robert early in the film, "A lie is a very heavy garment to carry around," displays her innocence; for everyone knows of her friendship with André. But her innocent sincerity ends abruptly when, as Renoir says, "her romantic vision of the world is brusquely replaced by a reality much more brutal . . . Then, in the unreal atmosphere of the fête, she feels a need, purely physical, for love, and turns to the first man she sees."[18]

Christine: a woman not too young, rather innocent, rather romantic.

In terms of Chamfort's definition, after the shock and hurt of her discovery of Robert's infidelity, she needs and seeks the contact with another skin and tries to create a fantasy to exchange for it. Hence her itinerary, from St. Aubin to André to Octave, and our doubt as to which, if any, she really loves.

André shares Christine's romanticism, but not her mystery—if anything, he seems too simple and romantic in all this complication. Falling in love, he disappears into the blue; rejected, like Coelio he swears he'll die. His way of love resembles that described by a Marivaux heroine: "He falls in love with me. Bang! he carries me off and never asks how I feel about it." André's declarations of love, to Octave and Robert, presume that these assertions— "Moi, je l'aime!" and "Mais moi, j'ai une excuse; j'aime Christine"—justify every action and settle every question about what should be done. And Renoir shoots these scenes so as to give André a look of idiotic, or angelic, certitude. Though his love may be a fantasy, he thinks his flight has been its proof and makes it real. For this lovelorn flyer drops into the bourgeois milieu from above, both spatially and spiritually, with a sort of angelic innocence that makes him the appropriate sacrificial lamb.

Though not unmindful of the rules, passion distracts him from them. His mad and ultimately fatal outburst of sincerity comes quite by chance.

"Moi, je l'aime."

His first response when landing at Le Bourget, "It's not me, you know—it's the machine," falls quite within your proper modest-heroic vein; then the accidental conjunction of Octave's arrival and a microphone, thrust at him, provokes his intemperate attack on Christine. At La Colinière he suffers Robert's attention to Christine with decent, civilized restraint; only the suggestion that she might prefer, to him, that "imbécile de St. Aubin" drives him to his most ungentlemanly intervention. His sense of propriety returns full force when Christine, in her distraction, avows her love. Several suggestions seem implicit here: For the true knight of courtly love, adoration suffices, worship at a distance is his forte—if the lady appears, he knows not what to do or, as with Coelio, knows but cannot do. Or, the happiness he feels so overwhelms him he wishes to prolong it by delaying the next phase of the affair—if love *is* eternal, why hurry? Or, most probably, he simply thinks himself a member of this class and wants to heed its rules, to act as a proper bourgeois gentleman should.

For though André must be ejected from the class for its preservation, his failure to belong is wholly spiritual and not material, hence hardly noticed by those inside. He does not arrive as an intruder at La Colinière; the guests already know him and think him "one of us." Unlike Octave, he joins in the hunt. Mme. La Bruyere, assured of his wealth, sees a fine catch for Jackie; Robert is thankful that Christine has "fallen for someone of our class."

But his romanticism makes André not of this milieu, and makes him a danger to it. The romantic always dreams of *doing* something, not of accumulating possessions. André's commitment to purposive action disturbs the balance of the clockwork order dear to this world. Yet Renoir takes care

not to allow this romantic hero to appear a hero. His sincerity may be a virtue missing in this crowd, but Christine describes him as "too sincere" and,
therefore, boring. He may suffer for his love, but Renoir also shows him to
be petulant, self-centered, rude, even—in a scene still missing from the reconstructed print—as big a snob as the marquis whom he contemns.

In short, this lover/hero appears as absurd, and as real, as those around
him, and equally an object of Renoir's cool and critical lens, which does not
encourage us to identify with André or sympathize with his plight. Above
all, Renoir will not allow us to grieve at André's death. Quite deliberately
he contrasts this death to that shattering image of a dying rabbit; André dies
a mere figure seen obscurely tumbling in the distant dark.

Renoir's decision to play Octave himself has sent critics searching the role
for autobiographical details or profound hints about the relation of the
director to his work. Thus Stanley Cavell writes of "self-pity" and takes
Octave/Renoir's absence as a "critical feature" of the final scene of *La Règle
du jeu*,[19] even though it seems, dramatically, very clear that Octave must be
absent no matter who had played the role. Renoir's life did resemble that he
created for Octave, insofar as he had lingered on the bohemian fringe of the
French upper-class milieu, but, if anything, he seems to use Octave to display a sort of life he had refused to live, that of a hanger-on of the *haute
bourgeoisie*.

The name, Octave, provides a clue; though Renoir began with four characters from *Les Caprices de Marianne*, only one, Octave, retains the name
provided by Musset, and only one, Octave, retains essentially the characteristics found in Musset's play. The clown's facade masking a melancholy
soul, the self-doubt and self-pity, the sense of failure and the final despair,
all already exist in *Les Caprices de Marianne*. No doubt Renoir felt a certain
kinship with this Octave; he had had his moments of failure and periods of
doubt, and would again, but when he made *La Règle du jeu* his mastery was
unquestioned; *La Grande Illusion* had won international acclaim; *La Bête
humaine* was a great success and he had achieved in several ways that
"contact avec le public" that Octave speaks of so regretfully. Hence what
transpired was not that Renoir used the role of Octave to display his own
wounds to the world, but rather that his own experiences enabled him to
enter sympathetically into this character's skin.

Figaro's joy in meddling in other's affairs, a touch of Batala, an echo of
those other would-be artists, Legrand and M. Lange, help build Musset's
character into Renoir's Octave. And Renoir adds that inimitable style that
Jean Jay deplored, but which now seems so right for the role—a manner of
acting that sets Octave apart, clumsy, effusive, idiosyncratic. Where Dalio's
overstated gestures tend to create a character whose façade is false, Renoir's
define the authenticity of Octave.

Christine, Robert, André, all fit somewhat uneasily into the bourgeois mold; each has a flaw. But Octave does not fit at all. Like André he does not share the acquisitive ideal of accomplishment—he dreams of doing things. Failing to conform in manner, dress or speech, he doesn't hunt and seems not to join in any of the games. And, amid the inattentive, the self-centered and self-satisfied, he exhibits more concern and self-awareness, a more critical perception of the world. He resists the formalized view; for him André is not the contemporary hero, but a troubled friend: "Ah. How happy I am— oh, not about your flight; I don't give a damn about that—but just to see you there." Christine is not for him Madame la Marquise but a girl from Salzburg among strangers. For this oddness, the others treat Octave as if he doesn't really belong—or, perhaps, the failure to belong has made him odd. His pleas for help with his bearskin reveal his status; no one responds. Berthelin, putting on his death's head, says: "I have something else to do. Let's talk about serious things." St. Aubin tells him, "I don't have time." Throughout the film, except for André and Christine, no one takes Octave seriously, including Marceau and Schumacher, who would not be quite as ready to shoot any other guest, or to believe any other guest a seducer of Lisette.

All this may be Renoir's view of the plight of artists in the bourgeois world—trapped in the bearskin of "entertainment" while the public hasn't time to release or discover what's inside. But in the film it's love that suffers, not art.

Octave early on admits he loves Christine "in my fashion," a fashion not in vogue in Christine's world, for it rests on neither fantasy nor skin but partakes more of concern and care than infatuation: "I can look after her, and I will look after her. And she needs it." Christine's confession of love for Octave comes at the end of her string, when anything she says of love must be suspect. But her route to this confession, and its manner, may give us pause.

It starts with the third solo performance of the film, the third time a man, alone, has acted out the realization of his desire. The first two were actual and found their proper outcome in the plaudits of a crowd—but without Christine. This one begins as jest and ends in self-awareness; it plays to a single spectator, Christine. Its initial consequence is to move Christine, for the first time in this wild night, to think of someone but herself, and thus be freed of thinking of herself as loving André. Then, when Lisette appears, Christine can talk about herself and state her self-perception, "for three years my life has been based on a lie." Octave then describes the world she lives in, a world where everyone lies—which leaves her, we might say, as une femme comme une autre. They walk. Octave reveals his self-perception: "If I didn't have some friends who support me, well, I'd starve to death. And still, you know, when I was young, I too thought I'd have my word to say. The contact with the public, you see—that's the stuff I'd like to

Begins as jest and ends in self-awareness.

know. That, that must be . . . that must be staggering, eh? When I think that I've been passed by . . . well, that does something to me. Then I try to . . . to fool myself into imagining it's happened. Only for that, I've got to drink a bit, eh?" They walk again; then, in the greenhouse, in her most lucid moment of the film, which resembles not at all her impulsive pairings with André and St. Aubin, Christine discovers an object for her care and finds she loves Octave—and in words that closely echo his: "You only need someone to look after you. I'm going to look after you."

Thus, this love may be genuine, since not in vogue; hence Lisette's objections make no impression on Octave: "For living together I think you should leave the young with the young and the old with the old . . . And then, you haven't any money. A woman like Madame, she needs a lot of things and if you haven't any money, how will you do it?" What have those words to do with concern or care? But the mirror is more deadly. Lisette just lives the bourgeois life, at one remove; the mirror reflects it, blindingly— that is, blinding Octave to the genuiness of Christine's love by showing him himself through bourgeois eyes, which cannot believe a *femme du monde* could prefer his concern to a hero's passion.

That sounds obscure, and this critical moment demands clear under-standing. Octave's concern and his vulnerability, Christine's disillusion and her capacity for care, come together and give promise that each may change the other's life. In the greenhouse, this seems like love. In the chateau, Oc-tave once more finds himself surrounded by the trappings of the bourgeois world. The life he wants to change reclaims him; even his hat, lost and bat-tered among more elegant apparel, becomes a symbol of his lowly status in that milieu. His search for it does allow him to avoid looking at Lisette and being recaptured, by her look, back into his jester's role. Having found it, he still avoids her eye, but in that effort inadvertently catches his own and can see only a disheveled misfit and not the needful, caring soul that Chris-tine saw.

Thus, despite Renoir's reading of Marivaux, *La Règle du jeu* concludes not by revealing any truth of the heart but by denying the truth it has revealed. Octave cannot face Christine, for in refusing to betray André he has been false to her, implicitly denying the love he's just avowed, as well as his belief in her avowal. Christine, abandoned, returns to the chateau, Madame la Marquise, more cool and elegant than ever, we presume, and ready now, perhaps, to take lessons in fashionable infidelity from Lisette, or even Geneviève.

These two, Lisette and Geneviève, each in her sphere, represent complete assimilation to the bourgeois life and hence seem the most shallow of the major characters in the film. In this society, love gets its definition from them: Geneviève repeats Chamfort's mot; Lisette denies the possibility of friendship with a man. Thus every encounter of a man and a woman becomes a part of the game, and Lisette and Geneviève treat each encounter as such. Geneviève, clever, poised, cynical, chic, with her expensive apartment overlooking the place du Trocadero, embellished with exotic objects d'art, seems the embodiment of the idle rich, even objecting to Robert's request to see her at 10:00 A.M. "Oh, no, no, no, not ten o'clock. That's better, eleven; let's be reasonable." Her belief in the superiority of the life of elegant hypocrisy shows in her remark about Christine's foreignness: "A Parisienne would understand. Not her!"

Geneviève plays the game of love to its limit, even proposing to tell all to Christine just to hurt Robert: "It annoys me to suffer alone. Yes, I have the impression that if we all suffer together it would be less boring." Yet this life seems so natural to Geneviève that her actions wear the look of innocence beside Lisette's conscious duplicity. For Lisette plays a double-edged game, using her position as Madame's personal maid to keep Schumacher at a distance while leaving herself free for flirtation with whatever man may catch her eye. She is insincere even with Christine when she talks about children. Yet the openness of her infidelity seems to reflect position as much as character. A defender of Madame's right to have lovers, as Madame's maid Lisette feels entitled to the same privilege, an attitude that Christine does not discourage. An odd misperception may be suggested here, with Lisette seeing her own conduct as an emulation of the grande monde she serves, while Christine thinks it the sort of thing one finds among the servants, much as Robert later confesses to André that he had always though the sort of battle they had just engaged in occurred only among working-class foreigners—"an Italian ditch-digger and a Polish laborer."

Wholly self-centered, Lisette responds to André's death as if it were completely external to her actions. While everyone else is devastated, she becomes entirely professional, thus rejecting any personal implication of Octave's despairing cry, "Lisette, why didn't you let me go down there?" Renoir once remarked: "Sometimes I wonder what might become of my characters. I can see Lisette as the proprietor of a very smart shop in Paris."

Poor Schumacher, patrolling the woods at La Colinière, has no chance to absorb Parisian manners, hence his wife shows only scorn for his practical, old-fashioned ways. Some critics have called Schumacher "the terrible Alsatian," yet he , like everyone, has his reason, "I love her," and both his love and his provocation may be more genuine than any other in the film. Others talk of suffering for their love, but Schumacher's face, wet with tears, displays his pain. In describing André as "too sincere," Christine surely also expresses Lisette's view of Schumacher, whose earnestness embarrasses everyone engaged in the high frivolity of life at the top.

Musset's Claudio, when told by his valet that a death sentence is a superb thing to read aloud, replies wistfully, "It's not the judge who reads it, it's the clerk." Schumacher, Renoir's Claudio, has it both ways; he is, in effect, Claudio reduced to the status of a clerk, who thus can pronounce his death sentences for himself. And he does so with fervor and frequency, avowing openly that streak of violence that the others conceal. But being by profession a guardian of convention against nature, Schumacher's violence defends the rules. If he seems barbaric in importing the rule of the woods into the chateau, he may be no more confused than the marquis, who exports the capriciousness of Paris to the woods when he hires Marceau, or Lisette, who presumes that her position with Madame makes her as independent of Schumacher at La Colinière as it did in Paris. An inability to perceive the dissonance of one's own actions is pervasive in *La Règle du jeu* and in the world it portrays—if we acknowledge the volcano, we might stop dancing. Yet Schumacher's failure may be more excusable and more poignant than the others', for his attitude is purely practical and protective, and the institutions he protects, property and marriage, were once, at least, the bulwarks of society. If the collapse of one of these institutions drives him mad, this may mitigate his violation of the other.

Some critics interpret the final scene of *La Règle du jeu* as a triumph for Schumacher: "In taking the gamekeeper back into his service and conspiring to cover the accident, the marquis places himself at the mercy of the gamekeeper . . . he has submitted himself to the gun's dominion."[20] But precisely the opposite interpretation seems equally plausible. Schumacher's gun has run wild through the chateau, in defence of his own honor, but in "accidentally" shooting the wrong poacher, he has placed himself at the mercy of the marquis—his gun is finally, firmly, under the marquis's domain. That is, he is no longer a defender of traditional values, but subject to the capriciousness and indecision that marks the life of the haute bourgeoisie. Was this, in 1939, a reflection on the domination of the bourgeois mentality among the French and British, which kept them from going to the aid of the Czechs?

Gaston Modot's performance as Schumacher is a high point in one of the most memorable careers in French cinema. Originally an artist, painting with Picasso and Modigliani on the butte of Montmartre, Modot became in 1909 one of Jean Durand's troupe of "Pouics," who inspired Mack Sennett to make comedies; he also played in Joe Hamman's "Arizona Bill" French westerns, shot in the Camargue. Thereafter, Modot performed in films of every sort, from the most commercial to the most avant-garde, including the central role in Bunuel's infamous *L'Age d'or*. From *La Vie est à nous* in 1936, Modot became the most faithful of Renoir's secondary players, appearing in half a dozen more Renoir films and making his last appearance before the cameras in *Le Testament du Dr. Cordelier* in 1959. As Schumacher he is flawless, an upright servant with pride in his profession, a man of principle, baffled and outraged by a world from which principles have disappeared—comic, tragic, ludicrous, pitiful—the major symbol in *La Règle du jeu* of the impact of the haut bourgeois style on traditional mores.

The dramatic lineage of Marceau, the poacher, includes both Harlequin and Figaro. Hence those who look for inside jokes may find one in Marceau's plea that he is really a chairmender fallen on hard times. For Moliere's entry into the royal court came through his father's profession of upholsterer, while Beaumarchais' duties in the court of Louis XV included that of prosecutor of rabbit poachers on the king's preserves. In addition to these ancient ancestors, Marceau's more proximate forebears include Boudu and Rodolphe of *Une Partie de campagne*. He is, in *La Règle du jeu*, the incarnation of that nature god so often found in Renoir films. In a world in which "nothing is natural," it is only appropriate that the nature god should appear as a little poacher in disguise and be pursued with deadly intent by a gamekeeper through that effete version of the Bacchanal, the fête de La Colinière. But his influence remains the same; when he appears, erotic impulses stir in human hearts. Note, for example, that Christine and Octave acknowledge their love only after Marceau has begun to watch. That these impulses are destructive rather than creative becomes one more Renoir comment on the corruption of this world.

André drops into the bourgeois world from above; Marceau sneaks in from below. In a world in which everyone lies, he seems completely at home, gaining entry by claiming that he'd be safer in the chateau, away from Schumacher; whereas it is only by disguising himself as a servant that he can continue to be a poacher, with only a change in the game. Against the bourgeois enslavement to convention and ceremony, Marceau opposes a purely practical outlook; he makes use of all those elements that have become merely expressive for the upper-class world. He uses the rabbits for food, not ceremonial slaughter (even the servants sneer at eating rabbit). He uses Robert's mechanical doll as an aid in his pursuit of Lisette. Perhaps Robert's instant attraction to the poacher is sound, recognizing as he does in Marceau exactly what he most needs, the ability to turn merely ceremonial elements of his life into productive ones. Yet he cannot incorporate Marceau into his world without inviting destruction, for the ceremonial weapons can also have practical uses, as the death of André shows.

Like Gaston Modot, Julien Carette was one of those fine character actors, the pride of French cinema of the 1930s, who became a regular in Renoir films. Of his performance as Marceau, I can only repeat, "Carette, once more, is perfect."

For me, Octave's farewell to Marceau has a poignance beyond that of the film. *La Règle du jeu* is the last Renoir film of this period and the last film Renoir would make in France for fifteen years. And thirty years later Renoir would say: "What I most regret about leaving France in 1940 is that I was never able to make a film with Carette in the lead. I think we could have done something interesting."

Style and Form

Gerald Mast writes, "the film is built in five acts—like any traditional French play."[21] The roots of *La Règle du jeu* in classical comedy are unmistakable; yet I think Mast's view also reflects the recent insistence that theatre plays as large a role as life or nature in Renoir's films. And indeed, from the opening shot of *Nana* elements of theatre, fragments of spectacle, have appeared in Renoir's work, often in conjunction with characters, like Nana or Emma Bovary, who dramatize their lives. But through the 1930s these aspects of theatre are always absorbed into the flow of images and subordinated to the life that Renoir creates—the lives may be theatrical, but the films are not. And *La Règle du jeu* is an untheatrical, or antitheatrical, as any film of its period. Hence, I doubt that any ordinary viewer would describe it as a five-act comedy, for that suggests a mode of perception and a clarity of articulation we do not experience in the film.

If anything, our experience on first viewing may be of a complete lack of

The mirror is more deadly.

clear articulation through the last forty-five minutes of the film, when everything seems jumbled together chaotically, with abrupt changes of pace and mood and only a gradual transition from interior to exterior and to the darker, quieter tone of the final moments. There is, of course, a clear spatial disjunction between the first quarter of the film and the remainder, and almost every writer has noted how Renoir removes his characters from the relatively open Paris milieu to the closed world of the chateau, where the orderly and idle life of the eighteenth-century aristocracy may be simulated. However, our confinement in the chateau does not begin with the departure from Paris, but, more appropriately, only when Marceau, the nature god of *La Règle du jeu*, asks to be confined. The next shot takes us with Geneviève to the door of the chateau, where games and gossip have already begun. Then, with the nature god in service, the woods become part of the closed, rule-governed world in the formalized slaughter of the hunt, while Marceau's presence in the chateau soon reduces its order to chaos. Freedom and disorder return to the outdoors only when Robert reluctantly dismisses Marceau.

If *La Règle du jeu* were a play, perhaps its acts would end at the points Mast chooses. But, as a film, its effective overall structure seems rather different. My experience suggests a three-part structure, imposed by both the power and form of the hunt, which separates itself from the surrounding scenes, while both all that precedes and all that follows the hunt are felt as continuous wholes.

The separateness of the hunt should be obvious. It begins and ends with the full stop of a fade out-fade in, and Renoir sets it off with a matched pair that brackets a hiatus in the intrigue. The preceding pages have made it abundantly clear, I hope, that the formal pattern which Renoir had made central in *La Bête humaine*, the matched opposing pairs, has a similar predominance in *Le Règle du jeu*, beginning with the initial doubling of Musset's characters to produce two matched sets of husband, wife, lover, and friend. I suggest that this pattern of matched pairs also forms the overall structure of this film, consisting of two opposing members of such a pair, flanking the hurt, a central section which both divides and illuminates this pair.

But if these two large segments, each running about fifty minutes, are to be seen as a pair, then each must have an internal unity and contrast with or oppose the other. Most apparent in this regard, a different quality pervades each segment: a feeling of order and unity precedes the hunt; disorder, disunity, and conflict follow it: A repeated pattern underlies this opposition in tone and provides the basis for my claim about the overall structure of the film. Each scene before the hunt begins with some sort of confusion, conflict, or separation and moves toward unity; after the hunt, almost every scene begins in unity and moves to disorder and conflict. These movements may be either formal or dramatic; I find them surprisingly consistent.

Marceau. The nature god appears as a poacher in disguise.

Thus, before the hunt: (1) The scene at Le Bourget begins with the confused and random movement of the crowd and ends with three friends, Octave, André, and the mechanic, walking together out of the frame. Intercut with this is (2) the scene at La Chesnaye's, which begins with Christine and Robert in separate rooms, each feeling dishonest toward the other; when it ends they have come together, expressed mutual confidence, and Robert has decided to be true to Christine. (3) At Geneviève's the first scene begins with Geneviève and the card players at opposite sides of the room and ends with them all together; while (4) the second scene begins with Rob-

ert and Geneviève both spatially and emotionally apart, then brings them together. (5) The crash of André's car leads Octave to announce that André can go his way without him, but by the scene's end Octave has made André's unhappiness "mon affaire." (6) Octave's entry into the hôtel de La Chèsnaye leads to a series of minor discords, Octave with Lisette, Octave with Robert, Robert with Lisette, Octave with Christine; but then everyone agrees to invite André to La Colinière, and Octave gaily chases Lisette around the room.

At La Colinière the generally harmonious arrival has an undertone of conflict between Schumacher and both Robert and Lisette. Then the scene in the fields (7) begins with Robert's denial of Schumacher's request, moves to the clash of Schumacher and Marceau, then ends with the mutual admiration of Robert and Marceau. (8) In the chateau, Geneviève arrives in a downpour and the general confusion finds focus only in the embarrassing arrival of André, but Christine's little speech brings everyone together and prompts Robert to propose the fête. (9) In the kitchen the servants disagree about the propriety of Christine's treatment of André and about Robert's status as a *métèque*, but this scene ends with the instant mutual attraction of Marceau and Lisette. (10) The final scene before the hunt opens with general confusion in the hall, then, as the hall empties, becomes a series of warm and friendly two-person exchanges.

After the hunt three scenes precede the fête de La Colinière. (1) In the first, Christine visits Geneviève to discover the truth about Robert, and her deception creates a false unity with Geneviève; the scene ends in the hall with general complaint and confusion about the disappearance of the shoes. (2) A scene just 22 seconds long follows, beginning with Schumacher hopefully taking the tag from the cape he has given Lisette and ending with his look of pain and dismay at her response. (3) Then, in the kitchen, Lisette and Marceau come happily together only to be angrily parted by Schumacher, who is then scolded by Corneille and threatens to shoot Marceau.

When the fête begins, scenes grow progressively more complex, but the recurrent movement from unity to conflict or disorder continues. (4) The

fête opens with the unity of a performance on stage, the Boulangist song with its appreciative audience. This scene ends with Christine gone, André and Robert searching for her, and Octave looking unsuccessfully for help with his bearskin. (5) Again, a performance on stage starts a scene, the danse macabre, which ends with André still searching, Robert and Geneviève arguing, and Octave on the floor as Geneviève tugs at his bearskin. (6) Marceau stops Robert in the hall, they act and talk amicably, but this scene continues on to the fight of André and St. Aubin and ends with Christine and André arguing. Here the flow of action pauses as (7) Robert presents his Limonaire. This solo scene does not repeat the unity-to-discord movement, but does contain, as Renoir has said, a mixture of humility and pride, success and doubt. (8) The next scene begins with an embrace, Marceau and Lisette in the kitchen. Schumacher arrives; the chase erupts again, leading to Robert's fight with André and the total chaos at the end of the scene when Corneille finally captures Schumacher. Into this scene Renoir cuts (9) four shots of Octave and Christine on the terrace, with Octave comforting Christine, then finally sitting on the step, telling her to leave him alone.

To this point the scenes of the fête inside the chateau have grown progressively longer—running approximately 2½, 4, 5½, and 7 minutes, with the repeated pattern of order-to-disorder reaching its crescendo when all of the guests are drawn into the whirl and the Limonaire goes wild before Schumacher is subdued. There then follows one large movement, nearly eighteen minutes, in which three separate scenes of unity—Robert with André, Marceau with Schumacher, and Octave with Christine—all run together to end in the same ultimate expression of disorder: the shooting of André. The final five minutes of La Règle du jeu then function as an epilogue whose movement reverses that which has prevailed after the hunt and repeats that of the first half of this overarching pair; for the movement here runs from the disorder following Schumacher's shot to the unity and formalized order of the final moments. The film then ends with the completion of the ultimate pair: the orderly movement of shadows across the dark façade of the

chateau matching the random movement of the crowd in darkness at Le Bourget. With this epilogue, the structure of matched opposing pairs achieves its closure, allowing Renoir to return his bourgeois characters to the relationships that held when the film began, but without recourse to the cyclical form he had used in *Boudu* and *Toni*. But, as in *Boudu*, the self-knowledge these survivors should have gained leaves the future open and in doubt.

I have taken space to list every scene in order to show how pervasive these patterns are. My division of scenes follows my perception of continuity; to some degree I take the occurrence of the order-to-disorder pattern as a clue in itself to the identification of a scene.

If these two large segments do form a pair, they are both separated and joined by the central section, the hunt, which itself repeats in minor key the tripartite form of the whole. The shooting itself, the powerful center of this scene and the film, is preceded by small repetitions of the discord-to-unity pattern and followed by small instances of the movement from unity to discord. The first exchange between La Bruyère and St. Aubin goes from embarrassment to amity. The scene between Octave and André begins with André denouncing Robert and Christine and ends, in the lost fragment, with the two joined in laughter over Octave's penchant for maids. A warm scene between Robert and Christine follows the shooting. They exit with Robert's arm around Christine as Geneviève enters, sees them, and raises her head in a gesture of vexation; the next shot sees St. Aubin and La Bruyère squabbling over a pheasant. A scene with André and Jackie has him kiss her twice but ends with Jackie's remark: "Oh, don't try to laugh. You are sorrowful and so am I." But the most significant movement of this latter part of the hunt scene brings together the essentially discordant scene of Robert and Geneviève with the essentially happy scene of Christine, Octave, and the others in Christine's disconcerting discovery of Robert and Geneviève in their farewell embrace.

Though the hunt occupies almost the exact center of the film, and both this scene and the film have a similar tripartite form, neither is symmetrical. The epilogue, with its reversal of the order-to-disorder pattern, upsets the symmetry of the whole; the hunt achieves its balance by weighing the intensity of the shooting against the much greater length of the following episode. In fact, symmetry, a form Renoir had used extensively before, even making it the predominant form in *Les Bas Fonds*, is notably absent in *La Règle du jeu*. Two or three scenes are roughly symmetrical—for example, that one which begins with André and Robert, ends with Octave and Robert, and has as it center Octave's search for his hat while Lisette tries to dissuade him from running off with Christine—but no scene has the carefully crafted symmetry often seen in earlier Renoir films. In *La Règle du jeu* Renoir achieves his balance by more complex forms.

The central, shooting segment of the hunt remains, with the opening sequence of *La Bête humaine*, Renoir's primary exploitation of the power of editing. In a film whose shots often run for a minute or more, here fifty-one shots take just three minutes, forty seconds, in a mounting rhythm of cutting and movement which culminates in that awesome barrage of gunfire as, in twenty-two shots—fifty-three seconds—twelve animals die.

The impact of this barrage is carefully prepared. The sequence begins in quiet beauty with two long shots of the fields and trees, the beaters' white smocks, Schumacher in his dark velour, the hunters waiting in a line—two shots dominated by the vast and cloudy sky. Then that fine and powerful shot of the beaters beginning to move; with Schumacher in the foreground, they stretch in a line away from the camera, which, to the tap, tap of sticks on trees, travels slowly left to right with them through the woods. Then, three short, still, close shots of immobile animals in the field; two longer shots, a rabbit and a pheasant, with some slight movement right to left. A rabbit runs and two shots cut together into a single ten-second rush across the field, left to right. The beauty of the woods dominates a shot of beaters coming toward the camera, then five brief shots of hunters, guns at hand— Robert, La Bruyère, the general, Geneviève, St. Aubin. In a two-shot, Christine breaks the growing tension by asking Jackie, "You like to hunt?"

After five shots of grim readiness, her shrug of indifference punctuates the scene. Perhaps the rhythm of this segment can be conveyed by merely listing the length, in seconds, of the successive shots: 6, 6, 15, 2, 2, 2, 4, 4, 5, 5, 18, 3½, 4, 4½, 4, 3, 8.

A breath before the storm, Christine's shrug precedes the longest shot of the sequence: twenty-six seconds of slow, steady, movement by camera and beaters, left to right, as Schumacher shouts commands and rabbits scurry away. Two rabbits run and the screen explodes in a blur of motion; five shots cut together into a single rapid flow; one brief shot with a motionless camera and the blur of a running rabbit—two-thirds of a second—then, a rabbit runs beneath the camera, which follows him for a blurred second; a gun fires; he tumbles end over end; the shot concludes with both rabbit and camera still as death. Cut to Robert, the softest and gentlest character in the film, sighting down his gun barrel as the barrage begins.

The shot form of a rapid movement stopping, to end in twelve or twenty completely motionless frames, expressing the finality of an animal death, repeats several times in this fifty seconds. The uniform left-to-right movement gives way to varied—left, right, left, down (falling with a wounded bird)—camera movements. In twenty-two shots the longest lasts four and a half seconds as a lucky bird escapes.

A bird falls; the camera withdraws to a long shot of the field—another puntuating shot, ten seconds, with the camera panning from beaters to hunters as a bird flies across the field. Then the final, agonizing death: a blur of rabbit for one second, a shot, in another second both rabbit and camera stop; for five seconds, more than twice the length of the average shot in the barrage, we watch in close-up as the rabbit stretches, his legs stiffen, his tail quivers, quivers, stops. A horn sounds. Cut to a completely still shot of the empty field, strewn with dead game; after sixty frames the beaters enter to gather the kill. Two quiet shots match those that began the scene. The shooting has ended.

Through the barrage the animals, quick and dead, have riveted our attention. Life and death at close range. Through the scene, Renoir has contrasted the formalized ritual of the hunt with the frightened, spontaneous life of the animals, destroyed by the numbers in this game. Still, the beauty and the precise rhythm of the images that convey this spontaneity may suggest that order need not kill, that the ultimate matching pair, nature and convention, need not be opposed but may work together to further life. But not in *La Règle du jeu*, a world where everyone lies. Only shadows return to the chateau.

Within the tripartite structure, matching pairs abound. I add two comments to what has gone before: First, Stanley Cavell has noted that Christine's discovery through Berthelin's telescope is itself a kind of shooting accident.[22] It is, in fact, the matching counterpart to the shooting of André

but its opposite in that Christine's "shot" is an accident which leads to a misconception and destroys the social life of the shooter, whereas Schumacher shoots quite deliberately as a result of a misconception and destroys the physical life of his target. Second, Robert's final scene before the chateau matches Octave's sad pantomime, but Robert's speech has two other counterparts, one in form, one in meaning. In form, as a public statement it matches André's public statement over the radio—a deliberate unifying lie to conclude the process begun by that spontaneous, disruptive truth. In meaning, its match is not a public statement, but Octave's talk with Christine after André's auto crash. There Octave defines the crash as a suicide attempt, that is, *not* an accident, for the purpose of declaring Christine responsible. Robert defines André's death as an accident precisely in order to deny anyone's responsibility.

This multiplicity of matched pairs contributes to our sense of complexity and intricacy in *La Règle du jeu*, but a prevailing puzzlement about the film's form has a further source. A precisely structured vision of disorder, *La Règle du jeu* presents a rule-governed world in process of disintegration. And just those formal means which help Renoir express the disorder of that world also obscure the sureness and firmness of his form. He avoids symmetry, that most obvious type of order. As he had often done, he omits any

A kind of shooting accident. *Upper right*, Berthelin (Tony Corteggiani) with Octave and Christine. *Lower left*, Christine, Octave, St. Aubin (Pierre Nay), the general (Pierre Magnier).

introduction to most of his scenes, simply thrusting us into the midst of an ongoing action, without establishing shots or explanation, leaving us to find our way as the scene unfolds. But in this film several strands of action, though in the same closed world, develop quite independently—seeing one gives us no clue to the others. Even when we do see the beginning of some interaction, Renoir abandons it in midstream, then switches back some time later in the affair. Hence disorientation becomes a recurrent element in our experience. The strands converge through Pre-established Harmony, not connecting causation; hence the strict order seems random. Perhaps this prompted Bazin's claim that Renoir "has succeeded in dispensing entirely with dramatic structures."[23]

The style Renoir had developed through the 1930s reaches it culmination in *La Règle du jeu*. Special lenses were made to maximize the depth of field. The corridors and large rooms of Lourié's sets provided those long spaces in which Renoir loved to range his characters in depth. His camera moves more freely than ever through this space, sometimes abandoning an action in mid-movement to follow another, sometimes catching two or three actions simultaneously at different depths in the field, often through a door which frames another receding space. Fully half the film's 336 shots have some camera movement. The degree to which this fluid camera allows Renoir to extend the duration of his shots may be indicated by these facts: of fifteen shots that run for about one minute or longer, only two have no camera movement; of sixty-eight shots which run for 30 seconds or more, only eleven have none. The camera stops and starts, reverses its direction, changes direction several times in a single shot, circles, breaking most of the rules of the day, yet so smoothly integrated with the action and so natural in its rhythm that it never announces its virtuosity. Not unusual for Renoir, but here the contrast with the rapid cutting of the hunt accentuates these long, flowing shots.

Close-ups of a single head are rare, and again Renoir avoids the conventional shot-countershot treatment of conversations. His preference for two-shots even leads him, when Robert and Geneviève are too far apart to be in the same frame, to give each a placid Buddha to complete the pair. But such terms as "two-shot," "close-up," "full shot," developed to describe more highly fragmented films, have no clear application to a large proportion of the shots in this film. With both camera and actors moving so frequently and freely, and half the shots in the film, apart from the central four minutes of the hunt, running from 17 to 110 seconds, the composition within a shot changes so rapidly and so radically that the standard labels hardly fit.

Jean Prat describes the sound track as "of a perfection never equaled by any French film."[24] Rich, dense, clear, remarkable in its fidelity and variety, this sound track plays a major role in building the world of *La Règle du jeu*. At Le Bourget the sound creates a surging crowd from a few visible figures. In the Sologne the recurrent background gun fire makes the hunt scene more bearable by identifying it as characteristic of the region. The complete chaos of the climax of the fête exists in an overwhelming mélange of screams, shouts, laughter, gunfire, and the rhythmic, grating clamor of the Limonaire. Talk abounds in the film, but it is often delivered very rapidly or shouted, sometimes with two or three voices heard at once; again, intonation, pace, and gesture are frequently more significant than the spoken words.

For music Renoir returns to his practice of the earlier thirties; apart from the overture and finale, all of the music of *La Règle du jeu* is internal to the world of the film—produced by the radio, Robert's mechanical instruments, or the musicians at La Colinière. For the first twenty-five shots (8½ minutes), the radio broadcast from Le Bourget ties all the scenes together and shows that no time elapses between scenes; the continuity of the radio sound defines the temporal flow of the action. Later, the music of the fête plays a similar role, but with a more remarkable effect. Once the fête begins, its music, interspersed with applause, provides a continuous background for fifteen minutes. After a two-minute pause it begins again and continues for five minutes more until the Limonaire goes wild. Thus, all the events from the first performance on stage to the capture of Schumacher have been timed by the music, which gives them a semblance of complete continuity while also dimly conveying to us the fact of an audience watching several more acts performed on the little stage, then dancing, wholly oblivious of the mêlée we have seen. When the guests come upstairs to retire, we have shared the long evening they have spent; only twenty-three minutes have elapsed since the first frame of the fête, but the music has created an impression of continuous time. The independence of the pursuits and encounters we see intermittently makes it difficult to conceive clearly the temporal flow of action, but the music solves the difficulty by providing a background continuity into which we presume the action fits. A sort of invisible condensation of time occurs in some transitions. For example, after Christine has told André she loves him, the song "Nous avons l'vé l'pied" begins in the background a few seconds before the cut to the salon where the four bearded singers finish their act and Robert appears to present the Limonaire. The music is continuous, but lasts only perhaps thirty seconds— hardly enough for the whole of the act whose beginning we have heard and whose end we have seen.

In almost every respect, the style of *La Règle du jeu* is simply a perfection and extension of that which Renoir had been developing since *Tire au flanc*. The complete failure of the film in 1939 and the fact that it was not seen whole for twenty years kept it from having any immediate impact on the cinema world. A few French critics sensed something of the value of this disturbing film, "a copious work, even too much so, very complex and profoundly intelligent from one end to the other,"[25] but their voices were drowned in the flood of anger and disapprobation that quickly swept *La Règle du jeu* off the screen.

While making the film Renoir had planned to show it at the New York World's Fair of 1939, but its crushing failure in Paris terminated such dreams. Frantic efforts to recoup something from the debacle led to a final cut to eighty-five minutes, so the film would fit in double-feature programs. Banned by the French censors in October, its career seemed at an end.

In 1942 British and American planes bombed Boulogne-sur-Seine, destroying the G. M. Film Laboratories where the negative of *La Règle du jeu* had been stored. At the end of the war, in September 1945, the film had a short new run in Paris, but with no more success than in 1939. A few eighty-five- and ninety-minute prints, in poor condition, began to circulate, though hardly anyone cared. The complete disappearance of the film seemed near.

The rebirth of *La Règle du jeu* began in northern France in 1946 when an exhibitor happened upon a forgotten film box he had hidden when the Nazis occupied France. Opened, the box revealed a brand new print of the eighty-five-minute version of *La Règle du jeu*, which he had received from Paris just before the Germans arrived. From this copy a new eighty-minute negative was made. A new life in ciné-clubs and the Cinémathèque began; even though the film is nearly incomprehensible in its eighty- and ninety-minute versions, it began to build a reputation among film lovers—enough to have a New York premiere in April 1950, where its reception was hardly better than in Paris in 1939.

In 1956, two film buffs who directed a ciné-club in Paris, Jean Gaborit and Jacques Marechal, formed the Société des Grands Films classiques, hoping to restore and distribute forgotten or neglected masterpieces, among them *La Règle du jeu*. After much effort they persuaded Camille François to sell them what remained of the film—the eighty-minute negative and a few prints—and all of his records. Restoration of the ninety-minute print seemed the most to hope for, but somewhere among Camille François's papers a letter from the G.T.C. Laboratories turned up, reporting that 224 boxes had been recovered from the bombed G.M. lab, containing positives, negatives, dupes, and sound mixes from *La Règle du jeu*. In fact, two hun-

dred boxes were found at the Lilas warehouse, and the process of restoration began. With the collaboration of Jacques Durand and the advice of Jean Renoir, a nearly complete version of the original 113-minute print finally emerged, to have its first public presentation at the Venice Film Festival in 1959. Still, memories of the disaster of 1939 delayed its commercial premiere in Paris until April 1965.

Since 1959 *La Règle du jeu* has steadily grown in esteem. Few now question its stature as one of the masterworks of cinema and it has had a profound influence on a new generation of film-makers. Three quotations will summarize the career of this last prewar film of Jean Renoir:

> Exactly what Jean Renoir had in mind when he wrote, performed in and directed "The Rules of the Game" . . . is anybody's guess . . . The new arrival is really one for the buzzards . . . . The distributors claim that the picture . . . was banned by the Occupation on grounds of immorality. Rest assured it wasn't immortality. . . . If the game is supposed to be life, love or hide-and-seek, which makes more sense, it's M. Renoir's own secret. At any rate, the master has dealt his admirers a pointless, thudding punch below the belt. (HHT, *New York Times*, April 10, 1950.)

> Twenty-two years after "The Rules of the Game" was made, and twelve years after a mutilated print was exhibited here, the full version of Jean Renoir's study of the manners and mores of Pre-war France opened yesterday . . . and completely justified its European reputation . . . The technique is admirable throughout, with at least two sequences emerging as classics of their kind . . . Admirers of the director's work . . . will discover a deeply personal statement of unusual richness and complexity. M. Renoir obviously set out to make a masterpiece . . . For discerning audiences, "The Rules of the Game" affords a memorable experience. (Eugene Archer, *New York Times*, January 19, 1961.)

> It remains, I think, the single most overwhelming experience I have ever had in the cinema. When I first came out of the theatre, I remember, I just had to sit on the edge of the pavement; I sat there for a good five minutes, and then I walked the streets of Paris for a couple of hours. For me, everything had been turned upside down. All my ideas about the cinema had been changed. While I was actually watching the film, my impressions were so strong physically that I thought that if this or that sequence were to go on for one shot more, I would either burst into tears, or scream, or something. Since then, of course, I've seen it at least fifteen times—like most film-makers of my generation. (Alain Resnais)[26]

Epilogue
1940

Stunned by the violent public reaction to *La Règle du jeu*, Jean Renoir felt only doubt and confusion during the early summer of 1939. Much later he wrote, "The failure of *La Règle du jeu* so depressed me that I resolved either to give up the cinema or to leave France."[1] Certainly, any dream of future productions by Nouvelles Editions Françaises lay dead. No doubt if circumstances had been normal he would have shaken off his depression and returned to work. But circumstances were far from normal in the summer of 1939.

Renoir has said that reading Marivaux had made him think of Italy: "All my work on *La Règle du jeu* had brought me closer to Italy, in a fantastic mode. I wanted to see the baroque statues, the angels on bridges, their garments with too many folds, their wings with too many feathers." Yet that seemed an unlikely destination for French cinema's spokesman for the Left, whose anti-Fascist activities had included writing and speaking the narration for the French version of Joris Ivens' *Spanish Earth*. But Benito Mussolini thought otherwise. Though his government had banned *La Grande Illusion* in Italy, it is said that he admired the film enough to have his own personal copy. Now he sent through diplomatic channels an invitation for Jean Renoir to come to Italy to make a film and to lecture to the film students at the Centro Sperimentale. Perhaps this was one of those fortunate accidents of which Renoir talks. The film was to be *La Tosca*, and Renoir's old assistant, Luchino Visconti, would work with him on it.

In mid-August, Renoir and Dido Freire went to Rome, but the outbreak of the war on September 3 seemed to bring that venture to an early conclusion. They returned to France, where Renoir was mobilized as a captain in the cinematographic services of the French army. As the "phony war" began, he led his small camera crew to front-line villages to photograph the idle troops.[2]

But Mussolini had not hastened to join in the war, and soon the invitation to Renoir to work in Rome was renewed. Renoir says: "I was not anxious to

Captain Renoir, 1939.

go; in fact I refused. But at that time the French government was willing to do anything to keep Italy neutral, to dissuade Mussolini from entering the war on Hitler's side. I was in uniform; the French government decided I should go. So I went."

In Rome, Jean and Dido were joined by Karl Koch, who was a German citizen. For several months Renoir worked with Koch and Visconti on an adaptation of *La Tosca* and roamed about the city looking for locations for the film. Renoir says that he tried not to have the action of his script stray too far from that of Sardou's play and Puccini's opera, which was, of course, very popular in Italy. He also remarked that he had the idea then of using Puccini's music to form a sort of background structure for the film, though this would be a very different use of music from that in his French films.

The lectures at the Centro Sperimentale he did not later remember in any detail: "I think I must have gone there about twenty times. I lectured to a large group, one hundred or more, on the fundamentals of film-making, and to a small group of fifteen or twenty on the direction of actors. I don't remember who any of the students were. But Visconti was with me everywhere in Rome, and when Antonioni visited us here a little while ago he said he had heard me lecture at the Centro Sperimentale."

The phony war ended abruptly on May 10, 1940, when German Panzer divisions attacked the lowlands. The vaunted Maginot line, flanked, would offer little effective resistance, and France would fall in six weeks. In Rome, Renoir was nearly ready to begin shooting *La Tosca*. Viviane Romance, who had made her screen debut in a bit part in *La Chienne*, was cast as Tosca, with Georges Flamant scheduled to come from France with her to take a role in the film. Michel Simon, a Swiss citizen, came to Rome to play Scarpia and to renew his work with Renoir after eight years. In early June the opening scene of the film was shot at the Chateau Saint-Ange and in the streets of Rome. Renoir did not make more than a few of the shots in *La Tosca*, none of them involving the principal actors. Whether he had shot one or four shots he did not remember, though the whole opening scene seems very much a part of a Renoir film. The first images recall the opening shot of *La Marseillaise*, with a squad of uniformed guards marching in the Chateau Saint-Ange, then horsemen ride from the chateau and gallop through the dark streets in images which seem to anticipate Fellini's *Roma*.

But by then, early June, Rome was filling with Germans, and the French

Renoir in Rome, 1940.

ambassador advised Renoir to leave by the first train. Dido, a Brazillian citizen, stayed in Rome a few days longer. On June 10, 1940, Mussolini announced to a cheering throng that Italy was at war with France; Dido caught the last train before the border was closed.[3]

Karl Koch and Michel Simon remained in Rome to complete *La Tosca*, but without French actors, of course. Imperio Argentina took over the title role. I do not know what work Visconti did in completing the film. Renoir was never to see him again. The names of neither Renoir nor Visconti appear in the credits of the print I have seen, which lists Carlo Koch as director. Visconti is reported to have regarded the film as falling far short of what Renoir might have done.[4] Jean Renoir never saw the finished film until March 1978, when a print of *La Tosca* from the UCLA Film Archive was projected for him. He said then that he was happy to finally see the outcome of that project, and that he thought it a good film, with some very moving moments. But when I asked if the film was very close to the script he had written, he replied: "I don't think so. The first thing I taught my assistants, Koch and Visconti, was that you have to improvise. And I think they did."

However *La Tosca* may be judged—and my perception is that it seems to become progressively less like a Renoir film as it goes along—this odd project seems strangely fitting for its time. From dancing on the volcano, Renoir had nearly plunged into it—amid the phony war, a left-wing French director, rather disillusioned with the Communist Party after the Hitler-Stalin pact, worked quietly in the fascist capital; then, while Nazi legions smashed across France, he began to shoot a story about revolutionaries and corrupt Italian officials in Roman streets that swarmed with German agents. These months of writing and preparation and few days of shooting would be the end, for many years, of Renoir's European career; yet the crossing of borders, the multinational cast and crew, the mixture of opera, stage, and screen, all make *La Tosca* seem an appropriate beginning for what will henceforth be an international film career and one in which the influence of the theatre will become much more apparent.

The exact degree of Jean Renoir's influence on the Italian neorealist cinema is impossible to state, though it must be considerable.[5] But his relation to Visconti and the realism of his early work seems clear. Visconti had been exhilarated by the freedom of working with Renoir's *équipe* in France in the days of the Popular Front. He was Renoir's constant companion in Rome in 1939-40 and has said that Renoir taught him the way to work with actors. And when he was ready to make his own first film and his proposal to adapt a Verga story had been rejected by the fascist censor, Visconti found among his papers the typescript of a French translation of James M. Cain's brutal novel *The Postman Always Rings Twice*, which had been given to him by Renoir while they were making *Une Partie de campagne*—Renoir then having suggested it as an interesting subject for a film. This became the source of Visconti's first film, now regarded as the precursor of neorealism, *Osses-*

Dido Freire and Jean Renoir, Italy, 1940.

sione (1942)—relocated in Italy and shorn of all the crude violence of Cain's novel. Both thematically and stylistically, *Ossessione* exhibits the influence of Renoir, from a plot and setting that resemble those of *Toni* to opening images that might have been taken from *La Nuit du carrefour* and several shots that seem directly modeled on shots from *La Bête humaine*. The Renoir style does not long persist in Visconti's films, but the operatic character of Visconti's later work may have its roots in those months he spent working with Renoir on the adaptation of *La Tosca*.

Renoir returned to Paris from Rome two weeks before the fall of France, which surrendered to the German armies on June 22. As the Germans approached Paris, Jean and Dido went to join the Cézannes at Marlotte, then began with them a flight to the south, stopping in a village off the main track in the middle of France, where they all lived in a big barn surrounded by Cézanne paintings.[6]

Early in 1939, Robert Flaherty had been in Paris, and Dido Freire had been introduced to him by some journalist friends. One day Dido and Flaherty went to the movies, to see *La Bête humaine*, then in its first run. Flaherty loved the film and remarked that he would like to meet its director. "Nothing easier," Dido replied, for she had known Renoir for many years. So she arranged a meeting. "It was love at first sight. They adored each other," she says. In a few hours they had become old friends—a friendship which now, in the midst of a collapsing France, beckoned Renoir to the new world. A letter from Flaherty urged Renoir to come to the United States and informed him that a visa awaited him at the American consulate in Nice.

The rest of 1940, for Jean and Dido, was a story of delays. They waited for months at Les Colletes in Cagnes while the French authorities hesitated over giving Jean an exit visa. Meanwhile, some representatives of Nazi cultural institutions came to call and to urge Jean to begin making films for the New France—an experience similar to that Fritz Lang had had seven years earlier in Berlin, and with an identical resolution: a decision to leave the country as soon as possible. Finally, allowed to leave France, they traveled to Marseilles, to Algeria, to Morocco, with more delays at every stop. Late in November, they arrived in Lisbon, where Jean was welcomed by the film community and interviewed as a celebrity—interviews that would become a center of controversy after the war,[7] when Renoir's politics became a matter of debate.

In mid-December Jean and Dido secured passage on an American liner sailing from Lisbon to New York. On December 31, 1940, Jean Renoir landed in New York. He would not make another film in France until 1954.

Notes

Bibliography

Acknowledgments

Index

Notes

Where references are French sources, the translations have been made by the author.

Abbreviations

B: André Bazin, *Jean Renoir*, ed. François Truffaut (Paris: Éditions Champ Libre, 1971).
CDC: *Cahiers du Cinéma* (Paris).
E: Jean Renoir, *Écrits 1926-1971*, ed. Claude Gauteur (Paris: Pierre Belfond, 1974).
L: Pierre Leprohon, *Jean Renoir* (Paris: Seghers, 1967).
LAS: *L'Avant-scène du Cinema* (Paris).
MLMF: Jean Renoir, *My Life and My Films*, tr. Norman Denny (New York: Atheneum, 1974).
ORTF: Office de Radiodiffusion-télévision francaise.
PP: Bernard Chardère, ed., *Jean Renoir*, Premier Plan, nos. 22-24 (Lyons: Serdoc, 1962).

Prologue

1. *MLMF*, p. 37.
2. Ibid., p. 17.
3. Ibid., p. 18.
4. Ibid., p. 282.
5. Jean Renoir, *Renoir, My Father*, trans. Randolph and Dorothy Weaver (Boston: Little, Brown, 1962), p. 3.

1. First Films: *Catherine and La Fille de l'eau*

1. "Souvenirs," *Le Point*, no. 18 (December 1938). Reprinted in *B*, pp. 144-145.
2. *Cinéa-Ciné*, January 5, 1926. Cited in *B*, p. 201.
3. *MLMF*, p. 50.
4. Pierre Philippe, "Catherine Hessling, Ou Retouches a un Renoir," *Cinéma 61*, no. 57 (June 1961).

5. *PP*, p. 56.

6. Ibid.

7. Jacques B. Brunius, *En Marge du Cinéma Français* (Paris: Arcanes, 1954), p. 168.

8. "Souvenirs." *B*, p. 146.

2. *Nana*

1. "Souvenirs." *B*, p. 146.

2. *PP*, p. 62.

3. Emile Zola, *Oeuvres complètes*, vol. 4 (Paris: Cercle du Livre Précieux, 1967), pp. 40-42.

4. See also *MLMF*, pp. 81-83.

5. See also *MLMF*, p. 83.

6. Renoir's account of *Nana*'s reception is given in *MLMF*, p. 84.

3. *Charleston* and *Marquitta*

1. *MLMF*, p. 85.

2. *Pour Vous*, no. 204 (October 1932).

3. "Souvenirs." *B*, p. 147.

4. *La Petite Marchande d'allumettes*

1. *L*, p. 31.

2. For example, *CDC*, vol. 13, no. 78 (December 1957), pp. 18-20.

5. *Tire au flanc*

1. *PP*, p. 88.

2. *B*, p. 74.

3. *CDC*, vol. 13, no. 78 (December 1957), p. 65.

4. *B*, chapter 5, "Renoir français."

6. *Le Tournoi* and *Le Bled*

1. *Pour Vous*, May 2, 1929. Cited in *L*, p. 33.

7. *On purge bébé*

1. *PP*, p. 102.

2. "Souvenirs." *B*, p. 151.

3. *PP*, p. 102.

8. *Le Chienne*

1. "Souvenirs." *B*, pp. 151-152.

2. Cited in *LAS*, no. 162 (October 1975), p. 30. This issue of *LAS* contains a rather accurate account of the dialogue of *La Chienne*.

3. *MLMF*, p. 108.

4. *PP*, p. 122.

9. *La Nuit du carrefour*

1. André Brunelin, "Jacques Becker ou la trace de l'homme." *Cinéma 60*, no. 48 (July 1960).
2. *CDC*, vol. 13, no. 78 (December 1957), p. 68.
3. Brunius, *En Marge du Cinéma Français*, p. 165.

10. *Boudu sauvé des eaux*

1. *B*, p. 79.
2. Review by Paul Schrader, *Los Angeles Free Press*, March 21, 1969, p. 26.

12. *Madame Bovary*

1. *PP*, p. 150.
2. *CDC*, vol. 13, no. 78 (December 1957), p. 32.
3. Ibid., p. 31.
4. *PP*, p. 149.
5. "Love in Three Dimensions," *Sight and Sound*, vol. 34, no. 2 (1965), pp. 71-75.
6. *PP*, pp. 151-152.
7. Armand-Jean Cauliez, *Jean Renoir* (Paris: Éditions universitaires, 1962), p. 43.

13. *Toni*

1. *CDC*, vol. 13, no. 78 (December 1957), p. 32.
2. Ibid., p. 33.
3. *Les Lettres françaises*, June 6, 1956.
4. Ibid. Or also Cauliez, *Jean Renoir*, p. 44.
5. "*Toni* et le classicisme," *CDC*, vol. 12, no. 60 (June 1956). Reprinted in *E*, p. 237.
6. Jean Quéval, *Jacques Becker* (Paris: Seghers, 1962), pp. 196-198.
7. Cauliez, *Jean Renoir*, p. 46.
8. *CDC*, vol. 13, no. 78 (December 1957), p. 38.

14. *Le Crime de M. Lange*

1. Renoir's journalistic writings in the left-wing press in 1936-1938 have been reprinted in *E*.
2. Thorold Dickinson, *A Discovery of Cinema* (London: Oxford University Press, 1971), p. 69.
3. *L*, p. 59.
4. *L*, p. 60.
5. *B*, p. 154.
6. *CDC*, vol. 13, no. 78 (December 1957), p. 35.
7. *B*, chapter 5.
8. Ibid., p. 42.
9. *L*, p. 62.
10. *Encyclopédie du cinéma*, ed. Roger Boussinot (Paris: Bordas, 1967), p. 1268.

15. *La Vie est à nous*

1. Quoted by Michel Capdenac, "Le Réalisme polémique, le realisme poétique," *Les Lettres françaises*, no. 1308 (November 12, 1969).

2. *PP*, p. 190.

3. Capdenac, *Les Lettres françaises*. See also "*La Vie est a nous, Film Militant*," *CDC*, vol. 26, no. 218 (March 1970), p. 46.

4. Ibid.

5. *PP*, pp. 186-188.

6. *PP*, p. 176.

7. The opening scene of *La Vie est à nous* was edited by Jacques Brunius. See his account in *En Marge du Cinéma Français*, p. 131.

8. Capdenac, *Les Lettres françaises*.

16. *Une Partie de campagne*

1. *CDC*, vol. 13, no. 78 (December 1957), p. 36.

2. *PP*, p. 225.

3. Ibid.

4. Op. cit. *L*, p. 69.

5. Louis Chauvet, *Le Figaro*, December 18, 1946. Cited in *LAS*, no. 21 (December 15, 1962), p. 42.

6. Leo Braudy, *Jean Renoir: The World of His Films*. (Garden City: Doubleday, 1972), p. 34.

7. Ibid.

17. *Les Bas Fonds*

1. *PP*, p. 233.

2. *L*, p. 73.

3. Donald Richie, *The Films of Akira Kurosawa* (Berkeley: University of California Press, 1965), p. 129.

4. In "The Cinema of the Popular Front (1934-1938)," *Screen*, vol. 13, no. 4 (1972-73), pp. 5-58.

5. Ibid., p. 39.

6. Poulle, *Renoir 1938*, p. 103.

18. *La Grande Illusion*

1. *CDC*, vol. 13, no. 78, (December 1957), p. 38.

2. *B*, pp. 169-181.

3. "Jacques Becker, ou la trace de l'homme," *Cinéma 60*, no. 48 (July 1960).

4. Francoise Giroud, "Souvenirs," *L'Express*, October 9, 1958.

5. *CDC*, vol. 13, no. 78, p. 40.

6. *E*, p. 240.

7. James Kerans, "Classics Revisited: *La Grande Illusion*," *Film Quarterly*, vol. 14, no. 2 (1960), pp. 10-17.

8. See the excerpts from Italian critics in *PP*, pp. 246-250.

9. Jean Fayard in *Candide*. Cited in *LAS*, no. 44 (January 1965), p. 43.

10. Charles Baudelaire, *Le peintre de la vie moderne* (Paris: Editions de la

Pleiade), p. 1178. Cited in Henri Agel, "Le dandy a l'écran," *Revue d'esthétique*, nos. 2-3 (1967), p. 156.

11. Ibid.

12. *B*, p. 57.

13. *LAS*, no. 44 (January 1965), p. 16.

14. Giroud, "Souvenirs."

15. "La Grande Illusion de 1937," *L'Écran français*, September 4, 1946.

16. Giroud, "Souvenirs."

19. *La Marseillaise*

1. *PP*, p. 282.

2. "La marche de l'idée," *CDC*, vol. 23, no. 196 (December 1967), p. 17.

3. *CDC*, vol. 13, no. 78 (1957), p. 40.

4. Claude Beylie, "Jean Renoir ou les jeux du spectacle et de la vie," *Cinéma d'aujourd'hui*, no. 2 (May-June 1975), p. 71.

5. *CDC*, vol. 23, no. 196 (1967), p. 14.

6. *PP*, p. 251.

7. *CDC*, vol. 23, no. 196 (1967), p. 17.

8. Ibid., p. 21.

9. Leo Braudy, *Jean Renoir*, p. 43.

10. *CDC*, vol. 23, no. 196 (1967), p. 21.

11. Georges Champeaux in *Gringoire*, December 1, 1938. Cited in *PP*, p. 261.

12. Ibid.

13. *CDC*, vol. 23, no. 196 (1967), p. 21.

14. Ibid.

20. *La Bête humaine*

1. *Pour Vous*, no. 451 (August 7, 1937). Reprinted in *E*, p. 36.

2. *PP*, p. 263.

3. *Ce Soir*, February 24, 1938. *E*, p. 154.

4. *E*, p. 162.

5. *Ce Soir*, August 9, 1938. *E*, p. 256.

6. *Ce Soir*, September 3, 1938. *E*, p. 258.

7. "Ah! qu'on est fier d'etre français quand on contemple la colonne!" *Ce Soir*, October 7, 1938. *E*, pp. 177-178.

8. Zola, *Oeuvres complètes*, vol. 6, p. 302.

9. *Cinémonde*, no. 529 (December 7, 1938). *E*, p. 263.

10. Ibid. *E*, p. 267.

11. *Ce Soir*, September 3, 1938. *E*, p. 259.

12. *B*, p. 75.

13. Raymond Durgnat, *Jean Renoir* (Berkeley: University of California Press, 1974), p. 172.

14. *L*, p. 79.

15. *Cinémonde*, no. 529. *E*, p. 264.

16. *Cinémonde*, no. 529. *E*, p. 264.

17. *Cinémonde*, no. 537, February 1, 1939. *E*, pp. 268-269.

18. *Ce Soir*, August 9, 1938. *E*, p. 256.

19. Francois Vinneuil. Cited in *PP*, p. 270.

21. *La Règle de jeu*

1. *MLMF*, p. 140.

2. The most complete account of the making of *La Règle du jeu* will be found in André Brunelin, "Histoire d'une malédiction," in *Cinéma 60*, no. 43 (February 1960), pp. 36-64. Jean Renoir has said of this account that it is not, generally, incorrect, but that it represents the point of view of essentially one man, Camille François.

3. *E*, pp. 177-178.

4. *Pour Vous*, January 25, 1939. *B*, p. 183.

5. From an interview filmed by ORTF in 1961. Part of this interview has been published in Jean Renoir, *The Rules of the Game* (New York: Simon and Schuster, 1970), pp. 9-12.

6. *CDC*, vol. 6, no. 34 (May 1954), p. 6.

7. *CDC*, vol. 2, no. 8 (January 1952), p. 8.

8. *MLMF*, p. 172.

9. *ORTF*.

10. *MLMF*, p. 169.

11. *ORTF*.

12. *ORTF*.

13. Stanley Cavell, "More of *The World Viewed*," *Georgia Review*, vol. 28, no. 4 (Winter 1974), p. 625.

14. *ORTF*.

15. A. Brunelin, "Histoire d'une malédiction," p. 47.

16. *ORTF*.

17. *MLMF*, p. 171.

18. *ORTF*.

19. Cavell, "More of the World Viewed," pp. 624, 630.

20. Ibid., pp. 623.

21. Gerald Mast, *Filmguide to The Rules of the Game* (Bloomington: Indiana University Press, 1973), p. 24.

22. Cavell, "More of *The World Viewed*," p. 624.

23. *B*, p. 76.

24. *Analyse des Films de Jean Renoir* (Paris: IDHEC, 1966), p. 104.

25. Nino Frank in *Pour Vous*, reprinted in *PP*, p. 289.

26. Cited in Jean Renoir, *The Rules of the Game*, p. 14.

Epilogue

1. *MLMF*, p. 173.

2. See Renoir's account of this in *MLMF*, pp. 174-175.

3. Cf. *MLMF*, p. 177.

4. G. Nowell-Smith, *Visconti*, (Garden City: Doubleday, 1968), p. 15.

5. See Roy Armes, *Patterns of Realism* (New York: A.S. Barnes, 1971), pp. 48-51.

6. See *MLMF*, pp. 180-183. for Renoir's account of these days.

7. See Claude Beylie's careful account of these interviews in *Jean Renoir, Cinéma d'aujourd'hui*, no. 2 (1975), p. 30.

Bibliography

Extensive bibliographies of articles and interviews are contained in Christopher Faulkner, *Jean Renoir: A Guide to References and Resources;* Raymond Durgnat, *Jean Renoir;* Claude Beylie, *Jean Renoir;* and Pierre Leprohon, *Jean Renoir.*

Books by Jean Renoir

Les Cahiers du Capitaine Georges. Paris: Gallimard, 1966.

Le Coeur a l'aise. Paris: Flammarion, 1978.

Ecrits 1926-1971, ed. Claude Gautier. Paris: Pierre Belfond, 1974.

Ma Vie et mes films. Paris: Flammarion, 1974. Published in English as *My Life and My Films,* trans. Norman Denny. New York: Atheneum, 1974.

Orvet. Paris: Gallimard, 1955.

Renoir. Paris: Hachette, 1962. Published in English as *Renoir, My Father,* trans. Randolph and Dorothy Weaver. Boston: Little, Brown, 1958.

Film Scripts

La Chienne, in *L'Avant-Scène du cinéma,* no. 162 (October 1975).

La Grande Illusion, in *L'Avant-Scene du cinéma,* no. 21 (December 1962). Published in English under the same title, trans. Marianne Alexander and Andrew Sinclair. London: Lorimer, 1968. Published as a book with frames from every shot, Paris: Balland, 1974.

Une Partie de campagne, in *L'Avant-Scène du cinéma,* no. 21 (December 1962).

La Règle du jeu, in *L'Avant-Scène du cinéma,* no. 52 (October 1965). Published in English as *The Rules of the Game,* trans. John McGrath and Maureen Teitelbaum. New York: Simon and Schuster, 1970.

Books about Jean Renoir

Bazin, André. *Jean Renoir,* ed. Francois Truffaut. Paris: Editions Champ Libre, 1971. Published in English under the same title, trans. W. W. Halsey II and William H. Simon. New York: Dell, 1974.

Beylie, Claude. *Jean Renoir.* Cinema d'aujourd'hui, no. 2. Paris: FilmEditions, 1975.

Braudy, Leo. *Jean Renoir: The World of his Films*. Garden City: Doubleday, 1972.

Cauliez, Armand-Jean. *Jean Renoir*. Paris: Editions Universitaires, 1962.

Chardère, Bernard, ed. *Jean Renoir*. Premier Plan, nos. 22-24. Lyon: SERDOC, 1962.

Durgnat, Raymond. *Jean Renoir*. Berkeley: University of California Press, 1974.

Faulkner, Christopher. *Jean Renoir: A Guide to References and Resources*. Boston: G. K. Hall, 1979.

Gilliatt, Penelope. *Jean Renoir*. New York: McGraw-Hill, 1975.

Gregor, Ulrich, ed. *Jean Renoir und seine Filme*. Berlin: Deutschen Filmclubs, 1970.

Institut des hautes études cinématographiques. *Analyse des films de Jean Renoir*. Paris: IDHEC, 1966.

Leprohon, Pierre. *Jean Renoir*. Paris: Editions Seghers, 1967. Published in English under the same title, trans. Brigid Elson. New York: Crown, 1971.

Mast, Gerald. *Filmguide to The Rules of the Game*. Bloomington: Indiana University Press, 1973.

Poulle, Francois. *Renoir 1938*. Paris: Editions du Cerf, 1969.

Viry-Babel, Roger. "La Grande Illusion de Jean Renoir." Dissertation, Université de Nancy, 1973.

Acknowledgments

For whatever I have achieved in this work I am most indebted to Jean and Dido Renoir—not merely for the obvious reason that my subject is Renoir films, but more directly for the many hours they allowed me to spend with them, in Beverly Hills and in Paris, viewing and discussing these films, watching Renoir at work during the shooting of *Le Petit Théâtre de Jean Renoir*, even becoming, in a small way, one of Renoir's "accomplices" when we worked together to translate the dialogue of *Le Petit Théâtre* into English subtitles. Jean Renoir read my manuscript as it emerged and saved me from occasional errors; he also kindly allowed me to copy from his prints most of the frame enlargements which illustrate this book and to rummage among his souvenirs in search of photos from this earlier period of his life.

A critical event in the development of this work was the Renoir retrospective at the Los Angeles County Museum of Art in February 1969, arranged by Philip Chamberlin, who has aided and encouraged me throughout the years of my work. Henri Langlois and his staff at the Cinémathèque française made it possible for me to see films not then available in the United States and allowed me to copy frames from Cinématheque prints sent to the Los Angeles County Museum of Art. Mme. Claude de Ste. Phalle, then Ginette Courtois-Doynel, of the Compagnie Jean Renoir, has provided information, encouragement, and understanding. David Bradley played a large role in mounting the Renoir retrospective, then allowed me to browse in his library, and has helped in other ways.

Many students, both in and out of classrooms, have helped me to see more clearly. Among these Carol Brownson deserves special mention as one of the first to share my interest in Renoir and one whose critical opinions have been most valuable. Among others who have shared their perception of some of these films I remember Timothy Lyons, Scott Larson, Robert Curry, Phyllis Walder, Randy Moore, Tom Roberson, Steven Cloud, Patrice Dally, and Toni McCarty. I hope those whose names I have forgotten will forgive me if they find an idea of their own somewhere in my text.

Helen D. Willard of the Harvard College Library provided microfilm of the Renoir manuscripts in the Harvard collection. Stanley Cavell gave invaluable support. Ronald Gottesman and William Rothman made many valuable suggestions.

Typists who worked on my manuscript include June Kelley, Dennis Aubry, and Patti O'Hara.

Chapter 14 was first published as "Jean Renoir as Moralist: *Le Crime de M. Lange*," in *The Journal of Aesthetic Education*, vol. 8, no. 1 (January 1974). It is reprinted here with the permission of the University of Illinois Press. Chapter 18 was first published as "Jean Renoir's *La Grande Illusion*" in *The Georgia Review*, vol. 29, no. 1 (Spring 1975). Quotations from Jean Renoir's interviews and articles in *Cahiers du Cinema* are translated and reprinted with the permission of the editors of *Cahiers du Cinema*. Quotations from Francoise Giroud's memories of the production of *La Grande Illusion* are translated and reprinted by permission of *L'Express*.

My wife, Sally Sesonske, read every chapter as it emerged and corrected many an infelicitous phrase; she also insisted on clarity whenever I tended to be obscure. Her presence has sustained me through all the years of this work.

Index

Page numbers in italics indicate photographs.